THE DAWN OF ISRAEL

THE DAWN OF ISRAEL

A HISTORY OF CANAAN IN THE SECOND MILLENNIUM BCE

Lester L. Grabbe

t&tclark
LONDON • NEW YORK • OXFORD • NEW DELHI • SYDNEY

T&T CLARK
Bloomsbury Publishing Plc
50 Bedford Square, London, WC1B 3DP, UK
1385 Broadway, New York, NY 10018, USA
29 Earlsfort Terrace, Dublin 2, Ireland

BLOOMSBURY, T&T CLARK and the T&T Clark logo
are trademarks of Bloomsbury Publishing Plc

First published in Great Britain 2023

Copyright © Lester L. Grabbe, 2023

Lester L. Grabbe has asserted his right under the Copyright, Designs and Patents Act, 1988, to be identified as Author of this work.

Cover image: Replica of the Merneptah Stele (Israel Stele or the Victory Stele)
© World History Archive / Alamy Stock Photo

All rights reserved. No part of this publication may be reproduced or transmitted in any form or by any means, electronic or mechanical, including photocopying, recording, or any information storage or retrieval system, without prior permission in writing from the publishers.

Bloomsbury Publishing Plc does not have any control over, or responsibility for, any third-party websites referred to or in this book. All internet addresses given in this book were correct at the time of going to press. The author and publisher regret any inconvenience caused if addresses have changed or sites have ceased to exist, but can accept no responsibility for any such changes.

A catalogue record for this book is available from the British Library.
Library of Congress Cataloging-in-Publication Data:
Names: Grabbe, Lester L., author.
Title: The dawn of Israel : a history of Canaan in the Second Millennium BCE / by Lester L. Grabbe.
Description: London ; New York, NY : T&T Clark, 2022. | Includes bibliographical references and index. | Summary: "Lester L. Grabbe provides a comprehensive history of the main ancient Near Eastern peoples and empires, drawing on insights from archaeology, iconography and the social sciences"-- Provided by publisher.
Identifiers: LCCN 2022003685 (print) | LCCN 2022003686 (ebook) |
ISBN 9780567663221 (hardback) | ISBN 9780567663214 (paperback) |
ISBN 9780567663238 (pdf) | ISBN 9780567663245 (epub)
Subjects: LCSH: Israel--History. | Palestine--History--To 70 A.D. | Palestine--Antiquities.
Classification: LCC DS121 .G73 2022 (print) | LCC DS121 (ebook) |
DDC 956.94--dc23/eng/20220307
LC record available at https://lccn.loc.gov/2022003685
LC ebook record available at https://lccn.loc.gov/2022003686

ISBN:	HB:	978-0-5676-6322-1
	PB:	978-0-5676-6321-4
	ePDF:	978-0-5676-6323-8
	ePUB:	978-0-5676-6324-5

Typeset by: Trans.form.ed SAS
Printed and bound in Great Britain

To find out more about our authors and books visit www.bloomsbury.com and sign up for our newsletters.

TO

Nadav Na'aman
Israel Finkelstein
Ernst Axel Knauf
Aren M. Maeir
Hermann Michael Niemann

Contents

Preface	xi
Abbreviations	xiii

Part I
INTRODUCTION

Chapter 1
INTRODUCTION — 3
  1.1 Aims — 3
  1.2 Principles of Historical Method — 4
  1.3 Chronology — 6
  1.4 Terminology and Other Technical Matters — 11

Chapter 2
THE THIRD-MILLENNIUM CONTEXT — 12
  2.1 Egypt — 12
  2.2 Mesopotamia — 16
  2.3 Anatolia — 18
  2.4 Syria-Palestine — 18
    2.4.1 Archaeology — 20
    2.4.2 Ebla — 22
    2.4.3 Byblos — 23
    2.4.4 Palestine — 23
  2.5 Writing, Scribes and Literature — 27
  2.6 Conclusions — 31

Part II
MIDDLE BRONZE AGE (*C.* 2000–1600 BCE)

Chapter 3
ANCIENT NEAR EASTERN CONTEXT — 35
  3.1 Egypt — 35
    3.1.1 Middle Kingdom — 36
    3.1.2 Second Intermediate Period — 38

3.2 Mesopotamia	40
3.2.1 The Isin and Larsa 'Intermediate Period'	41
3.2.2 Old Assyrian Period (*c.* 2000–1750 BCE)	42
3.2.3 Old Babylonian Period (*c.* 2000–1600)	43
3.2.4 Mari	44
3.2.5 Elam	45
3.3 Anatolia	45
3.3.1 Hittite Old Kingdom	45
3.3.2 Mitanni	48
3.4 Conclusions	48

Chapter 4
SYRIA AND PALESTINE

	51
4.1 Sources	51
4.2 History of Syria	53
4.2.1 Ugarit	54
4.2.2 Byblos (Gubla)	56
4.2.3 Amorites	56
4.2.4 Yamhad	60
4.3 History of Palestine/Canaan	62
4.3.1 Archaeology	62
4.3.2 Egyptian Textual References	65
4.3.3 The Hyksos	65
4.4 The Question of the Patriarchs	71
4.5 Conclusions	78

Part III
LATE BRONZE AGE (*C.* 1600–1200 BCE)

Chapter 5
ANCIENT NEAR EASTERN CONTEXT, INCLUDING SYRIA

	83
5.1 Egypt	83
5.1.1 From the Hyksos to Amenhotep IV (Akhenaten)	85
5.1.2 The First Part of the 19th Dynasty	88
5.1.3 Table of Egyptian Kings	**89**
5.2 Mesopotamia	90
5.2.1 Middle Assyrian Kingdom	90
5.2.2 Kassite Babylonia	92
5.3 Anatolia	93
5.3.1 Hittite (Middle and) New Kingdom (1500–1200)	93
5.3.2 The Mitanni Kingdom (1600–1350) and Nuzi	96

5.4 Syria	100
5.4.1 Amurru	100
5.4.2 Ugarit	103
5.4.3 Phoenicia	111
5.5 Conclusions	111

Chapter 6
PALESTINE 114

6.1 Sources	115
6.2 Archaeology	116
6.3 The Search for Israel	122
6.3.1 Egyptian Incursions into Canaan	122
6.3.2 Canaan as Depicted in the Amarna Letters	128
6.3.3 Ethnic and Other Groups	136
6.3.3.1 'Nomads' and Pastoralists	137
6.3.3.2 Canaan/Canaanites	139
6.3.3.3 *'Apiru/Ḫaberu*	142
6.3.3.4 *Shasu (Shosu, Š3św, Sutu)*	143
6.3.3.5 'Nomadic' Copper Producers	145
6.3.3.6 Conclusions about Ethnic and Other Groups	147
6.3.4 The Origins of Israel and the Merenptah Stela: Where Did Israel Come from?	148
6.4 The Question of the Exodus	153
6.4.1 Issues relating to Historicity	155
6.4.2 Conclusions on the Exodus	160
6.5 Conclusions	162

Part IV
EARLY IRON AGE (*C.* 1200–900 BCE)

Chapter 7
ANCIENT NEAR EASTERN CONTEXT, INCLUDING SYRIA
AND TRANSJORDAN (1200–900 BCE) 167

7.1 Egypt	167
7.2 Sea Peoples	169
7.3 Mesopotamia and Anatolia	178
7.3.1 Elam, Babylonia and Assyria	178
7.3.2 Neo-Hittite States	180
7.4 Phoenicia	181
7.5 Aramaeans	183
7.6 Transjordan	184
7.7 Conclusions	188

Chapter 8
PALESTINE (1200–900 BCE) — 190

- 8.1 Sources — 190
- 8.2 Archaeology — 191
  - 8.2.1 Archaeological Survey — 194
  - 8.2.2 Analysis and Conclusions on Archaeology — 202
- 8.3 Coming of the Philistines — 204
- 8.4 The Settlement (of 'Israel'?) — 213
  - 8.4.1 Who Settled in the Hill Country? — 213
  - 8.4.2 Recent Models for the Settlement — 216
  - 8.4.3 Israelite Tribes — 219
  - 8.4.4 Israel versus Judah — 223
  - 8.4.5 The Book of Judges and the 'Song of Deborah' (Judges 5) — 223
  - 8.4.6 The Settlement: An Overview — 227
- 8.5 Rise of the Israelite State — 235
  - 8.5.1 Models of Statehood — 235
  - 8.5.2 Beginnings of the Kingdom of Israel — 240
  - 8.5.3 Samuel — 243
  - 8.5.4 Saul — 244
  - 8.5.5 Eshbaal — 247
  - 8.5.6 David — 247
    - 8.5.6.1 Origin/Early Life of David — 249
    - 8.5.6.2 David's Wars — 249
    - 8.5.6.3 Jerusalem — 251
    - 8.5.6.4 Archaeology — 251
    - 8.5.6.5 Relationship of Saul and David Traditions — 253
    - 8.5.6.6 Conclusions about David — 254
  - 8.5.7 Solomon — 255
  - 8.5.8 Shoshenq I's Palestinian Raid(s) — 259
  - 8.5.9 Reversion to Two Kingdoms — 264
- 8.6 Conclusions — 265

Part V
CONCLUSIONS

Chapter 9
THE ORIGINS OF ISRAEL – A HOLISTIC PERSPECTIVE — 271

Bibliography — 283
Index of References — 327
Index of Authors — 333
Index of Subjects — 340

Preface

When I first contemplated the present study, I was reminded of a book I had seen as a student: Emmanuel Anati's *Palestine before the Hebrews*. A number of questions were begged by this title, but I thought of calling mine, *Canaan before Israel*. Yet since I wanted to include the beginnings of Israel – indeed, the end point was to be the rise of Israel – that title did not quite fit!

In addition to the debt I owe to many predecessors and colleagues for their labours on the history of early Palestine, I must thank especially the following for their help in writing this book: Christian Frevel for a gift of his history of Israel; Axel Knauf and Hermann Michael Niemann, for their history; Alexander Andrason and Juan-Pablo Vita for their article on the Amorite language; Ido Koch for an article on Egypt and Canaan; Jesse Michael Milleck for several articles on the Sea Peoples; Dennis Pardee for articles relating to Ugarit; Louis C. Jonker for articles on Saul and Solomon. No doubt I have missed some people, for which I apologize and add my thanks to them.

The amount that I owe to archaeologists should be clear from the place of that discipline in this study. For that reason, I am grateful for the friendship or acquaintance with a number of archaeologists: Eric Meyers, Amihai Mazar, David Ussishkin, Oded Lipschits, Shlomo Gibson, Ronny Reich. Margreet Steiner, Bill Dever, Ann Killebrew, Zvi Lederman, Beth Alpert Nakhai, Alex Fantalkin, Norma Franklin, Elizabeth Bloch-Smith, Omer Sergei. Again, I am bound to have missed one or more people.

There are two further archaeologists to whom I owe a special debt, as well as to three historians. The prolific studies of Israel Finkelstein have been an inspiration, as have those of Aren Maeir, not only on Tell el-Ṣafi-Gath but also on other important topics. I have known and worked with Axel Knauf on history for many years, especially with regard to the European Seminar in Historical Methodology; Hermann Michael Niemann also contributed to volumes of the Seminar but in addition provided many studies that made me think. Most of all, however, I have been inspired by Nadav Na'aman, whether in the work of the Seminar or in his many other studies. He has shown how to combine the three vital areas of archaeology, Near Eastern texts and biblical studies into a proper historical synthesis. I have found him the model of the historian that I have aspired to. To these five individuals I dedicate this volume.

Lester L. Grabbe
Kingston upon Hull
13 October 2021

Abbreviations

AASOR	Annual of the American Schools of Oriental Research
AB	Anchor Bible
ABC	A. K. Grayson (1975) *Assyrian and Babylonian Chronicles*).
ABD	David Noel Freedman (ed.) (1992) *Anchor Bible Dictionary* (6 vols).
ACEBT	*Amsterdamse Cahiers voor Exegese van de Bijbel en zijn Tradities*
ADPV	Abhandlungen des Deutschen Palästina-Vereins
AEL	Miriam Lichtheim (1973–80) *Ancient Egyptian Literature* (3 vols).
AfO	*Archiv für Orientforschung*
AGAJU	Arbeiten zur Geschichte des antiken Judentums und des Urchristentums
AJA	*American Journal of Archaeology*
ALGHJ	Arbeiten zur Literatur und Geschichte des hellenistischen Judentums
AnBib	Analecta biblica
ANET	James B. Pritchard (ed.) (1969) *Ancient Near Eastern Texts Relating to the Old Testament* (3rd ed. with Supplement).
ARE	J. A. Breasted (1906–7) *Ancient Records of Egypt: Historical Documents from the Earliest Times to the Persian Conquest, Edited and Translated with Commentary* (vols 1–5).
ASOR	American Schools of Oriental Research
ATD	Das Alte Testament Deutsch
AuOr	*Aula Orientalis*
AUSS	*Andrews University Seminary Studies*
BA	*Biblical Archeologist*
BAR	*Biblical Archaeology Review*
BASOR	*Bulletin of the American Schools of Oriental Research*
BBB	Bonner biblische Beiträge
BCE	Before the Common Era (= BC)
BETL	Bibliotheca Ephemeridum Theologicarum Lovaniensium
BHS	*Biblia Hebraica Stuttgartensis*
Bib	*Biblica*
BibOr	Biblica et orientalia
BJRL	*Bulletin of the John Rylands Library*
BN	*Biblische Notizen*
BO	*Bibliotheca Orientalis*
BWANT	Beiträge zur Wissenschaft vom Alten und Neuen Testament

BZ	*Biblische Zeitschrift*
BZAW	Beihefte zur *ZAW*
CBC	Century Bible Commentary
CBET	Contribution to Biblical Exegesis and Theology
CBQ	*Catholic Biblical Quarterly*
CBQMS	*Catholic Biblical Quarterly* Monograph Series
CE	Common Era (= AD)
CIS	Copenhagen International Seminar
CML	J. C. L. Gibson (1978) *Canaanite Myths and Legends*.
ConBOT	Conjectanea biblica, Old Testament
CRAIBL	Comptes rendus de l'Academie des inscriptions et belles-lettres
CR: BS	*Currents in Research: Biblical Studies*
CTH	Standard reference to Hittite texts, from E. Laroche (1971) *Catalogue des textes hittites*.
DDD	K. van der Toorn, B. Becking, and P. W. van der Horst (eds) (1999) *Dictionary of Deities and Demons in the Bible*.
DtrH	Deuteronomistic History
EA	El-Amarna text; the same numbering system is followed in the standard editions of J. A. Knudtson (1907–15); W. L. Moran (1992); A. F. Rainey (2015).
EB(A)	Early Bronze (Age)
Erman-Grapow	A. Erman and H. Grapow (1926–50) *Wörterbuch der ägyptischen Sprache* (6 vols)
ESHM	European Seminar in Historical Methodology
EsIr	*Eretz-Israel*
ET	English translation
EvT	*Evangelische Theologie*
FAT	Forschungen zum Alten Testament
FOTL	Forms of Old Testament Literature
FRLANT	Forschungen zur Religion und Literatur des Alten und Neuen Testaments
Fs	Festschrift
HAT	Handbuch zum Alten Testament
HdA	Handbuch der Archäologie
HeBAI	*Hebrew Bible and Ancient Israel*
HSM	Harvard Semitic Monographs
HSS	Harvard Semitic Studies
HTR	*Harvard Theological Review*
HUCA	*Hebrew Union College Annual*
IA	Iron Age
ICC	International Critical Commentary
IDB	G. A. Buttrick (ed.) (1964) *Interpreter's Dictionary of the Bible* (4 vols)
IDBSup	Supplementary volume to *IDB* (1976)
IEJ	*Israel Exploration Journal*
JAEI	*Journal of Ancient Egyptian Interconnections*
JANES	*Journal of the Ancient Near Eastern Society of Columbia University*
JAOS	*Journal of the American Oriental Society*
JARCE	*Journal of the American Research Center in Egypt*
JBL	*Journal of Biblical Literature*

JCS	*Journal of Cuneiform Studies*
JEA	*Journal of Egyptian Archaeology*
JESHO	*Journal of the Economic and Social History of the Orient*
JNES	*Journal of Near Eastern Studies*
JNSL	*Journal of Northwest Semitic Languages*
JQR	*Jewish Quarterly Review*
JSOT	*Journal for the Study of the Old Testament*
JSOTSup	Supplements to *Journal for the Study of the Old Testament*
JSS	*Journal of Semitic Studies*
JTS	*Journal of Theological Studies*
KAI	H. Donner and W. Röllig (eds) (1962–64) *Kanaanäische und aramäische Inschriften, Mit einem Beitrag von O. Rössler* (vols. 1–3).
KAT	Kommentar zum Alten Testament
KTU	Manfried Dietrich, Oswald Loretz, and Joaquín Sanmartín (eds) (1995) *The Cuneiform Alphabetic Texts from Ugarit, Ras Ibn Hani and Other Places (Second, Enlarged Edition)*.
LAPO	Series Littératures anciennes du Proche-Orient, cited by volume and text number: (Volume) 14: André Caquot, Jean-Michel de Tarragon, and Jesús-Luis Cunchillos (1989) *Textes ougaritiques, Tome II: Textes religieux et rituels; Correspondance*. (Volume) 16: Jean-Marie Durand (1997) *Documents épistolaires du palais de Mari, 1*. (Volume) 17: Jean-Marie Durand (1998) *Documents épistolaires du palais de Mari, 2*. (Volume) 18: Jean-Marie Durand (2000) *Documents épistolaires du palais de Mari, 3*. (Volume) 20: Sylvie Lackenbacher (2002) *Textes akkadiens d'Ugarit: Textes provenant des vingt-cinq premières campagnes*.
LB(A)	Late Bronze (Age)
LC	Low Chronology (see §1.3).
LdÄ	Wolfgang Helck and Eberhard Otto (eds) (1975–92) *Lexikon der Ägyptologie* (vols. 1–7).
LHBOTS	Library of Hebrew Bible/Old Testament Studies
LXX	Septuagint version of the Old Testament
MB(A)	Middle Bronze (Age)
MCC	Modified Conventional Chronology (see §1.3)
MK	Egyptian Middle Kingdom
MT	Masoretic text
NEAEHL	Ephraim Stern (ed.) (1992) *New Encyclopedia of Archaeological Excavations in the Holy Land* (4 vols); (2008) (vol. 5).
NEB	Neue Echter Bibel
NK	Egyptian New Kingdom
OBO	Orbis Biblicus et Orientalis
OEAE	Donald B. Redford (ed.). 2001. *Oxford Encyclopedia of Ancient Egypt* (3 vols).
OEANE	Eric M. Meyers (editor-in-chief) (1997) *The Oxford Encyclopedia of Archaeology in the Near East* (5 vols).
OJA	*Oxford Journal of Archaeology*

OK	Egyptian Old Kingdom
Or	*Orientalia*
OT	Old Testament/Hebrew Bible
OTL	Old Testament Library
OTS	*Oudtestamentische Studiën*
PAPS	*Proceedings of the American Philosophical Society*
PEQ	*Palestine Exploration Quarterly*
PJb	*Palästina-Jahrbuch*
RdA	*Revue d'Assyriologie et d'archéologie orientale*
RDSO	*Rivista degli Studi Orientali*
RevB	*Revue Biblique*
RI 1	K. A. Kitchen (1993) *Ramesside Inscriptions: Translated and Annotated: Translations Volume I: Ramesses I, Sethos I and Contemporaries.*
RI 2	K. A. Kitchen (1996) *Ramesside Inscriptions: Translated and Annotated: Translations Volume II: Ramesses II, Royal Inscriptions.*
RIME	Royal Inscriptions of Mesopotamia: Early Periods
RlA	Erich Ebeling, Bruno Meissner, et al. (eds) (1932–2018) *Reallexikon der Assyriologie und Vorderasiatischen Archäologie* (vols 1–16).
RSO	Monograph series Ras Shamra-Ougarit: RSO 4: Pierre Bordreuil (ed.) (1991) *Une bibliotheque au sud de la ville: les textes de la 34e campagne (1973).* RSO 7: Dennis Pardee (ed.) (1988) *Les textes para-mythologiques de la 24ᵉ Campagne (1961).*
SAAS	State Archives of Assyria Studies
SAK	*Studien zur altägyptischen Kultur*
SANE	Studies on the Ancient Near East
SAOC	Studies in Ancient Oriental Civilization
SBL	Society of Biblical Literature
SBLASP	SBL Abstracts and Seminar Papers
SBLBMI	SBL Bible and its Modern Interpreters
SBLDS	SBL Dissertation Series
SBLMS	SBL Monograph Series
SBLSBL	SBL Studies in Biblical Literature
SBLSBS	SBL Sources for Biblical Study
SBLSCS	SBL Septuagint and Cognate Studies
SBLTT	SBL Texts and Translations
SBT	Studies in Biblical Theology
SEL	*Studi epigrafici e linguistici*
SHANE	Studies in the History of the Ancient Near East
SHCANE	Studies in the History and Culture of the Ancient Near East
SJOT	*Scandinavian Journal of the Old Testament*
SMEA	*Studi Micenei ed Egeo-Anatolici*
SWBA	Social World of Biblical Antiquity
TA	*Tel Aviv*
TRu	*Theologische Rundschau*
TSSI	J. C. L. Gibson (1973–81) *Textbook of Syrian Semitic Inscriptions* (vols 1–4).

TZ	*Theologische Zeitschrift*
UF	*Ugarit-Forschung*
Urk.	G. Steindorff (1906–58) *Urkunden des ägyptischen Altertums* (4 vols).
VT	*Vetus Testamentum*
VTSup	Supplements to *Vetus Testamentum*
WBC	Word Bible Commentary
WMANT	Wissenschaftliche Monographien zum Alten und Neuen Testament
WO	*Welt des Orients*
ZA	*Zeitschrift für Assyrologie*
ZAH	*Zeitschrift für Althebräistik*
ZAR	*Zeitschrift für altorientalische und biblische Rechtsgeschichte*
ZAW	*Zeitschrift für die attestamentliche Wissenschaft*
ZDPV	*Zeitschrift des Deutschen Palästina-Vereins*
ZTK	*Zeitschrift für Theologie und Kirche*
§	Marks the sections of the text for cross referencing

Part I

Introduction

CHAPTER 1

Introduction

C. Frevel (2016) *Geschichte Israels*; **L. L. Grabbe** (2007) *Ancient Israel: What Do We Know and How Do We Know It?*; **idem** (2017) *Ancient Israel: What Do We Know and How Do We Know It?* (2nd edn); **N. Grimal** (1992) *A History of Ancient Egypt*; **E. Hornung, R. Krauss, and D. A. Warburton (eds)** (2006) *Ancient Egyptian Chronology*; **E. A. Knauf and P. Guillaume** (2016) *A History of Biblical Israel: The Fate of the Tribes and Kingdoms from Merenptah to Bar Kochba*; **E. A. Knauf and H. M. Niemann** (2021) *Geschichte Israels und Judas im Altertum*; **A. E. Kuhrt** (1995) *The Ancient Near East c. 3000–300 BC, Volumes 1-2*; *LdÄ*; **G. Lehmann** (2003) 'The United Monarchy in the Countryside: Jerusalem, Judah, and the Shephelah during the Tenth Century B.C.E.', in A. G. Vaughn and A. E. Killebrew (eds), *Jerusalem in Bible and Archaeology: The First Temple Period*: 117–62; **M. Liverani** (2014) *The Ancient Near East: History, Society and Economy*; **M. Van De Mieroop** (2003) *A History of the Ancient Near East, ca. 3000-323 BC*; *NEAEHL*; *OEAE*; **A. Ofer** (1994) '"All the Hill Country of Judah": From a Settlement Fringe to a Prosperous Monarchy', in I. Finkelstein and N. Na'aman (eds), *From Nomadism to Monarchy: Archaeological and Historical Aspects of Early Israel*: 92–121; **D. B. Redford** (1992a) *Egypt, Canaan, and Israel in Ancient Times*; *RlA*; **M. Steiner and A. E. Killebrew (eds)** (2014) *The Oxford Handbook of the Archaeology of the Levant, c. 8000–332 BCE*; **H. Weippert** (1988) *Palästina in vorhellenistischer Zeit*.

1.1 AIMS

The earliest mention of the name 'Israel' in history is found in an inscription by Merenptah from about 1208 BCE (§6.3.4). We know, therefore, that an entity called Israel had its origins already in the second millennium BCE. If that entity in Merenptah's inscription had anything to do with the historical kingdom of Israel – which most scholars accept – then Israel (in some form) originated probably as early as the mid-second millennium and perhaps even earlier. It is part of the purpose of the present study to explore these roots.

The biblical text of course has the ancestors of Israel active already by this time. In the text only a few generations separate Abraham from the worldwide flood (Gen. 11:10-26), and a past generation of scholars commonly dated Abraham to about 2000 BCE. As we shall see, the biblical text cannot be taken at face value in this case (§1.2), but it illustrates that were we to be guided by the text, much of Israel's prehistory would fit quite comfortably into the second millennium BCE. We shall see whether this is ultimately likely to be historical, but it gives us reason to want to know more about what was happening in the ancient Near East during this important millennium.

The aim of the present study is to give a survey of ancient Near Eastern history as a context for events in Canaan where the kingdoms of Israel and Judah existed in the first millennium BCE. The focus will be on the area of Canaan, often referred to – and this is a neutral geographical term without political or ideological implications – as Palestine. Primary sources (archaeology, inscriptions and contemporary texts) will be emphasized as the basis for any history of the time, though the views of present-day scholars will be considered where possible. The present study will thus link up with *Ancient Israel: What Do We Know and How Do We Know it?* (Grabbe 2017), which is primarily set in the first millennium BCE, though the contents relating to the earlier chapters of that book will be considered here in more detail.

As noted above, the emphasis for the history of Canaan will be on primary sources. This means that the chapters on Syria and Canaan will have a discussion of original sources. This is not the case with other areas of ancient Near Eastern history, mainly Egypt and Mesopotamia. Original sources are often used and will be cited, but much background history depends on standard scholarly references, some of which can be noted here. A. Kuhrt (1995) surveys the whole of the ancient Near East, including Egypt. Otherwise, works tend to specialize either on Egypt or on Mesopotamia or on Asia Minor (where relevant, Syria-Palestine is often included in both sorts of reference). For Egypt, important are the *Lexikon der Ägyptologie* (*LdÄ*, 1975–92), *The Oxford Encyclopedia of Ancient Egypt* (*OEAE*, 2001), and the works of Grimal 1992; Redford 1992a; Hornung/Kraus/Warburton 2006. For Mesopotamia and Asia Minor, this includes the *Reallexikon der Assyriologie und Vorderasiatischen Archäologie* (*RlA*, 1932–2018), and the works of Liverani 2014 and Mieroop 2003. Histories of Israel include Knauf/Guillaume 2016, Frevel 2016, and Knauf/Niemann 2021. For archaeology which will be discussed primarily with regard to the Levant, Steiner/Killebrew 2014 is the primary reference source, followed by Weippert 1988, though the *NEAEHL* is used for individual sites. Many specialized works on individual nations, empires, periods, and topics will be cited at the appropriate places.

1.2 PRINCIPLES OF HISTORICAL METHOD

G. G. Iggers (1997) *Historiography in the Twentieth Century: From Scientific Objectivity to the Postmodern Challenge*; **E. A. Knauf** (1991a) 'From History to Interpretation', in D. V. Edelman (ed.), *The Fabric of History: Text, Artifact and Israel's Past*: 26–64.

INTRODUCTION

The main considerations in writing a history of this period are the same as those laid out for a history of ancient Israel and of the Jews: Grabbe 2007: 3–18; Grabbe 2017: 4–38. Only a brief summary will be given here, rather than a repetition of the points already discussed in detail in the works cited. The principles guiding the present study include the following:

- All potential sources should be considered. Nothing should be ruled out *a priori*. After a full critical evaluation has been undertaken, some sources might be excluded, but this is only *a posteriori*.
- Preference should be given to primary sources, i.e., those contemporary or nearly contemporary with the events being described (a concept expounded by L. von Ranke [Iggers 1997: 24; Knauf 1991a: 46]). This means mainly archaeology and inscriptions, but also the many cuneiform and hieroglyphic texts that are roughly contemporary with the events they refer to. The biblical text is almost always a secondary source, written and edited long after the events ostensibly described. In some cases, the text may depend on earlier sources, but these sources were edited and adapted; in any case the source has to be dug out from the present context.
- The context of the *longue durée* must always be recognized and given an essential part in the interpretation. One of the factors often forgotten is the difference between Israel in the north and Judah in the south. There was a considerable disparity of natural resources and economy between the two, with Judah continually the poorer. There are reasons for this (Lehmann 2003: 149–62; Ofer 1994: 93–5). In Judah the agriculture was largely subsistence and disadvantaged by lack of good soil for grain growing and rainfall of 300–500 mm per annum. The better soils around Hebron had their value reduced by low rainfall. This meant that pastoralism was an important pursuit. In competition with Israel, Judah definitely came off second best. When Palestine enters the inscriptions of other nations, such as the Assyrians, in the first millennium BCE, there is already a division between Israel and Judah. This long-term division is also hinted at in a number of biblical passages (2 Sam. 2:4; 5:4; Judges 5), in spite of a supposed twelve-tribe nation.
- Each episode or event has to be judged on its own merits. Even secondary sources have their uses, while primary sources may well contradict one another. Historical reconstruction requires all data to be used, critically scrutinized, evaluated, and a judgment made as to the most likely scenario in the light of all that is known.
- All reconstructions are provisional. New data, new perspectives, new theories may suggest other – better – ways to interpret the data. This openness to new ways of thinking and new configurations of events always needs to be there.
- All reconstructions have to be argued for. There can be no default position. You cannot just follow the text unless it can be disproved (sometimes expressed in the nonsensical phrase, 'innocent until proved guilty' – as if the text were a defendant in court; if there is a forensic analogy, the text is a witness whose veracity must be probed and tested). The only valid arguments are historical ones. Ideology, utility, theology, morality, politics, authority – none of these has a place in judging how to reconstruct an event. The only argumentation allowed is that based on historical principles. Naturally, subjectivity is inevitable in the process, and

all historians are human and have their weaknesses and blind spots. This is why each must argue for their viewpoint and then subject the result to the judgment of peers, who are also human and subjective.

1.3 CHRONOLOGY

P. S. Ash (1999) *David, Solomon and Egypt: A Reassessment*; **G. Barkay** (1992) 'The Iron Age II–III', in Amnon Ben-Tor (ed.), *The Archaeology of Ancient Israel*: 302–73; **N. Coldstream** (2003) 'Some Aegean Reactions to the Chronological Debate in the Southern Levant', *TA* 30: 247–58; **I. Finkelstein** (1995b) 'The Date of the Settlement of the Philistines in Canaan', *TA* 22: 213–39; **idem** (1996a) 'The Archaeology of the United Monarchy: An Alternative View', *Levant* 28: 177–87; **idem** (2005a) 'A Low Chronology Update: Archaeology, History and Bible', in T. E. Levy and T. Higham (eds), *The Bible and Radiocarbon Dating: Archaeology, Text and Science*: 31–42; **idem** (2005b) 'High or Low: Megiddo and Reḥov', in T. E. Levy and T. Higham (eds), *The Bible and Radiocarbon Dating: Archaeology, Text and Science*: 302–9; **I. Finkelstein and E. Piasetzky** (2003) 'Wrong and Right: High and Low – ^{14}C Dates from Tel Reḥov and Iron Age', *TA* 30: 283–95; **P. James** (1991) *Centuries of Darkness: A Challenge to the Conventional Chronology of Old World Archaeology*; **P. James and P. G. van der Veen** (2015) *Solomon and Shishak: Current Perspectives from Archaeology, Epigraphy, History and Chronology*; **P. James, I. J. Thorpe, N. Kokkinos, R. Morkot, and J. Frankish** (1992) 'Centuries of Darkness: A Reply to Critics', *Cambridge Archaeological Journal* 2: 127–44; **A. E. Killebrew** (2008) 'Aegean-Style Pottery and Associated Assemblages in the Southern Levant: Chronological Implications Regarding the Tradition from the Late Bronze Age II to the Iron I and the Appearance of the Philistines', in L. L. Grabbe (ed.), *Israel in Transition: From Late Bronze II to Iron IIA (c. 1250–850 BCE): The Archaeology*: 54–71; **P. L. Kohl** (1995) Review of P. James, *Centuries of Darkness*, *Journal of Interdisciplinary History* 26: 274–5; **A. Mazar** (2004) 'Greek and Levantine Iron Age Chronology: A Rejoinder', *IEJ* 54: 24–36; **idem** (2005) 'The Debate over the Chronology of the Iron Age in the Southern Levant: Its History, the Current Situation, and a Suggested Resolution', in T. E. Levy and T. Higham (eds), *The Bible and Radiocarbon Dating: Archaeology, Text and Science*: 15–30; **idem** (2007) 'The Spade and the Text: The Interaction between Archaeology and Israelite History Relating to the Tenth–Ninth Centuries BCE', in H. G. M. Williamson (ed.), *Understanding the History of Ancient Israel*: 143–71; **idem** (2008) 'From 1200 to 850 BCE: Remarks on Some Selected Archaeological Issues', in L. L. Grabbe (ed.), *Israel in Transition: From Late Bronze II to Iron IIA (c. 1250–850 BCE): The Archaeology*: 86–120; **A. Mazar, H. J. Bruins, N. Panitz-Cohen, and J. van der Plicht** (2005) 'Ladder of Time at Tel Reḥov: Stratigraphy, Archaeological Context, Pottery and Radiocarbon Dates', in T. E. Levy and T. Higham (eds), *The Bible and Radiocarbon Dating: Archaeology, Text and Science*: 193–255; **E. Piasetzky and I. Finkelstein** (2005) '^{14}C Results from Megiddo, Tel Dor, Tel Reḥov and Tel Hadar', in T. E. Levy and T. Higham (eds), *The*

Bible and Radiocarbon Dating: Archaeology, Text and Science: 294–309; **I. Sharon, A. Gilboa, and E. Boaretto** (2008) 'The Iron Age Chronology of the Levant: The State-of-Research at the ¹⁴C Dating Project, Spring 2006', in Lester L. Grabbe (ed.), *Israel in Transition: From Late Bronze II to Iron IIA (c. 1250–850 BCE): The Archaeology*: 177–92; **I. Sharon, A. Gilboa, E. Boaretto, and A. J. T. Jull** (2005) 'The Early Iron Age Dating Project: Introduction, Methodology, Progress Report and an Update on the Tel Dor Radiometric Dates', in T. E. Levy and T. Higham (eds) *The Bible and Radiocarbon Dating: Archaeology, Text and Science*: 65–92; **A. J. Shortland** (2005) 'Shishak, King of Egypt: the Challenges of Egyptian Calendrical Chronology', in T. E. Levy and T. Higham (eds), *The Bible and Radiocarbon Dating: Archaeology, Text and Science*: 43–54; **D. Ussishkin** (2007a) 'Samaria, Jezreel and Megiddo: Royal Centres of Omri and Ahab', in L. L. Grabbe (ed.), *Ahab Agonistes: The Rise and Fall of the Omri Dynasty*: 293–309; **R. Wallenfels** (2019) 'Shishak and Shoshenq: A Disambiguation', *JAOS* 139: 487–500.

The dating of persons and events in the second millennium is fraught with problems, and a variety of chronological schemes have been used by ancient Near Eastern specialists, which are usually divided into two or three versions: the high, the middle (which some eliminate), and the low dating (this has little or nothing to do with the debate over Israel Finkelstein's 'low chronology' for the early first millennium BCE [Grabbe 2017: 83–5]). There is a tendency to favour the middle dating, but this may be more from an instinct to go for the moderate middle rather than compelling scientific arguments. In any case, there seems to be no consensus for one system as opposed to another overall, though in some areas there is more agreement than in others. The following will be the guide used here unless otherwise referenced:

Egyptian chronology: especially Hornung/Kraus/Warburton 2006; also Grimal 1992; Kuhrt 1995.
Mesopotamian chronology: Liverani 2014; Mieroop 2003; Kuhrt 1995.
Chronology of Canaan: all of the above.

However, the chronological calculations and estimates by specialists for the third millennium and much of the second for Egypt and Mesopotamia still vary by as much as half a century or even more; there is certainly no agreed-on scheme among Near Eastern scholars at the moment. Therefore, dates given here are often rounded off and should be considered only as a general guide. For more exact estimates (yet still with wide differences!) see the works cited above.

From an archaeological perspective, the third and second millennium BCE is conventionally divided into several eras, which will be roughly dated as follows:

Early Bronze Age (EBA): *c.* 3200–2000 BCE.
Middle Bronze Age (MBA): *c.* 2000–1600 BCE.
Late Bronze Age (LBA): *c.* 1600–1200 BCE.
Iron Age I (IA I): *c.* 1200–1000 BCE.
Iron Age IIA (IA IIA): *c.* 1000–900 BCE.

Because the present study needs to take in the early Israelite monarchy, it will take in the time from about 3000 to 900 BCE, though it is the second millennium BCE that receives the most attention. These are only rough guides and archaeological divisions do not always map easily onto those based on texts. This means that there is not a watertight division between the sections and chapters of this book. Some topics spill across the chronological divisions and may need to be discussed outside the boundaries given above.

For the period of the early monarchy, the invasion of Shoshenq has been used extensively to date specific sites with a destruction layer. Yet whether Shoshenq's topographical list relates an actual invasion of his or is only a traditional compilation is very much a debatable point (§8.5.8). In any case, a widespread destruction by Shoshenq is by no means a certainty. Also, as D. Ussishkin points out, Shoshenq's treatment of various sites may have differed; e.g., the stela erected in Megiddo suggests a site occupied rather than destroyed. Recently, however, there have been challenges to Shoshenq's dating and to general Egyptian chronology as a guide, primarily from P. James and his followers. First came his initial study (James 1991, with contributions by others), which challenged Greek, Egyptian, and ancient Near Eastern chronology in a sweeping fashion. Its main point was downgrading the change from the Late Bronze to Iron I from about 1200 BCE to about 950 BCE, which put David and Solomon about the time of the reign of Ramesses II. Reviewers (e.g., Kohl 1995) generally commended his willingness to challenge a widespread consensus, but pointed out the major weakness of the study: it focuses on revising chronology but does not adequately address the problems this revision creates for a full history of the period.

James and his fellow contributors replied to critics (James/Thorpe/Kokkinos/Morkot/Frankish 1992), but the next main contribution was the collection of essays edited by P. James and P. G. van der Veen (2015) which focused on the time of Solomon and Shishak. This is too recent to be reviewed by many, though it was given a cautious welcome by R. Wallenfels (2019). In the collection, James and others defend the identification of Shishak with Ramesses III; however, the essayists do not take a uniform point of view, and a number depend on the traditional equation of Shishak with Shoshenq I (e.g., A. M. Dodson, S. Ben-Dor Evian, and T. L. Sagrillo). While the problems with Shoshenq's invasion are clear, as discussed in a subsequent chapter (§8.5.8), the solution does not appear to be redating Egyptian history by two and a half centuries.

One of the most controversial but also potentially important developments is Israel Finkelstein's 'low chronology' (LC). It does not generally affect the time period covered in the present volume but is mentioned in passing a few times (especially in chap. 8). This thesis, advanced in its first full form in the mid-1990s, dated most of the events and finds of the Iron I and Iron IIA about a century later than had been common among archaeologists. Finkelstein's original study (Finkelstein 1996a) argued that conventional chronology is based on the twin pillars of the stratigraphy of Megiddo and the Philistine Bichrome ware. Since then the debate has widened considerably to take in radiocarbon dating, correlation with the Aegean, the context of the Assyrian expansion in the ninth century, and other factors. A major opponent of the 'low chronology' has been Amihai Mazar (2005) who has developed what he calls the 'modified conventional chronology' (MCC). This is similar to the traditional chronology but extends the Iron IIA from 980 to 830, that is, covering most of both the tenth and the ninth centuries. This allows three major pottery periods (Iron IB, Iron IIA, Iron IIB), each lasting about 150 years, in the 450 years between approximately 1150 and 700 BCE. The following are some of the main issues around which the arguments – pro and con – have revolved:

- I. Finkelstein (e.g., 2005a: 34) points out that conventional dating is strongly – if not always explicitly – influenced by the biblical text. This sometimes leads to circular arguments in which the argument depends on the biblical text but then moves around to arguing that the data support the biblical text. A good example is Shoshenq's invasion (see next point). Yet all parties have appealed to the biblical text in the discussion of the two key sites of Samaria and Jezreel (Ussishkin 2007a; Finkelstein 2005a: 36–8).
- The invasion of Shoshenq has been a central benchmark for dating historical and archaeological data, yet the dating of when it happened has depended on the biblical text, since 1 Kgs 14:25-28 puts it in the fifth year of Rehoboam (Finkelstein 1996a: 180). A recent Egyptological evaluation has dated the event to 917 BCE (Shortland 2005), but P. S. Ash (1999: 30–1) has shown that it could be anytime in the period 970 to 915 BCE. Yet this is not the end of the matter, because it is not clear exactly what sort of measures were taken by Shoshenq. It had been assumed that his invasion resulted in widespread destruction of sites, but it has been argued that if Shoshenq planned to use Megiddo as the place to plant his royal stela, he would hardly have destroyed the site (Ussishkin 2007a). In fact, it 'has not been proven that any sites were destroyed by Shishak in 925 B.C.E., and the attribution of destruction layers to the end of the tenth century at many sites is mere conjecture' (Barkay 1992: 306–7). For further discussion, see §8.5.8.
- N. Coldstream (2003: 256) argues that the 'low chronology' best fits the situation in the Aegean, but A. Mazar (2004) stands against this. Yet Killebrew (2008) also relates the situation in Philistia to the broader Mediterranean pottery context and agrees that the low chronology 'with some minor revisions' would best fit the situation elsewhere in the Mediterranean: see next point.
- It seems to be generally agreed that Philistine Monochrome (or Mycenaean IIIC:1b or Mycenaean IIIC Early to Middle) appears in the late twelfth century, developing from imported Mycenaean IIIC:1a (Mycenaean IIIC Early or Late Helladic IIIC Early). The Egyptian 20th Dynasty and the Egyptian presence in Palestine came to an end about 1140/1130 (Mazar 2007). Yet no Philistine Monochrome ware appears together with Egyptian pottery of the 20th Dynasty, not even in nearby sites such as Tel Batash and Tel Mor, which suggests that Philistine Monochrome is post-1135 BCE, and the Philistine Bichrome is even later – the eleventh and perhaps much of the tenth century (Finkelstein 1995b: 218–20, 224; 2005a: 33). A. Mazar (2008) responds: (1) Canaanite pottery assembly in Ashdod XIII and Tel Miqne is typical of the thirteenth and beginning of the twelfth centuries BCE, and Lachish VI must have been contemporary; (2) local Mycenaean IIIC is inspired by the Mycenaean IIIC pottery in Cyprus but this disappears after the mid-twelfth century; (3) although D. Ussishkin and Finkelstein claim it is inconceivable that locally made Mycenaean IIIC did not reach contemporary sites in Philistia and the Shephelah, this ignores cultural factors that could limit it to a few urban centres; the early stage of Philistine settlement lasted perhaps only a generation, and Lachish is at least twenty-five km from the major Philistine cities which is sufficient to create a cultural border; (4) the Philistine settlement was possible perhaps because of the state of the Egyptian domination of Canaan at this time, and Philistine Bichrome pottery slowly emerged as a hybrid style later, probably during the last quarter of the twelfth century.

- Yet in a thorough study of the Aegean-style pottery A. E. Killebrew (2008) argues that the high chronology (two-wave theory) would date the Philistine Monochrome (Mycenaean IIIC:1b) to about 1200 BCE as the result of an early proto-Philistine wave of Sea Peoples, while the middle chronology would date this pottery to about 1175 BCE, with the Bichrome developing from it in the mid-twelfth century. Such datings are becoming more problematic in light of the increasing consensus that Mycenaean IIIC:1b should be equated to Mycenaean IIIC Early (into Middle) which is dated to the mid-twelfth. With some revisions (such as dating the initial appearance of Mycenaean IIIC Early phase 2 to about 1160 BCE), the low chronology would best fit the dating of Mycenaean IIIC Early to Middle at other sites in the eastern Mediterranean and would also provide a more reasonable dating of Bichrome to the eleventh continuing into the tenth, based on LB II–Iron I stratigraphic sequences at both Tel Miqne and Ashdod.
- Pottery assemblages and the dating of various strata: here there is a surprising difference of interpretation between professional archaeologists whom one would expect to agree about the facts in the ground: the relationship between the strata in the sites of Hazor, Samaria, Jezreel and Megiddo; the interpretation of Jerusalem; the dating of Lachish; the dating of the Negev destruction.
- Current dating leaves a strange gap in the ninth century in the dating of archaeological remains (Finkelstein 1996a). We have much in the tenth and the eighth centuries but not the ninth, leaving a very thin stratigraphy over 350 years. For example, Tel Miqne and Tel Batash have thick accumulations related to Philistine Bichrome ware, a ninth-century gap, then limited Iron II remains. Other sites show a similar gap: Tell Halif, Tel Mor, Tell Beit Mirsim, Ashdod, Tel Haror, Gezer, Jerusalem. The LC closes the unexplained gap between monumental architectures of the tenth century and evidence of public administration for the late ninth to the eighth centuries BCE.
- The monuments previously associated with the United Monarchy are redated from the second half of the tenth century to the early ninth. It strips the United Monarchy of its monumental buildings, including ashlar masonry and proto-Ionic columns. We have evidence of fortifications in the tenth century, but the main mounds in the north (Megiddo and Gezer) and the south (Beersheba and Lachish) only date to the ninth century or later. This means that the strong and historically attested Omri kingdom is the first state in Palestine and preceded the geographically weaker Judah. Taking a global perspective, this is what one would expect rather than the anomalous Jerusalem-centred and Judah-dominated kingdom of David and Solomon.

The most recent attempt to find a way to pin down the matter of dating involves radiocarbon dates. Yet a database of radiometric dates from a wide variety of sites is needed; such is now being developed and may resolve the issue (Sharon et al. 2005; Sharon et al. 2008). In the meantime, there are significant differences in interpretation. The reasons for this have been well laid out by A. Mazar:

The many stages of selecting the samples, the pre-treatment, the method and process of dating, and the wide standard deviation of Accelerator Mass Spectrometry dates may create a consistent bias, outliers or an incoherent series of dates. The calibration process adds further problems, related to the nature of the calibration curve in each period. In our case, there are two difficulties: one is the many wiggles and the shape of the curve for the twelfth–eleventh centuries BCE. This leads to a wide variety of possible calibrated dates within the twelfth–eleventh centuries BCE. The other problem is the plateau between 880 and 830 BCE, and the curve relating to the last third of the tenth century BCE, which in certain parts is at the same height as the ninth century BCE plateau. In many cases the calibrated dates of a single radiocarbon date is in both the tenth and the ninth centuries BCE, and in the ninth century BCE more precise dates between 880 and 830 BCE are impossible. These limitations are frustrating, and make close dating during this time frame a difficult task. It seems that in a debate like ours, over a time-span of about 80 years, we push the radiometric method to the edges of its capability, and perhaps even beyond that limit. [Mazar 2005: 22]

The result is that a variety of radiocarbon dates has been made at key sites, with some arguing that they support the 'modified conventional chronology' (Mazar 2005: 22–3; Mazar et al. 2005); and others, that they support the 'low chronology' (Finkelstein and Piasetzky 2003; Piasetzky and Finkelstein 2005; Finkelstein 2005b; Sharon et al. 2005; Sharon et al. 2008).

1.4 TERMINOLOGY AND OTHER TECHNICAL MATTERS

- The transliteration of Hebrew will be clear to scholars who work in that language, generally following the standard forms; however, I have used *v* and *f* for the non-*dagesh*ed forms of *bet* and *pe*, while *w* is always used for *waw* (or *vav*, even though now pronounced *v* by most modern users of Hebrew).
- Proper names generally follow the conventional forms used in English Bibles or by Near Eastern scholars where they are not biblical names.
- Translations are normally my own, unless the source of the translation is explicitly given.
- The term 'Judaean' is normally restricted to those who live in Judaea or were at least born there. Otherwise, the term 'Jew' is used for anyone in the Jewish ethnic community or who is labelled יהודי/יהדי/Ἰουδαῖος/Iudaeus in the historical sources.
- 'Palestine' is purely a geographical term, used because it has been widely accepted for many years and because it is sometimes difficult to find a suitable substitute.

CHAPTER 2

The Third-Millennium Context

H. Klengel (1992) *Syria 3000 to 300 B.C.: A Handbook of Political History*; **A. Kuhrt** (1995) *The Ancient Near East c. 3000–300 BC*; **M. Liverani** (2014) *The Ancient Near East: History, Society and Economy*; **D. B. Redford** (1992a) *Egypt, Canaan, and Israel in Ancient Times*.

What has been called 'history' or the historical period, versus 'pre-history', began about 3000 BCE (or perhaps a couple of centuries earlier). That is, writing was invented about then which eventually made possible the writing of historical narratives, as opposed to reconstructing history from material remains. 'Pre-history' is of course history, just of a different kind, and the earliest writings were not historical narratives in any case. Yet the invention of writing at approximately the same time in both Egypt and Mesopotamia (and perhaps also elsewhere in the world, such as China and Meso-America) made possible written records which could recount certain sorts of information not easily gleaned from archaeology. The ability to write represented an important step forward in communication and developing culture but also in preserving knowledge for later generations.

From the point of view of the historian of ancient Near Eastern peoples the third millennium marks a significant advance. It was also the time when many of the major historical actors arose in some form or other. We can use a quick survey of its history to form the initial bookend for the history of the second millennium. At this stage in history Egypt, Mesopotamia, and Anatolia had little interaction, but each was undergoing internal developments that were noteworthy for the history to come in the second millennium. Some of these are laid out under the individual regions below.

2.1 EGYPT

J. Baines (1995) 'Kingship, Definition of Culture, and Legitimation', in D. O'Connor and D. P. Silverman (eds), *Ancient Egyptian Kingship*: 3–47; **B. Bell** (1971) 'The Dark Ages in Ancient History. I. The First Dark Age in Egypt', *AJA* 75: 1–26; **N. Grimal** (1992) *A History of Ancient Egypt*; **W. Helck** (1956) *Untersuchungen zu Manetho und* *den Ägyptischen Königslisten*; **idem** (1971) *Die Beziehungen Ägyptens zu Vorderasien im 3. und 2. Jahrtausend v. Chr.*; **E. Hornung, R. Krauss, and D. A. Warburton (eds)** (2006) *Ancient Egyptian Chronology*; **M. Lichtheim** (1973) *Ancient Egyptian Literature, Volume 1: The Old and Middle Kingdoms*; **idem** (1988) *Ancient Egyptian Autobiographies, Chiefly of the Middle Kingdom: A Study and an Anthology*; **M. Nuzzolo and J. Krejčí** (2017) 'Heliopolis and the Solar Cult in the Third Millennium BC', *Ägypten und Levante* 27: 357–80; **D. B. Redford** (1986a) *Pharaonic King-Lists, Annals and Day-Books: A Contribution to the Study of the Egyptian Sense of History*; **idem** (1986c) 'Egypt and Western Asia in the Old Kingdom', *JARCE* 23: 125–43; **A. Schlott** (1989) *Schrift und Schreiber im Alten Ägypten*; **W. G. Waddell** (1940) *Manetho*.

For centuries the main source of information on ancient Egypt was the Greek account of the Egyptian priest Manetho from around 300 BCE, called *Aegyptiaca* (Waddell 1940). Unfortunately, the original was lost, and what survives are quotations, primarily from Josephus and from Julius Africanus and Eusebius. Once the Egyptian language was deciphered in the nineteenth century and the preserved inscriptions could be read, new information was forthcoming from Egyptian inscriptions that allowed Manetho's account to be checked, at least in part (Redford 1986; Helck 1956). The shortcomings of Manetho's account are clear. Apart from scribal copying errors and the epitomizing of those who preserved his writing, it included legendary material, stylized accounts of the past that were created long before Manetho's time, and dynasties in linear order which were actually contemporaneous. Yet there is still much in Manetho's account that is useful, not least the 30-dynasty scheme that continues to be used (in appropriately modified form) by Egyptologists today.

Egyptian hieroglyphic writing originated about 3000 BCE in what is conventionally referred to as the *Early Dynastic Period*, about 3150 to 2700 BCE, including Dynasties 1-2. (Hornung/Krauss/Warburton [2006] go against others in including Dynasties 1-3, which they date from 2900 to 2545 BCE). The first king of Dynasty 1, according to Manetho, was Menes who united Upper (southern) and Lower (northern and the Delta) Egypt by military action. This looks to be a stereotyped tradition. Whether there was a single ruler behind Menes (such as Nar-mer, the first king, or Aha, the second king, of Dynasty 1 according to the inscriptions) or whether he is a composite figure, it appears that Upper Egypt gradually annexed Lower Egypt over a long period of time, rather than by a single unifying conquest. It was during this period that the main characteristics of Egyptian rule and civilization took shape. These especially included the ideology/theology of the ruler or pharaoh (the title originally meant the 'palace' [from *pr* 'house' and *ꜣ* 'great') and the bureaucracy which became the backbone of Egyptian administration and the main strength of Egyptian culture.

The king was the mediator between the human and the divine realm (see the discussion in Baines 1995). He was the personification of Horus while alive (each king had a Horus name), while the dead king became personified as Osiris, god of the underworld. It was his duty to keep the cosmos operating, to maintain *maat* ('order') against the forces of chaos. The dead king had the responsibility of protecting the sun Re in its nightly passage through the underworld from its setting in the west to reach the place of its rising in the east. This journey of the sun god's boat was threatened at various points by demonic forces (especially the serpent Apophis) that had to be fended off by the sun's protectors, which included the deceased king in the persona of Seth. If they failed, the world would be plunged into darkness, and all life would come to an end. In the Old Kingdom only the king and his family had access to an afterlife, but eventually (perhaps at the end of the Old Kingdom) eternal life became available also to high officials. Hence, the emphasis on the mortuary cult.

Although the priest of the gods, the king could not be everywhere at once, which meant that he had to have representatives to perform cultic duties at various temple sites. Originally, this seems to have meant that administrators also had religious duties; however, a professional priesthood developed to serve permanently in temples. The solar cult appears to have reached its height perhaps in the 4th Dynasty, but solar temples of several Old Kingdom rulers have been excavated (Nuzzolo/Krejčí 2017).

The bureaucracy developed with writing and the emergence of the pharaonic state. This assisted the king in his duties to the nation and the people. It is well documented over three millennia and more (Schlott 1989). In Egyptian inscriptions 'scribe' and 'administrator' are often used interchangeably. Briefly, scribes were initially in the service of the king and also took care of the affairs of the administration. They had a variety of different functions, just as the higher officials in the administration had functions different from the ordinary scribe at the bottom of the ladder, as their titles show (Schlott 1989: 93–4). At the lower level were those scribes who recorded the numbers of cattle or the yield of the harvest (primarily for tax purposes) and perhaps wrote letters for the illiterate at the village level. At the top were the high officials next to the king: they were often members of the pharaoh's family or individuals from the leading families of the aristocracy who were trained as scribes. But they employed a 'middle level' of scribes who did the actual work of writing, recording, and translating. There was a certain egalitarianism, since a scribe could sometimes rise through the ranks by ability and intellect and not just by birth alone. Yet, although there are examples in which scribes rose in status in the hierarchy, generally the sons of those at the bottom of the hierarchy themselves remained also at the bottom, and so on.

Dynasty 3 conventionally initiated what is referred to as the *Old Kingdom*, which traditionally included Dynasties 3-6, though some make it Dynasties 4-8 (*c.* 2700 to 2200 BCE; Hornung/Krauss/Warburton [2006] date Dynasties 4-8 [their Old Kingdom] to 2545 to 2120). The Old Kingdom was the 'pyramid age': the king traditionally had a mortuary temple where he would be buried, with a monument of some sort. This latter developed into the pyramid. The first pyramid was the Stepped Pyramid of Djoser, of Dynasty 3, which still survives near Saqqara. A number of other pyramids were built – or were started but not finished – during Dynasties 2-6, though some continued to be built into the Second Intermediate Period (§3.1.2). This included the famous pyramids of Giza, with the Great Pyramid of Khufu, but many others were built elsewhere up and down the Nile, especially in the vicinity of Memphis and Saqqara (more than a hundred are known of). The later pyramids were often largely or entirely of mud brick and have not survived as well as those entirely of stone.

Trade routes to Nubia and to Syria and Palestine (especially with the city Byblos) were cultivated, though there were also military expeditions to Nubia, Libya, and Sinai. Sinai was the source of turquoise and other precious stones and metals, but Egypt did not try to occupy it on a permanent basis: hence, the periodic raids into the region. Nubia was a source of many luxuries but also some needed products that were not found in Egypt itself, such as gold and fine-grained stone. The desert peoples were a permanent problem, since they might encroach on Egyptian territory at any time (Redford 1986c). It is difficult to know how many actual military campaigns took place, since even peaceful trips to collect tribute might use the language of confrontation and conquest. A number of officials left inscriptions in the form of an autobiography. This was a literary genre that arose in the Old Kingdom and became quite popular among the king's high officials (cf. Lichtheim 1988). They would compose a narrative of their life, with its achievements and accomplishments as faithful servants of the king, to be inscribed in their mortuary chapel (later, these autobiographies could be left on statues and other sites).

One of these was Weni (or Uni) of Dynasty 6 whose autobiography is especially notable (*AEL* 1:18–23). It tells of leading a campaign against the 'Dwellers-across-the-Sand': usually taken to be somewhere in Syria-Palestine (though some see it as no further north than the Delta). He states that this army 'of many tens of thousands' had been assembled by the king from all over Egypt, and he led it not once but five times, whenever the 'Dwellers-across-the-Sand' rebelled. Another was by Pepy-Nakht (*ARE* 1: 163–4), under Pepy II (c. 2216–2153 BCE), who had to retrieve the body of a commander who was building a boat for Punt when he was killed by Asiatics (*Amu*). One presumes this was somewhere on the shores of the Red Sea. Egypt made use of a large labour force of foreigners. Some of these appear to have immigrated peaceably and were ready to work for the Egyptians as a means of making a living. Others, however, appear to have been captives of war enslaved to work for the pharaoh (Redford 1992a: 53). In short, interaction with the peoples of Syria-Palestine seems to have been a regular thing, though how often this was peaceful and how often hostile is difficult to determine.

The enormous monuments to the (dead) king took their toll on resources. The builders were not slaves but ordinary Egyptians who had to contribute their labour during the agriculturally slack time of year. Nevertheless, they had to be fed and housed, and some may have received wages. (This may have led to the impoverishing of the country by the end of the Old Kingdom, though this interpretation remains controversial.) The cult of the sun god reached its peak in Dynasty 4, and the kings all assumed the title *sa Re* ('son of the sun god'). The Pyramid Texts and later the Coffin texts were written during this period (or at least survive from that time), which gives us insight into the contemporary religion and society.

The latter part of Dynasty 6 saw the power of local officials in general increasing. The result was for the pharaoh's hold on Upper Egypt to weaken considerably. The dynasty ended with the first ruling queen, Nitocris, who had the title of 'King of Upper and Lower Egypt' (though the 'King of Upper Egypt' in her title seems to have been wishful thinking). Dynasty 7 was composed of several ephemeral rulers (one quotation from Manetho says '70 kings of Memphis who ruled for 70 days'), and some Egyptologists omit it entirely. In any case, Dynasties 7-8 are included by some as part of the Old Kingdom, but many include them in the *First Intermediate Period* (c. 2120 to 1980 BCE), which also encompasses Dynasties 9-10 (and even Dynasty 11 according to some). The First Intermediate Period was a time of disunity, with several rival dynasties ruling at the same time in the cities of Memphis (Dynasties 7-8), Heracleopolis (Dynasties 9-10), and Thebes (Dynasty 11), though different Egyptologists construct the chronology of the period differently.

Causes of the collapse of the Old Kingdom and the First Intermediate Period are probably multiple (Redford 1992a: 57–63). The amount of resources that went into the tombs of the kings seems – surprisingly – only a minor factor: royal prosperity seems to have been maintained for some of the time before the collapse. A key cause was apparently a long series of low Nile floods, with subsequent poor crops and famine (Bell 1971). Since the king was regarded as the one upholding order not only in society but also in the wider cosmos, the failure of the Nile flood was viewed as in some way his fault. This might explain the many ephemeral rulers that are alleged for this time in the sources, as noted above. A standing feature of descriptions about chaos in society is the entry of Asiatics into the Delta region, but this may have been the result of disorder leading to lack of border control rather than an invasion as such. Asiatics came in because they could, not because they forced themselves.

From a literary point of view the First Intermediate Period seems to have been a productive one, with a number of writings originating in this period (at least according to some scholars, though the writings are given different dates by different scholars). The *Admonitions of Ipuwer* is often assigned to this time (though some put it in the Second Intermediate Period [§3.1.2]). It laments the state of society in which chaos reigns and no one observes the societal rules, restraints, and morality. Some see it as a description of a particular episode in society, but others see it as a paradigmatic lament over what happens when the ruler does not maintain order as he should. Other possible writings are *The Dispute of a Man with his Ba* and *The Eloquent Peasant*. In the first a man asks whether life is worth living (it is not a dialogue on suicide as it has sometimes been labelled). In the second a wealthy steward tries to defraud a poor peasant on the way to market; the peasant first appeals to the local magistrate and eventually to the king, and is successful in the end.

2.2 MESOPOTAMIA

A. Archi (2015) *Ebla and its Archives: Texts, History, and Society*; **G. Buccellati** (1966) *The Amorites of the Ur III Period*; **T. Jacobsen** (1939) *The Sumerian King List*; **M. Liverani (ed.)** (1993) *Akkad: The First World Empire: Structure, Ideology, Traditions*; **P. Matthiae, F. Pinnock, and M. d'Andrea (eds)** (2018) *Ebla and Beyond: Ancient Near Eastern Studies after Fifty Years of Discoveries at Tell Mardikh: Proceedings of the International Congress Held in Rome, 15th–17th December 2014*.

The history of Mesopotamia begins with Sumer, the southern area extending north along the Tigris and Euphrates rivers from the Persian Gulf. It was here that the first city-states arose and where writing was invented. The first part of the third millennium marked the *Early Dynastic Period*, lasting until about 2350 BCE. It had been preceded by the *Uruk Period* (or *Uruk* and *Jemnet Nasr Periods*), starting about 4000 BCE, in which the city of Uruk seems to have been dominant. The *Sumerian King List* (Jacobsen 1939) covers this period, though the early parts are legendary, and it seems to have been compiled from several sources. It is also known in several different versions, the best-known beginning with kings who are said to have ruled before the flood. Kingship was given from heaven but moved around the various cities of Sumer. The ruling kings are listed with their lengths of reign: some of the early ones ruled for fantastically long periods of time, comparable to the long lives of pre-flood patriarchs of Genesis. The *Sumerian King List* can be used as a historiographic text only with caution.

In the Early Dynastic several city-states dominated the region, though none controlled the others: Uruk, Ur, Lagash, Larsa, and Adab in Sumer and Kish in Akkad. Other sites included Umma-Gisha in Sumer and such cities as Akshak and Mari in Akkad. The culture and language were Sumerian, though we begin to find Semitic names in the texts from Akkad in the north. The Sumerian city-states generally had a single ruler for each state, though major temples seem to have been central in most of them with a significant function in the economy. The economy was based on the irrigation of crops from the rivers. One of the important functions of the administration was to oversee the maintenance of the irrigation canals. Some important literature arose during this period, such as the *Epic of Gilgamesh*, which seems to be based on a king of that name over Uruk (in the period *c.* 2700–2500 BCE).

The *Akkadian Empire* was centred on Akkad (Sumerian Agade) in the area north of Sumer. It was initiated by the dynamic king Sargon I (*c.* 2300 BCE) who conquered the region of Sumer and established his rule over both the northern and southern areas. He also reorganized the trade routes, reaching as far as Dilmun (on the western shore of the Persian Gulf in the Bahrain region) and the Indus Valley. A major rival was Elam in the southeast (part of modern Iran), with its capital of Susa. Sargon's grandson Naram-Sin (*c.* 2250 BCE) expanded the empire to reach in theory from 'the Upper Sea to the Lower Sea' (i.e., from the Mediterranean to the Persian Gulf). This included a favourable treaty with Elam. He later moved west to take Ebla. This empire was brought to an end by the Gutians, peoples in the Zagros Mountains (described stereotypically in Akkadian literature as uncultured barbarians). The language of the Akkad region was the Eastern Semitic language of Akkadian, though the Sumerian writing system was adapted by Akkadian scribes to fit their speech (see §2.5 on language and writing).

The *Ur III period*, which succeeded the Akkadian Empire, was the continuation of the Early Dynastic in Sumer, with Ur as the main centre. At first it was under Gutian domination, but a number of the Sumerian cities seemed to have gained independence, including Ur, Uruk, Umma, and Lagish. Finally, Utu-Hegal of Uruk (*c.* 2120 BCE) defeated the Gutians after about a century of their rule and briefly established dominance over the other Sumerian cities. But then Ur-Nammu of Ur (*c.* 2100 BCE) united the cities and established his rule over Sumer and Akkad. His son Shulgi (*c.* 2050 BCE) campaigned to the north, into Assyrian and Hurrian territory. Although his direct rule may not have been imposed, he was able to take control of trade routes that extended from Susa to the east, from Assyria into Anatolia, and from Mari into Syria.

The fall of the Northern Kingdom is frequently ascribed to the 'Amorites'; unfortunately, the term Amorite was often applied indiscriminately by both ancient and modern scholars. Amorites were an important part of Ur III urban society (Buccellati 1966), though there were also pastoral Amorites who were outside settled Sumerian society (on the Amorites generally, see §4.2.3). Bands of marauders – whatever their ethnic identity – were an increasing problem for the Ur III rulers, but the end came with an invasion from a coalition of Elam and the region of Shimashki about 2000 BCE. Yet there had been a weakening of Ur's control over Sumer and Akkad, and a famine from low river floods exacerbated the general situation.

Mari was an important actor from both the Mesopotamian and Syrian point of view. Its main interest relates to the MB period (§3.2.4), the time to which most of its texts are dated, but we now have information on it as early as the third millennium BCE, thanks primarily to the Ebla texts (§2.4.2). Although in Mesopotamia, Mari was on the western extreme and had many contacts with Syria. The Ebla texts cover only a relatively short period of time, but during much of that time Ebla and Mari, though rivals, had friendly relations, with records preserved of the couriers that carried messengers and gifts back and forth between the two powers (cf. §2.4.2). Archaeology has revealed a palace and several temples in Mari in the Early Dynastic III period; the general culture suggests it was a Sumerian centre; however, it was apparently not settled by Sumerians, judging by the linguistic evidence. For a time Mari ruled over the whole Middle and Upper Euphrates region and later conquered Ebla. Not long afterward it was destroyed in turn by Sargon. It was subordinate to Akkad and later to the Ur III kings.

2.3 ANATOLIA

G. Beckman (2001) 'Sargon and Naram-Sin in Hatti: Reflections of Mesopotamian Antiquity among the Hittites', in D. Kuhn and H. Stahl (eds), *Die Gegenwart des Altertums: Formen und Funktionen des Altertumsbezugs in den Hochkulturen der Alten Welt*: 85–91; **T. Bryce** (2005) *The Kingdom of the Hittites*; **M. Van De Mieroop** (2000) 'Sargon of Agade and his Successors in Anatolia', *SMEA* 42: 133–59; **S. Tinney** (1995) 'A New Look at Naram-Sin and the "Great Rebellion"', *JCS* 47: 1–14.

We have little information from the Early Bronze Age, with records really becoming available in the second millennium. This especially includes the Old Assyrian period when Assyria established trading networks with kingdoms in Asia Minor (see further §3.2.2). For the EB period, the indication is that a linguistic group known as the Hatti had early settled in the region, judging from language elements that influenced and were borrowed into later Hittite. Already in the EBA there is evidence of three Indo-European linguistic groups: the Luwian, the Nesite, and the Palaian. Yet there is no clear agreement on whether the Indo-Europeans migrated into the region in the third millennium (as many believe) or were even native to Anatolia from about 7000 BCE (as others argue). Unfortunately, archaeology has not settled the matter. What we can say is that Indo-Europeans were there by the end of the third millennium, and an Indo-European dialect (called Nesite) became the dominant language of the Hittite texts.

References to Anatolia are found in the texts of the Akkadian Empire kings Sargon and Naram-Sin (Mieroop 2000; Beckman 2001; cf. Tinney 1995). One of the reasons Akkad was interested in Anatolia was copper, because of ore deposits and their smelting which developed there. Knowledge of bronze working is also attested, though tin had to be imported since there were no tin deposits in Asia Minor. As a footnote, a few early *Hurrian* inscriptions appear in the late third millennium. Some Hurrian states managed to control territory that had once belonged to the Akkadian Empire but had not been taken over by the Ur III Dynasty. The Hurrians became quite important in the second millennium BCE (§3.3.1).

2.4 SYRIA-PALESTINE

A. Archi (2015) *Ebla and its Archives: Texts, History, and Society*; **A. Ben-Tor** (1982) 'The Relations between Egypt and the Land of Canaan during the Third Millennium B.C.', *JJS* 33: 3–18; **idem** (1986) 'The Trade Relations of Palestine in the Early Bronze Age', *JESHO* 29: 1–27; **idem** (1991) 'New Light on the Relations between Egypt and Southern Palestine during the Early Bronze Age', *BASOR* 281: 3–10; **A. Ben-Tor (ed.)** (1992) *The Archaeology of Ancient Israel*; **B. Couroyer** (1971)

'Ceux-qui-sont-sur-le-sable: Les Hériou-Shâ', *RevB* 78: 558–75; **M. Dunand** (1937) *Fouilles de Byblos: tome 1, 1926–1932: Atlas*; **Erman-Grapow**; **R. O. Faulkner** (1962) *A Concise Dictionary of Middle Egyptian*; **A. H. Gardiner** (1909) *The Admonitions of an Egyptian Sage from a Hieratic Papyrus in Leiden (Pap. Leiden 344 recto)*; **idem** (1947) *Ancient Egyptian Onomastica: Text and Plates*; **A. H. Gardiner, T. E. Peet, and J. Černý** (1955) *The Inscriptions of Sinai, Part II Translations and Commentary*; **R. Gophna** (1976) 'Egyptian Immigration into Southern Canaan during the First Dynasty?', *TA* 3: 31–7; **idem** (1984) 'The Settlement Landscape of Palestine in the Early Bronze Age II–III and Middle Bronze Age II', *IEJ* 34: 24–31; **H. J. Greenfield et al.** (2020) 'Evidence for Movement of Goods and Animals from Egypt to Canaan during the Early Bronze of the Southern Levant: A View from Tell Eṣ-Ṣâfi/Gath', *Ägypten und Levante* 30: 377–97; **W. C. Hayes** (1949) 'The Career of the Great Steward Ḥenenu under Nebḥepetrē' Mentuḥotpe', *JEA* 35: 43–9; **W. Helck** (1971) *Die Beziehungen Ägyptens zu Vorderasien im 3. und 2. Jahrtausend v. Chr.*; **J. Huehnergard and C. Woods** (2004) 'Akkadian and Eblaite', in R. D. Woodard (ed.), *The Cambridge Encyclopedia of the World's Ancient Languages*: 218–80; **M. Krebernik** (1996) 'The Linguistic Classification of Eblaite: Methods, Problems, and Results', in J. S. Cooper and G. M. Schwartz (eds), *The Study of the Ancient Near East in the Twenty-First Century: The William Foxwell Albright Centennial Conference*: 233–51; **J. Leclant** (1984) 'T. P. Pépi Ier VII: Une nouvelle mention des *FNḪW* dans Les Textes des Pyramides', *SAK* 11: 455–60; **T. E. Levy (ed.)** (1998) *The Archaeology of Society in the Holy Land*; **D. Lorton** (1973) 'The So-called "Vile" Enemies of the King of Egypt (in the Middle Kingdom and Dyn. XVIII)', *JARCE* 10: 65–70; **P. Matthiae** (2020) *Ebla: Archaeology and History*; **A. Mazar** (1993) *Archaeology of the Land of the Bible 10,000–586 B.C.E.*; **P. Matthiae, F. Pinnock, and M. d'Andrea (eds)** (2018) *Ebla and Beyond: Ancient Near Eastern Studies after Fifty Years of Discoveries at Tell Mardikh: Proceedings of the International Congress Held in Rome, 15th–17th December 2014*; **P. Montet** (1928) *Byblos et l'Égypte: Quatre campagnes de fouilles à Gebeil, 1921–1922–1923–1924: Texte*; **A.-L. Mourad** (2015) *Rise of the Hyksos: Egypt and the Levant from the Middle Kingdom to the Early Second Intermediate Period*; **L. Nigro et al.** (2019) 'Jericho and the Chronology of Palestine in the Early Bronze Age: A Radiometric Re-Assessment', *Radiocarbon* 61: 211–41; **E. D. Oren** (1973) 'The Overland Route between Egypt and Canaan in the Early Bronze Age (Preliminary Report)', *IEJ* 23: 198–205; **R. B. Parkinson** (1997) *The Tale of Sinuhe and Other Ancient Egyptian Poems 1940–1640 BC.*; **G. Pettinato** (1991) *Ebla: A New Look at History*; **D. B. Redford** (1986) 'Egypt and Western Asia in the Old Kingdom', *JARCE* 23: 125–43; **P. Saretta** (2016) *Asiatics in Middle Kingdom Egypt: Perceptions and Reality*; **M. L. Steiner and A. E. Killebrew (eds)** (2014) *The Oxford Handbook of the Archaeology of the Levant, c. 8000–332 BCE*; **C. Vandersleyen** (1987) 'L'étymologie de Phoïnix, "Phénicien"', in E. Lipiński (ed.), *Phoenicia and the Eastern Mediterranean in the First Millennium B.C.*: 19–22; **A. Vassiliev** (2020) 'Upper Retenu and Lower Retenu', in C. Graves (ed.), *BEC 4: Proceedings of the Fourth British Egyptology Congress University of Manchester, 7–9 September 2018*: 159–67; **W. A. Ward** (1961) 'Egypt and the East Mediterranean in the

Early Second Millennium B. C.', *Orientalia* 30: 22–45; 129–55; **idem** (1963) 'Egypt and the East Mediterranean from Predynastic Times to the End of the Old Kingdom', *JESHO* 6: 1–57; **H. Weippert** (1988) *Palästina in vorhellenistischer Zeit*.

Apart from archaeology our knowledge of Syria and the Levant in the third millennium is episodic. The Ebla texts (see below) impart a valuable insight by providing a brief window onto some of the commercial and political movements in Syria in the mid-third millennium. Byblos also furnishes vase inscriptions that refer to the pharaoh Pepi I and other kings of the 4th and 6th Dynasties. The city was an important trade link for part of the Egyptian Old Kingdom for products that Egypt lacked, especially wood. Ugarit (§5.4.2) had existed since the seventh millennium BCE, but it does not seem to be significant at this time.

2.4.1 Archaeology

Most of our information on Palestine-Canaan at this time comes from archaeology (see especially Steiner/Killebrew 2014; also Levy [ed.] 1998; Weippert 1988; Mazar 1993; and Ben-Tor 1992). The term 'Early Bronze Age' is an archaeological characterization, which does not always map easily onto Near Eastern historical periods as reconstructed from written texts; unfortunately, even archaeologists are not agreed on how to divide up EBA. The following schema is fairly conventional, but it should be noted that slightly different divisions of time are used by some scholars. Also, certain divisions fit the developments in some regions, while those in other regions are better handled by different dividing lines between periods. The following are those suggested in Nigro et al. (2019):

EB I: *c*. 3500–3000 BCE
EB II: *c*. 3000–2700 BCE
EB III: *c*. 2700–2300 BCE
EB IV=Intermediate Bronze: *c*. 2300–2000 BCE

For the last phase, EB IV now seems to be the standard convention, though in the past a number of other terms were used, including Intermediate Bronze Age, Early Bronze/Middle Bronze Transition, EB IV/MB I, Intermediate Early Bronze/Middle Bronze Age, and even MB I (which made MB II equal to what most now call MB I).

Broadly speaking, the Early Bronze Age is characterized by movement toward urbanization. This was especially true of Sumer, Akkad, and Egypt, of course, but was also true of other regions, including Syria. The beginnings of the EBA marked a break with the preceding Chalcolithic culture, which seems to have ended in a general collapse of settlement from north to south: 'By all accounts, the complete disintegration of the Chalcolithic settlement system in Canaan after a long and prosperous existence entailed a severe demographic and sociocultural crisis' (Levy [ed.] 1995: 272). This new situation included the development of mixed agriculture (cereals, olives and vineyards, and animal husbandry) and a village society in the Levant and also burial in large cemeteries. Specialization in crafts and long-distance trade was limited; however, metallurgy made great progress in producing implements of copper. We must not forget that Egypt was already establishing links with the Levant even at this early stage.

Around 3000–2800 BCE a transition to walled towns and cities and larger, denser communities occurred, possibly stimulated by the temporary withdrawal of the Egyptian presence. The first large fortified sites with urban characteristics in the southern Levant included Megiddo, Ai, and Yarmuth. The EB II represented the high point of urbanization in Palestine. Some EB I villages had been abandoned, as the population became more concentrated in fortified cities. Some of the main sites were Tel Bareqet, Tell el-Farah (North), and Qiryat Ata in EB II, and Tel Yarmuth, Beth Yerah, and Jericho in EB III (Steiner/Killebrew [eds] 2014: 316). Many of these settlements were located in the Shephelah and the mountain regions rather than the plains and valleys as was once conventional (Gophna 1984). Abydos Ware was widespread in EB II. Khirbet Kerak Ware seems to have originated in the northern Levant from whence it spread to south Canaan. Another type was the Cross-Combed Ware or Metallic Ware, especially found in the coastal areas. It seems to have been popular in Palestine in the EB II, after which it declined in use, at the same time as it was becoming more widespread in northern Syria in the EB III.

The northern Levant lagged behind but began to see urbanization (e.g., Byblos and Ebla) about the time that the same culture was declining in the southern region. The development in northern Syria was no doubt stimulated by interest from states in Mesopotamia, though the Egyptian trade with the northern Syrian coast and Byblos was also a factor. Egyptian connections with southern Canaan were important in the EB II, but declined considerably in EB III with Egyptian focus on the extensive trade through Byblos.

About the middle of the third millennium, at the end of EB III, EB Palestine collapsed. Many of the EB III cities were abandoned, some never to be resettled. The populated areas were composed primarily of villages; areas of low rainfall were inhabited by pastoralists. This return to the earlier rural conditions affected the whole region. That is why this transition to the MB was often designated by some form of the appellation 'Intermediate Bronze Age'. The cause(s) is (are) uncertain. A climate catastrophe has been seriously argued: 'Societies responded to the abrupt climate change with political collapse, regional abandonment, nomadization, and habitat tracking to sustainable agriculture regions' (H. Weiss in Steiner/Killebrew 2014: 367–87, quote from p. 378), but there may have been a combination of factors. Yet some large sites continued to function, including Megiddo, Hazor, and Jericho. As so often in real life, this crisis was diffuse, affecting various areas differently.

This crisis in the Levant was once associated with the Ur III downfall in Mesopotamia, but the present view is that the Levant decline began while the Akkad Empire was still at its height. An 'Amorite invasion' was once popular as a hypothesized cause of many of the changes at the end of EB III, but this hypothesis has been largely given up (see further at §5.4.2). There is no evidence of an invasion, though some less drastic population movement is not ruled out. It is estimated that the population of Palestine was about 150,000 in EB II and EB III but dropped to 10,000–15,000 during EB IV (R. Gophna in Ben-Tor 1992: 156). Western Syria seems to have remained prosperous throughout the third millennium, but a significant breakdown occurred in eastern Syria toward the end of this time. As well as climate upheavals (suggested above), this may have been partly the result of Assyrian incursions.

2.4.2 Ebla

The important Syrian city of Ebla first came to the attention of ancient Near Eastern and especially biblical scholars about half a century ago, amid some sensational claims about information in the Ebla texts coinciding – and allegedly confirming – elements of the stories about the patriarchs of Israel (see further at §4.4). Many of these claims turned out to be premature, and Ebla receded from the headlines. Nevertheless, from the point of view of ancient Near Eastern history in general and Syrian history in particular, it remained important, with the Ebla texts providing a much-welcomed window into the history of Syria in the mid- to late third millennium BCE (see especially Matthiae 2020, Matthiae et al. [ed.] 2018, and Archi 2015).

Ebla, modern Tell Mardikh, is about fifty-five km (thirty-four miles) southwest of Aleppo in Syria. At fifty hectares, with perhaps 15,000 or so inhabitants, the site was quite large for the region (though not in comparison with some Mesopotamian sites); 17,000 or so tablets from about 2350 BCE were discovered here in the 1970s. The language of Ebla has been much debated. The writing system was basically Sumerian, apparently borrowed from Mari, and was introduced during the reign of Igriš-Ḥalab (the third to last king). The local language of the city and region seems to have been Semitic, however, and most of the personal names and also many of the topographical names attested in the texts are Semitic. Because of the complications of the writing system (evolved to express Sumerian), trying to classify Eblaite has been difficult. It clearly has Akkadian grammatical features, but some of its vocabulary and even its grammar look more like Northwest Semitic, though these could represent borrowing or influence from Amorite. The closest thing to a consensus is that it was a form of East Semitic, in the same group as Akkadian (Huehnergard/Woods 2004; Krebernik 1996; Archi 2015: 32–50). In any case, the initial classification of it by G. Pettinato (1991: 50–1, 171–5) as 'Paleo-Canaanite' now looks to be universally rejected.

Eblaite usage seems to differ from that in Mesopotamia at a number of points. For example, the word LUGAL, Sumerian for 'king' (= Akkadian *šarru*), at Ebla refers to viziers, city governors, or some other government officials, while the Sumerian EN (*malikum*) is used for the king. We have lists that give the names of more than thirty kings. Sadly, the dates of reign are not listed, and we can calculate this only for the last three kings to rule: Igriš-Ḥalab (*c.* 12 years); Irkab-Damu (*c.* 11 years), Išar-Damu (35 years). Depending on how many average years of reign one gives to the other rulers, the dynasty must have begun about 2700 or 2800 BCE. The society seems to have been organized along tribal and familial lines. It is interesting that several of the kings have -*dāmu* ('[ties of] blood'; cf. Hebrew דם) as the last part of their name.

The kingdom worked as a redistributive system in which a large number of officials were provided with food by the palace. The basis of Ebla's economy was agrarian: the bulk of its inhabitants were engaged in growing grain, though wine and olive oil production and some fruit trees were also part of agriculture. Livestock raising, however, seems to have been mainly in the domain of the palace. Trade was also important to Ebla's economy. It especially exported wool and textiles, but the products of a large number of wood and metal workers, as well. Ebla had a trade network, though it was in competition with other trade networks (e.g., of Mari) which led to conflict.

The available texts unfortunately give us a detailed history of events only for the last four decades or so of the Ebla kingdom. These show that its power waxed and waned, though it sometimes controlled the Euphrates Valley and the Taurus foothills. This made it a rival to Mari at the western edge of Mesopotamia, with violent conflicts at times, but both were part of an extensive trade network. Mari under its king Iblul-Il (*c.* 2375 BCE) first dominated Ebla, but then Ebla's dynamic vizier Ibrium and his son Ibi-Zikir defeated Mari and forced an alliance. Eventually, Mari seems to have destroyed Ebla about 2300 BCE, though Naram-Sin a bit later claims to have destroyed the city (perhaps a rebuilt phase of the city).

2.4.3 Byblos

A few Egyptian objects are found in Byblos already in the early EB, showing trade between the two kingdoms as early as that time. Byblos was an important trading partner for Egypt. It was too far away to attempt to make it subject to Egyptian control, but it provided important products for Egypt, especially cedar wood. An early Egyptian term for a boat able to sail on the Mediterranean Sea was 'Byblos ship'. Not only objects but architectural technique shows Egyptian influence. The name of Pharaoh Khaʿsekhemwy of the 2nd Dynasty is the first Egyptian royal name attested in Byblos, but hieroglyphic inscriptions and the names of later pharaohs of the Old Kingdom are well represented, showing considerable Egyptian influence. It was customary for the Egyptian king to honour the chief goddess of Byblos:

> Hardly an Old Kingdom monarch, beginning with Khaʿsekhemwy, failed to send some object, inscribed with his name, as a present to the shrine of the 'Mistress of Byblos', the patron goddess of the town [apparently = Aṭtart/Aštart (Astarte), identified by the Egyptians with Hathor]. Menkaure of the 4th, Unas of the 5th, and Pepy I of the 6th Dynasties are very well represented by votives.... [Redford 1992a: 41]

2.4.4 Palestine

Most of our information on Palestine-Canaan at this time comes from archaeology (see especially Steiner/Killebrew 2003: 269–400; also Weippert 1988: 140–200). Already in the Egyptian Old Kingdom a number of terms were used of those who inhabited the regions to the north and northeast of Egypt, most of them rather generic (Redford 1986; Giveon 1975; Mourad 2015: 194–6; Saretta 2016: 18–21). Some of the main terms can be summarized as follows:

Amu (*ʿ3mw*): 'Asiatic', a term widely used from the Old Kingdom on (ERMAN-GRAPOW 1:167–8; Faulkner 1962: 38).

Fnḫw: from the Old Kingdom, the name of a people in Syria-Palestine (ERMAN-GRAPOW 1:577; Faulkner 1962: 98; Leclant 1984); Phoenicians? (cf. Vandersleven 1987); however, Vissiliev (2020: 162–4) rejects identification with Phoenicians and thinks it is a rather vague designation for 'Asian countries' in general.

ḥq3w.ḫ3swt: 'kings of foreign lands', usually rendered as 'Hyksos' (cf. ERMAN-GRAPOW 3:173–4; Faulkner 1962: 178; see further at §4.3.3), from the Middle Kingdom.

ḥryw-šʿ: beginning with the Old Kingdom, 'dwellers-across-the-sand', 'Bedouin' to the northeast of Egypt; the translation 'sand-dwellers', while perhaps a literal rendering, does not seem to capture the lifestyle of those described (ERMAN-GRAPOW 3:135; Faulkner 1962: 175; Redford 1986: 126; Couroyer 1971).

i3btyw: 'Easterners' (ERMAN-GRAPOW 1:31; Faulkner 1962: 8).

iwntyw: 'bowmen, tribesmen' (ERMAN-GRAPOW 1:55; Faulkner 1962: 13).

mḥtyw: 'Northerners, foreigners living in the north of Egypt; Delta dwellers' (ERMAN-GRAPOW 2:126; Faulkner 1962: 114).

mnṯw: Montu, inhabitants of Sinai ('wild men') (ERMAN-GRAPOW 2:92; Faulkner 1962: 110).

nmiw šʿ: 'those who traverse the sand, sandfarers', 'bedouin' (ERMAN-GRAPOW 2:265; Faulkner 1962: 133).

pḏtyw: 'bowmen, foreigners', from the Middle Kingdom (ERMAN-GRAPOW 1:570; Faulkner 1962: 97).

Rṯnw: from the Middle Kingdom, 'Syria-Palestine' (cf. ERMAN-GRAPOW 2:460; Faulkner 1962: 154; Gardiner 1947: 1:142*–9*); yet the most recent treatment of the term argues:

> The most complete geographical representation of Upper Retenu is contained in the list of towns defeated by Thutmose III on his first victorious campaign. The superscription of this list presents it as 'the list of countries of Upper Retenu' (*Urk.* IV: 780: 4, 16). It includes only Canaanite cities (with the exception of Qadesh) and covers almost all territory of Canaan.... Today, it can be argued that, in addition to this list, Yenoam (*Urk.* IV 744: 3-5) and the land of Takhsi (*Urk.* IV 1296: 13-1297: 4) are the only locatable toponyms situated 'in Upper Retenu'. Thus, Upper Retenu should be located in Palestine and southern Syria, that is, in the land of Canaan. [Vassiliev 2020: 160]

He goes on to make Reṯenu equivalent to Canaan, and Lower Reṯenu a designation for the Phoenician coast.

sṯtyw: since the 11th Dynasty, the inhabitants of the lands to the northeast of Egypt; 'Asiatic' (ERMAN-GRAPOW 4:348; Faulkner 1962: 255).

Listed here are some examples of statements about 'Asiatics' in Egyptian literature of the Old Kingdom or that seem to refer to the First Intermediate Period, even if our extant versions are from a slightly later time:

Ipuwer 15.1: 'What has happened...is to cause the Asiatics [*sṯtyw*] to know the condition of the land' (Gardiner 1909: 91).

THE THIRD-MILLENNIUM CONTEXT 25

Prophecy of Neferti:

[The sage Neferti] recalls the sad state of the East [*i3btt*], the Asiatics [*'3mw*] journeying in their strength, terrorizing the hearts of the harvesters, and seizing the cattle from ploughing.... Enemies have arisen in the East [*i3btt*]! Asiatics [*'3mw*] have come down to Egypt; a secure stronghold is lacking; ...the flock of the foreign countries will drink at the river of Egypt. ...a king from the south will come, called Ameny.... Asiatics [*'3mw*] will fall to his slaughtering and Libyans will fall to his flame.... And The Walls of the Ruler will be built. There will be no letting Asiatics [*'3mw*] come down to Egypt, so they will ask for water as suppliants do, to let their flocks drink. [Parkinson 1997: 135–9]

Sinuhe:

[When Sinhu flees to Syria in fear for his life, he first comes to the (B18-19)] 'Walls of the Ruler', which were made to repel the Asiatics [*styw*] and to crush the Sand-farers [*nmiw š'*].... (B29-31) I traveled to Byblos; I returned to Qedem [in Lebanon].... Then Ammunenshi, the ruler of Upper Retenu, took me to him.... [(B63) He praises the Egyptian king:] The Bowmen [*pdt*] flee before him... (B97-99) When Asiatics [*styw*] conspired to attack the Rulers of Hill-Countries, I opposed their movements.... [(B264-65) Sinuhe is brought into the presence of the Egyptian king, who says,] 'Here is Sinuhe, come as an Asiatic [*'3m*], a product of nomads [*styw*]!' [*AEL* 1:224–32]

Stela of Khu Sobek:

His majesty proceeded north to fell the *Mntw*-people of Asia. When his majesty reached the foreign country whose name is *Skmm*, his majesty made a good beginning in proceeding (home) to the Residence of life, prosperity, and health. *Skmm*, it fell, together with *Rtnw ḫst* [defeated *Rtnw*], while I was acting as the rear-guard of the army. [Lorton 1973: 67]

Instructions of Weni (officer of Pepy I of the 6th Dynasty):

His majesty made war on the Asiatic Sand-dwellers (*'3m-ḥryw-š'*) and his majesty made an army of many ten thousands.... This army returned in safety, (after) it had hacked up the land of the Sand-dwellers; this army returned in safety (after) it had overturned its strongholds; this army returned in safety, (after) it had cut down its figs and its vines; this army returned in safety, (after) it had thrown fire in all its [troops]; this army returned in safety, (after) it had slain troops therein, in many ten thousands; this army returned in safety (after) [it had carried away] therefrom a great multitude as living captives.... His majesty sent me to despatch [this army] five times, in order to traverse the land of the Sand-dwellers at each of their rebellions.... When it was said there were revolters because of matter among these barbarians in the land of Gazelle-nose [often thought to be the Mt Carmel ridge], I crossed over in troop-ships with these troops, and I voyaged to the back of the height of the ridge on the north of the Sand-dwellers. When this army had been brought in the highway, I came and smote them all and every revolter among them was slain. [*ARE* 1.142–4, texts 311-15]

Inscription of Pepi-nakht (an officer of Pepi II of the 6th Dynasty):

Now the Majesty of my lord sent me to the land (ḫ3st) of the '3mw to bring him the (corpse of) the sole friend (the shipwright K3-'pr) and the superintendent of aliens '.(i)-n-'nḫ, who had been building a 'Byblos'-boat there for Pwenet, when the '3mw who are across the sand had slain him together with the military troops who were with him […]; those '3mw were put to flight, and I slew some of them, I and the military troops that were with me. [Redford 1986: 127]

P. Saretta (2016) argues at length that '3mw should be equated with the Amorites; indeed, she sometimes translates '3mw with 'Amorite'. She points to some remarkable parallels between the descriptions and lifestyle of the '3mw and the Amorites, which are certainly interesting. Yet she is not able to point to any statement in the extant writings of Egypt and Mesopotamia that equate the two. The facts seem to be that the Amorites were at home in northern Syria and western Mesopotamia (though many of them also lived in the Sumerian area), whereas the '3mw could refer to anyone from the Syro-Palestinian region. If there were Amorites in Palestine by this time (for which we have no information), the Egyptians might well have referred to them as '3mw, but there is no evidence that the Egyptian term referred solely or largely to Amorites. See further at §4.2.3.

Movements of people (as well as goods and information) between Egypt and the southern Levant in antiquity have long been documented through textual and archaeological data (Greenfield et al. 2020; Ward 1963; Redford 1992a: 20–70). Already in pre-dynastic times turquoise seems to have been imported from Sinai. How early Egypt was directing mining in the Sinai is debated, but it seems to be an early source of copper. We know of the sporadic appearance of Egyptian artifacts at southern Palestinian sites in the Chalcolithic period. These greatly increased during Dynasties 1-2 (Ben-Tor 1982), mainly Egyptian pottery (some local imitations but mostly genuine imports). This seems to be mostly due to Egyptian 'colonies' in southern Canaan (Gophna 1976), yet Canaanite artifacts are also found at Egyptian sites, especially pottery vessels used to import Canaanite products. Indeed, a Canaanite jar became the hieroglyphic determinative sign for 'oil' in Egyptian texts.

An archaeological survey of northern Sinai seems to have discovered evidence of a trading route between the Nile Delta and southern Canaan in the Early Bronze period (Oren 1973). On the one hand were the considerable Egyptian pottery and other artifacts in the Sinai, extending into Canaan; on the other hand, Canaanite pottery and artifacts are found not only in the northern Sinai but also in Egyptian tombs. The excavations show permanent Egyptian settlements in northern Sinai extending on into the Negev area, which suggests that these are more than features of trade. An Egyptian population (civilian rather than military, judging from the tools found) seems to have settled in the southern Shephelah and western Negev alongside the native population (Ben-Tor 1986: 12–16; 1991: 8). Contacts appear to have begun in pre-dynastic times, became more intensive during the 1st Dynasty, were considerably reduced during the 2nd Dynasty, only to resume again with the rise of the Old Kingdom. This resumption looks to have bypassed the Sinai trade route (judging by the dearth of Egyptian pottery in Sinai and the Negev after the 1st Dynasty), however, but was focused on the sea trade route further north, such as to Byblos. The many small settlements seem to have declined sharply as well. Yet from the 3rd Dynasty on the Egyptians appear to have been mining copper in the Sinai as a major source of this metal.

Trade goods moving from Palestine to Egypt in the third millennium seem to have included mainly wine, oil, and honey, carried in jars. Also exported to Egypt were cosmetic articles such as perfumed oils, resins of various sorts, and bitumen (Ben-Tor 1986: 10). There may also have been 'invisible' exports that were less likely to leave detectable remains in the archaeological record, i.e., products made of organic material not packed in pottery jars but transported in bulk or in organic containers (those made of straw, leather, or cloth). As noted above, during the late EB period Egyptian artifacts are relatively rare throughout the southern Levant in general (Greenfield et al. 2020). This was apparently due to a shift in the focus of the Egyptian trade networks (away from the southern Levant to the northern). Trade with southern Canaan does not seem to have stopped, but it lessened or possibly moved to goods that were less visible in the archaeological record.

Small ivory tablets from 1st Dynasty tombs indicate hostilities already with the Asiatic and Libyan tribes on the eastern and western borders of the Delta (Ward 1963: 9). For Dynasties 1-2, but especially for Dynasty 3-6, raids against 'Asiatics' of various sorts are recorded (Gardiner/Peet/Černý 1955: 52–64; Helck 1971: 12–24). We get a brief insight into the interaction between Egypt and Canaan through the *Autobiography of Weni*, from Dynasty 6 (*AEL* 1:18–23). Weni was an official of the king sent at the head of a campaign against the land of the 'Dwellers-across-the-Sand', which many think is a reference to southern Canaan (Ben-Tor 1982: 13). We also have written sources that speak of the dangers from 'Asiatics'. The *Admonitions of Ipuwer*, the *Instructions of Merkare*, and the *Prophecy of Neferti* all mention them. In the 11th Dynasty the king's steward Henenu conducted a campaign against the Dwellers-across-the-Sand and brought back tribute, though this might have been a commercial rather than a strictly military venture; he also apparently cut trees in Lebanon and brought back cedar wood (Hayes 1949). By this time, the trading hub had moved further north, to Byblos, and Canaan was useful only for whatever spoils could be seized for Egypt.

2.5 WRITING, SCRIBES AND LITERATURE

S. M. Burstein (1978) *The Babyloniaca of Berossus*; **I. Finkelstein** (2020) 'The Appearance and Dissemination of Writing in Judah', *Semitica et Classica* 13: 269–82; **idem** (2022b) 'The Appearance and Dissemination of Writing in Israel and Judah' [revised version], in I. Finkelstein, *Essays on Biblical Historiography: From Jeroboam II to John Hyrcanus*: 25–43; **I. Finkelstein and B. Sass** (2013) 'The West Semitic Alphabetic Inscriptions, Late Bronze II to Iron IIA: Archeological Context, Distribution and Chronology', *HBAI* 2: 149–220; **idem** (2021) 'The Exceptional Concentration of Inscriptions at Iron IIA Gath and Rehob and the Nature of the Alphabet in the Ninth Century BCE', in T. Römer, H. Gonzalez, L. Marti, and J. Rückl (eds), *Oral et écrit dans l'Antiquité orientale: les processus de rédaction et d'édition: Actes du colloque organisé par le Collège de France, Paris, les 26 et 27 mai 2016*: 127–73; **D. Fleming**

and **S. J. Milstein** (2010) *The Buried Foundation of the Gilgamesh Epic: The Akkadian Huwawa Narrative*; **E. Frahm** (2011) *Babylonian and Assyrian Text Commentaries: Origins of Interpretation*; **S. N. Kramer** (1949) 'Schooldays: A Sumerian Composition Relating to the Education of a Scribe', *JAOS* 69: 199–215; **C. J. Lucas** (1979) 'The Scribal Tablet-House in Ancient Mesopotamia', *History of Education Quarterly* 19: 305–32; **N. Na'aman** (2015) 'Literacy in the Negev in the Late Monarchical Period', in B. Schmidt (ed.), *Contextualizing Israel's Sacred Writing: Ancient Literacy, Orality, and Literary Production*: 47–70; **L. E. Pearce** (1995) 'The Scribes and Scholars of Ancient Mesopotamia', in J. M. Sasson (ed.), *Civilizations of the Ancient Near East*: 4: 2265–91; **B. B. Powell** (2009) *Writing: Theory and History of the Technology of Civilization*; **A. Robinson** (2007) *The Story of Writing: Alphabets, Hieroglyphs and Pictograms*; **B. Sass and I. Finkelstein** (2016) 'The Swan-Song of Proto-Canaanite in the Ninth Century BCE in Light of an Alphabetic Inscription from Megiddo', *Semitica et Classica* 9: 19–42; **A. Schlott** (1989) *Schrift und Schreiber im Alten Ägypten*; Å **W. Sjöberg** (1976) 'The Old Babylonian Eduba', in *Sumerological Studies in Honor of Thorkild Jacobsen on his 70th Birthday*: 159–79; **J. H. Tigay** (1982) *The Evolution of the Gilgamesh Epic*; **B. G. Trigger** (2003) *Understanding Early Civilizations: A Comparative Study*.

The notable advance made by the introduction of writing was mentioned at the beginning of this chapter. Writing made possible the keeping of long-term records (even if most writing at this time was used for short-term functions such as sales receipts). With written records come scribes, and scribes are the backbone of bureaucracy. Bureaucracy, in turn, is usually taken as evidence of a full-fledged state, and the earliest states in Egypt and Sumer certainly had scribes and bureaucracies. We should be aware, however, that a state can exist without the existence of writing (Trigger 2003: 595–8), a good example being the Inca empire of South America. Bureaucracy can exist without writing, and a state does not need a enormously complicated bureaucracy to be a state.

Yet more can be said about the development of writing which was parallel in Egypt and Mesopotamia, specifically in Sumer. (One could bring in China and perhaps Meso-America at this point, since writing arose and developed in these regions in similar fashion as in the Near East. This is beyond our scope, but see such histories of writing as B. B. Powell [2009] and A. Robinson [2007].) In both Egypt and Sumer the first writing consisted of pictures. This was easily recognized with Egyptian hieroglyphs because their pictorial representation was plain and they continued to be used. But in Sumer they wrote on clay tablets, and drawing pictures was not easy. The earliest writing consists of pictures, as some of the earliest tablets show. But scribes soon found that it was easier to jab the rectangular point of the stylus into the clay, to produce wedge-shaped marks (cuneiform), rather than trying to draw with it. At first the wedge shapes still outlined the original picture, but the result was soon a stylized form that bore little resemblance to the picture from which it had originated.

In Egypt the hieroglyphs were gradually simplified over a long period to yield a more cursive effect, known as hieratic, and eventually a very cursive form to use in writing the late dialect, Demotic. (In its final stage, Coptic, the surviving Egyptian language came to be written in Greek uncial script with a few extra symbols.) In Mesopotamia the original cuneiform word and syllable symbols fitted the phonetic and phonemic structure of Sumerian. But as the original culture of southern Mesopotamia spread north, it encountered the Semitic-speakers of Akkad. The cuneiform symbols were picked up and used by Akkadian scribes to write their Semitic language; however, it did not always fit the sounds or structure of Akkadian and had to be adapted. Even then some aspects of the Akkadian language were not well represented by the cuneiform writing system, but it did a tolerable job. Also, it represented vowels which many of the Semitic scripts (as well as Egyptian) did not.

The beginnings of scribalism and the bureaucracy in Egypt were described above (§2.1). In the New Kingdom a number of high scribes were responsible for recruiting for the army and even leading it as generals (Schlott 1989: 217–37). (Cf. the Israelite 'scribe of the army' who had a similar function of 'recruiting the people of the land [for the military]' [2 Kgs 25:19; Jer. 52:25].) Because their tombs have been preserved, we have the 'autobiographies' of some Egyptian high officials who designate themselves as scribes (e.g., Rechmire [*LdÄ* 5:180–2]). Military campaigns required a number of ordinary scribes to keep the 'palace day book' in which the deeds of the king were recorded with regard to military operations (e.g., Thutmose III [*AEL* 2:29–35). When we look at the literature produced, we find a variety of genres. An important scribal product is the range of writings produced or selected as useful for teaching apprentice scribes (Schlott 1989: 196–208). In the First Intermediate Period we find writings, such as the *Admonitions of Ipuwer* or the *Prophecies of Neferti*, which have been interpreted as an expression of the consternation felt by many during those troubled times (Schlott 1989: 182–96), though not everyone agrees.

The scribal tradition in Mesopotamia is well documented, including the training of scribes (Pearce 1995; Lucas 1979; Sjöberg 1976; Kramer 1949). As elsewhere scribal duties and positions ranged from the ordinary scribe with the duties of copying texts and perhaps involved in local (village) administration and the lowest level of the bureaucracy up to the ministers of state next to the king. The composing of literature was not in the remit of most scribes, but we have documentation that some scribes had duties of teaching and enhancing scribal skills and knowledge of philology: bilingual word lists needed to be compiled, in part to help apprentice scribes learn to read and copy Sumerian (which had apparently become only a learned language among scholars by about the end of the third millennium BCE). But there were other texts that presented problems, such as divinatory texts and even literary wisdom texts that made use of rare and archaic vocabulary. Thus, one scribal enterprise was to compile commentaries on certain texts (Frahm 2011). We also have evidence that some texts were edited to produce new versions for political and perhaps theological reasons. This is documented for the *Enuma Eliš*, the Babylonian creation epic, with its hero Marduk. Under the Assyrian ruler Sennacherib, the *Enuma Eliš* (as well as some other texts) was edited to make Aššur the hero of the epic and the chief city Baltil (= Aššur) rather than Babylon (Frahm 2011: 347–54).

One of the texts that – perhaps surprisingly – does not have commentaries is the *Epic of Gilgamesh*. One possible reason for this is that it was not just passed down unchanged but underwent a variety of developments and edits from its origins (perhaps in the mid-third millennium BCE). There are still gaps that have to be filled, but its development over perhaps 1500 years can be observed in ways that Hebrew Bible scholars can only dream of because the many copies have given us variant versions, some of which seem to be intermediate between others. Therefore, even though the process of editing is nowhere described, it can be inferred from the various copies of the epic over the centuries. (This suggests that the editing of Gilgamesh might be a model for postulating how the biblical tradition was edited and developed over time.) The development of the Gilgamesh story has been analysed at least twice in recent decades.

First was the investigation by Jeffrey Tigay (1982) who argues that the story begins with Sumerian texts (perhaps written in the Ur III period in the late third millennium) that narrate individual episodes about Gilgamesh, such as *Gilgamesh and the Land of the Living*, *Gilgamesh and the Bull of Heaven*, *The Deluge*, *The Death of Gilgamesh*, *Gilgamesh and Agga*, and *Gilgamesh, Enkidu, and the Netherworld*. Some of these Sumerian episodes were translated into Akkadian. At some point, an author (apparently a single individual) took either the Sumerian tales or Akkadian translations of the Sumerian material and created the unified Gilgamesh epic in the Old Babylonian period. He did not just compile the epic but edited and rewrote existing material and perhaps even invented material to make a coherent single narrative subordinate to a single primary aim: 'The plan of the integrated epic thus testifies to the working of a single artistic mind' (Tigay 1982: 42). After the developments in the Old Babylonian period, the epic continued to develop in a Middle Babylonian version, a late version that contains the flood story (*ANET* 72–99, probably dated to the late second millennium) and the version in Berossus (Burstein 1978, late fourth century BCE).

More recently D. Fleming and S. Milstein (2010) argue that the 'Huwawa narrative' is at the core of the epic's growth. They do not appear to rule out an oral stage, but an earlier Sumerian version of the tale was turned into an Akkadian version in the Old Babylonian period (early second millennium BCE). This Akkadian version was not, however, a simple translation of the Sumerian but a new independent creation. This had material added before and after it, with some re-editing of the Huwawa narrative itself, to create the fuller Gilgamesh epic in the Old Babylonian period. Their study stops at this point and does not trace the further development of the epic after the Old Babylonian period.

In spite of the differences of the two analyses just outlined, there are substantial agreements. It seems clear that there was an oral stage of Gilgamesh traditions in the half millennium between a historical Gilgamesh, who seems to have been king of Uruk somewhere in the period 2700–2500 BCE, and the earliest Sumerian written texts with these traditions in the Ur III period. How the oral tradition was passed down and how it came to be written down are questions to which we have no answer. But it does seem that such an oral period of the various Gilgamesh traditions did exist. After the developments in the Old Babylonian period (as discussed above), the epic continued to evolve, with a Middle Babylonian version, a late version that contains the flood story, and finally the version in Berossus.

Composition of literature was not the main duty of scribes, whose primary job focused on administrative documents relating to the function of government. But over the centuries, various pieces of literature were created and passed down, and compositions such as law codes also came into existence that were not strictly necessary for the business of government as such. Yet already from the third millennium BCE kings had their deeds recorded in various media, including statues and monuments, and the biographies of important Egyptian officials became fashionable. These records have historiographic potential, even if some of the claims are not credible or at least need sceptical interpretation.

The aim of this section has been to discuss the origin and development of writing and scribalism. One might legitimately wonder, however, how writing developed in ancient Israel. This was much later than the third millennium BCE and has been discussed elsewhere, with references (Grabbe 2017: 150–4). Yet this discussion now needs updating, with particular notice of several recent studies which have attempted to document the development of writing by archaeology (Finkelstein 2020;

2022b; Finkelstein/Sass 2013; 2021; Na'aman 2015; Sass/Finkelstein 2016). The ostraca from the site of Arad have often been used as evidence for writing in Judah perhaps as early as the tenth century BCE; however, the stratigraphic analysis of the original excavator has been challenged, with recognition that later Hellenistic building damaged the older remains.

An examination of the extant ostraca indicates that 'of the ca. 200 ostraca known from Judah, almost all originated from seventh century (mainly late seventh century) contexts; only two to four ostraca (at Tel Beer-sheba and possibly Lachish) can be securely dated to the late eighth century BCE' (Finkelstein 2002b: 32). The fact is that writing suddenly appears in Judah in the late eighth century BCE in several different forms (ostraca, inscriptions, etc.). One argument is that writing was used on papyri at an earlier time, but that this material did not survive archaeologically. It has been assumed that plaster inscriptions, such as the Deir 'Alla and Kuntillet 'Ajrud inscriptions, portray the written texts that would have been found on papyri. But no such inscriptions have been found in Judah. It should be noted that the writing of short administrative documents is not the same as the creation of extensive literary works. The material evidence so far indicates that this was a late development in both Israel and Judah. To summarize, recent analysis (such as given in the articles cited) concludes that the ability to compose literary texts arose in Israel in the first half of the eighth century BCE. At that time, Israel seems to have dominated Judah, though this might have allowed writing technology and bureaucracy in Israel to transfer to the Southern Kingdom. In any case, writing of literary texts in Judah is not attested until the late eighth or even the seventh century.

2.6 CONCLUSIONS

This chapter has discussed the third millennium BCE, not part of the stated period of coverage, but this period of time served as a bookend to events of the second millennium (which ends with a second bookend about 900 BCE in our coverage). Egypt was already important for Syria-Palestine as it remained throughout the second millennium. The Early Dynastic Period (*c.* 3150–2700 BCE: Dynasties 1-2) was succeeded by the Old Kingdom (*c.* 2700–2200 BCE: Dynasties 3-6). This was followed by a period during which Egypt was fragmented among several ruling cities and dynasties, called the First Intermediate Period (*c.* 2200–2000 BCE: Dynasties 7-11). The end of the First Intermediate Period and the beginning of the Middle Kingdom was about 2000 BCE, roughly coming at the same time as the end of the Ur III period in Mesopotamia.

In Mesopotamia the Uruk Period (or Uruk and Jemnet Nasr Periods) began about 4000 BCE and lasted until about 3000 BCE, after which was the Early Dynastic Period (*c.* 3000–2350 BCE) dominated by Sumerian city-states. The Akkadian Empire (*c.* 2350–2200 BCE) saw the centre move north to Akkad, effected by Sargon I (*c.* 2300 BCE) who established his rule over Sumer and the Akkadian region. This was brought to an end by a mountain people, the Gutians. But the Sumerian cities recovered and threw off their yoke, bringing in the Ur III period (*c.* 2100–2000 BCE). We have little information on Asia Minor at this time, but Mesopotamia and Anatolia seem to have had little effect on Syria and the west in the third millennium BCE.

It is writing that stands out as the Egyptian and Mesopotamia contribution to culture. This was initially for commercial and economic purposes, to inventory possessions and record sales. But with time the deeds of the rulers began to be recorded and celebrated in public inscriptions. It is from these inscriptions that we know about the history of the civilizations of the Nile and of the Tigris and Euphrates. Although archaeology has been of great benefit, written records give us information not easily available from archaeology alone. One of the contributions is the world literature arising out of the third millennium BCE. In these two centres of civilization we have the initiation of literary development and the beginnings of historiography. Unfortunately, the ability to record events in writing did not reach Canaan for many centuries.

Syria-Palestine is known mainly from archaeology in the third millennium BCE. The Ebla texts have given us an important insight on a major player in Syria about the middle of the third millennium, though only for some decades. After an initial flurry of excitement in the mid-1970s when many parallels with the text of Genesis were supposed, the interest in Ebla from biblical scholars has mainly disappeared, once those parallels evaporated. The city remains important to historians of the period, however. It was a rival with the city of Mari, on the western extreme of Mesopotamia, but the two also had trade links. From archaeology we know that the Palestine of the early third millennium experienced a period of urbanization, with some large fortified sites. The high point came in the EB II (*c.* 3000–2700 BCE). A collapse came at the end of EB III (about 2400–2300 BCE), with a move back to small villages and pastoralism, though some large sites remained. But population dropped from perhaps 150,000 in EB II and III to 10,000–15,000 in EB IV. The cause is not certainly known, though climatic upheavals may have played an important part.

The link between Syria-Palestine and Egypt is a significant area to explore. Syria-Palestine and its people (referred to under a variety of names, including Retenu, *Amu*, and Dwellers-across-the-Sand) are generally seen negatively as a threat. Occasional campaigns were made to the north and east, though it is not always possible to know when these were genuine military incursions and when they were peaceable trade delegations or missions to collect 'gifts' (tribute). But we do have a description of at least one military expedition under Weni, apparently the general of Pepy I (*c.* 2276–2228 BCE).

Yet commercial trade was an import feature of Egyptian and Syro-Palestinian relations. This began early with southern Canaan but gradually shifted north, with Byblos becoming one of the main trading partners, especially for wood which Egypt lacked. Sinai became important for mining, primarily turquoise but also other products such as copper. There were even some Egyptian 'colonies' in Sinai and southern Canaan. Products not produced in quantity in Egypt were imported from Palestine, such as wine, oil, and honey, as well as resins and bitumen. This connection via trade and royal campaigns into the interior was to characterize Egyptian and Syro-Palestinian relations for many centuries.

Part II

Middle Bronze Age (*c.* 2000–1600 BCE)

CHAPTER 3

Ancient Near Eastern Context

H. Klengel (1992) *Syria 3000 to 300 B.C.: A Handbook of Political History*; **A. Kuhrt** (1995) *The Ancient Near East c. 3000–300 BC*; **M. Liverani** (2014) *The Ancient Near East: History, Society and Economy*.

The Middle Bronze Age in the ancient Near East encompasses the Egyptian Middle Kingdom and Second Intermediate Period and several different eras in Mesopotamia (some use 'Intermediate Period' even here). The extent to which these areas are relevant for Palestine can be debated, but the 'Patriarchal Period' (§4.4) has been alleged to relate to events or at least the cultural background of both Egypt and Mesopotamia.

3.1 EGYPT

W. Adler and P. Tuffin (ed.) (2002) *The Chronography of George Synkellos: A Byzantine Chronicle of Universal History from the Creation*; **K. Baer** (1963) 'An Eleventh Dynasty Farmer's Letters to his Family', *JAOS* 83: 1–19; **J. von Beckerath** (1964) *Untersuchungen zur politischen Geschichte der Zweiten Zwischenzeit in Ägypten*; **idem** (1984) *Handbuch der ägyptische Königsnamen*; **D. Ben-Tor, S. J. Allen, and J. P. Allen** (1999) 'Seals and Kings' [review of K. S. B. Ryholt, *The Political Situation in Egypt during the Second Intermediate Period c. 1800–1550 B. C.*], *BASOR* 315: 47–74; **L. L. Grabbe** (2003) 'Of Mice and Dead Men: Herodotus 2.141 and Sennacherib's Campaign in 701 BCE', in L. L. Grabbe (ed.), *'Like a Bird in a Cage': The Invasion of Sennacherib in 701 BCE*: 119–40; **N. Grimal** (1992) *A History of Ancient Egypt*; **E. Hornung, R. Krauss, and D. A. Warburton (eds)** (2006) *Ancient Egyptian Chronology*; **M. Lichtheim** (1973) *Ancient Egyptian Literature, Volume 1: The Old and Middle Kingdoms*; **K. Michałowski** (1968) 'The Labyrinth Enigma: Archaeological Suggestions', *JEA* 54: 219–22; **A.-L. Mourad** (2015) *Rise of the Hyksos: Egypt and the Levant from the Middle Kingdom to the Early Second Intermediate Period*;

R. B. Parkinson (1991) *Voices from Ancient Egypt: An Anthology of Middle Kingdom Writings*; **idem** (1997) *The Tale of Sinuhe and Other Ancient Egyptian Poems 1940–1640 BC*; **S. G. J. Quirke** (2001) 'Second Intermediate Period', in *OEAE* 3:260–5; **K. S. B. Ryholt** (1997) *The Political Situation in Egypt during the Second Intermediate Period c. 1800–1550 B. C.*; **W. G. Waddell** (1940) *Manetho*.

The section of Egyptian history that encompasses the 500-year period of the Middle Kingdom and the Second Intermediate Period (*c.* 2050–1550 BCE) is perhaps one of the most important, but also one of the least known. The literature, language, and culture of the Middle Kingdom became something of a 'classical age' in Egyptology (cf. Grimal 1992: 171). The Second Intermediate Period also brought in the Hyksos who have become so important in subsequent discussions about Egypt and Israel.

3.1.1 Middle Kingdom

The Middle Kingdom (*c.* 2050–1750) was made up of the latter part of Dynasty 11 and Dynasty 12; some also include the first part of Dynasty 13 to Merneferre Aya, whereas others simply include Dynasty 13 in the Second Intermediate Period. The question is whether Egypt remained more or less unified until Merneferre Aya (*c.* 1684–1661 BCE). As noted in the previous chapter (§2.1) the first part of Dynasty 11 is usually assigned to the First Intermediate Period. It was the Theban Nebhepetre Mentuhotep II (*c.* 2009–1959 BCE) who is credited with beginning the Middle Kingdom, since he became sole ruler of Egypt after the century and a half of divided rule that constitutes the First Intermediate Period.

Somewhere around 2000 BCE Mentuhotep II intervened in a revolt of the Thinite nome against the 10th Dynasty (ruling in Herakleopolis) and conquered what had been seen as an independent territory in Asyut. He established his capital in Thebes, but it took a further number of years in his long reign of fifty years to bring the rest of Egypt under his control. He secured the Egyptian borders with campaigns into Libya and the Sinai. He also extended Egyptian rule in the south by taking some of the northern parts of Nubia, though he did not attempt to take over the country.

His successor, Mentuhotep III (*c.* 1958–1947 BCE), was noted for two activities. He established control over the eastern part of the Delta and built fortresses that protected against the incursions of so-called 'Asiatics' that were the traditional barbarian threat to Egypt. The other achievement was an expedition to Punt. To assist such trade with Punt, a series of wells were dug between Koptos on the Nile and the Red Sea (under a later pharaoh a regular port for expeditions to Punt was established at Mersa Gawasis). It is from sometime during his reign that we have the archive of a minor official named Heqanakht who was servant to the vizier. Heqanakht's letters give us an insight into Egyptian society and economy of the time (cf. Baer 1963; Parkinson 1991: 101–7).

The reign of the next king, Mentuhotep IV (*c.* 1947–1940 BCE), was regarded as years of chaos, but his vizier seems to have been the one who became Amenemhet (or Ammenemes) I (*c.* 1939–1910 BCE) and the founder of Dynasty 12 (*c.* 1950–1750 BCE). The 12th Dynasty was one of the most famous, reaching a height of power and culture. It consisted mainly of four Amenemhets (Amenemhet I–IV) and three Sesostrises (Senwosret I–III). Amenemhet I seems to have had opposition to his rise to the throne, as indicated by the support of his kingship by the *Prophecies of Neferti* which supposedly predicted his divine choice (*AEL* 1:139–45). He ordered the construction of the 'Walls of the Prince' at Wadi Tumilat on the eastern edge of the Delta. One interpretation is that it was a fortress or set of fortresses erected as a barrier to invasion from the northeast. He established at new capital near el-Lisht called Itj-tawy and resumed trade with Byblos. His reign ended with his assassination.

Amenemhet's son (apparently co-regent by this time) became Sesostris I (*c.* 1920–1875 BCE). Two important writings of the Middle Kingdom seem to have been composed to help legitimate his rule: the *Instruction of Ammenemes I* and the *Tale of Sinuhe* (*AEL* 1:135–9, 222–35; Parkinson 1997: 21–53, 203–11). Of interest are his trade links with the Levantine coast as far north as Ugarit. Amenemhet II (1878–1843 BCE) and his son Sesostris II (1845–1837 BCE) continued to expand trade (e.g., to Punt) and Egypt's borders. A chest of silver 'tribute' was discovered as a foundation deposit, and Egyptian objects from this time have been found in Crete, Byblos, and Ras Shamra. Some have suggested that 'Asiatics' began to move into the Delta during this time, following Egyptian use of 'foreign' workers.

Sesostris II and III were known for their building projects and internal developments in Egypt (e.g., development of the Fayum region). They also cut back the developing powers of the local rulers that had been increasing during the 12th Dynasty. In addition to expeditions to push back an expanding Nubia, Sesostris III (*c.* 1837–1819 BCE) sent an expedition into Palestine which apparently captured Shechem (see further at §4.3.3). We also find the deeds of an Egyptian king called *Sesōstris* in classical sources (e.g., Herodotus 2.102-11). We can briefly note that the king is said to have done the following things:

- Sailed with a fleet from the Arabian Gulf and subdued all those who dwelt by the Red Sea.
- Took an army overland and subdued all peoples through Asia as far as Europe, including the Scythians and Thracians.
- Set up pillars describing his exploits (one of which Herodotus claims to have seen in Palestine).
- Left some of his army at Phasis (Colchis).
- His brother attempted to murder him and his family by setting fire to a house, but Sesostris escaped by sacrificing two children.
- Made captives of his campaigns drag blocks of stone to build the temple at Hephaestus and dig canals.
- Divided the land and gave an equal parcel to each Egyptian.
- Established a yearly tax on the land.
- Became the only Egyptian king who also ruled Ethiopia, setting up statues of himself and his family before the temple of Hephaestus to commemorate this.

Do any of the three kings named Sesostris (Senwosret or Senusret: *S-n-wsr.t*) fit with the Greek Sesostris legend? The answer is no; however, if the activities of all three Sesostris kings are taken into account, there are a number of coincidences that match the main features found in the Herodotus account:

- Conquest and rule over Nubia (I and III).
- Water projects and land reclamation (II).
- Temple building (I, II, III).
- Administrative re-organization (III).

Thus, the Sesostris of Herodotus and other classical writers is probably a composite based on the activities of all three rulers but of course developed in a legendary way. (A further discussion of the history behind the classical figure can be found in Grabbe 2003.)

Amenemhet III (c. 1818–1773 BCE) was another famous king of what became one of the most prosperous periods of ancient Egypt. He continued to strengthen the frontiers, as his predecessors had done. Judging from the inscriptions at Serabit el-Khadim he developed turquoise and copper mining in the Sinai. There were other major building projects, including in the Fayum. His work there was remembered under the name Lacharēs or Lamarēs/Lamaris (in Manetho, apud Syncellus: Adler/Tuffin 2002: 84–5; Waddell 1940: 68–9). To enable these projects he is said to have brought in a large number of workers from abroad. His mortuary temple at Hawara became the basis of the Labyrinth of Graeco-Roman writers (Lloyd 1970; Michałowski 1968). He was followed by Amenemhet IV (c. 1772–1764 BCE), who was not his son but apparently a high official in the administration. It may be that already during his reign the 'Asiatics' of the Delta established their independence (Ryholt 1997: 294). It was not one of the sons of Amenemhet IV but rather a daughter of Amenemhet III, Sobekneferu/Sebekkare' (Nefrusobk) (c. 1763–1760 BCE), who succeeded him (with the full pharaonic titles) to become the last ruler of the 12th Dynasty.

The 13th Dynasty (c. 1750–1625 BCE) ruled much of Egypt during the first part of its existence. It has been suggested that Dynasty 12 ended in violence with the assassination of Sobeknefern/Sebekkare', but this is very uncertain. K. S. B. Ryholt (1997: 294–5) argues that a civil war in the late Dynasty 12 was the opportunity for the Asiatic inhabitants of the Delta to set up their own ruler and the 14th Dynasty. What we do know is that archaeology shows a cultural continuum between the 12th and 13th Dynasties, and the literary evidence indicates that 'Asiatics' continued to move peacefully into northern Egypt, which was to lead to a new political force in the Second Intermediate Period (§4.3.3). The alleged '60 kings' of the 13th Dynasty came and went at a brisk tempo, and little is known about many of them. Neferhotep I (c. 1721–1710 BCE) seems to have ruled all of southern Egypt and most – if perhaps not all – of the Delta. Byblos was still paying tribute in his time. If correct, this part of the 13th Dynasty therefore belongs to the Middle Kingdom, while the Second Intermediate Period formally began perhaps sometime after Neferhotep I.

3.1.2 Second Intermediate Period

The dynasty that arose in the Delta and broke the unified rule of the 13th Dynasty, was the 14th, often referred to as 'ephemeral'. The reason is that it is alleged to have had many rulers (76 kings in less than two centuries, according to one version of Manetho [Waddell 1940: 74–5]), yet only two of them seem to be referred to in any contemporary monuments or documents. This has led some to question Dynasty 14 or to dismiss it altogether from their reconstruction (e.g., Hornung/Krauss/Warburton 2006: 492). More important was Dynasty 15, the 'Hyksos dynasty'. This dynasty is discussed in greater detail below (§4.3.3). Dynasty 16 also presents problems and is differently treated in various reconstructions.

The Second Intermediate Period (*c.* 1750-1550) encompassed Dynasties 13–17 according to most Egyptologists. During the first part of the 13th Dynasty, however, all of Egypt seems to have been ruled from Itj-tawy; if correct, this makes that first part of Dynasty 13 a constituent of the Middle Kingdom, with Dynasty 13 straddling the divide between the Middle Kingdom and the Second Intermediate Period. A major question is when the rival Dynasty 14 arose to dominate part of the Delta, which is really the beginning of the Second Intermediate Period. As noted above (§3.1.1), Ryholt thinks Dynasty 14 already arose during the last part of Dynasty 12, which would make the Second Intermediate Period begin already then. Because of the uncertainties, a variety of reconstructions of this period have been put forward by Egyptologists. The length of the individual dynasties is uncertain, but some of them were contemporaneous. In many cases we have nothing more than the names of the kings within the dynasties, though even here there are questions.

S. G. J. Quirke's reconstruction is fairly conventional (2001: 260–1). In his phase 1 the 13th Dynasty, ruling at Itj-tawy, became paralleled by the 14th Dynasty (perhaps ruling from Tell ed-Dab'a). The 13th was succeeded by the 17th Dynasty, ruling from Thebes, in his phase 2, while the 15th ('Hyksos') Dynasty replaced the 14th (still with the capital at Tell ed-Dab'a); however, the relationship of the 14th Dynasty to the 15th is unclear. Also, exactly where to put Dynasty 16 is a problem; it may be an invention of Manetho. Phase 3 represents the last part of the period, in which the 15th and 17th Dynasties were at war (leading to the defeat and expulsion of the Hyksos by Kamose and Ahmose).

One of the most radical reconstructions is that of K. S. B. Ryholt (1997). According to Ryholt, as already noted, the 14th Dynasty (composed of Canaanite kings ruling from Avaris) was established toward the end of the 12th Dynasty and ruled in parallel with the 13th (which was a continuation of the 12th). The 15th Dynasty arose when the Hyksos from the north invaded and conquered Avaris and ended the 14th. He sees the '16th Dynasty', not as part of the Hyksos sphere as many do, but uses the term for a set of Theban kings who ruled after the 13th Dynasty but which was overturned by the 15th Dynasty which conquered Thebes but only after about half a century of conflict (making the 16th rule in parallel with much of the 15th Dynasty). He also argues for a short-lived 'Abydos Dynasty', which arose at the same time as his 16th Dynasty (in the vacuum created by the fall of the 13th) but was defeated by the invading 15th Dynasty (who moved on to attack the southern Egypt of the 16th).

Dynasty 17 succeeded the 16th, arising suddenly and establishing an independent state (though details are obscure). The 15th Dynasty withdrew (or was driven) from Thebes, ruling in parallel with the last part of Dynasty 17. The 15th Dynasty may have lost Thebes because of an internal conflict caused by the accession of Apophis; also, there may have been a Hurrian invasion into Palestine that seemed a threat to the Delta kingdom. The 17th Dynasty attempted to retake the territory of Lower Egypt under several kings. It appears to have failed under Ta'o Seqenenre, but Kamose led successful campaigns both into Nubia and the north. It was his successor Ahmose I who succeeded in taking Avaris and ending the rule of Dynasty 15 over the Delta.

Critics of Ryholt (Hornung/Kraus/Warburton 2006: 168–96; Ben Tor/Allen/Allen 1999: 65–6) acknowledge the value of his challenges but differ from him at various points. His work allows the period to be divided into three distinct phases (cf. Quirke above). The first of these comprises most of the 13th Dynasty which is a direct continuation of the 12th Dynasty (and thus really belongs to the Middle Kingdom). The second phase consists of Dynasty 14 (with its Asiatic rulers) and the six Hyksos kings of Dynasty 15. Most of these rulers are attested only by scarabs. In contrast with Ryholt, however, they doubt whether Dynasty 14 was so early. Dynasty 14 does seem to overlap the 13th, but (contrary to Ryholt) this appears to have occurred toward the end of Dynasty 13 rather than at its beginning. Some think it was about the time of Merneferre Aya (of Dynasty 13) that the 14th Dynasty came to rule part of the Delta (*c.* 1700 BCE). The third phase consists of Dynasty 16 and its Theban successor Dynasty 17.

The following broad reconstruction appears to summarize something of a consensus. The first part of Dynasty 13 belongs to the Middle Kingdom, as still a time of basic unity; however, the rise of a new rival Dynasty 14 in the Delta region, contemporary with the last part of Dynasty 13, marks the beginning of the Second Intermediate Period. Many think the 14th Dynasty was composed of Canaanite kings. It was ended and succeeded by the 15th Dynasty, made up of Hyksos rulers (some would see a relationship between the 15th and 14th Dynasties as both made up of Canaanite rulers, but this is not certain). The 13th Dynasty also seems to have ended about the time that the 15th began, and the 17th Dynasty succeeded it, ruling contemporary with the 15th (the relationship of the 17th Dynasty to the 13th is still unclear). The 16th Dynasty is difficult because we have little information. (It may have been Hyksos and thus related in some way to the 15th, but some omit it entirely.) It was the last king of the 17th (Kamose) and the first of the 18th Dynasty (Ahmose) who ended Hyksos rule.

The Second Intermediate Period was thus dominated by the Hyksos, who are discussed at length in the next chapter (§4.3.3).

3.2 MESOPOTAMIA

S. Dalley (2002) *Mari and Karana: Two Old Babylonian Cities*; **G. Dossin** (1938) 'Les Archives épistolaires du Palais de Mari', *Syria* 19: 105–26; **idem** (1939b) 'Les archives économiques du palais de Mari', *Syria* 20: 97–113; **idem** (1955) 'L'inscription de fondation de Iaḫdun-Lim, roi de Mari', *Syria* 32: 1–28; **J.-M. Durand** (1997–2000) *Documents épistolaires du palais de Mari, 1-3* (= LAPO 16-18); **idem** (2012) 'Sargon a-t-il détruit la ville de Mari ?', *RdA* 106: 117–32; **J. J. Finkelstein** (1961) 'Ammiṣaduqa's Edict and the Babylonian "Law Codes"', *JCS* 15: 91–104; **idem** (1969) 'The Edict of Ammiṣaduqa: A New Text', *RdA* 63: 45–64; **D. R. Frayne** (1990) *Old Babylonian Period (2003–1595 BC)*; **I. J. Gelb** (1954) 'Two Assyrian King Lists', *JNES* 13: 209–30; **L. L. Grabbe** (2004) *A History of the Jews and Judaism in the Second Temple Period 1: Yehud: A History of the Persian Province of Judah*; **A. K. Grayson** (1972) *Assyrian Royal Inscriptions, Volume I: From the Beginning to Ashur-resha-ishi I*; **W. Heimpel** (2003) *Letters to the King of Mari: A New Translation, with Historical Introduction, Notes, and Commentary*; **K. A. Kitchen** (1967) 'Byblos, Egypt, and Mari in the Early Second Millennium B.C.', *Or* 36: 39–54; **M. T. Larson** (1976) *The Old Assyrian City-State and its Colonies*; **W. F. Leemans** (1960) 'The Trade Relations of Babylonia and the Question of Relations with Egypt in the Old Babylonian Period', *JESHO* 3: 21–37;

A. Malamat (1971) 'Syro-Palestinian Destinations in a Mari Tin Inventory', *IEJ* 21: 31–8; **M. Van De Mieroop** (2003) *A History of the Ancient Near East, ca. 3000–323 BC*; **A. Poebel** (1942a) 'The Assyrian King List from Khorsabad', *JNES* 1: 247–306; **idem** (1942b) 'The Assyrian King List from Khorsabad (Continued)', *JNES* 1: 460–92; **idem** (1943) 'The Assyrian King List from Khorsabad (Concluded)', *JNES* 2: 56–90; **J. M. Sasson** (2015) *From the Mari Archives: An Anthology of Old Babylonian Letters*; **Wu Yuhong** (1994) *A Political History of Eshnunna, Mari and Assyria during the Early Old Babylonian Period (from the End of Ur III to the Death of Šamši-Adad)*; **G. D. Young (ed.)** (1992) *Mari in Retrospect: Fifty Years of Mari and Mari Studies*.

The period in Mesopotamia from about 2000–1600 BCE is generally known as the 'Old Babylonian Period', because Babylon came to dominate the region. Nevertheless, Babylon arose to prominence only after a time, and there were other cities and regions of importance. It was apparently about this time that Sumerian ceased to be a living language, though Sumerian culture continued to have major influence and Sumerian persisted as the 'classical language' of scribal texts (much as Latin was in the Middle Ages). There was increased use of Akkadian in texts, though Sumerian ideogrammes were widely used since they could be read as either Sumerian or Akkadian. Except for the Assyrian area, the dominant form of Akkadian was the Babylonian dialect.

Many of the preserved texts in this period are in letter form. Letters were important in business dealings and also in communication between the ruling elite and other parts of the bureaucracy. It is thus both private archives and official documents that provide information on the period. In the sphere of justice the Old Babylonian Period is characterized by a number of 'law codes': Lipit-Ishtar, Eshnuna, Hammurabi. The term 'law code' is a bit of a misnomer: the document in each case is in the form of a law code, but it would be wrong to think of it as a body of legal regulation or a rule book or constitution in the modern sense. These seem to have been scribal documents meant to show that the king was just and pious (since justice was seen to come from the divine sphere). Nowhere are these law codes cited as precedent for rulings in the legal judgments so far preserved. Yet where they can be checked, they do seem to summarize to a large extent the juridical tradition extant at the time of their writing (for further on law, see Grabbe 2004: 173–83).

At this time the Amorites exerted a great deal of influence, and many city-states were ruled by an Amorite dynasty. Amorite rulers tended to control the north. They have been of especial interest because many scholars have seen them as somehow among the ancestors of Israel (the Amorites as a group will be discussed in the next chapter: §4.2.3).

3.2.1 The Isin and Larsa 'Intermediate Period'

After the fall of the Ur III Dynasty Sumer ceased to have major control over southern Mesopotamia, but some Sumerian cities established dominance over their surrounding regions for a time. The *Sumerian King List* tells us that Isin, under the leadership of Ishbi-Erra, initially attempted to become the heir of Ur. For about a century (*c.* 2000–1900 BCE) Isin endeavoured to maintain and expand an empire. Sometimes it succeeded in taking various cities, especially in the old region of Ur (e.g., Nippur; cf. the *Lamentation of Nippur*). Yet a number of city-states managed to keep their independence part or all of this time: Mari, Assyria, Elam, Eshnuna, Uruk, Babylon. Around 1900

BCE Larsa, under command of Gungunum, became a rival to Isin and took some of the cities it had controlled, though Isin itself remained independent for quite a long time. (Although much further south than the normal Amorite domain, Larsa seems to have been ruled by an Amorite dynasty.) Isin finally fell to Larsa just before 1800 BCE under Rim-Sin I.

In the Babylonian region a number of cities, such as Kish, became independent after the fall of Ur III. But about 1900 Babylon began to unify neighbouring cities under the rule of its king Sumu-abum, including Sippar, Dilbat, and Kish. Sumu-abum claimed to be king of the whole of Akkad, and his name heads the Babylonian king list. This led to a dual hegemony, with Larsa dominating the southern area of Sumer but Babylon being supreme over the northern area of Akkad.

3.2.2 Old Assyrian Period (c. 2000–1750 BCE)

The main features of this period can be stated as (1) Assyria's becoming independent of Ur about 2000 BCE, (2) the commercial network it developed by about 1900 BCE, and (3) its conquest by Shamshi-Adad I about 1800 BCE (Kuhrt 1995: 86). Much of our knowledge of the Assyrian area of the early second millennium BCE relates to the Assyrian trading network with Anatolia. According to the Assyrian King List the first 17 kings 'dwelled in tents' (Gelb 1954: 210: *a-ši-bu-tu kúl-ta-ri*). Although the list is not reliable for the early kings, it indicates the tribal origins of the Assyrian ruling dynasty. At least, the composition under the ruler Shamshi-Adad I (c. 1800 BCE) seems to want to connect his dynasty with the earlier kings to legitimate his position.

Shamshi-Adad was an older contemporary of Hammurabi and (like Hammurabi) apparently of Amorite ancestry (see §4.2.3 on the Amorites) who became the king of Ekallatum, a city-state somewhere south of Ashur. He conquered Ashur and Nineveh and brought the variety of Assyrian city-states under his control. He also fought with Eshnunna, which had been trying to expand as well. He defeated Mari, and its ruler Yahdun-Lim fled to Yamhad (and was replaced by his son). But then he conquered Mari outright and made his son Yasmah-Addu its ruler. He continued to expand his territory but was eventually forced to sign a treaty with Eshnunna. He also ran up against Yamhad and sought help against it by making treaties with other Syrian city-states, such as Carchemish and Qatna. Shamshi-Adad ruled for 33 years, though his empire collapsed after his death.

The two main cities of Assyria were already leading centres in this period: Ashur and Nineveh. Assyria had been under the dominance of Ur until the end of the Ur III period. Toward the end of the nineteenth century BCE Assyria, under Ilushuma (the first king about whom we have much information), turned the tables and raided as far as Sumer. It was about this time that a commercial network was created between Ashur and Kanesh in Anatolia, over a travel distance of approximately 800 km (c. 500 miles). This was done mainly by merchants who set up trading colonies in different cities by agreement with the city rulers (Larson 1976). Although essentially private enterprise (by leading families of Ashur rather than the government), the government assisted in certain ways. Charters were drawn up giving the merchants certain rights, some of which have been preserved. The trade was mainly in textiles and tin (needed to make bronze, the principle metal of this time). In return they were paid in silver and gold. One of the figures who promoted this sort of trading empire was Shamshi-Adad himself (Ilushuma's successor); however, he introduced greater state control of the trading process.

Although Kanesh was the main Anatolian centre, a number of other city-states were part of the overall network, about 30 in all. The term for such a commercial centre was *kārum* (originally meaning 'harbour'). There were also trade routes to the south (to Ur and Babylon) and to the east (to Elam and Iran). The treaties and letters relating to this trade give us an insight into the economy and society of the various city-states, as well as about Assyria as a whole. A partial disruption came about from Pithana of Kussara (*c.* 1750 BCE) who conquered Kanesh (= Nesa). He was succeeded by his son Anitta who conquered Hattusa (see further at §3.3.1). Their dominance did not last more than a few decades, Kanesh was rebuilt, and trade resumed (or continued). For the best part of a century, this trade continued in relative peace, but it eventually collapsed when local conflicts developed between some of the Anatolian entities (see further at §3.3.1). For the next two or three centuries, we know little about Assyria.

3.2.3 Old Babylonian Period (c. 2000–1600)

The height of Babylonian greatness came in the early second millennium, not to be equalled until the brief Neo-Babylonian empire (605–539 BCE). There were several rival states, but the area was united by Hammurabi of Babylon. He conquered many cities of the region, including Mari on the Euphrates. The date of his reign is very important for chronology of this period but varies widely between those advocating the High, Middle, or Low Chronology: his dates vary from *c.* 1850/1800 to 1800/1750 to 1730/1680 BCE. The date of *c.* 1800–1750 will be used here.

The rival states were primarily Larsa in the south and Babylonia in the north. Larsa established the first hegemony, with Rim-Sin I (*c.* 1800) uniting the region. Uruk and Isin were allied with Babylonia, but Rim-Sin conquered them and took control of the entirety of Sumer. He borrowed a number of social practices from Babylonia and the northern regions, especially the debt release (*mīšarum, andurārum*), the clearest example of which is perhaps the Edict of Ammisaduqa (Finkelstein 1961, 1969). At this time, there were several rival kingdoms, including not only Babylon but also Eshnunna and Assyria.

One of Hammurabi's first acts was to take Isin and Uruk, forcing Rim-Sin to become his supporter. The death of Shamshi-Adad removed the threat of Assyria. Eventually, toward the end of his reign Hammurabi conquered Larsa, Eshnunna, and Mari. He also fought against Assyria which now became a marginal power, but it and Elam remained independent of Babylon. Hammurabi had now united much of Mesopotamia – the 'Lands of Sumer and Akkad' – under his control. The area under his domain was mainly that of the earlier Ur III period, but the age of the city-state was coming to an end, to be replaced by the territorial state.

Hammurabi also included Amorites explicitly under his rule (he had the title, 'king of the Martu'). The Amorites retained their identity for the moment, though they were eventually assimilated to general Babylonian society. Hammurabi is famous for his 'law code', though as already noted these were not law codes in a modern sense (see the introductory paragraphs under §3.2). Although the regulations more or less coincided with those current in the legal sphere, they were propaganda on behalf of the king to demonstrate that he was 'just' and 'righteous', caring for his people as a king was meant to do. They were scribal products and are almost never cited in legal decisions. Judges applied customary law and common sense, though many of the regulations in the law codes seem to have been conventional at the time.

After the death of Hammurabi, Babylonia declined over the next 150 years. There were periodic rebellions by subordinate peoples, though his successor Samsu-iluna (*c.* 1725) managed to keep things in check. A dynasty arose in the far south of Sumer, known as the Sealand, and blocked Babylon's access to the sea for a time. One of those he fought were the Kassites from Zagros mountains. Babylon was finally devastated by a Hittite attack under Mursili I about 1600 BCE. This weakened the state considerably and allowed it to be taken over by the Kassites, who were usually seen in much the same way as the barbarian tribes who destroyed Rome. Babylonia was controlled by the Kassites for the next three centuries until about 1150. The Kassite rule is discussed at §5.2.2.

3.2.4 Mari

Although Mari was an important city in the Old Babylonian period, its fame among present-day scholars is no doubt because of the quantity of texts found there (still in the process of publication), dating mainly to the eighteenth century BCE. These texts give us a remarkable insight not only on Mari directly but on other political states and entities in the region and many aspects of Mesopotamian society of the time. The economy of Mari depended partly on Euphrates-based agriculture but also heavily on the extensive pastoral activities set on the steppe area away from the Euphrates. The city-state was also important as an intermediate centre between Mesopotamia and Syria, as it had been in the third millennium BCE. Various Amorite groups or tribes were important to its administration and society (§4.2.3), and it had an Amorite ruling dynasty from about the nineteenth century BCE (the Lim dynasty that succeeded the Shakkanakku dynasty of the late third/early second millennium BCE). The dominant city was not always Mari but sometimes Shubat-Enlil, which Shamshi-Adad used as his capital after his conquest of Mari (probably because it was closer to Assyria than Mari).

As noted, pastoral groups were widespread in Mari territory and also important for the economy. These were not nomads in the sense of wandering from place to place with no fixed abode. Rather, in most cases the people had permanent or semi-permanent settlements but moved their flocks and herds seasonally to gain the best pasturage and also protection from the weather. This 'dimorphic' lifestyle was maintained for many centuries, apparently (cf. §6.3.3.1). These pastoral groups were often identified in part (or mostly) as 'Amorites'. The Mari ruling dynasty was said to be Amorite in the texts, and the Mari population was divided between several Amorite tribes, primarily the Yaminites, the Sim'alites, and the Sutians (on the Amorites, see further at §4.2.3). This gave two aspects to Mari society: the palace and city, with their administrative apparatus, and the tribe with its traditional structure. The tribes were also an important source of military troops for the state.

Mari had declined during the latter part of the third millennium but revived under Yahdun-Lim I (*c.* 1800 BCE). It seemed to be engaged in constant conflict with its neighbours, partly because of expansionist endeavours, but also alliances to aid it against its opponents. A number of small states were under its control, including Terqa and Karana. Governance was achieved through a combination of the two modes of working, the palace/city and the tribal. Yahdun-Lim I made Mari into a major power during the reign of Shamshi-Adad I in Assyria. Yahdun-Lim was of the Sim'al tribe, and brought a number of Yaminite areas under his control. His empire spread to include several neighbouring cities (including Terqa) but also some further away, including Tuttul and Emar.

Yamhad of Syria (§4.2.4) was seen as a rival during much of Yahdun-Lim's reign, and Mari formed an alliance with Qatna against Yamhad, though the two did not come into open conflict as far as we know. Indeed, at first Yahdun-Lim made an alliance with Yamhad, as well as with Eshnunna. But when some Yaminite tribes rebelled against Yahdun-Lim, he blamed Sumu-epuh, the ruler of Yamhad, for provoking their revolt. While this gave rise to tensions between the two, they still did not actually come to blows. Yahdun-Lim's son Sumu-Yaman apparently continued peaceful relations with Yamhad, but Sumu-Yaman was evidently assassinated after a short reign, and Shamshi-Adad I of Assyria defeated Mari and placed his son Yasmah-Addu as puppet ruler over the city.

Shamshi-Adad made an alliance with Qatna against Yamhad (which had its own allies in Eshnunna and Babylon). During Shamshi-Adad's latter years he had threats both from rebellions of subordinate peoples and neighbours (such as Eshnunna and Yamhad which were both under new rulers). After Shamshi-Adad's death Mari was able to throw off the rule of Yasnah-Addu, and Zimri-Lim (who claimed to be son of Yahdun-Lim, though this is questionable) came to the throne (*c.* 1775 BCE). His ally and protector was Yamhad under Yarim-Lim I: with Yamhad's help Zimri-Lim eventually drove Ishme-Dagan (Shamshi-Adad's successor over Assyria) out of the Upper Mesopotamian region. Zimri-Lim apparently even journeyed to Yamhad and Ugarit with Yarim-Lim (see further at §4.2.4). Zimri-Lim made alliances with a number of states, including Babylonia. Eshnunna presented a problem now, because it had resumed its expansion. With the help of Yamhad and Babylon Zimri-Lim resisted Eshnunna who eventually abandoned many of the cities it had conquered. After a period of peace, Mari was threatened again, this time by Elam. With allied help he succeeded in stopping this threat, but his end came with the invasion of Hammurabi of Babylon (§3.2.3).

3.2.5 Elam

The *Sukkal-maḫ* dynasty came to power about 1900 BCE. The *Sukka-maḫ* was head of a confederation that was administered through a coalition of brothers in subordinate offices. The succession by brothers (rather than sons) was maintained for a couple of centuries but began to break down in favour of more conventional inheritance of property and office. Elam maintained its independence during the OB period and was never conquered by Babylon. Nevertheless, there was considerable Babylonian influence, not least in the writing of cuneiform texts: Akkadian was the standard written language at this time, even in legal texts, although Elamite was evidently the spoken language.

3.3 ANATOLIA

3.3.1 Hittite Old Kingdom

G. M. Beckman (1995) 'The Siege of Uršu Text (CTH 7) and Old Hittite Historiography', *JCS* 47: 23–34; **idem** (1996) *Hittite Diplomatic Texts*; **T. R. Bryce** (1981) 'Ḫattušili I and the Problems of the Royal Succession in the Hittite Kingdom', *AS* 31: 9–17; **idem** (2005) *The Kingdom of the Hittites*; **M. W. Chavalas (ed.)** (2006) *The Ancient Near East: Historical Sources in Translation*; **F. Cornelius** (1976) *Geschichte der Hethiter: mit besonderer Berücksichtigung der geographischen Verhältnisse und* *der Rechtsgeschichte*; **A. M. Dinçol, B. Dinçol, J. D. Hawkins, and G. Wilhelm** (1993) 'The "Cruciform Seal" from Boğazköy-Hattusa', *Istanbuler Mitteilungen* 43: 87–106; **J. Freu** (2003) *Histoire du Mitanni*; **H. Genz and D. P. Mielke (eds)** (2011) *Insights into Hittite History and Archaeology*; **A. Götze** (1933) *Die Annalen des Muršiliš*; **O. R. Gurney** (1990) *The Hittites*; **W. Helck** (1984) 'Die Sukzija-Episode im Dekret des Telepinus', *WO* 15: 103–8; **H. A. Hoffner, Jr** (2009) *Letters from the Hittite Kingdom*; **F. Imparati** (1965) 'L'Autobiografia di Ḫattušili I', *Studi Classici e Orientali* 14: 40–76; **A. Kempinski and S. Košak** (1982) 'CTH 13: The Extensive Annals of Hattušili I (?)', *TA* 9: 87–116; **H. Klengel** (1998) *Geschichte des Hethitischen Reiches*; **C. Saporetti** (1965) ['L'Autobiografia di Ḫattušili I:] Versione Accadica', *Studi Classici e Orientali* 14: 77–85; **O. Soysal** (1989a) *Mursili I – Eine historische Studie*; **idem** (1989b) '"Der Apfel möge die Zähne nehmen!"', *Or* 58: 171–92.

Although we have some inklings from the third millennium BCE (cf. §2.3), the history of the Hittites begins with data from the early second millennium. But even here there are problems with lack of sources: 'It is only from *c.* 1650 on that we can begin to reconstruct Hittite history' (Kuhrt 1995: 229). What we have in the Hittite Old Kingdom are bits and pieces, some very interesting and allowing for comment on some important episodes, but no continuous reconstruction or convincing chronology. We know that at this time an Indo-European people, the Hittites, became the ruling class in their region. They developed their own writing system, Hittite hieroglyphic, but also used Akkadian cuneiform writing. What little we know of their early history begins in many ways with the trading network of the Old Assyrian Period, although the Hittites do not seem to have been very well plugged into it.

According to the *Anitta Inscription* (*CoS* 1:182–4) about 1750 BCE Pithana of Kussara (a city probably south of the main trading hub Kanesh) conquered Nesa (= Kanesh), though he seems not to have sacked the city. Pithana's son Anitta is believed to have made Kanesh his base to continue the expansion of territory. Eventually, he took Hattusa, destroyed it, and sowed it with cress, cursing anyone who rebuilt it. Anitta's conquests seem to have taken place mainly in central Anatolia. The unity he established temporarily apparently allowed the trading network with Assyria to continue (or resume) its activity. But after the death of Anitta, the dominance by Kussara collapsed. The disunity that resulted eventually led to the cessation of the trade between Assyria and the Kanesh hub.

The Hittite Old Kingdom straddled the line between the Middle and Late Bronze Age (*c.* 1650–1500). As suggested above, Hittite history really begins about a century after Anitta with the first documented king, Hattusili I (*c.* 1625 BCE). The city of Hattusa seems to have been refounded, either by him or an ancestor (in spite of Anitta's curse). The much later *Edict of Telipinu*, by a successor from about 1500 BCE (*CTH* 19; *CoS* 1:194–8), names an ancestor of Hattusili known as Labarna. Some scholars accept this (e.g., Bryce 2005: 66–8), but others doubt that such an individual existed. They (e.g., Liverani 2014: 256–8) argue that the figure is an ideal creation from a much later time, noting that 'Labarna' was a title used by many of the Hittite rulers. It has also been argued that a cuneiform seal lists not only Labarna but also an individual named Huzziya as a predecessor of Hattusili (Dinçol/Dinçol/Hawkins/Wilhelm 1993).

Regardless of alleged ancestors of Hattusili I, Hittite history at present still begins basically with him. The *Annals of Hattusili* (*CTH* 4: Chavalas [ed.] 2006: 219–22; Imparati 1965; Saporetti 1965; cf. *CTH* 13 [Kempinski/Košak 1982], though this text may relate to Mursili I [Soysal 1989a: 136–9; 1989b: 189–92]) list a series of conquests over six years; however, rather than this all happening in the first six years of his reign, it is likely that these accomplishments were simply excerpted from a more complete chronicle and happened over a much longer period of time. For example, he led a campaign into Syria that destroyed Alalakh, but this implies control already over the region to the north of Yamhad. This is unlikely to have happened in the first few years of his reign. He did not in fact conquer Yamhad, though he did take control of many cities in the area that became part of the Hittite realm. Nevertheless, Hattusili encountered considerable opposition. His main opponent seems to have been the Hurrians, with a number of small Hurrian states uniting against him. This does not mean that he confronted Yamhad directly, but Yamhad appears to have supported some of those city-states in his area that rebelled against him.

Other texts may relate to his conquests. The historical value of the *Siege of Usha* text (*CTH* 7; Beckman 1995) is uncertain; it looks like an ironic text in support of the Hittite king, but may be based on an actual siege of Usha. A letter to Tunip-Teshub of Tikunani (Hoffner 2009: 75–80), apparently from Hattusili, might suggest that Hattusili expanded his empire well to the east of the Euphrates, but the interpretation of this document is controversial. In his latter years Hattusili fought several engagements against Aleppo, though apparently without success. Indeed, it is possible that Hattusili was himself wounded or killed in one of these raids, since Mursili is said to have 'avenged [the blood?] of his father' (*CTH* 11; Soysal 1989: 57, 102; Klengel 1998: 53).

Hattusili was succeeded by Mursili I (*c.* 1600 BCE), as described in *Hattusili's Testament* (*CTH* 6: *CoS* 2:79–81). This is a strange document, addressed to the military commanders and officials. It tells how Hattusili's son, as his appointed successor, refused to listen to his father and take responsibility for acting as a ruler should; indeed, other sons and other members of his family conspired against the king. It would be a mistake to take the *Testament* as an accurate historical document: rather, it is an apology that explains how Hattusili was succeeded not by his own son but by Mursili who was not a son of the king. According to a much later treaty (between Muwatalli and Aleppo: *CTH* 75; Beckman 1996: 88–90), Mursili was the grandson of Hattusili. Regardless, what the 'Testament' and other texts do is show how the competition within the royal family helped to fuel disunity within the community. In spite of Hattusili's conquests the kingdom itself was far from unified, and rebellions of various elements within it evidently frequent.

Few historical texts have survived from this period (another which might relate to Mursili I is *CTH* 13 [Soysal 1989a: 136–9; 1989b: 189–92]). According to the *Testament of Hattusili*, Mursili I conquered Aleppo and Babylon. Unfortunately, a detailed account of neither episode is extant. For Mursili to feel the need to take Aleppo is understandable, since Hattusili had not succeeded in doing so. There is also the possibility that he was seeking vengeance for the injury or death of Hattusili in the fight with Yamhad, as noted above. More puzzling is the destruction of Babylon (*CTH* 10: Soysal 1989a: 53–4, 100–102, 147–60; also Bryce 2005: 97–100; Klengel 1999: 65). This involved a 500-mile (800 km) march, and an aim of doing it for booty alone seems unlikely. Babylon was on friendly terms with Yamhad, which might have had something to do with it. One possible reason is that Mursili wanted to accomplish something great like his predecessor Hattusili had done, and taking Babylon could be seen in this light. But what it did to Babylon was to enable the Kassites to take control, which they then maintained for several centuries (§5.2.2). Furthermore, his expedition to Babylon brought him into conflict with the Hurrians who had become a traditional enemy of the Hittites (Soysal 1989a: 136–9).

Mursili's brother-in-law Hantili was a cup-bearer married to his sister Harapshi. The text is broken at this point, but Hantili seems to have become involved with a man named Zidanta, and they formed a conspiracy to assassinate Mursili (*Testament of Hattusili* §11). Once this was done, he became king as Hantili I. He embarked on military campaigns, but the 'gods sought revenge' (*Testament* §13). A broken text makes a precise picture difficult, but his wife and two sons were delivered to the city of Shukziya (cf. Helck 1984; Soysal 1990). Was this for their protection, or were they taken there as captives of the Hurrians? It is not clear, but the Hittite queen Harapshi apparently then became ill. She and her sons died or were killed. Later, the queen of the city and her family were executed in revenge (by the Hittites?). Hantili lost his fight against the Hurrians who proceeded to take control of northern Syria.

When Hantili's life was coming to an end, Zidanta killed another of Hantili's sons, named Pisheni, and took the throne. Again, the gods were said to take revenge for the shed blood: they made Zidanta's own son Ammuna his enemy. Ammuna killed his father and became king himself (*Testament* §20), but again the gods visited the blood of his father on him: his various military campaigns were unsuccessful. After his death, various members of the royal family – apparently potential heirs to the throne – were assassinated. Huzziya became king, with Telipinu as his brother-in-law (*Testament* §22). Huzziya is said to have threatened Telipinu and/or his family, but he successfully resisted. Telipinu then somehow, it seems, deposed Huzziya and became king (*c.* 1500 BCE).

Telipinu campaigned successfully against certain cities, but some of the court officials conspired to assassinate Huzziya and his family, without Telipinu's knowledge. Telipinu now embarked on a policy of resisting blood-for-blood revenge, allowing the assassins to live and become farmers. At this point, he issued his *Testament* that laid down laws of succession and also attempted to regulate punishment for acts of treason, as well as other administrative regulations. He enacted a treaty with the kingdom of Kizzuwatna, to the south of the Hittite realm, although they had earlier been rivals. Telipinu's death (*c.* 1500 BCE) brought the Hittite Old Kingdom to an end.

3.3.2 Mitanni

Mitanni's history seems to begin toward the end of the Old Babylonian period. The history of Mitanni for both the MBA and the LBA is given at §5.3.2.

3.4 CONCLUSIONS

The Middle Bronze Age took up the first part of the second millennium BCE. This was the time of the Egyptian Middle Kingdom and the Second Intermediate Period. The situation in Mesopotamia is more complicated to describe: the Isin and Larsa 'Intermediate Period', followed by the Old Assyrian and Old Babylonian Periods in parallel. But the city-state of Mari deserves its own treatment because the texts found there are so important a source for much going on not only in Mesopotamia but also in Syria. In Anatolia was the Hittite Old Kingdom, which interacted with both the Syrian and the Mesopotamian peoples and states.

Egypt became reunited under the 11th Dynasty king Mentuhotep II around 2000 BCE. Egypt began once again to expand its borders into Nubia and the Delta and to establish trade links with Punt, Byblos, and Sinai. This continued under the 12th Dynasty with its four Amenemhets and three Sesotrises. The achievements of Sesostris I, II, and III became so well known that the Greek writer Herodotus was acquainted with a legend of Sesostris more than a thousand years later, while a building project of Amenemhet III seems to have given rise to the Labyrinth legend. In the meantime, 'Asiatics' appear to have been migrating peacefully into the Delta and settling there. The country became disunified once more, apparently during the 13th Dynasty. Some assign the first part of Dynasty 13 to the Middle Kingdom, while others put the whole of it under the Second Intermediate Period.

The Second Intermediate Period (*c.* 1750–1550) was a time of chaos not only in Egypt at the time but also for modern Egyptologists who are trying to reconstruct its history and rule. Some think the 14th Dynasty broke the unified rule of the 13th, but others dismiss the existence of the 14th all together. Most make the 13th Dynasty straddle the line between the Middle Kingdom and the Second Intermediate Period. Particularly important is the 15th or 'Hyksos' Dynasty, though whether it succeeded the 14th which was already an 'Asiatic' rule or whether it had no connections with the alleged 14th Dynasty is a matter of debate. The 17th Dynasty seems to have succeeded the 13th, but the 16th Dynasty also remains a problem (some think it was invented by Manetho). What seems accepted by most is that the Second Intermediate Period came to a close with the last king of Dynasty 17 and the first of Dynasty 18 defeating the Hyksos in their capital of Avaris and driving them out of Egypt (though probably only some of the ruling class).

The Old Assyrian Period (*c.* 2000–1750 BCE) is notable mainly for the trading network it established with Anatolia and the trading colonies it set up there, covering the best part of a century before interference not only from hostile powers but also the Assyrian king Shamshi-Adad brought the enterprise to an end. It was Hammurabi (*c.* 1775) who made Babylon great during the Old Babylonian Period (*c.* 2000–1600 BCE), though his empire did not long outlive him. But he is the one who brought Mari independence to an end and made it only another component in his domain. Yet in spite of its relatively small size and its position on the edge of Mesopotamia, it deserves much more than a footnote in the history of this period. The thousands of texts found there give us insight into all aspects of Mesopotamian culture and also about the history of Mesopotamia and Syria, since she had connections both with the east and the west. Interaction with Syria, however, is dealt with in the next chapter.

Although the history of the Hittites begins in the third millennium BCE, we know little about them. It is also true that we know little even in the second millennium before about 1650 BCE. We have some information from about 1750 of a conquest of the city of Kanesh, called Nesa (which was the hub of the Assyrian trading route). The son of the conqueror was named Anitta who continued to expand, including into Hattusa which he destroyed. The first documented Hittite king was Hattusili I (*c.* 1625 BCE) who refounded Hattusa as his capital and expanded west into cities north of Yamhad (though apparently avoiding a confrontation with Yamhad itself). His successor Mursili

I conquered Aleppo and even went on a 500-mile expedition to take Babylon (he did not occupy it but his destruction allowed the Kassites to take over). Mursili was assassinated, and a number of his successors shared the same fate. But finally (*c.* 1500) Telipinu became king. He brought stability to the throne and issued a famous *Testament* that attempted to regulate the succession. His rule ended the Hittite Old Kingdom.

Of the data catalogued in this chapter, two have implications for the history of Syria and Palestine (described in the next chapter): the migration of 'Asiatics' into the Nile Delta and the establishment of the Hyksos 15th Dynasty, and the Mari texts which tell us about the Amorites and Syria.

CHAPTER 4

Syria and Palestine

L. L. Grabbe (2017) *Ancient Israel: What Do We Know and How Do We Know it?*;
H. Klengel (1992) *Syria 3000 to 300 B.C.: A Handbook of Political History*; **A. Kuhrt**
(1995) *The Ancient Near East c. 3000–300 BC*; **M Liverani** (2014) *The Ancient Near
East: History, Society and Economy*; **A.-L. Mourad** (2015) *Rise of the Hyksos: Egypt
and the Levant from the Middle Kingdom to the Early Second Intermediate Period*;
D. B. Redford (1992a) *Egypt, Canaan, and Israel in Ancient Times*; **M. L. Steiner and
A. E. Killebrew (eds)** (2014) *The Oxford Handbook of the Archaeology of the Levant,
c. 8000–332 BCE*.

The present chapter is concerned with the various states and groups that made up the Middle Bronze Levant. It begins with a review of the sources before treating first the area of Syria and then the area of Palestine/Canaan, ending with the important question of whether the history of Israel might begin with the patriarchal narratives as some have assumed.

4.1 SOURCES

J. Baines (1982) 'Interpreting *Sinuhe*', *JEA* 68: 31–44; **L. L. Grabbe** (1994)
'"Canaanite": Some Methodological Observations in Relation to Biblical Study', in
G. J. Brooke, A. H. W. Curtis, and J. F. Healey (eds), *Ugarit and the Bible: Proceedings
of the International Symposium on Ugarit and the Bible, Manchester, September 1992*:
113–22; **idem** (1997) 'The Book of Leviticus', *CR:BS* 5: 91–110; **idem** (2004) *A History
of the Jews and Judaism in the Second Temple Period 1: Yehud: A History of the Persian
Province of Judah*; **idem** (2006b) 'The Law, the Prophets, and the Rest: The State of the
Bible in Pre-Maccabean Times', *DSD* 13: 319–38; **W. Helck** (1971) *Die Beziehungen
Ägyptens zu Vorderasien im 3. und 2. Jahrtausend v. Chr.*: 44–67; **S. B. Parker** (1997)
Ugaritic Narrative Poetry; **G. Posener** (1940) *Princes et pays d'Asie et de Nubie:
Textes hiératiques sur des figurines d'envoûtement du Moyen Empire*; **A. F. Rainey**
(1972) 'The World of Sinuhe', *IOS* 2: 369–408; **D. B. Redford** (1992b) 'Execration

and Execration Texts', *ABD* 2:681–2; **R. Rendtorff** (1997) 'Directions in Pentateuchal Studies', *CR:BS* 5: 43–65; **S. J. Seidlmayer** (2001) 'Execration Texts', in D. B. Redford (ed.), *Oxford Encyclopedia of Ancient Egypt*: 1:487–9; **K. Streit** (2017) 'A Maximalist Interpretation of the Execration Texts – Archaeological and Historical Implications of a High Chronology', *JAEI* 13: 59–69; **R. N. Whybray** (1987) *The Making of the Pentateuch: A Methodological Study*.

We have a variety of sources for the MBA, primarily archaeology but also texts preserved in several different sites around the ancient Near East, though not in Palestine itself. The sources noted here concern both Syria and Palestine; however, archaeology and some others will chiefly relate to Palestine. Archaeology is primary, though the information it gives is often different from that found in texts (cf. Grabbe 2017: 6–29). The textual sources are the following:

Apart from archaeology, the situation in Palestine is known mainly through Egyptian texts, though Egyptian texts also give information on other parts of the Levant. The Egyptian Execration Texts (Streit 2017; Helck 1971: 44–67; Seidlmayer 2001; Redford 1992b; *ANET* 328–9; *CoS* 1:50–2; Posener 1940) were ceramic objects on which the names of enemies or potential enemies to be cursed were written. The object was then broken to effect the curses. Two sets of broken pieces, dated to the 12th or 13th Dynasty (nineteenth or eighteenth centuries BCE) have been found which included names in the Palestinian area. The main value of these is topographical, to show which cities existed in Palestine in particular periods, since only names and no other information is given. The *Story of Sinuhe*, although taken as an actual account of personal experiences by some, seems rather to be a piece of literature (*AEL* 1:222–35; Baines 1982). Its main theme has been taken to focus on the disadvantages of being removed from one's country of Egypt, but it makes reference to a number of data relating to Syria and Palestine that seem to represent a contemporary description (Rainey 1972).

The city-state of Ugarit on the Mediterranean coast opposite Cyprus has become quite important for study of the Hebrew Bible. The city was known of through the Amarna letters but was not discovered until about 1928 in the area of Ras Shamra in Syria. Tablets written in an unknown language and script were unearthed quite quickly. The script was written on clay tablets in wedge shapes but, unlike Mesopotamian cuneiform, was clearly an alphabet of 29 letters. The script and language were deciphered within a couple of years, and some of the important tablets were already translated before World War II. The language was found to belong to Northwest Semitic, the sub-family which also includes Hebrew, Aramaic, and Phoenician. Ugarit already existed as an independent entity in the eighteenth century, but it reached its height during the Amarna period (fourteenth century).

We have correspondence between Egypt and Ugarit in the Amarna tablets and in texts from Ugarit. The city was apparently destroyed sometime about 1200 BCE, whether by the Sea Peoples (as often alleged) or others. When the Ugaritic texts were first deciphered about 1930, their importance for the mythology and literary world of the Israelites was quickly recognized. Many of the texts are in alphabetic cuneiform and the Ugaritic language (*KTU*; *CML*; Parker 1997). But other texts were in Akkadian and even Hurrian, and some of these have more direct relevance for the history of the eastern Mediterranean in the second millennium BCE. Although Ugarit and the Ugaritic texts have often been used to reconstruct Canaanite culture, mythology, and religion, Ugarit seems to have been considered outside of Canaan (Grabbe 1994). The Ugaritic texts provide some historical information for the Amarna age, though this is usually in the way of general background since they do not usually mention Palestine directly.

The Mesopotamia texts for Syria are limited, but the main ones are the Mari tablets (see §3.2.4 for a discussion of Mari and the Mari texts). Most of the Mesopotamian texts do not mention Palestine, though there seems to have been trade between Hazor and Mari. These texts are mainly important for northern Syria, though they have been invoked in the past for information relating to the patriarchs. From northern Syria we have the Alalakh tablets which give us information on activity of the states in that region (§4.2.4). In the Mitanni region the Nuzi tablets (§5.3.2) mainly relate to the legal and business spheres but are often brought into the discussion about the patriarchs.

Our main secondary written source is the book of Genesis. It is really the only biblical book that purports to describe events in the first part of the second millennium BCE. The question is how much the author or compiler knew about the events it describes. Not long ago, it was a strong consensus of scholarship that Genesis was compiled mainly from three sources: the Yahwist (J), the Elohist (E), and the priestly writer (P). Many would still agree with that, but opinion is much more divided. Basically, the old consensus that had developed around the Documentary Hypothesis has gone, though there is nothing to take its place (Rendtorff 1997; Whybray 1987). Some still accept the Documentary Hypothesis in much its original form, but many accept only aspects of it or at least put a question mark by it. There has also been much debate around the J source (Rendtorff 1997: 53–5) and the P source (Grabbe 1997).

It seems clear that the Pentateuch was put together in the Persian period (Grabbe 2004: 331–43; 2006b). If so, it is unlikely that a substantial memory of second-millennium events is to be found in Genesis. True, many traditions in the Pentateuch are accepted to be pre-exilic (for example, Deuteronomy is still widely dated to the seventh century BCE), but that is still well over a thousand years later than a conventional dating for the patriarchs. An evaluation of the patriarchal tradition on its own terms confirms this *a priori* position (§4.4).

4.2 HISTORY OF SYRIA

M. Broshi and R. Gophna (1986) 'Middle Bronze Age II Palestine: Its Settlements and Population', *BASOR* 261: 73–90; **M. E. Buck** (2019) *The Amorite Dynasty of Ugarit: Historical Implications of Linguistic and Archaeological Parallels*; **S. Bunimovitz and Z. Lederman** (2013) 'Solving a Century-Old Puzzle: New Discoveries at the Middle Bronze Gate of Tel Beth-Shemesh', *PEQ* 145: 6–24; **P. M. Fischer** (1999) 'Chocolate-on-White Ware: Typology, Chronology, and Provenance: The Evidence from Tell Abu al-Kharaz, Jordan Valley', *BASOR* 313: 1–29; **I. J. Gelb** (1984) 'The Inscription of Jibbiṭ-Lîm, King of Ebla', *Studia Orientalia* 55: 213–29; **L. L. Grabbe** (1994) '"Canaanite": Some Methodological Observations in Relation to Biblical Study', in G. J. Brooke, A. H. W. Curtis, and J. F. Healey (eds), *Ugarit and the Bible: Proceedings of the International Symposium on Ugarit and the Bible, Manchester, September 1992*: 113–22; **W. Helck** (1971) *Die Beziehungen Ägyptens zu Vorderasien im 3. und 2. Jahrtausend v. Chr.*; **M. L. Pruitt** (2019) *Cultural Identity, Archaeology, and the Amorites of the Early Second Millennium BCE: An Analytical Paradigmatic Approach*.

As was indicated under sources (§4.1), the history of the Levant in the MBA is known primarily from texts preserved at various sites. We begin with some general remarks before surveying the individual kingdoms. Ebla was important about the middle of the third millennium BCE, but was destroyed about 2300 BCE. After its destruction, Ebla had risen from the ashes, but it was not a major player, now being a minor and often subordinate kingdom. It continued to exist in the Middle Bronze Age and apparently did function as an economic centre. We know of at least one ruler, Ibbit-Lim (or Jibbit-Lîm), about 1950 BCE who has been analysed as having an Amorite name (Gelb 1984). Most of the Syrian centres seem to have had Amorite dynasties (see further at §4.2.3). The indication is that there was brisk trade involving the city-states of Byblos, Ugarit, Ebla, Aleppo, and Mari – with each other but also further afield: the names of Crete and Cyprus are mentioned in texts from about 1800 BCE.

4.2.1 Ugarit

D. Arnaud (1998) 'Prolégomènes à la rédaction d'une histoire d'Ougarit II: Les bordereaux de rois divinisés', *SMEA* 41: 153–73; **M. E. Buck** (2019) *The Amorite Dynasty of Ugarit: Historical Implications of Linguistic and Archaeological Parallels*; **A. Caquot, J.-M. de Tarragon, and J.-L. Cunchillos** (1989) *Textes ougaritiques, Tome II: Textes religieux et rituels; Correspondance* (= LAPO 14); **S. Lackenbacher** (2002) *Textes akkadiens d'Ugarit: Textes provenant des vingt-cinq premières campagnes* (= LAPO 20); **D. Pardee** (1988) *Les textes para-mythologiques de la 24ᵉ Campagne (1961)* (= RSO 4); **idem** (2002) *Ritual and Cult at Ugarit*; **J. A. Sasson** (1984) 'Zimri-Lim Takes the Grand Tour', *BA* 47: 246–51; **idem** (2008) 'Text, Trade, and Travelers', in J. Aruz (ed.), *Beyond Babylon: Art, Trade, and Diplomacy in the Second Millennium B.C.*: 95–100; **idem** (2015) *From the Mari Archives: An Anthology of Old Babylonian Letters*; **I. Singer** (1999) 'A Political History of Ugarit', in W. G. E. Watson and N. Wyatt (eds), *Handbook of Ugaritic Studies*: 603–733; **P. Villard** (1986) 'Un roi de Mari à Ugarit', *UF* 18: 387–412; **D. J. Wiseman** (1953) *The Alalakh Tablets*.

This important city on the Syrian coast opposite to Cyprus existed already in the third millennium BCE (though not mentioned in the Ur III texts), and some of its texts seem to date to the early second millennium, though most are later. Because much of its known history relates to the Late Bronze Age, most of our discussion of Ugarit will be delayed until that chapter (§5.4.2 below). A huge corpus of literature relates to the Ugaritic myth and ritual texts but less is available on the history of the city-state. Of particular importance here is the survey of I. Singer (1999). Although some of the most important literary texts are written in the Ugaritic language and the unique Ugaritic alphabet, texts important for its history are more often in Akkadian cuneiform (see especially Lackenbacher 2002 [LAPO 20], but also Caquot/de Tarragon/Cunchillos 1989: 239–421 [LAPO 14]). Toward the end of the third millennium BCE, the site of Ugarit was deserted, but sometime in the early second millennium it was resettled again, with an Amorite ruling dynasty (Buck 2020).

An Alalakh text from Level VII mentions Ugarit (Wiseman 1953: 99, text *358), as do some of the Mari texts. It has been argued that two temples on the acropolis and the 'Hurrian temple' in the palace area were built shortly after the city was refounded; however, some now date these constructions to the end of the MB or later (Singer 1999: 609). Ugarit was central to the trade network linking Mesopotamia to Crete, Cyprus, and the Aegean. The importance of the trade in tin for the Mesopotamian and Syrian region has been noted (§3.2.2). Ugarit was part of this exchange, and a number of Mari texts mention tin for Ugarit as well as other recipients or intermediaries (e.g., Sasson 2015: 50–1, text 23.556). Tin was of course a constituent of bronze, and copper from Cyprus moved eastward through Ugarit, as tin moved westward. Of interest is the mention of interpreters to assist in the process of trading (Klengel 1992: 77).

For much of the Middle Bronze Age, the Ugaritic city-state seems to have been under the domination of Yamhad (§4.2.4). We have Mari texts that describe a state journey to Ugarit made by Yarim-Lim I of Yamhad; he was apparently accompanied by his son-in-law Zimri-Lim of Mari (*c.* 1765 BCE: Villard 1986; Sasson 1984, 2008; 2015: 73 [text A.2966]; Klengel 1992: 56–7, 77). Why Zimri-Lim would have made this journey is not certain, but it would have given him an opportunity to engage with his father-in-law, interact with trading partners such as Yamhad and Ugarit, see some of his daughters who had been married off to other royalty, and perhaps to claim he had reached the 'Great Sea', as other rulers had boasted. Like Byblos, Ugarit appears to have had contacts with Egypt, judging from Egyptian artifacts with hieroglyphic inscriptions, found there for this period (Helck 1971: 68).

No king is mentioned for Ugarit in any of the MB texts, though a later king list may give us the succession (or partial succession) of rulers of Ugarit (RS 24.257 = CTA 1.113: Pardee 1988: 165–78; 2002: 192–210). The text (in the Ugaritic language and alphabet) is only partially preserved, and its reading and interpretation has occasioned much discussion (§5.4.2). There is general agreement that it is a list of 'divinized' kings of Ugarit, i.e., kings who (after death) had assimilated to the ranks of the lower group of divine beings called *Rephaim*. The preserved text contains 16 names that can be reconstructed but clearly listed many more. Another Ras Shamra text (RS 94.2518) in Akkadian cuneiform apparently overlaps it, with 26 names (Arnaud 1998; Pardee 2002: 203–4). Pardee suggests that the original list had about 49 names. If so, they apparently stretched from the (mythical) founder of the dynasty Ditanu to perhaps the final king to rule Ugarit. Pardee (2002: 201) suggests that the 'text may reflect a musical rite in honor of the deceased kings, perhaps repeated regularly, perhaps repeated only on the death of a king'. Thus, we probably have a substantial list of the kings of Ugarit beginning already in the Middle Bronze Age, though the exact dates are uncertain (see the proposed list and rough dates in Arnaud 1998: 163). A number of these names are, however, known from LB sources.

M. E. Buck (2020) developed a 'hybrid model' to explain the material culture, involving both exogenous and endogenous forces. That is, about 1800 BCE Amorite migratory groups immigrated into both northern and southern Levant and settled some of the main sites abandoned in the late EBA. They built a number of monumental constructions in the city of Ugarit, including fortifications, two large temples, and a massive palace. This indicated a centralized command of large labour and financial resources. They interacted with the indigenous inhabitants and developed a hybrid material culture. They also brought Amorite religious rites and deities. According to her reconstruction, the Amorite heritage continued to be important to Ugarit throughout its history and was a factor in its flourishing culturally and commercially.

4.2.2 Byblos (Gubla)

W. F. Albright (1964) 'The Eighteenth-Century Princes of Byblos and the Chronology of Middle Bronze', *BASOR* 176: 38–46; **idem** (1965) 'Further Light on the History of Middle-Bronze Byblos', *BASOR* 179: 38–43; **G. Dossin** (1939b) 'Les archives économiques du palais de Mari', *Syria* 20: 97–113; **K. A. Kitchen** (1967) 'Byblos, Egypt, and Mari in the Early Second Millennium B.C.', *Or* 36: 39–54; **G. T. Martin** (1968) 'A New Prince of Byblos', *JNES* 27: 141–2.

Artifacts found at Byblos, as well as some mentions in Egyptian inscriptions, indicate that trading contacts existed between Egypt and Byblos in the MBA. The Execration Texts refer to 'Asiatics' (*'Amu*) of this city but without the name of a ruler. Byblos is repeatedly mentioned in the Mari texts where fabrics from the city (*Gu-ub-la^{ki}*) were especially appreciated (Dossin 1939b: 111). We know of several Byblos rulers who were contemporary with the Egyptian late Middle Kingdom and the Mesopotamian Old Babylonian epoch. K. A. Kitchen (1967) reconstructs the king list of Byblos as follows (based mainly on hieroglyphic inscriptions on seals and tombs):

Ib-dadi ruler of Byblos under Amar-Suen of the 3rd Dynasty of Ur.
Abishemu I, apparently time of Amenemhet III.
Yapi-shemu-abi, associated with Amenemhet IV.
Yakin-ilu, contemporary of a Sehetepibrē' (either II or III in the early 13th Dynasty).
Yakin.
Yantin or Entin, known on a broken relief that also names Neferhotep I.
Yantin-Ammu (-Ḫammu in cuneiform script), contemporary of Zimri-lim of Mari and probably identical with the Yantin who was ruling under Neferhotep I (above).
Ilima-yapi(i), possibly son of Yantin.
Hasrurum son of Rum; labelled 'ruler of the land of Byblos', but evidently not ruler of metropolitan Byblos (like the others in this list); possibly a contemporary of Sihathor of the 13th Dynasty.
Abishemu II, considered later than Abishemu I; probably the same as the father of the next two.
Yapa'-shemu-abi, son of an Abishemu (II?).
'Egel (*'kr*), also son of an A[bish]emu (II?); identical with next?
'Egliya (*'k3i*), restoring work of an unnamed father; identical with previous?

There is much uncertainty here, but the connections between Byblos and Egypt are clear.

4.2.3 Amorites

M. Anbar (1991) *Les tribus amurrites de Mari*; **A. Andrason and J.-P. Vita** (2018) 'Amorite: A Northwest Semitic Language?', *JSS* 63: 19–58; **A. Archi** (1985) 'Mardu in the Ebla Texts', *Or* 54: 7–13; **G. Buccellati** (1966) *The Amorites of the Ur III Period*; **idem** (1997) 'Amorites', *OEANE* 1:107–11; **M. E. Buck** (2020) *The Amorite Dynasty of Ugarit: Historical Implications of Linguistic and Archaeological Parallels*; **A. A. Burke** (2021) *The Amorites and the Bronze Age Near East: The Making of a Regional*

Identity; **D. Charpin and J.-M. Durand** (1986) '"Fils de Sim'al": Les origines tribales des rois de Mari', *RdA* 80: 141–83; **G. Dossin** (1956) 'Une lettre de Iarîm-Lim, roi d'Alep, à Iašûb-Iaḫad, roi de Dîr', *Syria* 33: 63–9; **D. E. Fleming** (2016) 'The Amorites', in B. T. Arnold and B. A. Strawn (eds), *The World around the Old Testament: The Peoples and Places of the Ancient Near East*: 1–30; **A. H. Gardiner** (1947) *Ancient Egyptian Onomastica: Text and Plates*; **I. J. Gelb** (1961) 'The Early History of the West Semitic Peoples', *JCS* 15: 27–47; **idem** (1980) *Computer-Aided Analysis of Amorite*; **V. Golinets** (2018) *Das amurritische Onomastikon der altbabylonischen Zeit: Band 2 Verbalmorphologie des Amurritischen und Glossar der Verbalwurzeln*; **W. Helck** (1971) *Die Beziehungen Ägyptens zu Vorderasien im 3. und 2. Jahrtausend v. Chr.*; **H. B. Huffmon** (1965) *Amorite Personal Names in the Mari Texts: A Structural and Lexical Study*; **K. A. Kamp and N. Yoffee** (1980) 'Ethnicity in Ancient Western Asia during the Early Second Millennium B.C.: Archaeological Assessments and Ethnoarchaeological Prospectives', *BASOR* 237: 85–104; **M. Liverani** (1973) 'The Amorites', in D. J. Wiseman (ed.), *Peoples of Old Testament Times*: 100–133; **M. L. Pruitt** (2019) *Cultural Identity, Archaeology, and the Amorites of the Early Second Millennium BCE: An Analytical Paradigmatic Approach*; **P. Saretta** (2016) *Asiatics in Middle Kingdom Egypt: Perceptions and Reality*; **I. Singer** (1991) 'Appendix III: A Concise History of Amurru', in S. Izre'el, *Amurru Akkadian: A Linguistic Study*: 2:135–95; **M. P. Streck** (2000) *Das amurritische Onomastikon der altbabylonischen Zeit: Band 1 Die Amurriter, die onomastische Forschung, Orthographie und Phonologie, Nominalmorphologie*; **H. Tadmor** (1958) 'Historical Implications of the Correct Rendering of Akkadian *dâku*', *JNES* 17: 129–41.

The Amorites are often thought to be important for the early history of Israel (Buccellati 1966, 1997; Gelb 1961). The Bible presents them as a pre-Israelite people in the Palestinian region (e.g., Gen. 15.21; Exod. 13.5), sometimes associated with the hill country (Num. 13.29; Deut. 1.7, 44) but also with the Transjordanian region (Num. 21.13, 26). For example, they are mentioned as being among Israel's ancestors in Ezek. 16.3, though interestingly they were also supposedly one of the peoples opposing Israel on its way to Canaan (Num. 21.21-32). They are known mainly from two sorts of information: (1) their names in cuneiform sources and also a certain number of Amorite words borrowed into cuneiform texts (Streck 2000; Huffmon 1965; Gelb 1980); (2) references to them in cuneiform sources, by the Sumerogram MAR.TU or Akkadian *Amurru*. As far as archaeology is concerned, however, nothing distinctive has been found to relate to them (Buccellati 1966: 13–14).

The so-called 'Amorite Hypothesis' was a thesis made popular by such well-known advocates as K. M. Kenyon and W. F. Albright. It found its way into the standard *Cambridge Ancient History* (*CAH²* II, Parts 1 and 2) and dominated thinking in the 1950s to 1970s. This was the view that nomadic Amorites moved from the Amorite homeland east into Mesopotamia and south into Palestine, and served to explain the acknowledged Amorite influence and even Amorite ruling dynasties in a number of Syrian and Mesopotamian city-states. It came to be widely questioned in the 1980s and 1990s and is mainly discounted today in the sense of an invasion and mass migration of Amorite tribes from Syria into Palestine and Mesopotamia. The old thesis depended on the view that 'pots equal people' – that material culture can be associated with specific ethnic groups – which has now been generally rejected by archaeologists. A strong change in material culture, which was once assigned to the arrival of a new population, is now recognized to be possible in a settled population for a variety of reasons.

Yet some, even while ostensibly rejecting the Amorite Hypothesis, still theorize a widespread Amorite cultural incursion into the region, including into southern Palestine and even the Delta region of Egypt. A. A. Burke asserts this in his contribution to the archaeological handbook of Steiner/ Killebrew (2014: 403–13; see also in more detail his recent monograph Burke 2021). Similarly, P. Saretta (2016) argues that where Middle Kingdom and Second Intermediate Period Egyptian texts refer to *Amu*, normally translated generically as 'Asiatics', it in fact refers specifically to Amorites. The problem is that the label 'Amorite' is not used of Canaanites or those called *Amu* in the extant Egyptian texts. The term 'Amurru' apparently first appears in the texts of the New Kingdom pharaoh Sety I (Gardiner 1947: 1:188*; Helck 1971: 287) but refers to the small kingdom in northern Syria on the border between Egypt and Mitanni/Hatti (see further at §5.4.1). The argument that makes Canaan an Amorite area depends primarily on cultural similarities.

The recent study by M. E. Buck (2020: 116–84) looks at five key elements of material culture in her argument that Ugarit had an Amorite dynasty: fortifications, palace organizational system, *migdāl* temple construction, glyptic usage on seals, and evidence for the ritual sacrifice of donkeys (cf. above §4.2.1). Her investigation is very important, for she finds that only a few sites have four or five of these key elements (including Hazor and Megiddo), while in the area of Canaan itself only a few have two or three of the elements. More important are the number of sites which do not have these key elements, being most of the Palestinian sites. This indicates that Canaan as a whole was not dominated by Amorites, according to her criteria. Three of the key elements are found in Tell ed-Dab'a, the Hyksos capital. This would suggest that the ruling Hyksos dynasty might indeed have been Amorite, but the bulk of the Canaanites were not. The Egyptian term *Amu* seems to have referred to a variety of different West Semitic groups. We should not hypothesize an 'Amorite *koine* culture' for the region, as Burke seems to do.

The Amorites are already attested for the third millennium BCE, but treatment of them was postponed until here. G. Buccellati (1966) has examined the information available in the Ur III sources, which are an important reservoir of data on the Amorites. He finds that individuals labelled by the Sumerian term MAR.TU seem to fall into two categories. First, there are 'foreign' Amorites, usually with Amorite names who are said to come from the 'land of the Amorites' (*kur* MAR.TU) or the 'mountain of the Amorites' (*ḫursag* MAR.TU). In some cases these seem to refer to envoys operating between the Amorite country and Sumer, or they are individuals temporarily in the Babylonian region. References to them are mostly found in connection with the cities of Drehem (near Nippur) and Isin. But sometimes they are presented as hostile forces who are a danger to the 'civilized' country of Sumer. In their eyes, many Amorites were uncivilized barbarians foreign to their country and culture (see further below).

Yet there is a second group, also labelled Amorite, that seems to be settled in Sumerian cities. They generally have non-Amorite (i.e., Sumerian) names and tend to be associated with the cities of Lagaš and Umma. They occupy a variety of positions and professions, some fairly low in social position but others apparently high up in the social hierarchy (e.g., royal envoy and city mayor). The indication is that some of these have been settled for several generations and had assimilated to the Sumerian city culture.

A number of questions immediately rise as one looks into the matter of the Amorites. First, since language has played a large role in identifying Amorites, the question of the classification of Amorite is important. It has been widely analysed as a form of Northwest Semitic. Yet the matter is not so simple. A recent study by A. Andrason and J.-P. Vita (2018) has examined the question carefully and finds that while some features coincide with what would be associated with Northwest Semitic, other features (e.g., the verbal system) are more in line with East Semitic (various forms of Akkadian). They conclude, 'the evidence available currently does not enable us to equivocally determine the position of Amorite within the Semitic family' (Andrason/Vita 2018: 55). The extant data could link it with Northwest or East Semitic; especially important is the fact that various pieces of essential evidence are missing or their interpretation is uncertain. Since many arguments depend on the linguistic classification of Amorite, this means that such arguments are considerably weakened. This applies to the frequent assumption (usually unargued) that the Amorites are (North) west Semitic peoples.

The home of the Amorites according to the Ur III texts seems to be in northern Syria, in the mountainous region known as Jebel Bišri, to the northeast of Palmyra (Buccellati 1966: 235–42). This appears to be labelled the 'mountain of *Ba-sa-ar*' (alternatives include *Ba-ša-ar*, Ba_{11}-*sal-la*, *Bi-su-ru*, *Bi-ši-ir*) of some texts, which looks to be the equivalent of the 'mountain of MAR.TU' of other texts. From the late third millennium (2500–2000) the Amorites are referred to in texts from Ebla (Archi 1985) and the Ur III period of southern Mesopotamia (usually by the Sumerian designation MAR.TU). In spite of the decline of the Ur III regime, there is a basic continuity of references into the Old Babylonian period (1900–1600). Many names are found in OB texts and are identified as 'Amorite' by their structure, though the individual who bore them is seldom said to be Amorite. They are especially associated with the city-state of Mari on the Euphrates. Here we come to a major debate about how the Amorites came into Mesopotamia: some have argued that the Amorites invaded many of the Mesopotamian centres and established themselves by force; others have maintained that they were a dimorphic society who lived on the margins of Mesopotamian cities but gradually infiltrated and settled among the Akkadian population (Anbar 1991: 9–26). M. Anbar sets out to try to settle the question in his monograph.

The texts refer to 'Amorites' (MAR.TU, *Amurri*) during the first part of the MBA, but this usage gradually dies out. The last reference to the people seems to be about 1600 BCE (Liverani 1973: 115). After this Amorites are identified only by the Amorite form of their names or by reference to their tribes, with names such as Yaḥmadu, Did(a)num, Yamūtum, and Yaḥmuṭum (the last two might be the same); other names in the texts include Amurrum, Amnanūm, Yamina, Sim'al, Yariḫūm. We have the curious fact that the tribes are never called 'Amorite' in the extant texts, but we identify them as Amorite because they seem to have lived in the area labelled as Amorite in earlier texts. Amorite tribes include the 'sons of the south' (or 'southerners') and 'sons of the north' (or 'northerners'). The name of the first attracted attention since it was equivalent to 'Benjaminites'; however, the reading has been disputed. The last part of the name, *Yamīna*, apparently referring to the right-hand (or southern) bank of the Euphrates, is clear, but the first part of the name is written in Sumerograms DUMU.MEŠ 'sons (of)'. The question is whether it should be read as Akkadian *mārū(-yamīna)* or as Northwest Semitic *bini(-yamīna)* (Tadmor 1958; Anbar 1991: 83–4 n. 324). Gelb (1961: 37–8) suggests that 'sons' is only a semantic indicator of a tribal name and that it is appropriate to refer only to Yaminites. In any case, there is the parallel tribe of DUMU.MEŠ-*si-im-a-al* 'sons of the north' (or 'northerners'). The similarity to the biblical Benjaminites seems coincidental, even if the name is read *Bini-Yamīna* and not *Mārū-Yamīna* or just *Yamīna*.

Many of the descriptions make them nomadic pastoralists, and one text refers to the Amorite as a 'tent dweller [buffeted?] by wind and rain…the one who digs up mushrooms at the foot of the mountain, who does not know how to…bend his knee, who eats uncooked meat, who in his lifetime does not have a house, who on the day of his death will not be buried' (Buccellati 1966: 324–30, quote from 92–3). These were plainly exaggerated views but were nevertheless stated at various times in texts and seemed to represent a widespread concept of Akkadian peoples. Although many of the Amorites were tribal and engaged in pastoralism, this was not true of all of them (Kamp/Yoffee 1980: 89–94). As already discussed above, there are texts which refer to Amorites in an urban setting. Also, rather than being seen always as unruly, wild, and hostile, many seem to have been well blended into Sumerian society.

Already in the Ur III period many Amorites were 'fully integrated in every facet of the Mesopotamian social landscape. Amorites were pastoralists, agriculturalists, country dwellers and city dwellers' (Kamp/Yoffee 1980: 98). By the Late Bronze Age references to Amorites (*Amurru*) disappear from the Mesopotamian texts except as a general reference for the region to the west. However, a 'Kingdom of Amurru' in Syria is known from references in the Amarna letters, Ugaritic texts, and the texts from the Hittite capital at Boğazköy in Anatolia (Gelb 1961: 41–2); some Mari texts suggest that it already existed several centuries earlier than the Amarna period (Gelb 1961: 47). It was located west of the Euphrates, in Syria between Lebanon and Damascus; apparently a section of the territory extended as far as the Mediterranean (Gelb 1961: 42).

There are disagreements over Amorite origins. In the past it has been common to label them nomads on the fringes of civilization in the Euphrates region, and some texts seem to give support to this picture. Others think they were originally farmers in a narrow region of the mid-Euphrates who expanded their territory by moving into the steppe and taking up sheepbreeding. There is also the biased view in some cuneiform texts that considered them as uncultured, semi-wild people of the wilderness. There is also the position of M. E. Buck (2020) who argues for a 'hybrid model' which suggests a union between migrating Amorites into areas of the Levant and an integration with the culture of the indigenous inhabitants. Many texts already noted suggest such an integration in areas of Sumer and Mesopotamia.

4.2.4 Yamhad

M. C. Astour (1963) 'Place-Names from the Kingdom of Alalaḫ in the North Syrian List of Thutmose III: A Study in Historical Topography', *JNES* 22: 220–41; **G. Dossin** (1938) 'Les Archives épistolaires du Palais de Mari', *Syria* 19: 105–26; **idem** (1939a) 'Iamḫad et Qatanum', *RdA* 36: 46–54; **idem** (1955) 'L'inscription de fondation de Iaḫdun-Lim, roi de Mari', *Syria* 32: 1–28; **W. Heimpel** (2003) *Letters to the King of Mari: A New Translation, with Historical Introduction, Notes, and Commentary*; **B. Kienast** (1980) 'Die altbabylonischen Kaufurkunden aus Alalaḫ', *WO* 11: 35–63; **J. Sasson** (2015) *From the Mari Archives: An Anthology of Old Babylonian Letters*; **D. J. Wiseman** (1953) *The Alalakh Tablets*.

Yamhad was a northern Syrian city-state that we first hear of in the early second millennium BCE; it seems to have continued for about 200 years. There are only scattered references, but these indicate a substantial state during the Old Babylonian period, strong enough to resist the moves of Shamshi-Adad I of Assyria to take control. Its capital was Aleppo (Halab), but it dominated a number of neighbouring cities, including Ebla and Alalakh. About 500 texts were found in the excavations of Alalakh, mainly from two periods: about 1700 BCE and the fifteenth century (see the important collection of Wiseman 1953). They are mostly lists of various sorts: inventories, rations, landholdings, loans, etc. They thus tell us mainly about social, legal, and economic aspects of the people, though there are some documents about historical events. Carchemish also came under its control for a time, as did Emar and even Ugarit. We know of a number of its rulers, especially from the Mari texts. This was an Amorite dynasty, composed of those from the tribe Sim'al. The overall picture is not always clear because the same names occur over several generations and as governors over different vassal cities. The texts do not always distinguish one person from one with the same name a generation or so later or perhaps in a position of leadership over a vassal city. The following summarizes essentially what we know of Yamhad's history and rulers (Klengel 1992: 49–64).

The first recorded ruler is Sumu-epuh (*c.* 1800 BCE). He ruled about the same time as Yahdun-Lim of Mari. When Yahdun-Lim was attacked by a coalition of small kingdoms of the Euphrates Valley, Sumu-epuh evidently provided troops to aid this coalition against him (Dossin 1955), probably because Yahdun-Lim was seen as trying to expand Mari's power into Syria. Yamhad's neighbour Qatna was hostile toward her. After Shamshi-Adad conquered Mari, he formed an alliance against Sumu-epuh with Qatna but also including some other city-states (some of whom had previously been allies of Yamhad) such as Carchemish. The intent was apparently to capture Sumu-epuh and deliver him to Qatna, but the plan evidently failed. Qatna controlled the southern route between Mesopotamia and the Syrian coast, perhaps through Tadmor, but bypassing Yamhad to the north. No battle between Yamhad and Shamshi-Adad's alliance is discussed in the texts, suggesting that the alliance was primarily meant to put pressure on Sumu-epuh. Although Sumu-epuh did not die in battle, his death is mentioned in a letter of Shamshi-Adad after he conquered Mari.

Yarim-Lim I (*c.* 1775 BCE), Sumu-epuh's son, had quite an eventful reign. Shamshi-Adad continued to oppose Yamhad, allied with Qatna and Mari (which was ruled by one of Shamshi-Adad's sons); however, Yamhad had allies in Eshnuna and Babylon. A few years after Yarim-Lim came to the throne, Shamshi-Adad died (possibly killed in a conflict with Yamhad). The result was that Zimri-Lim from the traditional dynasty was able to take back rulership of Mari from the Assyrians. Yarim-Lim had hosted Zimri-Lim in Aleppo at an earlier time, which allowed Yamhad to establish a good relationship with Mari (cf. Dossin 1939; Heimpel 2003: 321); indeed, some texts (e.g., *ARM* 28.16 [Sasson 2015: 81–2]) state that Yarim-Lim assisted Zimri-Lim to the throne. According to a 'declaration of war' (Dossin 1956; Sasson 2015: 184) Yarim-Lim 'saved' (*ú-še-zi-bu*) the city of Babylon (though not everyone agrees that the letter is historical: e.g., Sasson 2015: 184). All this, plus the fact that Yamhad either prevailed or held its own (as with Shamshi-Adad) in conflicts with its regional enemies, indicates that it was a powerful state at this time. Yarim-Lim's influence reached widely into Mesopotamia.

Hammurabi I of Yamhad (*c.* 1750 BCE) came to the throne in Zimri-Lim's ninth year (year 28 of Hammurabi of Babylon). He maintained good relations with Mari and also Ugarit. Also, apparently acceptable relations with the traditional enemy Qatna were established, and the regular conflicts between these two neighbours appear to have ceased. Yamhad also seems to have remained on good terms with Hammurabi of Babylon (even though the latter conquered Mari and deposed Zimri-Lim). Abba-el I (*c.* 1725 BCE) was probably the son of Hammurabi I, though this is not certain. He seems to be referred to in an Old Babylonian letter by the successor of Hammurabi of Babylon, Samsuiluna (Klengel 1992: 60). Alalakh remained subordinate to Yamhad, evidently ruled by Abba-el's brother. He put down a rebellion and destroyed the town of Irride but gave Alalakh to his brother as compensation for Irride which his brother would otherwise have ruled (Frayne 1990: 799–800). Emar and Carchemish were under Abba-el's control, though it is not clear that Ugarit was also. Abba-el is a witness in a sale document (Kienast 1980).

Little is known of the next king, Yarim-Lim II (*c.* 1710 BCE). He was succeeded by his son, Niqmi-epuh (*c.* 1700 BCE), who was responsible for the conquest of Arazik on the Euphrates (Wiseman 1953: 35, text *7). This fighting at Arazik might suggest that Yamhad's control of the regions east of the Euphrates was endangered. He is also associated with the city of Nishin (if that is the correct reading [Wiseman 1953: 38, text *11]) within the territory of Yamhad, a site evidently also mentioned in the topographical list of Thutmose III as Egyptian *ntn* (Astour 1963: 230). Irkabtum (*c.* 1675 BCE) was the son of Niqmi-epuh (Wiseman 1953: 113, text *443, if the reading is correct). During his reign a document was dated to the time that he 'returned from Nashtarbi' (Wiseman 1953: 43, text *33), which could be a reference to a rebellion in that city. If so, this may relate to the rise of Hurrian power in this region to the east once controlled by Yamhad.

Next was Yarim-Lim III (*c.* 1650 BCE), the brother of Irkabtum, who was succeeded by his son Hammurabi II (*c.* 1625 BCE). Again, we know little of them, but we at least have the names of rulers in Aleppo covering a period of about 200 years. Yamhad's end as a major power in Syria came with the expansion of the Hittite Old Kingdom about 1600 BCE. Hattusili I (*c.* 1625 BCE) invaded Syria and destroyed Alalakh, Urshu, and other sites in the region. Yamhad territory may have been violated, and her troops may have assisted some of the besieged cities. Yet a direct assault on Aleppo seems not to have taken place, at least not a successful one. It was Hattusili's successor Mursili I who conquered Yamhad about 1600 BCE (see further at §3.3.1).

4.3 HISTORY OF PALESTINE/CANAAN

4.3.1 Archaeology

W. F. Albright (1961) 'Abram the Hebrew: A New Archaeological Interpretation', *BASOR* 163: 36–54; **S. Bunimovitz** (1998) 'On the Edge of Empires – Late Bronze Age (1500–1200 BCE)', in T. E. Levy (ed.), *The Archaeology of Society in the Holy Land*: 320–31; **W. M. Clark** (1977) 'The Patriarchal Traditions: The Biblical Traditions', in J. H. Hayes and J. M. Miller (eds), *Israelite and Judaean History*: 120–48; **W. G. Dever** (1977) 'The Patriarchal Traditions: Palestine in the Second Millennium BCE: The Archaeological Picture', in J. H. Hayes and J. M. Miller (eds), *Israelite and Judaean History*: 70–120; **idem** (1987) 'The Middle Bronze Age – The Zenith of the Urban Canaanite Era', *BA* 50: 148–77; **I. Finkelstein** (1988) *The Archaeology of the Israelite Settlement*; **idem** (1992c) 'The Middle Bronze Age "Fortifications": A Reflection of

Social Organization and Political Formations', *TA* 19: 201–20; **idem** (1993) 'The Sociopolitical Organization of the Central Hill Country in the Second Millennium B.C.E.', in A. Biran and J. Aviram (eds), *Biblical Archaeology Today, 1990. Proceedings of the Second International Congress on Biblical Archaeology*: Supplement: *Pre-Congress Symposium: Population, Production and Power, Jerusalem, June 1990*: 110–31; **idem** (1998) 'The Rise of Early Israel: Archaeology and Long-Term History', in S. Aḥituv and E. D. Oren (eds), *The Origin of Early Israel – Current Debate: Biblical, Historical and Archaeological Perspectives*: 7–39; **I. Finkelstein and N. A. Silberman** (2001) *The Bible Unearthed: Archaeology's New Vision of Ancient Israel and the Origin of its Sacred Texts*; **Z. Herzog** (1997) 'Beersheba', *OEANE* 1:287–91; **D. Ilan** (1998) 'The Dawn of Internationalism – The Middle Bronze Age', in T. E. Levy (ed.), *The Archaeology of Society in the Holy Land*: 297–319; **Ø. LaBianca** (1997) 'Palestine in the Bronze Age', *OEANE* 4:212–17; **A. F. Rainey** (1984) 'Early Historical Geography of the Negeb', in Z. Herzog (ed.), *Beer-Sheba II: The Early Iron Age Settlements*: 88–104; **H. Weippert** (1988) *Palästina in vorhellenistischer Zeit*.

The Middle and Late Bronze Ages cover much of the second millennium BCE, MB extending over approximately 2000–1500 BCE. These divisions are not exact and are to some extent artificial, but they broadly represent significant differences in culture and society, as well as historical background. As noted in an earlier chapter, terminology for archaeological periods is not consistent (§2.4.1). The scheme used here (cf. Dever 1987: 149–50; Ilan 1998: 297) is:

MB I (*c.* 2000–1800 BCE)
MB II (*c.* 1800–1650 BCE)
MB III (*c.* 1650–1500 BCE)

These dates are in part based on historical events, whereas the cultures recorded by archaeology do not always follow the historical periods marked off by events. Needless to say, there is much disagreement, with many ending the MB in 1550 or even 1600 BCE.

Middle Bronze Age I–III in Palestine has become better known in recent years (Dever 1977, 1987; Finkelstein 1993: 110–31; LaBianca 1997; Ilan 1998; Steiner/Killebrew [eds] 2014: 401–94). It seems to have been an era of considerable urbanism: one estimate puts the urban population at half as great again as the rural population (Ilan 1998: 305). Many sites were fortified (Finkelstein 1993), and 'a proliferation of massive fortifications is the single most characteristic feature of the fully developed phases of the period' (Dever 1987: 153): an estimated 65 per cent of the population lived in a few fortified sites of 20 hectares or more. In MB I an unprecedented surge in settlement swept the hill country, large sites including Shechem, Dothan, Shiloh, Tell el-Far'ah North, Hebron, Beth-zur and Jerusalem (Finkelstein 1993: 117–18). About 75 per cent of the population seems to have lived between Shechem and the Jezreel Valley. In the areas of Ephraim and Manasseh there was a definite extension into the western part of the regions. But settlement in the central hill country began only later, in MB II. In MB II–III almost every site seems to have been fortified, down to as small as 8–16 dunums.

W. G. Dever (1987: 153) suggests that the larger sites were in fact city-states. How one is to relate this conclusion with S. Bunimovitz's (1998: 323) argument that, following the Rank Size Index, the southern coastal plain and the Jezreel Valley were more integrated in MB than LB is not clear. D. Ilan (1998: 300–301) suggests that the cultural changes coming about in MB were in part caused by immigration of a new population into Canaan (possibly the Amorites and perhaps others such as the Hurrians), even though the 'diffusionist' explanation has ceased to be very popular (on the Amorites, see §4.2.3). There is evidence of trade with Syria and Mesopotamia, with Hazor as the main 'gateway' for Canaan (Ilan 1998: 306–8). There was also extensive trade with Egypt, the main trading centre being Tell el-Dab'a. At first most commerce was with the northern Syrian coast (especially Byblos), but it gradually shifted south.

The Middle Bronze Age ended with widespread collapse, often ascribed to the conquest of Avaris and the expulsion of the Hyksos from Egypt (*c.* 1550 BCE), and/or subsequent campaigns by Thutmose III and other 18th Dynasty rulers (Ilan 1998: 314–15). There is now a tendency to see other causes (or additional causes) and also to recognize that the collapse was complex and spread over a considerable period of time. Also, there was substantial cultural continuity with the following LBA. The socio-cultural changes at the end of the MBA 'reshaped the social landscape of Palestine and had a profound, long-term impact on Canaanite society' (Bunimovitz 1998: 320). Although some have seen a major shift away from urbanism in the LBA, Bunimovitz (1998: 324) argues against this: urbanism was different in scale but the balance between urban and rural remained much the same. The urban centres were considerably smaller but so was the rural sector.

One issue concerns the cities or sites mentioned in Genesis in connection with the patriarchs (Dever 1977). W. F. Albright (1961) had argued that the patriarchal narratives fitted what is commonly called the EB IV period (2200–2000 BCE, though he attempted to date it as late as 1900 or even 1800 BCE). Unfortunately, neither his placement of the patriarchs nor that of others who have tried to situate them in the early second millennium BCE can be supported:

> A date in MB I [= EB IV or Intermediate Bronze] is ruled out for the patriarchs simply because the latest evidence shows that the main centres traditionally associated with their movements, *pace* Albright, are conspicuously lacking in MB I remains…. To date, not a single MB IIA [=MB I] site has been found in all of southern Transjordan or the Negeb – one of the principal arenas of patriarchal activities in Genesis. [Dever 1977: 99, 102]

At Beersheba (Genesis 21–22) there was a settlement gap between the Chalcolithic and Iron I – no MB remains at all (Herzog 1997; Rainey 1984: 94). Attempts to find the 'cities of the plain' (Gen. 19.24-29) have failed (Dever 1977: 101). It is difficult to find a period in the early or middle second millennium BCE when all sites in the patriarchal narratives were settled; on the contrary, it appears to be not until Iron I that this was so (Clark 1977: 147). On the other hand, many of the main cities known to have existed in the MBA are completely absent from the patriarchal narratives (Finkelstein/Silberman 2001: 321–3). For further information on the patriarchs, see §4.4.

4.3.2 Egyptian Textual References

W. C. Hayes (1949) 'The Career of the Great Steward Ḥenenu under Nebḥepetrē' Mentuḥotpe', *JEA* 35: 43–9; **N. Na'aman** (1992b) 'Canaanite Jerusalem and its Central Hill Country Neighbours in the Second Millennium B.C.E.', *UF* 24: 275–91; **D. B. Redford** (1992b) 'Execration and Execration Texts', *ABD* 2:681–2.

The main source here is the Execration Texts (discussed above [§4.1]). Their primary value is topographical, to show which cities existed in Palestine in particular periods, since only names and no other information is given. Included are apparently sites in Phoenicia (Byblos, Tyre), Syria (Damascus), some sites in Transjordan (such as Pella), but in Cis-Jordan are Aphek, Ashtaroth, Akko, Laish, Hazor, Rehov, Megiddo, Beth-Shean, Ekron, Beth-Shemesh, Lod, and Ashkelon; Shechem and Jerusalem are the only two highland sites in the extant texts. Some doubt the reference to Jerusalem (e.g., Na'aman 1992b). Some personal names also occur, 'Amorite' in form, with apparently no Hurrian or Indo-Iranian ones. An argument has been made that the two sets of texts attest a gradual sedentarizing and urbanizing of the countryside, but this view has been challenged (Redford 1992b). We do know that the Ephraimite hill country, as well as extensive sections of Syria, are absent from the texts.

Other texts give information on the coming of the Hyksos, their rule, and their ultimate demise, discussed in the next section on the Hyksos (§4.3.3). There was some interaction with Canaan in pre-Hyksos times. For example, in the 11th Dynasty the king's steward Henenu conducted a campaign against the Dwellers-across-the-Sand and brought back tribute, though this might have been a commercial rather than a strictly military venture; he also apparently cut trees in Lebanon and brought back cedar wood (Hayes 1949). Sesostris III (*c.* 1825 BCE) sent an expedition into Palestine which apparently captured Shechem (see further in the next section on the Hyksos).

4.3.3 The Hyksos

J. von Beckerath (1984) *Handbuch der ägyptische Königsnamen*; **P. P. Betancourt** (1997) 'Relations between the Aegean and the Hyksos at the End of the Middle Bronze Age', in E. D. Oren (ed.), *The Hyksos: New Historical and Archaeological Perspectives*: 429–32; **M. Bietak** (1996) *Avaris, the Capital of the Hyksos: Recent Excavations at Tell el-Dab'a*; **idem** (1997) 'Avaris, Captial of the Hyksos Kingdom: New Results of Excavations', in E. D. Oren (ed.), *The Hyksos: New Historical and Archaeological Perspectives*: 87–139; **idem** (2001) 'Hyksos', *OEAE* 2:136–43; **idem** (2011) 'The Aftermath of the Hyksos in Avaris', in R. Sela-Sheffy and G. Toury (eds), *Culture Contacts and the Making of Cultures: Papers in Homage to Itamar Even-Zohar*: 19–46; **G. Farino** (1938) *Papiro dei re, restaurate*; **H. Goedicke** (1986) 'The End of the Hyksos in Egypt', in L. H. Lesko (ed.), *Egyptological Studies in Honor of Richard A. Parker*: 37–47; **P. E. McGovern and G. Harbottle** (1997) '"Hyksos" Trade Connections between Tell el-Dab'a (Avaris) and the Levant: A Neutron Activation Study of the Canaanite Jar', in E. D. Oren (ed.), *The Hyksos: New Historical and Archaeological Perspectives*: 141–57; **A.-L. Mourad** (2013) 'Asiatics and Abydos: From the Twelfth Dynasty to the Early Second Intermediate Period', *Bulletin of the Australian Centre* *for Egyptology* 24: 31–58; **idem** (2015) *Rise of the Hyksos: Egypt and the Levant from the Middle Kingdom to the Early Second Intermediate Period*; **E. D. Oren (ed.)** (1997) *The Hyksos: New Historical and Archaeological Perspectives*; **E. Peet** (1914) *Stela of Sebek-khu: The Earliest Record of an Egyptian Campaign in Asia*; **G. Posener** (1957) 'Les Asiatiques en Égypte sous les XIIe et XIIIe dynasties (À propos d'un livre récent)', *Syria* 34: 145–63; **A. F. Rainey** (1993) 'Sharḫân/Sharuhen – The Problem of Identification', in *Eretz-Israel 24: Avraham Malamat Volume*: 178*–87*; **D. B. Redford** (1970b) 'The Hyksos in History and Tradition', *Or* 39: 1–51; **idem** (1997a) 'Textual Sources for the Hyksos Period', in E. D. Oren (ed.), *The Hyksos: New Historical and Archaeological Perspectives*: 1–44; **D. B. Redford and J. M. Weinstein** (1992) 'Hyksos', *ABD* 3:341–8; **C. A. Redmount** (1995) 'Ethnicity, Pottery, and the Hyksos at Tell El-Maskhuta in the Egyptian Delta', *BA* 58: 181–90; **K. S. B. Ryholt** (1997) *The Political Situation in Egypt 'during the Second Intermediate Period c. 1800–1550 B.C.*; **S. N. Saleen and Z. Hawass** (2021) 'Computed Tomography Study of the Mummy of King Seqenenre Taa II: New Insights Into His Violent Death', *Frontiers in Medicine* (21 February 2021); **P. Saretta** (2016) *Asiatics in Middle Kingdom Egypt: Perceptions and Reality*; **T. Säve-Söderbergh** (1951) 'The Hyksos Rule in Egypt', *JEA* 37: 53–71; **G. J. Shaw** (2009) 'The Death of King Seqenenre Tao', *JARCE* 45: 159–76; **C. Stantis et al**. (2020) 'Who were the Hyksos? Challenging Traditional Narratives Using Strontium Isotope (^{87}Sr/^{86}Sr) Analysis of Human Remains from Ancient Egypt', *PLoS One* 15/7: 1–14; **J. Van Seters** (1966) *The Hyksos: A New Interpretation*; **W. G. Waddell** (1940) *Manetho*; **J. M. Weinstein** (1997a) 'Hyksos', *OEANE* 3:133–6.

In the eyes of the Egyptians the regions outside Egypt were made up of barbarians and nomads. We already noted relations between Egypt and the Levant in the third millennium BCE (§2.1): there were trading relations but also violent confrontation. The Middle Kingdom shows a more complex relationship and also set of attitudes, as discussed in several studies on the question (Redford 1992a; Mourad 2015; Saretta 2016; Posener 1957). It is true that the famous Execration Texts of the nineteenth or eighteenth century BCE see potential enemies in various cities and areas of the Levant to the northeast of Egypt (§4.1), but this was not the only view of 'Asiatics'.

'Asiatics' began to settle in the Delta region toward the beginning of the second millennium. There were also hostile relations with the *Amu*, with various hints in the documents and inscriptions of the 12th and 13th Dynasties about Egyptian attacks on them (Redford 1992a: 76–80). Many of the Asiatics serving in Egyptian households were probably there through enslavement, but others – free individuals – seem to have been imported to work on building projects. There were also free individuals living at various places in Egypt (some no doubt descendants of former slaves), some well integrated, even taking Egyptian names. But others came by immigration, with Asiatics coming with their cattle and families, sometimes temporarily but at other times permanently. As Egypt was descending into the Second Intermediate Period, the Levant was reaching its zenith, including the continuing migration into the Delta region.

A.-L. Mourad (2015) has studied the relations between the Levant and Egypt in the Middle Kingdom, with the aim of illuminating the rise of the Hyksos dynasty. The Hyksos were a group of people who became temporary rulers of Egypt but were said to be foreigners associated with Asia

(Weinstein 1997a; Oren [ed.] 1997; Redford/Weinstein 1992; Redford 1970b; the monograph of Van Seters [1966] marked a milestone in study of the Hyksos but appeared before major archaeological data were available from Egypt). They ruled during the Second Intermediate Period, making up the 15th Dynasty of the traditional Manethan king list. The Hyksos might not have been a single group, though they are treated as such by the Egyptian sources. One of the main textual sources remains Manetho, as mediated by Josephus and Julius Africanus (Waddell [ed.] 1940), but some native Egyptian sources are also available (Redford 1997a), as is archaeology (Bietak 1997; Redmount 1995). The Egyptian name *ḥq3w ḫ3swt* means 'rulers of foreign lands' and seems to have been their name for the actual Hyksos rulers, whereas the people are often referred to as *'3mw* 'Asiatics'. The names known from scarabs and other written sources appear to be Northwest Semitic.

The Hyksos could be said to belong mainly to Egyptian history, but since they seem to represent a group or groups that came from the Palestinian region, they are treated in this chapter. According to Manetho, as quoted in Josephus (*Ag. Ap.* 1.14 §§73-92),

> Tutimaeus. In his reign, for what cause I know not, a blast of God smote us; and unexpectedly, from the regions of the East, invaders of obscure race marched in confidence of victory against our land.... Finally, they appointed as king one of their number whose name was Salitis.... Their race as a whole was called Hyksôs, that is 'king-shepherds': for *hyk* in the sacred language means 'king', and *sôs* in common speech is 'shepherd' or 'shepherds'.... In another copy the expression *hyk*, it is said, does not mean 'kings': on the contrary, the compound refers to 'captive-shepherds'. [translation from Waddell 1940: 83, 85]

Josephus goes on to say (supposedly quoting Manetho) that when they left Egypt, the Hyksos built Jerusalem. He also says (probably drawing his own conclusions rather than quoting Manetho) that they were 'our ancestors' (ἡμέτεροι πρόγονοι [*Ag. Ap.* 1.16 §103]), i.e., the ancestors of Israelites who were in Egypt but left to move into Palestine. He thus seems to be identifying them with the exodus group (*Ag. Ap.* 1.26 §228).

Josephus looks to be mistaken on several accounts. The name Hyksos appears to come from the Egyptian *ḥq3w.ḫ3swt* 'kings of foreign lands' (Redford 1970b: 10–15). While the Hyksos might be among the ancestors of Israel, they would have been much earlier than any alleged 'exodus group' (see further §6.4 on the exodus). As far as we can tell, Jerusalem was already attested before the time of the Hyksos (§6.3.2); they certainly did not found the city. Therefore, even though Josephus's account was long followed (because there was nothing else), it can no longer serve as our main guide about the origin of Israel. It does, however, provide some information on the Hyksos, even if this picture needs correction from contemporary Egyptian sources.

The origins of the Hyksos remain a matter of controversy even to the present (cf. Mourad 2015: 9–11). Archaeology indicates a population largely (at least in the core Hyksos area) made up of those heavily influenced by Canaanite culture (Bietak 1997; McGovern and Harbottle 1997; Redmount 1995) and evidently originating in the Palestinian area. Excavations at Tell ed-Dab'a, the site of the Hyksos capital Avaris, show a culture with a mixture of Levantine and Egyptian elements. Neutron Activation Analysis indicates that many amphora with imported goods were manufactured in southern Palestine (McGovern and Harbottle 1997). It was once widely believed that there was a

'Hyksos invasion', even part of a large Amorite (§4.2.3 above) population movement from north to south (e.g., *CAH²* II, Parts 1 and 2). M. Liverani notes, on the contrary:

> A thorough investigation of the archaeological, onomastic, historical and political evidence, however, shows that the Hyksos' arrival in Egypt, despite not being entirely painless, was neither a mass movement, nor a military conquest. [Liverani 2014: 237]

A similar conclusion was reached by T. Säve-Söderbergh (1951) and J. Van Seters (1966: 121–6). Yet D. B. Redford (1970b: 3–15) and K. S. B. Ryholt (1997: 301–4) were somewhat more cautious, accepting that the violence alleged in the Egyptian sources (including Manetho) could not be excluded. Their view seems currently to be a minority one. In any case, the mass movement of peoples, especially the Hurrians, and an accompanying conquest of Egypt by them now needs to be modified or even discounted. The Hurrian cultural elements appear to be primarily the result of cultural diffusion rather than mass migration (Liverani 2014: 237).

A strontium isotope analysis was recently done on burials in the Tell ed-Dabʻa area to attempt to determine the geographical origin of the Hyksos rulers (Stantis et al. 2020). The conclusions were as follows:

> Although the Levantine origin of these rulers is not in question due to their rulers' names, architecture, and material culture, these results challenge the classic narrative of the Hyksos as an invading force. Instead, this research supports the theory that the Hyksos rulers were not from a unified place of origin, but Western Asiatics whose ancestors moved into Egypt during the Middle Kingdom, lived there for centuries, and then rose to rule the north of Egypt. [Stantis et al. 2020: 10]

An invading force would tend to show a predominance of non-local males, but the researchers actually found a larger proportion of non-local females. They also found that the rulers apparently were mostly those whose ancestors had come from the 'Asian' area but had lived in the Delta for several generations.

So, it is more commonly argued today that 'Asiatics' gradually settled in the eastern part of the delta during the later Middle Kingdom and the Second Intermediate Period, many as slaves or mercenaries in some cases but no doubt also coming from a variety of backgrounds in the Levant. These settlers in many cases integrated into the community. Here is where Mourad's thesis (2015: especially 124–30), which consolidates archaeological, textual, and iconographic data, comes into its own. She argues that in the first part of Dynasty 12 there were many conflicts with Asiatics, though the Egyptian administration also used them as mercenaries. Beginning already with Amenemhet I subjection of the *ʼ3mw* and the *sṯtyw* (see §2.4.4 for these terms), capture of their forts, and enslavement of many individuals is claimed by a number of the 12th Dynasty pharaohs. But inscriptions and archaeology show that they were also allies and trading partners. The non-royal tombs indicate an expanding community of Egyptian-Asiatic mixed descent, sometimes over many generations. These individuals of mixed Egyptian-Asiatic heritage are often depicted uniquely in murals, different both from native Egyptians and Asiatics. Individuals labelled 'Asiatic' often have completely Egyptian names and occupy a variety of posts, including officials in the administration.

In the second half of the 12th Dynasty the situation continued and expanded. An inscription describing a campaign against Retenu (Syria-Palestine) under Sesostris III (*c.* 1825 BCE) mentioned the place *Skmm*, which is often thought to be Shechem (Mourad 2013: 53 n. 21). This description is found on the Sebek-khu Stela (or the Stela of Khu-sobek): 'His majesty reached a foreign country of which the name was Sekmem.... Then Sekmem fell, together with the wretched Retenu' (*ANET* 230; text in Peet 1914). By Dynasty 13 the Delta capital Avaris (originally Hutwaret [*ḥwt-wʿrt*]; modern Tell el-Dabʿa) shows considerable evidence of Levantine material culture, both imported Syro-Palestinian ware and locally made pots showing knowledge of the craft practised further north. The city seems to have been a trading and cultural hub, with Levantine products and imitations moving as far as Upper Egypt. Asiatics apparently continued to migrate into the Delta, as indicated by some Semitic names. But there is also evidence of eastern Delta local turbulence with a high mortality rate indicated by the burials, a destruction layer caused by fire in Tell el-Dabʿa, and the burning of the mayor's residence at Tell Basta.

But new building took place, including a major temple complex at Tell el-Dabʿa that used the architecture tradition of the northern Levant. Those of Asiatic descent seemed to feel free to express their ethnic identity through their own religion and also mode of dress. They freely mixed with the Egyptian population, which included intermarriage. The elite looked to have connections mainly with the northern Levant, but this period saw increasing ties with and immigration from the southern Levant. Asiatics were found in a variety of social positions, from household servants and lowly workers to military personnel to higher positions within the administration.

The 15th Dynasty is the so-called 'Hyksos dynasty', the kings in it being labelled 'foreign rulers' (*ḥq3w-ḫ3swt*). Not only is this term used in the Turin Canon, but seems to have been used (at least initially) by the Hyksos themselves, as indicated by scarabs and other objects originating with the Hyksos. The heavily 'Asiatic' population of the northeastern Delta apparently broke away from control of Dynasty 13 and founded their own state which became the 15th Dynasty (possibly even the 14th earlier). They came to extend their rule over much of Lower Egypt, though whether this was a gradual process or a sudden coup is still debated, as discussed above. Some argue that the 16th Dynasty might also have been a vassal of Avaris (cf. Bietak 2001: 136).

The religion of the Hyksos shows connections with the Levant. From the Egyptian point of view, they were particularly devoted to the god Seth, though it is clear from the royal titularies and votive objects that they also worshipped some of the standard Egyptian gods. Seth seems to have been the pre-Hyksos city god of Avaris. Seth was in turn identified with the Baal widely worshipped in Canaan, and the Northwest Semitic goddess Anat appears to have been identified with the Egyptian goddess Hathor. These equations are well documented for the period of the New Kingdom; the question is whether this was also true in the Middle Kingdom/Second Intermediate Period. Although Ryholt (1997: 148–50) is sceptical, several specialists argue that it was already the case earlier (Redford 1992a: 116–28; Bietek 2001: 138).

During the time of control by the 15th Dynasty, the capital evidences extensive trade with the Levantine coast, Cyprus, and possibly even the Aegean (Betancourt 1997; Bietak 2001: 138, though Redford [1992a: 121–2] is sceptical of trade with the Aegean). We must distinguish, however, between the general settled population and those who began to dominate and eventually take over rule of the Delta. Although 'Asiatics' infiltrated the Delta region over a long period of time in the Middle Bronze Age, as already noted, the current evidence seems to support the view of Bietak

(1997: 98–9) and others that the ruling elite among the Hyksos came from the northern Levant (Mourad 2015: 217). The argument for this revolves particularly around the relationship of the Avaris architecture with that known from Byblos but also Ugarit, Alalakh, and Tell Brak.

The text in Manetho (Waddell 1940) lists six rulers for the 15th (Hyksos) Dynasty. Josephus (*Ag. Ap.* 1.14 §§79-92) and Syncellus give the names of Manetho's six kings; unfortunately, the names are missing for all but the last one in the Turin Canon (Farina 1938: 56), though it gives a total of 108 years, which seems more likely than the exaggerated figure in Josephus of 511 years (*Ag. Ap.* 1.14 §84). Josephus (as quoted in Waddell 1940: 79–99; cf. also Syncellus) gives us:

Salitis
Bnōn
Apachnan
Apōphis
Iannas
Assis

Although scarabs and seals suggest a number of other names, the monuments and the Turin king list attest the following (Ryholt 1997: 383–8, 410; Hornung/Krauss/Warburton 2006: 192–5; cf. Beckerath 1984: 77–8):

Ryholt	Hornung et al.
??Šamuqēnu??	Sarā-Dagan (*Š3rk[n]*)
??ʻAper-'Anati??	*Bin-ʻAnu
Sakir-Har	Jinaśśi'-Ad
Khayan	Sikru-Haddu
Apophis	Apapi
Khamudi, *c.* 1550–1540 BC	Ḥālmu'di

The details of Hyksos rule remain obscure, though it appears that their actual area of control was only the eastern Delta and did not extend south of Hieropolis; however, there are some indications of influence, if not actual control, as far south as Cusae. Whether they ruled the area of Thebes is a question to which there is no certain answer at the moment. But after about a century of Hyksos rule, the 17th Dynasty decided to take steps to extend its rule over Lower Egypt again. This apparently began with Seqenenreʻ Taʻo. His mummy has been discovered and shows that he died from several blows of an axe and other weapons to the head, ascribed to battle with the Hyksos, though G. J. Shaw (2009) has recently argued it was probably a ceremonial execution by the victorious Hyksos king on the battlefield (supported by the tomographic study by Saleen/Hawass 2021). Some have connected this with the New Kingdom tale of the *Quarrel of Apophis and Seqenenre*, which claims that the Hyksos ruler Apepi/Apophis demanded that Taʻo remove a pool of hippopotamuses from near Thebes because of the noise they made, though this is clearly a fictional wisdom tale rather than a historiographic text. But a contemporary inscription in the Deir el-Ballas region may also refer to hostilities between Seqenenra and Apophis (Shaw 2009: 160).

Ta'o's failure was only a temporary setback. His successor Kamose (the last king of Dynasty 17) went on to continue the attack, taking Avaris. Finally, Ahmose (the first king of Dynasty 18) followed up by besieging the Hyksos in Sharuhen where they had withdrawn from the Delta (see especially the autobiography of Ahmose, an official of King Ahmose with the same name as the king [*AEL* 2:12–15]). This site has been variously identified with Tell el-Far'ah South, Tell el-'Ajjul, and Tel Haror/Tell Abû Hureirah (Oren [ed.] 1997: 253–5; Rainey 1993). Although E. D. Oren (in Oren [ed.] 1997: 253–5) does not specify the exact location of the fortress, he postulates a 'Kingdom of Sharuhen' which covered this region of the Negev. Despite the fact that its precise relationship with the Hyksos is not clear, it seems to have had some association with them for them to retreat there after their defeat in Avaris.

According to the Ahmose autobiography, the siege of Sharuhen lasted three years (or three campaigns?) but ended in defeat for the Hyksos. Yet we should not assume that the bulk of Avaris's Asiatic population was driven out of the Avaris region; on the contrary, the archaeological evidence indicates that it (or much of it) continued where it was, though now under rule from Thebes (Bietek 2011). It may be that the ruling elite decamped to southern Palestine when defeated, but there was no break in the material culture: a movement of a large population from Avaris would have left a visible mark since the material culture in Canaan was very different from that in the eastern Delta.

The 15th Dynasty and Hyksos rule finally came to an end after more than a century. A.-L. Mourad gives a summary that many specialists would probably agree with:

> The rise of the Hyksos was due to a gradual infiltration of Northern and Southern Levantines across the Middle Kingdom and the early Second Intermediate Period. The Levantines entered Egypt as captives, warriors, expedition members and individuals searching for vocational, diplomatic and commercial opportunities. Escalating trade within the Levant for prized and prestigious commodities developed a lucrative and strategically positioned hub of culture activity at Tell el-Dab'a, the officials of which became more powerful and affluent as significant ties with the Northern Levant were maintained. Following internal conflict in the Delta, perhaps related to this increasing power and/or other political shifts in Dynasty 13, the Northern Levantine-influenced elite gradually began to secede from Thirteenth Dynasty rule.... On the whole, the examined evidence suggests that the Hyksos dynasty was a result of the Egyptian rulers' own persistent relations with the Levant from the very beginning of Dynasty 12 to the Second Intermediate Period. [Mourad 2015: 217]

For information on the subsequent Egyptian New Kingdom, see §5.1.

4.4 THE QUESTION OF THE PATRIARCHS

A. Alt (1966) 'The God of the Fathers', in *Essays on Old Testament History and Religion*: 1–77; **A. Archi** (1979) 'The Epigraphic Evidence from Ebla and the Old Testament', *Bib* 60: 556–6; **J. Bright** (1980) *A History of Israel*; **B. S. Childs** (1970) *Biblical Theology in Crisis*; **W. M. Clark** (1977) 'The Patriarchal Traditions: The Biblical

Traditions', in J. H. Hayes and J. M. Miller (eds), *Israelite and Judaean History*: 120–48; **R. E. Clements** (1974) 'אברהם *'abhrāhām*', *TDOT* 1:52–8; **B. J. Collins** (2007) 'The Bible, the Hittites, and the Construction of the "Other"', in D. Groddek and M. Zorman (eds), *Tabularia Hethaeorum: Hethitologische Beitrage, Silvin Kosak zum 65. Geburtstag*: 153–61; **J. S. Croatto** (1966) '*'Abrek* "Intendant" dans Gén. XLI 41, 43', *VT* 16: 113–15; **W. G. Dever** (1977) 'The Patriarchal Traditions: Palestine in the Second Millennium BCE: The Archaeological Picture', in J. H. Hayes and J. M. Miller (eds), *Israelite and Judaean History*: 70–120; **A. Gilan** (2013) 'Hittites in Canaan? The Archaeological Evidence', *BN* 156: 39–52; **H. Donner** (1969) 'Adoption oder Legitimation? Erwägungen zur Adoption im Alten Testament auf dem Hintergrund der altorientalischen Rechte', *Oriens Antiquus* 8: 87–119; **C. H. Gordon** (1958) 'Abraham and the Merchants of Ura', *JNES* 17: 28–31; **idem** (1962) *Before the Bible*; **B. L. Eichler** (1977) 'Another Look at the Nuzi Sistership Contracts', in M. de Jong Ellis (ed.), *Essays on the Ancient Near East in Memory of Jacob Joel Finkelstein*: 45–59; **S. Greengus** (1975) 'Sisterhood Adoption at Nuzi and the "Wife-Sister" in Genesis', *HUCA* 46: 5–31; **H. A. Hoffner** (1969) 'Some Contributions of Hittitology to Old Testament Study', *Tyndale Bulletin* 20: 27–55; **J. Joosten** (2005) 'The Distinction between Classical and Late Biblical Hebrew as Reflected in Syntax', *Hebrew Studies* 46: 327–39; **idem** (2019) 'The Linguistic Dating of the Joseph Story', *HBAI* 8: 1–20; **H. Petschow** (1965) 'Die neubabylonische Zwiegesprächsurkunde und Genesis 23', *JCS* 19: 103–20; **G. W. Ramsey** (1981) *The Quest for the Historical Israel*; **D. B. Redford** (1970a) *A Study of the Biblical Story of Joseph (Genesis 37–50)*; **L. Sapir-Hen and E. Ben-Yosef** (2013) 'The Introduction of Domestic Camels to the Southern Levant: Evidence from the Aravah Valley', *TA* 40: 277–85; **B. U. Schipper** (2011) 'Gen 41:42 and the Egyptian Background to the Investiture of Joseph', *RevB* 118: 331–8; **idem** (2018) 'Joseph, Ahiqar, and Elephantine: The Joseph Story as a Diaspora Novella', *JAEI* 18: 71–84; **N. Schneider** (1952) 'Patriarchennamen in zeitgenössischen Keilschrifturkunden', *Bib* 33: 516–22; **I. Singer** (2006) 'The Hittites and the Bible Revisited', in A. M. Maeir and P. de Miroschedji (eds), '*I will Speak the Riddles of Ancient Times': Archaeological and Historical Studies in Honor of Amihai Mazar on the Occasion of His Sixtieth Birthday*: 723–56; **J. A. Soggin** (2000) 'Dating the Joseph Story and Other Remarks', in F. W. Golka and W. Weiß (eds), *Joseph: Bibel und Literatur: Symposion Helsinki/Lathi 1999*: 13–24; **E. A. Speiser** (1964) *Genesis: A New Translation and Commentary*; **H. Tadmor** (1958) 'Historical Implications of the Correct Rendering of Akkadian *dâku*', *JNES* 17: 129–41; **T. L. Thompson** (1974) *The Historicity of the Patriarchal Narratives: The Quest for the Historical Abraham*; **G. Tucker** (1966) 'Legal Background of Genesis 23', *JBL* 85: 77–84; **J. Van Seters** (1975) *Abraham in History and Tradition*; **P. Wapnish** (1997) 'Camels', *OEANE* 1:407–8; **G. E. Wright** (1950) *The Old Testament Against its Environment*; **idem** (1952) *The God Who Acts*; **J. Zarins** (1978) 'The Camel in Ancient Arabia: A Further Note', *Antiquity* 52: 44–6.

Since it is with Abraham and the patriarchs that some think Israel's history first begins to be recorded, a discussion of the patriarchal narratives is needed. A proper full discussion would take a book – indeed, whole books have been devoted to the subject – but an outline can be given here to show that confidence in finding history in Genesis 11–50 is misplaced. Critical scholars have long tended to view the early chapters of Genesis – the stories of creation, Adam and Eve, the flood, the Tower of Babel – as Hebrew legend. Yet suddenly about Gen. 11.26 it was once common even for critical scholars to see the start of Israelite historiography (which then continued on through the Pentateuch to the end of 2 Kings). A few still take this view, though that is now very much the exception.

To understand the evolution of thinking on the subject, note that this outlook was a key perspective of what has been called the Biblical Theology Movement (described by B. Childs [1970], whose study also in a sense wrote the epitaph of it). This was not a fundamentalist reading, but one of the central pillars of the Biblical Theology Movement was the 'revelation of God in history', which meant that the Bible should be 'taken seriously' as history. This included the so-called patriarchal period. There was of course a debate, with North American scholars tending to give more credence to the narratives while the Europeans were more sceptical, but a variety of views was advanced on both sides of the Atlantic.

The Biblical Theology Movement was embraced by scholars from a variety of religious traditions, but some of the prominent representatives were from the 'Albright school', notably G. E. Wright (cf. 1950, 1952). Wright was not a fundamentalist – indeed, neither was Albright – but their language at times seemed to espouse a literal interpretation of the Bible, which tended to be welcomed by conservative Christians. As it turned out, despite their language Wright and others did not believe that 'the acts of God' really involved literal miracles, such as the sea opening up before the Israelites for them to walk through dry shod. Yet a version of the 'patriarchal period', which saw some sort of history beginning with Gen. 11.26, was accepted by many scholars in the 1950s, 1960s, and into the 1970s.

One of the problems immediately encountered was what period of history the patriarchal narratives were supposed to represent. The Albright school seemed to follow a version of inner-biblical chronology and put Abraham about 2000 BCE, which would make the 'patriarchal period' roughly coincide with the Middle Bronze Age. But considering the unreliability of the biblical numbers in Genesis, there was no reason to follow biblical chronology, and others who gave credence to the patriarchal narratives as in some way history were happy to date them at a different time. In fact, a number of other scholars dated the patriarchs many centuries later than Albright and Bright: later in the MB, in the LB, and even in the Iron I (cf. Dever 1977: 93–6; Clark 1977: 143–8).

For example, O. Eißfeldt and H. H. Rowley argued for the fifteenth century BCE. A. Alt and his student M. Noth had followed Wellhausen's dictum that the contents of the texts reflected the history of the age in which they were composed. Alt's interest in the patriarchal texts was mainly in the religion that might be reflected there (cf. Alt 1966). Perhaps the most exotic dating was that of C. H. Gordon who argued that Abraham was a 'merchant prince; a *tamkârum* from the Hittite realm' (Gordon 1958: 31; 1962), who lived in the Amarna period (fourteenth century BCE), for which he found parallels in the ancient Near Eastern texts. But the Albright school was particularly effective in promoting the idea that the patriarchal traditions contained 'substantial historicity' from around 2000 BCE; the following statement by J. Bright (1980: 77) is exemplary:

When the traditions are examined in the light of the evidence, the first assertion to be made is that already suggested, namely, that the stories of the patriarchs fit authentically in the milieu of the second millennium, specifically in that of the centuries sketched in the preceding chapter [twentieth to seventeenth centuries BCE], far better than in that of any later period. The evidence is so massive and many-sided that we cannot begin to review it all.

Yet this consensus began to come unravelled in the 1970s, with the publication of two independent studies, with quite different approaches, that nevertheless came to similar conclusions.

These were the monographs of T. L. Thompson (1974) and J. Van Seters (1975). They argued that the content of the biblical patriarchal narratives were filled with anachronistic data and could hardly represent genuine history of the early second millennium BCE. Albright had died in 1971 and was no longer around to dominate the discussion, and the studies of Thompson and Van Seters had a significant impact. Yet shortly after they appeared, a new discovery seemed to give considerable support to the more conservative view. This was the discovery and initial decipherment of the Ebla archives at Tell Mardikh in Syria, beginning in 1975 (see above §2.4.2).

Soon after the textual discovery the epigrapher, G. Pettinato, began to give interviews – sometimes to fellow scholars but also to the popular press – in which he presented astonishing Eblaite parallels to texts from the patriarchal chapters of Genesis. These were eagerly seized on by some to support conservative conclusions about the historicity of the patriarchal narratives. One of the most provocative claims was that not only the names of Sodom and Gomorrah but also the other cities of the plain were found on a single tablet from Ebla listed in the same order as in the Bible (e.g., *New York Times*, 16 January 1979; see also Archi [1979: 562–3] and the references given there).

On the basis of what he was (allegedly) told by Pettinato, D. N. Freedman (1978) wrote a rather polemical article in which he attacked Thompson and Van Seters. In it he referred to the 'recent archaeological discoveries' which he asserted had supported the basic historicity of the patriarchal narratives 'while effectively under-cutting the prevailing skepticism and sophistry of the larger contingent representative of continental and American scholars' (Freedman 1978: 144). While admitting that the narratives contain an 'admixture of the legendary and the mythical', they give us information that allows us to say something about the dates (at least, of some of them), the places from which they came and to which they went, their work, and even about their legacy of faith and practice (Freedman 1978: 145). He went on to refer to a tablet with the names of the five cities of the plain – in the same order as in the Bible – though he admitted he had not seen the tablet and was relying on a conversation with Pettinato. But on that basis he concluded that Thompson, Van Seters, and others who placed the narratives in the first millennium BCE had jumped in the wrong direction – they should now be placed in the Early Bronze Age, the third millennium BCE.

But just as the article was going to press, Freedman received some disturbing news: Pettinato had apparently retracted some of his identifications. Freedman's article was printed as he had written it, but an introductory text did bring the readers' attention to Pettinato's alleged retraction. The result was that the article's defence of historicity, based on the biblical text, was essentially negated. It took a while to settle down, but within a few years the use of Ebla as a defence of the patriarchal narratives had been silenced. When Pettinato's book (1991) appeared in English, there was no mention of Sodom and Gomorrah or the cities of the plain. A whole host of claims about Ebla and the

Bible simply evaporated. The *Washington Post* (9 December 1979) interviewed the Assyriologists R. Biggs about the Ebla tablets just about the same time as Freedman's article appeared:

> 'In my opinion, parallels with the Bible are quite out of the question at this stage', Biggs told a recent gathering of science writers sponsored by the Council for the Advancement of Science Writing. 'People who are looking to the Ebla tablets for proof of the authenticity of the Bible are going to be sorely disappointed'.

> 'At least one well-known biblical scholar took the early interpretation as evidence of the historical reality of the two cities', Biggs said. 'But alas, it turned out that corrections in reading the names have eliminated the names of the patriarchs and that in any case they did not occur on the same tablet with what was supposed to be Sodom and Gomorrah'.

Today there continues to be lively interest in and discussion about Ebla among scholars, but they seldom relate to the biblical text. Ebla has ceased to appear in standard scholarly discussions about Genesis.

The basic problem with finding history in the 'patriarchal age' is that the only information preserved has been what could be found in the text of Genesis – there was no direct external confirmation, either epigraphic or literary. None of the patriarchs has been found attested in extant sources. This means that the arguments in favour of historicity have generally attempted to present a circumstantial case for regarding the Genesis narratives as containing historical data. We can now briefly survey some of the main arguments used to support the historicity of the patriarchal narratives or, contrariwise, arguments and data that undermine that claim of historicity. This is only a summary, but more information can be found in Ramsey (1981) and some of the other studies cited above. As already noted, few are any longer willing to defend the historicity of the patriarchal stories because of new evidence and arguments that have arisen since 1970.

Archaeology has sometimes been drawn on in support of 'substantial historicity', but the most recent study is mainly negative. To summarize the discussion above (§4.3.1), the main centres of Transjordan and the Negev that are associated with the patriarchs in the text lack remains for the MB I. At the important site of Beersheba (Genesis 21–22) there are no MB remains, while investigation of the 'cities of the plain' (Gen. 19:24-29) have also found nothing. On the one hand, many of the main cities known to have existed in MB are absent from the text; on the other hand, no period in the early or middle second millennium BCE is known when all sites in the patriarchal narratives were settled: it was not until Iron I that this complete settlement of those sites took place.

Chronology is a significant issue: if the patriarchs are historical, when did they live? If the narratives are reliable, reliable for when? Some writers act as if the chronology can be taken for granted, but it cannot be. Having asserted how well the narratives fit the early second millennium (as quoted above), Bright nevertheless went on to admit:

> Granting the above, does the evidence allow us to fix the date of the patriarchs with greater precision? Unfortunately, it does not. The most that can be said, disappointing though it is, is that the events reflected in Genesis chs. 12–50, for the most part, fit best in the period already described, i.e., between about the twentieth and seventeenth centuries

(MB II). But we lack the evidence to fix the patriarchs in any particular century or centuries and we have, moreover, to face the possibility that the patriarchal stories combine the memory of events that took place over a yet wider span of time. [Bright 1980: 83]

Nomadic mode of life. It was once assumed that the patriarchs were nomadic and that this was uniquely in line with the early second-millennium BCE context (Ramsey 1981: 34–6). Much discussion has taken place in the past few decades, undermining this argument; see the discussion at §6.3.3.1.

Names. Many parallels can be found to the names in the patriarchal narratives. Bright asserted that they fitted the early second millennium, but a number of his examples actually came from later than the first few centuries of the second millennium. Names cannot be proof, of course, because the patriarchal names can all be found in the telephone book of almost any large Western city today; however, it is interesting that a number of the names do not recur in the Israelite tradition until the Graeco-Roman period. But as Thompson (1974: 35) points out, most of the names have a typical Northwest Semitic structure. Some of the names for Abraham's ancestors in Gen. 11:20-32 are actually topographical names in the region of Haran, as known from Mesopotamian texts (Schneider 1952): Peleg, Serug, Nahor, Terah, Haran are the names of places, not persons. On the name Benjamin, supposedly known from the Mari texts, see §4.2.3.

Customs in society. Customs have been one of the main pieces of evidence. A good example of this is E. A. Speiser's commentary on Genesis (1964). Drawing extensively on the Nuzi texts, he used them to illustrate many passages in the patriarchal narratives. Yet at times his argument was that the biblical custom could be found in the Nuzi texts but that the custom was not understood by the biblical writer – a rather strange way of arguing for authenticity and reliability! For example, he cites three specific examples where he argues that the actual event was not understood by the biblical writer who distorted the situation (Speiser 1964: xl–xliii). In fact, many of the alleged Nuzi customs are not parallel to the biblical passage, or either the Nuzi text or the biblical text have been misunderstood or misrepresented: for example, the idea that Eliezer was an heir because he was an adopted son of Abraham but would not inherit once Isaac was born was actually contrary to the Nuzi custom (Donner 1969; Thompson 1974: 203–30). Abraham's and Isaac's passing of their wives off as sisters (Gen. 12:10-20; 20:1-2; 26:1-11) was said to reflect a Hurrian custom of adopting the wife as a sister. The biblical text does not actually suggest such an adoption (Speiser argued that the Genesis writer no longer understood this custom), but the Nuzi practice was actually misapprehended by some modern scholars (Greengus 1975; Eichler 1977).

Genesis 23 gives the story of how Abraham purchased a cave at Hebron to bury Sarah his deceased wife. It was argued that this reflected intimate knowledge of Nuzi custom and practice. But specialists and others have not found the arguments convincing. H. A. Hoffner (1969: 33–7; 1973: 214) contests the alleged Nuzi parallels and concludes that 'the customs in real estate transactions and feudal dues [alleged for Genesis] are unlike anything known among the Hittites of Asia Minor'. The best parallel to Genesis 23 actually seems to come from the Neo-Babylonian period, more or less a millennium after the supposed Nuzi parallels (Tucker 1966; Petschow 1965; cf. Hoffner 1969: 34–7). In the end, none of the alleged customs demonstrating an early second-millennium background for the patriarchal stories seems to have stood up to careful scrutiny.

Late traditions. Except for Jacob/Israel the references to the patriarchs are attested in Israelite tradition only late. Apart from the Genesis texts, Abraham (1 Kgs 13.36; 2 Kgs 13.23; Isa. 29.22; Mic. 7.20) and Isaac (1 Kgs 18:36; 2 Kgs 13:23; Amos 7:9, 16; Jer. 33:26) are little mentioned. R. E. Clements expressed the view, 'In the preexilic prophets, there is no authentic reference to the Abraham traditions. Micah 7:20 is a postexilic oracle, as is also probably Isa. 29:22' (*TDOT* 1:57).

Joseph story. The main study remains that of D. B. Redford (1970a). He investigated the Egyptian parallels and references in the account. Some of them occur as early as the Middle Kingdom, but the potentially early elements also occur in later Egyptian history. Furthermore, a number can be found only late, in the Saite and later periods. This suggests that the narrative was written in the seventeenth to fifth centuries BCE (Redford 1970a: 252–3; cf. also Schipper 2018). A. Soggin (2000) would date it even later. Some examples of late or anachronistic elements include the following:

- Gen. 41:43: *Abrek* (אברך) is thought to be from an Akkadian word *abarakku*, one of whose meanings is 'chief steward of a private or royal household' (*CAD*, vol. 1 A, part I, 32-35), sometimes written (or confused with) *abriqqu*; cf. Croatto 1966; Soggin 2000: 166; Redford 1970a: 226–8). There is also the Phoenician word הברך (Karatepe Ai 1 [discussed in *SSI* 3:56]), which some interpret as 'vizier' or similar, and may also be a borrowing from Akkadian. Although Egyptian words have been proposed, this looks the most likely solution. But Egyptian officials are unlikely to be using an Akkadian word in the Middle Kingdom.
- The name Potiphar (פוטיפר) is clearly of Egyptian origin; it means, 'he whom Re gives' (*P3-di-p3-Rʿ*) and is attested from the Saite to the Ptolemaic period (Redford 1970a: 228–31).
- Gen. 40:15: 'land of the Hebrews [העברים]' as a designation for Palestine would not have been used in the early second millennium, especially considering the origin of the term (§6.3.3.3). Naturally, no such usage occurs in Egyptian texts of the Middle and New Kingdoms. It apparently occurs in texts from the Saite, Persian, and Ptolemaic periods (Redford 1970a: 201–3).
- Gen. 41:42: 'gold chain around his neck' (Schipper 2011; Redford 1970a: 208–26). The Egyptian phrase 'gold of honour' (*nbw n[.y] ḥsw.t*) is attested from the New Kingdom. What is significant about the Joseph example, however, is that foreigner is invested with honour and given an administrative position. This is not so far known in the New Kingdom or earlier, but Schipper (2011: 334–6) cites an example in the time of Psammetichus I (seventh century BCE) in which a foreigner (a Greek) is granted a 'golden collar' (ΨΙΛΟΝ ΤΕ ΧΡΥΣΕΟΝ) for his neck and given command of a city.
- A word should be said about linguistic dating. J. Joosten (2019) has pointed out that the Joseph story is in Standard Biblical Hebrew (also called Classical Biblical Hebrew) rather than Late Biblical Hebrew and suggests that the story is pre-exilic. It should be noted that Redford's assigning the book to the Saite and Persian periods, however, allows the story to be dated to include the period of Standard Biblical Hebrew, even according to Joosten's dating (he thinks Standard Biblical Hebrew was used to about 500 BCE, while Late Biblical Hebrew was established by the middle of the fifth century [Joosten 2005]). This would not allow for a later Persian or a Ptolemaic date, but Redford's arguments seem to permit a date of about 700 to 500 BCE; it looks as if the book does not have to be pre-exilic even by Joosten's standards, and Redford's dating is not ruled out by linguistic considerations.

Anachronisms. The patriarchal narratives in Genesis in their present form reflect a later time, with many anachronistic details: the Philistines in the land long before the migration of the Sea Peoples; Aramaeans (Gen. 22:21; 24:10) who are first attested about 1100 BCE in an inscription of Tiglath-pileser I; Arabs who first occur about the ninth century (Gen. 26:12-18); the Chaldeans (Gen. 11:28) who are attested after 1000 BCE but are mainly important in the Neo-Babylonian period (Ramsey 1981: 40–2) – while the migration from Ur has an interesting parallel to the return from exile. There has been something of a debate over the presence of camels in Genesis: Albright had argued that this was anachronistic and made Abraham a donkey caravaneer, but Gordon and also some conservatives had claimed evidence for the domestication of camels at an earlier time. The most recent evidence for the domesticated camel in Palestine, however, seems to be no earlier than the Iron Age, with the concentration of bones at Tell Jemmeh, apparently a caravan centre, focusing on the seventh century BCE (Sapir-Hen/Ben-Yosef 2013; Wapnish 1997; Zarins 1978; Na'aman 1994c: 225–7; Finkelstein/Silberman 2001: 37). The most recent research concludes as follows:

> Current data from copper smelting sites of the Aravah Valley enable us to pinpoint the introduction of domestic camels to the southern Levant more precisely based on stratigraphic contexts associated with an extensive suite of radiocarbon dates. The data indicate that this event occurred not earlier than the last third of the 10th century BCE and most probably during this time.... The observations from the Aravah Valley are in accordance with reports from the Negev and the settled land, which demonstrate high frequency of camel remains only from the Iron IIA onward. [Sapir-Hen/Ben-Yosef 2013: 282–3]

4.5 CONCLUSIONS

This chapter has concentrated on Syria and Palestine in the Middle Bronze Age. This was an important period to consider for the ancestry of the Israelites, especially because the biblical text as well as some scholars want to place the contents of the patriarchal narratives (Genesis 11–50) in the early second millennium BCE. But before considering the biblical material, a survey of the history of Syria-Palestine as known from contemporary records would be appropriate. In northern Syria the city of Ugarit was an important city-state on the coast already in the third millennium BCE, though we know little about it. More information is available from the MBA, but contemporary records are available only sporadically. Most of this time it seems to have been under the rulership of Yamhad. The only possible list of kings comes from a text of the LBA, and there is no consensus on a sequence of kings for the MBA. What we know of Ugarit at this time comes mainly from Mari and similar cuneiform texts.

An important but somewhat enigmatic group were the Amorites. They are mentioned already in texts from Ebla and the Ur III period and were clearly important in the MBA. References seem to be of two sorts: references to (primarily) pastoralist tribes on the steppes either side of the Euphrates and in the region of Jebel Bišri who are often presented as uncultured barbaric peoples; but many references were to people who live in Sumerian and Akkadian cities and were assimilated to Mesopotamian city culture. In some cases they are known only by their names, not by being labelled as Amorites. Much of the information, especially about their language, comes from the Amorite names plus a few words borrowed into cuneiform texts. Although this has often been designated as Northwest Semitic, the most recent analysis states that there is not sufficient data to classify the language: it has some features in common with Northwest Semitic but other important ones are more like East Semitic (Akkadian). The old hypothesis that there was a mass migration of Amorites south into south Syria and Palestine has been largely given up. Thus, the Amorites remain a puzzle, and their relevance for Israelite origins is very uncertain.

Yamhad is an important state in northern Syria for a couple of centuries in the MBA. With a capital at Aleppo, it had a number of smaller states under its domain, including Alalakh and, at times, Carchemish and Ugarit. It was opposed by the neighbouring state of Qatna but most importantly by Shamshi-Adad I of Assyria; however, it had allies in Eshnuna and Babylon and survived Shamshi-Adad's attacks. Whereas Yamhad had been opposed by Mari, with the death of Shamshi-Adad the new ruler Zimri-Lim formed an alliance with Yamhad. We know the names of a number of rulers over the 200 years. About 1600 BCE Mursili I of Hatti brought the Syrian kingdom to an end.

As usual, Palestine is known primarily from archaeology, though Egyptian texts (including the Execration Texts) give us some names of cities in Canaan. The MBA was a period of intense urbanization, with the urban population estimated as about one and a half times as great as the rural. Many sites were fortified. A surge of settlement took place in the hill country, especially in MB I, though the central hill country was mainly settled in MB II and III. Large sites include such well-known names as Shechem, Shiloh, Hebron, and Jerusalem. Hazor was an important conduit for trade with Syria and even Mesopotamia. Trade with Egypt was also important, especially with Byblos initially, but it gradually shifted south. The MBA ended with a widespread collapse.

Dynasty 15 of the Second Intermediate Period was the 'Hyksos' dynasty, though some argue that Dynasty 14 was also composed of some or all 'Asiatic' rulers. The argument that the Hyksos formed an invasion force who set up their rule through violence is now largely abandoned. Genetic study and archaeology suggests that the people who made up the Hyksos population around their capital of Avaris had lived there for some time, several generations. They did not have a single place of origin but seem to be a group of Western Asiatics who had lived in Egypt for several centuries before setting up rule over a section of the Delta. We have reports of 'Asiatics' migrating to Egypt temporarily or permanently from the third millennium BCE. Yet their culture and religion, as well as their genetics, indicate a connection with the Levant. It is suggested that the elite had connections primarily with the northern Levant.

After about a century of rule the Hyksos dynasty came to an end. One of the last kings of Dynasty 17 might have been killed fighting the Hyksos, but the last king of the dynasty made headway by taking Avaris, while the first king of Dynasty 18 pursued them to Sharuhen (perhaps Tell el-'Ajjul or Tel Haror/Tell Abû Hureirah). Actually, most of the population probably remained where they were, with only some of the elite fleeing into Canaan, but even there they were attacked and defeated. After that we have no further information, but presumably they simply merged back into the population of Canaan. It is possible that some of them were among Israel's ancestors, but we have no way of knowing.

The question, finally, is whether the Israelite ancestors can be found in the stories about the patriarchs in Genesis. In English-speaking scholarship it was common during the 1950s and 1960s to ascribe 'substantial historicity' to the patriarchal narratives. That has now ceased to be the case because of a series of studies beginning in the mid-1970s. It is true that a brief blip occurred when the initial decipherment of the Ebla texts led to the claim that remarkable parallels with the Genesis events could be found in the Ebla archives. But these turned out to be premature wishful thinking, and with more careful study the alleged parallels were found simply not to be there. Several considerations now undermine any claim to substantial historicity: the Genesis narratives appear to reflect the eighth century or so; the Joseph story seems set in the Saitic period (seventh–sixth century BCE); a number of Abraham's supposed ancestors and relatives are actually the names of cities and towns; the best parallels for customs and practices in the stories seems to be from later times, including the Neo-Babylonian period; and archaeology has not found evidence for the sites in the stories to have been settled in the MBA, while some of the sites known to have been inhabited then are not mentioned.

For the MBA, then, there is very little that can be considered as part of the Israelite ancestry. The patriarch stories now appear to have been composed very late (eighth century BCE or later) and show little evidence of knowledge of the early second-millennium BCE context. What is more promising is that 'Asiatic' peoples migrated into the Egyptian Delta over several centuries, and a dynasty of Hyksos even ruled there for a century or so. It is very possible that some of the ancestors of Israel were among these peoples, but beyond that we cannot go.

Part III

Late Bronze Age
(c. 1600–1200 BCE)

CHAPTER 5

Ancient Near Eastern Context, Including Syria

H. Klengel (1992) *Syria 3000 to 300 B.C.: A Handbook of Political History*; **A. Kuhrt** (1995) *The Ancient Near East c. 3000–300 BC*; **M. Liverani** (2014) *The Ancient Near East: History, Society and Economy*.

Unlike the previous sections, the content of this chapter is divided differently. In order to make as much room as possible in the next chapter, which will be a long one, Syria (including Ugarit and Amurru) are included in the present chapter which surveys the Near Eastern neighbours outside Palestine.

5.1 EGYPT

B. Bryan (1991) *The Reign of Thutmose IV*; **E. H. Cline and D. O'Connor (eds)** (1998) *Amenhotep III: Perspectives on his Reign*; **idem** (2006) *Thutmose III: A New Biography*; **idem** (2012) *Ramesses III: The Life and Times of Egypt's Last Hero*; **R. Giveon** (1971) *Les bédouins Shosou des documents égyptiens*; **idem** (1984) 'Scharuhen', *LdÄ* 5:532; **N. Grimal** (1992) *A History of Ancient Egypt*; **E. Hornung, R. Krauss, and D. A. Warburton (eds)** (2006) *Ancient Egyptian Chronology*; **T. G. H. James** (2002) *Ramesses II*; **D. Kahn** (2011) 'One Step Forward, Two Steps Backward: The Relations between Amenhotep III, King of Egypt and Tushratta, King of Mitanni', in S. Bar, D. Kahn, and J. J. Shirley (eds), *Egypt, Canaan and Israel: History*: 136–54; **K. A. Kitchen** (1982) *Pharaoh Triumphant: The Life and Times of Ramesses II, King of Egypt*; **M. Lichtheim** (1976) *Ancient Egyptian Literature: Volume 2: The New Kingdom*; **J. Lipinska** (2001) 'Hatshepsut', *OEAE* 2:85–7; **G. D. Mumford** (1998) *International Relations between Egypt, Sinai, and Syria-Palestine during the Late Bronze Age to Early Persian Period (Dynasties 18-26: c. 1550–525 B.C.)*; **D. B. Redford** (1984) *Akhenaten: The Heretic*

King; **idem** (1992a) *Egypt, Canaan, and Israel in Ancient Times*; **idem** (2003) *The Wars in Syria and Palestine of Thutmose III*; **H. D. Schneider** (2001) 'Horemheb', *OEAE* 2:114–16; **J. Tyldesley** (1996) *Hatchepsut: The Female Pharaoh*; **I. Velikovsky** (1952) *Ages in Chaos*.

The Egyptian New Kingdom, consisting of Dynasties 18-20 (*c.* 1550–1050 BCE), was a high point in the history of Egypt. Dynasty 18 was responsible for the 'expulsion' of the Hyksos (see §4.3.3 for the complications to what had happened). They first secured their northern and southern borders and then began to expand into Nubia and Syro-Palestine. This brought them into conflict with the Hittites and the kingdom of Mitanni in the north. Eventually Thutmose IV (*c.* 1400 BCE) reached an agreement with Mitanni. One pharaoh of the 19th Dynasty is quite famous because of being a woman. When Thutmose II (*c.* 1500 BCE) died with a minor son, his wife took the throne and ruled as Hatshepsut (Tyldesley 1996); she apparently took on the persona of a man in certain contexts and is sometimes so represented. The son reached maturity, and took the throne as Thutmose III at Hatshepsut's death.

One of her descendants was Amenhotep IV (*c.* 1353–1336 BCE) who is one of the most famous of the ancient Egyptians (Redford 1984). The priesthood and temples were dominated by the cult of Amen Re, but Amenophis promoted the cult of Aten (the sun disk). This 'religious reform' is still debated by modern scholars, though the idea that it was the first example of monotheism is probably exaggerated. Amenhotep changed his name to Akhenaten and built an entirely new city as his capital, what is now Tell el-Amarna, giving the name 'Amarna period' to the mid-fourteenth century BCE. After Akhenaten's short reign of about 17 years, his name was blackened and even erased from inscriptions and monuments. The powerful priesthood of Amen Re seems to have been partly behind this. In any case, his capital was abandoned, leaving a unique find for archaeologists when it was excavated in the late 1800s (because it was built on a new site and nothing was built on top of it). Of particular importance were the archives abandoned there, the Amarna letters (§6.1).

When the last king of Dynasty 18 had no offspring, he appointed his vizier as his successor: Ramesses I who initiated Dynasty 19 (*c.* 1300 BCE). Perhaps the most famous pharaoh of this dynasty – and one of the most famous of all the Pharaohs – was Ramesses II who ruled for 66 years (*c.* 1279–1213 BCE; James 2002; Kitchen 1982). The expansion of the Hittites had brought them and Egypt into conflict. A famous battle (still studied by military strategists) took place at Qadesh in northern Syria, with both sides claiming victory. Ramesses then concluded a treaty with the Hittites. (It was once common to make Ramesses the pharaoh of the exodus, which is rather strange considering that far from being destroyed, Egypt was at its height under his reign; on the exodus see §6.4) His son was Merenptah who set up the victory stela known as the Merenptah Stela or Israel Stela (§6.3.4). Merenptah apparently had to put down a number of rebellions in Palestine and elsewhere.

The Egyptian background to the history of Canaan in the Late Bronze Age is very important, since Palestine was under Egyptian rule almost continually during this period. Egypt had interactions and interconnections with Palestine through a good portion of the second millennium BCE. One of the best ways of assessing the historicity of the biblical text in the early history of Israel is by a close examination of Egyptian history, since it seems unlikely that this history would have had no implications for the biblical text. Only a survey can be given here, but it will give a context for the more detailed survey of Egyptian interaction with the Palestinian region during this period of about half a millennium that is given in the next chapter (§6.3.1).

5.1.1 From the Hyksos to Amenhotep IV (Akhenaten)

The end of the Second Intermediate Period and the Hyksos time marked the start of the Egyptian New Kingdom. The Hyksos ruled over northern Egypt, including the Delta region, for a little more than a century (forming the 15th Dynasty and possibly the 16th). The end of Hyksos rule began under Kamose (?–c. 1540 BCE), who was the last king of Dynasty 17 which ruled over Thebes, parallel with Dynasty 15 over northern Egypt. This would bring us roughly to about 1550 BCE.

The process of expelling the Hyksos was continued by Ahmose (c. 1539–1515 BCE), who may have been Kamose's brother. He is conventionally the founder of the New Kingdom and first king of the 18th Dynasty. We have the mortuary autobiography of an individual named Ahmose son of Abana (a different individual from the pharaoh, even though he had the same name) who gives brief descriptions of campaigns by Pharaoh Ahmose and some of his successors because he served on them:

> Now when I had established a household, I was taken to the ship 'Northern', because I was brave. I followed the sovereign on foot when he rode about on his chariot. When the town of Avaris [the Hyksos capital] was besieged, I fought bravely on foot in his majesty's presence. Thereupon I was appointed to the ship 'Rising in Memphis'. Then there was fighting on the water in 'Pjedku' of Avaris. I made a seizure (10) and carried off a hand. When it was reported to the royal herald the gold of valor was given to me.... Then Avaris was despoiled, and I brought spoil from there: one man, three women; total, four persons. His majesty gave them to me as slaves. [*AEL* 2:12–13]

Ahmose son of Abana goes on to give information on a follow-up campaign, this time into southern Palestine:

> Then Sharuhen was besieged for three years. His majesty despoiled it and I brought spoil from it: two women and a hand. Then the gold of valor was given me, and my captives were given to me as slaves. [*AEL* 2:13]

Sharuhen seems to be the city mentioned in Josh. 19:6 and is often identified with Tell el-Far'ah South, about twenty-four km (fifteen miles) south of Gaza in the Negev; another suggested site is Tell el-'Ajjul in the same general area but only about six km from Gaza and almost on the coast (Giveon 1984). The significance of this conquest was pointed out by Donald Redford:

> The capture of Sharuhen by Ahmose and the disintegration of its polity has been correctly seen as a significant opening shot in the weakening of Canaan. Its reduction meant that the early 18th Dynasty had nothing immediately to fear across the Sinai.... Geopolitically the Negeb, Shephelah and the southern hill-country, when viewed over

time, can only sustain a large and powerful state when Egypt is either weak or occupied by a congenial regime. With Sharuhen gone, there was no other metropolitan state of significance south of Hazor. [Redford 2003: 190 + n. 24]

Some reference books mention expeditions by other New Kingdom rulers, such as Amenhotep I, Thutmose II, and Hatshepsut. These campaigns are deduced from small amounts of information. Redford (1992a: 149) is dubious of all but the excursion of Thutmose I in the period of 70 or 80 years between Ahmose's expulsion of the Hyksos and Thutmose III's taking of Megiddo. What we find is that for the next three-quarters of a century after the expulsion of the Hyksos, the Egyptian pharaohs concentrated on extending their borders south into Nubia. However, during this period the new state of Mitanni was developing its strength and extending its territory. Egypt ignored it for the time being, but Thutmoses I (c. 1493–1483 BCE) may have begun to see a danger (so Redford 1992a: 146–9) and responded with an expedition to the Euphrates and the Mitanni territory. We know little about this, though he apparently set up a stela on the Euphrates. According to the mortuary autobiography of Ahmose son of Abana, who was on the expedition:

> After this (his majesty) proceeded to Retjenu [Palestine], to vent his wrath throughout the lands. When his majesty reached Nahrin, his majesty found that foe marshalling troops. Then his majesty made a great slaughter of them. Countless were the living captives which his majesty brought back from his victories. Now I was in the van of our troops, and his majesty saw my valor. I brought a chariot, its horse, and him who was on it as a living captive. When they were presented to his majesty, I was rewarded with gold once again. [*AEL* 2:14]

For the next 40 years, however, the Mitanni threat seems to have been neglected. A razzia against the Shasu is sometimes ascribed to Thutmose II, based on another mortuary autobiography, this time by an individual named Ahmose Pennekheb:

> I followed king 'Akheperenre' (Thutmose II), triumphant; there was brought off for me in Shasu (*Š'-sw*) very many living prisoners; I did not count them. [*ARE* 2 §124; Giveon 1971: 10]

The famous queen Hatshepsut (c. 1479–1458 BCE; Tyldesley 1996) ruled jointly as regent with her son Thutmose III, though she claimed sole rulership at times. She was not the Queen of Sheba, and Punt was not Palestine (*pace* Velikovsky 1952), though there is the possibility that she sent one excursion into Syria-Palestine (Lipinska 2001: 2:86). Because of his habit of having his various activities recorded in day-books, we happen to know a lot about Thutmose III's activities (see Redford 2003; Cline/O'Connor 2006). His long reign covered a good portion of the fifteenth century (c. 1479–1425). He already began his campaigns into Palestine during his co-rulership with his mother and made many expeditions when he became sole ruler. A couple of his campaigns to the north can be mentioned in which he exhibited brilliance as a battlefield strategist. Perhaps the most famous exploit of Thutmose III was in his twenty-second year (the first year of sole reign) where he took Megiddo by the bold move of leading his army directly through a narrow pass in the Carmel ridge. This was followed in year 33 by an exploit in which he defeated Mitanni by prefabricating boats on the Mediterranean, disassembling them and taking them by wagon to the Euphrates, where he was then able to attack the Mitanni army stationed on the other side of the river. It was under Thutmose III that the Egyptian empire reached its farthest expansion to the north.

He was followed by Amenhotep (Amenophis) II (*c.* 1425–1400 BCE) who continued to keep the pressure on the northern frontier. He made forays into Syria-Palestine during his 3rd, 7th, and 9th regnal years. In his seventh year, he came against Mitanni and its allies, including Ugarit. Following him, however, there seems to be a hiatus for several rulers, though this could be because the internal administrative system in Canaan and Syria was working reasonably well. For example, there were apparently no expeditions to the north under either Thutmose IV (1400–1390 BCE) or Amenhotep III (1390–1353 BCE), and Thutmose IV made a treaty with Mitanni (for Thutmose IV, see Bryan 1991; for Amenhotep III, see O'Connor and Cline 1998). But this was supposedly because these territories had been brought thoroughly into line. Redford sums up the situation in this way:

> The long reign of Amenophis III reaped the fruits of the labor expended in subduing Asia during the three preceding generations. A Pax Aegyptiaca had been forcibly imposed on Canaan, and Amenophis III had no need to go on campaign. Taxes and benevolences poured in at Pharaoh's behest, caravans from and to Egypt passed peacefully along the routes through Palestine, and merchant shipping around the eastern Mediterranean increased greatly. The ties with Mitanni grew tighter, and frontier problems largely ceased.... Babylon and Cyprus also courted Pharaoh, dispatching gifts and concluding diplomatic marriages. In a word, the habitable world was at Egypt's feet. [Redford 1992a: 169]

The reign of Akhenaten (Amenophis IV: 1353–1336 BCE) covers much of the Amarna period (which is discussed in detail at §6.3.2). Some of the Amarna tablets were written during the reigns of the last Amarna kings, but apart from Horemhab, these pharaohs seem to have accomplished little. These kings were

Smenkhkare' (1336–1334 BCE)
Nefernefruaten (1334–? BCE)
Tut'ankhaten/Tut'ankhamun (?–1324 BCE)
Aya (1323–1320 BCE)

Horemheb (1319–1292 BCE) was apparently the real leader of the country when Tutankhamun came to the throne as a boy. Reliefs in his tomb (found in 1975) indicate that he undertook campaigns into Syria and Nubia on Tutankhamun's behalf. He claims that 'his name was famous in the land of the Hittites' (Schneider 2001). He was outmanoeuvred by others at the end of Tutankhamun's life, and Aya succeeded Tutankhamun. It was only when Aya's short reign ended that Horemheb took the throne, though we know of no campaigns to the north after this.

5.1.2 The First Part of the 19th Dynasty

The founder of the new 19th Dynasty was Ramesses I (1292–1291 BCE), though Horemheb is credited with guiding the transition. Ramesses I was aged and reigned only a year or so before Sety I (1290–1279 BCE) took over to act as a new Thutmoses III. The thirteenth century is dominated by active pharaohs who exerted themselves in maintaining their northern possessions. To begin, Sety led an expedition against the Shasu in southern Palestine:

> Regnal year one, third month of the third season…. On this day, one came to tell His Majesty, 'The vile foe that is in the town of Hammath has gathered unto himself many people and has seized the town of Beth Shan and, having joined (?) those of Pella (*Pḥr*), does not allow the prince of Rehob to go out'. Then His Majesty sent the first army of Amun, (called) 'Powerful of Bows', against the town of Hammath; the first army of Pre, (called) 'Abounding in Valor', against the town of Beth Shan; and the first army of Seth, (called) 'Mighty of Bows', against the town of Yenoam. After the duration of a day had passed, they were felled through the power of His Majesty. [Murnane 1990: 42–3]

This campaign took place as part of one directed at Tyre, which was also subdued, and brought the chiefs of Palestine in general into line. He later attacked Amurru and retook the town of Qadesh. In another campaign he marched against the Hittites in the Orontes Valley of northern Syria.

His successor Ramesses II (1279–1213 BCE) had a long reign of 66 years and was a great military leader, at least in his younger years (on him, see Tyldesley 2000; Kitchen 1982). He had a campaign up the Mediterranean coast to Phoenicia and perhaps to Amurru in his fourth year. The next year was the famous battle of Qadesh. Although Ramesses retrieved the battle from a Hittite ambush and it was more or less a standoff, on balance it was probably a defeat for the Egyptians. The result was that Palestine rebelled against Egyptian rule; however, after three years he retaliated and took many towns, some of which we know of:

> Town which His Majesty plundered: 'Ain Na'am (*'n-N'm*).
> Town which His Majesty plundered [on] the Mountain of Bayt-'Anath:
>   Karpu[n/m]a (*Krp[n/m]*).
> Town which His Majesty plundered in Year 8: Qana (*Qn*)….
> Town which His Majesty plundered in Year 8: Marom (*Mrm*)….
> Town which His Majesty plundered in Year 8: Shalamu (*Šrm*).
>
> [*RI* 2.26-27]

He continued to pacify his northern territories in year 10 and also in some undated expeditions. In year 21 Hatti proposed a treaty, which Ramesses accepted, but Egypt never recovered Qadesh, Amurru, or Ugarit. Strangely, though, it is often proposed that the exodus and/or conquest of Canaan by the Israelites took place under his reign – apparently overlooking that he was one of the strongest of the pharaohs who had a firm hold of the whole region well into Syria and reigned for so much of the thirteenth century – and did not drown in the Red Sea. One cannot imagine an Egypt devastated by plagues, with a huge population leaving the country and an army destroyed in the wilderness near the Red Sea, as compatible with everything we know about this ruler.

Ramesses II's long life meant that he outlived several of his sons who had been designated his successor. He was succeeded by his 13th son Merenptah (1213–1203 BCE) who was already middle aged. Merenptah had been a successful military leader, but this was behind him. However, Egypt suffered a Libyan invasion allied with a number of the Sea Peoples (Lebu, Meshwesh, Akawash, Turash, Luka, Shardana, Shekelesh), in the fifth year of his reign. They were met in the western Delta region and defeated. Merenptah's inscription is mainly devoted to the Libyan victory but also includes some Palestinian cities plus Israel at the end. How they relate to the Libyan invasion – if at all – is unclear.

5.1.3 Table of Egyptian Kings

The dates in Hornung/Krauss/Warburton (2006) have been followed.

Kamose (?–c. 1540 BCE): last king of 17th Dynasty; began expulsion of Hyksos.

Ahmose (c. 1539–1515 BCE): founder of New Kingdom; first king of the 18th Dynasty; completed expulsion of Hyksos.

Amenhotep (Amenophis) I (c. 1514–1494 BCE).

Thutmose (Tuthmosis) I (c. 1493–1483 BCE).

Thutmose (Tuthmosis) II (c. 1482–1480 BCE): raid against the Shasu.

Hatshepsut (c. 1479–1458 BCE): ruled jointly as regent with Thutmose III, though she claimed sole rulership at times.

Thutmose III (c. 1479–1425 BCE): his long reign covered a good portion of the fifteenth century BCE.

Amenhotep (Amenophis) II (c. 1425–1400 BCE): continued keeping northern territories under control.

Thutmose (Tuthmosis) IV (c. 1400–1390 BCE): no raids into Syria but probably unnecessary.

Amenhotep (Amenophis) III (1390–1353 BCE): no raids because Palestine and much of Syria under Egyptian control.

Amenhotep (Amenophis) IV, better known as Akhenaten (1353–1336 BCE): most of Amarna letters written during his rule.

[*Akhenaten to Tutankhamun are often referred to as the 'Amarna pharaohs'.*]

Smenkhkare' (1336–1334 BCE).

Nefernefruaten (1334–? BCE).

Tutankhamun (Tut'ankhaten/Tut'ankamun) (?–1324 BCE).

Aya (1323–1320 BCE).

Horemheb (1319–1292 BCE).

Ramesses I (1292–1291 BCE): founder of 19th Dynasty.

Sety (Seti, Sethos) I (1290–1279 BCE): began recovery of the territories where control was weakened under the last of the Amarna pharaohs; like another Thutmose III.

Ramesses II (1279–1213 BCE): one of greatest pharaohs; an unlikely ruler for the exodus!

Merenptah (1213–1203 BCE): apparently the first mention of Israelites in history.

5.2 MESOPOTAMIA

A. Bartelmus and K. Sternitzke (eds) (2017) *Karduniaš: Babylonia under the Kassites, Volumes 1-2*; **G. M. Beckman** (1996) *Hittite Diplomatic Texts*; **O. Boivin** (2018) *The First Dynasty of the Sealand in Mesopotamia*; **J. A. Brinkman** (1968) *A Political History of Post-Kassite Babylonia 1158–722 B.C.*; **idem** (1976) *Materials and Studies for Kassite History, Vol. 1: A Catalogue of Cuneiform Sources Pertaining to Specific Monarchs of the Kassite Dynasty*; **idem** (1980) 'Kasitten (*Kaššû*)', *RlA* 5:464–73; **idem** (1997) 'Meerland (Sealand)', *RlA* 8:6–10; **I. J. Gelb** (1954) 'Two Assyrian King Lists', *JNES* 13: 209–30; **J.-J. Glassner** (2004) *Mesopotamian Chronicles*; **A. K. Grayson** (1972) *Assyrian Royal Inscriptions, Volume I: From the Beginning to Ashur-resha-ishi I*; **H. O. Malko** (2014) *Investigation into the Impacts of Foreign Ruling Elites in Traditional State Societies: The Case of the Kassite State in Babylonia (Iraq)*; **S. Paulus and T. Clayden (eds)** (2020) *Babylonia under the Sealand and Kassite Dynasties*; **A. Poebel** (1942a) 'The Assyrian King List from Khorsabad', *JNES* 1: 247–306; **idem** (1942b) 'The Assyrian King List from Khorsabad (Continued)', *JNES* 1: 460–92; **idem** (1943) 'The Assyrian King List from Khorsabad (Concluded)', *JNES* 2: 56–90; **U. Seidl** (1989) *Die babylonischen* Kudurru-*Reliefs: Symbole mesopotamischer Gottheiten*; **I. Singer** (1985) 'The Battle of Niḫriya and the End of the Hittite Empire', *ZA* 75: 100–123; **W. Sommerfeld** (1995) 'The Kassites of Ancient Mesopotamia: Origins, Politics, and Culture', in J. M. Sasson (ed.), *Civilizations of the Ancient Near East*: 2:917–30; **E. Weidner** (1963) 'Assyrische Epen über die Kassiten-Kämpfe', *AfO* 20: 113–16.

The Late Bronze Age brought about what is often termed the 'middle' kingdoms of Assyria, Babylonia, and the Hittites (the Old Babylonian and Old Assyrian kingdoms belong to the Middle Bronze Age in a previous chapter [§3.2.2, §3.2.3]).

5.2.1 Middle Assyrian Kingdom

In Assyria there was a 400-year 'dark age' from about 1750 to the beginning of the Middle Assyrian Kingdom (*c.* 1350–1050 BCE) during which time we have little information on Assyria. There seems to have been little opportunity for expansion, however. The expansion of Mitanni had brought about the loss of Assyrian independence (*c.* 1450). The Assyrian King List covers this period, which suggests that it continued to be updated, regardless of the kingdom's general political weakness (Gelb 1954; Poebel 1942a, 1942b, 1943). About 1450 BCE the Mitannian king Shaushtatar made Assyrian a vassal. But later the defeat of Mitanni by the Hittite king Suppiluliuma I (*c.* 1350 BCE) gave Assyria its chance to regain independence and begin to exert itself again.

The Assyrian king who began to exercise power and expand was Ashur-uballit (*c.* 1350 BCE). His first move was to seek control of Hanigalbat, the territory of Mitanni. Artatama II was forced into submission. This was followed by correspondence with Egypt's Amenhotep IV/Akhenaten (EA 15-16). The Assyrian king sent a gift of two chariots and horses to make first contact with Egypt, but then the second letter complains that Akhenaten has not reciprocated adequately with gold as

Ashur-uballit expected! There was clearly a lack of diplomatic finesse on the Assyrian's part. Ashur-uballit got involved with Babylonia, marrying his daughter to the heir of the throne. When the latter was assassinated, the Assyrian king invaded and made king an infant son, Kurigalzu II. When this individual became a man, he nevertheless confronted Assyria and was not a willing patsy of the Assyrians.

Assyria had now become a major power. But various forces were in its way of expansion: the Hittites across the Euphrates and disputing control of Mitanni, the Kassite kingdom of Babylon to the south, and the Zagros mountain tribes to the north. The next major Assyrian ruler was Adad-nirari I (*c.* 1300). He fought Nazi-Marutash of Babylon and expanded the Assyrian frontier further north. This Assyrian king turned his attention to Mitanni and made it a vassal under its king, Shattura I. The latter's son Wasashatta rebelled against Assyrian rule but received no help from Hatti, and the whole of the region came under Assyrian control. Adad-nirari also used diplomacy and proposed a treaty with the Hittites. One letter from the Hittite king (Hattusili III? Urhi-Teshub?) gives the proposal a brush-off (*CTH* 171; Beckman 1996: 138–9); however, another letter – definitely from Hattusili III – is more conciliatory toward Adad-nirari (*CTH* 173: Beckman 1996: 139–40); apparently they made an agreement.

Shalmaneser I (*c.* 1250) fought against the Mitanni king, Shattura II. Evidently, Mitanni had managed to slip out of the Assyrian orbit for a time, but this battle returned it to Assyria. The native Hurrian dynasty was cut off and replaced with Assyrian governors. This brought the Assyrian and the Hittite empires into direct contact, with only the Euphrates separating them. Assyria wanted to expand west, and Hatti wanted to retake the territory of Hanigalbat, but neither had sufficient superior power to move the border. Nevertheless, there was a victory against Hatti, either by Shalmaneser or Tukulti-Ninurta I. This battle was over Nihriya on the Euphrates (*c.* 1240 BCE): the decisive defeat of Tudhaliya IV meant that Mitanni became unquestionably an Assyrian possession, and the Assyrian king even wrote a letter to the king of Ugarit about it (Singer 1985; see further at §5.4.2).

The last major Middle Assyrian king was Tukulti-Ninurta I (*c.* 1225 BCE). He tamed the tribes and small states ('forty kings of the lands of Nairi') in the Zagros area, which formed a constant irritant to the Assyrian kingdom (Grayson 1972: 108 [text 715]). This also made available certain natural resources to the Assyrians (e.g., timber and copper). His major 'accomplishment' was the conquest of Babylonia *c.* 1200 BCE. He claims to have captured the Babylonian king, Kashtiliash, and 'trod with my feet upon his lordly neck' (Grayson 1972: 108 [text 716]). He then attempted to take possession of Akkad down to the Persian Gulf. He also built a new capital, Kar-Tukulti-Ninurta. In these various endeavours, Tukulti-Ninurta seems to have outrun his resources: ultimately, after a rule of about seven years he lost Babylon from Assyrian possession and was himself assassinated.

The next several Assyrian kings – Ashur-nadin-apli, Ashur-nirari III, Enlil-kudurri-usur, and Ninurta-apil-Edur – had ephemeral reigns. But then came Ashur-Dan I (*c.* 1150 BCE) who ruled for about 40 years and plundered Babylonia. This was not the end of the Middle Assyrian kingdom, but the rest of its history, and its general decline, are discussed at §7.3.1. Toward the end of this period the Aramaeans became a threat by launching raids on Assyrian territory and even taking some of it temporarily (§7.5).

5.2.2 Kassite Babylonia

The famous Old Babylonian king Hammurabi had unified Babylonia under his rule (§3.2.3), but soon after his death his empire began to break up. Larsa, under Rim-Sin II, and Eshnunna both rebelled against Hammurabi's son Samsu-iluna. He was able to contain the rebellions, but his inscriptions indicate further unrest and defensive measures, including the building of walls and fortifications at various cities, and even a line of fortresses to the south of Babylonia. Already under his rule we begin to hear about a threat from the peoples of the Zagros mountain region, called the Kassites, and his claimed defeat of them.

The Babylonian King Lists catalogue a new dynasty, said to rule in the southern region (along the coast of the Persian Gulf), originally a part of the Sumerian area, as the Sealand – KUR A.AB.BA/*māt tâmti(m)*. It apparently became established shortly after the death of Hammurabi in an area seen as marginal marshy land from the perspective of Babylon. The preserved data suggest that the first king ruled about 1750 BCE and was an opponent of Samsu-iluna. Some have thought that one or more kings of Sealand ruled all of Babylonia, but this is not clear. There may have been as many as 11 kings ruling for more than 350 years, but we know little about them. Information independent of the king lists is not found until about 1475 BCE. Sometimes the Sealand came back under Babylonian and Assyrian control, but the inaccessible nature of much of its territory meant that its rulers could often maintain an independent or semi-independent status until about 400 BCE. At different times rebel rulers took refuge in this area, perhaps the most famous being Marduk-apla-iddina II (the Merodach-baladan of 2 Kgs 20:12//Isa. 39:1).

The period of Kassite rule in Babylon was a lengthy one (1600–1150). Not much is known, though the older view that the Kassites were seen as foreigners and illegitimate probably requires revision. Interestingly, the rulers were designated as 'kings of Babylonia', i.e., the whole region, whereas previous kings had been kings of a particular city-state (the title, 'king of the land of Karduniash' is sometimes used, which might be a Kassite title). The King Lists give several names (Gandash, Agum I, and Kashtiliash I) that do not appear in actual Babylonian inscriptions. It is possible that they did not rule in Babylon but only in the Kassite homeland.

Hana and Hatti had apparently joined forces late in the Old Babylonian period (seventeenth century BCE). The Hittite king Mursili I destroyed Babylon and carried off the famous Marduk statue to Hana, during the reign of one of the last native Babylonian kings, Samsu-ditana (*c.* 1600). This evidently provided the opportunity needed for the Kassites to intervene and establish a Kassite dynasty. But one of the first Kassite kings, Agum II (*c.* 1550), was able to defeat Hana and take back the Marduk statue to Babylon. It apparently took time for the Kassites to take complete control: how this happened and which king is to be credited with the deed for first taking the city is not currently known. But Babylonia was all under Kassite rule by the first part of the fifteenth century BCE. They also held the Sealand.

The Amarna archives contain communications between Egypt and Babylonia, indicating that Kassite Babylon was an international power. These letters mainly concern dynastic marriages between Egypt and Babylonia. The Babylonian king Kara-indash (*c.* 1425 BCE) was the one who began the process, establishing contact with Amenhotep II, according to a later letter (EA 10). But the Assyrian king Ashur-uballit did the same, though his rather tactless opening of communication with Akhenaten had the effect of forcing the Kassite king Burna-Buriash II (*c.* 1350 BCE) to try to counter any Assyrian influence in his own letters to Egypt. Nevertheless, Assyria and Babylonia were able to reach an agreement, with Ashur-uballit sending a daughter to marry Burna-Buriash's son, apparently Kadashman-Harbe who was meant to take the Babylonian throne.

Unfortunately, there was a violent reaction in the Babylonian court against Kadashman-Harbe who was assassinated. Ashur-uballit could not ignore this insult to his family and invaded Babylonia, placing Kadashman-Harbe's infant son Kurigalzu II (*c.* 1325 BCE) on the throne. When Kurigalzu reached maturity, however, he was not a willing instrument in the hands of Assyria, but confronted the next Assyrian king, Enlil-nirari, in battle to establish the territorial boundary between the two. The Synchronistic Chronicle states that Kurigalzu was defeated, but the Chronicle of Kassite Kings (also known as Chronicle P) makes Kurigalzu the victor (Glassner 2004: 178–9, 280–1; Grayson 1972: 53–4 [Paragraphs 345-47]). Whatever the case with Assyria, Kurigalzu defeated the king of Elam, Hurba-tilla, though this Elamite king is not in the standard king lists. He was probably also the builder of Dur-Kurigalzu. His son, Nazi-Marutash (*c.* 1300 BCE), also fought the Assyrians (under their new king, Ark-den-ili).

It was under the next Assyrian king, Adad-nirari I (*c.* 1300), that the Assyrian frontier was pushed further south by defeating Nazi-Marutash at a place called Kar-Ishtar of Ugarsallu (Glassner 2004: 78–9; Grayson 1972: 78–9 [Paragraph 520]; Weidner 1963). The change was not very great, however, and Adad-nirari imposed on Nazi-Marutash a new border. In spite of problems from the Assyrians, Kadash-Enlil II (*c.* 1250 BCE) seems to have managed good trade relations with the Hittites. The border was still a sore point, however, and when the new Assyrian king Tukulti-Ninurta I was being crowned, Kashtiliash IV of Babylonia (*c.* 1225 BCE) took the opportunity to push the border further north. Tukulti-Ninurta reacted quickly and went against Kashtiliash, not only defeating him but also taking him personally captive. The Assyrians then went on to take the city of Babylon.

For seven years Babylon was ruled by Tukulti-Ninurta who took the title, 'King of Babylon', and the statue of Marduk was deported once again. But then Tukulti-Ninurta was assassinated, and Kashtiliash's son Adad-shum-usur (*c.* 1200 BCE) was put on the throne. He continued the struggle with Assyria, defeating the Assyrian ruler Enlil-kudurri-usur, but the success of Babylonia for the next decades was only moderate against a weak Assyria. Also, Elam was asserting itself, especially against Babylonia. Rule by the Kassite dynasty did not long outlive Adad-shum-usur. The Assyrian king Ashur-Dan I (*c.* 1150 BCE) plundered Babylonia, but it was the Elamite ruler Shutruk-Nahhunte who particularly damaged eastern and northern Babylonian cities. His son, Kutir-Nahhunte, took control of the north of Babylonia, alongside Kassite rule in the south. But within a few years, the Elamite conquered Babylon and brought an end to the Kassite dynasty about the middle of the twelfth century BCE.

5.3 ANATOLIA

5.3.1 Hittite (Middle and) New Kingdom (1500–1200)

G. M. Beckman (1995) 'The Siege of Uršu Text (CTH 7) and Old Hittite Historiography', *JCS* 47: 23–34; **idem** (1996) *Hittite Diplomatic Texts*; **idem** (2001) 'Sargon and Naram-Sin in Hatti: Reflections of Mesopotamian Antiquity among the Hittites', in D. Kuhn and H. Stahl (eds), *Die Gegenwart des Altertums: Formen und Funktionen des Altertumsbezugs in den Hochkulturen der Alten Welt*: 85–91; **S. R. Bin-Nun** (1974) 'Who Was Tahurwaili, the Great Hittite King?', *JCS* 26: 112–20; **T. Bryce** (2005) *The Kingdom of the Hittites*; **idem** (2012) *The World of the Neo-Hittite Kingdoms: A Political and Military History*; **F. Cornelius** (1976) *Geschichte der Hethiter: mit besonderer Berücksichtigung der geographischen Verhältnisse und der Rechtsgeschichte*; **H. Genz and D. P. Mielke (eds)** (2011) *Insights into Hittite History and Archaeology*; **A. Gilan** (2008) 'Were There Cannibals in Syria? History and Fiction in an Old Hittite Literary Text', in E. Cingano and L. Milano (eds), *Papers on Ancient Literatures: Greece, Rome and the Near East*: 267–84; **A. Goetze** (1957a) 'On the Chronology of the Second Millennium B. C.', *JCS* 11: 53–61; **idem** (1957b) 'On the Chronology of the Second Millennium B. C. (Concluded)', *JCS* 11: 63–73; **O. R. Gurney** (1990) *The Hittites*; **H. G. Güterbock** (1967) 'The Hittite Conquest of Cyprus Reconsidered', *JNES* 26: 73–81; **idem** (1983) 'The Hittites and the Aegean World: Part 1, The Ahhiyawa Problem Reconsidered', *AJA* 87: 133–8; **H. A. Hoffner** (2009) *Letters from the Hittite Kingdom*; **A. Kempinski and S. Košak** (1982) '*CTH* 13: The Extensive Annals of Hattušili I (?)', *TA* 9: 87–116; **H. Klengel** (1998) *Geschichte des Hethitischen Reiches*; **I. Singer** (1985) 'The Battle of Niḫriya and the End of the Hittite Empire', *ZA* 75: 100–123; **idem** (2000) 'New Evidence on the End of the Hittite Empire', in E. D. Oren (ed.), *The Sea Peoples and their World: A Reassessment*: 21–33; **O. Soysal** (1989a) *Mursili I – Eine historische Studie*; **idem** (1989b) '"Der Apfel möge die Zähne nehmen!"', *Or* 58: 171–92; **idem** (1990) 'Noch einmal zur Šukziya-Episode im Erlaß Telipinus', *Or* 59: 271–9.

The period following Telipinu's death (*c.* 1500 BCE; §3.3.1) is often referred to as the 'Hittite Middle Kingdom', though many now reject this concept and lump all the subsequent history of the Hittite empire under the term 'Hittite New Kingdom' (confusingly, Bryce [2005: xv] includes these kings under the 'Old Kingdom'). Unfortunately, we know little about the history of the so-called Middle Kingdom, encompassing approximately a century. Its succession of rulers are little more than names, and Hatti was only one of many states in Asia Minor. Two neighbouring states and major rivals were Arzawa to the west (a former vassal) and Kizzuwatna to the south. The Hittite regime was also threatened by Kaska to the north and Mitanni to the east. Following Telipinu his son-in-law Aluwamna (*c.* 1500 BCE) apparently gained the throne because of his marriage to Telipinu's daughter (Goetze 1957a: 57). Somewhere in there we should probably fit Tahurwaili (Bin-Nun 1974) who renewed the treaty with Kizzuwatna; his name is known from a seal but does not appear in the lists of kings. He might have died after a short reign or might have been removed by Aluwamna. Over the next century were several other kings, who names are known mainly from offering lists but also some from (fragments of) treaties: Hantili II, Zidanta II, Huzziya II, Muwattalli I. This last is said to have murdered his predecessor and to have been assassinated in turn.

It was about 1400 BCE that the Hittite New Kingdom is thought by many to commence. The fortunes of the kingdom began to revive under Tudhaliya II (some think he was actually the first king by this name). He began a series of military campaigns against his neighbours, conquering Arzawa and Aleppo, and countering the Kaska threat. He also brought Kizzuwatna under his control, though this was by treaty. The Hittite expanded territory had only begun unification, however, and his successor, Arnuwanda I, had to deal with a series of revolts. As the Hittite strength grew, Egypt and Mitanni attempted to counter it. Mitanni took back control of Kizzuwatna and Aleppo (during the reign of Hattusili II?). Under Tudhaliya III, Kaska invaded and burned the Hittite capital Hattusa (*c.* 1360 BCE; *CTH* 88: Bryce 2005: 146). The various kingdoms of Anatolia menaced the Hittite state. This was the situation when Tudhaliya's son Suppiluliuma I, perhaps the most famous king of Hatti, came on the scene.

Half a century separates Tudhaliya II from Suppiluliuma I (*c.* 1350 BCE). The conquests of the latter are found in the 'Deeds of Suppiluliuma' (*CTH* 40; *CoS* 1: 185–92). He brought Kizzuwatna once more under Hittite sovereignty, made Mitanni into a protectorate, and eventually took Carchemish. He moved into northern Syria, first gaining the loyalty of Amurru and Qadesh and then conquering the other small kingdoms (later, Ugarit submitted to Hittite authority). He stopped short of making major inroads into the Egyptian sphere, but the attempt to establish good relations with Egypt was thwarted. The conflict with Egypt eventually culminated some decades later (see below). After 30 years of campaigning, Suppiluliuma's reign ended in a plague spreading within the whole of Anatolia. His successor Arnuwanda II died not long afterward.

The next ruler, Mursili II (*c.* 1300 BCE), had to deal with rebellions in Arzawa and Syria, as well as the plague ravaging the land. By a combination of military force and treaties, he brought these areas back under Hittite domination (Amurru had not rebelled). About this time Adad-Nirari I (*c.* 1300 BCE) began to expand the Assyrian realm. He made Mittani into a vassal, and his son Shalmaneser I (*c.* 1275 BCE) transformed it into an even tighter possession. Whatever the Hittites did to defend their vassal was not enough. In the meantime, to the Hittite north Kaska continued to be a thorn in the side. It fell to the next ruler, Muwatalli II (*c.* 1275), to deal with the continual danger from Kaska. Muwatalli delegated the task to his brother Hattusili (his later successor). Muwatalli had to respond to another threat, once again from Egypt. First, Sety I campaigned in northern Syria, then Ramesses II. This finally culiminated in the battle of Qadesh between Ramesses and Muwatalli (*c.* 1275 BCE). Although Ramesses claimed victory, the Hittites were able to take over Qadesh and Amurru and hold them for the rest of the Egyptian 19th Dynasty.

Muwatalli's son Urhi-Teshub succeeded him, but Hattusili had established his ability as a military leader and would not accept Urhi-Teshub's attempts to limit his power. Eventually, the former rebelled and replaced Urhi-Teshub on the throne, as Hattusili III (*c.* 1250 BCE; see his *Apology* [*CTH* 81: *CoS* 1:199–204]). He established peace with Egypt by a treaty between himself and Ramesses (*CTH* 91: Beckman 1996: 90–5), which was sealed by Ramesses taking his daughter as a wife. Hattusili also established relations with the Kassite Babylonia, but Assyria remained an opponent. The border between Hatti and Assyria had been set at the Euphrates. The next Hittite king, Tudhaliya IV (*c.* 1225 BCE), battled with the Assyrians over this border, but neither side could prevail. Tudhaliya needed to suppress revolts on the Aegean coast of Anatolia that had been encouraged by 'Ahhiyawa', often identified with the Mycenaean Greeks (see the 'Letter of Milawata' [*CTH* 182: Hoffner 2009: 313–21]). This included a campaign even as far as Cyprus (Alashiya).

Two more kings followed Tudhaliya: Arnuwanda III and Suppiluliuma II (*c.* 1200 BCE). Suppiluliuma showed some of the spirit of his namesake by capturing Cyprus through sea and land action (*CTH* 121: Güterbock 1967). Yet the wider Hittite empire was disintegrating, with various vassals and possessions falling away from Hittite control. The kingdom seems to have come to an end primarily by internal decline, though raids from the Sea Peoples might have had a destructive effect on the Hatti as well as on Ugarit. Nevertheless, the downfall of the Hittite empire was in the context of a decline all over the ancient Near East at this time. It was succeeded by a series of Neo-Hittite states that carried on for another 500 years (§7.3.2).

5.3.2 The Mitanni Kingdom (1600–1350) and Nuzi

M. C. Astour (1972) 'Ḫattušiliš, Ḫalab, and Ḫanigalbat', *JNES* 31: 102–9; **idem** (1981) 'Ugarit and the Great Powers', in G. D. Young (ed.), *Ugarit in Retrospect: Fifty Years of Ugarit and Ugaritic*: 3–29; **G. M. Beckman** (1995) 'The Siege of Uršu Text (CTH 7) and Old Hittite Historiography', *JCS* 47: 23–34; **idem** (1996) *Hittite Diplomatic Texts*; **B. M. Bryan** (1991) *The Reign of Thutmose IV*; **idem** (2000) 'The Egyptian Perspective on Mitanni', in R. Cohen and R. Westbrook (eds) *Amarna Diplomacy: The Beginnings of International Relations*: 71–84; **E. Cancik-Kirschbaum, N. Brisch, and J. Eidem (eds)** (2014) *Constituent, Confederate, and Conquered Space; The Emergence of the Mittani State*; **M. W. Chavalas (ed.)** (2006) *The Ancient Near East: Historical Sources in Translation*; **R. Drews** (1988) *The Coming of the Greeks: Indo-European Conquests in the Aegean and the Near East*; **J. Freu** (2003) *Histoire du Mitanni*; **A. Gilan** (2004) 'Der Pūḫanu Text – Theologischer Streit und politische Opposition in der Althethitischen Literatur', *AoF* 31: 263–96; **idem** (2008) 'Were There Cannibals in Syria? History and Fiction in an Old Hittite Literary Text', in E. Cingano and L. Milano (eds), *Papers on Ancient Literatures: Greece, Rome and the Near East*: 267–84; **A. Goetze** (1957) 'On the Chronology of the Second Millennium B. C.', *JCS* 11: 53–73; **F. Imparati** (1965) 'L'Autobiografia di Ḫattušili I', *Studi Classici e Orientali* 14: 40–76; **D. Kahn** (2011) 'One Step Forward, Two Steps Backward: The Relations between Amenhotep III, King of Egypt and Tushratta, King of Mitanni', in S. Bar, D. Kahn, and J. J. Shirley (eds), *Egypt, Canaan and Israel: History*: 136–54; **A. Kempinski and S. Košak** (1982) 'CTH 13: The Extensive Annals of Ḫattušili I (?)', *TA* 9: 87–116; **E. R. Lacheman and M. P. Maidman (eds)** (1989) *Joint Expedition with the Iraq Museum at Nuzi VII: Miscellaneous Texts*; **E. R. Lacheman, M. A. Morrison, and D. I. Owen (eds)** (1993) *The Eastern Archives of Nuzi and Excavations at Nuzi 9/2*; **M. P. Maidman** (1994) *Two Hundred Nuzi Texts from the Oriental Institute of the University of Chicago, Part I*; **idem** (1995) 'Nuzi: Portrait of an Ancient Mesopotamian Provincial Town', in J. M. Sasson (ed.), *Civilizations of the Ancient Near East*: 2:931–47; **M. Mayrhofer** (1982) 'Welches Material aus dem Indo-arischen von Mitanni verbleibt für eine selektive Darstellung?', in E. Neu (ed.), *Investigationes philologicae et comparativae: Gedenkschrift für Heinz Kronasser*: 72–90; **M. Monier-Williams** (1899) *A Sanskrit-English Dictionary*; **M. A. Morrison and D. I. Owen (eds)** (1981) *In Honor of Ernest R. Lacheman on His Seventy-fifth Birthday, April 29, 1981*; **W. J. Murnane** (1995) *Texts from the Amarna Period in Egypt*; **N. Na'aman** (1994) 'The Hurrians and the End of the Middle Bronze Age in Palestine', *Levant* 26: 275–91; **D. I. Owen** (1995) *General Studies and Excavations at Nuzi 9/3*; **D. I. Owen and M. A. Morrison (eds)** (1987) *General Studies and Excavations at Nuzi 9/1*; **P. Raulwing** (2005) 'The Kikkuli Text (CTH 284). Some Interdisciplinary Remarks on Hittite Training Texts for Chariot Horses in the Second Half of the

2nd Millennium B.C.', in A. Gardeisen (ed.), *Les Équidés dans le monde méditerranéen antique: Actes du colloque organisé par l'École française d'Athènes, le Centre Camille Jullian, et l'UMR 5140 du CNRS, Athènes, 26-28 Novembre 2003*: 61–75; **idem** (2009) 'The Kikkuli Text: Hittite Training Instructions for Chariot Horses in the Second Half of the 2nd Millennium B.C. and Their Interdisciplinary Context'; **P. Raulwing and R. Schmitt** (1998) 'Zur etymologischen Beurteilung der Berufsbezeichnung *aššuššanni* des Pferdetrainers Kikkuli von Mittani', in P. Anreiter et al. (eds), *Man and the Animal World: Studies in Archaeozoology, Archaeology, Anthropology and Paleolinguistics in memoriam Sándor Bökönyi*: 675–704; **D. B. Redford** (1982) 'Mitanni', *LdÄ* 4:149–52; **idem** (1992a) *Egypt, Canaan, and Israel in Ancient Times*; **idem** (2003) *The Wars in Syria and Palestine of Thutmose III*; **C. Saporetti** (1965) ['L'Autobiografia di Ḫattušili I:] Versione Accadica', *Studi Classici e Orientali* 14: 77–85; **O. Soysal** (1989a) *Mursili I – Eine historische Studie*; **idem** (1989b) '"Der Apfel möge die Zähne nehmen!"', *Or* 58: 171–92; **A. Spalinger** (1978) 'New Reference to an Egyptian Campaign of Thutmose III in Asia', *JNES* 37: 35–41; **D. L. Stein** (1989) 'A Reappraisal of the "Sauštartar [sic] Letter" from Nuzi', *ZA* 79: 36–60; **P. Thieme** (1960) 'The "Aryan" Gods of the Mitanni Treaties', *JAOS* 80: 301–17; **I. Wegner** (2007) *Einführung in die hurritische Sprache*; **G. Wilhelm** (1987–90) 'Marijannu', *RlA* 7:419–21; **idem** (1989) *The Hurrians*; **G. Wilhelm and D. L. Stein** (1993–97) 'Mittan(n)i, Mitanni, Maitani', *RlA* 8:286–99; **idem** (1998–2001) 'Nuzi', *RlA* 8:636–47; **M. Witzel** (2001) 'Autochthonous Aryans? The Evidence from Old Indian and Iranian Texts', *Electronic Journal of Vedic Studies* 7, no. 3: 1–93.

We first hear of a people called the Hurrians as early as the late third millennium BCE (§3.3.2). It seems clear now that their name also gave us the 'Horites' (חרים) of the Hebrew Bible. It was only in the mid-second millennium that a kingdom of Mitanni arose. The Hurrian language is related neither to Indo-European nor Semitic (cf. Wegner 2007). The main part of the population was apparently made up of the Hurrian speakers, a people especially attested in northern Mesopotamia and Syria in the early second millennium BCE. We know that Hurrians were found among the populations of many cities across Asia Minor and northern Syria. But there is evidence of an elite component of the population with an Indo-Aryan background.

Some have seen a significant incursion of the Hurrians and their Indo-Aryan overlords into southern Syria and northern Palestine as early as the sixteenth century, perhaps even before Mitanni was founded (Redford 1992a: 134–8; 2003: 191–4; Na'aman 1994; Astour 1981: 9; Wilhelm 1989: 18). Mitanni's taking control of northern Syria and the former realm of Yamhad is well documented; however, M. Liverani (2014: 272–3) is sceptical of a mass migration, especially one extending as far as southern Syria and Palestine or even Egypt. Mitanni seems to have a connection with the Qedesh-led coalition against Thutmose III at Megiddo, but the named members of the alliance are mostly sites within the area of Canaan (§6.3.1). Mitanni's influence seems to have been more indirect.

The Mitanni leaders were believed to be Indo-Aryan rather than Hurrian, however, perhaps some of the ancestors of the people migrating from southern Russia and eventually reaching northern India. This is based on what seem to be Indo-Aryan borrowings in some of the texts: their names and especially some of the terms in technical areas (Mayrhofer 1982; Witzel 2001). This can be seen in names (Witzel 2001: 53–4; Wilhelm 1989: 18): personal names, such as *ar-ta-aš-šu-ma-ra* (Artashumara, Sanskrit **Ṛta-smara*), (Tushratta [Tuišeratta] = Vedic *tveṣá-ratha-*), and *ar-ta-ta-a-ma* (Artatama, Sanskrit *Ṛta-dhāman*), and names of deities (Thieme 1960), which include *a-ru-na, ú-ru-wa-na* (Sanskrit Varuṅa), *mi-it-ra* (Sanskrit Mitra), *in-da-ra/in-tar* (Sanskrit Indra), and *na-ša-at-ti-ya-an-na* (Sanskrit Nāsatya). A number of terms relating to horses and chariotry seem to have been borrowed from Indo-Aryan, especially in the Kikkuli treatise on training chariot horses found among the Hittite texts (Raulwing 2005, 2009; Raulwing/Schmitt 1998). One word borrowed into many languages across the region was *maryannu* 'charioteer', a word that has been compared with Sanskrit *marya* ('a mortal, man, (esp.) young man': Monier-Williams 1899: 791). It has been noted that 'most scholars accepted that Kikkuli's profession title *aššu-ššanni* contains the Indo-Aryan word **aśva-* for "horse" as its first element' (Raulwing/Schmitt 1998; Raulwing 2009: 7–8; cf. Monier-Williams 1899: 114–15). Several of the numbers in the text also seem to be borrowings, in Vedic form.

When it is argued that Indo-Aryan influence has been exaggerated, and claims are made that the word *maryannu* is Hurrian in origin, the arguments do not seem to stand up. G. Wilhelm (1987–90) documents these claims and then refutes them. It seems that the question of Indo-Aryan influence stands. Yet there are still many questions about how this came about and what this says about Mitanni society. The Indo-Aryan names look to be those of the royal family or upper-class individuals, while the technical terms relate to the chariotry core of the military. It could be that Hurrians and Indo-Aryans met up in the Transcaucasian region before migrating to the Anatolian area, or a fragment of the broad Indo-Aryan migration south moved further west into Anatolia (Wilhelm 1989: 17–18). At this point, there are a number of possibilities.

The kingdom of Mitanni (called Hanigalbat in some texts) was made up of a union of Hurrian states which coalesced about 1600 BCE (cf. Astour 1972: 103–5). The decline of Yamhad, the failure of the Hittites to take control of its territory, and the crisis in Assyria after the death of Ishme-Dagan all contributed to the rise of Mitanni. The capital of the kingdom was Washshukkanni (Tell Fekheriye). The bi-lingual *Annals of Hattusili I* (*CTH* 4: Chavalas [ed.] 2006: 219–22; Imparati 1965; Saporetti 1965) already mention Hurrian attacks on the Hittites during the reign of the Hittite king Hattusili I (*c.* 1625 BCE); also, the *Siege of Usha* text (*CTH* 7: Beckman 1995), depending on how seriously one takes this text as history. But another text (*CTA* 13) is thought to mention conflict with the Hurrians as well, though whether it is from the time of Hattusili I (Kempinski/Košak 1982) or Mursili I (Soysal 1989a: 136–9; 1989b: 189–92) is debated. In any case, it seems likely that Mursili I (*c.* 1600) was opposed by the Hurrians. This is indicated by *CTH* 16 (Gilan 2004; cf. *CoS* 1:184–5) and the so-called cannibal text (*CTH* 17: Gilan 2008: 272): these texts, which seem to straddle the line between legend and historiography, are not easy to interpret but may give us some insight into events of the period. The later *Edict of Telipinu* (*CTH* 19: *CoS* 1:194–8) also speaks of Hittite conflict with the Hurrians *c.* 1550.

The first royal name mentioned is Barattarna (*c.* 1475, also known as Parshatatar, Paršatar, Barrattarna, or Parattarna), who occurs in the Idrimi inscription (*CoS* 1:479–80). Idrimi was a member of the royal family ruling Alalakh. As a child he had to flee to Emar; as a young man he took refuge in Canaan. He returned to Alalakh and was made ruler but was opposed by Barattarna king of the Hurrians. Eventually, they made an agreement, and Idrimi became a vassal of Barattarna. The first mention of Mitanni in an Egyptian text is in the biography of the court astronomer Amenemhet who served under both Amenhotep I and Thutmose I. The inscription is unfortunately fragmentary but contains the phrase: 'the land which they call Mitanni' (Helck 1971: 115; Redford 1982: 4:149). Am3enemhet was apparently a commander in the force that accompanied Tuthmosis I (c. 1493–1483 BCE) when he marched as far as the Euphrates. A more complete inscriptional reference is given to the campaign by another officer of the king, Ahmose, though he mentions only the name of the region ('Retenu', 'Naharin' [*nhrn*]) and not Mitanni specifically (*AEL* 2:14; Bryan 2000: 72). Yet this seems to have been an invasion of Mitanni territory, and Barattarna may have been the ruler who opposed him with troops (Redford 1992a: 153–5). In this encounter Mitanni seems to have acquitted herself adequately or better.

Another royal name attested (on a seal impression: *RlA* 8:296) is that of Shuttarna, son of Kirta. Whether to put him before or after Barattarna is a question. One suggestion is to put him earlier (c. 1575 BCE) and make him the possible founder of the dynasty and the capital (Liverani 2014: 291). In any case, we shall refer to him as Shuttarna I (c. 1460 BCE). The next attested Mitanni king was Shaushtatar (c. 1450), much later than the founding of the dynasty. A letter with his seal was once used to date one of the archaeological strata of Nuzi (Stein 1989), but it is now argued that the letter could have come from one of four different Mitanni rulers (Shaushtatar, Barattarna II, Artatama I, or Shuttarna II). Shaushtatar had to support Ugarit militarily when Thutmose III (c. 1479–1425) marched to the Euphrates, where the Mitannian army was allegedly defeated (Redford 2003: 224–5; 1992a: 159–62). Thutmose's Gebel Barkal stela describes how the pharaoh took prefabricated boats to the Euphrates to cross it and was thus able to outflank the enemy (Redford 2003: 103–16, especially 106–7), but it is suggested that it 'was more in the nature of a draw and that in fact the Egyptians were fought to a standstill' (Redford 2003: 229–32; cf. Redford 1992a: 161–2). In any case, Shaushtatar clearly recovered and went on to make vassals of Assyria and Kizzuwatna (Cilicia).

Under the rule of the Egyptian king Amenhotep II (c. 1425–1400 BCE) things seem to have been quiet with Mitanni: although he conducted a campaign into Syria-Palestine, there was little fighting and his inscriptions contain no hostile comments against Mitanni (Bryan 2000: 76–7; Redford 1992a: 162–3). It is even possible that Amenhotep and Mitanni made a treaty; in any case, after decades of enmity a treaty between Mitanni and Thutmose IV (c. 1400–1390 BCE) was concluded (EA 29:16–18; Helck 1971: 163–4; Bryan 1991: 336–40). The good relations were sealed by dynastic marriages (though Egypt did not usually share its woman with other states). The information about these also provides a list of the next sequence of Mitanni kings and their approximate chronology: Artatama I, his daughter married by Tuthmosis IV (EA 29.16-20); Shuttarna II, his daughter married by Amenhotep III (1390–1353 BCE; EA 19-20); Tushratta I, his daughter married by Amenhotep IV (also known as Akhenaten [1353–1336 BCE]; EA 29; Murnane 1995: 9, 210–11).

Tushratta I engaged in civil strife with his brother. He was killed and the brother became Artatama II. He was succeeded by his son Shuttarna III who was conquered by the Hittite king Suppiluliuma; the latter made Mitanni into a protectorate (c. 1350), which allowed Assyria to gain independence and expand. Not long afterward (c. 1250?), Mitanni was destroyed by the Assyrians who took control of their territory, despite its being a supposed Hittite possession.

5.4 SYRIA

5.4.1 Amurru

A. Altman (1977) 'The Fate of Abdi-Ashirta', *UF* 9: 1–11; **G. M. Beckman** (1996) *Hittite Diplomatic Texts*; **W. Helck** (1963) 'Urḫi-Tešup in Ägypten', *JCS* 17: 87–97; **S. Izre'el** (1991) *Amurru Akkadian: A Linguistic Study*; **S. Izre'el and I. Singer** (1990) *The General's Letter from Ugarit: A Linguistic and Historical Evaluation of RS 20.33 (*Ugaritica V*, No. 20)*; **J. M. Millek** (2021) 'Just What did They Destroy? The Sea Peoples and the End of the Late Bronze Age', in J. Kamlah and A. Lichtenberger (eds), *The Mediterranean Sea and the Southern Levant: Archaeological and Historical Perspectives from the Bronze Age to Medieval Times*: 59–98; **D. B. Redford** (2003) *The Wars in Syria and Palestine of Thutmose III*; **I. Singer** (1991a) 'Appendix III: A Concise History of Amurru', in S. Izre'el, *Amurru Akkadian: A Linguistic Study*: 2:135–95; **idem** (1991b) 'The "Land of Amurru" and the "Lands of Amurru" in the Šaušgamuwa Treaty', *Iraq* 53: 69–74; **A. Spalinger** (1977) 'A Critical Analysis of the "Annals" of Thutmose III (Stücke V-VI)', *JARCE* 14: 41–54.

Although some texts from the LBA continue to mention the MAR.TU/*Amurru* with special reference to a people, our main statements for this period relate especially to the country of Amurru of the Amarna letters (Singer 1991b; Klengel 1992: 160–74; Redford 2003). This was an area mainly stretching between Ugarit and Byblos, bound on the west by the Mediterranean coast and on the east by the Orontes River. While it was thus not far from the original Amorite home (centring on Jebel Bišri [§4.2.3]), it was located further to the west. It fitted the general designation of earlier *Amurru*, however, in being located in northwestern Syria. This was only its core area, of course, with the boundaries shifting back and forth over a couple of centuries. To what extent the population was descended from the Amorites of the Early and Middle Bronze Ages is question which seems not to be answerable at the present.

The first we hear of this Amurru is in EA 60-62, a letter of its ruler Abdi-Ashirta (*c.* 1350 BCE); however, the region had already come under Egyptian control probably with the campaigns of Thutmose III, especially those in his nineteenth to thirty-first years (Redford 2003: 156–60; Spalinger 1977). We know nothing of Abdi-Ashirta's origins; indeed, much of the little we know comes from the letters of Rib-Hadda of Byblos (EA 66-96, 101-38, 362) who is hardly the most objective source. It seems clear, though, that Abdi-Ashirta drew his strength from connections with the *Apiru* in the mountainous region, not the urban centres. He turned the *Apiru* into an army and attacked the coastal cities, taking Ardata, Irqata, Ammiya, Shigata, Bitarha, and Batruna.

He appears to have made Sumur on the coast his headquarters for a time but apparently had no capital city as such. Eventually, he promoted uprisings in the Phoenician cities of Tyre, Sidon, and Beirut, and threatened Byblos. But then Abdi-Ashirta was killed (EA 101; by whom is uncertain, possibly an Egyptian task force: cf. Altman 1977), and Byblos was safe for the time being. In his letters Abdi-Ashirta claimed to be a loyal servant of the pharaoh, but his actions said otherwise: his taking control of the Phoenician coast was not what Egypt expected of its vassal states, and the Egyptian king's tolerance seems finally to have come to an end. Abdi-Ashirta is also alleged by

Rib-Hadda to have been attempting to join up with Mitanni (EA 86, 90, 95, 101), though whether this is true can be debated.

Abdi-Ashirta had at least three sons whose names are known, and they set about renewing domination of the Amurru territory that had been lost after their father's death. This included Ardata, Wahliya, Ambi, Shigata, and Ullasa (EA 104, 105, 109); now all of Amurru except for Irqata and Sumur had been taken (EA 103). Sumur was under siege, while some of the other coastal cities (e.g., Arwad) appear to have thrown in their lot with the sons of Abdi-Ashirta (EA 104, 105, 106, 109, 114, 118). Aziru (c. 1325 BCE) emerged as the dominant brother and became the focus of correspondence. In spite of rebuking letters from the Egyptian king about his activities (e.g., EA 162), Aziru protests his loyalty (e.g., EA 156-61, 165, 168, 171). Yet he captured Sumur and apparently threatened Irqata (EA 100). At one point, Aziru promised to rebuild Sumur, indicating that there was damage to the city involved in its capture (EA 159).

Pressure from Aziru eventually forced Rib-Hadda to leave Byblos and take refuge in Beirut (EA 136-38). His own brother turned against him and helped to drive him out. Rib-Hadda even claims that his brother was delivering Byblos to Aziru, but there is no evidence that Aziru actually brought the city under his rule (cf. EA 140). On the other hand, there is no evidence that Rib-Hadda was ever able to return to his city. Yet Aziru's continued actions caused the pharaoh to order him to come to Egypt. Aziru was able to postpone this trip for a time (cf. EA 162) but eventually made his way south to give an account of himself before his sovereign (EA 169-70). In spite of the accusations against him, he seems to have convinced the Egyptian king to let him return to Amurru which was under attack by troops from Nuhashe and Hatti (EA 169-70). This probably led him to make a treaty with Niqmaddu II of Ugarit (*CTH* 54; RS 19.68: LAPO 20: 64–6; Izre'el 1991: 88–9). But there is also evidence that he resumed encroaching on the territory of his neighbours, such as Tunip (EA 59).

Aziru had long affirmed his allegiance to the pharaoh, but he then made a treaty with Suppiluliuma I (*CTH* 49; Beckman 1996: 32–7; Izre'el/Singer 1990: 144–50). This was probably in response to threats of a Hittite invasion (EA 161, 164-67). To what extent this was a continuation of the attack while Aziru was in Egypt and to what extent it was a new campaign is not clear, but in the middle of the treaty it states that Aziru had approached the Hittite king 'of his own free will' (iii 4'-5'), which seems ironic. In any case, Aziru appears to have remained loyal to his new overlord (cf. the 'historical' remarks at the beginning of the Hittite treaty with his grandson: *CTH* 62; Beckman 1996: 54–9), but that did not prevent his continuing to send placating letters to Egypt (EA 160, 161, 164, 171); although the dating of the various letters is not easy, some of them may be subsequent to his treaty with Suppiluliuma (cf. EA 126).

In spite of his suspect activities, Aziru seems to have lived to an old age. At this point, the Amarna letters come to an end, and we are thrown back on Hittite and Ugaritic sources, which do not give us the detail of Amurru history that is found in the Amarna texts. Aziru was succeeded by Ari-Teshub (c. 1310 BCE) who appears to have reigned only briefly, though he fought for the Hittite king against various rebel kingdoms (the 'historical prologue' to *CTH* 62; Beckman 1996: 54–9). But during his reign we have a number of indications of good relations with Ugarit, such as the marriage of (his daughter?) Princess Ahat-Milku to Niqmepa, king of Ugarit (cf. the inventory of her possessions: RS 16.146 + 161: LAPO 20: 289–91; Izre'el 1990: 68–72). The next king, Duppi-Teshub (c. 1300 BCE), was said to have been ill when he ascended the throne (the 'historical prologue' to *CTH* 62; see above). The treaty specifically forbids him from paying tribute to Egypt: is this because Egypt was active in trying to get Amurru to return to her fold? We know that Sety I led a campaign against Qadesh and Amurru (§6.3.1). A later treaty refers to the fact that Amurru came once more under Egyptian rule, apparently during Sety's reign (see the 'historical prologue' to *CTH* 105; Beckman 1996: 98–102). Whether this was while Duppi-Teshub was still king of Amurru or whether it happened under his successor is uncertain.

The next king was Benteshina (first reign: *c.* 1275 BCE). Regardless of which ruler was on Amurru's throne when Sety attacked, it was clearly during Benteshina's period of rule that the crucial battle of Qadesh between the Egyptians and Hittites took place. In spite of Ramesses's claims to victory, Qadesh and Amurru returned to Hittite control and were to remain so for the rest of the New Hittite Empire. After this battle, Muwattilli II removed Benteshina from the throne and deported him to Hattusa. No reason is stated, but something in Benteshina's actions must have been interpreted as disloyalty to the Hittites: perhaps it was simply because Amurru had submitted to Egypt again for a time (however difficult it would have been to resist!). He was replaced by Shapili (*c.* 1260 BCE), about whom we know little, except that he seems to have reigned about a decade. Benteshina was taken as a client of Muwattilli's brother Hattusili, who treated the exile well. Muwattilli was succeeded briefly by his son Urhi-Teshup, but his uncle soon displaced him to become Hattusili III. Benteshina had of course supported him and was rewarded by being reinstated on the throne of Amurru.

Benteshina (second reign: *c.* 1250 BCE) now had a long further reign. He was given the daughter of Hattusili in marriage, while Benteshina's daughter became the wife of Hattusili's son. This information is laid out in the historical prologue to the treaty made between Hattusili and Benteshina (*CTH* 92; Beckman 1996: 95–8). It seems that shortly afterward, Hattusili and Ramesses II signed a peace treaty that settled the relationship of Egypt and Hatti and also the division of the border territories. Amurru appears to have been an important conduit of messengers and transactions between the two. For example, according to a Hittite text (KUB XXI 38) the Hittite princess who was to become a bride of Ramesses as part of the deal was accompanied to Amurru by her mother where she was then picked up by her Egyptian escort (Helck 1963). A long letter from Hattusili III to Kadashman-Enlil II of Babylon mentions that the Babylonians were concerned about their merchants killed in Ugarit and Amurru and also about Benteshina's cursing of Babylon (*CTH* 172; Beckman 1996: 132–7). Hattusili is clearly trying to smooth things over: the matter of the merchants is being dealth with, and Benteshina had a claim of three silver talents against Babylon which had apparently not been paid. It was a daughter of Benteshina who married Ammittamru II and later caused a scandal (§5.4.2).

The final king of Amurru looks to have been Shaushgamuwa (*c.* 1225 BCE). His reign was marked by several negative situations: the Assyrians becoming a serious enemy to Hatti, the scandal of the Amurru princess married to Ammittamru II, and the attacks by contingents of the Sea Peoples. The Hittite king by this time was Tudhaliya IV, whose sister was given in marriage to Shaushgamuwa. One of the sources of his reign is the treaty between the two kings (*CTH* 105; Beckman 1996: 98–102). It clearly states that Assyria was already the enemy of Hatti. Amurru is not to allow his merchants to trade with Assyria nor Assyrian merchants to travel through his land nor ships from Ahhiyawa (Mycenae) to connect with Assyria. Because of Hatti's war with Assyria, Shaushgamuwa must raise an army and a unit of chariotry. Yet we know that the struggle between Assyria and Hatti ended in a defeat for the latter, with consequences for Amurru.

The Ugaritic queen's scandalous affair, and Shaushgamuwa's place in it is discussed elsewhere (§5.4.2). As for the Sea Peoples, it looks as if they were already threatening Amurru – as they were Ugarit – while Shaushgamuwa was still reigning, as a letter from an individual named Parsu seems to indicate (RS 20.162: LAPO 20: 184–5; Izre'el 1990: 98–100). As noted above, Assyria's defeat of the Hittites ended Hittite protection of Amurru. There is no evidence that the Assyrians launched attacks on Amurru, but the Syrian kingdom was left vulnerable to depredations from other aggressors. The question is whether the Sea Peoples brought about the end of the kingdom of Amurru. A recent study by Millek allows this possibility, but with strong caveats:

> Taking both the textual and archaeological sources together, *Tell Kazel*, the possible capital of Amurru, is the only site which might have been destroyed by the Sea Peoples. From the textual side, Amurru is described as destroyed by the Sea Peoples in Ramesses III's Year 8 and from the archaeological side at *Tell Kazel*, its Area IV, the temple complex, was destroyed shortly after 1200 BC which would coincide with the traditional historical dates for the movements of the Sea Peoples. However, even here, there is no conclusive evidence that the site was destroyed by the Sea Peoples as Handmade Burnished ware appeared at the site prior to this destruction event representing a peaceful intrusion of Sea Peoples' material culture. Therefore, there is no certain evidence that this destruction event was brought on by the Sea Peoples over another local group or even Ramesses III himself. It remains a possibility that *Tell Kazel* was destroyed by the Sea Peoples, but this is all it remains as, a possibility. [Millek 2021: 84]

We can conclude that a case can be made for the destruction of Amurru by the Sea Peoples, but it still remains a subject for further study and certainty is not currently possible.

5.4.2 Ugarit

A. Altman (2001) 'EA 59:27-29 and the Efforts of Mukiš, Nuḫašše and Niya to Establish a Common Front against Šuppiluliuma I', *UF* 33: 1–25; **idem** (2008) 'Ugarit's Political Standing in the Beginning of the 14th Century BCE Reconsidered', *UF* 40: 25–64; **D. Arnaud** (1997) 'Prolégomènes à la rédaction d'une histoire d'Ougarit 1. Ougarit avant Suppiluliuma 1er', *SMEA* 39: 151–61; **idem** (1998) 'Prolégomènes à la rédaction d'une histoire d'Ougarit II: Les bordereaux de rois divinisés', *SMEA* 41: 153–73; **G. M. Beckman** (1996) *Hittite Diplomatic Texts*; **P. Bordreuil and D. Pardee** (1982) 'Le rituel funéraire ougaritique RS. 34.126', *Syria* 59: 21–8; **G. J. Brooke** (1979) 'The Textual, Formal and Historical Significance of Ugaritic Letter RS 34.124 (= *KTU* 2.72)', *UF* 11: 69–87; **G. J. Brooke, A. H. W. Curtis, and J. F. Healey (eds)** (1994) *Ugarit and the Bible: Proceedings of the International Symposium on Ugarit and the Bible, Manchester, September 1992*; **M. Dietrich** (2001) 'Der Brief des Kommandeurs Šumiyānu an den ugaritischen König Niqmepa' (RS 20.33): Ein Bericht über Aktivitäten nach der Schlacht bei Qadeš 1275 v. Chr.', *UF* 33: 117–91; **J. Freu** (2006) *Histoire politique du royaume d'Ugarit*; **L. L. Grabbe** (1994) '"Canaanite": Some

Methodological Observations in Relation to Biblical Study', in G. J. Brooke, A. H. W. Curtis, and J. F. Healey (eds), *Ugarit and the Bible: Proceedings of the International Symposium on Ugarit and the Bible, Manchester, September 1992*: 113–22; **M. Heltzer** (1976) 'Mortgage of Land Property and Freeing from It in Ugarit', *JESHO* 19: 89–95; **J. Huehnergard** (1991) 'Remarks on the Classification of Northwest Semitic Languages', in J. Hoftijzer and G. van der Kooij (eds), *The Balaam Text from Deir 'Alla Re-evaluated: Proceedings of the International Symposium Held at Leiden 21-24 August 1989*: 282–93; **J. Huehnergard and N. Pat-El** (2019) 'Introduction to the Semitic Languages and their History', in J. Huehnergard and N. Pat El (eds), *The Semitic Languages*: 1–21; **S. Izre'el** (1991) *Amurru Akkadian: A Linguistic Study*; **S. Izre'el and I. Singer** (1990) *The General's Letter from Ugarit: A Linguistic and Historical Evaluation of RS 20.33 (Ugaritica V, No. 20)*; **S. Lackenbacher** (1982) 'Nouveaux documents d'Ugarit: I. Une lettre royale', *RdA* 76: 141–56; **G. A. Lehmann** (1979) 'Die Šikalāju – ein neues Zeugnis zu den "Seevölker"-Heerfahrten im späten 13. Jh. v. Chr. (RS 34.129)', *UF* 11: 481–94; **I. Márquez Rowe** (1996) 'An Akkadian Letter of the Amarna Period at Ugarit', *Aula Orientalis* 14: 107–26; **idem** (2000) 'The King of Ugarit, his Wife, her Brother, and her Lovers: The Mystery of a Tragedy in Two Acts Revisited', *UF* 32: 365–72; **J. M. Millek** (2020–21) '"Our City Is Sacked. May You Know it!" The Destruction of Ugarit and its Environs by the "Sea People"', *Archaeology and History in the Lebanon* 52–53: 102–32; **idem** (2021) 'Just What did They Destroy? The Sea Peoples and the End of the Late Bronze Age', in J. Kamlah and A. Lichtenberger (eds), *The Mediterranean Sea and the Southern Levant: Archaeological and Historical Perspectives from the Bronze Age to Medieval Times*: 59–98; **N. Na'aman** (1996b) 'Ammishtamru's Letter to Akhenaten (EA 45) and Hittite Chronology', *AuOr* 14: 251–7; **D. Pardee** (1983–84) 'Ugaritic', *AfO* 29-30: 321–9; **idem** (1988) *Les textes para-mythologiques de la 24ᵉ Campagne (1961)* [= RSO 4]; **idem** (2002) *Ritual and Cult at Ugarit*; **I. Singer** (1985) 'The Battle of Niḫriya and the End of the Hittite Empire'. *ZA* 75: 100–123; **idem** (1999) 'A Political History of Ugarit', in W. G. E. Watson and N. Wyatt (eds), *Handbook of Ugaritic Studies*: 603–733; **W. H. van Soldt** (2014–16) 'Ugarit. A. Geschichte und Literatur', *RlA* 14: 280–3; **J. Vidal** (2000) 'King Lists and Oral Transmission: From History to Memory', *UF* 32: 555–66; **W. G. E. Watson and N. Wyatt (eds)** (1999) *Handbook of Ugaritic Studies*.

As already mentioned, this city-state already existed in the third millennium BCE and is named in early second-millennium texts, though most of the Ugaritic texts are from the LBA. Its history is best known for the Amarna period when the city was flourishing. Ugarit was not in the area of Canaan, and the use of the term 'Canaanite' for matters relating to Ugarit is generally incorrect. Although there is definitely Canaanite influence, and some of its myths might have originated in the area of Canaan, it is a mistake to confuse 'Canaanite' with 'Ugaritic' (Grabbe 1994). The same also holds true for its language: Ugaritic does not seem to be appropriately classified as a Canaanite dialect (Huehnergard 1991; Huehnergard/Pat-El 2019; Grabbe 1994), but takes its place as a separate language in Northwest Semitic, alongside the Canaanite dialects (including Hebrew and Phoenician) and Aramaic (for the classification of Amorite, see §4.2.3).

A huge bibliography of primary and secondary studies has accumulated for Ugarit (see Watson/Wyatt [eds] 1999 for a helpful overview), but our focus here will be on the history of the city-state rather than on the literature as such.

D. Arnaud (1998) has reconstructed a table of Ugaritic kings, based on lists of deceased 'divine' kings (especially *KTU* 1.113 [= RS 24.257] and RS 94.2518); see Pardee (1988: 165–78; 2002: 195–210) for a different transliteration of some of the names:

		1. Ugarānu
eighteenth century BCE	1800	2. Amqūnu
		3. Rap'ānu
		4. Lim-il-Malik
		5. Ammu-harrāšï
		6. Ammu-šamar
seventeenth century BCE	1700	7. Ammistamru I (if he existed)
		8. Niqmepa I
		9. Mabu'u
		10. Ibirānu I
		11. Ya'dur-'Addu, alias Ehli-Tešub
sixteenth century BCE	1600	12. Niqmepa II
		13. Ibirānu II
		14. Ammurapi 1
		15. Niqmepa III
		16. Ibirānu III
fifteenth century BCE	1500	17. Niqmepa IV
		18. Ibirānu IV
		19. Niqmadu I (if he existed)
		20. Yaqaru
		21. Ibirānu V
fourteenth century BCE	1400	22. Niqmadu II (or 'I')
		23. Niqmepa V
		24. Ammistamru II (or 'I')
		25. Niqmadu III (or 'II')
		00. Ar-Halba
thirteenth century BCE	1300	26. Niqmepa VI (or 'I')
		27. Ammistamru III (or 'II')
		28. Ibiranu VI (or 'I')
		29. Niqmadu IV (or 'III')
		30. Ammurapi II (or 'I')
twelfth century BCE	c. 1190	Destruction of Ugarit

Although the list is based on texts, we cannot be certain that these texts give a reliable list of the kings of Ugarit in the late third/early second millennium BCE. Arnaud argues that the combined texts give a complete list, but D. Pardee (2002: 196–9) disagrees, arguing that the original list could have contained as many as 49 names. J. Vidal (2000: 560) even suggests that two founding traditions are found in the different texts. Thus, the list of Arnaud, intriguing as it is, must be considered hypothetical.

The last few kings, however, are known from contemporary inscriptions and relate more solidly to the history of the city-state. Thus, while this reconstructed list is too hypothetical to be taken account of, the following discussion will focus on those kings actually attested in extant documentary sources (the kings below the line: those numbered 24-30). The numbering of kings (I, II, III, etc.) with the same name only follows the documented kings, which is why they do not seem to fit with their hypothetical counterparts (though Arnaud has also given this latter numbering in brackets). N.B.: the dates given here are those of Singer (1999) unless otherwise indicated.

A dynastic seal of Yaqaru son of Niqmaddu has been preserved (Arnaud 1997: 158–61). Some think he was the founder of the dynasty, because his name comes at the end of the list in *KTU* 1.113, the argument being that the list is retrograde, making him the dynastic originator. Yet in the list in RS 94.2518 his name comes as the 20th in a list of 26 names, which means that he is likely a fifteenth-century ruler, not an early one (Arnaud 1998: 153–63; Pardee 2002: 196–8). We can only say that he seems to be earlier than Ammittamru I, though his exact dates are not known. We also have a letter from a King Ibira to Alalakh (RS 4.449: LAPO 20: 191). Is this Ibiranu, and is he to be equated with the Ibiranu who succeeds Yaqaru in the list above (Vidal 2000: 563–6)? Vidal suggests that the historical dynasty might therefore begin with Yaqaru in the middle of the fifteenth century BCE. But much remains uncertain.

We begin with Ammittamru (Ammištamru) I (*c.* 1350 BCE) who wrote the letter (EA 45) to the king of Egypt (Amenhotep III? Akhenaten?). He may have been threatened by the Hittite king (Suppiluliuma I) for having detained some messengers which he intended to send to the pharaoh (Na'aman 1996b). Now in Suppiluliuma's bad books, he appealed to the Egyptian king for help. The fragmentary state of the letter makes interpretation uncertain, however, though it is clear that Ammittamru was loyal to Egypt. He apparently had difficulties with Abdi-Ashirta of Amurru, judging by a later treaty between Ugarit and Amurru (see below).

The first Ugarit king known from his own inscriptions is Niqmaddu II (*c.* 1350–1315 BCE). At some point, he looks to have been the one who wrote to the king of Egypt, asking for a physician among other things (EA 49). At that time, he seems to have had good relations with Egypt. But in spite of this, relations with his neighbour Amurru were apparently not good; to resolve this he made a treaty with Abdi-Ashirta (RS 19.68: LAPO 20: 64–6; Izre'el 1991: 2:88–92). It was probably later that Suppiliuluma I the Hittite king wrote him a letter (*CTH* 45; RS 17.132: LAPO 20: 69–71; Beckman 1996: 119–20), which notes that Niqmaddu was being pressed by Mukish and Nuhashe and urges him to fight them. Ugarit was attacked by them and appealed for Hittite help. This was provided, but it meant becoming a vassal of the Hittites as is made clear by a treaty with Suppiliuluma (*CTH* 46; RS 17.340; 17.369: LAPO 20: 71–3; Beckman 1996: 30–2). This treaty establishes the borders of Ugarit.

Another document sets down the tribute that Ugarit was to pay to Hatti (*CTH* 47; RS 17.227; 11.732: LAPO 20: 74–6; Beckman 1996: 151–4). Thus, his ties with Egypt were severed. At a time when a number of Hittite vassals arose in rebellion against the new king Mursili II, Niqmaddu apparently remained loyal (cf. Altman 2001). Yet when the king of Carchemish (Mursili's brother and deputy) proposed that he attack one of these rebels, Nuhashe (*CTH* 77; RS 17.334: LAPO

20: 77; Beckman 1996: 120–1), the response of Niqmaddu or his successor seems to have been lukewarm. This judgment is based partly on the fact that Niqmaddu II's successor Ar-ḫalba ruled only a short time (*c*. 1315–1313 BCE), suggesting that he was removed from office by Mursili.

Regardless of how he came to the throne, Niqmepa (*c*. 1313–1260 BCE) seems to have been on good terms with his overlord Mursili II who established a treaty with him (*CTH* 66; RS 17.338, etc.: LAPO 20: 78–85; Beckman 1996: 59–64). The treaty emphasizes that Mursili placed Niqmepa on the throne and returned his father's land to him, which may indirectly support the idea that Ar-halba had been removed and replaced by Niqmepa. At some point, the region of Siyannu was removed from Ugaritic control to that of Carchemish, reducing Ugaritic territory by a third (*CTH* 65; RS 17.335 + 379 + 381 + 235; 17.382 + 380; 17.368 : LAPO 20: 135–9; Beckman 1996: 160–2). At the request of Ugarit, Mursili reduced the tribute proportionally to the territory lost. Also, Mursili seems to have ruled in Ugarit's favour with regard to the frontier with Mukish (*CTH* 64; RS 17.62 + 17.237: LAPO 20: 134–5; Beckman 1996: 159–60). Niqmepa was married to the princess Ahat-Milku from Amurru (RS 16.146 + 161: LAPO 20: 289–91; Izre'el 1991: 2:68–72).

Merchants and trade were an important factor of life in Ugarit, and some issues arose during Niqmepa's reign. A regulation was written by the later Hittite king, Hattusili III, in response to a complaint from Niqmepa about the activities of merchants from Ura in Kizzuwatna (*CTH* 93; RS 17.130: LAPO 20: 154–5; Beckman 1996: 162–3): the decree allowed the merchants to carry on their trade in the summer but required them to vacate Ugarit in the winter; they were also prohibited from buying property in Ugarit. Trading was evidently a dangerous profession for merchants, with deaths being reported and even regulated, because another judgment of Hattusili related to merchants killed apparently in Ugaritic territory (RS 17.229: LAPO 20: 158). The dangers were outlined in a letter of Hattusili III to the king of Babylon who had complained that merchants of his had been killed in Ugarit and other lands subject to the Hittites (*CTH* 172; Beckman 1996: 132–7). Hattusili III also issued a decree relating to people who sought refuge in Ugarit from the Hittite territory or vice versa, indicating that this was a current problem (*CTH* 94; RS 17.238: LAPO 20: 85–6; Beckman 1996: 163). In one of Niqmepa's tablets transferring property by gift, he mentions that someone has committed a great sin by forging the king's seal and using it to falsify ownership documents (RS 16.249: LAPO 20: 226–7).

One of the continuing puzzles is the so-called General's Letter (RS 20.33: LAPO 20: 66–9), found at Ugarit. It is a report by the commander of a company of soldiers in the border area (Amurru?) between the Egyptian and Hittite areas of influence. He requests military equipment, with which he is confident he can prevail. He complains of the poor weather and other conditions affecting him and his men. After a broken section he appears to describe a skirmish (the taking of a fortress?) that his troops won, capturing an enemy prisoner who informed them that an Egyptian force was moving against them. The first problem with interpreting the letter has to do with dating (see the summary of discussion in Izre'el/Singer 1990: 14–16; Dietrich 2001: 172–7). The original publication argued that the letter was from the Amarna period in the fourteenth century and has been followed by a number of commentators (Izre'el/Singer 1990; Márquez Rowe 1996). Yet M. Liverani apparently dated it around the time of the battle of Qadesh (1275 BCE), and the most recent studies also argue for this dating (Dietrich 2001; Freu 2006: 80–6).

In line with their dating Izre'el and Singer (1990) place the letter in the context of Aziru of Amurru's activities, when he was an Egyptian vassal but was seriously negotiating with the Hittites to join them. This would make the letter most likely to have the Hittite king as the addressee, with the sender expecting an Egyptian attack because his lord Aziru had defected to the Hittites. The letter was sent via Ugarit, where it was archived, though a copy (translated into Hittite?) was forwarded to Hattusa. I. Márquez Rowe (1996) follows Izre'el/Singer in many ways, but argues that the addressee was the king of Amurru (Abdi-Ashirta or Aziru), who received the letter when he happened to be in Ugarit; the 'General' was leading Amurrite troops. M. Dietrich (2001; also Freu 2006: 81) gives a different dating, shortly after the battle of Qadesh about the middle of the thirteenth century BCE. The troop contingent is stationed in Amurru but is from Ugarit, and the letter is addressed to Niqmepa king of Ugarit. In the end, much remains uncertain about this intriguing letter.

In spite of Ugarit's being allied with Hatti, she seems to have maintained trade ties with Egypt (Klengel 1992: 137). An important matter is whether Ugarit was a vassal of Egypt before she became a vassal of the Hittite king. A recent study by A. Altman (2008) argues that the Hittite documents indicate that Ugarit remained independent of Egypt and that the Amarna letters are compatible with this conclusion: 'together they…have undermined eventually and conclusively the possibility of Ugarit having been subordinated to Egypt under the 18th Dynasty Pharaohs' (Altman 2008: 58). After the Battle of Qadesh, Ramesses II and Hattusili III made a treaty in due course and established what has sometimes been called the *Pax Hethitica*, since it brought relative peace to northern Syria. The borders and areas of control were established between Egypt and Hatti. This meant that Ugarit remained under Hittite dominion.

The next king, Ammiṭṭamru II (c. 1260–1235 BCE), seems to have had problems with his brothers over the royal succession (RS 17.352; 17.35: LAPO 20: 106–8; Beckman 1996: 164–5). Two of his brothers, sons of the Amurrite princess Ahat-Milku like himself, had committed an offence (apparently relating to possession of the throne) and had been banished to Cyprus by their mother. They were given their inheritance and sent away with all their possessions, perhaps in many ways a mild punishment at a time when would-be usurpers were often executed. Ammiṭṭamru gained a favourable judgment from Tudhaliyah IV that Ugarit did not have to provide troops to assist the Hittites in their war with Assyria; instead, they contributed a supplement to their tribute to support the Hittite military (*CTH* 108; RS 17.59: LAPO 20: 101–2; Beckman 1996: 167–8). Yet a further communication from the king of Carchemish seems to demand troops (LAPO 20: 102–3). Another judgment by the Hittite king relates to a suit over the destruction of a boat in Ugarit's harbour, apparently by a citizen of Hatti (*CTH* 95; RS 17.133: 20: 158–9; Beckman 1996: 164). The decision is given by the indefinite 'his Majesty', but the letter has the seal of Queen Puduhepa who seems to have acted at various times for both Hattusili III and Tudhaliyah IV.

Ammiṭṭamru also had marriage problems, ending up with the scandal of having to divorce his wife (LAPO 20: 108–26: *CTH* 107; RS 17.159; 17.396; Beckman 1996: 165–7). Like his father, he had also taken an Amurrite princess as his wife, the daughter of Benteshina king of Amurru. At some point, the queen had committed 'a great sin'. Ammiṭṭamru divorced her and let her return to Amurru, taking only the property she had brought with her to the marriage. All other property became his. Her son Utri-Sharrumma was allowed to remain as crown prince but only if he had no further contact with his mother. A whole dossier of about 15 documents was apparently preserved by the king, though some aspects of the incident are still obscure. The lady in question is not named, and the 'great sin' is nowhere delineated. Speculation has proposed adultery, a political act, or even incest. It has been proposed that Ammiṭṭamru eventually requested the extradition of his former wife for execution, and that she was subsequently put to death by her brother Shaushgamuwa who was now king of Amurru (see Brooke 1979, who summarizes earlier studies; Singer 1999: 681).

I. Márquez Rowe (2000) gives a rather different interpretation. He agrees that her husband did wish to punish her with death, but argues that it did not take place. Instead, both her brother and the Hittite king Tudhaliya IV calmed Ammittamru down by persuading him to accept the 'blood money' of 1400 minas (*sic*! an impossible sum; most interpret it as '1400 [sheqels] of gold') for her life. He also argues from RS 16.270 (LAPO 20: 118–19), lines 22-25, that the sin of the queen constituted 'dallying' with members of the court while her husband was away (the verb *te-eṣ-ṣe-ni-iḫ* [*ṣâḫu*] implying sexual looseness), i.e., serial adultery.

The next king was not Utri-Sharrumma, which suggests that the crown prince in some way took his mother's part and was disqualified. Instead, Ibiranu (*c.* 1235–1225/1220) became king of Ugarit, but he seems to have done little; however, our skimpy documentation has improved in recent decades. He appears to have had border problems. Several documents indicate difficulties over the borders with Siyannu (LAPO 20: 140–4), which included explicitly the time of Ibiranu's reign (RS 17.292: LAPO 20: 141–2). A number of destructive incidents apparently occurred (RS 17.341: LAPO 20: 143–4). A letter from Pihawalwi (presumably the son of the Hittite king) to Ibiranu admonishes him for (a) not appearing before the Hittite king (to pay his respects after having been put on the throne?) and (b) for not sending his 'presents' (tribute) as he was supposed to (*CTH* 110; RS 17.247: LAPO 20: 94; Beckman 1996: 121). Another letter in the name of the Hittite king (sent by the ruler of Carchemish) informs Ibiranu that one of the Hittite king's sons is coming to visit him, and he is to treat him well (RS 17.423: LAPO 20: 94). A further letter asks for two seasoned juniper tree trunks of a certain length and diameter (RS 17.385: LAPO 20: 176). The various preserved items of correspondence suggest that the Hittite rulership was less than happy with Ibiranu.

A letter also seems to have been written to Ibiranu by the Assyrian king (Shalmaneser I or Tukulti-Ninurta I) about the taking of the city of Nihriya by the Assyrians from the Hittites (RS 34.165: RSO 7: 90–100; Lackenbacher 1982; Singer 1985; Dietrich 2003). Why the Assyrian king should have written this letter is unclear, but it may have been a move to detach Ugarit from the Hittite sphere. This interpretation might be supported by correspondence from the Hittite king or his representative about the supplying of military assistance by Ugarit, perhaps against the Assyrians (RS 17.189: LAPO 20: 100–101; RS 20.237: LAPO 20: 101; RS 34.138: RSO 7: 31–2; RS 34.150: RSO 7: 35–6; RS 32.204: RSO 7: 50–1; RS 17.18); one of these states that it is a matter of 'life and death'! (RS 17.189). Some of these letters suggest that Ibiranu has been negligent, or at least less than enthusiastic in supplying the required resources. One letter (apparently from Ibiranu, though this is debated) insists that he has supplied the required (copper points for arrows?) as requested (RS 15.14: LAPO 20: 175). His queen may have been Sharelli (Ugaritic Ṭryl) who is mentioned in several texts (e.g., *KTU* 1.161, line 32; RS 34.126: RSO 7: 151-63; *KTU* 2.16; RS 15.08: LAPO 14: 297–302). She was once thought to be the spouse of Ammurapi, Ugarit's last king, but new textual finds put her with Ibiranu – she was evidently Ammurapi's grandmother! (Singer 1999: 690–1).

Niqmaddu III (*c.* 1225/1220–1215) was Ibiranu's son; again, we know little about him. It appears that the Hittite queen Puduhepa wrote a letter to him (*KTU* 2.36+2.73+2.37+2.74; LAPO 14: 387–421; Pardee 1983–84), but the identity of the sender Puduhepa and the recipient Niqmaddu are debated. The letter seems to be about tribute, however, and reminds one of the letter to Ibiranu about not sending 'gifts' (RS 17.247). Another document records a transfer of property by and in the presence of Niqmaddu son of Ibiranu (RS 18.21: LAPO 20: 251; Helzer 1976: 92–4).

Niqmaddu was apparently married to a Hittite princess (RS 34.136); some have suggested that this was Ehli-Nikkalu (Soldt 2014–16: 281; Singer 1999: 701–4). This statement goes contrary to the standard assumption that Ehli-Nikkalu was the wife of the last king of Ugarit, Ammurapi, and that he divorced her and returned her dowry so that she could marry the king of another land (RS 17.226; 17.355; 20.216: LAPO 20: 128–30; Beckman 1996: 168–70; cf. Klengel 1992: 148). Singer (likewise Lackenmacher in LAPO 20: 126–7) makes the argument that Ehli-Nikkalu is indeed named in some texts relating to Ammurapi, but it could well be that she is here the widow of his father Niqmaddu; nothing requires her to be the (ex-)wife of Ammurapi. Her receiving back her dowry could be for reasons other than divorce. Important is the fact that in this correspondence there is no suggestion of a scandal. Rather, she returned the property not a part of her dowry to the king of Ugarit, received her dowry, and left the city and country for reasons unknown but apparently peaceably and without any hint of dishonour. Nevertheless, J. Freu (2006: 159–62) disagrees with this interpretation and reaffirms that Ammurapi divorced his wife who was Ehli-Nikkalu.

The last king of Ugarit appears to have been Ammurapi (c. 1215–1190/85); he was apparently the son of Niqmaddu since some ritual texts connect him with that dynasty (e.g., *KTU* 1.161; Bordreuil/ Pardee 1982; see above on the list of Ugaritic kings). He was evidently married to a princess, but whether she was Ehli-Nikkalu or whether Ammurapi divorced her is a matter of current debate (see above). His reign was marked by two crises: food shortage and the incursions of the Sea Peoples (Singer 1999: 707). He also received a number of rebukes from his Hittite masters (e.g., *KTU* 2.39; RS 18.38: *CoS* 3: 94–5). Another letter to the king of Ugarit (probably Ammurapi) takes him to task for not following orders to send grain to the Hittite port of Ura: 'a matter of life or death' (RS 20.212: LAPO 20: 103–4). A letter (from a citizen?) describes famine in pitiful terms (RS 34.152: RSO 7: 84–6).

During Ammurapi's reign Ugarit was taken and much of it destroyed. This is conventionally ascribed to the Sea Peoples. The incursions of the Sea Peoples is a complicated matter (discussed in a later chapter [§7.2]), but some important histories of Ugarit argue that the city-state fell to their depredations (Liverani 2014: 386; Singer 1999: 730). A letter from the king of Ugarit to the king of Cyprus mentions enemy boats which have set fire to his villages; unfortunately, his troops are in Hatti and his ships are in Lycia (Lukka) and thus apparently unable to defend Ugarit, or so he claims (RS 20.238: LAPO 20: 193–4). Another letter written on behalf of the Hittite king rebukes the king of Ugarit for not providing military assistance in the way that was earlier demanded (RS 34.143: RSO 7: 27–9): his force is camped in the wrong place and not where he (the king of Ugarit) has stated; furthermore, the chariots and soldiers he has sent are inferior, and the horses ill-fed, while he has kept the best troops for himself. A letter from someone who seems to be the commander of a city reports that his troops have been defeated and his city sacked, their grain burned and their vineyards destroyed (*KTU* 2.61; RS 19.11: *CoS* 3: 109–10). One letter identifies one of the problem raiders as belonging to the Shikila(yu), probably the same as the Shekelesh known from other sources about the various Sea Peoples (RS 34.129: RSO 7: 38–9; cf. Lehmann 1979; see further at §7.2). But did the Sea Peoples destroy Ugarit and some of its neighbours, such as Amurru?

While the Sea Peoples have been blamed for the destructions in the northern coastal Levant, the evidence is not so clear-cut. There is strong evidence suggesting that some sites experienced a destruction by warfare, such as Ras Shamra [Ugarit], Ras Ibn Hani, and Tell Kazel [capital of Amurru]; yet these destruction events were not complete, as buildings were left unscathed, nor were they necessarily concurrent with one another.... there was far less destruction on the northern Levantine coast than previously assumed. This is in line with the rest of the Levantine coast, as no sites on the Lebanese coast, such as Tyre, Sidon, and Sarepta, were destroyed.... Generally speaking, there is far less evidence for destruction on the Levantine coast than recent assessments of the transition from the Late Bronze Age to the Iron Age have claimed. [Millek 2020–21: 121–2]

Thus, the exact cause of the demise of Ugarit remains an area of investigation. Also, the exact year of Ugarit's destruction is not certain, though it was the early twelfth century BCE. Whoever the aggressor, archaeology shows that the city was consumed by a massive conflagration, and many arrowheads have been found in the destruction layer (Singer 1999: 729–31). The city was not resettled, and its identity eventually lost until 1929.

5.4.3 Phoenicia

Byblos was a major centre in the Levant already in the third millennium (§2.4.3), but most of the other Phoenician city-states did not exist at that time. In the MBA we also hear mainly about Byblos; however, in the LBA the Amarna letters have many references to Phoenician cities, as will be noted in the discussion of the Amarna texts in the next chapter (§6.3.2). Finally, see the comments relating to Phoenicia and the Early Iron Age (§7.4).

5.5 CONCLUSIONS

This chapter has surveyed the history of the various actors on the world scene outside Palestine/Canaan. In the LBA there was a lively interaction between various states and kingdoms. These included the states of Egypt (the New Kingdom), Syria (including Amurru and Ugarit), Anatolia (the Hittite New Kingdom and Mitanni), and Mesopotamia (primarily Assyria and Babylonia). Palestine was a small, marginal territory but it became important to a number of the rulers of the larger entities and was caught up in the interactions, intrigues, and struggles between the various empires and larger players. Within the chapter each state or people and its history were looked at separately; therefore, an attempt will be made here to synthesize the data to give an integrated picture of events during the LBA, though this will not be easy since chronology is often a problem.

The Hittite Old Kingdom began about 1650 BCE with Hattusili I. He was succeeded by Mursili I who attacked Babylon, a destruction which allowed the Kassite takeover of the Babylonian throne for the next several centuries. We also know little about Assyria for several hundred years at the beginning of the LBA. It was about 1600 BCE that a union of Hurrian states coalesced to form the kingdom of Mitanni (called Hanigalbat in some texts). Although the people seem to have been primarily Hurrian, the indication is that the ruling elite were Indo-Aryan, judging by their names and their obsession with chariots and horses. Some of the Hittite rulers had to fight the Hurrians. But by the time the kingdom of Mitanni arose, the Old Hittite empire had vanished. The final king of the Hittite empire was Telipinu, with the Hittite Old Kingdom coming to an end about 1500 BCE.

Around 1550 BCE the Second Intermediate Period came to an end, and Egypt was reunited under one ruler. The Hyksos were defeated and expelled from Avaris, which initiated the powerful 18th and 19th Dynasties that had some of the most dynamic pharaohs in history. The first Mitanni ruler attested seems to be Barattarna (*c.* 1475). A clash soon developed between this new state of Mitanni and Egypt: Thutmoses I (*c.* 1485) led an expedition to the Euphrates and Mitanni territory, evidently at a time when Barattarna ruled. It was Thutmoses III (*c.* 1450) who met Mitanni in battle on the Euphrates, probably commanded by Shaushtatar. Things seem to have calmed down under Amenhotep II (*c.* 1425–1400 BCE), and he may even have made a treaty with Mitanni; in any case, one was made with Thutmoses IV (*c.* 1400–1390 BCE), sealed by marriages of Mitanni women to Thutmoses IV, and subsequently to Amenhotep III (1390–1353 BCE) and Akhenaten. This brings us to the Amarna period (*c.* 1350 BCE, perhaps 1360–1330 BCE, though the exact years are very uncertain), specifically the pharaohs Amenhotep III (but toward the end of his reign), Akhenaten (1353–1336 BCE), and perhaps the first year or so of Tutankhamun (*c.* 1330 BCE).

We first hear of Amurru from a letter of its ruler Abdi-Ashirta (*c.* 1350 BCE), though the region had already come under Egyptian control probably with the campaigns of Thutmose III. Abdi-Ashirta seems to have had dealings only with his neighbours, but his son Aziru – in spite of protestations of loyalty to the Egyptian king – made a treaty with Suppiluliuma I. Sety I (*c.* 1290–1279 BCE) may have brought Amurru back into the Egyptian fold. Benteshina, who had two periods on the throne (*c.* 1275 and *c.* 1250), may have been removed from rule by Muwattilli II after the battle of Qadesh (perceived disloyalty?); however, he was taken as client to Hattusa and made friends with the man who became Hattusili III, who put him back on the throne. The last king of Amurru appears to have been Shaushgamuwa (*c.* 1225 BCE). He made a treaty with the Hittite king Tudhaliya IV which indicates that Assyria was a major enemy of the Hittites. The capital of Amurru may have been destroyed by some of the Sea Peoples, but there are other possibilities.

What is often referred to as the Hittite Middle Kingdom occupied the time between about 1500 and 1400 (some reject the term and begin the Hittite New Kingdom at 1500 BCE). Little is known of this period, except a few names of rulers. Many begin the Hittite New Kingdom about 1400, with Tudhaliya II. Hatti was threatened by Kaska and others, and the capital Hattusa was burned by Kaska under Tudhaliya III. Suppiluliuma I (*c.* 1350 BCE), perhaps the greatest Hittite ruler, expanded his realm, making Mitanni a protectorate. He brought Amurru, Qadesh, and eventually Ugarit under the Hittite wing, though he was careful not to challenge Egypt directly; however, attempts to establish good relations with Egypt were rejected. This standoff eventually culminated about 1275 BCE when the armies of Ramesses II and Muwatalli II clashed at Qadesh. Both claimed victory, but Hatti took and held Amurru and Qadesh for the rest of the LBA; however, Ramesses sealed a treaty with the new Hittite king Hattusili III (*c.* 1250 BCE).

The first king of Ugarit attested by contemporary documents is Ammiṯtamru (Ammištamru) I (*c.* 1350 BCE) who wrote a letter (EA 45) to the king of Egypt (Amenhotep III? Akhenaten?). Next was Niqmaddu II (*c.* 1350–1315 BCE) who was the author of EA 49. Because of problems with Amurru, he made a treaty with Abdi-Ashirta. But then he appealed to Suppiluliuma, because of being attacked by Mukish and Nuhashe, and made a vassal treaty with the Hittites. Niqmepa (*c.* 1313–1260) made a treaty with the Hittite king Mursili II and had good relations with him. One of the issues that comes up more than once is the question of providing military assistance to the Hittites. Ugarit paid tribute, of course, but military assistance was a problematic obligation. Some of the later Ugaritic kings were not in Hatti's good books, apparently in part because of this question of providing military resources. The last king appears to have been Ammurapi (*c.* 1215–1190/85 BCE), but the extent to which some of the Sea Peoples attacked the city is debated. In any case, the city was destroyed and was not rebuilt.

About 1350 Assyria became to rise again, under Ashur-uballit (*c.* 1350 BCE). He forced Artatarna II of Mitanni into submission and got in touch with Egypt, though his letter to Akhenaten was not very diplomatic. He also became involved with Babylonia and intervened in its royal succession. The Assyrian Adad-nirari I (*c.* 1300 BCE) brought Mitanni (under Shattura I) into subjection and seems to have made a treaty with the Hittite king Hattusili III. Mitanni seems to have slipped out of Assyrian control, but his son the next Assyrian king Shalmaneser I (*c.* 1275 BCE) defeated Shattura II and replaced the ruling dynasty with Assyrian governors. There was an attempt by the Hittite Tudhaliya IV (*c.* 1225 BCE) to retake Hanigalbat territory, but he was defeated. The Hittite New Kingdom came to an end about 1200 BCE, mainly through internal decay. The last major Middle Assyrian king was Tukulti-Ninurta I (*c.* 1225 BCE), and the next several kings seem to have had only brief undistinguished reigns. Kassite Babylonia had a long period of existence (*c.* 1600–1150). As noted, Assyria became involved in her kingly succession with Ashur-uballit, because of an assassination, and continued to dominate Babylonia during the rest of Kassite rule.

CHAPTER 6

Palestine

J. A. Knudtson (1907–15) *Die El-Amarna Tafeln*; **W. L. Moran** (1992) *The Amarna Letters*; **A. F. Rainey** (2015a) *The El-Amarna Correspondence: A New Edition of the Cuneiform Letters from the Site of El-Amarna based on Collations of all Extant Tablets*, Volume 1; **idem** (2015b) *The El-Amarna Correspondence: A New Edition of the Cuneiform Letters from the Site of El-Amarna based on Collations of all Extant Tablets*, Volume 2; **D. B. Redford** (1992a) *Egypt, Canaan, and Israel in Ancient Times*.

The previous chapter was extended to include the area of Syria in its coverage so that the present chapter could focus on Palestine/Canaan. This chapter covers a critical period for Israel's origins, since the name 'Israel' first appears in tangible form at the very end of the LBA. One suspects, however, that events or actors earlier in the LBA relate to the rise of what became the Israelite people and kingdom in the Iron Age. In this chapter, therefore, a good deal of focus will be on extant sources and the data they provide. In addition to the Amarna letters, we have a good many inscriptions from the Egyptian New Kingdom, as well as texts from Ugarit and other kingdoms in the Near East. We shall of course concentrate on those sources that specifically relate to Palestine/Canaan. It begins with a survey of sources before treating archaeology at length. It then proceeds to cover various historical issues, culminating in the naming of Israel in the Merenptah stela. It is in LB Palestine that we certainly begin the history of the people we call 'Israel'. That puts this chapter, along with chap. 8, at the centre of our study.

Although the present chapter concentrates on Cisjordan Palestine, its history is critically affected by Egypt and other entities of the Near East which will be discussed here when relevant. Because so much has to be dealt with in this chapter, a number of topics important for Palestine in the LBA were included in the previous chapter. The LBA in the Levant is dominated by the Amarna letters, which will be discussed in the first main section of the chapter (§6.1).

6.1 SOURCES

A variety of sources are available for the history of Palestine in the LBA. They will be briefly surveyed here, though additional information may be available in the following sections (with cross references given here). First is archaeology, which is sketched out below (§6.2).

Several Egyptian inscriptions and writings are also important for the history of this time. One interesting text is the *Report of Wenamun*, about a journey to the Phoenician and Palestinian area (*AEL* 2:224–30). The text is usually dated to the early eleventh century BCE, allegedly before Egypt lost its hold on the region. It appears to give useful insights into the relationship between Egypt and the Phoenician area and contains many useful incidental details. Another important source is the 'Israel stela' of Merenptah, discussed in detail below (§6.3.4).

Our most extensive information on Canaan comes from the fourteenth century BCE, in the Amarna letters, which give us a unique insight into events in Palestine during this period (see especially §6.3.2). At this time, Palestine was a part of the Egyptian New Kingdom. The letters belonged to the archive of Akhenaten (*c.* 1353–1336 BCE) in the capital that he built on a new site, whose ruins were later named by the Arabs as Tell el-Amarna. After his death, the capital was abandoned, which is probably why the archive was not eventually discarded. The letters are written in Akkadian which seems to have been the language of international communication at the time. When the city was excavated in the nineteenth century, among the recovered archives were copies of correspondence between the Egyptian administration and their vassals in other regions. This valuable cache of letters in Babylonian cuneiform mainly consists of dispatches from the city-state kinglets of the Levant to their overlord the Egyptian king. However, there is also some international correspondence with 'friends' in Mesopotamia, as well as a set of letters relating to the kingdoms north of Canaan: Amurru, Byblos and other Phoenician cities, and Ugarit.

Among those who wrote letters to the Pharaoh was the king of Jerusalem (Urusalim). We have six letters from him (EA 285-90), plus a couple of other letters that refer to him (EA 284, 366). The king of Jerusalem is called 'Abdi-Ḫeba. Other kings include Suwardata of Gath and Lab'aya of Shechem. Other cities mentioned are Gaza (EA 129, 287, 296), Ashkelon (EA 187, 320-21, 322, 370), Gezer (EA 253, 254, 287, etc.), and Lachish (EA 287, 288, 328, 329, 335). One term that appears several times is *Apiru* (§6.3.3.3). Although the Amarna letters relate only to a few decades in the fourteenth century, they provide an aperture into Palestine that gives a panoramic view, unprecedented until well into the first millennium BCE. This makes them one of the most important sources for the second millennium BCE. We are fortunate to have the recent edition and translation from A. F. Rainey (2015a, 2015b), the English translation of W. L. Moran (1992), as well as the older text and German translation of J. A. Knudtson (1907–15; see also *ANET* 483–90; *CoS* 3:237–42), not to mention many studies.

Most of the biblical texts of potential relevance to this time period are from the Pentateuch. Scholarly consensus regards this as a late compilation, and thus a secondary source, but possibly having early material in certain sections. The scholarship around the Pentateuch was briefly discussed at §4.1. The main texts relevant for Israel's history in this period are the books of Exodus and Numbers. These revolve around the exodus which is discussed below (§6.4).

6.2 ARCHAEOLOGY

S. Ahituv (1984) *Canaanite Toponyms in Ancient Egyptian Documents*; **D. A. Aston** (2004) 'Amphorae in New Kingdom Egypt', *Ägypten und Levante* 14: 175–213; **D. Ben-Ami** (2001) 'The Iron Age I at Tel Hazor in Light of the Renewed Excavations', *IEJ* 51: 148–70; **idem** (2014) 'Notes on the Iron IIA Settlement in Jerusalem in Light of Excavations in the Northwest of the City of David', *TA* 41: 3–19; **A. Ben-Tor** (1998) 'The Fall of Canaanite Hazor – The "Who" and "When" Questions', in S. Gitin, A. Mazar, and E. Stern (eds), *Mediterranean Peoples in Transition: Thirteenth to Early Tenth Centuries BCE, in Honor of Professor Trude Dothan*: 456–67; **E. Bloch-Smith** (2003) 'Israelite Ethnicity in Iron I: Archaeology Preserves What Is Remembered and What Is Forgotten In Israel's History', *JBL* 122: 401–25; **E. Bloch-Smith and B. A. Nakhai** (1999) 'A Landscape Comes to Life: The Iron I Period', *NEA* 62: 62–92, 101–27; **S. Bunimovitz** (1998) 'On the Edge of Empires – Late Bronze Age (1500–1200 BCE)', in T. E. Levy (ed.), *The Archaeology of Society in the Holy Land*: 320–31; **S. Bunimovitz and A. Faust** (2003) 'Building Identity: The Four Room House and the Israelite Mind', in W. G. Dever and S. Gitin (eds), *Symbiosis, Symbolism, and the Power of the Past: Canaan, Ancient Israel, and their Neighbors from the Late Bronze Age through Roman Palaestina*: 411–23; **S. Bunimovitz and Z. Ledermann** (2008) 'A Border Case: Beth-Shemesh and the Rise of Ancient Israel', in L. L. Grabbe (ed.), *Israel in Transition: From Late Bronze II to Iron IIA (c. 1250–850 BCE), Volume 1, The Archaeology*: 21–31; **E. H. Cline** (2014) *1177 B.C.: The Year Civilization Collapsed*; **J. A. Dearman** (1992) 'Settlement Patterns and the Beginning of the Iron Age in Moab', in P. Bienkowski (ed.), *Early Edom and Moab: The Beginning of the Iron Age in Southern Jordan*: 65–75; **W. G. Dever** (1987) 'The Middle Bronze Age – The Zenith of the Urban Canaanite Era', *BA* 50: 148–77; **idem** (2003) *Who Were the Early Israelites and Where Did They Come From?*; **R. Drews** (1993) *The End of the Bronze Age: Changes in Warfare and the Catastrophe ca. 1200 B.C.*; **I. Finkelstein** (1988) *The Archaeology of the Israelite Settlement*; **idem** (1988–89) 'The Land of Ephraim Survey 1980–1987: Preliminary Report', *TA* 15-16: 117–83; **idem** (1998a) 'The Great Transformation: The "Conquest" of the Highlands Frontiers and the Rise of the Territorial States', in T. E. Levy (ed.), *The Archaeology of Society in the Holy Land*: 349–65; **idem** (1998b) 'The Rise of Early Israel: Archaeology and Long-Term History', in Shmuel Aḥituv and Eliezer D. Oren (eds), *The Origin of Early Israel – Current Debate: Biblical, Historical and Archaeological Perspectives*: 7–39; **idem** (1999) 'State Formation in Israel and Judah: A Contrast in Context, a Contrast in Trajectory', *NEA* 62: 35–52; **idem** (2003) 'City-States to States: Polity Dynamics in the 10th–9th Centuries B.C.E.', in W. G. Dever and S. Gitin (eds), *Symbiosis, Symbolism, and the Power of the Past: Canaan, Ancient Israel, and their Neighbors from the Late Bronze Age through Roman Palaestina*: 75–83; **I. Finkelstein and N. A. Silberman** (2001) *The Bible Unearthed: Archaeology's New Vision of Ancient Israel and the Origin of its Sacred Texts*; **I. Finkelstein, D. Ussishkin, and B. Halpern**

(eds) (2000) *Megiddo III: The 1992–1996 Seasons*; **S. Gibson** (2001) 'Agricultural Terraces and Settlement Expansion in the Highlands of Early Iron Age Palestine: Is There any Correlation between the Two?', in A. Mazar (ed.), *Studies in the Archaeology of the Iron Age in Israel and Jordan*: 113–46; **R. Gonen** (1984) 'Urban Canaan in the Late Bronze Period', *BASOR* 253: 61–73; **L. G. Herr** (2001) 'The History of the Collared Pithos at Tell el-'Umeiri, Jordan', in S. R. Wolff (ed.), *Studies in the Archaeology of Israel and Neighboring Lands in Memory of Douglas L. Esse*: 237–50; **Z. Herzog** (1994) 'The Beer-Sheba Valley: From Nomadism to Monarchy', in I. Finkelstein and N. Na'aman (eds), *From Nomadism to Monarchy: Archaeological and Historical Aspects of Early Israel*: 122–49; **B. Hesse and P. Wapnish** (1997) 'Can Pig Remains Be Used for Ethnic Diagnosis in the Ancient Near East?' in N. A. Silberman and D. B. Small (eds), *The Archaeology of Israel: Constructing the Past, Interpreting the Present*: 238–70; **D. Ilan** (1998) 'The Dawn of Internationalism – The Middle Bronze Age', in T. E. Levy (ed.), *The Archaeology of Society in the Holy Land*: 297–319; **D. Kaniewski, E. Van Campo, J. Guiot, S. Le Burell, T. Otto, and C. Baeteman** (2013) 'Environmental Roots of the Late Bronze Age Crisis', *PLoS ONE* 8, issue 8: 1–10; **A. E. Killebrew** (2001) 'The Collared Pithos in Context: A Typological, Technological, and Functional Reassessment', in Samuel R. Wolff (ed.), *Studies in the Archaeology of Israel and Neighboring Lands in Memory of Douglas L. Esse*: 377–98; **idem** (2005) *Biblical Peoples and Ethnicity: An Archaeological Study of Egyptians, Canaanites, Philistines, and Early Israel 1300–1000 B.C.E.*; **idem** (2007) 'The Canaanite Storage Jar Revisited', in S. White Crawford (eds), *'Up to the Gates of Ekron': Essays on the Archaeology and History of the Eastern Mediterranean in Honor of Seymour Gitin*: 166–88; **K. A. Kitchen** (1992a) 'The Egyptian Evidence on Ancient Jordan', in P. Bienkowski (ed.), *Early Edom and Moab: The Beginning of the Iron Age in Southern Jordan*: 21–34; **R. Kletter** (2006) 'Can a Proto-Israelite Please Stand Up? Notes on the Ethnicity of Iron Age Israel and Judah', in A. M. Maeir and P. de Miroschedji (eds), *'I Will Speak the Riddles of Ancient Times': Archaeological and Historical Studies in Honor of Amihai Mazar on the Occasion of his Sixtieth Birthday*: 573–86; **Ø. S. LaBianca and R. W. Younker** (1998) 'The Kingdoms of Ammon, Moab and Edom: The Archaeology of Society in Late Bronze/Iron Age Transjordan (ca. 1400–500 BCE)', in T. E. Levy (ed.), *The Archaeology of Society in the Holy Land*: 399–415; **T. E. Levy** (2009a) 'Ethnic Identity in Biblical Edom, Israel, and Midian: Some Insights from Mortuary Contexts in the Lowlands of Edom', in J. D. Schloen (ed.), *Exploring the* Longue Durée: *Essays in Honor of Lawrence E. Stager*: 251–61; **idem** (2009b) 'Pastoral Nomads and Iron Age Metal Production in Ancient Edom', in J. Szuchman (ed.), *Nomads, Tribes, and the State in the Ancient Near East: Cross-Disciplinary Perspectives*: 147–77; **T. E. Levy, R. B. Adams, and A. Muniz** (2004) 'Archaeology and the Shasu Nomads: Recent Excavations in the Jabal Hamrat Fidan, Jordan', in R. E. Friedman and W. H. C. Propp (eds), *Le-David Maskil: A Birthday Tribute for David Noel Freedman*: 63–89; **J. M. Miller** (1992) 'Early Monarchy in Moab?' in P. Bienkowski (ed.), *Early*

Edom and Moab: The Beginning of the Iron Age in Southern Jordan: 77–91; **N. Na'aman** (1997) 'The Network of Canaanite Late Bronze Kingdoms and the City of Ashdod', *UF* 29: 599–626; **A. Raban** (2001) 'Standardized Collared-Rim Pithoi and Short-Lived Settlements', in S. R. Wolff (ed.), *Studies in the Archaeology of Israel and Neighboring Lands in Memory of Douglas L. Esse*: 493–518; **J. A. Sauer** (1986) 'Transjordan in the Bronze and Iron Ages: A Critique of Glueck's Synthesis', *BASOR* 263: 1–26; **S. Sherratt** (2003) 'The Mediterranean Economy: "Globalization" at the End of the Second Millennium B.C.E.', in William G. Dever and Seymour Gitin (eds), *Symbiosis, Symbolism, and the Power of the Past: Canaan, Ancient Israel, and their Neighbors from the Late Bronze Age through Roman Palaestina*: 37–62; **E. van der Steen** (2004) *Tribes and Territories in Transition: The Central East Jordan Valley in the Late Bronze Age and Early Iron Ages: A Study of the Sources*; **idem** (2016) 'The Archaeology of the Late Bronze Age in Palestine', in L. L. Grabbe (ed.), *The Land of Canaan in the Late Bronze Age*: 159–75; **C. W. Tyson** (2014) *The Ammonites: Elites, Empires, and Sociopolitical Change (1000–500 BCE)*; **D. Ussishkin** (2003) 'Solomon's Jerusalem: The Text and the Facts on the Ground', in A. G. Vaughn and A. E. Killebrew (eds), *Jerusalem in Bible and Archaeology: The First Temple Period*: 103–15; **D. Ussishkin (ed.)** (2004) *The Renewed Archaeological Excavations at Lachish (1973–1994)*; **W. A. Ward and M. S. Joukowsky (eds)** (1992) *The Crisis Years: The 12th Century B.C. from Beyond the Danube to the Tigris*.

The Late Bronze Age covers a good portion of the second millennium, from *c.* 1600/1500 to 1200 BCE. As already noted (§2.4.1), these archaeological divisions are not exact and are to some extent artificial, but they broadly represent significant differences in culture and society, as well as historical background. Terminology for archaeological periods is not consistent even among professionals (§2.4.1). The scheme used here (cf. Dever 1987: 149–50; Ilan 1998: 297) is

LB I (*c.* 1600–1400 BCE)
LB IIA (*c.* 1400–1300 BCE)
LB IIB (*c.* 1300–1200 BCE)

These dates are in part based on historical events, whereas the cultures recorded by archaeology do not always follow the historical periods marked off by events. Needless to say, there is much disagreement, with many beginning the LB in 1500 but others in 1550 or 1600 BCE.

The MB had ended with widespread collapse. The causes have been debated, and there were probably several of them. But a recent study suggests that an environmental crisis was a significant factor:

> By combining data from coastal Cyprus and coastal Syria, this study shows that the LBA crisis coincided with the onset of a ca. 300-year drought event 3200 years ago. This climate shift caused crop failures, dearth and famine, which precipitated or hastened socio-economic crises and forced regional human migrations at the end of the LBA

in the Eastern Mediterranean and southwest Asia. The integration of environmental and archaeological data along the Cypriot and Syrian coasts offers a first comprehensive insight into how and why things may have happened during this chaotic period. [Kaniewski et al. 2013: 9]

The accompanying sociocultural changes 'reshaped the social landscape of Palestine and had a profound, long-term impact on Canaanite society' (Bunimovitz 1998: 320). Although some have seen a major shift away from urbanism in the LB, Bunimovitz (1998: 324) argues against this: urbanism was different in scale but the balance between urban and rural remained much the same. The urban centres were considerably smaller but so was the rural sector, according to his interpretation. As the urban areas declined in size, the rural areas might have gained in influence (Steiner/Killebrew 2014: 545). In general the Canaanite city-states were underpopulated and short of manpower (Bunimovitz 1998: 326–7). This is no doubt to be related to the frequent mention in the Amarna letters of the *Apiru* and other groups on the margins of society: the rural decline left a vacuum that *Apiru* and *Shasu* moved into (Steen 2016: 173). It seems that areas important to Egypt thrived, while those more remote from Egyptian centres declined (Steen 2016: 161–2).

It was at this time that 'the empires of Egypt, the Mitanni, the Hittites, and later also Assyria endeavoured to establish themselves politically in the economically important area of the Levant' (Steiner/Killebrew 2014: 536). In the area of Lebanon the culture was one of urbanism (especially Arqa, Beirut, Kamid el-Loz [Damascus], Tyre, Sidon, Byblos), with most large sites fortified (Steiner/Killebrew 2014: 525–6). Many of the goods were imported or were local imitations of foreign originals. Imports came from Egypt, Crete, Mycenae, Cyprus, and also Syria and Anatolia further north. Ceramics from Egypt seem to have been acquired primarily by the elite, whereas those from the Mycenae and Cyprus seem to have been possessed by a larger set of citizens.

In the upper Galilee the ceramic continuity from the LB II to IA I indicates that the population was indigenous rather than immigrants as pictured by the biblical text (Josh. 19:24-48; Bloch-Smith/Nakhai 1999: 81). Settlement of the Jezreel and Beth-shean valleys flourished in the LB, with a significant Egyptian presence at the administrative centres of Megiddo and Beth-Shean. The collapse of Egyptian dominance resulted in a general decline, with an impoverished culture (Bloch-Smith/Nakhai 1999: 81–8). LB II Megiddo (strata VIII/VIIB-VIIA), with an estimated area of 11 ha, was one of the most prominent cities of Palestine (Finkelstein/Ussishkin/Halpern 2000: 593). With its monumental buildings it appears to have been the city-state centre for the local king and his elite supporters. Megiddo thus seems to provide a good example of the nature of the main city-states in Canaan during the later part of LB (over 30 sites were apparently subordinate to Megiddo), though the LB city was generally unfortified.

The absolute dating of the LB II strata is not clear: according to Finkelstein, stratum VIII can hardly post-date the mid-fourteenth century; it is unlikely that there was no palace during the Amarna period. Stratum VIIB alone would represent the city of the thirteenth. Stratum VIIA was then built in the late thirteenth century and destroyed in the second half of the twelfth. Strata VIII-VIIA therefore all represent one phase of urban continuity. Ussishkin agrees that Megiddo was continuously settled throughout the LB, including the Amarna period, but the character of settlement was not uniform throughout the time. Significantly, most or all of the monumental buildings were constructed after the Amarna period, while the Amarna settlement was relatively modest. The conclusion seems to be that the stratum VIII royal palace and gatehouse and some other public buildings were constructed in the thirteenth century.

A region of major interest, because of its implications for the Israelite settlement, is the Palestinian highlands (coincidentally, they were more remote from Egyptian centres). The highlands contained hardly any settlement throughout much of the LB (Finkelstein 1988: 339–45). The argument is that pastoralists were the main inhabitants of the hill country on both sides of the Jordan (Finkelstein 1988: 339–45; 1993: 119; 1998b; Bunimovitz 1998: 324; Ilan 1998: 304). In the LB and early IA I, a clear difference separated the north and south in the central hill country between the Jezreel and Beersheba valleys (Finkelstein 1998a: 361; 1999: 43–4). The north experienced significant continuity, with most of the main sites continuing from the LB into IA I.

S. Bunimovitz (1998: 323) applied rank-size distribution and found that the coastal plain and the Jezreel Valley had a cluster of semi-autonomous city-states and exhibited a low degree of socio-political integration. On the other hand, the central hill country showed a greater degree of integration than in the MB III, with large LBA territorial polities. He does not suggest why, but the dominance of Shechem might have been a factor. The Negev and Judaean hills had hardly any sedentary sites in the LB. Indeed, large parts of Palestine appear to have remained sparsely settled in the LBA: Upper and Lower Galilee, Golan Heights, central hill country, lower Jordan Valley, and the Negev (Na'aman 1997: 606; Gonen 1984). This included a settlement gap throughout the LB in the Negev. This long settlement gap came to an end in the early IA I. In the northern highlands most of the LB sites continued to be inhabited in IA I, in contrast to the Judaean highlands which had almost no LB settlements (Finkelstein 1999: 43–4).

Jerusalem is a particular puzzle since we have the Amarna letters providing evidence for a chieftain of Jerusalem. Some small LB remains have been found, especially tombs. Also, some of the Amarna tablets seem to have been created from clay deposits near Jerusalem: 'Five of the seven letters of 'Abdi-Ḫeba, the ruler of Jersusalem belong to a petrographic group that is…in the vicinity of Jerusalem' (Goren/Finkelstein/Na'aman 2004: 265–9, quote from p. 269). This seems to confirm that Abdi-Heba indeed had some sort of headquarters at Jerusalem. Yet no LB remains of Abdi-Heba's city or fortress seem to have been found so far. The argument that the Middle Bronze wall was used as a city wall in the LB, IA I, and IA IIA and IIB has no archaeological support: Jerusalem lacked a fortification wall until the mid- or late eighth century when the MB IIB wall was partially built over and partially reused for a new fortification wall (Killebrew 2003: 334; Ussishkin 2003: 110–11).

This is supported by recent excavations, such as the one at the Givati parking lot, which showed that there were no IA IIA fortifications on the southeast ridge ('City of David' settlement); rather, 'all Iron Age fortification components unearthed in Jerusalem are the outcome of one comprehensive building operation that took place at the close of the 8th century BCE' (Ben-Ami 2014: 17). The lack of other finds relating to fortification suggests that Jerusalem was unwalled and unfortified between the LB and IA IIB (sixteenth to mid-eighth centuries), and thus Jerusalem was 'at best modest' (Killebrew 2003: 334). Also, the elaborate water system of MB IIB went out of use until the eighth/seventh centuries (Warren's shaft never served as a water system), as shown by the excavations of Reich and Shukron (Killebrew 2003: 334–5).

Transjordan is discussed in a later chapter (§7.6) and is omitted here. However, archaeological interest has recently focused on the copper workings and the large cemetery in the Feinan region (Levy/Adams/Muniz 2004; Levy 2009a, 2009b). All seem to agree that in the LB the inhabitants were nomadic groups whom the Egyptians referred to as *Shasu* (but see below on the lifestyle of this group).

Returning to Canaan as a whole, the material culture shows a great range with regard to socio-economic considerations, from evidence of wealth in burial deposits, patrician houses, and ceramic and luxury imports, but also indications of poverty in the dominance of local technology for ceramic production and the small amount of monumental architecture (large administrative buildings or palaces). This raises questions of whether Canaan was prosperous or impoverished. To what extent was Egyptian administration responsible one way or the other? Did the Egyptians exploit Canaan or did they bring development and opportunities for enrichment? These matters continue to be debated, but it seems clear that Egypt deepened its involvement in Canaanite affairs and engagement with the inhabitants of the region during the 19th Dynasty (Steiner/Killebrew 2014: 547–8).

Canaan was very much a part of the wider Mediterranean trade network which included overseas participants such as Cyprus and Mycenaen Greece. Canaan was famous for its merchants in the first millennium BCE, but the roots of this expertise may lie in the LBA when Canaanite amphorae and storage jars were widely used to contain products for trading and storage (Killebrew 2007; Aston 2004). In any case, we find Canaanite jars at various sites not only in Egypt and Syria-Palestine but also in the eastern Mediterranean more widely. Conversely, Cypriot ceramics and other imported products are found widely in Canaan.

To summarize, the end of the LB saw a general collapse of trade and communication, with many cities destroyed along the Mediterranean coast and sometimes further inland. This breakdown seems to have affected the whole of the eastern Mediterranean (Cline 2014; Drews 1993; Ward and Joukowsky [eds] 1992). The LB had been what S. Sherratt unapologetically refers to as a period of 'globalization' (Sherratt 2003), which means that the collapse had a far-reaching effect on the various cultures in the region from about 1200 BCE, with the destruction of the main centres: Hazor, Akko, Megiddo, Beth-Shean, Lachish, Ashdod. It was around this time that Egypt withdrew from Palestine, now thought by many to be about 1130 BCE. Concomitant with this was a remarkable increase in settlement in the highlands, mainly small sites.

Yet the 'conventional wisdom' that the Palestinian city-state system came to an end at this time oversimplifies what happened (Finkelstein 2003: 75–9). Some city-states evidently did decline or disappear with the destruction of their urban centres, but the rural sector generally experienced continuity, both demographically and culturally, as is indicated by such sites as Tel Menorah, Tell el-Wawiyat, and 'Ein Zippori. The peasants in the vicinity of the ruined LB cities lived as they already had, and the northern valleys remained densely settled. Then, in the Iron I (eleventh century, according to Finkelstein) the primary centres began to recover, the main exceptions being Lachish and Hazor. This 'new Canaan' was prosperous because of stability in the rural sector and trade with Phoenicia, Cyprus, and even further afield, as will be discussed in a later chapter (§8.2).

6.3 THE SEARCH FOR ISRAEL

6.3.1 Egyptian Incursions into Canaan

P. J. Brand (2000) *The Monuments of Seti I: Epigraphic, Historical and Art Historical Analysis*; **E. H. Cline and D. O'Connor (eds)** (2012) *Ramesses III: The Life and Times of Egypt's Last Hero*; **D. P. Davies** (2003) *The Taking of Joppa*; **E. Elmar** (1953) 'Die Stelen Amenophis' II. aus Karnak und Memphis mit dem Bericht über die asiastischen Feldzüge des Königs', *ZDPV* 69: 97–176; **C. Epstein** (1963) 'A New Appraisal of Some Lines from a Long-Known Papyrus', *JEA* 49: 49–56; **ERMAN-GRAPOW**; **R. O. Faulkner** (1962) *A Concise Dictionary of Middle Egyptian*; **A. H. Gardiner** (1947) *Ancient Egyptian Onomastica*; **H. Goedicke** (1968) 'The Capture of Joppa', *Chronique d'Egypte* 43: 219–33; **W. Helck** (1971) *Die Beziehungen Ägyptens zu Vorderasien im 3. und 2. Jahrtausend v. Chr.*; **K. A. Kitchen** (1964) 'New Light on the Asiatic Wars of Rameses II', *JEA* 50: 47–70; **idem** (1982) *Pharaoh Triumphant: The Life and Times of Ramesses II, King of Egypt*; **idem** (1993) *Ramesside Inscriptions: Translated and Annotated: Translations Volume I: Ramesses I, Sethos I and Contemporaries*; **idem** (1996) *Ramesside Inscriptions: Translated and Annotated: Translations Volume II: Ramesses II, Royal Inscriptions*; **G. D. Mumford** (1998) *International Relations between Egypt, Sinai, and Syria-Palestine during the Late Bronze Age to Early Persian Period (Dynasties 18-26: c. 1550–525 B.C.)*; **W. J. Murnane** (1990) *The Road to Kadesh: A Historical Interpretation of the Battle Reliefs of King Sety I at Karnak*; **D. O'Connor and E. H. Cline (eds)** (1998) *Amenhotep III: Perspectives on his Reign*; **D. B. Redford** (1973) 'New Light on the Asiatic Campaigning of Ḥoremheb', *BASOR* 211: 36–49; **idem** (1979) 'A Gate Inscription from Karnak and Egyptian Involvement in Western Asia during the Early 18th Dynasty', *JAOS* 99: 270–87; **idem** (1984) *Akhenaten: The Heretic King*; **idem** (2003) *The Wars in Syria and Palestine of Thutmose III*; **A. Spalinger** (1979) 'The Northern Wars of Seti I: An Integrative Study', *JARCE* 16: 29–47; **A. Vassilev** (2020) 'Upper Retenu and Lower Retenu', in C. Graves (ed.), *BEC 4: Proceedings of the Fourth British Egyptology Congress University of Manchester, 7-9 September 2018*: 159–67; **K. R. Weeks (ed.)** (1986) *Reliefs and Inscriptions at Karnak, Volume 4: The Battle Reliefs of King Sety I*; **S. Yeivin** (1967) 'Amenophis II's Asianic Campaigns', *JARCE* 6: 119–28.

In the previous chapter the Egyptian contacts with Palestine were surveyed, along with other historical data on Egyptian history (§5.1). Here the specific information on Egyptian incursions into the region is summarized in more detail (especially useful for this survey is Mumford 1998: 50–331).

It is important to be aware of the terms used in the Egyptian texts. Some of the terms used for 'Asiatic peoples' were considered earlier (§2.4.4). Here we must note the geographical terms used. Two frequent terms are related: 'Upper Reṭenu' and 'Lower Reṭenu'. *Rtnw* is taken to refer generally to the region of 'Syria-Palestine', excluding Mitanni (Helck 1971: 266–7). The term 'Upper Reṭenu (ḥrt Rṯnw)' seems to refer to a mountainous area to the north (ḥrt means 'upland, highland' [Gardner 1947: 142*]), which would be the hill country in Palestine; 'Lower Rṯnw' may refer to lowlands, which seems to be used of the Euphrates area in some texts (ERMAN-GRAPOW 2:460; Faulkner 1962: 154; Gardiner 1947: 1:142*–9*). The most recent study argues that 'Retenu' refers to Canaan, while 'Lower Retenu' designates the Phoenician coast (Vassiliev 2020); if so, this gives the name a narrower territory than often thought. The name Lotan (לוטן) in Gen. 36:20 seems to be the Hebrew form of the Egyptian name Rṯnw.

This traditional term became replaced by the more recent Ḏahy (sometimes written Djahy or even Ṣa-hi) (Ḏ3hy: Faulkner 1962: 319). According to one text which mentions the 'maryannu of Ḏahy', the Palestinian sites of Megiddo, Kinneret, Achshaph, Shimron, Taanach, Mishal, Tienni(?), Sharon, Ashkelon, Hazor, and Ham(?) are then named (Epstein 1963; Helck 1971: 268). This would seem to relate the name to the area of Palestine, the towns being in the Galilean region except for Ashkelon, though the locations of Tienni and Ham are uncertain (though see the next section [§6.3.2] which suggests that Tienni – if read correctly [perhaps Tienna?] – might be Ashdod).

Ahmose (c. 1539–1515 BCE): captured Avaris from the Hyksos; later besieged their city (fortress? stronghold?) of Sharuhen (perhaps Tell el-Farʿah South or Tell el-ʿAjjul), said to be for 'three years'. It is doubtful that a three-year siege can have taken place; perhaps a series of attacks over a three-year period. There were also some scattered references to military activity in Djahi (Syria) against the Fenkhu (a Syrian people), according to texts quoted by Breasted (ARE 2:10-13).

Amenhotep I (1514–1494 BCE): it is often thought that he took no campaigns into 'Asia', but Redford (1979: 275) has suggested that there may have been one or more, based on the fragmentary Gate Inscription from the Amun Temple at Karnak that seems to mention 'God's land' (Palestine) and places in northern Syria: 'Qedem', 'Upper Retenu', and 'Tunip'.

Thutmose I (1493–1483 BCE): he made a campaign to the Euphrates; this was apparently through Palestine (Retenu), but no details are given of any activities there.

Thutmose II (1482–1480 BCE): inscriptional references seem definitely to relate to at least one campaign: the tomb inscription of a court official named Ahmose Pen-Nekhbet describes a campaign into Upper Retenu against the Shasu (ARE 2:50–1).

Thutmose III (1479–1425 BCE) and Hatshepsut (1479–1458 BCE): under Hatshepsut's 'regency' tribute was received from various areas, including the North; however, there is no clear evidence for any military campaigns into this area. This may have emboldened the subject people of these areas to think of rebellion; indeed, the Armant stela (ANET 234; CoS 2:18–19) suggests that rebellion had actually taken place. In any case, once Thutmose III assumed full rulership (c. 1457 BCE) he conducted 16 or 17 expeditions into northern areas:

[Not included here is the alleged capture of Joppa by the commander Djehuty under Thutmose III (Goedicke 1968; Davies 2003). This is a legendary text (possibly with a historical core), probably composed later than Thutmose III, perhaps during the reign of Ramesses II.]

Year 23, first campaign: the ruler of Qadesh had assembled a coalition at Megiddo, with participants from as far away as Mitanni (though most of the sites names in Thutmose's inscriptions seem to be sites within Palestine). Thutmose surprised the enemy by taking the narrow passage through the Carmel range and won a great victory (*CoS* 2:8–13). In addition to taking many spoils, he captured the wives and children of a number of the leaders of the rebellion (*ARE* 2:236). Finally, he apparently established an Egyptian fortress in Lebanon (*ANET* 238).

(There are no specific references to the second, third, and fourth campaigns [Redford 2003: 210]; these would have fallen in years 24-29. There are several episodes that might fall into this period:

Year 24: Breasted (*ARE* 2:190–2) proposes a second campaign, though all that the inscriptions mention is tribute, including the daughter of a chief in Reṯenu. The king of Assyria also sent gifts.

Year 25: third campaign?; there is mention of plants from Reṯenu, though it is not clear that there was an actual campaign (cf. *ARE* 2:192–3).

(If there was a fourth campaign, no record of it seems to be currently known.)

Year 29, fifth campaign: Thutmose went further north this time, well into Syria (Djahy), attacking such towns as Wartet (on the coast?) and Ardata (to the east of modern Tripoli).

Year 30, sixth campaign: he captured and destroyed Qadesh and took Ardata once again.

Year 31, seventh campaign: captured Ullaza on the Syrian coast and collected tribute from Reṯenu.

Year 33, eighth campaign: took the city of Qatna, then marched to the Euphrates and into the country of Mitanni (Naharin), setting up an inscription on the Euphrates beside that of his grandfather Thutmose I (Redford 2003: 73–8).

Year 34, ninth campaign: said to have captured some towns in Djahy and took tribute from Reṯenu (Redford 2003: 78–83; *ARE* 2:205–6). The reference to 'tribute' (i.e., probably gifts) from Cyprus must now be given up, though *Asy* in the text remains unidentified (Redford 2003: 82–3).

Year 35, tenth campaign: marched through Djahy against Naharin (Mitanni), where he took the town of Ar'anu (location unknown; near Aleppo?). Thutmose's defeat of the Mitannians seems to have used a particular battlefield tactic, though precisely what that was is not clear (Redford 2003: 85–6).

Years 36 and 37: records are mostly lost.

Year 38, thirteenth campaign: captured towns in Nukhashshe (a district east of the Orontes between Qatna and Ebla [Redford 2003: 81, 87–90]).

Year 39, fourteenth campaign: attacked the Shasu and collected tribute from Reṯenu (Redford 2003: 90–3).

Year 41(?), fifteenth campaign: much of the record is damaged, but reference is made to taking tribute from Reṯenu (Redford 2003: 93–4).

Year 42, sixteenth(?) campaign (perhaps seventeenth): reference is made to the lands of the Fenkhu (coastal region north of Carmel) and the destruction of towns such as Irkata, Tunip, and Qadesh (Redford 2003: 94–8, 131 n. 129). Troops of Naharin are mentioned, as are gifts from Tanaya (a site in the Aegean?).

Amenhotep II (1425–1400 BCE): there seems to be a contradiction between Amenhotep's inscriptions, two putting his first campaign in his third year and two putting it in his seventh year (Cumming 1992: 22–35). It seems clear that there were three campaigns to the north, but for some reason (various explanations have been offered) the first seems to have been ignored later. S. Yeivin

(1967: 120–1) has suggested that this was only a punitive raid, taken while Amenhotep was still co-ruler, which is why it was given little attention later in his reign.

Year 3(?), a campaign: to Upper Retenu where he reports the killing of seven chieftains in the district of Takhsy or Tekhsy (Tahash [תחש] of Gen. 22:24?), an area in Syria east of Sidon and Byblos (Mumford 1998: 143), and displayed their bodies.

Year 7, 'first campaign': G. D. Mumford summarizes the events of this campaign as follows:

> (1) Amenhotep II's departure for Retjenu, (2) his capture of Shamash-Edom, (3) his crossing of the River Orontes in Lebanon, (4) the subjugation of Niy to the south, (5) the execution of disloyal officials in the coastal city of Ugarit, (6) the subjugation of the villages of Mendjat in the vicinity of Tjalkhi, (7-8) the peaceful affirmation of Egypt's suzerainty over Hetjera and Kadesh. (9) the subjugation of the town of Hashabu. (10) the capture in the plain of Sharon of a messenger belonging to the chieftan [sic] of Naharin (Mitanni), (11) the king's return by chariot to Memphis, and (12) the listing of all the booty obtained during this campaign. [Mumford 1998: 144–5]

Another inscription clarifies that some 'Asiatics' in Ugarit were plotting to expel the troops and overthrow the chieftain who was loyal to Egypt. S. Yeivin (1967: 122–4), however, rejects the identification as Ugarit. E. Edel (1953: 149–50) is also uncertain, but most recent discussions have still accepted this identification (e.g. Helck 1971: 158). Thus, although the city in question was not certainly Ugarit, the consensus is that it probably was. The site of Shamash-Edom has been identified with Qurn-Ḥaṭṭin in Lower Galilee (Aharoni 1960: 177–81; cf. Ahituv 1984: 174–6) but the consensus now seems to be on the west bank of the Orontes near Qatna (Helck 1971: 157; Singer 1988: 1). Hashabu may be *Tell Ḥašbe* near Baalbek (Edel 1953: 155 n. 61a; Helck 1971: 159; Singer 1988: 1). The place of the capture of the Mitanni messenger is widely accepted as the Sharon, though I. Singer (1988) has argued for the Beqaʿ Valley.

Year 9, the 'second' campaign: this did not go north of the Galilee. His first stop was the southern Aphek (near Jaffa) which welcomed him; he then moved to the Samarian region, to Jemma, which was near Socho, and plundered some surrounding villages (cf. Ahituv 1984: 197–8). Next, he took the towns of Ituryn and Mektilyn (apparently north of Socho: Goedicke 1992; Ahituv 1984: 142). Finally, he journeyed into the Jezreel Valley where he plundered Anaharath. At Hu'aket (in the Jezreel Valley?) he deposed the chieftain of Giboa-Saman (modern Kfar Hasidim near Haifa?: Rainey 1973: 74–5; cf. Ahituv 1984: 100–101; Helck 1971: 163) and replaced him. He then returned to Memphis, whether overland or by sea is not specified.

Year ?: Amenhotep did not campaign into Syria after his ninth-year expedition, perhaps because he had concluded a treaty with Mitanni. This was apparently agreed already by Amenhotep II, though we have no certain reference to it in his inscriptions.

Thutmose IV (1400–1390 BCE): for reasons which are probably somewhat complicated, Mitanni offered to make a treaty with Egypt, perhaps as early as the time of Amenhotep II (as noted above). In any case, we know that Thutmose had a treaty, which was sealed by his taking a daughter of Artatama I in marriage (cf. EA 29.16-18).

Yet there are references to an expedition into Syria, mentioned only in passing or in fragmentary passages: 'the testimony we do have refers to the king's exploits only circumstantially.... It is probable that this "monumental" silence is actually the reflection of reality' (Bryan 1991: 336; also Mumford 1998: 168–73). Although some have wanted to restore *Naharin* as the defeated foe in the major inscription (Karnak statue dedication text), this seems unlikely (Bryan 1991: 337–40). Yet Syria-Palestine (Djahy) is mentioned in inscriptions (Bryan 1991: 339–47), and a mortuary temple inscription refers to taking plunder from Gezer (*Urk.* 4:1556; Cumming 1984b: 258). An Amarna letter apparently to Amenhotep III notes that his 'father' (Thutmose IV) had visited Sidon (EA 85.69-71). Thus, Thutmose IV does seem to have conducted some sort of campaign into Syria, but this does not appear to have affected his relationship with Mitanni, a princess from which he had married (Redford 1992a: 165–6; Bryan 1991: 346–7).

[NB: this campaign of Thutmose IV 'terminated Egypt's military adventures in western Asia for sixty-five years' (Redford 1992a: 166).]

Amenhotep III (1390–1353 BCE): in spite of traditional titles and other statements having Amenhotep 'smite the Asiatics', as well as lists of tribute and gifts to the king (cf. Mumford 1998: 176–224), Egyptologists are clear that he conducted no campaigns into Syria-Palestine (O'Connor/Cline [eds] 1998: 224).

Akhenaten (Amenhotep IV 1353–1336 BCE): although the Amarna letters show that Akhenaten's regime was very much in charge of Palestine and Syria, there is no indication of any campaigns by this pharaoh into the region. Discipline against unruly subordinates seems to have been dispensed by summoning them to Memphis and dealing with them there (e.g., Aziru of Amurru [EA 162]). Important is the fact that the border between Egypt and the Hittites seems to have been established at this time and continued more or less at the same place for the next century and a half (Redford 1973: 40–1).

[The question of the rule of Smenkhkare and/or Nefernefruaten still seems uncertain. In any case, there appears to have been no Syria-Palestinian connection.]

Tutankhamun (?–1324 BCE): he coordinated with Assyria for a two-pronged attack against Suppiluliuma the Hittite king; however, the Hittite armies defeated both of the attackers (Redford 1984: 213–15), including capturing Qadesh back from the besieging Egyptians. Otherwise, he may have conducted another campaign into Syria-Palestine, though this is only hinted at, perhaps led by Horemheb (Mumford 1998: 255).

Ay (1323–1320 BCE); in spite of maintaining control over much of Syria and Palestine, no campaigns as such were conducted.

Horemheb (1319–1292 BCE): in addition to any campaigns undertaken while Tutankhamun was on the throne, Horemheb seems to have conducted a campaign to Byblos and Carchemish in his sixteenth year (Redford 1973).

Ramesses I (1292–1291 BCE): like Ay and Horemheb, Ramesses was an aged general who succeeded to the throne, but he was the founder of a new dynasty, the 19th Dynasty. In his short reign he apparently put Sety in charge of one expedition to Syria-Palestine (Fenkhu: Mumford 1998: 277; Kitchen 1993: 93–4).

Sety I (1290–1279 BCE): already in his first year he embarked on 'foreign' campaigns: first, was an attack on the Shasu who were apparently disrupting communications between Egypt and southern Palestine (Spalinger 1979: 29–35; Murnane 1990: 40–2; Brand 2000: 120–5;

Kitchen 1993: 6–9). This included action in the hill country: 'the hills of the rebels…. His Majesty captured them entirely' (Weeks [ed.] 1986: 14). They were defeated between Raphia and Gaza. Sety then moved to pacify Beth-Shean, Hamath, and Yenoam, after which he went on to return Acre and Tyre to Egyptian control. Finally, he returned to capture Pella on his way back to Egypt. The Second Beth-Shean Stela describes an action against *Apiru* in the region of Beth-Shean (Kitchen 1993: 12–13), though the relationship of this skirmish to the previous campaign is uncertain. A later campaign (years 5 or 6?) was against northern Syria, specifically Qadesh and Amurru (Kitchen 1993: 19–20; Murnane 1990: 51–65; Mumford 1998: 279–80). There may have been an encounter with Hittite forces at this time, though this is not certain (Spalinger 1979: 33–5; Mumford 1998: 280).

Ramesses II (1279–1213 BCE):

Year 4: his first campaign into Syria-Palestine went through Canaan, Phoenicia, and into Amurru where he defeated the small force of Benteshina and made Amurru his vassal (Kitchen 1982: 51; 1996: 1, 78).

Year 5: the main battle that has so often characterized his reign: to recapture Qadesh for Egypt (Kitchen 1982: 53–64; Lichtheim 1976: 57–72; Kitchen 1996: 2–26). The Egyptian army marched up the through the Jordan Valley, the Huleh Valley, and the Beqa to Qadesh. We know about the battle in much more detail than many others. The final result was basically a standoff with the Hittite army under Mawatalli. Both sides claimed victory (as one might expect), but Qadesh remained under Hittite control, and Mawatalli appointed a new ruler of Amurru which was also back as a Hittite vassal. He also moved to take the territory of Upi.

Years 6/7: the Egyptian failure at Qadesh led to several rebellions in Syria-Palestine, which required Ramesses to take action (Kitchen 1982: 67–8). His goal was the Shasu (§6.3.3.4) in the Transjordan region. He split his army to attack on the east of the Dead Sea, advancing from the north against Moab and the south against Seir-Edom, after which the united forces moved against Heshbon and Damascus and then Kumidi. The Egyptians were once more in charge of Upi.

Years 8/9: this time he took the army to Akko, then up the Phoenician coast to Tyre, Sidon, Byblos, Irqata, then to Dapur and Tunip (Kitchen 1982: 68–9; 1996: 26–7). This seems to have returned Qadesh and Amurru to Egyptian control.

Year 10: he again marched through Phoenicia to Dapur (Kitchen 1982: 69–70; 1996: 45–7). There was apparently no response from the Hittites who were experiencing internal conflicts. After Mawatalli's death, Mursili II took the throne but was dethroned and exiled by his uncle who became Hattusili III. Eventually, Mursili sought refuge with Ramesses II (in the latter's eighteenth year). Although Hattusili demanded his return at first, things changed when Assyria under its new king Shalmaneser I conquered Mitanni. Now Hattusili proposed a treaty with Egypt.

Year 21: Ramesses II and Hattusili III signed a treaty in Gaza that brought peace between the two countries, with Qadesh and Amurru remaining under Hittite control but Egypt having access all along the coast as far as Ugarit (Kitchen 1982: 73–95). Ramesses married first one daughter of Hattusili, then another. Hattusili may even have visited Egypt in person (he was invited), but this is not certain. The two powers seem to have remained at peace with each other until the end of the Hittite empire (*c.* 1200 BCE).

Merenptah (1213–1203 BCE): early in his reign he apparently experienced unrest in the Syria-Palestine part of his empire; the Delta was also attacked by a coalition of Libyans and some of the Sea Peoples (Mumford 1998: 312). Merenptah writes of his victory over these various groups in the famous Israel stela of his fifth year (discussed at §6.3.4). Whether this represents one campaign or perhaps several, even over several years, is uncertain. Egypt was also at peace with the Hittites during this time.

What becomes clear is that in the period between Ahmose and Akhenaten, the kinglets of Canaan were brought into vassalage to the Egyptian king. Exactly when and how this came about is not clear from the extant records, but the Amarna letters paint a picture in which the chieftains of the Canaanite city-states are visibly in subjection to Akhenaten, even if some attempt to establish a certain independence (e.g., Abdi-Ashirta and Aziru of Amurru [§6.3.2]). We can assume that this general situation continued through the rest of the New Kingdom, in spite of rebellions and challenges (such as the invasion of the Sea Peoples [§7.2]). This seems to have been more or less the state of Canaan when Merenptah claims to have subdued Ashkelon, Gezer, Yenoam, and Israel about 1209 BCE (§6.3.4).

6.3.2 Canaan as Depicted in the Amarna Letters

S. Bunimovitz and Z. Lederman (2013) 'Solving a Century-Old Puzzle: New Discoveries at the Middle Bronze Gate of Tel Beth-Shemesh', *PEQ* 145: 6–24; **I. Finkelstein** (1996) 'The Territorial-Political System of Canaan in the Late Bronze Age', *UF* 28: 221–55; **I. Finkelstein and N. Na'aman** (2005) 'Shechem of the Amarna Period and the Rise of the Northern Kingdom of Israel', *IEJ* 55: 172–93; **Y. Goren, I. Finkelstein, and N. Na'aman** (2004) *Inscribed in Clay: Provenance Study of the Amarna Tablets and Other Ancient Near Eastern Texts*; **N. Na'aman** (1979) 'The Origin and Historical Background of Several Amarna Letters', *UF* 11: 673–84; **idem** (1985) 'Geographical-Historical Aspects of the Amarna Tablets', in *Proceedings of the World Congress of Jewish Studies: Panel Session Bible Studies and Ancient Near East*: 17–26; **idem** (1992a) 'Amarna Letters', *ABD* 1:174–81; **idem** (1992b) 'Canaanite Jerusalem and its Central Hill Country Neighbours in the Second Millennium B.C.E.', *UF* 24: 275–91; **idem** (1997) 'The Network of Canaanite Late Bronze Kingdoms and the City of Ashdod', *UF* 29: 599–626; **idem** (2005) *Canaan in the Second Millennium B.C.E.: Collected Essays, Volume 2*; **J.-P. Vita** (2005) 'The Town of Mušiḫuna and the Cities of the "Beqaʻ Alliance" in the Amarna Letters', *SEL* 22: 1–7.

The Amarna letters serve as an important source on the divisions and administrative districts and entities for Syria and Palestine in the LBA. It is clear that most of this territory was under the domination of Egypt, though Mitanni and later the Hittites sought to take control of some of the border kingdoms. N. Na'aman has summarized the various divisions that arise from study of the Amarna texts. At one time Na'aman (e.g., 1985, 1986b) attempted to make use of biblical data, especially Joshua and Judges, to help draw a picture of territories and boundaries, but he later abandoned this approach, as he himself noted:

In the light of these examples, it is important to emphasize that there is a profound difference between the reconstructed network of Canaanite entities and the system of tribal boundaries as described in the book of Joshua. The first set of borders represents the actually delineation of historical units functioning politically for hundreds of years.... The system of tribal borders, on the other hand, is a work of historiographic character, recorded as part of the description of the conquest and settlement in the book of Joshua and served as a kind of legitimation of the Israelite hold on their newly conquered territories. [Na'aman 1985: 25]

More than a decade later, he further renounced his earlier conclusions:

However, it is clear now that the descriptions of tribal allotments is a late, non-historical composition and was written hundreds [of] years after the final collapse of the system of Canaanite kingdoms. I, therefore, withdraw all my former reconstructions of boundaries of Canaanite kingdoms based on the tribal allotments, as well as the identifications of towns as city-states on the basis of the biblical text. [Na'aman 1997: 601]

In opposition to I. Finkelstein (1996), Na'aman (1997: 606–7) argues that large parts of Palestine were unsettled in the LBA. This included Upper and Lower Galilee, the Golan Heights, the central hill country, the lower Jordan Valley, and the Negev. This makes drawing precise boundaries very uncertain in many cases, and not all territory can be included in the territory of the city-states. Na'aman's judgment seems to be the correct one here. The following draws on the reconstructions of Na'aman (1992a: 1:177–8; 1997) but also that of Finkelstein (1996) and Goren/Finkelstein/Na'aman (2004), as well as the map in Helck (1971: 188). The readings of names is based on a comparison of Na'aman, Moran (1992), and Rainey (2015).

The Amarna archive begins with ***international correspondence*** (EA 1-50, 189-90): between Amenhotep III, Akhenaten, and Tutankhamun of Egypt and kings Kadashman-enlil and Burraburiash of Babylon, Ashur-uballit of Assyria, and Tushratta of Mitanni (EA 1-11, 13-25, 27-29); this includes a love letter from a Babylonian princess to a king of Egypt (EA 12), a letter from Tushratta to Teye, wife of Amenhotep III, after the king's death (EA26), and a letter from the king of Mitanni (Tushratta?) to the kinglets of Canaan, asking them to let his messenger go through their country without hindrance (EA 30). Other letters were between Amenhotep III and Tarhundaradu, king Arzawa (a region in southwest Anatolia: EA 31-32); from the king of Alashia (Cyprus?: EA 33-40); from Suppiluliuma, king of Hatti (also his brother Zidan), to 'Huriya', king of Egypt (thought to be Akhenaten, Tutankhamun, or Smenkhkare: EA 41-44).

We begin the geographical survey with ***Northern Syria***. The city of Ugarit is mentioned in the Amarna letters (e.g., EA 1, 45, 89, 98, 126, 151), though it appears not to have been a vassal of Egypt. There are letters from Ammiṯṯamru I and Niqmaddu II, kings of Ugarit; also, from Heba, queen of Ugarit, and a daughter of the king of Ugarit (to the queen of Egypt) (EA 45-50). Ugarit interacted with both Egypt and Mitanni but seems to have remained autonomous. But we know of a number of the northern polities in Syria that were south of Ugarit and under Egyptian control, including Amurru (EA 60-62, 73-76, etc.), Byblos (Gubla: EA 67-140, etc.), Sidon (Ṣiduna: EA 83, 85, 92, 101, 103, 114, 144-49, etc.), and Tyre (Ṣurru: EA 77, 89, 92, 101, etc.). Qadesh, another

Syrian city-state, was a vassal of Mitanni most of the time; however, we have a letter from Etakkama of Qadesh which affirms his loyalty to the king of Egypt and protests against the alleged excursions of Biryawaza (see below) against the territory of Qadesh (EA 189). A letter from Egypt to Qadesh is too fragmentary to make much sense except to admonish Etakkama to guard his cities (EA 190).

Moving from north to south, we come to **Central Syria** or Lebanon (EA 51-62, 66-214): our information for the area of Phoenicia and Syria is more extensive than that for Canaan, because of the voluminous correspondence of Rib-Hadda of Byblos (most of the letters in EA 67-140). These letters tell us especially about the activities of Abdi-Ashirta (EA 60-62) and his son Aziru (EA 156-71), who were opposed by Rib-Hadda (Rib-Eddi) of Byblos (EA 66-96, 101-38, 362). Amurru is treated in the previous chapter (§5.4.1) and will not be discussed further here. Qadesh was mentioned above. We have letters from the 'mayors' of a number of known places: Addu-Nirari of Nuhasse (EA 51), Akizzi of Qatna (EA 52-57), Ili-Rapih of Byblos (EA 139-40), Ammunira of Beirut (EA 141-43), Yapah-Hadda apparently also of Beirut (EA 97-98), Zimreddi of Sidon (EA 144-45), Abimilki of Tyre (EA 146-55), Ildayyi (Ilu-Dayyani) and Mayarzana of Hasi (Tell Hizzin in the Beqa [Goren/Finkelstein/Na'aman 2004: 127]; EA 175, 185-86), and Arasha of Kumidi (EA 198). Biryawaza of Damascus was an important actor in this region (EA 194-97). He proclaimed his loyalty to the Pharaoh, with his *Apiru* and Sutaeans at the king's disposal, and he was guarding Kumidi; however, the rulers Biridashwa (of Ashtartu) and Arsawuya (of Ruhizzi), as well as the cities of Yanuamma, Busruna, and Halunnu – all of these loyal to the Hittite king – had allied against him and were taking over Apu (Upi). As discussed elsewhere (§6.3.3.3), the term *Apiru* is not an ethnic term but a social one. The word seems originally to mean someone outside the social system or an outcast or a refugee. However, in the Amarna Letters it always seems to have a pejorative connotation along the lines of 'outlaw' or 'bandit', perhaps because banditry was one of the few ways that those outside the system could survive. Some of these *Apiru* seem, however, to have served as mercenaries.

Letters from *cities* include Ammiya (EA 99; also 73, 75, 81, 88, 95, 139-40), Irqata (EA 100) and Tunip (EA 59). Letters from rulers of places not yet identified include Shutarna of Mushihuna (perhaps in the Beqa [Vita 2005]; EA 182-84), Arsawuya of Ruhizzi (on the border between Qadesh and Upi? [Goren/Finkelstein/Na'aman 2004: 98]; EA 191-92; also 53, 56), Tiwati of Labana (on the border between Qadesh and Upi? [Goren/Finkelstein/Na'aman 2004: 98]; EA 193), Shatiya and Abdi-Resha of Eni-Shasi (in the Beqa? [Goren/Finkelstein/Na'aman 2004: 127]; EA 187, 363), Artamanya of Siribashani (possibly Bashan or Ezra in Hauran [Goren/Finkelstein/Na'aman 2004: 215]; EA 201), Amawashe (of Byblos? or Bashan?; EA 202); Abdi-Milki of Shashimi (unknown [Goren/Finkelstein/Na'aman 2004: 215]; EA 203). Leaders of cities not otherwise specified or known include Tehu-Teshupa (EA 58), Ipte (EA 207), Zishamimi (EA 209-10), Zitriyara (EA 211-14). Letters without a specified sender or location include EA 188, 199-200, 208.

However, our concern is not primarily with the area of Lebanon and Syria but the area of **Canaan** (EA 63-65, 215-337). Fortunately, we have quite a few letters from the area of Canaan itself. We know of the main city-states of Hazor, Megiddo, Shechem, Jerusalem, Gezer, Gath, Ashkelon, Lachish. The Amarna letters describe a situation in which the various city-states are jockeying for position, whether to gain power and territory or to defend themselves against takeover by neighbouring city-states or perhaps even a combination of both. We begin with **northern Palestine**, which was dominated by Hazor. We have letters from Abdi-Tirshi/Abdi-Shullim of that city

(EA 227-28). A number of city-states were based in the Jezreel Valley and associated areas: Akko, with letters from Surata and Satatna (EA 232-35 + 236? + 327); Megiddo ruled by Biridiya (EA 242-47); Achshaph, led by Endaruta/Intaruta (EA 366-67; also EA 272 [Goren/Finkelstein/Na'aman 2004: 231–3]); Pella, with leader Mut-Ba'lu (EA 255-56); Taanach, under Yashdata (EA 248; also 245). In the Galilee was Shamu-Adda of Shamhuna (Shim'on [Goren/Finkelstein/Na'aman 2004: 233–7]: EA 224-25). Ayyab and Biridashwa seem to have been from Ashtarot/Ashtartu (Goren/Finkelstein/Na'aman 2004: 218; EA 364; also EA 196-97).

We know of a number of rulers from places not certainly identified: Yanuamma (Yenoam, in the vicinity of Beth-Shean?: EA 197), Qanu (Qanawat, below Jebel ed-Druz [Goren/Finkelstein/Na'aman 2004: 215]: EA 204), Tobu (eṭ-Ṭayibeh?; EA 205), Amayashe of Nasiba (Naṣib in region of Der'a? [Goren/Finkelstein/Na'aman 2004: 215]: EA 206), Rusmanya of Sharuna (Galilee or Bashan? [Goren/Finkelstein/Na'aman 2004: 220–1]: EA 241), Dagantakala (of northern Canaan?; EA 317-18); Zuḫra/Suhra (Bashan? [Na'aman 1997: 607; Goren/Finkelstein/Na'aman 2004: 219–20]: EA 334). Letters EA 249-50, 257-60 have a 'mayor' whose name is various rendered as Ba'lu-Meher and Ba'lu-UR.SAG. These are identified as the same individual by Rainey (2015: 1:1565) but considered separate by Goren/Finkelstein/Na'aman (2004: 249–50) who associate Ba'lu-UR.SAG with EA 249-50 (and EA 263) and Ba'lu-Meher with EA 257-60. They suggest Ba'lu-UR.SAG's city was Rehov but agree with Rainey that Ba'lu-Meher was from Gath-Padalla. But where was Gath-Padalla? They argue from clay composition and archaeology that it was Tel Yokneam/Yoqne'am (Goren/Finkelstein/Na'aman 2004: 249–55). With regard to EA 319, Na'aman and Moran read Surashar's capital as Ahtiashna/Ahtirumna, somewhere in the south of Canaan (Goren/Finkelstein/Na'aman: 2004: 302–3). This is objected to by Rainey and others who read the name as Ginti-Ashna; although no specific identification is proposed, this would be somewhere in the Jezreel Valley.

The main city of *central Palestine* was Shechem, one of the more powerful kingdoms in Canaan at this time (whereas Jerusalem was a rather smaller, minor state [Na'aman 1992b: 288–9]). This kingdom was commanded by the notorious figure of Lab'ayu (EA 252-54; also mentioned in EA 237, 244-46, 250, 255, 263, 280, 287, 289). Another figure associated with Lab'ayu was Tagi (EA 264-66). No place is given for him in his letters, but according to EA 288 (cf. EA 289 and 290), Ginti-Kirmil was his town. It now seems likely that this is to be identified with the site of Jatt in the Sharon (Goren/Finkelstein/Na'aman 2004: 256–9), where a modern Israeli Arab town by the same name exists.

Lab'ayu protested his loyalty to the Egyptian king, but Abdi-Heba and others accused him of aggressive tactics (EA 244):

> Thus says Biridiya, the loyal servant of the king…. May the king, my lord, be apprised that since the regular army went back (to Egypt), Lab'ayu has made war against me so that we are unable to pluck the sheep (or) complete the harvest. We can't even go out the city gate because of Lab'ayu since he found out that regular troops are not c[oming fo]rth. And no[w] he is determin[ed] to take Megiddo. So may the king please rescue his city; let not Lab'ayu seize it! [Rainey 2015: 1, no. 244]

After Lab'ayu's death, his sons are alleged to have carried on the same way (EA 246, 250, 287, 289). What we appear to have here is a coalition of city-states, led by Shechem, which was seeking to seize control of territory that would allow them to control the main trade routes through Palestine: the coastal route connecting Egypt to Lebanon, Syria, and beyond and the King's Highway that extended from the Gulf of Aqaba through the Jordan Valley and on up to Damascus (Finkelstein/ Na'aman 2005).

With Lab'ayu were Gezer, Ginti-kirmil, Tel Yoqne'am, Anaharath, and eventually Pehel or Pella (Piḫilu), Ashtaroth, and the city of the kinglet Yashdata (perhaps Taanach). Opposing them (perhaps simply for self-defence) was another coalition of Megiddo, Rehov, Achshaph, Akko, Gath, and perhaps Hazor. The thrust of the Lab'ayu axis threatened to divide the rest of Egyptian Canaan into two disconnected parts, a northern grouping (the anti-Shechem alliance listed above) and a southern one of Jerusalem, Gath, Ashkelon, and Lachish. Lab'ayu apparently intended to take Shim'on or Shimron (Shamḫuna) in the Jezreel Valley, which would allow him to encircle those opposing him in the rest of the Jezreel Valley, including the Egyptian centre at Beth-Shean. If he had been able to achieve his evident territorial ambitions, this would have given him a base from which he could manipulate trade and might even endanger Egyptian control of the region. Eventually, Egypt acted to sort out Lab'ayu's rebellion and apparently executed him (cf. EA 245, 250, 253, 254, 280).

When Shechem's ruler Lab'ayu died, Abdi-Heba of Jerusalem evidently took the opportunity to try to expand his territory to the west. This was at the expense of the kingdom whose ruler was Shuwardata, probably Gath (see below). This was why the latter complained to the Egyptian king that Abdi-Heba had become another Lab'ayu throwing his weight around, as EA 280 indicates:

> Mes[sage] of Šuwardata, [yo]ur servant, the dirt at your feet…. The king, my lord, permitted me to wage war against Qeltu…. Why did 'Abdi-Ḫe[b]a write to the men of Qeltu, '[Ac]cept silver and follow me'? Moreover, may the king, my lord, conduct an inquiry. If I took a man, or a single ox, or an ass, from him, then he is in the right! Moreover, Lab'ayu, who used to take our towns, is dead, but now [an]other Lab'ayu is 'Abdi-Ḫeba, and he seizes our town. [Moran 1992: 321]

Another figure was this Shuwardata, though his city appears to be Gath (Finkelstein 1996: 232–3; Finkelstein and Na'aman 2005: 178–80; Rainey 2015b: 1586). Moran thinks it might be Keilah (Ginta?); while Helck makes it Hebron (*LdÄ* VI: 112), a city not otherwise identified in the Amarna texts; indeed, it is doubtful at the moment that there was a Late Bronze city on the site. But whatever city he represented, he was sometimes in league with Lab'ayu – or at least, accused of being such.

However, in the political manoeuvrings and shifting alliances that one expects of the region at this time, Shuwardata and Abdi-Heba were able to make common cause when they were both threatened by *Apiru*, as indicated in EA 366 (letter from Shuwardata):

> May the king, my lord, be informed that the 'Apiru that rose up…against the lands, the god of the king, my lord, gave to me, and I smote him. And may the king, my lord, be informed that all my brothers have abandoned me. Only 'Abdi-Ḫeba and I have been at war with (that) 'Apiru. Surata, the ruler of Akka, and Endaruta, the ruler of Akšapa,

(these) two also have come to my aid...with 50 chariots, and now they are on my side in the war. [Moran 1992: 364]

The primary cities of *southern Palestine* were Ashkelon, Lachish, Gath (Tell es-Safi), Gezer, and Jerusalem (with Debir). We have several named rulers from Gezer: Milkilu (EA 267-71); Ba'lu-Dani/Ba'lu-Shipti (EA 272, 292-93, 295); and Yapai (EA 297-300). From Lachish we know of three rulers: Zimredda (EA 294 + 329), Yabni-Ilu (EA 328), and Ba'lu-Shipti (EA 330-32). We know of Shuwardata of Gath (EA 278-84), but it has been argued that Abdi-Ashtarti (EA 63-65 + 335) was a successor of his (Na'aman 1979: 676–82). We also know of Abdi-Heba of Jerusalem (EA 285-91), and Yidya of Ashkelon (EA 320-26). Although the name Ashdod does not occur in the Amarna texts, it was noted that an 'Ashdad' is found in contemporary Ugaritic and Akkadian texts; however, Na'aman (1997: 609–15) argued that this is a city in Cyprus (perhaps Enkomi). In the same article Na'aman proposed that Ashdod appears in the Amarna letters under the name Tianna (or Tianni: EA 298, 306, 284). This interpretation was rejected by Rainey (2003: 193*–4*) whose collation of the tablets in question eliminated the reading 'Tianna'. Now Goren/Finkelstein/Na'aman (2004: 292–4) propose that two Amarna letters originated in Ashdod (EA 294, 296) based on the clay composition and their textual contents. The location of the capital of some writers is not clear, such as Pu-Ba'lu of Yurza (Tell Jemmeh? [Finkelstein 1996: 231–2]; EA 314-16).

As discussed above, the residence of Surashar (EA 319) is given as Ahtiashna/Ahtirumna by some, which would place it somewhere in the south of Canaan (Goren/Finkelstein/Na'aman 2004: 302–3), but others read Ginti-Ashna, which would be somewhere in the Jezreel Valley. A number of letters that seem to be from the south do not have an identifiable residence for the writer: Bayawa (EA 215-16); Wiktasu/Yiqdasu (EA 221-22); Bayadi (EA 237? + 238); Baduzana (EA 239); Yashdata (EA 248); Dashru (EA 261-62); 'Lady of the Lions' (ᶠNIN.UR.MAḪ.MEŠ) (EA 273-74); Yahzib-Hadda (EA 275-77); Yatiri (EA 296-300); Shubandu (EA 301-6 + 313?); Pa'api (an Egyptian official; EA 333); Hizziri (EA 336-37). Letters without either a writer or place of origin identified include EA 240, 251, 263, 307-12, 338-39.

Exactly how many city-states existed in Palestine is uncertain. Estimates vary from 13-14 to 22-27; a good compromise estimate is about 20 (Steiner/Killebrew 2014: 544–5). Several sites not mentioned in the Amarna archive are considered capitals of city-states by Na'aman (1997: 619–18) but rejected by Finkelstein (2016: 228–31): Anaharath (Tel Rekhesh), Rehov (Tell eṣ-Ṣarem), Mishal. Others rejected by Finkelstein are only considered possibilities by Na'aman: Debir (Khirbet Rabud), Bethel, Tel Goded (Tell Judeideh), Tell Beit Mirṣim, Tel 'Eton. Beth-Shemesh is interesting because its excavators regard it as a city-state capital (Bunimovitz/Lederman 2013: 23). Na'aman (1997: 618) thinks some other names missing from the Amarna letters might also have been the seats of local rulers: Tel Dor, Tel Jokneam, and Tell Qarnei-Ḥiṭṭin.

Among those who wrote letters to the Pharaoh from the southern part of Canaan was the king of Jerusalem (Urusalim), Abdi-Heba (EA 285-91). N. Na'aman (1992b: 275–8; 1997: 601–3) has noted that the impression given in the Amarna letters is that the city-state of Jerusalem dominated the Judaean hill country, but that this is misleading because of the incomplete nature of the archive. Many of the letters, especially the recent ones, were taken to Memphis when the capital was relocated back there from Akhetaten (Tell el-Amarna), leaving only a portion of the archive, the 'outdated' correspondence, to be slowly buried and finally discovered millennia later. He also argues that the

Rwš3mm of the Execretion Texts was not Jerusalem (Na'aman 1992b: 278–9), though I am not yet convinced. As he notes, 'Jerusalem' is normally transliterated with an initial *waw/yod* in most sources, but it sometimes has an *alef* (e.g., in Arabic and Syriac) which could easily be dropped. Na'aman makes a reasonable case and may be right, in which case Jerusalem would have become important after the eighteenth century BCE (when the later Execration Texts were produced), though before the fourteenth when it appears in the Amarna letters. But one cannot help feeling that those who see Jerusalem in the Execration Texts are correct.

The name Abdi-Heba means 'servant of the (Hurrian) goddess Heba'; however, as far as we can tell he was a native Canaanite, one of the many kinglets of the Canaanite city-states. In the passages that follow, the term used for the head of the various city states is usually *ḫazannu* which normally means 'mayor' or chief administrator of a city; however, it is used here of the petty kings of the city-states. The Akkadian term for king, *šarru*, seldom occurs for the rulers of the city-states. We have six letters from Abdi-Heba (EA 285-90), plus a couple of other letters that refer to him (EA 284, 366). Here is one (EA 287):

> May the [kin]g know (that) all the lands are [at] peace (with one another), but I am at war. May the king provide for his land. Consider the lands of Gazru, Ašqaluna, and L[akis]i. They have given them food, oil, and any other requirement. So may the king provide for archers and the mayors will belong to the king, my lord. But if there are no archers, then the ki[ng] will have neither lands nor mayors. Consider Jerusalem! This neither my father nor m[y] mother gave to me. The [str]ong hand: …(arm) [of the king] gave it to me. Consider the deed! This is the deed of Milkilu and the deed of the sons of Lab'ayu, who have given the land of the king <to> the 'Apiru. [Moran 1992: 328]

As will be clear, we need to keep in mind that only Abdi-Heba's side of the story is given in his letters. His claims to loyalty and being a victim of treacherous neighbours need to be considered alongside other letters, letters from those very same neighbours who accuse him of treachery, aggression, and disloyalty toward the Pharaoh (e.g., EA 280)!

To summarize this discussion, what we can find from the various letters is that there were a number of competing city-states: they squabble among themselves and complain to the Pharaoh, each manoeuvring for position and seeking advantage for itself in competition with its neighbours, constantly playing off one another in relation to the Egyptian king. A combination of the Amarna letters, archaeology, and a recent petrographic examination of the clay composition of the letters allows us to reconstruct some of the interactions of the various city-states at this time (Goren/Finkelstein/Na'aman 2004). Two of those who have written on the city-states in Canaan are N. Na'aman (e.g., 1992b, 1997) and I. Finkelstein (e.g., 1996; 2013: 13–22). Although Na'aman and Finkelstein have a number of differences in their reconstruction of the system of city-states, the general picture they paint is still remarkably similar (in addition to Goren/Finkelstein/Na'aman 2004, see Finkelstein/Na'aman 2005). They agree that there were about 20-25 city-states in Canaan (not to mention other city-states in Lebanon and Syria). They also disagree about whether the city-state boundaries included all the land (so Finkelstein) or omitted a certain amount of 'no-man's-land' (Na'aman). Some of the main city-states of Canaan are listed in the following table:

Jerusalem	Abdi-Ḫeba	EA 285-90; also 280, 366
Shechem (Šakmu)	Lab'ayu	EA 252-54; also 237, 244-46, 250, 255, 263, 280, 287, 289
Megiddo (Magidda)	Biridiya	EA 242-46, 365; also 248
Lachish (Lakiša)	Zimredda/Zimreddi	EA 329; also 288, 333
	Yabni-Ilu	EA 328
Hazor (Haṣura)	Abdi-Tirši	EA 227-28; also 148, 364
Gezer (Gazru)	Milkilu	EA 267-71, 369; also 249, 250, 253, 254, 287, 290, 292
	Yapaḫu	EA 297-300, 378
	Adda-Danu	EA 292-94
Gath (Gimtu)	Šuwardata, Šuardatu	EA 278-84, 366; also 271, 290
Ashkelon (Ašqaluna)	Yidya/Idiya	EA 320-26, 370; also 287
Ginti-kirmil	Tagi	EA 263-66; also 249, 289
Tel Yoqneʻam	Baʻlu-meḫir	EA 257-59; also 245
Anaharath	Bayadi	EA 237-38
Pella (Piḫilu)	Mut-Baḫlu	EA 255-56
Ashtaroth (Aštartu)	Ayyab	EA 364; also 256
	Biridashwa?	cf. EA 196-197
Taḫnaka (Taanach?)	Yašdata	EA 248; also 245
Shimʻon/Shimron (Šamḫuna)	Šamu-Adda/Šum-Adda	EA 225-26; also 8
Rehov (Reḥob)	Baʻlu-UR.SAG, Baʻlu-Meher (?)	EA 249-50
Achshaph (Akšapa)	Endaruta	EA 223, 366, 367
Acco (Akka)	Surata/Šaratu	EA 232-35; also 8, 85, 88, 111, 245, 366

The contribution of the Amarna letters to the origins of Israel can be summarized as follows:

- Although the Amarna age was only about a quarter of a century, the letters give us a unique insight into the situation at the time. The picture that emerges from them seems to have encompassed Syria and Palestine for most of the LBA.
- We know the names and even the main territorial limits of some of the city-states in Syria and Palestine. Yet the precise number of such entities, and especially their boundaries, are still very much the subject of debate.
- From the Amarna letters, we know of several rulers of city-states and their activities:

  Northern Syria: Ugarit seems to have retained its independence most of the time. But the border territories such as Amurru and Qadesh were fought over and ended up under Mitanni and later the Hittite domination part of this time. In any case, they often tried by surreptitious or even open rebellion against Egyptian rule to control other city-states in their region. Tyre, Sidon, Byblos remained under Egyptian control, though Amurru sometimes attempted to take them over. Other small states were Ruhizzi and Lapana.

Southern Syria (Northern Canaan): Damascus (surprisingly hardly mentioned in the Amarna correspondence: EA 53.63; 107.28; 197.21) was the main player and the capital of Upi. The cities of Kumidi, Hashabu, Enishazi, Hasi, Tubihu, and probably Tushultu were subordinate to it.

Northern Palestine: Hazor was the main city-state. A number of smaller territories of Bashan, the Galilee, and the Jezreel Valley in the region were Akko, Achshaph, Ashtaroth, Busruna, Gath-padalla, Halunnu, Shim'on, Anaharath, Megiddo, Pehel, Yanuamma (Yenoam), and probably Rehov.

Central Palestine: Shechem was the leading power.

Southern Palestine: Gezer, Ashkelon, Lachish, Gath (Tell es-Safi), and Jerusalem seem to have been the most important kingdoms. Other city states were (in the Sharon), Yurza, and perhaps Tianna (= Ashdod?).

- When the Amarna correspondence is fully taken into account, it becomes obvious that nothing like the exodus and settlement of Israel as described in Exodus to Joshua could have taken place in the fourteenth or thirteenth century BCE, as some propose (§6.4, §8.4), or indeed in the fifteenth. The Canaan of the Amarna letters bears no resemblance to the Israelite settlement described in Joshua, while a large body of people could not have moved out of Egypt and through the Sinai and Negev wildernesses – after a series of devastating plagues – without leaving any trace in the Amarna texts, the Egyptian inscriptions, or the archaeology of the regions in question.

6.3.3 Ethnic and Other Groups

B. C. Benz (2016) *The Land before the Kingdom of Israel: A History of the Southern Levant and the People Who Populated It*; **H. Goedicke** (1987) 'Anastasi VI 51-61', *SAK* 14: 83–98; **N. Gottwald** (1979) *The Tribes of Yahweh: A Sociology of the Religion of Liberated Israel, 1250–1050 B.C.E.*; **M. G. Hasel** (1998) *Domination and Resistance: Egyptian Military Activity in the Southern Levant, ca. 1300–1185 BC.*; **A. E. Killebrew** (2005) *Biblical Peoples and Ethnicity: An Archaeological Study of Egyptians, Canaanites, Philistines, and Early Israel 1300–1000 B.C.E.*

This section looks at groups that are mentioned in LB sources. Groups in Egyptian sources were already discussed for the EB (§2.4.4) and MB (§3.1.1), but as will soon be clear, here we are not dealing with ethnic groups, or at least not for the most part. Canaan/Canaanite deals with territorial terms, while *Apiru* and *Shasu* (at least sometimes) are designations for social groups with particular lifestyles. Nevertheless, these groups will need to be considered when discussing the origins of Israel, as will be very evident in that section below (§6.3.4).

6.3.3.1 'Nomads' and Pastoralists

M. L. Chaney (1983) 'Ancient Palestinian Peasant Movements and the Formation of Premonarchic Israel', in D. N. Freedman and D. F. Graf (eds), *Palestine in Transition: The Emergence of Ancient Israel*: 39–90; **W. Irons and N. Dyson-Hudson (eds)** (1972) *Perspectives on Nomadism*; **K. A. Kamp and N. Yoffee** (1980) 'Ethnicity in Ancient Western Asia during the Early Second Millennium B.C.: Archaeological Assessments and Ethnoarchaeological Prospectives', *BASOR* 237: 85–104; **A. M. Khazanov** (1984) *Nomads and the Outside World*; **N. P. Lemche** (1985) *Early Israel: Anthropological and Historical Studies on the Israelite Society before the Monarchy*; **A. Mohammed** (1973) 'The Nomadic and the Sedentary: Polar Complementaries – Not Polar Opposites', in C. Nelson (ed.), *The Desert and the Sown: Nomads in the Wider Society*: 97–112; **C. Nelson (ed.)** (1973) *The Desert and the Sown: Nomads in the Wider Society*; **P. C. Salzman** (1980a) 'Introduction: Processes of Sedentarization as Adaptation and Response', in P. C. Salzman (ed.), *When Nomads Settle: Processes of Sedentarization as Adaptation and Response*: 1–19; **idem** (1980b) 'Processes of Sedentarization Among the Nomads of Baluchistan', in Philip Carl Salzman (ed.), *When Nomads Settle: Processes of Sedentarization as Adaptation and Response*: 95–110; **idem** (2002) 'Pastoral Nomads: Some General Observations Based on Research in Iran', *Journal of Anthropological Research* 58: 245–64; **idem** (2004) *Pastoralists: Equality, Hierarchy, and the State*; **P. C. Salzman (ed.)** (1980) *When Nomads Settle: Processes of Sedentarization as Adaptation and Response*; **I. Sharon and A. Gilboa** (2013) 'The *SKL* Town: Dor in the Early Iron Age', in A. E. Killebrew and G. Lehmann (eds), *The Philistines and Other 'Sea Peoples' in Text and Archaeology*: 393–468; **T. Staubli** (1991) *Das Image der Nomaden im Alten Israel und in der Ikonographie seiner sesshaften Nachbarn*; **J. Szuchman (ed.)** (2009) *Nomads, Tribes, and the State in the Ancient Near East: Cross-Disciplinary Perspectives*.

Several of the groups in Palestine and more widely in the ancient Near East at this time have been described as nomads or given some similar designation. Through much of the twentieth century many biblical scholars saw the origin of Israel from a nomadic lifestyle (or 'semi-nomads', whatever that meant). The assumption of the Alt–Noth school (§8.4.2), but also others, was that a nomadic existence explained much about the early Israelite traditions. One of the critiques coming from those who embraced the Mendenhall–Gottwald thesis was that nomadism was not the key to understanding early Israel (Chaney 1983), but the place of 'nomads' (or 'pastoralists') in the origins of Israel has not been given up (see further at §8.4.2). Now, however, there is a much more sophisticated understanding of the question, though some of the anthropological studies one still sees cited have been superseded.

Earlier discussions especially focused on the work of J. R. Kupper, J. T. Luke, and M. B. Rowton (see the summary in Kamp and Yoffee 1980: 90–2). Unfortunately, models were developed on these studies by biblical scholars who were apparently unaware of the wide range of nomadic/pastoralist modes of living (Irons and Dyson-Hudson [eds] 1972; Nelson [ed.] 1973; Kamp and

Yoffee 1980: 92–4; Lemche 1985: 84–163; Khazanov 1994; Staubli 1991; Salzman 1980a, 1980b, 2002, 2004; Szuchman [ed.] 2009). The main problem was the assumption of bipolar opposites: sedentary/nomadic, agriculturalist/pastoralist, rural/urban, village/city (Mohammed 1973; Kamp and Yoffee 1980: 93; Lemche 1985: 198–201). This is despite the fact that a number of researchers recognized that pastoralists and farmers generally had a mutually beneficial relationship and usually lived together in harmony.

What was often forgotten was that 'pastoral nomad' covers a wide spectrum of living modes, from those who grow crops alongside their animal husbandry and have close contacts with the settled community to those who live away from the settled areas and have a very mobile way of life. Philip Salzman summarizes the situation, by saying that we must reject an evolutionary view that

> would not at all correspond to life in the Middle East and North Africa, where nomadization and sedentarization have been ongoing complementary processes for millennia.... People settled when it seemed beneficial to do so and became nomadic for the same reason.... We must also keep in mind that 'settled' and 'nomadic', rather than being two types, are better thought of as opposite ends of a continuum with many gradations of stability and mobility. [Salzman 2004: 34]

He suggests a model of sedentarization that is much more nuanced to the realities of actual groups studied by modern anthropologists:

> it is necessary to propose a further model…in which sedentarization is seen not so much as a forced, coerced, unavoidable process, to which no conceivable alternative but annihilation could exist, but rather as (in very many cases) a voluntary, uncoerced shift from one available pattern to another in response to changing pressures, constraints, and opportunities both internal and external to the society.

Salzman (2004: 23–41) went on to make a number of proposals that give a perspective rather different from that found in many writings on the subject. Listed here are some of the ones that seem most relevant (my own formulation):

- Nomadism is a way of coping with a situation of scarce and unpredictable resources.
- Nomads do not usually concentrate on only one activity of production such as pastoralism but combine it with other activities such as grain cultivation, arboriculture, viticulture, fishing, or trading. There are nomadic agriculturalists as well as nomadic pastoralists.
- Nomadism is not necessarily connected to political structure or economic situation. The nomads' relationship to the political and economic situation varies greatly from community to community.
- Nomads vary considerably in structure, from egalitarian, acephalus, decentralized peoples to weak chiefdoms to very hierarchical and centralized entities. Nomadic pastoralists tend to be the former (decentralized) and in the more remote regions, while the more centralized and hierarchical tend to be sedentary or associated with agricultural settlements, cities, etc.

- Nomads are not a particular kind of people but a variety of peoples who use a particular strategy (household mobility) to carry out productive activities and to defend themselves. Nomadism is not their life goal or *raison d'être*: they migrate to live. Given other circumstances they might choose a non-nomadic way of life.
- Those that we call 'nomads' might in other contexts go by a variety of other names: peasants, warriors, tribal people, peaceful civilians. The label 'nomad' (or 'pastoralist') captures only a portion of their way of life, characteristics, and identity.
- If, as will be argued in a later chapter (§8.4), Israel and Judah developed from a variety of indigenous peoples who settled in the highlands, it is likely that this mixture included pastoralists and transhumants. Thus, the study of 'nomads' in its broadest sense is still relevant to early Israel, but the great variety of types, lifestyles, and combinations has to be recognized.

6.3.3.2 Canaan/Canaanites

B. J. Collins (2007) 'The Bible, the Hittites, and the Construction of the "Other"', in D. Groddek and M. Zorman (eds), *Tabularia Hethaeorum: Hethitologische Beitrage, Silvin Kosak zum 65. Geburtstag*: 153–61; **A. Gilan** (2013) 'Hittites in Canaan? The Archaeological Evidence', *BN* 156: 39–52; **L. L. Grabbe** (1994) '"Canaanite": Some Methodological Observations in Relation to Biblical Study', in G. J. Brooke, A. H. W. Curtis, and J. F. Healey (eds), *Ugarit and the Bible: Proceedings of the International Symposium on Ugarit and the Bible, Manchester, September 1992*: 113–22; **R. S. Hess** (1998) 'Occurrences of "Canaan" in Late Bronze Age Archives of the West Semitic World', in S. Izre'el, I. Singer and R. Zadok (eds), *Past Links: Studies in the Languages and Cultures of the Ancient Near East*: 365–72; **H. A. Hoffner** (1969) 'Some Contributions of Hittitology to Old Testament Study', *Tyndale Bulletin* 20: 27–55; **idem** (1973) 'The Hittites and Hurrians', in D. J. Wiseman (ed.), *Peoples of Old Testament Times*: 197–228; **N. P. Lemche** (1991) *The Canaanites and Their Land: The Tradition of the Canaanites*; **idem** (1996) 'Where Should We Look for Canaan? A Reply to Nadav Na'aman', *UF* 28: 767–72; **idem** (1998) 'Greater Canaan: the Implications of a Correct Reading of EA 151:49-67', *BASOR* 310: 19–24; **N. Na'aman** (1988a) 'Canaanites and Perizzites', *BN* 45: 42–7; **idem** (1994a) 'The Canaanites and their Land: A Rejoinder', *UF* 26: 397–418; **idem** (1994b) 'The Hurrians and the End of the Middle Bronze Age in Palestine', *Levant* 26: 275–91; **idem** (1994c) 'The "Conquest of Canaan" in the Book of Joshua and in History', in I. Finkelstein and N. Na'aman (eds), *From Nomadism to Monarchy: Archaeological and Historical Aspects of Early Israel*: 218–81; **idem** (1999) 'Four Notes on the Size of Late Bronze Canaan', *BASOR* 313: 31–7; **A. Rainey** (1996) 'Who Is a Canaanite? A Review of the Textual Evidence', *BASOR* 304: 1–15; **I. Singer** (2006) 'The Hittites and the Bible Revisited', in A. M. Maeir and P. de Miroschedji (eds), *'I will Speak the Riddles of Ancient Times': Archaeological and Historical Studies in Honor of Amihai Mazar on the Occasion of His Sixtieth Birthday*: 723–56; **J. Van Seters** (1972) 'The Terms "Amorite" and "Hittite" in the Old Testament', *VT* 22: 64–81.

The biblical text uses 'Canaan' and 'Canaanite' in a variety of ways. The Hebrew language is once referred to as the 'lip of Canaan' (Isa. 19:18). The 'land of Canaan' is the common way of referring to the area on the western side of the Jordan, even after Israel had supposedly taken over and settled that region. The 'Canaanites' are sometimes the inhabitants of the land of Canaan, but sometimes they are just another tribe among the tribes who inhabit the land of Canaan (Exod. 23:23, 28; 33:2; 34:11; Josh. 12:8; 24:11; Ezra 9:1; Neh. 9:8). The Canaanites (sometimes listed as several different tribes [see below]) are the traditional enemies of the Israelites and also the bad example of the traits and practices that they are to avoid (Lev. 18:3; Deut. 12:29-31; 18:9). N. P. Lemche (1991) makes a good case for the biblical picture of the Canaanites being a literary construct, based on certain ideologies. If he is correct, one cannot rely on the Bible for information on the historical Canaanites.

Lemche goes on to argue that in other sources as well the term 'Canaan/ites' had no precise geographical or ethnic content. Contrary to Lemche, however, original sources from the second millennium BCE and elsewhere indicate a geographical content to Canaan and Canaanite that is as specific and meaningful as many other such names in the texts (Na'aman 1994a, 1999; Hess 1998; Killebrew 2005: 93–148; Rainey 1996; cf. the response in Lemche 1996, 1998). There appears to be no difference in the many references in the Amarna letters to 'Canaan/ites' and to other geographical or ethnic entities. Many passages are not very specific, of course, but a 'passport' from the king of Mitanni to the 'kings of Canaan' to allow his messenger to pass (EA 30) must have had some practical purpose. Similarly, a number of the texts available are legal texts, such as a note of indebtedness in which the debtor is identified as a 'man of Canaan' (LÚ URU $Ki\text{-}in\text{-}a\text{-}ni_7{}^{\text{KI}}$: Rainey 1996: 3; Na'aman 1999: 32). A letter to Amenhotep IV from the king of Babylon addresses the issue of some of his merchants that were killed in Canaan (EA 8). Finally, the phrase 'cities of Canaan' seems to be parallel to the 'cities of the king' and also 'lands of the king' and 'mayors of the king' (EA 131, 137, 227, 237, 272, 281, 286, 326, 362). There is no question, from the Amarna letters, that Canaan was a known geographical entity.

Lemche (1991: 152) makes the point that no one would have referred to himself as a Canaanite. Whether that is true is debatable (cf. Na'aman 1994a: 408), though it might be true if the term was primarily a geographical designation. But there are many examples in history of a group of people who are known mainly by a name – even a pejorative name – given to them by outsiders (for example, the names given to the Sioux Indians and the Eskimos in North America meant 'enemy'). The present-day trend to call aboriginal groups by their own designation does not negate the fact that the group had an identity – even an ethnic identity – in spite of the use of a name that they themselves might have rejected. Also, we do not have to know precise borders to a geographical area or territory before the name has meaning. How many of us could give a precise delineation of the Sahara, even though we all know basically what it refers to?

From the indication in the Egyptian, Ugaritic, and Mesopotamian sources 'Canaan' referred to what we call Palestine and Phoenicia (Killebrew 2005: 94). In the LBA sources Canaan corresponded to the Egyptian 'province' in Asia, which encompassed the territory south of the Eleutherus River (Nahr el-Kebir), including Palestine and Phoenicia, to a line just north of Berytus/Beirut (Na'aman 1994). To the east it went as far as Damascus. The territory excluded Ugarit, but Qadesh and Amurru initially fell into it, though they later came under Mitanni and then Hittite rule.

The biblical text's references to Canaanites sometimes appears to be generic, including all the inhabitants of the land of Canaan (Gen. 12:6; Deut. 11:30; 21:1; Josh. 3:10; 5:1; 17:16, 18; Judg. 1:9-17, 27-33). At other times, the Canaanites seem to be just one of a number of peoples living in the land: Kenites, Kenizzites, Kadmonites, Hittites, Perizzites, Rephaim, Amorites, Canaanites, Girgashites, Jebusites (Gen. 15.19-21); Canaanites, Hittites, Amorites, Perizzites, Hivites, Jebusites (Exod. 3:8; 23:23; 34:11; Deut. 20:17; Josh. 9:1; Judg. 3:5); Hittites, Girgashites, Amorites, Canaanites, Perizzites, Hivites, Jebusites (Deut. 7:1; Josh. 24:11); Canaanites, Hittites, Perizzites, Jebusites, Ammonites, Moabites, Egyptians, Amorites (Ezra 9:1). Also of interest are the Horites, though these are associated with Seir/Edom and do not feature in the other lists (Gen. 14:6; 36:20-30; Deut. 2:12, 22). How are we to understand these lists? Na'aman (1994b; 1994c: 239–43) argues that a major displacement of peoples occurred at the end of the LBA, at which time a number of 'northerners' migrated into Palestine, including a number of peoples from Anatolia, such as the Hittites, Hivites, Girgashites, and Jebusites (the Perizzites are so far unattested outside the Bible). If so, far from being enemies of Israel, they may have been one of the constituents of the developing ethnic group in the Palestinian highlands (see next section: §6.3.4).

But other scholars are very sceptical of such a migration (cf. Collins 2007: 160–1; Hoffner 1969: 30–2; 1973: 214–16; Van Seters 1972). Part of the problem is that all these 'Hittites' have Semitic names (Hoffner 1969: 32–3; 1973: 214). On the other hand, a number of figures do seem to have Hurrian names: Abdi-Heba of Jerusalem in the Amarna period (EA 285-90), Araunah (2 Sam. 24:16-24), possibly Uriah 'the Hittite' (2 Samuel 11). B. J. Collins (2007: 160) argues that there was no actual memory of the Anatolian peoples of the LBA in these lists: what they evidence is not historical accuracy but a 'shared literary patrimony'. These were just names remembered as enemies of Israel who had to be displaced. Forming a 'negative counter-identity', they were peoples 'against which a collective Israelite identity could be constructed' (Collins 2007: 160). After surveying the archaeological evidence, I. Singer (2006: 754) concludes, 'The archaeological evidence seems hardly sufficient to prove the presence of northern Hittites in Palestine' (cf. also Gilan 2013). What little there is seems to relate to diplomacy and gift exchange.

In any case, we can be sure that within that territory of Canaan was a variety of ethnic groups. Perhaps all the inhabitants of this region had a tribal or ethnic name for themselves, in which case 'Canaanite' was an outsider's term for any inhabitant of the region. If so, our term 'Canaanite' as a contrast with 'Israelite' is nonsense: Israelites were as much Canaanite as anyone else (Grabbe 1994). Most of the references to Canaanite/Canaanites seem to be geographical and support Killebrew's decision to use it as a purely geographical term. Yet the term seems to be ethnic in the biblical text (and this might also be the case in a few ancient Near Eastern passages). It is easy to explain this as a misunderstanding, especially in the light of other biblical distortions with regard to the historical Canaanites. But there is enough imprecision in our data to make us back away from dogmatic statements. 'Canaan/ite' had meaning in antiquity, but whether we yet have the precise usage pinned down might still be debated. The ironic thing is that probably our most extensive example of Canaanite literature is the Hebrew Bible (Grabbe 1994).

From present data the most certain conclusion is that 'Canaan' and 'Canaanite' were geographical terems and designated anyone in that region. It is also archaeological convention to use 'Canaanite' to refer to the material culture in Palestine that preceded the Phoenician (Sharon/Gilboa 2013).

6.3.3.3 'Apiru/Ḫaberu

> **M. Greenberg** (1955) *The Ḫab/piru*; **N. P. Lemche** (1992) 'Ḫabiru, Ḫapiru', *ABD* 3:6-10; **O. Loretz** (1984) *Habiru-Hebräer: Eine sozio-linguistische Studie* über *die Herkunft des Gentiliziums* 'ibrî *vom Appellativum* ḫabiru; **N. Na'aman** (1986) 'Ḫabiru and Hebrews: The Transfer of a Social Term to the Literary Sphere', *JNES* 45: 271–88; **idem** (1988) Review of O. Loretz, *Habiru-Hebräer, JNES* 47: 192–4.

One term that appears several times in second millennium texts is '*Apiru* or possibly *Ḫapiru* or *Ḫaberu* (Greenberg 1955; Na'aman 1986; Lemche 1992; Gottwald 1979: 397–409; Loretz 1984 [but see the review of Na'aman 1988]), often written in cuneiform with the Sumerograms SA.GAZ; Ugaritic: *'pr*; Egyptian *'prw*. When these texts were first studied a century or so ago, it was assumed that it was an ethnic term related to 'Hebrew'. As has become clear in recent years, the word is not an ethnic term but a social one (Na'aman 1986; Lemche 1992). The word seems originally to mean someone outside the social system or an outlaw (Gottwald 1979: 401, 404) or a refugee or migrant (Na'aman 1986; Lemche 1992).

Many modern scholars agree that the term *Apiru* and 'Hebrew' are cognate, but that neither was originally an ethnic term but a social designation. In the early texts it appears to have a merely descriptive meaning of 'migrant'. People were always temporarily in this category because they would soon be integrated into the (new) society and location. Yet migrants often took on employment that might be considered marginal by the natives, such as becoming mercenaries. Or on occasion they might become brigands as the easiest or even the only way to survive. Idrimi, king of Alalakh, joins the *Apiru* when he himself becomes a refugee (*ANET* 557; Greenberg 1955: 20):

> An evil deed happened in Halab, the seat of my family, and we fled to the people of Emar…. (So) I took with me my horse, my chariot, and my groom, went away and crossed over the desert country and even entered into the region of the Sutian warriors…. but the next day I moved on and went to the land of Canaan. I stayed in Ammia in the land of Caanan [*sic*]; in Ammia lived (also) natives of Halab, of the country Mukishkhi, of the country Ni' and also warriors from the country Ama'e…. There I grew up and stayed for a long time. For seven years I lived among the Hapiru-people. [*ANET* 557]

In the Amarna letters many of those labelled *Apiru* seem to have sold themselves as mercenaries to the highest bidder, while others turned to raiding or stealing. Therefore, the term not infrequently has a pejorative connotation along the lines of 'outlaw' or 'bandit', and was used of one's enemies, regardless of whether they were truly *Apiru* (EA 68; 185; 186). In some cases, the writer accuses fellow kings of city-states of siding with the *Apiru* or employing them against the Pharaoh's interests (EA 286; 287; 288, 289) or asserts that the *Apiru* would take over (EA 366) or even that the rulers themselves are becoming *Apiru* (EA 67; 288). In the biblical text the word has become an ethnic term, used by Israelite and Judahite writers only for themselves, or by outsiders such as the Philistines, perhaps as a way of satirizing the outsiders (Na'aman 1986). In some passages in the laws, however, it seems to have much of the original base meaning of one who was likely to be vulnerable and poor and in need of legal protection, perhaps even a slave (Exod. 21:2; Deut. 15:12; Jer. 34:9, 14).

6.3.3.4 Shasu (Shosu, Š3św, Sutu)

B. C. Benz (2016) *The Land before the Kingdom of Israel: A History of the Southern Levant and the People Who Populated It*; **R. Giveon** (1965) 'The Shosu of Egyptian Sources and the Exodus', *Proceedings of the World Congress of Jewish Studies, 1965, Volume 1*: 193–6; **idem** (1971) *Les bédouins Shosou des documents égyptiens*; **H. Goedicke** (1987) 'Anastasi VI 51-61', *SAK* 14: 83–98; **M. G. Hasel** (1998) *Domination and Resistance: Egyptian Military Activity in the Southern Levant, ca. 1300–1185 BC*; **J. K. Hoffmeier, T. W. Davis, and R. Hummel** (2016) 'New Archaeological Evidence for Ancient Bedouin (Shasu) on Egypt's Eastern Frontier at Tell el-Borg', *Ägypten und Levante* 26: 285–311; **T. E. Levy** (2009b) 'Pastoral Nomads and Iron Age Metal Production in Ancient Edom', in J. Szuchman (ed.), *Nomads, Tribes, and the State in the Ancient Near East: Cross-Disciplinary Perspectives*: 147–77; **T. E. Levy, R. B. Adams, and A. Muniz** (2004) 'Archaeology and the Shasu Nomads: Recent Excavations in the Jabal Hamrat Fidan, Jordan', in R. E. Friedman and W. H. C. Propp (eds), *Le-David Maskil: A Birthday Tribute for David Noel Freedman*: 63–89; **A. F. Rainey** (2001) 'Israel in Merenptah's Inscription and Reliefs', *IEJ* 51: 57–75; **D. B. Redford** (1990) *Egypt and Canaan in the New Kingdom*; **idem** (1992a) *Egypt, Canaan, and Israel in Ancient Times*; **W. A. Ward** (1972) 'The Shasu "Bedouin": Notes on a Recent Publication', *JESHO* 15: 35–60.; **idem** (1992a) 'Shasu', *ABD* 5:1165–7; **M. Weippert** (1974) 'Semitische Nomaden des zweiten Jahrtausends: Über die Š3św der ägyptischen Quellen', *Bib* 55: 265–80, 427–33.

A group referred to in a number of Egyptian texts (Giveon 1971; Hasel 1998: 217–36) are the *Š3św*, usually transcribed as *Shasu* or *Shosu* (Redford 1990: 68–75; 1992a: 269–80; Weippert 1974; Ward 1972, 1992); Akkadian texts, such as the Amarna tablets, seem to refer to the same group as *Sutu* (EA 16; 122; 123; 169; 195; 297; 318; however, Benz [2016] has reservations as to whether they should be equated). Sety I conducted an Asian campaign in which he defeated the *Shasu* from the fortress of Sile to (the city of) Canaan (= Gaza?) (*ANET* 254). In a frontier report from the Papyrus Anastasi VI (*ANET* 259; Giveon 1971: text 37) the *Shasu* tribes are allowed to pass the fortress with their cattle (see further below).

Several texts mention geographical areas associated with the *Shasu* (Giveon 1971: texts 6a; 16a): 'the land of the Shasu Samath' (*t3 š3św smt*; *šsw smt*), 'the land of the Shasu Yahu' (*t3 š3św Yh*[*w*]; *šsw yhw*), 'the land of the Shasu Trbr' (*t3 š3św trbr*); 'Seir (in the land of) the Shasu' (*šsw s'rr*); 'Laban (in the land of) the Shasu' (*šsw rbn*); *šsw psps* 'Pyspys (in the land of) the Shasu'; *šsw wrbwr* 'Arbel (?) (in the land of) the Shasu'. They are often associated with the area of southern Transjordan in Egyptian texts (Redford 1992a: 272–3). Ramesses II claimed to have destroyed the land of the *Shasu* and captured the mountain of Seir (Giveon 1971: text 25). These texts seem to concentrate the location of the *Shasu* in the area of Edom, Seir, and Transjordan east of the Arabah, but it is also clear that *Shasu* came from all over Canaan. Reference is often made to a text which mentions *Shasu* of Edom bringing their cattle into the Delta for water and pasturage (Giveon 1971: text 37). Without going into discussion of when and how such nomadic herdsmen were allowed across the border, there is a question of whether they could have driven their animals across 500 km from the Dead Sea region to Egypt. This has led H. Goedicke (1987) to argue that the 'Edom' in this text must refer to a location much closer to the border with Egypt. Goedicke has a point; on the other hand, we have little context: these *Shasu* might possibly have been driving their livestock over such a long distance because of conditions in their home area of Edom and hope of better pasturage, etc., in the Delta.

But the question is complicated by the fact that *Shasu* are mentioned in lists that include toponyms from other areas, some as far away as Mesopotamia (Giveon 1971: texts 4, 5, 6, 7, 48). Also, Ramesses II's version of the battle of Qadesh refers to the capture of two *Shasu* who were spying for the Hittites (Giveon 1971: text 14). None of these examples proves that Shasu came from other regions, since the topographical lists have diverse names, and the spies accompanying an army would not necessarily remain in their home territory. But another list seems to include mainly names from northern Palestine or northern Syria (Giveon 1971: text 13; cf. text 12); however, since not all sites can be identified, it is not decisive. From the data so far known, it is argued that the *Shasu* tend to be associated (though not exclusively) with a specific area around the southern and eastern part of the Dead Sea (Redford 1992a: 272–3).

This raises an important question: do the *Shasu* simply represent groups with a particular lifestyle (i.e., herding and transhumance nomadism), or is this a designation for a particular ethnic group? For example, we have Ward's statement (1992) that the *Shasu* represent 'not an ethnic group but rather a social class'. Some texts seem to refer to a particular lifestyle of pastoralism. Yet as just noted, some texts seem to refer to an ethnic group centring on a particular region. In this case, a social class is not usually said to be a people and to have their own country, while the text and the normal determinative used with the *Shasu* indicate both a people and a territory.

It also often seems to be assumed that the *Shasu* were all pastoral nomads (or just labelled 'nomads' or 'semi-nomads'). The question of nomads generally was discussed above (§6.3.3.1), but as noted in the discussion, nomadic pastoralism covers a wide-ranging spectrum and can include those who raise crops, engage in trade, or even go raiding or robbing caravans, alongside their livestock husbandry. A nomadic lifestyle would have been best suited to the desert fringe around the southern end of the Dead Sea, but the *Shasu* may also have inhabited more fertile areas and engaged in farming, arboriculture, raiding, trade, and perhaps even copper smelting (see §6.3.3.5). One Egyptian inscription does say that Ramesses III destroyed the 'tents' (*ihrw*) of the *Shasu*, using the common Semitic term *'hl* 'tent' (Hebrew אהל; Giveon 1971: text 38; Hasel 1998: 224). But it is not at all established from the few texts that we have of the *Shasu* that their lifestyle was exclusively nomadic: we do not appear to have enough information from texts or archaeology to be definitive. The *Shasu* did not just wander around indiscriminately but made up a *Shasu* country or territory (though, as we saw above, nomadic pastoralists do not just 'wander' but migrate purposefully). Although we know that pastoralism was characteristic of some or possibly even most *Shasu*, we cannot say that this was the sole means of livelihood for all of them: pastoralism is part of the general way of living among settled peoples as well. But some inscriptions seem to suggest that the *Shasu* also lived in towns (Giveon 1971: 114–15 [text 32]; 240–1).

Perhaps the hottest debate has to do with whether the Israelites arose from the *Shasu*. Such has been proposed by Rainey (2001) and Redford (1990: 73–5; 1992a: 267–80). This origin for Israel is partly based on the reliefs associated with Merenptah's supposed conquests (§6.3.4). Some argue that the 'Israel' of the inscription is to be identified with the *Shasu* of the reliefs. Yet F. J. Yurco

(1986; 1997: 28–42) argues that the fourth panel shows Egyptians fighting the Israelites who are distinguished in dress and appearance from the *Shasu*. Both conclusions go far beyond the evidence. It seems that the texts distinguish the Israelites, Canaanites, and Shasu. This does not mean that both *Shasu* and Canaanites could not have joined the settlers who became Israel, but once Israel had its own identity (as indicated by the Merenptah reference) it was seen as separate from both the Canaanites and *Shasu*. See further the discussion in relation to the Merenptah inscriptions in the next main section (§6.3.4).

6.3.3.5 'Nomadic' Copper Producers

E. Ben-Yosef (2010) *Technology and Social Process: Oscillations in Iron Age Copper Production and Power in Southern Jordan*; **idem** (2012) 'Environmental Constraints on Ancient Copper Production in the Aravah Valley: Implications of the Newly Discovered Site of Khirbet Manaʻiyah in Southern Jordan', *TA* 39: 186–202; **idem** (2019) 'The Architectural Bias in Current Biblical Archaeology', *VT* 69: 361–87; **E. Ben-Yosef, T. E. Levy, T. Higham, M. Najjar, and L. Tauxe** (2010) 'The Beginning of Iron Age Copper Production in the Southern Levant: New Evidence from Khirbat al-Jariya, Faynan, Jordan', *Antiquity* 84: 724–46; **E. Ben-Yosef, R. Shaar, L. Tauxe, and H. Ron** (2012) 'A New Chronological Framework for Iron Age Copper Production at Timna (Israel)', *BASOR* 367: 31–71; **P. Bienkowski** (1992) 'The Beginning of the Iron Age in Southern Jordan: A Framework', in P. Bienkowski (ed.), *Early Edom and Moab: The Beginning of the Iron Age in Southern Jordan*: 1–12; **I. Finkelstein** (1995) *Living on the Fringe: The Archaeology and History of the Negev, Sinai and Neighbouring Regions in the Bronze and Iron Ages*; **idem** (2005) 'Khirbet en-Nahas, Edom and Biblical History', *TA* 32: 119–25; **I. Finkelstein and E. Piasetzky** (2008) 'Radiocarbon and the History of Copper Production at Khirbet en-Naḥas', *TA* 35: 82–95; **L. G. Herr and M. Najjar** (2001) 'The Iron Age', in B. MacDonald, R. Adams, and P. Bienkowski (eds), *The Archaeology of Jordan*: 323–45; **T. Higham, J. van der Plicht, C. B. Ramsey, H. J. Bruins, M. A. Robinson, and T. E. Levy** (2005) 'Radiocarbon Dating of the Khirbat en-Nahas Site (Jordan) and Bayesian Modeling of the Results', in T. E. Levy and T. Higham (eds), *The Bible and Radiocarbon Dating: Archaeology, Text and Science*: 164–78; **E. A. Knauf** (1988) *Midian: Untersuchungen zur Geschichte Palästinas und Nordarabiens am Ende des 2. Jahrtausends v. Chr.*; **idem** (1992) 'The Cultural Impact of Secondary State Formation: The Cases of the Edomites and Moabites', in Piotr Bienkowski (ed.), *Early Edom and Moab: The Beginning of the Iron Age in Southern Jordan*: 47–54; **T. E. Levy** (2009b) 'Pastoral Nomads and Iron Age Metal Production in Ancient Edom', in J. Szuchman (ed.), *Nomads, Tribes, and the State in the Ancient Near East: Cross-Disciplinary Perspectives*: 147–77; **T. E. Levy, R. B. Adams, and A. Muniz** (2004) 'Archaeology and the Shasu Nomads: Recent Excavations in the Jabal Hamrat Fidan, Jordan', in R. E. Friedman and W. H. C. Propp (eds), *Le-David Maskil: A Birthday Tribute for David Noel Freedman*: 63–89; **T. E. Levy, R. B. Adams, M. Najjar, A. Hauptmann, J. D. Anderson, B. Brandl, M. A. Robinson, and T. Higham** (2004) 'Reassessing the Chronology of Biblical Edom: New Excavations and ^{14}C Dates from Khirbat en-Nahas (Jordan)', *Antiquity* 302: 865–79; **T. E. Levy, M. Najjar, J. van der Plicht, N. G. Smith, H. J. Bruins, and T. Higham** (2005) 'Lowland Edom and the High and Low Chronologies: Edomite State Formation, the Bible and Recent Archaeological Research in Southern Jordan', in T. E. Levy and T. Higham (eds), *The Bible and Radiocarbon Dating: Archaeology, Text and Science*: 129–63; **T. E. Levy and T. Higham (eds)** (2005) *The Bible and Radiocarbon Dating: Archaeology, Text and Science*; **T. E. Levy, M. Najjar, and E. Ben-Yosef (eds)** (2014) *New Insights into the Iron Age Archaeology of Edom, Southern Jordan: Surveys, Excavations, and Research from the University of California, San Diego & Department of Antiquities of Jordan, Edom Lowlands Regional Archaeology Project (ELRAP)*; **E. J. van der Steen and P. Bienkowski** (2005) 'Radiocarbon Dates from Khirbat en-Nahas: A Methodological Critique'; **idem** (2005–6) 'How Old Is the Kingdom of Edom?'; **idem** (2006) 'Radiocarbon Dates from Khirbat en-Nahas: A Methodological Critique', *Antiquity* 80 (no. 307): [no pagination].

At first glance it might seem strange to include a section on copper production in the list of 'groups', but recent study indicates that copper was being produced by nomadic groups at the southern end of the Dead Sea, possibly in the Late Bronze, but especially in the early Iron Age. An important aspect of the economy at this time was copper production and the regional commerce involving it. Therefore, at this point we need to discuss those who produced copper in this region. This centred primarily on the Arabah around the sites of Khirbat en-Nahas and Wadi Faynan (or Feinan). Yet copper was also produced elsewhere, including Khirbet Manaʻiyah in southern Transjordan and Timna in the southern Negev (Ben-Yosef 2012; Ben-Yosef et al. 2012). According to several hypotheses, control of the copper supply was the primary driver behind a number of events in the Late Bronze/Iron I (see further at §7.6).

The excavations at Khirbat en-Nahas and the application of ^{14}C analysis to samples taken from slag heaps have given a new perspective (Levy/Najjar/Ben-Yosef [eds] 2014; Levy et al. 2004; Levy et al. 2005; Higham et al. 2005). They point to two crucial physiographic attributes: (1) an abundant ore deposit that allowed major copper mining and production, and (2) a landscape divided between highlands, with some sections having sufficient rainfall to provide fertile agricultural land, and lowlands that could be farmed only with irrigation but also containing the copper deposits. Copper from the Negev became important in Iron Age I when the disruption of international trade stopped Egypt and the Levant from receiving the metal from Cyprus. The debate about early Edomite chronology seems to have been partially settled by radiocarbon dating (so Levy et al. [2004] argue) because their sampling shows that copper working at Faynan took place at least as early as the tenth century BCE, with an expansion from about 950 BCE (Higham et al. 2005: 177). This metal production occurred over a century or a century and a half but ceased by the end of the ninth century.

I. Finkelstein (2005; Finkelstein/Piasetzky 2008) argued against Levy et al. (2004), who had concluded that Edom became a state as early as the tenth century BCE; Finkelstein sets this event in the late eighth century at the earliest. He dates the beginning of copper production at Khirbat en-Nahas to the late twelfth century BCE, after the collapse of trade in copper with Cyprus. Levy et al. (2005: 160) replied to Finkelstein, making the point that the fortress at the site associated with metal production was to be dated to the mid-ninth century at the latest and thus pre-Assyrian (with contemporary radiocarbon dates found at satellite sites) and that the fortress at Khirbat en-Nahas did not exist in the eighth century when the Assyrian palace was extant at Busayra. But their argument relates primarily to Finkelstein's low chronology thesis in general (though they admit that the sample size is too small to resolve the issues of the low chronology [Levy et al. 2005: 158]). In fact, the early dating of metal working at Faynan seems to provide some support for Finkelstein in his debate with Bienkowsky over whether Edom was settled in the early Iron period (Levy et al. 2005: 158).

Also, some of the conclusions of Levy et al. have been strongly critiqued by E. J. van der Steen and P. Bienkowski (2005, 2005–6, 2006). One area of particular focus is the technical side of ^{14}C dating and Bayesian analysis. They argue that the figures of Levy et al. look to be skewed to give a result about a century earlier than normal calibration would lead to. Attempts to clarify by Levy et al. have not laid these concerns to rest. A further question relates to the conclusion from the Khirbat en-Nahas excavations that 'perhaps the emergence of the kingdom of Edom…began some 200–300 years earlier than previously assumed' (Levy et al. 2005: 157). This seems to ignore the level of settlement evidence known from actual excavations and surveys (Herr/Najjar 2001: 338; Bienkowski 1992: 3). The existence of metalworking does not contradict the other archaeology nor necessarily imply a complex social organization in Edom at this time. E. A. Knauf (1992: 49) – who had anticipated some of the Khirbat en-Nahas Project's findings – argued that the Faynan mining concern was controlled from west of the Wadi Arabah during the Iron I, a point also made by van der Steen and Bienkowski (2005, 2005–6). Neither do the new radiocarbon dates have to confirm the statement about Edomite chiefs in Gen. 36:31 (Levy et al. 2005: 158; similarly Finkelstein 1995: 136). The argument that Genesis 36 is a description of the situation in the seventh or sixth century is still a strong one (e.g., Knauf 1992: 49).

Now we come to the important question of who was producing this copper. Archaeologists have been reluctant to credit nomadic peoples with this technology, but the evidence suggests that it is justified in this case (cf. Ben-Yosef 2019). Granted that nomads often leave few archaeological remains in the areas where they move, studies show that they can still have sophisticated technical knowledge and skills. In the case of copper production, it appears that some of those labelled Shasu by the Egyptians may have been the ones who were selling them copper at the end of the Late Bronze Age, after the copper supply from Cyprus dried up (Ben-Yosef 2014: 207, 371; Levy/Adams/Muniz 2004). The new information from Khirbat en-Nahas is to be welcomed and will no doubt have implications for the history of Edom, but it has to be evaluated with other evidence.

6.3.3.6 Conclusions about Ethnic and Other Groups
These groups were mostly non-ethnic, though there is still a question about the *Shasu*. 'Canaan/ite' was a territorial term, designating the territory of what later would be Palestine and Phoenicia (but did not take in Ugarit). Anyone living in that region could be called a Canaanite. Israelites were originally Canaanites, only later rejecting that designation for themselves; the Hebrew Bible represents the largest piece of Canaanite literature, in spite of its negative picture of that group. The term *Apiru* was used to refer to those outside the accepted social sphere and could refer to migrants and marginal people and uprooted individuals, including those who fled the civilized area to live in wilderness areas. It was a term also used of outlaws and bandits and frequently had a negative connotation. This was because such people might find it necessary to live by stealing and raiding inhabited areas. On the other hand, they could be found useful to hire as mercenaries or to carry out

questionable activities. The term *Shasu* (sometimes *Sutu*) was usually applied to pastoralists who often inhabited marginal territory. Yet some references to them suggest cities and settled territory, and some even suggest tribes and other identity reminiscent of ethnic groups. The curious thing is that those in copper production in the Arabah seem originally to have been nomadic pastoralists, perhaps even being called *Shasu* in other contexts. As we shall see (§8.4.1), these various groups all look to have fed into those settling in the hill country who were eventually to become the kingdom of Israel.

6.3.4 The Origins of Israel and the Merenptah Stela: Where Did Israel Come from?

M. R. Abbas (2017) 'The Town of Yenoam in the Ramesside War Scenes and Texts of Karnak', *Cahiers de KARNAK* 16: 329–41; **idem** (2020) 'The Canaanite and Nubian Wars of Merenptah: Some Historical Notes', *Égypte Nilotique et Méditerranéenne* 13: 133–49; **S. Ahituv** (1984) *Canaanite Toponyms in Ancient Egyptian Documents*; **W. G. Dever** (2001) *Who Were the Early Israelites and Where Did They Come From?*; **M. Dijkstra** (2011) 'Origins of Israel between History and Ideology', in B. Becking and L. L. Grabbe (eds), *Between Evidence and Ideology: Essays on the History of Ancient Israel read at the Joint Meeting of the Society for Old Testament Study and the Oud Testamentisch Werkgezelschap, Lincoln, July 2009*: 41–82; **idem** (2016) 'Canaan in the Transition from the Late Bronze to the Early Iron Age from an Egyptian Perspective', in L. L. Grabbe (ed.), *The Land of Canaan in the Late Bronze Age*: 59–89; **O. Eissfeldt** (1975) 'Palestine in the Time of the Nineteenth Dynasty: (a) The Exodus and Wanderings', in I. E. S. Edwards, C. J. Gadd, N. G. L. Hammond and E. Sollberger (eds), *The Cambridge Ancient History: Volume II, Part 2 History of the Middle East and the Aegean Region c. 1380-1000 B.C.*: 307–30; **M. Görg** (2001) 'Israel in Hieroglyphen', *BN* 106: 21–7; **M. G. Hasel** (1994) 'Israel in the Merneptah Stela', *BASOR* 296: 45–61; **idem** (1998) *Domination and Resistance: Egyptian Military Activity in the Southern Levant, ca. 1300–1185 BC*; **idem** (2003) 'Merenptah's Inscription and Reliefs and the Origin of Israel', in B. A. Nakhai (ed.), *The Near East in the Southwest: Essays in Honor of William G. Dever*: 19–44; **idem** (2004) 'The Structure of the Final Hymnic-Poetic Unit on the Merenptah Stela', *ZAW* 116: 75–81; **idem** (2008) 'Merenptah's Reference to Israel: Critical Issues for the Origin of Israel', in R. S. Hess, G. A. Klingbell, and P. J. Ray Jr (eds), *Critical Issues in Early Israelite History*: 47–59; **idem** (2009) 'Pa-Canaan in the Egyptian New Kingdom: Canaan or Gaza?', *JAEI* 1.1: 8–17; **I. Hjelm and T. L. Thompson** (2002) 'The Victory Song of Merneptah, Israel and the People of Palestine', *JSOT* 27: 3–18; **J. K. Hoffmeier** (2007) 'What Is the Biblical Date for the Exodus? A Response to Bryant Wood', *JETS* 50: 225–47; **K. A. Kitchen** (2004) 'The Victories of Merenptah, and the Nature of their Record', *JSOT* 28: 259–72; **O. Margalith** (1990) 'On the Origin and Antiquity of the Name "Israel"', *ZAW* 102: 225–37; **N. Na'aman** (1977) 'Yeno'am', *TA* 4: 168–77; **idem** (1994c) 'The "Conquest of Canaan" in the Book of Joshua and in History', in I. Finkelstein and N. Na'aman (eds), *From Nomadism to Monarchy: Archaeological and Historical Aspects of Early Israel*: 218–81; **D. Nestor** (2015) 'Merneptah's "Israel" and the Absence of Origins in Biblical Scholarship',

CBR 13: 293–329; **A. Niccacci** (1997) 'La stèle d'Israël: grammaire et stratégie de communication', in M. Sigrist (ed.), *Études égyptologiques et bibliques à la mémoire du Père B. Couroyer*: 43–107; **A. F. Rainey** (2001) 'Israel in Merenptah's Inscription and Reliefs', *IEJ* 51: 57–75; **D. B. Redford** (1986b) 'The Ashkelon Relief at Karnak and the Israel Stela', *IEJ* 36: 188–200; **A. R. Schulman** (1987) 'The Great Historical Inscription of Merenptah at Karnak: A Partial Reappraisal', *JARCE* 24: 21–34; **I. Singer** (1988) 'Merneptah's Campaign to Canaan and the Egyptian Occupation of the Southern Coastal Plain of Palestine in the Ramesside Period', *BASOR* 269: 1–10; **P. van der Veen** (2012) 'Berlin Statue Pedestal Reliefs 21687 and 21688: Ongoing Research', *JAEI* 4.4: 41–2; **P. van der Veen, C. Theis, and M. Görg** (2010) 'Israel in Canaan (Long) before Pharaoh Merneptah? A Fresh Look at Berlin Statue Pedestal Relief 21687', *JAEI* 2.4: 15–25; **F. J. Yurco** (1986) 'Merenptah's Canaanite Campaign', *JARCE* 23: 189–215; **idem** (1997) 'Merenptah's Canaanite Campaign and Israel's Origins', in E. S. Frerichs and L. H. Lesko (eds), *Exodus: The Egyptian Evidence*: 27–55.

The name 'Israel' first occurs in the Merenptah Stela (so far, at least, though some have proposed earlier appearances; see below). The question naturally arises: what was the origin of the group called Israel? Was it to be identified with one of the groups found elsewhere in the Egyptian and other texts or did it have a separate origin? This remains an important question and one that still lies at the core of a major debate. It is also one of the fundamental questions being considered in the present study. Various researchers have attempted to equate Israel with one of the groups known from Bronze Age sources. First of all, we can note that one identification now seems obvious, though it was once resisted and still is by some: Israel was a Canaanite entity. 'Canaanite' was not an ethnic term but a geographical one. All the inhabitants of Canaan, regardless of their ethnic origin, were Canaanites: from all we can see, in the light of present evidence, is that the Israel in the Merenptah inscription was a Canaanite group.

The Merenptah inscription was found at Karnak and dates to that pharaoh's fifth year (conventionally dated to 1207 BCE, though Kitchen insists it is 1209/1208). It has the only reference to Israel until the ninth-century Assyrian inscriptions. Recently, it has been claimed that the name 'Israel' also occurs in other Egyptian inscriptions, the Berlin Statue Pedestal Reliefs 21687 and 21688, which are variously dated to Ramesses II or even earlier, in the 18th Dynasty (Görg 2001; Veen 2012; Veen/Theis/Görg 2010). The names 'Ashkelon' and 'Canaan' occur, as in the Merenptah inscription. The problem is that the name identified as 'Israel' is partially obliterated. The proponents attempt to reconstruct the name as *i͗-3-š3-i-r*. The final *r* may stand for *l*, as is often the case with foreign words and names that have an *l* in them. The main problem is that the third element should be *-šr-*. The sign *3* in these names normally stands for a vowel, but the proponents cite some examples where *3* seems to stand for *r*.

J. K. Hoffmeier (2007: 241–2) very much opposes this reading, arguing that the reconstructed name is 'plagued by serious linguistic and orthographic problems that preclude it from being Israel'. The proponents give examples that allow them to reconstruct the reading as *İ3-šr-il*, though some will question portions of their argument. But even then there are still problems with the second element in the name; their response is hardly convincing: they simply ask, what other name could it be? The other explanation is that Egyptian scribes might not have known how to pronounce the

Semitic name or how to write it. This is a patent case of speculation and circular reasoning. Granted, a plausible explanation is given for each anomaly in the reconstruction, but the whole adds up to an unconvincing case overall: a convincing identification would not have needed such elaborate explanations. It is always possible that the name 'Israel' will turn up in an earlier inscription, but so far no convincing case has been made for such.

Moving back to the Merenptah inscription, accompanying the Merenptah reference to Israel are reliefs from the Karnak temple that have been associated with some of the events described in the poem (on these, see below). Most of the inscription is about Merenptah's defeating the Libyans who attempted to conquer Egypt, along with help they received from a revolt in Nubia. It is only at the very end that statements are made about other peoples supposedly conquered by Merenptah, one of whom seems to be Israel (translation of Redford [1986b: 197]; textual quote from Niccacci 1997: 64):

> Tjehenu is seized, Khatte is pacified,
> Pekana'an (Gaza) is plundered most grievously
> Ashkelon is brought in and Gezer captured,
> Yeno'am is turned into something annihilated,
> Israel is stripped bare, wholly lacking seed!
> [*Ysr3r fk(w) bn prt.f*]
> Kharu has become a widow for Egypt
> And all lands are together at peace.

A number of points call for comment. The name read 'Pekana'an' above is often taken to be the region or land of Canaan, which may be the case, but in some inscriptions it refers specifically to the city of Gaza. It does not seem to be certain which is referred to here. 'Kharu' seems to be a synonym of Canaan and would be a sort of summing up of the previous lines. Ashkelon and Gezer are the known cities in southern Palestine. More of a problem is Yeno'am/Yenoam whose location is not certain. Several possibilities have been mooted (cf. Ahituv 1984: 198–200), including southern Lebanon or across the Jordan; however, much can be said for its being in the region of Beth-Shean (Abbas 2017; Na'aman 1977). What these all suggest is that 'Israel' is in the area of Canaan, though exactly where is not specified; also, Transjordan cannot be ruled out.

Although the reading 'Israel' (for Egyptian *Ysr3r*) has been widely accepted, not everyone agrees. For example, the name *Ysr3r* has been read as 'Jezreel', as well as some less credible renderings (Eissfeldt 1975; Margalith 1990: 228–30; Hasel 1998: 195–8; Hjelm/Thompson 2002: 13–16). From a philological point of view, this seems an unlikely reading, as do some of the other suggestions (Hasel 1998: 197–8; Kitchen 2004: 270–1). All in all, it seems that the reference to Israel is reasonably secure. Much debate has centred around the determinative (cf. Yurco 1986: 190 n. 3; Hasel 1998: 198–9). The other three names have the three-hills and throw-stick signs, which are normally used for a foreign territory, whereas Israel has a seated man and woman with the throw-stick, which suggests a people rather than a fixed geographical site. These data have been used in arguments about Israel's origins (§8.4). Another question concerns the phrase 'his seed is not' (*bn prt.f*). It has often been taken metaphorically to refer to 'descendants, offspring' (e.g., Niccacci 1997: 92–3), but recently it has been argued that this means 'grain', suggesting that Israel is a sedentary community of agriculturists at this time (Hasel 1998: 201–3). Rainey (2001) argues strongly that it should be understood as 'descendants', though this translation is then taken as evidence for his own interpretation of how Israel originated.

The question is, is this inscription only a piece of royal propaganda – a triumph-hymn – with little or no historical value (cf. Hjelm/Thompson 2002)? It is one of four sorts of royal inscription and includes extravagant praise of the king as a matter of course, but this by itself does not resolve the matter because factual material is also included at relevant points in such inscriptions (Kitchen 2004: 260–5). The argument – really, more of an assertion – that Israel is only an eponym ('analogous to Genesis' Israel: the patriarch of all Palestine's peoples') ignores the determinative, which is plural and which refers to a people. According to Kitchen (2004: 271) the oft-made statement that a number of errors in determinatives are found in the inscription is incorrect. As for Israel's being paired with Kharu, this is only one possible analysis. In fact, a number of different literary structures have been seen in the passage (summarized in Hasel 1998: 257–71). There is also the question of whether *Pekana'an* refers to 'Canaan' or 'Gaza'. In spite of Hjelm/Thompson, the conclusion that this inscription 'has been considered correctly as concrete proof of an Israel in Palestine around 1200 BCE' (Lemche 1998: 75) remains the most reasonable one.

More controversial are the reliefs (Redford 1986b; Yurco 1986; 1997: 28–42; Hasel 1998: 199–201). The reliefs in question give ten different scenes: the first four are the main ones, which picture the Pharaoh triumphant in battle; the fifth pictures bound Shasu prisoners; and the sixth shows Canaanite captives being led to a chariot. Redford (1986b) has argued that the inscriptions originally related to Ramesses II and have been altered to fit later rulers, and there is no reason to associate all of them with Merneptah who was in poor health and decrepit when he came to the throne. There 'is absolutely no evidence that Merneptah attacked all these places during his short reign. To the best of our knowledge, during his rule there occurred no triumph over Khatte…nor any defeat of Gaza or Yeno'am' (Redford 1986b: 197). He goes on to conclude that the '*Shasu*' in the inscriptions from the time of Ramesses II equate to the 'Israel' of Merenptah's stela (which does not use the name '*Shasu*').

F. Yurco has argued (against Redford) that the first four reliefs can be equated with the four names in the inscription (Yurco 1986; 1997: 28–42). In other words, scene 1 describes the conquest of Ashkelon; scene 2, of Gezer; scene 3, of Yano'am; and scene 4, of Israel. He concludes that the scenes pictured agree with the determinative that accompanies each name, with the first three shown as cities and the fourth (Israel) as a people but no city. Yurco's argument that the reliefs are to be ascribed to Merneptah seems to have won over some (cf. Kitchen 2004: 268–70) – though Redford maintains his position (1992a: 275 n. 85). But the equation of the reliefs with the four names in the inscription is rather less secure (Rainey 2001: 68–74). In only the first scene is the site named (Ashkelon), but no names are found in scenes 2–4. Also, it may be that there were once other scenes on the wall that are now missing because of deterioration of the structure. Thus, the relating of specific names to specific scenes is much more hypothetical than Yurco seems to allow.

The interpretation of the reliefs is important to the various scholarly antagonists primarily because of the identity of the peoples being defeated. Yurco's main concern seems to focus on the dress of those fighting the Egyptians. He argues that the defeated Israelites have the typical dress of the Canaanites, providing evidence that Israel was like (and thus arose from) the Canaanites. Rainey

(2001: 72–4) argues that, on the contrary, the Israelites are to be identified with another group who are pictured in scene 5: the Shasu (also Redford 1986b: 199–200). Although this seems to be a definite possibility, Redford's arguments for a positive identification seem to be no stronger than those of Yurco for the Canaanites.

M. Dijkstra (2011; 2016: 60–7) agrees with Redford that a succession of rulers copied or imitated reliefs of Ramesses II at Karnak, so that the reliefs are best seen as examples of long-term political claims about the Levant. The 'Victory' inscription is mainly about the Libyan war in which the Libyan leader used elements of the Sea Peoples as mercenaries. The Sea Peoples are not always easy to distinguish from the Shasu, and the lower register on the wall seems to picture a standard coalition of Asiatics, Shasu, and representatives of the Sea Peoples. There is considerable doubt about a clear parallelism between the reliefs and the text, and we cannot be sure that an attempt is being made to represent Israel. Israel was on the margin of Egypt's interest until at least 1100 BCE.

Finally, there is the question of where Israel is supposed to reside. A number have asserted that it refers to the hill country (e.g., Dever 2001: 118–19). Kitchen (2004) argues that each name refers to a section of Palestine: Ashkelon to the coast, Gezer to the inland area, Yanoʻam to the Galilee; therefore, Israel would refer to the hill country. This is far from cogent. There is nothing in the inscription to suggest that the individual names were meant to refer to a specific part of the country – Merneptah may just be listing sites and peoples (supposedly) conquered. Also, the sections of Palestine listed for the first three names by Kitchen do not cover all the territory except the hill country: what of the Valley of Jezreel, the Jordan Valley, the Negev, the Transjordanian region, the plain of Sharon, and so on? N. Na'aman (1994c: 247–9) points out that it is possible that the author mentioned the cities first and then the people, so there was no sequential listing. The conjectured location is highly speculative: some put 'Israel' in the area of Shechem, but the Egyptians called it 'the land of Shechem' or 'the mountain of Shechem'; putting Israel in Manasseh is nothing more than guesswork. In conclusion, it is 'best to refrain from building on this isolated reference any hypothesis concerning the location and formulation of Israel at that time' (Na'aman 1994c: 249). Thus, no argument so far presented has been able to pin down the exact location in the land of this entity Israel. Ultimately, the only thing we can say is that the inscription proves there was an entity called 'Israel' in Palestine about 1200 BCE. This is an important datum, but it does not allow us to be certain of where it was located (if indeed there was a single location) or the precise organization or status of this entity 'Israel'.

Therefore, we are thrown back on other considerations, many of which are inferential or speculative. But this pushes us back to Merenptah's statement (if it is his). He lists the names of three cities, each with a determinative for 'city' (throw-stick plus mountain symbol); however, 'Israel' has the determinative for 'people' (throw-stick plus a seated man and woman). As noted above, the argument that the scribe is inconsistent in his use of determinatives has been rejected by specialists. If so, then Israel is a people, not a city; it is, as some have argued, a kinship group rather than a group associated with a particular city (see further at §8.5.1 on Israel as a kinship group). If this 'people' had a specific territory, no indication is given in the inscription. Thus, all we can conclude is that Israel is a people but no specific location is indicated for it.

6.4 THE QUESTION OF THE EXODUS

R. Albertz (1994) *A History of Israelite Religion in the Old Testament Period*; **M. Bietak** (1987) 'Comments on the "Exodus"', in A. F. Rainey (ed.), *Egypt, Israel, Sinai: Archaeological and Historical Relationships in the Biblical Period.*: 163–71; **R. Cohen** (1981) 'Excavations at Kadesh-barnea 1976–1978', *BA* 44: 93–107; **idem** (1997) 'Qadesh-barnea', *OEANE* 4: 365–7; **F. M. Cross** (1973) *Canaanite Myth and Hebrew Epic*; **F. M. Cross and D. N. Freedman** (1955) 'The Song of Miriam', *JNES* 14: 237–50; **G. I. Davies** (1979) *Way of the Wilderness: A Geographical Study of the Wilderness Itineraries in the Old Testament*; **idem** (1983) 'The Wilderness Itineraries and the Composition of the Pentateuch', *VT* 33: 1–13; **idem** (1990) 'The Wilderness Itineraries and Recent Archaeological Research', in J. A. Emerton (ed.), *Studies in the Pentateuch*: 161–75; **idem** (2004) 'Was There an Exodus?', in J. Day (ed.), *In Search of Pre-exilic Israel: Proceedings of the Oxford Old Testament Seminar*: 23–40; **W. G. Dever** (1997) 'Is There any Archaeological Evidence for the Exodus?', in E. S. Frerichs and L. H. Lesko (eds), *Exodus: The Egyptian Evidence*: 67-86; **idem** (2003) *Who Were the Early Israelites and Where Did They Come From?*; **idem** (2009) 'Merenptah's "Israel", the Bible's, and Ours', in J. D. Schloen (ed.), *Exploring the* Longue Durée: *Essays in Honor of Lawrence E. Stager*: 89–96; **D. V. Edelman** (1998) 'The Creation of Exodus 14–15', in I. Shirun-Grumach (ed.), *Jerusalem Studies in Egyptology*: 137–58; **M. Fieger and S. Hodel-Hoenes** (2007) *Der Einzug in Ägypten: Ein Beitrag zur alttestamentlichen Josefsgeschichte*; **I. Finkelstein and N. A. Silberman** (2001) *The Bible Unearthed: Archaeology's New Vision of Ancient Israel and the Origin of the Sacred Texts*; **E. S. Frerichs and L. H. Lesko (eds)** (1997) *Exodus: The Egyptian Evidence*; **A. H. Gardiner** (1909) *The Admonitions of an Egyptian Sage*; **idem** (1918a) 'The Delta Residence of the Ramessides', *JEA* 5: 127–38, 242–71; **idem** (1918b) 'The Supposed Egyptian Equivalent of the Name of Goshen', *JEA* 5: 218–23; **idem** (1920) 'The Ancient Military Road between Egypt and Palestine', *JEA* 6: 99–116; **idem** (1924) 'The Geography of the Exodus: An Answer to Professor Naville and Others', *JEA* 10: 87–96; **idem** (1933) 'Tanis and Pi-Ra'messe: A Retraction', *JEA* 19: 122–8; **M. Görg** (1997) *Die Beziehungen zwischen dem Alten Israel und* Ägypten: *Von den Anfängen bis zum Exil*; **L. L. Grabbe** (1993) 'Comparative Philology and Exodus 15,8: Did the Egyptians Die in a Storm?' *SJOT* 7: 263–9; **idem** (2000) '*Adde Praeputium Praeputio Magnus Acervus Erit*: If the Exodus and Conquest Had Really Happened….', in J. C. Exum (ed.), *Virtual History and the Bible*: 23–32; **idem** (2014) 'The Exodus and Historicity', in T. B. Dozeman, C. A. Evans, and J. N. Lohr (eds), *The Book of Exodus: Composition, Reception, and Interpretation*: 61–87; **S. I. Groll** (1998) 'The Egyptian Background of the Exodus and the Crossing of the Reed Sea: A New Reading of Papyrus Anastasi VIII', in I. Shirun-Grumach (ed.), *Jerusalem Studies in Egyptology*: 173–92; **M. Haran** (1976) 'Exodus, The', *IDBSup* 304–10; **M. G. Hasel** (1998) *Domination and Resistance: Egyptian Military Activity in the Southern Levant, ca. 1300–1185 BC*; **idem** (2003) 'Merenptah's Inscription and Reliefs and the Origin of Israel', in B. A. Nakhai (ed.), *The Near East in the Southwest: Essays in Honor of William G. Dever*: 19–44; **W. Helck**

(1965) 'Ṯkw und die Ramses-Stadt', *VT* 15: 35–48; **I. Hjelm and T. L. Thompson** (2002) 'The Victory Song of Merneptah, Israel and the People of Palestine', *JSOT* 27: 3–18; **J. E. Hoch** (1994) *Semitic Words in Egyptian Texts of the New Kingdom and Third Intermediate Period*; **Y. Hoffman** (1989) 'A North Israelite Typological Myth and a Judaean Historical Tradition: The Exodus in Hosea and Amos', *VT* 19: 169–82; **idem** (1998) 'The Exodus – Tradition and Reality: The Status of the Exodus Tradition in Ancient Israel', in I. Shirun-Grumach (ed), *Jerusalem Studies in Egyptology*: 193–202; **J. K. Hoffmeier** (1997) *Israel in Egypt: The Evidence for the Authenticity of the Exodus Tradition*; **idem** (2005) *Ancient Israel in Sinai: The Evidence for the Authenticity of the Wilderness Tradition*; **J. S. Holladay, Jr** (2001) 'Pithom', *OEAE* 3: 50–3; **G. Hort** (1957) 'The Plagues of Egypt', *ZAW* 69: 84–103; **idem** (1958) 'The Plagues of Egypt', *ZAW* 70: 48–59; **K. A. Kitchen** (1992b) 'Exodus, The', *ABD* 2: 700–708; **idem** (1998) 'Egyptians and Hebrews, from Raʻamses to Jericho', in S. Aḥituv and Eliezer D. Oren (eds), *The Origin of Early Israel – Current Debate: Biblical, Historical and Archaeological Perspectives*: 65–131; **E. A. Knauf** (1988) *Midian: Untersuchungen zur Geschichte Palästinas und Nordarabiens am Ende des 2. Jahrtausends v. Chr.*; **idem** (2010) 'Exodus and Settlement', in L. L. Grabbe (ed.), *Israel in Transition: From Late Bronze II to Iron IIA (c. 1250–850 BCE): Volume 2, The Text*: 241–50; **C. R. Krahmalkov** (1994) 'Exodus Itinerary Confirmed by Egyptian Evidence', *BAR* 20, no. 5: 55–62, 79; **T. E. Levy, T. Schneider, and W. H. C. Propp (eds)** (2015) *Israel's Exodus in Transdisciplinary Perspective: Text, Archaeology, Culture, and Geoscience*; **B. MacDonald** (2000) *'East of the Jordan': Territories and Sites of the Hebrew Scriptures*; **A. Malamat** (1997) 'The Exodus: Egyptian Analogies', in E. S. Frerichs and L. H. Lesko (eds), *Exodus: The Egyptian Evidence*: 15–26; **E. F. Morris** (2005) *The Architecture of Imperialism: Military Bases and the Evolution of Foreign Policy in Egypt's New Kingdom*; **N. Na'aman** (1994) 'The "Conquest of Canaan" in the Book of Joshua and in History', in I. Finkelstein and N. Na'aman (eds), *From Nomadism to Monarchy: Archaeological and Historical Aspects of Early Israel.*: 218–81; **E. W. Nicholson** (1973) *Exodus and Sinai in History and Tradition*; **M. Noth** (1962) *Exodus*; **M. de Odorico** (1995) *The Use of Numbers and Quantifications in the Assyrian Royal Inscriptions*; **E. D. Oren** (1984) 'Migdol: A New Fortress on the Edge of the Eastern Nile Delta', *BASOR* 256: 7–44; **E. B. Pusch** (2001) 'Piramesse', *OEAE* 3:48–50; **I. Rabinowitz** (1956) 'Aramaic Inscriptions of the Fifth Century B.C.E. from a North-Arab Shrine in Egypt', *JNES* 15: 1–9; **G. von Rad** (1965) 'The Form-Critical Problem of the Hexateuch', in *The Problem of the Hexateuch and other Essays*: 1–78; **D. B. Redford** (1963) 'Exodus I 11', *VT* 13: 401–18; **idem** (1987) 'An Egyptological Perspective on the Exodus Narrative', in A. F. Rainey (ed.), *Egypt, Israel, Sinai: Archaeological and Historical Relationships in the Biblical Period*: 137–61; **idem** (1990) *Egypt and Canaan in the New Kingdom*; **idem** (1992a) *Egypt, Canaan, and Israel in Ancient Times*; **idem** (2009) 'The Land of Ramesses', in P. J. Brand and L. Cooper (eds), *Causing his Name to Live: Studies in Egyptian Epigraphy and History in Memory of William J. Murname*: 175–7; **C. A. Redmount** (1995) 'The Wadi Tumilat and the "Canal of the Pharaohs"', *JNES* 54: 127–35; **D. A. Robertson** (1972) *Linguistic Evidence in Dating*

Early Hebrew Poetry; **A. R. Roskop** (2011) *The Wilderness Itineraries: Genre, Geography, and the Growth of Torah*; **B. D. Russell** (2007) *The Song of the Sea: The Date of Composition and Influence of Exodus 15:1-21*; **S. C. Russell** (2009) *Images of Egypt in Early Biblical Literature: Cisjordan-Israelite, Transjordan-Israelite, and Judahite Portrayals*; **B. U. Schipper** (2015) 'Raamses, Pithom, and the Exodus: A Critical Evaluation of Ex 1:11', *VT* 65: 265–88; **B. E. Scolnic** (2004) 'A New Working Hypothesis for the Identification of Migdol', in J. K. Hoffmeier and A. Millard (eds), *The Future of Biblical Archaeology: Reassessing Methodologies and Assumptions*: 91–120; **W. H. Stiebing** (1989) *Out of the Desert? Archaeology and the Exodus-Conquest Narratives*; **E. P. Uphill** (1968) 'Pithom and Raamses: their Location and Significance', *JNES* 27: 291–316; **idem** (1969) 'Pithom and Raamses: their Location and Significance', 28: 15–39; **D. Ussishkin** (1995) 'The Rectangular Fortress at Kadesh-Barnea', *IEJ* 45: 118–27; **J. Van Seters** (2011) 'The Geography of the Exodus', in *Changing Perspectives I: Studies in the History, Literature and Religion of Biblical Israel*: 115–33; **J. Vergote** (1959) *Joseph en Égypte: Genèse Chap. 37–50 à la Lumière des Études Égyptologiques Récentes*; **W. A. Ward** (1992b) 'Goshen', *ABD* 2:1076–7; **J. Weinstein** (1997) 'Exodus and Archaeological Reality', in E. S. Frerichs and L. H. Lesko (eds), *Exodus: The Egyptian Evidence*: 87–103; **T. F. Wei** (1992) 'Pithom', *ABD* 5:376–7.

6.4.1 Issues relating to Historicity

For the final section in this chapter, we need to investigate the historicity of the exodus. The idea that the ancestors of Israel were in Egypt for a period, that they were oppressed, that they came out of Egypt 'with a high hand' (Exod. 14:8), and that they entered the Promised Land after a period in the wilderness is a major concept in the biblical text. According to the Bible the exodus and the 40 years in the wilderness were the prelude to the invasion and settlement of Canaan. This scenario is still given credence by some conservative scholars, and it is difficult to deal with the settlement while ignoring the exodus. Finally, the exodus tradition became a strong one in later parts of the Bible and has a powerful resonance in later Judaism and Christianity. This section will summarize some of the points and arguments made in Grabbe 2014, which should be consulted for further details (see also Levy/Schneider/Propp [eds] 2015). The basic question is, how historical is the exodus account. Several issues are involved:

1. The exodus tradition in the biblical text is late. The vast bulk of the Pentateuchal text describing the exodus and related events seems to be quite late (Albertz 1994: 23–4, 42–5: 'exilic or early post-exilic'). The question is whether the exodus is presupposed in early texts. It was once widely argued that the exodus was embodied in certain passages quoting an early Israelite 'credo' (von Rad 1965), but subsequent study suggested that some of these passages (e.g., Deut. 6:21-23; 26:5-9; Josh. 24:2-13) were actually late (Nicholson 1973: especially 20–7). Some point out that Hosea (12:1; 13:4), for example, presupposes the exodus tradition. Not everyone is confident any longer in such literary analysis; in any case, this would take us back only to the eighth century, long after the alleged event.

2. The tradition is clothed in a thick layer of mythical interpretation, and attempts to interpret it naturalistically generally fail. The Pharaoh is a generic figure, without a name. A series of ten miracles is enacted – and attempts to find naturalistic explanations (e.g., Hort 1957) miss the point: the aim of the narrative is to magnify the power of Yhwh and his servant Moses. According to the plain statement of the text, 600,000 men of military age came out; with the elderly, women, and children, the number would have been at least three or four million (Grabbe 2000). The crossing of the Red Sea seems to mix a more naturalistic account, in which an east wind moves the waters (Exod. 14:21), with a more miraculous one in which the sea divides and the water stands on either side like walls (Exod. 14:22-29). F. M. Cross (1973: 121–44) attempted to argue that a naturalistic account, in which the Egyptians died in a storm as they pursued the Israelites across the sea in boats, is reflected in Exod. 15:7, but his philological analysis is flawed (Grabbe 1993). Thus, even if Exodus 15 is an example of early poetry as some argue (e.g., Robertson 1972; Cross/Freedman 1955; Cross 1973: 121–44), it does not appear to give a picture different from the surrounding narrative (for the argument that Exodus 15 is not early, see Noth 1962). The biblical text does not provide any particular time for Israel's coming out of Egypt, and a number of the dates assigned to the event depend on data not really relating to the exodus itself (e.g., the settlement, the Merneptah stela).

3. Semitic peoples in Egypt. A number of Egyptian texts from the second millennium BCE mention peoples who were non-Egyptian and probably Semitic (see the survey in a previous chapter [§2.4.4; Malamat 1997]). None of the 'Asiatics' mentioned in Egyptian texts is referred to in such a way as to make one identify them with Israelites (though see the discussion above on the Shasu at §6.3.3.4). In the Old Kingdom, at least, they often settled in the northeastern part of the Delta, the general area where the family of Jacob was supposedly assigned land. On the other hand, there are several aspects of the biblical tradition that do not accord with a New Kingdom context:

- No Egyptian texts at this time suggest a subjected ethnic element because there was no threat of invasion from the east (as there was in the Late Period).
- The duties given to the Israelites, such as making bricks, do not match the types of work in which Asiatics were normally employed.
- The assimilation of Asiatics into Egyptian society, known from the late New Kingdom, has no place in the exodus narrative (Redford 1987: 146–8).

What it does indicate is that the idea of people from Syro-Palestine – including possibly ancestors of the Israelites – living for a time in Egypt is not in and of itself problematic.

4. The Merneptah stela (see §6.3.4 for a full discussion). Appeals to this text as evidence for the exodus are very problematic. The inscription provides no evidence for any sojourn in Egypt for those identified in the text as 'Israel'; on the contrary, this entity appears to be in Palestine.

5. Lack of references in Egyptian texts (Frerichs/Lesko 1997; Davies 2004). There is nothing in Egyptian texts that could be related to the story in the book of Exodus. It is not just a question of the official ignoring of defeats of the Pharaoh and his army. There is no period in the second half of the second millennium BCE when Egypt was subject to a series of plagues, death of children, physical disruption of the country, and the loss of huge numbers of its inhabitants. Occasionally, a scholar has seen a remarkable resemblance between Moses and an Egyptian official, but the arguments have not met widespread acceptance. At most, one could say that a memory of the Egyptian figure was used to create the figure of Moses in the biblical text. G. I. Davies (2004) surveys about all the evidence available, but little of it is very compelling; indeed, he finds the attempts to equate the exodus tradition with certain figures known from Egyptian sources as 'not very convincing'. Thus, his conclusion that the exodus 'tradition is apriori unlikely to have been invented' appears tacked on rather than arising from his data. The situation can be summarized as follows:

- No Egyptian document, inscription, or piece of iconography depicts, describes, or refers to an exodus as described in the Bible. The use of the Ipuwer Papyrus in some lay circles is completely misconceived (cf. §2.1), but it creates problems for anyone arguing for an exodus anything like that described in the biblical narrative. The Israelite narrator never puts a name to the pharaoh nor to any of the other Egyptians, a surprising omission if we were dealing with a contemporary historical document. As D. B. Redford (1987: 138–9) has pointed out, when Isaiah and Jeremiah refer to Egyptological matters, it has the feel of authenticity: 'it is at once familiar and precise'. This is not the case with the exodus narrative where the Egyptian colouring is almost entirely geographical.
- The Amarna texts do not describe a situation in Palestine anything like the narrative in Joshua or Judges (cf. §6.3.2). This rules out an exodus before the mid-fourteenth century BCE, contra some conservatives who still opt for a fifteenth-century date for the exodus.
- The reference to Israel in the Merenptah stela does not presuppose an Israel anything like that of Joshua or the Judges (§6.3.4). The 'Israel' mentioned there seems to be a people not yet settled, while the country is firmly under Egyptian control. Where this Israel is located is also unclear.

6. Egyptological elements in the exodus narrative. Some have argued that elements within the text fit the period of Ramesses II (Hoffmeier 1997), but this is not sufficient; one must show that they do not fit any other period in history (see nos. 7-9 below). It has been widely accepted that there are names and other references that suggest some knowledge of Egypt in the exodus narrative, but how early are they? What is notable is that there are few incidental or accidental references to Egypt, such as one might expect, unlike some other biblical passages such as found in Isaiah and Jeremiah; most of what is present is topographical (Redford 1987: 138). More important, a number of the Egyptian elements in the exodus story are anachronistic. There is no agreement among Egyptologists about elements that could only be dated to an early period.

7. The 'land of Goshen' occurs only in late texts (Gen. 45:20; 46:28, 29, 34; 47:1, 4, 6. 27; Exod. 8:22; 9:26; Redford 1987: 138–49; Vergote 1959: 183–7; Ward 1992b; Gardiner 1918b; Hoffmeier 1997: 121). No Egyptian name is known. It was once thought that it could be related to a geographical name found in Ptolemaic texts which was read as *Gsm.t*; however, this reading has now generally been rejected because of linguistic problems. It is thus somewhat disconcerting to have the theory revived by S. I. Groll (1998: 190), though in a somewhat different form, relating Goshen to the Egyptian word *gsm* (a body of water of some sort). This is speculative, of course, and no full argumentation is given to support it. More recently a number of scholars have agreed that the name derives at a late period from the name of the Qedarite leader whose area of control evidently related to the northern Egyptian and Delta area. The name 'Geshem' (cf. Neh. 2:19; 6:1-2, 6) seems to have been borne by several individual rulers (Rabinowitz 1956). The Septuagint of Gen. 45:10 and 46:34 translates Goshen with *Gesem Arabia*. Because of the linguistic differences between Goshen and Geshem, it would be necessary to postulate dialectic variation.

8. The cities Raameses (Pi-Ramesse) and Pithom (Exodus 1:11). These form a central issue regarding historicity (Schipper 2015; Redford 1963, 2009). The first problem is identification of the sites in question. Pi-Ramesse is widely identified with Qantir (Pusch 2001; Bietak 1987: 164; Hoffmeier 1997: 117), though Redford asked where the 'Pi' (Egyptian *pr* 'house') of Pi-Ramasse had gone (1963: 408–10; 1987: 138–9; but cf. Helck 1965). Contrary to some views, the name Ramesses and Pi-Ramesse are attested long after the city of Ramesses had disappeared about the mid-eleventh century BCE (Schipper 2015: 269–72). No agreement about the identity of Pithom (Egyptian *pr-'Itm* 'the house of Atum') had been reached for a long time (Wei 1992). Many have now argued for Tell el-Maskhuta (Schipper 2015: 270; Redford 1963: 403–8; Holladay 2001), but this site was not settled between the sixteenth and the seventh centuries. The nearby site of Tell el-Ratabah is another possibility, but it was reoccupied only about 1200 BCE (Wei 1992; Dever 1997: 70–1). It is therefore difficult to understand Davies' statement, 'they are more likely as a pair to belong to a tradition that originated in the Ramesside period than to a later time' (2004: 30). If Tell el-Maskhuta was known as 'Pithom' from about 600 BCE (Schipper 2015: 270–1; Davies 2004: 30) and topographical names with 'Ramesses' were also widespread in the first millennium BCE (Schipper 2015: 269–72; Redford 1987: 139), this argues that the tradition of Exod. 1:11 was likely to be late, rather than Ramesside.

A further consideration concerns the orthography of 'Ramesses' (רעמסס) in Exod. 1:11. Redford (1963, 2009) drew attention to the name as found in the Bible (Gen. 47:11; Exod. 12:37; Num. 33:3, 5): it is spelled with a *samek*, a late transliteration, whereas an early form would have had שׁ. He was opposed by Helck (1965), but the latter did not seem to negate one of Redford's main arguments: the transcription of Egyptian *s* (*ś*) with Hebrew *samek* occurs only at a later time, after about the ninth century BCE. Redford also had the support of J. E. Hoch's study on Semitic words in Egyptian texts of the New Kingdom and Third Intermediate Period. Hoch found that in the 500 words he investigated, gleaned from a wide range of Egyptian texts (mainly from the 18th to 24th Dynasty), Egyptian *s* (*ś*) was used to transcribe Semitic [ṯ], [š], and [ś] (= Hebrew שׁ), while ס (*samek*) was used to represent Egyptian *ṯ* (pronounced *č*). If the Egyptian name Ramesses (*R'-ms-sw*) had been written in Hebrew of the fifteenth to twelfth centuries BCE, it would have had שׁ, whereas the name in the biblical text has *samek*. This shows that the Egyptian name Ramesses entered the Hebrew text no earlier than the eighth century BCE. Schipper (2015: 272–5) has now looked at the philological argument and confirmed that 'the name Ramesses in Exod. 1:11 points to the first millennium BCE' (275).

In dating the time to which the textual data point one must consider not only the sites named but also any important ones that are omitted. Particularly notable for its absence is the site with the classical name of Sile. This was a strongly fortified frontier site and armoury built in the New Kingdom and still standing in the Saite period, though by then it was replaced by Migdol as the primary border entrance (Redford 1992a: 203, 457; Hoffmeier 2005: 90–4; Morris 2005: 509–11). The Egyptian name of Sile was *Ṯrw*, known already in the Middle Kingdom and as a fortress in the reign of Tutmose III (*c.* 1479–1425 BCE). Until recently it was identified with Tell Abu Sefeh, but archaeological excavations have found no remains earlier than the Persian period. On the other hand, the site of Hebua has yielded not only New Kingdom remains but also a votive statue with the name of *Ṯrw*. Yet *Ṯrw*/Sile seems to find no place in the biblical account. On the balance of historical considerations, the data in the narrative of Exodus – and probably the narrative itself in its present form – are no earlier than the Saite period or later (eighth to fifth century BCE).

9. The supposed route of the exodus from Egypt. Some have argued that the route of the Israelites' journeyings in the Bible matches the actual topography and Egyptian settlements on the ground (Hoffmeier 2005; Krahmalkov 1994). A more careful look shows, however, that the text does not reflect the fifteenth or thirteenth centuries BCE but the seventh or eighth (MacDonald 2000: 63–100; Dever 2003: 18–20). The largest portion of the Edomite Iron Age sites that have been excavated originated only in the seventh or eighth century (Dever 1997: 75). Overall, the Negev and Transjordanian sites and settlements are mainly later than the Late Bronze (see §7.6 for a summary of the archaeology). Some of the itineraries are rather vague, showing little actual knowledge of the topography supposedly being described (Deut. 2:1-25; Num. 21:10-20), with Num. 33:1-49 going the farthest in suggesting knowledge of a real travel route (MacDonald 2000: 98). Only at the end of Iron II (but not Iron I or early Iron II) were most of the sites that can be identified actually occupied. Most scholars argue that the itineraries in Exodus and in Numbers 33 are the result of late editing of several different traditions that do not presuppose the same route (Haran 1976; Davies 1990).

10. Conquest of the Transjordanian region. Trying to extract historical data from this tradition is difficult. There is some indication, for example, that at least some of the peoples listed in the tradition are simply creations from the names of mythical figures. Some of the most feared inhabitants of the land are the Anakim who are descended from the Rephaim (Num. 13:35; cf. Deut. 1:28; 2:10, 11, 21; 9:2; Josh. 11:21-22; 14:12, 15; 15:14). One of the main figures is Og of Bashan. He is said to be from the remnant of the Rephaim and dwells in Ashtarot and Edrei (Num. 21:33-35; Deut. 1:4; 3:10-11; Josh. 9:10; 12:4; 13:12; cf. Num. 13:33). These names are significant. Other passages (such as Job 26:5; Ps. 88:11-13; Isa. 26:14, 19; Prov. 9:18), as well as the Ugaritic texts, associate the Rephaim with the dead. The god Rapha'u of a Ugaritic incantation seems to dwell in Ashtarot and Edrei (*KTU* 1.108). Thus, it appears that myth has been historicized, and the shades of the dead have been turned into ethnographical entities. The writer seems at times to have taken traditional or mythical names and used them to create a narrative about ethnic groups. There is also some evidence that the writer has drawn on topographical knowledge of the eighth or seventh centuries to draw up his list of journeys.

11. Archaeological evidence. No event of the size and extent of the exodus could have failed to leave significant archaeological remains. Israel's itinerary has already been discussed (point #7 above). According to the book of Numbers (10:11; 12:16; 13:26; 20:1, 22; 33:36) much of the 40 years of 'wandering' was spent near Qadesh-barnea. This and related sites in Sinai and southern Palestine should yield ample evidence of a large population in this region. Yet we find nothing (Finkelstein/Silberman 2001: 62–4). Qadesh (Tell el-Qudeirat) itself has been extensively excavated but shows no habitation between the Middle Bronze and the tenth century BCE (Cohen 1981, 1997; Dever 2003: 19–20) or even later (Ussishkin 1995a).

12. The population of Israel. Numbers in the Bible, as well as many other ancient Near Eastern texts, is a fraught question (cf. Odorico 1995). The question is often dismissed, with the statement that the numbers are of course exaggerated, or that they need to be 'translated' into something more realistic. For example, it is often asserted that 'thousand' (אלף) really meant 'family' or 'clan'; while this is true in some cases, a clan can still be a thousand or so people. But those who say this want to make the '600,000', who were men capable of military muster (Exod. 12:37), really refer to a limited collection of families. Unfortunately, this attempt to reduce the number seems to miss the point of the original writer, who wanted to emphasize the great size of the people after only a few generations. The attempt to give 'thousand' another meaning also seems to founder on the later total of 603,550, excluding the Levites, given by the census of Israelites (Num. 2:32).

Opinions about the historicity of the exodus are divided. Despite the efforts of some fundamentalist arguments, there is no way to salvage the biblical text as a description of a historical event. A large population of Israelites, living in their own section of the country, did not march out of an Egypt devastated by various plagues and despoiled of its wealth and spend 40 years in the wilderness before conquering the Canaanites. On the other hand, this does not rule out the possibility that the text contains a distant – and distorted – memory of an actual event. Some feel that the tradition is so strong in the Bible that some actual event must lie behind it, though it might well be only a small group of (slave?) escapees fleeing Egypt (a view long and widely held). The general principle was appealing, especially in light of Anastasi 5 (19.2–20.6: translation in *ANET* 259; *CoS* 3: 16) that records the example of runaway slaves (though no miracle of waters). S. I. Groll (1998) has argued that Papyrus Anastasi VIII shows an ecological disaster in the 'Reed Sea' area during the reign of Ramesses II, with a major drought. During this time some slaves were able to escape across a former body of water that had temporarily dried up.

The previous thesis can be combined with the next one. E. A. Knauf (2010) has proposed that in the first half of the twelfth century BCE refugee Israelites returned to Canaan. They were descendants of prisoners of war taken captive by Merenptah. Knauf also notes that the subsequent removal of Egyptian rule from Canaan in the late twelfth century could be considered as 'coming out of Egypt'. It was this that gave rise to the tradition of an exodus from Egypt. How these former captives left Egypt, whether by being voluntarily released or by escaping, is not known, but the mode of their escape could be responsible for some of the details of the biblical account. This is accepted even by some of those proposing theories about the indigenous origin of Israel in Canaan (see §8.4.2). Some think it might even be a hazy remembrance of the Hyksos expulsion from Egypt in the sixteenth century BCE (e.g., the Egyptologist A. Gardner [1933]).

Yet others point out that there is no necessity for assuming there was an exodus in the early history of Israel (Dever 1997: 7–21). Many scholars now agree that there is little clear evidence that the biblical tradition is an early one. There is no external evidence for such an event, and any arguments must depend on the biblical tradition; however, since we know of many Egyptian connections with Israel and Judah at later times, from the time of the monarchy to the Persian and Hellenistic periods (cf. Isa. 19:19-25; Jeremiah 42–44), this could have been sufficient to give rise to the story in the biblical text.

6.4.2 Conclusions on the Exodus

One important conclusion about the exodus arises from the earlier survey of Egyptian history (§5.1): there were very few periods during the Late Bronze Age or the Egyptian New Kingdom when Palestine was not firmly under Egyptian control. Only for a period of about half a century between Ahmose and Thutmose III (in the fifteenth century BCE) was Egypt to neglect its northern frontier and concentrate on the southern one. Also briefly in the late Amarna period, several of the kings after Akhenaten seem to have done little about Syro-Palestine, but this was only a brief period. It is in that context that Israel is first mentioned about 1208 BCE by Merenptah (some have now argued that the name occurs in earlier inscriptions, but the arguments so far are not very convincing). This shows that Israel already existed by the end of the Late Bronze Age, but what exactly that entity consisted of is uncertain, and there is the important question of where it resided.

Those who want to revert to the 'traditional dating' of the exodus in the fifteenth century BCE have no place for anything like the exodus of the Bible. That is, only if it is completely reinterpreted and immensely scaled down to a few slaves escaping from Egypt can one place it in the interstices of Egyptian history. But then it is also difficult to fit an exodus into the thirteenth century where so many want to place it! This is especially the case when we consider that Merenptah claims to have destroyed 'Israel'. Either we completely disbelieve him or we accept that Israel was a small entity, not a great people who had left an Egypt ruined by plagues and an army decimated by a tsunami, and who entered the land with powerful military contingents and took it by force. An overview of Egyptian history at this time contradicts the biblical picture, but another sort of Israel was evidently in the process of developing, one which archaeology is starting to reveal.

Israel and the Jews had associations with Egypt through a good deal of their history during the First and Second Temple periods. If we want to find times when the story of the exodus might have arisen, we do not have to go back to the Bronze Age. The Bible itself does not refer to the 'Bronze Age', the 'Ramesside period', the 'Second Intermediate Period', the 'New Kingdom', or the 'fifteenth' or 'thirteenth' century BCE. When scholars attempt to situate the events of the Pentateuch in the second millennium BCE, this is only an interpretation – and not one well founded for some events or details of the text. No Egyptian king is named in the biblical text, and no reference to the exodus or associated events is found in Egyptian texts.

Thus, when some scholars relate the exodus story to the sixth century BCE or the Saite period or the Persian period, they are not necessarily being less true to the text than some conservative evangelicals – who incidentally also happily overlook or ignore aspects of the text when they try to find a place for it in the thirteenth or fifteenth centuries BCE. One of the first things they usually try to do is explain away the textual statements about 600,000 armed men, plus women, children, and animals, coming out of Egypt on the first Passover night. Reading the biblical text as literally and/or historically true is not necessarily a better way of reading it than is reading Shakespeare as literally and/or historically true. The following points summarize some of the main conclusions arising from the present study:

- It is not sufficient to point to early elements in a text to demonstrate an early date for it. Early elements can be found in late texts, but not vice versa. Ultimately, judging the date of a text depends on a variety of factors, but the final form of a text can be no earlier than the latest element in it. In some cases, it has been argued that an early text has 'only been updated'. But how is 'updating' different from editing or revising or rewriting that literary critics have traditionally appealed to? It means that the text has been interfered with and does not necessarily reflect the data or message of the original text. Thus, when Hoffmeier states, 'the terms correspond best to Egyptian toponyms of the thirteenth century B. C.', this is hardly surprising: he has consistently rejected any interpretations or identifications that did not fit that date! His statement is a tautology.
- There is no compelling reason that the exodus has to be rooted in any events in history. It is often assumed – and stated – that no people would have traced their origins from a condition of slavery if it was not true. Yet such statements are seldom argued in any detail.

- Each generation debates its past and re-creation of ethnic history goes on constantly. Divine deliverance from bad situations has been celebrated throughout Jewish history. In some cases, the bad situation was horribly true, in other cases not; unfortunately, divine deliverance was all too seldom a historical fact.
- Yet there are a number of scenarios which could have generated the foundation of the exodus story, since Israel has engaged with Egypt throughout its history. One is Merenptah's defeat of Israel, which would have led to captives (or their descendants) that may later have been released. Another is the classic explanation that a small number of Israelite slaves escaped (this might include – but does not require inclusion of – an accompanying story about a pursuit by an Egyptian force that was swallowed up in the treacherous terrain of the Suez peninsula). Another could have been the removal of 'oppressive' Egyptian rule at the end of the Late Bronze Age.
- There are no Egyptian references of any kind that relate to Joseph, the descendants of Jacob, Moses, the ten plagues, or the exodus. It does seem strange that there is not even a hint in Egyptian literature, iconography, or legend that any of this happened. It is even stranger that there is no early archaeology relating to the Israelites in the major areas of the exodus, especially around Qadesh-barnea or further north in the Transjordanian region.
- The exodus story has a place in the Israel of the eighth century BCE or perhaps a bit earlier. Some argue that the earliest version of the story is found in Exodus 15, yet it probably does not take us much further back in time. In any case, the exodus narrative of the Pentateuch is not so early, with influences and details from a much later time. The story as we have it is not a monolith but is made up of elements from a variety of periods and milieus.
- Although there may well be early elements within the exodus narrative, some perhaps even going back to Ramesside times, the form of the story as we presently have it in Exodus and Numbers contains data that are most closely associated with the Saite and Persian periods, or about the seventh to fifth centuries BCE. Only some of the details could fit the Egyptian New Kingdom, but almost all could have a home in the Late Kingdom.

6.5 CONCLUSIONS

It was in the time frame of this chapter that we began the history of Israel proper, for in many ways, we can say that 'Israel' begins with Merenptah. Something called Israel existed in the Palestinian region about 1200 BCE, at which point it is mentioned in an inscription of Merenptah, and it appears to have been a people. Exactly where this people lived, what/who constituted it, where it got its name, and it relationship to the Israel of the Bible are all questions. Some will say that the answer is obvious, but others will point out that this is not the same as proof. The settlement in Palestine will be discussed in chap. 8, but we can note here that the biblical text is of little help in writing the history of Israel at this point (on the exodus from Egypt, see below). Once the biblical text is eliminated, we are mainly dependent on archaeology (summarized at §6.2), but we do have some inscriptions, mostly from Egypt. Especially important are the Amarna letters that give us a brief glimpse of Syria-Palestine in a quarter of a century during the fourteenth century.

The history of the region in the LBA is the history of an Egyptian appendage. It is important to bear in mind that throughout the second millennium BCE, Palestine was mostly under Egypt's thumb, first through various raids but eventually as a province and/or a series of client city-states. The Execration Texts (§4.1) give the names of some cities. There are also a few texts describing individual episodes, such as the capture of Joppa by the commander Djehuty (perhaps a legend with a historical core). The accounts of military forays into Palestine and Syria by various Egyptian kings (e.g., the taking of Megiddo by Thutmose III or the campaigns of Seti I into Palestine and Syria) were surveyed at length (§6.3.1). The story of Sinuhe also offers insights (§6.1). It is the Amarna Letters, however, that give us a real look through the keyhole into the Palestine of the fourteenth century BCE (§6.3.2). The rulers of a number of cities are named and an account (often distorted, of course) of their activities is recorded for the pharaoh by their neighbours (and rivals). Of particular interest are the kings of Shechem and Jerusalem who seem to dominate the highlands.

The picture of Palestine arising from the Amarna letters does not include Israel; at least, it does not include an Israel anything like that pictured in the Bible. The texts do testify to various groups: some ethnic but mainly social and territorial. These groupings do have implications for the origin of Israel which is finally named at the end of the LBA. Indeed, they lead us to a conclusion that would have horrified many of the early biblical writers: ancient Israel and Judah were Canaanite peoples. The Hebrew Bible is the lengthiest piece of Canaanite literature extant! Although much of it was written after the Israelites disassociated themselves from the Canaanites, Israel was a part of Canaan when it is first attested in the Merenptah stela and seems to have arisen in Canaan (though this latter conclusion is still the subject of some debate). It seems unlikely that the bulk of the Israelites came from outside the Palestinian region, in spite of the biblical tradition, though some may well have been immigrants of one sort or another. But this will be further discussed in chap. 8.

Some still invoke the exodus tradition to explain how Israel eventually came into Palestine. There is still a widespread popular view that some of the Israelites may have come into the land after a temporary sojourn in Egypt. Unfortunately, the inscriptional and archaeological data do not support such a surmise. There is not a scrap of evidence for an exodus in Egyptian inscriptions – not a mention, not a hint, not a picture that would suggest the story found in the book of Exodus. A careful study of the references in the biblical text indicates that the exodus tradition is fairly late as a concept; the texts describing the exodus are demonstrably late, probably from the Saite period (eighth to fifth centuries BCE). In the past half century, mainstream scholarship has rejected the origin of Israel in the way described in the Bible, even if some still believe that a few Israelites were enslaved in Egypt but somehow escaped and made their way into Canaan (a possibility not ruled out but one quite different from the biblical picture).

We end our survey of the LBA with the existence of an Israel, an entity thought to be clearly attested by about 1200 BCE, but what exactly it was, how it originated, and where it resided are all still major questions. These questions will be taken up in the subsequent chapters of our study.

Part IV

Early Iron Age
(*c.* 1200–900 BCE)

CHAPTER 7

Ancient Near Eastern Context, Including Syria and Transjordan (1200–900 BCE)

E. H. Cline (2014) *1177 B.C.: The Year Civilization Collapsed*; **R. Drews** (1993) *The End of the Bronze Age: Changes in Warfare and the Catastrophe ca. 1200 B.C.*; **H. Klengel** (1992) *Syria 3000 to 300 B.C.: A Handbook of Political History*; **A. Kuhrt** (1995) *The Ancient Near East c. 3000–300 BC*; **J. M. Millek** (forthcoming) *The Fall of the Bronze Age*; **W. A. Ward and M. S. Joukowsky (eds)** (1992) *The Crisis Years: The 12th Century B.C. from Beyond the Danube to the Tigris*.

The Iron Age began with the Mediterranean-wide collapse at the end of the LBA. This chapter provides the background to, and context for, the settlement and rise to nationhood of Israel in Canaan. All the surrounding nations and peoples are surveyed in this chapter, even including the Transjordanian region. What is particularly interesting is that the Iron Age I in Palestine lay in a hiatus between major exertions of the great empires to the north and south.

7.1 EGYPT

E. H. Cline and D. O'Connor (eds) (2012) *Ramesses III: The Life and Times of Egypt's Last Hero*; **P. Grandet** (1993) *Ramsès III: Histoire d'un règne*; **N. Grimal** (1992) *A History of Ancient Egypt*; **E. Hornung, R. Krauss, and D. A. Warburton (eds)** (2006) *Ancient Egyptian Chronology*; **K. A. Kitchen** (1986) *The Third Intermediate Period in Egypt (1100–650 BC)*; **G. D. Mumford** (1998) *International Relations between Egypt, Sinai, and Syria-Palestine during the Late Bronze Age to Early Persian Period (Dynasties 18-26: c. 1550–525 B.C.)*; **A. Yasur-Landau** (2010) *The Philistines and Aegean Migration at the End of the Late Bronze Age*.

The 19th Dynasty through Merenptah was outlined in an earlier chapter (§5.1). Following Merenptah were several short-reigning figures of the 19th Dynasty, some perhaps ruling simultaneously: Sety II (1202–1198 BCE); Amenmesses (1202–1200 BCE); Siptah (1197–1193 BCE), who originally had the name Ramesses-Siptah but changed it to Merenptah-Siptah during his short reign. Towsre (1192–1191 BCE), one of the wives of Sethos II, was regent (along with the chancellor Bay) for her stepson Siptah and then ruled in her own right for a year or so after his death. She brought the 19th Dynasty to a close, though attempts were made by her successors to erase her rule from history.

The 20th Dynasty began with Sethnakhte (1190–1188 BCE), who was probably a military leader, when Towsre died without issue. His son became Ramesses III (1187–1157 BCE), the second king of the dynasty and one of the most successful rulers of it (on him, see Grandet 1993; Cline and O'Connor [eds] 2012). Ramesses was threatened almost at once by a Libyan invasion in his year 5. He defeated the Libyan army, but it came against him again in year 11. This time he took many prisoners and settled them, along with their families, in Egypt as mercenaries. However, Ramesses's reign is best known for at least two alleged defeats of the Sea Peoples in his eighth year (c. 1175 or 1180 BCE; on the Sea Peoples see §7.2). Ramesses III was succeeded by his fifth son (the others all having died) who became Ramesses IV (1156–1150 BCE).

By this time Egyptian power over Canaan was weakening, but Ramesses IV might still have maintained an Egyptian toehold since scarabs of him have been found in Beth-Shean and Lachish (Yasur-Landau 2010: 316). The problem is that scarabs of Ramesses III are not followed by those of Ramesses IV in Ashkelon XII (but instead by those of Ramesses VI). The Egyptians might even have clung on to some power until Ramesses VI (1145–1139 BCE) since, as well as scarabs of him in Ashkelon XII, a statue of him was found in Megiddo: it is hardly likely that a hostile population would have erected or maintained this statue. This is why some date the Philistine settlement to a time after Ramesses VI, though this may entail a simplistic view of the Sea Peoples' migration and settlement. Ramesses VI is the last pharaoh whose name is found in inscriptions in Sinai. About this time control over Palestine was gradually lost (probably by c. 1130 BCE).

The rest of Dynasty 20 was made up further kings named Ramesses, most with short reigns. One of those who ruled for any length of time was Ramesses IX who ruled for about 18 years (c. 1129–1111 BCE). It was under him that tomb robbery became a serious problem, with several trials of perpetrators whose records are still extant. This led to royal mummies being moved around and stored in different places, a number sometimes gathered together. Ramesses X is the last king of the dynasty attested to rule over Nubia. Ramesses XI (c. 1106–1077) was the second of the long-ruling pharaohs of the dynasty. By this time the chief priests had accumulated a great deal of power, to be almost equal to that of the kings. Another way to look at it is that the power of the king had greatly diminished. It was after the death of Ramesses XI that Egypt became once more divided into north and south. The end of the 20th Dynasty saw the close of the New Kingdom.

Next was the 21st Dynasty which began the Third Intermediate Period (c. 1076–723 BCE), a period of nearly four centuries when Egypt had lost its unitary rule and had rival dynasties. The standard treatment of this chaotic period is that of K. A. Kitchen (1986). From the point of view of Israel's history to about 900 BCE, one of the main pharaohs was Shoshenq I (c. 943–923 BCE). His invasion of Syria and Palestine is discussed at §8.5.8. He began Dynasty 22 which was made up of Libyan rulers, but this dynasty was instrumental in restoring Egyptian power.

Table of Egyptian Kings to the End of the New Kingdom
(Dates in Hornung/Krauss/Warburton 2006 have been followed.)

Sety II (1202–1198 BCE).

Amenmesses (1202–1200 BCE).

Siptah (1197–1193 BCE): father unknown; ruled as a minor, with Towsre as regent.

Towsre (Twosret, Tausret) (1192–1191 BCE): wife of Sety II, who took throne after Siptah.

Sethnakhte (1190–1188 BCE): founder of the 20th Dynasty.

Ramesses III (1187–1157 BCE): claims to have defeated invasions of the Sea Peoples.

Ramesses IV (1156–1150 BCE): scarabs of him found in Beth Shean, Lachish, and Ashdod.

Ramesses V (1149–1146 BCE).

Ramesses VI (1145–1139 BCE): left statue at Megiddo.

Ramesses VII (1138–1131 BCE).

Ramesses VIII (1130 BCE).

Ramesses IX (*c.* 1129–1111 BCE): by his reign Egypt seems to have given up any sovereignty over Palestine.

Ramesses X (*c.* 1110–1107).

Ramesses XI (*c.* 1106–1077).

7.2 SEA PEOPLES

T. J. Barako (2013) 'Philistines and Egyptians in Southern Coastal Canaan during the Early Iron Age', in A. E. Killebrew and G. Lehmann (eds), *The Philistines and Other 'Sea Peoples' in Text and Archaeology*: 37–51; **S. Ben-Dor Evian** (2016) 'The Battles between Ramesses III and the "Sea-Peoples": When, Where and Who? An Iconic Analysis of the Egyptian Reliefs', *ZÄS* 143: 151–68; **idem** (2017) 'Ramesses III and the "Sea-Peoples": Towards a New Philistine Paradigm', *OJA* 36: 267–85; **T. R. Bryce** (1979) 'The Role of the Lukka People in Late Bronze Age Anatolia', *Antichthon* 13: 1–11; **idem** (2005) *The Kingdom of the Hittites*; **S. Bunimovitz** (1990) 'Problems in the "Ethnic" Identity of the Philistine Material Culture', *TA* 17: 210–22; **E. H. Cline and D. O'Connor** (2003) 'The Mystery of the "Sea Peoples"', in D. O'Connor and S. Quirke (eds), *Mysterious Lands*: 107–38; **T. Dothan and D. Ben-Shlomo** (2013) 'Mycenaean IIIC:1 Pottery in Philistia: Four Decades of Research', in A. E. Killebrew and G. Lehmann (eds), *The Philistines and Other 'Sea Peoples' in Text and Archaeology*: 29–35; **T. Dothan and A. Zukerman** (2004) 'A Preliminary Study of the Mycenaean IIIC:1 Pottery Assemblages from Tel Miqne-Ekron and Ashdod', *BASOR* 333: 1–54; **R. Drews** (1998) 'Canaanites and Philistines', *JSOT* 81: 39–61; **idem** (2000) 'Medinet Habu: Oxcarts, Ships, and Migration Theories', *JNES* 59: 161–90; **C. S. Ehrlich** (1996) *The Philistines in Transition: A History from ca. 1000–730 B.C.E.*; **I. Finkelstein** (1995b) 'The Date of the Settlement of the Philistines in Canaan', *TA*

22: 213–39; **idem** (1996b) 'The Philistine Countryside', *IEJ* 46: 225–42; **A. Götze** (1933) *Die Annalen des Muršiliš*; **D. Groddek** (2002) 'Muršili II., die großen Feste und die "Pest" Überlegungen zur Anordnung der Fragmente der späteren Jahre seiner Regierung in den AM', in S. De Martino and F. Pecchioli Daddi (eds), *Anatolia antica: studi in memoria di Fiorella Imparati*: 1:329–38; **H. G. Güterbock** (1983) 'The Hittites and the Aegean World: Part 1, The Ahhiyawa Problem Reconsidered', *AJA* 87: 133–8; **H. A. Hoffner** (2009) *Letters from the Hittite Kingdom*; **A. E. Killebrew** (2000) 'Aegean-Style Early Philistine Pottery in Canaan during the Iron I Age: A Stylistic Analysis of Mycenaean IIIC:1b Pottery and its Associated Wares', in E. D. Oren (ed.), *The Sea Peoples and their World: A Reassessment*: 233–53; **idem** (2005) *Biblical Peoples and Ethnicity: An Archaeological Study of Egyptians, Canaanites, Philistines, and Early Israel 1300–1000 B.C.E.*; **idem** (2008) 'Aegean-Style Pottery and Associated Assemblages in the Southern Levant: Chronological Implications Regarding the Tradition from the Late Bronze Age II to the Iron I and the Appearance of the Philistines', in L. L. Grabbe (ed.), *Israel in Transition: From Late Bronze II to Iron IIA (c. 1250–850 BCE): The Archaeology*: 54–71; **A. E. Killebrew and G. Lehmann (eds)** (2013) *The Philistines and Other 'Sea Peoples' in Text and Archaeology*; **G. A. Lehmann** (1979) 'Die Šikalājū – ein neues Zeugnis zu den "Seevölker"-Heerfahrten im späten 13. Jh. v. Chr. (RS 34.129)', *UF* 11: 481–94; **O. Loretz** (1995) 'Les Šerdanū et la fin d'Ougarit: À propos des documents d'Égypte, de Byblos et d'Ougarit relatifs aux Shardana'; Annexe de Jochem Kahl: 'Les témoignages textuels égyptiens sur les Shardana', in M. Yon, M. Sznycer, and P. Bordreuil (eds), *Le pays d'Ougarit autour de 1200 av. J.-C.: Histoire et archéologie, Actes du Colloque International, Paris, 28 juin–1er juillet 1993*: 125–36; **A. Mazar** (2008) 'From 1200 to 850 BCE: Remarks on Some Selected Archaeological Issues', in L. L. Grabbe (ed.), *Israel in Transition: From Late Bronze II to Iron IIA (c. 1250–850 BCE): The Archaeology*: 86–120; **A. M. Maeir (ed.)** (2012) *Tell es-Safi/Gath I: The 1996–2005 Seasons: Part 1: Text*; **J. M. Millek** (2017) 'Sea Peoples, Philistines, and the Destruction of Cities: A Critical Examination of Destruction Layers "Caused" by the "Sea Peoples"', in P. M. Fischer and T. Bürge (eds), *'Sea Peoples' Up-to-Date: New Research on Transformations in the Eastern Mediterranean in the 13th–11th Centuries BCE*: 113–40; **idem** (2020–21) '"Our City Is Sacked. May You Know it!" The Destruction of Ugarit and its Environs by the "Sea People"', *Archaeology and History in the Lebanon* 52–53: 102–32; **idem** (2021) 'Just What did They Destroy? The Sea Peoples and the End of the Late Bronze Age', in J. Kamlah and A. Lichtenberger (eds), *The Mediterranean Sea and the Southern Levant: Archaeological and Historical Perspectives from the Bronze Age to Medieval Times*: 59–98; **E. F. Morris** (2005) *The Architecture of Imperialism: Military Bases and the Evolution of Foreign Policy in Egypt's New Kingdom*; **E. Noort** (1994) *Die Seevölker in Palästina*; **D. O'Connor** (2000) 'The Sea Peoples and the Egyptian Sources', in E. D. Oren (ed.), *The Sea Peoples and the World: A Reassessment*: 85–102; **E. D. Oren (ed.)** (2000) *The Sea Peoples and the World: A Reassessment*; **A. F. Rainey** (1982) 'Toponymic Problems (cont.)', *TA* 9: 130–6; **D. B. Redford** (2000) 'Egypt and Western Asia in the Late New Kingdom: An Overview', in E. D. Oren (ed.), *The Sea Peoples and their World:*

A Reassessment: 1–20; **D. Ussishkin** (2008) 'The Date of the Philistine Settlement in the Coastal Plain: The View from Megiddo and Lachish', in L. L. Grabbe (ed.), *Israel in Transition: From Late Bronze II to Iron IIA (c. 1250–850 BCE): The Archaeology*: 203–16; **S. Wachsmann** (1982) 'The Ships of the Sea Peoples' (*IJNA* 10.3: 187–220): Additional Notes', *The International Journal of Nautical Archaeology and Underwater Exploration* 11: 291–304; **idem** (2000) 'To the Sea of the Philistines', in E. D. Oren (ed.), *The Sea Peoples and their World: A Reassessment*: 103–43; **A. Yasur-Landau** (2010) *The Philistines and Aegean Migration at the End of the Late Bronze Age*.

A general account of the Sea Peoples is given here, though the Peleset or Philistines were one of the main tribes of the Sea Peoples. As will be clear here and also in the discussion of the Philistines in the next chapter (§8.3), it is difficult to separate treatment of the Sea Peoples from that of the Philistines, especially with regard to the Philistine settlement. Thus, the analysis here and that with regard to the Philistines will of necessity overlap to some extent. Our knowledge of the Sea Peoples comes from a number of sources, especially Egyptian ones. Ramesses III's temple at Medinet Habu is very important for reliefs and inscriptions that relate to their invasion and defeat (*ANET* 262–6; *ARE* IV, §§59–82; O'Connor 2000; Wachsmann 2000), along with a few other sources of lesser importance (Redford 2000: 8). These are not straightforward historical accounts but require a fully critical approach; nevertheless, with a careful reading much can be learned (Redford 2000). The essence of Ramesses III's claims occurs in the following excerpt:

(16) …The foreign countries made a *conspiracy* in their islands. All at once the lands were removed and scattered in the fray. No land could stand before their arms, from Hatti, Kode, Carchemish, Arzawa, and Alashiya on, being cut off *at* [*one time*]. A camp [was set up] in one place in Amor. They desolated its people, and its land was like that which has never come into being. They were coming forward toward Egypt, while the flame was prepared before them. Their confederation was the Philistines, Tjeker, Shekelesh, Denye(n), and Weshesh, lands united. They laid their hands upon the lands as far as the circuit of the earth…. I organized my frontier in Djahi, prepared before them: – princes, commanders of garrisons, (20) and *maryanu*. I have the river-mouths prepared like a strong wall, with warships, galleys and coasters…. [*ANET* 262, italics and square brackets in the original]

As C. Ehrlich (1996: 9–13; cf. also Morris 2005: 694–707) indicates, there are two main interpretations of the coming of the Sea Peoples (depending heavily on the Medinet Habu inscriptions and other documents but also bringing archaeological data into the question). The 'maximalist' interpretation argues that Ramesses III fought a coalition of Sea Peoples (Peleset [Philistines], Sherden, Tjeker, Shekelesh, Denyen, Tresh and Weshesh) in both sea and land battles, defeated them and forced (or allowed) them to settle in fortresses and cities in the Palestinian (Philistine) coastal plain (Dothan and Ben-Shlomo 2013). This would have been in his eighth year (roughly 1175 BCE). This view is still found in much of secondary literature. This interpretation has since been partially contradicted by archaeology, which shows that Egyptianizing material culture preceded the coming of the Philistines in the area but disappeared with their settlement.

A second or 'minimalist' interpretation argues that the nature of Pharaonic inscriptions needs to be taken into account. Ramesses III's claims are conventional propaganda, either created from a long literary tradition or a compilation building up a minor episode into an earth-shaking threat to Egypt from which the divine Pharaoh delivered her, as was his duty and function (cf. Morris 2005: 696–9). (It should be noted that at least two of Ramesses III's campaigns celebrated in Medinet Habu, his victories over the Nubians and Asiatics, are completely made up according to Noort [1994: 108], though Morris [2005: 782–85] accepts that there was minor military interaction with Nubia.) S. Ben-Dor Evian summarizes with a view from the 'minimalist' perspective:

> The Philistines, among other 'Sea-Peoples', were displaced populations from Anatolia, Cilicia, Cyprus and Syria. Some of them were previously affiliated to the great armies of the Hittite and Syrian kingdoms of the Late Bronze Age (known as *thr*). Various groups, in search of subsistence, raided the shores of the eastern Mediterranean in the early twelfth century BCE.... Once these populations presented a real threat on the northern frontiers of the Egyptian empire, clashes between them and the Egyptians began in Ramesses III's fifth year.... The Egyptian defence was successful in maintaining the Egyptian empire in the Levant under Ramesses III.... Only after Egypt's loss of control over the Levant did new populations occupy areas in southern Canaan that were now a 'no man's land'. These new populations came from established settlements across the Levant, thus bringing with them Syrian, Egyptian and Cypriot traditions, inducing the emergence of Philistine culture known as the Bichrome phase. [Ben-Dor Evian 2017: 278–9]

The main indication of the Sea Peoples/Philistines in the coastal plain of Palestine is the material culture. Important in this discussion is locally produced Mycenaean IIIC:1 pottery (sometimes referred to as 'Philistine monochrome'). It was not itself imported but was influenced by the LH IIIC:1 pottery of the Aegean and/or Cyprus. These indicators of Philistine settlement are generally found unmixed with Egyptianizing material remains. This is important because it strongly suggests that the Philistine settlement and Egyptian rule were opposed to one another. Recently, however, scholars have emphasized the need for a more nuanced reading of the sources, which recognizes the diversity of possibilities of interpreting Philistine origins.

These leave the interpretation much more open, ultimately taking into account the material culture from the archaeology. The result for some was to argue that rather than being the result of an invading force, the Aegeanizing material culture is the product of trade. Such a conclusion illustrates the need for re-evaluating the evidence, considering new ideas and possibilities. Yet, after a period of rethinking, most researchers at present reject purely trade influence (however important it may have been in the process) but favour the idea of an outside population coming to settle in the area of Philistia, as the Egyptian inscriptions suggest, though the process was probably a more complex one than indicated by a simple reading of the Egyptian material.

Although there are many problems of interpretation, several points about the Sea Peoples emerge with a reasonable probability from the reliefs and inscriptions (cf. Redford 2000: 12–13; Morris 2005: 691–715; Yassur-Landau 2010; Killebrew 2005: 197–245):

- They came from 'islands in the midst of the sea', which meant Crete and the Aegean archipelago to the Egyptians (cf. the biblical 'Caphtor' [Amos 9.7; Jer. 47.4], which seems to mean the same thing [Drews 1998]). But other considerations suggest a variety of Mediterranean and Anatolian origins.
- They seem to have been well organized and well led (though this does not appear in the reliefs, which, by their very nature, picture defeat and chaos); however, it was not necessarily a unified movement, but was made up of different groups at different times. Five (sometimes more) tribes are listed, of which the 'Philistines' (*prst*) are only one (see the list below).
- The presence not only of warriors (the only ones pictured in the sea battle) but also of families and livestock, with household goods in ox carts, suggests the migration of peoples rather than just an army of conquest. These migrants (women, children, and elders are depicted) may have come overland.
- As noted elsewhere (§5.4.1; §5.4.2), the Egyptian and other ancient Near Eastern texts have been interpreted to conclude that the Sea Peoples assisted in bringing an end to the Hittite empire, the kingdom of Ugarit, and the city state of Amurru. More recent study has been more sceptical, but whoever caused it, there does seem to have been some violence in bringing an end to (some of) these powers. In any case, there were probably multiple causes for the downfall or destruction of these civilizations (Kuhrt 1995: 386–93; Millek 2017, 2020–21, 2021). The archaeology shows no destruction for the Phoenician area, however, which leads to the proposal that at least any march south down the coast between Byblos and Dor was more or less peaceful (Yasur-Landau 2010: 168–71).
- A sea battle seems to have taken place in the region of the Nile Delta (as *r-ḥ3wt* 'river mouths' implies), but the land battle is more of a problem. Some (e.g. Redford 2000: 13) think the land battle was also in northern Egypt, but the inscription names Djahy, which can refer to the Phoenician coast. Three permutations concerning the relationship of the land and sea battles are possible (Ehrlich 1996: 9 n. 45), but the main question relates to the land battle. Ussishkin (2008) argues that since Egypt controlled Megiddo, the land part of the movement would have been stopped in northern Palestine. Ussishkin's view is supported in some ways by the recent book by E. Morris who comments in a footnote:

> There is nothing in either the reliefs or the texts that supports the supposition ... that the land battle had occurred near the mouth of the Pelusiac branch of the Nile. Indeed, Ramesses III's referral of the matter to vassals, garrison troops, and maryannu-warriors would argue strongly against an Egyptian locale. [Morris 2005: 697 n. 16]

The strength of the 20th Egyptian Dynasty is attested by Morris (2005: 703–5) who notes the number of Egyptian fortresses and sites, yet Yasur-Landau (2010: 340) still doubts that the Egyptian garrison severely hindered the movement of the migrating Sea Peoples. Ramesses III's 'victory' might have been an attack on a few contingents of migrating peoples but hardly the bulk of them.

- There is a debate over whether the Philistines were forcibly settled in the coastal plain by the Egyptians or whether they took the area by force in spite of what the Egyptians could do. T. J. Barako (2013: 51) has recently argued, primarily from archaeology, that the 'Egyptians were not in Philistia during this period because the Philistines were there instead; and not as garrisoned prisoners-of-war but, rather, as an intrusive population hostile to Egypt'. While Morris (2005: 698–709) presents both views, he also argues that Ramesses III may well have encouraged the Sea Peoples to settle in the Philistine plain. Ben-Dor Evian (2017: 278) concludes, 'There is no textual or archaeological evidence that Philistines were ever settled by the Egyptians in Canaan. There is, however, evidence of their settlement in Egypt and in Syria soon after the battles.'
- The immigration into the Philistine coastal plain may have been a prolonged one (Yasur-Landau suggests 'a time frame of fifty to seventy-five years' [2010: 320]; Killebrew [2005: 234] suggests a century or more). This is rather wide of the single invasion and battle in Ramesses III's eighth year that the textual data and some past interpretations have given us. In any case, by the later twelfth century BCE, Egypt no longer had the strength to prevent the Sea Peoples' migration.

Now we come to another pressing question: when did the Sea Peoples settle in Palestine? This question has been given three different answers (Yasur-Landau 2010: 315–20; Killebrew 2005: 232). One theory, the 'high chronology' (or two-wave theory), would date the Mycenaean IIIC Early (Mycenaean IIIC:1b) to about 1200 BCE, the result of an early proto-Philistine wave of Sea Peoples. However, with the finding of Myc IIIC:1 pottery, a variation on this view developed that a first wave of Philistine settlement appeared perhaps in the later thirteenth century BCE, but the main settlement (with Philistine Bichrome Ware) in the early twelfth century. This 'high chronology', which was favoured by the pioneers excavating the Philistine area, Moshe and Trude Dothan, has now been generally rejected (even by Trude Dothan [see Dothan and Zukerman 2004; Dothan and Ben-Shlomo 2013]).

The most widely followed theory, the 'middle chronology', depends on Ramesses III's inscription that he defeated the Sea Peoples in his eighth year or about 1175 BCE. This would date Mycenaean IIIC Early to about 1175 BCE and the Bichrome that developed from it to the mid-twelfth century BCE. This theory is becoming more problematic in light of the increasing consensus that Mycenaean IIIC:1b should be equated to Mycenaean IIIC Early to Middle, which should be dated to the mid-twelfth century (Killebrew 2005: 232). I. Finkelstein (1995b) and D. Ussishkin (2008), however, argued for a 'low chronology', which places the initial wave after about 1140 or 1130 BCE, after the Egyptian control of the area had effectively vanished. The low chronology theorizes that Mycenaean IIIC:1b appeared only after about 1140 BCE and the date of the bichrome pottery even later, into the eleventh century.

The choice at the moment seems to be between the 'middle' and the 'low' chronologies. A brief discussion of some of the arguments can be given here. Ussishkin (2008) has pointed out that, for all practical purposes, no Philistine pottery – Monochrome or Bichrome – was found at Lachish, even though such pottery was uncovered at the not-too-distant sites of Tell eṣ-Ṣafi-Gath and Tel Miqne-Ekron. This indicates that Philistine pottery post-dates the Lachish settlement, namely, 1130 BCE.

This argument (albeit, one from silence) goes against the Mazar-Singer-Stager hypothesis that lack of Philistine pottery is due to cultural factors. The inevitable conclusion (according to Ussishkin) is that the Philistine settlement of the coastal plain must post-date 1130 BCE.

A. Mazar (2008) responds that Ussishkin's and Finkelstein's arguments that contemporary sites should yield similar pottery assemblages in a geographical zone is correct in principle but should not be rigidly applied when dealing with specific cases such as this. They claim that it is inconceivable that local Mycenaean IIIC pottery did not reach contemporary sites in Philistia and the Shephelah but, according to Mazar, this ignores cultural factors that could limit particular pottery to a few urban centres. They think lack of such pottery means a settlement gap, but such a widespread occupational gap is infeasible and also negated by finds at such sites as Gezer. The early stage of Philistine settlement lasted perhaps only a generation. Lachish is at least 25 kilometres from the major Philistine cities, sufficiently distant to create a cultural border.

These differences between archaeologists may seem confusing, but they are no more significant than those between interpretations of the inscriptional data. What we have to recognize are some major divergences between the various models for understanding the settlement of the Sea Peoples and the early history of the Philistines. The archaeology is vital, but it is also very interpretative at certain points. Yet the archaeology also provides data that seem to give a much clearer picture in certain areas. To take an example, Finkelstein (1996b) has compared the settlement patterns in the coastal plain between the LB and the IA I, which appear to lead to more definitive conclusions: in the LB the area of the coastal plain that became Philistia seems to have been the most densely populated in Palestine, with many sites of a variety of sizes (*c.* 100, covering about 175 ha, though there were more sites in the Shephelah than in the coastal plain). About 80 per cent of the IA I sites had been settled in the LB, but there had been a drastic decline in numbers, down to about half the number in the LB. On the other hand, the proportion of large sites was up (from about half to three quarters), while medium-sized sites almost disappeared. Even though the number of sites was considerably reduced, it was mainly the smaller sites that no longer existed. Because there were proportionally larger sites (even though fewer in number), the total built-up area remained much the same. The result was a major reduction in rural sites but a considerable expansion in urban settlement. Finkelstein goes on to note that the major LB sites were Gezer, Gath, Lachish, Ashkelon, Gaza and Yurza. These continued into IA I, with two exceptions: Lachish was abandoned (as was Tel Harasim), but Tel Miqne-Ekron had grown considerably.

Ashdod and Ekron appear to have been the strongest towns in the region, with Ashkelon and Gath the weakest (unless Ashkelon controlled Jaffa). The estimated population was 35,000 for LB and 30,000 for IA I. This compares with 44,000 for the central hill country in IA I (but only 2200 of these were in the Judaean Hills). Considering that few new sites were established in IA I, and the total built-up area was also very similar, this suggests that the number of new settlers – the Philistines – was not great. This confirms what a number of scholars had been arguing: the Philistines settled among the indigenous Canaanite population, perhaps as an elite. One result of this is that the material culture in the region included both Philistine and Canaanite elements (Bunimovitz 1990). But if the Philistines were so few, this argues against a major invasion force that some postulate (as large as 25,000 or 30,000, according to some).

The recent studies of the pottery by A. E. Killebrew (2008; 2005: 219–30; cf. 2000) are an important addition to our knowledge of the period. At Tell Miqne-Ekron stratum VII shows the sudden appearance of quantities of locally produced Aegean-inspired Mycenaean IIIC Early and associated assemblages. In stratum VI Mycenaean IIIC and Bichrome appear together throughout, showing the development from Mycenaean IIIC to Bichrome. Finally, in Tell Miqne-Ekron stratum V, Mycenaean IIIC disappears and Bichrome becomes the predominant decorated ware. Killebrew concludes that, with 'some minor revisions', the low chronology would best fit the dating of Mycenaean IIIC Early-Middle at other sites in the Eastern Mediterranean and would also provide a more reasonable dating of Bichrome to the eleventh century (continuing into the tenth [Killebrew 2008: 64–5; 2005: 232]). This conclusion is based on the LB II to IA I stratigraphic sequences at both Tel Miqne-Ekron and Ashdod. This seems to provide some support for the interpretation of Finkelstein (1995b) and Ussishkin, that the Philistine settlement was later than Ramesses III's eighth year.

Yet, Killebrew emphasizes the complexity of the Philistine immigration process, which militates against a simple chronological reconstruction. T. J. Barako (2013) has tackled the problem by comparing the contiguous cities of Ashdod and Tel Mor (and Killebrew and Lehmann [2013: 9] cite it with approval). Ashdod shows a destruction layer at the end of the LB. The LB stratum (VIII) shows Egyptianizing pottery and other finds that suggest that the Egyptians were controlling a Canaanite population. The early IA I stratum (VII), however, is completely dominated by Philistine material culture, and without an Egyptianizing admixture. On the other hand, Tel Mor's remains in both LB and early IA I show Egyptianizing without any break. The solution may lie in the nature of the 'Philistine invasion' (as Killebrew already hinted at above). It appears that a certain violent element in them, at least in part, cannot be brushed aside, as Aren Maeir comments:

> The cause behind these destructions is very likely the Sea Peoples – even if this is not to be seen as a uniform conquest of Philistia. Thus, while I would hardly adhere to a 'D-Day like event'…, I believe that one cannot see the process of the arrival of the Philistines as a peaceful event in which foreign groups slowly arrived and were amicably accepted by the local Canaanites. Rather, this most probably was a complex process – including both violent interactions and peaceful integration. I would suspect that a likely scenario…would be that non-local leaders deposed the local Canaanite elites (and the destruction of the LB building in Area E which is most probably a public oriented building would fit in with this scenario) – while in most cases retaining connections and integrating with other elements of the original Canaanite population. This then would explain the evidence of partial destructions such as at Ekron and Ashdod, and the fact that the Philistine cities retained their original Canaanite names. [Maeir (ed.) 2012: 18]

At this point, we need to separate the initial movement and settlement of the Sea Peoples from the history of the Philistines, which is discussed in the next chapter (§8.3). We still need to consider the different 'tribes' of the Sea Peoples as they are delineated in the Egyptian sources. Some have given a straightforward origin of each of these tribes, while others have been more circumspect. For example, some of the first to write about the Sea Peoples in the nineteenth century identified them by their name resemblance with the following places: Peleset (Philistines) – Pelasgoi; Lukka – Lycia; Sherden – Sardinia; Tjeker – Treuci (people of Torias); Shekelesh – Sicily; Denyen – Danaoi

(Greek tribe); Teresh – Tyrsenia (Etruscans); and Weshesh/Ekwesh – Achaea (Yasur-Landau 2010: 18; Bryce 2005: 336–8). More recent writers have tended to be more cautious and more sceptical, but a number of the identifications are still accepted, with caveats, though other identifications have also been made (e.g., Cline/O'Connor 2003; Drews 2000). What these data do not tell us, however, is whether the connection with a particular geographical area shows origins or simply the place to which some the tribe migrated. The suggested identifications are given below (Killebrew/Lehmann [eds] 2013: 645–64; for further on the tribes, see §8.4.3):

Lukka (Lycia): allied with Hatti against Egypt; allied with Libya against Egypt; part of rebels in western Anatolia (*CTH* 142; *CTH* 181: Bryce 1979; Hoffner 2009: 296–313).
Sherden (Sardinia): among northerners allied with Libyans (*ARE* 3: 241–3, 248–50, 254–6). They are also part of mercenaries in the service of Egypt (*ARE* 3: 136–7). Individuals of this group (under the name *trtnm*) appear in the Ugaritic texts (Killebrew/Lehmann 2013: 651; Loretz 1995). Some Sherden lived in the Byblos city-state (EA 122-23).
Weshesh/Ekwesh (Achaea): allied with Libyans; references in Hittite texts are to Ahhiyawa (e.g., *CTH* 61: Götze 1933: 66–7; Güterbock 1983; Groddek 2002).
Shekelesh (Sicily): this might be connected with the name Sikil, found in a Ugaritic text (Killebrew/Lehmann 2013: 660 n. 15); Drews (2000) has argued that Shekelesh is equivalent to Tjeker (see further under Tjeker).
Tjeker (Sicily): the name is sometimes written Sekel or Sikil (e.g., Rainey 1982). This depends on how one transliterates the Egyptian name (*t3-k3-rw*), especially the first letter *t* (original pronunciation apparently [tj] or [tch]). The name is found in a letter in Akkadian from the Hittite king to Ugarit ($^{\text{lú.meš.kur.uru}}$*Ši-ka-la-iu-ú*: RS 34.129: RSO 7: 38–9). Drews (2000) has argued that Shekelesh and Tjeker are equivalent, simply two ways that the Egyptians found for writing the presumed Sea Peoples' own name. This is plausible, except that both names occur together in the Medinet Habu inscription. This would mean that the Egyptian scribes had lost knowledge of the origin of the two names. Some centuries later, *Wenamun* (1.8) states that the harbour of Dor was a possession of the Tjeker (see further at §8.3).
Teresh (Italy): this may be associated with the Greek name for Italy, Tyrsenia (Drews 2000); among the northerners allied with Libyans (*ARE* 3: 241–3, 248–50, 254–6).
Denyen – possibly Danuna of Asia Minor; alternatively, a form of *Tanaju*, 'Greek speakers' (Drews 2000). There was also a Danuna that seems to have been in Canaan (EA 151). Some want to connect with the biblical tribe of Dan.

The incoming Philistines and the other tribes of the Sea Peoples evidently settled to some extent independently along the coast and in the coastal plain. Trade links were no doubt a part of this process, but trade alone does not explain the southern settlement (the areas to the north may have a different history; see at the end of §8.3). There was some destruction of the earlier Canaanite settlement, but a massacre of the previous inhabitants and a wholesale destruction of their habitation was not to the Philistines' advantage. In many cases, the new settlers took their places without major violence, though they seem to have dominated the original population. The material culture shows this creative synthesis made up of elements from the two sides, the Canaanites and the Sea People.

7.3 MESOPOTAMIA AND ANATOLIA

J. A. Brinkman (1963) 'Provincial Administration in Babylonia under the Second Dynasty of Isin', *JESHO* 6: 233–42; **idem** (1968) *A Political History of Post-Kassite Babylonia 1158–722 B.C.*; **idem** (1998–2001) 'Nebukadnezar I', *RlA* 9:192–4; **M. W. Chavalas (ed.)** (2006) *The Ancient Near East: Historical Sources in Translation*; **J.-J. Glassner** (2004) *Mesopotamian Chronicles*; **A. K. Grayson** (1972) *Assyrian Royal Inscriptions, Volume I: From the Beginning to Ashur-resha-ishi I*; **idem** (1976) *Assyrian Royal Inscriptions, Volume II: From Tiglath-pileser I to Ashur-nasir-apli II*; **A. V. Kossian** (1997) 'The Mushki Problem Reconsidered', *SMEA* 39: 253–66; **W. G. Lambert** (1962) 'The Reign of Nebuchadnezzar I: A Turning Point in the History of Ancient Mesopotamian Religion', in W. S. McCullough (ed.), *The Seed of Wisdom: Essays in Honour of T. J. Meek*: 3–13; **M. Liverani** (2014) *The Ancient Near East: History, Society and Economy*; **M. Van De Mieroop** (2003) *A History of the Ancient Near East, ca. 3000–323 BC*.

7.3.1 Elam, Babylonia and Assyria

The Mesopotamian powers of Elam, Babylonia, and Assyria were in competition in the latter part of the Late Bronze and early Iron I periods. In general their activities did not affect Syria or Palestine (an exception is Tiglath-pileser I's campaign into northern Syria). This is really a continuation of events described earlier (§5.2.1), including the Middle Assyrian dynasty which had not come to an end. We can begin with Elam which was the first to establish dominance. Elam has been mentioned only in passing in previous chapters because it seemed to play a lesser role in Mesopotamia for the most part; however, the Middle Elamite kingdom became an effective aggressor from about 1200 BCE. Also the Assyrian king Ashur-Dan I had campaigned against Babylonia, seriously undermining the Kassite dynasty (§5.2.2).

Shutruk-Nahhunte (*c.* 1175 BCE) was the first of a new dynasty at Susa. Following the Assyrian attack, he now took the opportunity to invade Babylonia, take the city of Babylon, and establish his son Kutir-Nahhunte as its governor, effectively bringing down the Kassite dynasty. In the Elamite inscription he added to the 'Naram-Sin I Victory Stela' he boasts of having taken this ancient stela back to Susa from Akkad (it was apparently some of his ancestors that Naram-Sin had defeated). Kutir-Nahhunte soon had to return to Susa to take the throne (*c.* 1150 BCE). He was then replaced by Shilhak-Inshushinak (*c.* 1125 BCE) who led Elam to its largest control of territory and probably its highest point as an international power. He also instigated a major building programme of temples and public buildings. Yet this height of power did not last long, and even while Babylonia was partially in Elamite hands, southern Babylonia had come to be ruled by a new native dynasty, the Second Dynasty of Isin.

Assyria and Babylonia brought Elamite interference in Mesopotamian affairs to an end. The Second Dynasty of Isin had begun about 1150 BCE, even while Babylonia was under submission to the Elamites, replacing the long reign of the Kassites. It was under Nebuchadnezzar I (*c.* 1125 BCE) that Babylonia asserted its independence (Brinkman 1998–2001; 1968: 104–16). He took Susa and retrieved the statue of Marduk that had been deported by the Elamites. His battle-field defeat of Elam is described in detail in the so-called Shitti-Marduk Stela, named for the tribal chief who assisted and whose valour in combat is extolled; it also lists stipulations to be obeyed in the cities emancipated from Elamite rule (Chavalas [ed.] 2006: 160–4). The Shitti-Marduk Stela refers to him as 'conqueror of the Amorites', though we have no further information on this. It appears that it was under Nebuchadnezzar's reign that Marduk became head of the Assyrian pantheon (Lambert 1962). Whether the Babylonian creation epic *Enuma Elish* was written at this time is not certain.

Having disposed of Elam, Babylonia now had another opponent, Assyria. One of the main objects of this rivalry was control of trade routes. Already Nebuchadnezzar had military encounters with Assyria, though the Synchronistic Chronicle (a pro-Assyrian source) suggests that he was defeated (Glassner 2004: 178–81). The Synchronistic Chronicle lists the various interactions between the Assyrians and Babylonians. There were many battles and skirmishes, but there were also treaties and exchange of daughters to seal them (Glassner 2004: 180–1). Opposing Nebuchadnezzar included the Assyrian ruler Ashur-resh-ishi I (*c.* 1125 BCE), although he benefited from the former's reduction of Elam's power. But Ashur-resh-ishi had his own problems in the shape of Ahlamu Aramaeans who were infiltrating Assyrian territory.

Ashur-resh-ishi's successor was Tiglath-pileser I (*c.* 1100 BCE) who represented a high point amid the Middle Assyrian rulers. As it happens, we know much more about his exploits than for many of his predecessors, partly because a new form of royal inscription known as 'annals' first appears during his reign (Grayson 1976: 1–45). Elam had been tamed, primarily by the Babylonians, but there were threats from the Phrygians in the old area of Hatti, from the Aramaeans, and of course Babylonia itself. He pushed northwest and north into the mountains and also into the old area of the Hurrians and Hittites, and eventually further west into the border areas, including Amurru, and finally to the Mediterranean (Grayson 1976: 22–9). He cut timber in the mountains of Lebanon and took tribute from Amurru and the Phoenician cities of Byblos, Sidon, and Arwad. This was mainly symbolic, however, since he did not establish a permanent Assyrian presence there. But this brought him up against the Aramaeans whom he wanted to bring into submission. He crossed the Euphrates '28 times, twice in one year' in pursuit of Ahlamu Aramaeans. He also campaigned against Babylonia in the reign of Marduk-nadin-ahhe (*c.* 1090 BCE), taking Babylon itself along with other major cities. He did not remain there, however, and Babylonia continued to be independent. The 'Middle Assyrian Laws' seem to have been compiled during his reign.

After the death of Tiglath-pileser, the Middle Assyrian dynasty continued for another couple of centuries in a diminished state. The fortunes of Assyria began to rise again with Adad-nirari II (*c.* 900 BCE) who is often counted the first king of the Neo-Assyrian period. It was not until the ninth century and the rule of Shalmaneser III that Assyria once more made its presence felt in the Levant. Babylonia likewise existed but without any major effect on Palestine and the Levant. The Second Dynasty of Isin basically petered out about 1000 BCE or a bit later, to be succeeded by the 'Second Sealand Dynasty'. As already noted in a previous chapter (§5.2.2) the Sealand had come under Babylonian rule during the Kassite period; now, they established a short-lived dynasty of three kings that returned some stability to the kingdom. They were succeeded by another three rulers from an eastern tribe known as the Bazi, which brings us to the end of the time period covered in the present study. After that comes a period of about 20 rulers, about many of whom little is known, but this is part of the history of the first millennium BCE.

7.3.2 Neo-Hittite States

T. Bryce (2005) *The Kingdom of the Hittites*; **idem** (2012) *The World of the Neo-Hittite Kingdoms: A Political and Military History*; **F. Jacoby** (1926–58) *Die Fragmente der griechischen Historiker*; **A. V. Kossian** (1997) 'The Mushki Problem Reconsidered', *SMEA* 39: 253–66; **A. Payne** (2012) *Iron Age Hieroglyphic Luwian Inscriptions*.

The end of the Hittite New Kingdom occurred about 1200 BCE, the culmination of a long decline – and perhaps raids from the Sea Peoples, though this is debated (§5.3.1). The former empire broke up into about ten or so small Neo-Hittite states, depending on how you count them. According to T. Bryce (2012: 79–162) these include Carchemish, Malatya, Kummah, Masuwari/Til Barsip, Gurgum, Patin (Unqi), Hamath (including Luash), (Northern) Tabal, Atuna, Ishtunda, Shinutu, Tuwana, Hupishna, Adanawa, Hilakku. Each of these states tended to centre on a particular city, but much of the population was now living in villages. There was a distinction, however, in language and ethnic identity among these various states. The northern ones were Hittite speaking, or in the related language of Luwian. Many of their inscriptions were written in a particular hieroglyphic writing system (e.g., Payne 2012).

The southern Neo-Hittite states, mainly in northern Syria, tended to be Semitic in language and ethnicity. They included one of the main actors among these Neo-Hittite states: the kingdom of Carchemish. These kingdoms – or at least the ruling elite – had been subjected to Hittite influence, and Hittites lived (as a minority) among the population. These states bordered on the Aramaean region to the south of them and showed elements of both cultures. Indeed, some specialists label some of the Neo-Hittite kingdoms as Aramaean states. For example, Sam'al was in the Aramaean zone and not usually included among the Neo-Hittite states, but some have seen Hamath also as primarily Aramaean (see further at §7.5). For the two centuries following the fall of the Hittite empire, we know little about the region. Most of the Neo-Hittite kingdoms were in the state of development, and it is mainly about such previously existing entities like Carchemish that we have more detailed information.

The two kingdoms appearing early in the Middle Assyrian texts are Carchemish and Malatya. For the others there is little information until the inscriptions of Ashurnasirpal II (*c.* 875 BCE). This Assyrian king conducted campaigns against the Neo-Hittite, Aramaean, and Phoenician states. Luash was apparently the only one to resist and had appalling violence inflicted on it as a deterrence. The city-state of Carchemish was sometimes called 'great Hatti' by the Assyrians because of its prominence as a continuation of an older vassal kingdom of Hatti. Yet a number of the new kingdoms were in some sense heirs of older LB kingdoms such as Mukish and Kizzuwatna. Although the various kingdoms were independent of one another, as a group they controlled important key areas of geography, including fertile areas for agriculture, nodes of trade routes, and other natural resources. They were also outside the sphere of domination by the Assyrians until the time of Ashurnasirpal II and Shalmaneser III, which is after the chronological limits of the present volume.

There was another group who settled in the Hittite territories: the Phrygians. It was once believed – and still accepted by many – that the Phrygians migrated out of the Balkans, through the Hellespont, to central Anatolia, drawing on the statements of Herodotus (7.73) and Xanthus (*Lydiaka*: Jacoby 1926–58: text no. 765, frags. 14-15). More recently, the view seems to have prevailed that any migration was small scale – individual families and small units – rather than massive, because archaeology does not suggest a major new population (e.g., Drews 1993: 65–6). Whether the Phrygians were participants in the downfall of the Hittite empire is also debated. The Phrygians became an important opponent of the Assyrians, but this was not until later, the eighth and seventh centuries. It is not entirely clear whether the Phrygians were the same as the Mushki mentioned in Assyrian texts or whether these were two separate groups (cf. Kossian 1997). There is also a debate over whether two separate groups remained separate or united, though the consensus seems to be that they united (Bryce 2012: 40). The main activities under a King Mita (= Midas?) are in the eighth century BCE.

7.4 PHOENICIA

J. Elayi (2018) *The History of Phoenicia*; **Y. Goren I. Finkelstein, and N. Na'aman** (2004) *Inscribed in Clay: Provenance Study of the Amarna Tablets and Other Ancient Near Eastern Texts*; **H. J. Katzenstein** (1997) *The History of Tyre: From the Beginning of the Second Millenium B.C.E. until the Fall of the Neo-Babylonian Empire in 539 B.C.E.*; **M. Liverani (ed.)** (1998) *Le lettere di el-Amarna: vol. 1. Le lettere dei 'Piccoli Re'*; **S. Moscati (ed.)** (1988) *i Fenici*; **N. Na'aman** (1979) 'The Origin and Historical Background of Several Amarna Letters', *UF* 11: 673–84; **B. J. Peckham** (2014) *Phoenicia: Episodes and Anecdotes from the Ancient Mediterranean*; **A. F. Rainey** (2015a) *The El-Amarna Correspondence: A New Edition of the Cuneiform Letters from the Site of El-Amarna based on Collations of all Extant Tablets*, Volume 1; **G. Rawlinson** (1889) *History of Phoenicia*. **H. Sader** (2019) *The History and Archaeology of Phoenicia*; **W. H. van Soldt** (2002) 'Studies on the *sākinu*-Official (2): The Functions of the *sākinu* of Ugarit', *UF* 34: 805–28.

The history of Phoenicia has benefitted from several recent studies (Elayi 2018; Katzenstein 1997; Peckham 2014; Sader 2019). G. Rawlinson's study of 1889 is mainly of interest for the history of scholarship but was solidly based on the (mainly classical literary) sources then available. There are also studies on the later history of the Phoenician cities, but they are not listed here. The importance of Phoenicia as early as the third millennium BCE, especially Byblos, was noted in earlier chapters (§2.4.3). We also have a fair amount of information during the Amarna period because of the Amarna texts (§6.3.2), which is where most of the histories of Phoenicia begin (though H. Sader [2019] begins her history with IA I, except for archaeology). Letters are preserved from the rulers of Byblos, Beirut, Tyre, and Sidon, but not Arwad. What they show is a series of alliances, oppositions, and intrigues, especially relating to Amurru (§5.4.1).

First, the most prolific writer to the pharaoh was Rib-Hadda (Rib-Eddi) of Byblos (EA 66-96, 101-38, 362). He was under pressure from Amurru: from Abdi-Ashirta and then from Aziru and his brothers. He was eventually forced out of Byblos and had to take refuge in Beirut. After his death he was succeeded by Ili-Rapih who continued to complain about Aziru to Egypt (EA 139-40). Beirut had apparently had Yapah-Hadda as ruler initially (EA 97-98; cf. 83, 85, etc.), but he threw in his lot with Abdi-Ashirta and Aziru; however, he was succeeded by Ammunira (EA 141-43) who was loyal to Egypt and befriended Rib-Hadda and provided him sanctuary when things became too hot for him in Byblos.

A long-term rivalry between Tyre and Sidon surfaced in the Amarna texts. We can begin with EA 295 which has now been shown to be a letter from the ruler of Tyre (Na'aman 1979: 673–6; Goren/Finkelstein/Na'aman 2004: 168). The ruler is named as]DI.KUD whose name has been variously interpreted: Ba'lu-Dān (Soldt 2002: 811; accepted by Goren/Finkelstein/Na'aman 2004: 168), Ba'lu-dāni (Rainey 2015a: 1139), Baal-Shiptu (Elayi 2018: 75), –]-shipti (Liverani [ed.] 1998: 148). J. Elayi (2018: 75–6, 295, though unfortunately she gives no references) begins her rulers of Tyre with Baal-Shiptu I. He was apparently assassinated, along with his wife and children, according to Rib-Hadda. This ruler was succeeded by Abimilki, the main figure of Tyre who wrote a number of letters to the pharaoh (EA 146-55). Abimilki was loyal to Egypt and allies with Rib-Hadda but opposed by Aziru and his allies.

Those allies included Sidon whose king was Yabni- (EA 295). His full name is not preserved and has been variously given as Yab[(Liverani [ed.] 1998: 148), Yabni-Hadda/Ba'al? (Moran 1992: 207–8, 386), Yabni-ilu? (Rainey 2015a: 1139), Yabni[(Elayi 2018: 76). His successor was Zimreddi (EA 144-45; cf. 83, 103, 106, 146, 149, 151, 152, 154) who opposed Abimilki but worked closely with Aziru and became his spy. He seized the mainland site of Ushu, which supplied Tyre with water, and besieged Tyre. Abimilki at one point decided to journey to Egypt to present his case, but Zimreddi learned of this and sent forces to turn back the Tyrian entourage. Zimreddi's siege of Tyre seems to have been resolved at some point, however, since Tyre was back in control of Usha (though this was a century later). Although no letters from Arwad to the pharaoh are known, the city is mentioned in several (EA 98, 101, 104, 105, 149). It seems to have thrown its lot in with Amurru, which helped that kingdom become a naval power and use the ships of Arwad in attacking Tyre and other cities.

Commerce was an important activity of the Phoenician cities, though this tended to be local, i.e., with Egypt and along the Syrian coast. It was finally in the Early Iron Age, however, that Phoenician maritime trade managed to break free from its eastern Mediterranean sphere and expand to the whole of the Mediterranean. An important Phoenician product was textiles dyed purple, but they also produced and exported glass ware, carvings in various media, and the agricultural products of wine, oil, and figs. It is alleged that it was the purple dye that led the Greeks to give the name 'Phoenicia' (φοινίκη) to the people and cities along the Syrian coast. They were always independent cities, and to what extent they identified themselves as a single people is uncertain.

Unfortunately, the history of the Phoenicians from about 1200–800 BCE is largely unknown, at least from literary sources (Sader 2019: 33). It is only after 900 and the terminus of the present study that we start to find references in the Assyrian and other sources (including the Hebrew Bible). Many still give credence to a King Hiram of Tyre and his provision of materials to Solomon for the temple. More on this in the next chapter (§8.5.7). The archaeology gives a more enlightened position for the IA I period (Sader 2019: 48). Little is known about Byblos and Arwad, but further south the archaeology is much fuller (Sader 2019: 36–49). IA I seems to have no representation so far at Beirut, but it is fully represented at Sidon (a vase with the name of Queen Towsre of Egypt [1192–1191 BCE]), Sarepta (some of the best preserved evidence), Tyre (remains fragmentary; a cremation cemetery), Tell Abu Hawam, Tell Keisan (stratum 9A was destroyed; in 9B Philistine ware disappeared and Phoenician bichrome appeared), Akko (evidence for purple dye industry), and Dor (now shown to be a Phoenician site).

Most of the Phoenician sites continued to exist in the IA I, even those that were destroyed at the end of the LBA. At many sites evidence of trade with Cyprus, Egypt, and elsewhere can be found. As far as we can tell, the Phoenician cities were not bothered by the Sea Peoples, whatever their destructive activities might have been elsewhere. Several Middle Assyrian kings made raids to the west, as far as Phoenicia: Tiglath-pileser I (*c.* 1100 BCE) and Ashur-bel-kala (*c.* 1060 BCE). Then 150 years later the first Neo-Assyrian ruler Adad-nirari II (*c.* 900 BCE) carried a campaign as far as Cappadocia.

7.5 ARAMAEANS

P. E. Dion (1997) *Les Araméens à l'âge du fer: histoire politique et structures sociales*; **J. Dušek and J. Mynářová (eds)** (2019) *Aramaean Borders: Defining Aramaean Territories in the 10th–8th Centuries B.C.E.*; **W. G. Lambert** (1957–58) review of F. Gössmann, *Das Era-Epos*, *AfO* 18: 395–401; **E. Lipiński** (2000) *The Aramaeans: Their Ancient History, Culture, Religion*; **R. T. O'Callaghan** (1948) *Aram Naharaim: A Contribution to the History of Upper Mesopotamia in the Second Millennium B.C.*; **W. T. Pitard** (1987) *Ancient Damascus: A Historical Study of the Syrian City-State from Earliest Times until its Fall to the Assyrians in 732 B.C.E.*; **G. G. G. Reinhold** (1989) *Die Beziehungen Altisraels zu den aramäischen Staaten in der israelitisch-judäischen Königszeit*; **H. S. Sader** (1987) *Les états araméens de Syrie depuis leur fondation jusqu'à leur transformation en provinces assyriennes*; **K. L. Younger, Jr** (2007b) 'The Late Bronze Age/Iron Age Transition and the Origins of the Arameans', in K. L. Younger, Jr (ed.), *Ugarit at Seventy-Five*: 131–74; **idem** (2016) *A Political History of the Arameans: From their Origins to the End of their Polities*.

There is some debate over how early the name of Aram/the Aramaeans appears in the historical record (Lipiński 2000: 26–40; Younger 2016): arguments that it occurs as early as the third millennium in Ebla texts has not met general acceptance, nor have other attempts to find it in early second-millennium texts. Most recognize that the name clearly occurs in the inscriptions of Tiglath-pileser I, about 1100 BCE. There is also fairly wide agreement that the name may be found somewhat earlier, in inscriptions of Amenhotep III (*c.* 1375 BCE). The Aramaeans thus come into history in the late second millennium as an identifiable group. The Aramaeans were identified with the *Ahlamu* which seems to be a reference to pastoralists, though some interpret it as 'roving bands' of raiders. Another term applied to them is 'Sutaeans' (*Sutû*), which also seems to be a reference to the pastoralist lifestyle (Younger 2007b). The word is found in some of the Amarna letters (EA 16, 122, 123, 169, 195, 246, 297, 318), where it sometimes occurs alongside *Apiru* (EA 195, 246, 318) and suggests lawless individuals. But this seems to be a development of the term. The Aramaeans, sometimes alongside the Sutaeans and *Ahlamu*, are mentioned together in the inscriptions of such Assyrian rulers as Ashur-bel-kala (*c.* 1060 BCE), Ashur-dan II (*c.* 925 BCE), and Adad-nirari II (*c.* 900 BCE), and the Babylonian king Adad-apla-iddina (*c.* 1050 BCE) (Lipiński 2000: 409–16; Grayson 1976: 49, 53–4, 57–8, 62, 75–6, 80–1, 87–8; Glassner 2004: 284–5; Lambert 1957–58).

At one time it was argued that there was a mass migration of Aramaean groups into Mesopotamia and Syria, but this is now generally rejected. Instead, Aramaic-speaking tribes, mainly transhumance pastoralists, inhabited the steppe lands on the periphery of the dominant empires in Mesopotamia, Anatolia, and Syria during the Bronze Age. With the collapse of most of these major powers at the end of the Late Bronze, they moved into areas once controlled by the Hittites, Assyrians, and Babylonians. In other words, it was not a mass migration but a steady infiltration by settlers who were more or less local. The Aramaeans seem to have inhabited two main regions. Tiglath-pileser I and his successors encountered the Aramaeans along the middle Euphrates region and Jebel Bishri. This is a general region which Amorites had inhabited centuries earlier, a datum which has led some to see Aramaeans as descendants of the Amorites. But there does not seem to be a direct connection between the two peoples, though a more distant one is of course possible.

Certain of the Neo-Hittite kingdoms are identified as Aramaean states by some researchers (Sader 1987; Lipiński 2000), primarily Hamath. There were also Aramaean states in Syria outside the Neo-Hittite realm: Sam'al, Guzana (Tell Halaf), Bit-Agusi, Luash, Bit-Rehob and Sobah, Bit-Adini, and especially Damascus. We are primarily dependent on Assyrian texts for information on these states. The Assyrians apparently used ancient names if there had been known predecessors of the city-state in question, but otherwise they named the state after its alleged founder, hence *Bīt-* 'house/dynasty of'; however, this is an interpretation of what is often written as DUMU (= *mār*) 'son of' (Sader 1987: 272–3).

The Aramaean states become quite important to the history of Israel and Judah from the ninth century on; however, the biblical text also suggests that some of the Aramaean entities were already opponents of David. A closer investigation suggests that this was unlikely to be the case, but this will be examined in the next chapter (§8.5.6.2).

7.6 TRANSJORDAN

S. Ahituv (1984) *Canaanite Toponyms in Ancient Egyptian Documents*; **P. Bienkowski** (1992a) 'The Beginning of the Iron Age in Southern Jordan: A Framework', in P. Bienkowski (ed.), *Early Edom and Moab: The Beginning of the Iron Age in Southern Jordan*: 1–12; **idem** (1992b) 'The Date of Sedentary Occupation in Edom: Evidence from Umm el-Biyara, Tawilan and Buseirah', in P. Bienkowski (ed.), *Early Edom and Moab: The Beginning of the Iron Age in Southern Jordan*: 99–112; **P. Bienkowski (ed.)** (1992) *Early Edom and Moab: The Beginning of the Iron Age in Southern Jordan*; **E. Bloch-Smith and B. A. Nakhai** (1999) 'A Landscape Comes to Life: The Iron I Period', *NEA* 62: 62–92, 101–27; **J. A. Dearman** (1992) 'Settlement Patterns and the Beginning of the Iron Age in Moab', in P. Bienkowski (ed.), *Early Edom and Moab: The Beginning of the Iron Age in Southern Jordan*: 65–75; **D. V. Edelman (ed.)** (1995) *You Shall not Abhor an Edomite for he is your Brother: Edom and Seir in History and Tradition*; **I. Finkelstein** (1992a) 'Edom in the Iron I', *Levant* 24: 159–66; **idem** (1992b) 'Stratigraphy, Pottery and Parallels: A Reply to Bienkowsky', *Levant* 24: 171–2; **idem** (1995a) *Living on the*

Fringe: The Archaeology and History of the Negev, Sinai and Neighbouring Regions in the Bronze and Iron Ages; **L. T. Geraty and Ø. S. LaBianca (eds)** (1987–98) *Hesban*; **T. P. Harrison and C. Barlow** (2005) 'Mesha, the Mishor, and the Chronology of Iron Age Mādabā', in T. E. Levy and T. Higham (eds), *The Bible and Radiocarbon Dating: Archaeology, Text and Science*: 179–90; **S. Hart** (1992) 'Iron Age Settlement in the Land of Edom', in P. Bienkowski (ed.), *Early Edom and Moab: The Beginning of the Iron Age in Southern Jordan*: 93–8; **L. G. Herr et al. (eds)** (1989–2002) *Madaba Plains Project*; **K. A. Kitchen** (1992) 'The Egyptian Evidence on Ancient Jordan', in P. Bienkowski (ed.), *Early Edom and Moab: The Beginning of the Iron Age in Southern Jordan*: 21–34; **Ø. S. LaBianca and R. W. Younker** (1998) 'The Kingdoms of Ammon, Moab and Edom: The Archaeology of Society in Late Bronze/Iron Age Transjordan (ca. 1400–500 BCE)', in T. E. Levy (ed.), *The Archaeology of Society in the Holy Land*: 399–415; **T. E. Levy, M. Najjar, J. van der Plicht, N. G. Smith, H. J. Bruins, and T. Higham** (2005) 'Lowland Edom and the High and Low Chronologies: Edomite State Formation, the Bible and Recent Archaeological Research in Southern Jordan', in T. E. Levy and T. Higham (eds), *The Bible and Radiocarbon Dating: Archaeology, Text and Science*: 129–63; **B. MacDonald, R. Adams, and P. Bienkowski (eds)** (2001) *The Archaeology of Jordan*; **J. M. Miller** (1992) 'Early Monarchy in Moab?', in Piotr Bienkowski (ed.), *Early Edom and Moab: The Beginning of the Iron Age in Southern Jordan*: 77–91; **J. M. Miller (ed.)** (1991) *Archaeological Survey of the Kerak Plateau, Conducted during 1978–1982 under the Direction of J. Maxwell Miller and Jack M. Pinkerton*; **B. Routledge** (2004) *Moab in the Iron Age: Hegemony, Polity, Archaeology*; **idem** (2008) 'Thinking "Globally" and Analysing "Locally": South-Central Jordan in Transition', in L. L. Grabbe (ed.), *Israel in Transition: From Late Bronze II to Iron IIA (c. 1250–850 BCE): The Archaeology*: 144–76; **J. A. Sauer** (1986) 'Transjordan in the Bronze and Iron Ages: A Critique of Glueck's Synthesis', *BASOR* 263: 1–26; **J. F. A. Sawyer and D. J. A. Clines (eds)** (1983) *Midian, Moab and Edom: The History and Archaeology of Late Bronze and Iron Age Jordan and North-West Arabia*; **E. van der Steen** (2004) *Tribes and Territories in Transition: The Central East Jordan Valley in the Late Bronze Age and Early Iron Ages: a Study of the Sources*; **H. Tadmor** (1994) *The Inscriptions of Tiglath-Pileser III King of Assyria: Critical Edition, with Introductions, Translations and Commentary*; **C. W. Tyson** (2014) *The Ammonites: Elites, Empires, and Sociopolitical Change (1000–500 BCE)*; **U. Worschech** (1997) 'Egypt and Moab', *BA* 60: 229–36.

Until the coming of the Assyrians, most of our knowledge about the Transjordanian region derives from archaeology and the biblical text. A small amount of information occurs in Egyptian texts (Kitchen 1992; Worschech 1997; see also with regard to the Shasu [§6.3.3.4]), and beginning in the late ninth century or about 800 BCE we have some native inscriptions. The documentation is not great, but it is fortunate that several recent treatments of the archaeology are available (Routledge 2004; 2008; Steen 2004; MacDonald/Adams/Bienkowski [eds] 2001; Finkelstein 1995a; Bienkowski [ed.] 1992; Edelman [ed.] 1995; Miller [ed.] 1991; Sawyer/Clines [eds] 1983). This includes the important sites of Tall Hisbân (Geraty/LaBianca [eds] 1987–98) and Tall al-'Umayri (Herr et al.

[eds] 1989–2002). Much of what we know about the archaeology depends on surface surveys since only a relatively few sites in the areas of ancient Ammon, Moab, and Edom have been excavated. Surface surveys have certain limitations. This is evident in the Transjordan surveys since they have yielded surprisingly different results in some cases, especially disconcerting when this involves overlapping areas in the surveys. These can generally be explained (Miller 1992: 79–80), but it illustrates some of the problems.

In his well-known survey of the Transjordan, Nelson Glueck reached some conclusions that are still influential (see the references and discussion in Sauer 1986). His two main conclusions were (1) that the southern Transjordanian region showed a settlement gap between the EB and the end of the LB (also between the late IA II and the Persian period) and (2) that a chain of defensive forts marked the borders of the three kingdoms already in the IA I. Sauer questioned the first of these conclusions, arguing that more recent research showed major tell sites in the MB and LB in northern and central Transjordan, suggesting a system of city-states similar to those on the west side of the Jordan. The second of Glueck's conclusions has been widely criticized: the evidence for a chain of border fortresses is skimpy at best (Miller 1992: 79, 87–8; Steen 2004: 80–1).

In the three and a half decades since Sauer wrote, his conclusions have themselves been subjected to scrutiny, especially since, in the meantime, a number of surveys have reported. Many scholars now feel that Glueck had it largely correct: only a sparse sedentary population was present in the MB and LB but there was an explosion of settlements in the early Iron (Miller 1992: 80; Dearman 1992: 72–3; Steen 2004: 89–90). The problem seems to be the interpretation of the surface surveys, for the excavated sites have generally shown little in the way of LB settlement. The indications are that there was a greater sedentary population in the north: in general, the density of settlement decreases as one moves from north to south in Transjordan (LaBianca/Younker 1998: 406). Glueck's southern gap in the LB (south of the Wadi Mujib) largely remains: not that there were no inhabitants but that the population in that region was almost entirely nomadic.

Borders are usually difficult to determine from archaeology, and the borders indicated in the biblical text cannot be considered as necessarily accurate (MacDonald 1999: 30–9; Bloch-Smith/Nakhai 1999: 106–7). Yet the textual indications for the location of Ammon, Moab, and Edom are reasonably consistent around a core region in each case. New Kingdom Egyptian texts already have references to Moab (Ramesses II), Edom (Merenptah), and Seir (Ramesses II) (Kitchen 1992a; Miller 1992: 77–8; Aḥituv 1984). Ammon seems to appear first by name in an eighth-century inscription of Tiglath-pileser III (Tadmor 1994: 170–1 [Summary Inscription 7:10']), though it is now argued that there may already be a reference in the Kurkh Monolith inscription of Shalmaneser III a century earlier (*c.* 853 BCE; Tyson 2014: 72–5). Although it has been proposed that some Ammonite settlements are mentioned in Egyptian texts, this has also been doubted (Steen 2004: 11–12, 50); however, the archaeology suggests that the collapse of city-states toward the end of the LB II led to many rural villages with agricultural settlements (Steiner/Killebrew 2014: 573).

Ammon is associated with the section of the Transjordanian Plateau south of the Jabbok River (Wadi az-Zarqa) (Steen 2004: 50–1). At its largest extent it was perhaps the territory between the Jabbok and Arnon (Wadi al-Mujib) and between the Jordan and the desert to the east (MacDonald 1999: 38–9). The southern border probably fluctuated as the fortunes of Ammon and Moab waxed and waned. Although in Ammon the settlement gap inferred by Glueck has been shown not to exist, since several fortified sites have subsequently been excavated (Tall al-Umayri, Tall Sahab, Tall

Safrut, Khirbat Umm ad-Dananir), the LB settlement was nevertheless sparse (Bienkowski 1992: 5–6; Steen 2004: 51). The existing settlements centred on Amman and the Baqʻah Valley (Bloch-Smith/Nakhai 1999: 109–11); this area seems to have been at the end of a trade route and served as a trade market (Steen 2004: 297–8). The end of the LB saw an increase of settlements, but they tended to be small and fortified (Steen 2004: 304).

At the transition into IA I, however, some of the major sites were destroyed or suffered reduction, perhaps as a consequence of the collapse of the market system and trade with the Jordan Valley (Steen 2004: 305–6). Then, many sites were abandoned or even destroyed at the end of Iron I. For example, ʻUmayri was apparently destroyed by hostile attack and extensively reoccupied only in the seventh century BCE. Two-thirds of excavated sites show a gap in the late Iron I, though it has been suggested that this is a scholarly artifact resulting from poor pottery chronology or survey information (Bloch-Smith/Nakhai 1999: 111). Herr notes, 'The early centuries of Iron II are presently very difficult to document in all of Transjordan' (1997: 132). Little has been found that can be related to the tenth century, which has implications for the biblical passages relating to David and Ammon.

Moab looked focused on Wadi al-Mujib (Bienkowski 1992: 1). Its southern border is usually seen as Wadi al-Hasa, but most of the places associated with Moab are in fact north of the Mujib. Moab's northern border probably moved up and down, depending on the balance of power in Ammon and Moab's relationship. Although the settlement of the LB is meagre overall, there may have been an increase in settlement in the area south of Wadi Mujib; in any case, there was a sudden growth in fortified settlements at the beginning of IA I (Steen 2004: 305), with a steady increase of occupation through IA I to a peak in IA II (Bienkowski 1992: 5–6; Miller 1992: 80; Bloch-Smith/Nakhai 1999: 114). Others assert that walled settlements were infrequent in LB and IA I, but with fortified outposts and watchtowers reaching a high point in IA II (Dearman 1992: 73; LaBianca/Younker 1998: 407).

The area of Edom was originally south of Wadi al-Haba (perhaps down to Wadi Hisma) and east of the Wadi Arabah (Bienkowski 1992: 1). Sauer (1986) attempted to show that Glueck was wrong about the sparseness of settlement in this region in the Late Bronze and early Iron; his efforts have been both rejected (Hart 1992: 93) and accepted (Finkelstein 1995a: 135). MacDonald (1994: 242) noted that there was no LB evidence and also IA I evidence only in the northern part of the traditional Edomite territory to the east of the Wadi Arabah. Since the occupation of the main sites of Busayrah, Tawilan, and Umm al-Biyara showed no settlement before the seventh century BCE, it was possible that the 'Iron I' sherds were actually from Iron II (Bienkowski 1992b; Bloch-Smith/Nakhai 1999: 114). This has initiated an ongoing debate between Bienkowski and Finkelstein who has argued that Glueck was right and that there was continuous Iron Age settlement in southern Transjordan.

Bienkowski (1992b, 1992c) argues that Finkelstein has mistakenly dated sherds to Iron I by using parallels from Palestine and northern Transjordan, and that he has further ignored the fact that Iron II strata lie directly on the bedrock in many excavated sites (though Busayrah has not been sufficiently studied to say for certain). Finkelstein responds that the dating of Edomite sites has depended on C. M. Bennett's chronological sequence based on the find of a seal impression at Umm al-Biyara with the royal name 'Qos-Gabr', an Edomite ruler known from the inscriptions of Esarhaddon and Ashurbanipal (Finkelstein 1992a, 1992b; 1995a: 131–2; also Bienkowski 1992b: 99; Levy, et al. 2005: 132). The stratigraphy of Edomite sites is far from clear, and it was the highland custom to remove earlier material in order to establish walls on bedrock. The differences between these two scholars hinges a good deal on pottery assemblages, a debate for archaeologists to carry on. For example, a recent study of the collared-rim pithoi (a pottery type appealed to specifically by Finkelstein) concludes that the pithoi are found in Iron II at al-'Umayri and are thus not diagnostic for Iron I (Herr 2001). In any case, the two different interpretations lead to different reconstructions of early Edomite history:

All seem to agree that in the LB the inhabitants were nomadic groups whom the Egyptians referred to as *Shasu*. According to Bienkowski (1992a: 8) and others, this would have continued through the Iron I as well (except for some settlement in northern Edom) before a major process of sedentarization in the eighth or seventh centuries (though the extent of mountainous terrain meant that it did not become fully urban). The resumption of mining in Faynan may have helped with this, as well as the Arabian trade and the general conditions of peace and stability under Assyrian domination. According to Finkelstein (1995a: 135–7) settlement in Edom was parallel to the settlement of the hill country in Palestine and northern Transjordan, though the southern Transjordan was more marginal and yielded small sites. The Edomite state of Iron II had its roots in the sedentary occupation of Iron I. The settlement history was thus not particularly different from that of Moab and the northern Transjordan. All seem to agree that the peak of settlement was in the eighth to seventh centuries and allowed Edomite influence to spread west of the Wadi Arabah.

For a discussion of the mining and smelting of copper in Edom, see §6.3.3.5.

7.7 CONCLUSIONS

An important characteristic of Early Iron Age Canaan is that it was left largely alone to get on with its development. The major powers ceased to interfere for one reason or another. Babylon and Assyria were not primarily looking to the west, and Mitanni had ceased to exist. Egypt by and large withdrew from Palestine for a couple of centuries. The Hittite Empire had broken up into various small states. This left the Canaanites to pursue their own interests. They were not a unified group or unity, of course, and each tribe or city or even family unit did what it chose to do. This included the tribes that according to the biblical text and later history we refer to as Israel.

The one outside group was the Sea Peoples. They came on the scene at the beginning of IA I and, according to an older view, conquered their way down the Mediterranean coast before taking over the southern part of Canaan by violence. More recent study has rejected parts of this scenario and modified other parts. The Sea Peoples indeed came from a variety of places across the Mediterranean, even though they were called by the name of the single tribe 'Philistine' (*prst*) when they settled down. They were an important neighbour to the developing Israel, but they seem to have formed a minority of the population where they settled. Rather, they were perhaps an elite group who took control of the region, but the bulk of the population was made up of the local Canaanites, and together they created an 'entangled' material culture. The allegation that they destroyed many cities and states has come under increasing question. There was no doubt some violence, since piracy seems to have been one of their endeavours, and they may have raided some towns. But the charge of wholesale destruction is now looked at with a sceptical eye, though research is ongoing.

Phoenicia was important at this time, as it had been for centuries. It was never unified but consisted of several cities who sometimes competed. For two or three centuries after 1200 not much is known, though the various Phoenician cities apparently continued to develop their sea trade routes. They were another group who bordered on what was to become Israelite territory and had control of some of it. For example, Dor seems to have been a Phoenician city at this time. Similarly, we know of Aramaeans but do not know very much. The alleged warfare between David and various Aramaean groups was probably a literary invention (see §8.5.6.2). Transjordan also began to develop much as Cisjordan had, though the population was much sparser. IA I saw settlement growth, albeit more in the north than the south. Many of the inhabitants seem to still to have been pastoralists. A particular area of progress was copper smelting in the region of Edom.

CHAPTER 8

Palestine (1200–900 BCE)

C. Frevel (2016) *Geschichte Israels*; **L. L. Grabbe** (2017) *Ancient Israel: What Do We Know and How Do We Know it?*; **E. A. Knauf and P. Guillaume** (2016) *A History of Biblical Israel: The Fate of the Tribes and Kingdoms from Merenptah to Bar Kochba*; **E. A. Knauf and H. M. Niemann** (2021) *Geschichte Israels und Judas im Altertum*.

This chapter focuses on Iron I, which ended about 1000 BCE. Yet this is not sufficient for considering the 'dawn of Israel', since the period of its rise can be said to spill over into Iron IIA. For this reason, this chapter will take in the whole period of about 1200–900 BCE.

8.1 SOURCES

When we come to the Iron Age I, the political environment of Palestine had changed dramatically. As well as the general collapse that ended the Late Bronze Age, Egypt ceased to be a major factor: whereas Egypt had previously dominated the people and territory of Canaan and northern Syria, the situation was drastically altered with the removal of Egyptian hegemony about 1150 BCE or so. The coming and settlement of Sea Peoples was also a new element, but they did not take control in the way Egypt had. This means that the peoples of the region had much more freedom to develop according to their own lights, or so it seems. The main sources for Palestine/Canaan for this period can be summarized as follows.

Our foremost source for the Iron I is archaeology, which will be discussed in the next section (§8.2). Settlement patterns and evidence of invasion, destruction, or peaceful development become very important to determining what happened in the period 1200–900, especially when there is an absence of textual sources.

In spite of Egypt's general withdrawal from the region, we have two major Egyptian sources. One is an inscription of Rameses III on the coming of the Sea Peoples (discussed at §7.2). The other is the inscription of Shoshenq I supposedly describing a campaign through Palestine (§8.5.8 below).

The final potential source is the biblical text. This is less helpful than was usually considered in the past, even though some admittedly still use it as their ultimate guide to what was happening with Israel. But to the historian it is a secondary source, with much of the material of interest from a much later time than Iron Age I. As so often with the biblical text, its historical value varies considerably from passage to passage. The one biblical passage to be considered in its own right is the 'Song of Deborah' (Judges 5) which is thought to be one of the oldest passages in the Bible and one of the earliest examples of Hebrew language. This will be looked at below (§8.4.5). Joshua and Judges are discussed as sources at §8.4.5.

Finally, we have the books of Samuel and the first chapter of 1 Kings. These are historiographic works which seem to contain some authentic historical data. But as usual the question of how historical the narratives are is varied and debated. The problem is that the material to be considered here is not yet (as far as we know) based on information from royal chronicles that seem to be evident later on in 1 and 2 Kings. For bibliography and discussion of what these books tell us about the early monarchy, see §8.5.

8.2 ARCHAEOLOGY

D. Ben-Ami (2001) 'The Iron Age I at Tel Hazor in Light of the Renewed Excavations', *IEJ* 51: 148–70; **A. Ben-Tor** (1998) 'The Fall of Canaanite Hazor – The "Who" and "When" Questions', in S. Gitin, A. Mazar, and E. Stern (eds), *Mediterranean Peoples in Transition: Thirteenth to Early Tenth Centuries BCE, in Honor of Professor Trude Dothan*: 456–67; **idem** (2000) 'Hazor and the Chronology of Northern Israel: A Reply to Israel Finkelstein', *BASOR* 317: 9–15; **E. Bloch-Smith** (2003) 'Israelite Ethnicity in Iron I: Archaeology Preserves What Is Remembered and What Is Forgotten In Israel's History', *JBL* 122: 401–25; **E. Bloch-Smith and B. A. Nakhai** (1999) 'A Landscape Comes to Life: The Iron I Period', *NEA* 62: 62–92, 101–27; **S. Bunimovitz and A. Faust** (2003) 'Building Identity: The Four Room House and the Israelite Mind', in W. G. Dever and S. Gitin (eds), *Symbiosis, Symbolism, and the Power of the Past: Canaan, Ancient Israel, and their Neighbors from the Late Bronze Age through Roman Palaestina: Proceedings of the Centennial Symposium W. F. Albright Institute of Archaeological Research and the American Schools of Oriental Research Jerusalem, May 29–31, 2000*: 411-23; **S. Bunimovitz and Z. Lederman** (2008) 'A Border Case: Beth-Shemesh and the Rise of Ancient Israel', in L. L. Grabbe (ed.), *Israel in Transition: From Late Bronze II to Iron IIA (c. 1250–850 BCE), Volume 1 The Archaeology*: 21–31; **J. M. Cahill** (2003) 'Jerusalem at the Time of the United Monarchy: The Archaeological Evidence', in A. G. Vaughn and A. E. Killebrew (eds), *Jerusalem in Bible and Archaeology: The First Temple Period*: 13–80; **idem** (2004) 'Jerusalem in David and Solomon's Time', *BAR* 30, no. 6: 20–31, 62–3; **Y. Dagan** (2004) 'Results of the Survey: Settlement Patterns in the Lachish Regions', in D. Ussishkin (ed.), *The Renewed Archaeological Excavations at Lachish (1973–1994)*: 2672–90; **W. G. Dever** (2003) *Who Were the Early Israelites and Where Did They Come From?*; **A. Fantalkin and I. Finkelstein** (2006) 'The Sheshonq I Campaign and the 8th-Century BCE

Earthquake – More on the Archaeology and History of the South in the Iron I–IIA', *TA* 33: 18–42; **I. Finkelstein** (1988) *The Archaeology of the Israelite Settlement*; **idem** (1988–89) 'The Land of Ephraim Survey 1980-1987: Preliminary Report', *TA* 15-16: 117–83; **idem** (1996a) 'The Archaeology of the United Monarchy: An Alternative View', *Levant* 28: 177–87; **idem** (1998a) 'The Great Transformation: The "Conquest" of the Highlands Frontiers and the Rise of the Territorial States', in T. E. Levy (ed.), *The Archaeology of Society in the Holy Land*: 349–65; **idem** (1999a) 'State Formation in Israel and Judah: A Contrast in Context, A Contrast in Trajectory', *NEA* 62: 35–52; **idem** (1999b) 'Hazor and the North in the Iron Age: A Low Chronology Perspective', *BASOR* 314: 55–70; **idem** (2003) 'City-States to States: Polity Dynamics in the 10th–9th Centuries B.C.E.', in W. G. Dever and S. Gitin (eds), *Symbiosis, Symbolism, and the Power of the Past: Canaan, Ancient Israel, and their Neighbors from the Late Bronze Age through Roman Palaestina*: 75–83; **idem** (2005a) 'A Low Chronology Update: Archaeology, History and Bible', in T. E. Levy and T. Higham (eds), *The Bible and Radiocarbon Dating: Archaeology, Text and Science*: 31–42; **idem** (2013) *The Forgotten Kingdom: The Archaeology and History of Northern Israel*; **I. Finkelstein and A. Fantalkin** (2012) 'Khirbet Qeiyafa: An Unsensational Archaeological and Historical Interpretation', *TA* 39: 38–63; **I. Finkelstein, Z. Herzog, L. Singer-Avitz, and D. Ussishkin** (2007) 'Has King David's Palace in Jerusalem Been Found?', *TA* 34: 142–64; **I. Finkelstein, D. Ussishkin, and B. Halpern (eds)** (2000) *Megiddo III: The 1992–1996 Seasons*; **V. Fritz and A. Kempinski (eds)** (1983) *Ergebnisse der Ausgrabungen auf der Ḫirbet el-Mšāš (Tel Māśoś) 1972–1975: Teil I: Textband; Teil II: Tafelband; Teil III: Pläne*; **Y. Garfinkel** (2011) 'The Davidic Kingdom in Light of the Finds at Khirbet Qeiyafa', *City of David Studies of Ancient Jerusalem* 6: 14*–35*; **Y. Garfinkel and H.-G. Kang** (2011) 'The Relative and Absolute Chronology of Khirbet Qeiyafa: Very Late Iron Age I or Very Early Iron Age IIA?' *IEJ* 61: 171–83; **Y. Garfinkel, S. Ganor, and M. G. Hasel** (2012a) 'The Iron Age City of Khirbet Qeiyafa after Four Seasons of Excavations', in Gershon Galil, Ayelet Gilboa, Aren M. Maeir, and Dan'el Kahn (eds), *The Ancient Near East in the 12th–10th Centuries BCE: Culture and History*: 149–74; **idem** (2012b) 'Khirbat Qeiyafa 2010–2011', *Hadashot Arkheologiyot* 124: 1–12; **Y. Garfinkel, M. R. Golub, H. Misgav, and S. Ganor** (2015) 'The 'Išbaʿal Inscription from Khirbet Qeiyafa', *BASOR* 373: 217–33; **Y. Garfinkel, K. Streit, S. Ganor, and M. G. Hasel** (2012) 'State Formation in Judah: Biblical Tradition, Modern Historical: Theories, and Radiometric Dates at Khirbet Qeiyafa', *Radiocarbon* 54: 359–69; **S. Gibson** (2001) 'Agricultural Terraces and Settlement Expansion in the Highlands of Early Iron Age Palestine: Is There any Correlation between the Two?' in A. Mazar (ed.), *Studies in the Archaeology of the Iron Age in Israel and Jordan*: 113–46; **L. G. Herr** (2001) 'The History of the Collared Pithos at Tell el-ʿUmeiri, Jordan', in S. R. Wolff (ed.), *Studies in the Archaeology of Israel and Neighboring Lands in Memory of Douglas L. Esse*: 237–50; **Z. Herzog** (1994) 'The Beer-Sheba Valley: From Nomadism to Monarchy', in I. Finkelstein and N. Na'aman (eds), *From Nomadism to Monarchy: Archaeological and Historical Aspects of Early Israel*: 122–49; **idem** (2001) 'The Date of the Temple of Arad: Reassessment of the Stratigraphy and the

Implications for the History of Religion in Judah', in A. Mazar (ed.), *Studies in the Archaeology of the Iron Age in Israel and Jordan*: 156–78; **Z. Herzog and L. Singer-Avitz** (2004) 'Redefining the Centre: The Emergence of State in Judah', *TA* 31: 209–44; **B. Hesse and P. Wapnish** (1997) 'Can Pig Remains Be Used for Ethnic Diagnosis in the Ancient Near East?' in N. A. Silberman and D. B. Small (eds), *The Archaeology of Israel: Constructing the Past, Interpreting the Present*: 238-70; **D. W. Jamieson-Drake** (1991) *Scribes and Schools in Monarchic Judah: A Socio-Archeological Approach*; **A. E. Killebrew** (2001) 'The Collared Pithos in Context: A Typological, Technological, and Functional Reassessment', in S. R. Wolff (ed.), *Studies in the Archaeology of Israel and Neighboring Lands in Memory of Douglas L. Esse*: 377–98; **idem** (2003) 'Biblical Jerusalem: An Archaeological Assessment', in A. G. Vaughn and A. E. Killebrew (eds), *Jerusalem in Bible and Archaeology: The First Temple Period*: 329–45; **idem** (2005) *Biblical Peoples and Ethnicity: An Archaeological Study of Egyptians, Canaanites, Philistines, and Early Israel 1300–1000 B.C.E.*; **R. Kletter** (2006) 'Can a Proto-Israelite Please Stand Up? Notes on the Ethnicity of Iron Age Israel and Judah', in A. M. Maeir and P. de Miroschedji (eds), *'I Will Speak the Riddles of Ancient Times': Archaeological and Historical Studies in Honor of Amihai Mazar on the Occasion of his Sixtieth Birthday*: 573–86; **A. E. Knauf** (2000) 'Jerusalem in the Late Bronze and Early Iron Ages: A Proposal', *TA* 27: 75–90; **I. Koch** (2017) 'Settlements and Interactions in the Shephelah during the Late Second through Early First Millennia BCE', in O. Lipschits and A. M. Maeir (eds), *The Shephelah during the Iron Age: Recent Archaeological Studies*: 181–207; **G. Lehmann** (2003) 'The United Monarchy in the Countryside: Jerusalem, Judah, and the Shephelah during the Tenth Century B.C.E.', in A. G. Vaughn and A. E. Killebrew (eds), *Jerusalem in Bible and Archaeology: The First Temple Period*: 117–62; **G. Lehmann and H. M. Niemann** (2014) 'When Did the Shephelah Become Judahite?' *TA* 41: 77–94; **A. Mazar** (2005) 'The Debate over the Chronology of the Iron Age in the Southern Levant: Its History, the Current Situation, and a Suggested Resolution', in T. E. Levy and T. Higham (eds), *The Bible and Radiocarbon Dating: Archaeology, Text and Science*: 15–30; **idem** (2007) 'The Spade and the Text: The Interaction between Archaeology and Israelite History Relating to the Tenth-Ninth Centuries BCE', in H. G. M. Williamson (ed.), *Understanding the History of Ancient Israel*: 143–71; **idem** (2008) 'From 1200 to 850 BCE: Remarks on Some Selected Archaeological Issues', in L. L. Grabbe (ed.), *Israel in Transition: From Late Bronze II to Iron IIA (c. 1250–850 BCE): The Archaeology*: 86–120; **A. Mazar and E. Netzer** (1986) 'On the Israelite Fortress at Arad', *BASOR* 263: 87–91; **E. Mazar** (2006) 'Did I Find King David's Palace?' *BAR* 32, no. 1: 16–27, 70; **idem** (2009) *The Palace of King David: Excavations at the Summit of the City of David: Preliminary Report of Seasons 2005–2007*; **N. Na'aman** (1992c) 'Israel, Edom and Egypt in the 10th Century B.C.E.', *TA* 19: 71–93; **idem** (2008) 'In Search of the Ancient Name of Khirbet Qeiyafa', *Journal of Hebrew Scriptures* 8, no. 21; **idem** (2010) 'Khirbet Qeiyafa in Context', *UF* 42: 497–526; **idem** (2013) 'The Kingdom of Judah in the 9th Century BCE: Text Analysis versus Archaeological Research', *TA* 40: 247–76; **A. Ofer** (1994) '"All the Hill Country of Judah": From a Settlement Fringe to a Prosperous Monarchy', in

I. Finkelstein and N. Na'aman (eds), *From Nomadism to Monarchy: Archaeological and Historical Aspects of Early Israel*: 92–121; **idem** (2001) 'The Monarchic Period in the Judaean Highland: A Spatial Overview', in A. Mazar (ed.), *Studies in the Archaeology of the Iron Age in Israel and Jordan*: 14–37; **A. Raban** (2001) 'Standardized Collared-Rim Pithoi and Short-Lived Settlements', in S. R. Wolff (ed.), *Studies in the Archaeology of Israel and Neighboring Lands in Memory of Douglas L. Esse*: 493–518; **S. Schroer and S. Münster (eds)** (2017) *Khirbet Qeiyafa in the Shephelah: Papers Presented at a Colloquium of the Swiss Society for Ancient Near Eastern Studies Held at the University of Bern, September 6, 2014*; **I. Sharon, A. Gilboa, E. Boaretto, and A. J. T. Jull** (2005) 'The Early Iron Age Dating Project: Introduction, Methodology, Progress Report and an Update on the Tel Dor Radiometric Dates', in T. E. Levy and T. Higham (eds) *The Bible and Radiocarbon Dating: Archaeology, Text and Science*: 65–92; **L. Singer-Avitz** (2012) 'Khirbet Qeiyafa: Late Iron Age I in Spite of It All', *IEJ* 62: 177–85; **idem** (2016) 'Khirbet Qeiyafa: Late Iron Age I in Spite of It All – Once Again', *IEJ* 66: 232–44; **L. E. Stager** (1998b) 'Forging an Identity: The Emergence of Ancient Israel', in M. D. Coogan (ed.), *The Oxford History of the Biblical World*: 123–75; **M. L. Steiner** (1994) 'Re-dating the Terraces of Jerusalem', *IEJ* 44: 13–20; **idem** (1998) 'The Archaeology of Ancient Jerusalem', *CR:BS* 6: 143–68; **idem** (2001) 'Jerusalem in the Tenth and Seventh Centuries BCE: From Administrative Town to Commercial City', in A. Mazar (ed.), *Studies in the Archaeology of the Iron Age in Israel and Jordan*: 280–8; **idem** (2003a) 'Expanding Borders: The Development of Jerusalem in the Iron Age', in T. L. Thompson (ed.), *Jerusalem in Ancient History and Tradition*: 68–79; **idem** (2003b) 'The Evidence from Kenyon's Excavations in Jerusalem: A Response Essay', in A. G. Vaughn and A. E. Killebrew (eds), *Jerusalem in Bible and Archaeology: The First Temple Period*: 347–63; **D. Ussishkin** (2007a) 'Samaria, Jezreel and Megiddo: Royal Centres of Omri and Ahab', in L. L. Grabbe (ed.), *Ahab Agonistes: The Rise and Fall of the Omri Dynasty*: 293–309; **idem** (2007b) 'Archaeology of the Biblical Period: On Some Questions of Methodology and Chronology of the Iron Age', in H. G. M. Williamson (ed.), *Understanding the History of Ancient Israel*: 131–41; **D. Ussishkin (ed.)** (2004) *The Renewed Archaeological Excavations at Lachish (1973–1994)*; **A. Zarzeki-Peleg** (1997) 'Hazor, Jokneam and Megiddo in the 10th Century B.C.E.', *TA* 24: 258–88; **O. Zimhoni** (1985) 'The Iron Age Pottery of Tel 'Eton and its Relation to the Lachish, Tell Beit Mirsim and Arad Assemblages', *TA* 12: 63–90; **idem** (2004) 'Chapter 25 The Pottery of Levels V and IV and its Archaeological and Chronological Implications', in D. Ussishkin (ed.), *The Renewed Archaeological Excavations at Lachish (1973–1994)*: 4:1643–1788.

8.2.1 Archaeological Survey

Some mark the end of the LB and the beginning of Iron I with the end of Dynasty 19 and the beginning of Dynasty 20, a transitional phase covering roughly 1200–1150 BCE. This included the supposed invasion of the Sea Peoples and the fading away of the Canaanite city-states, to be replaced by a more disparate situation with some cities but mainly villages, especially in the highlands. We can survey the situation by moving roughly north to south, beginning with Hazor. The current excavators of Hazor have retained Y. Yadin's assignment of stratum X to the tenth century and stratum VIII to the Omride dynasty (Ben-Tor 2000; Mazar 2008). Although some ^{14}C dates contradict this, Mazar notes that it seems difficult to compress strata XB to VIII into 70 years in the ninth century, as required by the 'low chronology' (see Finkelstein's response in 2005a: 38).

The conventional view equates Megiddo VA-IVB, Hazor X, Gezer VIII, and Beersheba V – all seen as evidence for the United Monarchy (Finkelstein 1996a: 177). According to Mazar (2008), Yadin's thesis of Solomonic architecture at the three sites (Megiddo, Hazor, and Gezer) might still be correct. Finkelstein (1999b: 59) argues, however, that Yadin's equation of Hazor X with the time of Solomon creates chaos with strata IX, VIII, and VII, leaving no place for the important activities of Hazael in northern Israel. A. Zarzeki-Peleg's study (1997: 284) of the pottery assemblages connects Megiddo VIA with Jokneam XVII, while Hazor XB is later. Thus, Finkelstein (1999b: 60) argues, Hazor X was built by the Omrides. The recent overview by D. Ben-Ami has several important conclusions about Hazor, based on the recent excavations (Ben-Ami 2001, the numbering represents my formulation):

- The destroyers of LB Hazor (stratum XIII) left the site desolate and uninhabited. However, the 'impressive Late Bronze city of Hazor with its magnificence, monumentality, high status and influence...underwent a violent destruction that apparently cannot be related to the process of early Israelite settlement in Canaan' (Ben-Ami 2001: 168–9).
- There was a gap in settlement for a period of time.
- The settlement of IA I was a temporary encampment of a transient population whose presence was indicated by a large number of refuse pits; these settlers were not those who had destroyed Hazor.
- Although the identity of those in this encampment is unknown, the material culture is new, with substantial differences that suggest a different population.
- Yadin's identification of two separate settlement strata (XII and XI) is unsupported, and only one occupational phase is indicated by the remains.

Megiddo VIIA was destroyed in the second half of the twelfth century; rebuilt as VIB in Iron I it began to prosper again in stratum VIA (Finkelstein/Ussishkin/Halpern [eds] 2000: 594–5). This city was destroyed in a major conflagration. Megiddo VB was very different in character, with Iron Age traits in its material culture and layout (Finkelstein/Ussishkin/Halpern [eds] 2000: 595–6). In the transition from VIA to VB there is a change both in the pottery tradition and the layout of the city; nevertheless, it remained an imposing administrative centre (Finkelstein/Ussishkin/Halpern [eds] 2000: 597). Ussishkin (2007a) argues that Megiddo stratum VA-IVB or parts of it preceded the Omri dynasty and that this stratum (or the preceding stratum VB) was probably the city captured by Shoshenq in the late tenth century; however, Shoshenq did not destroy the city but intended to make it his administrative centre.

Settlement of the Jezreel and Beth-Shean valleys had flourished in the LB, but the collapse of Egyptian dominance resulted in a general decline, with an impoverished culture (Bloch-Smith/Nakhai 1999: 81–8). A number of small settlements existed in the Galilean area, the majority established in the twelfth and eleventh centuries, with a material culture suggesting continuity with the LB (Gal 1992: 84, 92). The ceramic continuity from the LB II to IA I indicates that the population was indigenous rather than immigrants as pictured by the biblical text (Josh. 19:24-48; Bloch-Smith/Nakhai 1999: 81). The suggestion that a new population took control appears to have little or no archaeological support (Bloch-Smith/Nakhai 1999: 83).

Thus, it seems that at least in the northern part of the country, Canaan rose again in the late eleventh and early tenth centuries from the blow of the mid-twelfth century (Finkelstein 2003a: 77). Other city-states seem to have emerged at that time, at Tel Kinneret, Tel Rehov, Tel Dor, and possibly Tel Keisan. IA I Kinneret replaced LB Hazor as the centre of the upper Jordan Valley, while IA I Tel Rehov was probably the focus of a territorial entity that covered the Beth-Shean and eastern Jezreel Valley. LB Tel Keisan continued to prosper and in the IA I seems to have served as the central site of the northern coastal plain (including Akko, and Tell Abu Hawam IVA as its port). IA I Dor dominated the coastal plain of the Carmel Ridge and possibly replaced LB Gath (Jatt) as the main centre of the region.

It has long been suggested that a number of innovations in technology took place in the central highlands: terracing, plastered cisterns, the 'Israelite house', collared-rim jars, and iron (Dever 2003a: 113–25). Unfortunately, it seems there is no list of technologies that is exclusive to this region and time or that can serve as 'Israelite ethnic markers' (Killebrew 2005: 171–81; Bloch-Smith 2003: 406–11; Kletter 2006: 579; Hesse/Wapnish 1997). Terracing was used as early as the EB; the early Iron Age settlers in the highlands made use of an existing technology (Gibson 2001). It is now argued that the collared-rim jar was already in use in the thirteenth century along the Levantine coast and is the product of a particular lifestyle or economy (such as the distribution of rations to employees) and is not exclusive to the Cisjordan highlands or Israel (Killebrew 2001; Raban 2001; Herr 2001). S. Bunimovitz and A. Faust (2003) recently argued that the four-room house was particularly Israelite, though they admit that a few such houses occur elsewhere, including in Transjordan. This seems to be more than just a few, while many presumed Israelite sites did not have such houses (Bloch-Smith 2003: 407–8). Iron seems to have been little used, despite the name 'Iron I': weapons and tools were mainly bronze (Bloch-Smith 2003: 417–20).

In this context of unique technologies, the question of pork consumption has also often been discussed, as an ethnic indicator. The subject is a complicated one, though there is a considerable drop in evidence for swine in the highlands during Iron I and Iron II, in contrast to the LB and also the IA I and II coastal plain where pigs remained a part of the diet. But Hesse and Wapnish conclude that 'no human behavioral evidence exists to indicate that pig avoidance was unique to any particular group in the ancient Near East.... Lots of people, for lots of reasons, were not eating pork' (1997: 261). S. Bunimovitz and Z. Lederman (2008) found that the total absence of pig bones in Beth-Shemesh in Iron I was consistent with the minimal percentage of pig bones in the hill country, in contrast to sites identified as Philistine. Beth-Shemesh became a sensitive seismograph for social changes between the regions, one such conspicuous boundary being pork avoidance. This allows that the pig taboo as an ethnic marker might have begun in the Shephelah and extended into the highlands, rather than the other way round.

For the area of Ephraim we have the preliminary survey results (Finkelstein 1988–89: especially 144–54; Finkelstein 1988: 121–204). The LB had seen a demographic decline, but the Iron I produced a 'settlement wave of unprecedented intensity', especially in the desert fringe and the northern central range (Finkelstein 1988–89: 146). This produced a pattern of major centres accompanied by a peripheral population. Finkelstein (1988–89: 148) argues that the population was densest in the east at the beginning of Iron I but then moved toward the west, with the cereal/animal husbandry economy also shifting toward a horticultural one; however, Bloch-Smith and Nakhai (1999: 71) assert that the archaeological data do not support either of these conclusions. Yet a comparison of Iron I and Iron II does indicate just such a population shift (Finkelstein 1998a: 357).

Regardless, it does appear that the Ephraimite and Manassite regions had the densest population of any region west of the Jordan. Settlement of the less favourable slopes and foothills, with trees and brush to be cleared, came later in the Iron I and continued into Iron II. In the Iron II almost all the regions of Ephraim were intensively settled (Finkelstein 1988–89: 151–4). Compared with Iron I, the population had shifted west, with some of the large sites in the east abandoned: Shiloh, 'Ai, and Khirbit Raddana. Sufficient grain was grown in some regions, apparently, to allow the western regions to concentrate on the important wine and oil production. In the southern central range of the Ephraimite hills some sites were abandoned and a fall in the population generally occurred in this region.

In the LB and early Iron I, a clear difference separated the north and south in the central hill country between the Jezreel and Beersheba valleys (Finkelstein 1998b: 361; 1999a: 43–4). The north experienced significant continuity, with most of the main sites continuing from the LB into Iron I. The Negev and Judaean hills had hardly any sedentary sites in the LB; this long settlement gap came to an end in the early Iron I. There was a large increase in small sites in the early Iron I, especially in the central hill country (Stager 1998: 134–7; Dever 2003a: 97–100). This increase was largely in the north, especially in the areas of Ephraim and Manasseh, and almost entirely north of Jerusalem. The Judaean hills had hardly any new sites in the early Iron I, and the region still remained highly pastoral (Finkelstein 1988: 52–3).

With regard to the Judaean Hills, however, we find a significant difference of opinion. Most of the early Iron I sites were between Jerusalem and Hebron, with hardly any south of Hebron. According to A. Ofer the mid-eleventh to the tenth centuries saw a rapid growth in the Judaean hills, including the more peripheral areas (Ofer 1994: 102–4). Based on his survey results Ofer (2001, 1994) argued that from the mid-eleventh to the eighth century the population nearly doubled in each century. To Iron IIA (a single identifiable ceramic stage) are to be assigned Tel Qasileh XI-IX, Izbet-Ṣartah II-I, Beersheba VIII-VI, Tel Edar III-II, Arad XII-XI (Ofer 2001: 30–1). We see the beginning of settlement in the pasture areas, and the first inhabitants of the desert fringe sites (e.g., Tekoah, ha-Qain, Ma'on, Carmel). The Shephelah only began to be populated at this date.

Some of Ofer's interpretation has been challenged. G. Lehmann (2003) criticized Ofer's survey from a methodological point of view (citing a recent publication of A. Faust). He noted that deciding between the conclusions of Ofer and Faust was currently impossible because the political situation prevented the necessary testing. Nevertheless, Lehmann (2003: 133, 141, 157) went on to argue, in contrast to Ofer, for a much smaller settled area and a population more like 10,000 in Iron I and 16,000 in Iron IIA Judah (including Jerusalem), but these are maxima: he reckoned Iron IIA at 5000 to 10,000, with Iron I correspondingly less. The built up area of the Shephelah was twice as large as Judah in Iron I and perhaps even three times as large in Iron IIA (2003: 134). Yet Z. Herzog and L. Singer-Avitz (2004: 220) critiqued Lehmann for nevertheless accepting too many of Ofer's data without question, though their study confirmed the view that the highlands of Judah (including Jerusalem – see below) were relatively sparsely settled, in contrast to the lowlands.

From a broader perspective the population density of the Judaean Hills was significantly less than the areas to the north. Ofer (1994: 107) notes the difference between the results of the Judaean Hills survey and those of the Manasseh hill country and the Land of Ephraim surveys. In Iron I Ephraim and Manasseh were four times that of the Judaean Hills, and twice that in Iron IIA. In the northern highlands most of the LB sites continued to be inhabited in Iron I, in contrast to the Judaean highlands which had almost no LB settlements (Finkelstein 1999a: 43–4). Many highland settlements disappeared in the later Iron I (Bloch-Smith/Nakhai 1999: 78). Growth in the Judaean hills was slow from Iron I to Iron IIA, in contrast, for example, with Benjamin where the growth was 243 per cent (Lehmann 2003: 134).

Penetration into the desert fringe and an increase in the population of the southern regions of the Judaean Hills in general characterized the Iron IIA (Ofer 1994: 104). The continuity of settlement from Iron I to Iron II was over 70 per cent, but the villages increased in Iron II, with 60 per cent new (Lehmann 2003: 147–50). Unlike Iron I, the sites were not at the highest elevation but tended to be in the middle slopes, suggesting that the settlers were feeling more secure. The more important settlements lined up with the north–south watershed in both the Iron I and IIA. The settlement peak came about in the eighth century (Ofer 1994: 105). This all suggests that developments in the central territory of Judah lagged significantly behind those of the north, which has implications for evaluating state development in general and the United Monarchy in particular.

Perhaps because of its ideological significance Jerusalem is probably the most contested site in Palestine. The main question is what kind of a settlement Jerusalem was in Iron IIA: was it a minor settlement, perhaps a large village or possibly a citadel but not a city, or was it the capital of a flourishing – or at least an emerging – state? Assessments differ considerably, with Ussishkin, Finkelstein, Steiner, Herzog, Lehmann, and Singer-Avitz supporting a minimal settlement; but many (including A. Mazar and, especially, J. M. Cahill) arguing for the latter. Using Rank Size Theory Ofer had argued that the graph of settled sites required Jerusalem to be included as the capital for the Judaean hill country to follow the expected pattern (1994: 97–8, 102–4); however, Lehmann's Rank Size analysis shows just the opposite (2003: 149–51). D. W. Jamieson-Drake (1991) was one of the first who queried the status of Jerusalem, concluding that it did not have the characteristics of a capital city, including monumental architecture, until the eighth century BCE. Jamieson-Drake has been much criticized for lacks in his data, but it seems that he was right as far as he went, even though he gave an incomplete description (Steiner 2001: 284).

J. M. Cahill (2003, 2004) has been one of the most vociferous voices arguing for a substantial city as early as the tenth century. She dates the 'stepped stone structure' to the Late Bronze/Early Iron transition, arguing that both the stepped mantle and the terraces below it were built together as a single architectural unit (Cahill 2003: 42). The fortification wall built during the Middle Bronze remained standing and was repaired and used until the Iron IIB (2003: 71). Cahill summarizes her conclusions for the tenth century (2004: 20):

> My own view is that the archaeological evidence demonstrates that during the time of Israel's United Monarchy, Jerusalem was fortified, was served by two complex water-supply systems and was populated by a socially stratified society that constructed at

least two new residential quarters – one located inside and the other located outside the city's fortification wall.

Reinforcing Cahill's interpretation, it has been argued that a building at the top of the 'stepped stone structure' dates to David's time and could be his palace (E. Mazar 2009, 2006); however, acceptance of her interpretation is by no means universal. See the criticisms by Finkelstein/Herzog/Singer-Avitz/Ussishkin (2007). They eventually conclude that the building is most likely late Hellenistic and that Mazar's interpretation was primarily based on the Bible and not the archaeology.

The 'stepped stone structure' is itself the subject of considerable dispute, with several positions being taken (Lehmann 2003: 134–6). In contrast to Cahill, Steiner (1994; 2003b: 351–61; 1998) argues from Kenyon's excavations that the stepped stone structure was quite different in extension and construction method from the terrace system. Where the terraces existed, only a mantle of stones was added, but where there were no terraces the structure was built up from bedrock. The dating and construction is confirmed by the pottery in the fill of the terraces which was Iron I, she argues, with no mix of later material. Steiner would date its construction to the tenth or early ninth century. In sum, the terrace and stepped structure systems do not have similar boundaries, identical pottery, or the same construction techniques. From Kenyon's excavations she feels there is enough evidence to show that the structure went out of use in late eighth or early seventh century BCE when a new city wall was built further down the slope.

As described by Steiner (2001, 2003a, 2003b), Jerusalem of the tenth and ninth centuries was a small town occupied mainly by public buildings, not exceeding 12 ha and approximately 2000 inhabitants (compare this with Lehmann's 2 ha and 300–600 inhabitants in Iron I, and 4 ha and 600–1200 in Iron IIA [Lehmann 2003: 135–6]). It exhibits the characteristics of a regional administrative centre or the capital of a small, newly established state, the towns of Megiddo, Hazor, Gezer, and Lachish showing similar characteristics at the same time. Excavations on the Ophel show the earliest buildings there date only from the ninth century. E. Mazar had argued that the fortified complex of this area south of the Temple Mount had been constructed as early as the ninth century, but they more likely date between the eighth and the early sixth centuries BCE (Killebrew 2003: 336). E. A. Knauf (2000) argues that the centre of the Davidic city has not been found because it would have been the area north of the Ophel, the area of the Temple Mount. Although it is not possible to test this hypothesis now, that section of the hill was a militarily strategic area and would have had to be incorporated into any settlement on the southeastern hill.

The argument that the Middle Bronze wall was used as a city wall in the LB, Iron I, and Iron IIA and IIB has no archaeological support: Jerusalem lacked a fortification wall until the mid-eighth century when the MB IIB wall was partially built over and partially reused for a new fortification wall (Killebrew 2003: 334; Ussishkin 2003: 110–11). The lack of other finds relating to fortification suggests that Jerusalem was unwalled and unfortified between the LB and Iron IIB (sixteenth to mid-eighth centuries), and thus Jerusalem was 'at best modest' (Killebrew 2003: 334). Also, the elaborate water system of MB IIB went out of use until the eighth/seventh centuries (Warren's shaft never served as water system), as shown by the excavations of Reich and Shukron (Killebrew 2003: 334–5).

The Shephelah in the LBA II displayed a gradual development of several sites, showing interaction with the Egyptian court (Koch 2017: 183). But in the transition from LB to Iron I the Shephelah suffered a massive demographic decline (perhaps related to the Egyptian withdrawal), with 67 sites in the LB but 25 in Iron I, and a reduction of settled area from 105 ha to 60 ha (Finkelstein 1999a: 44). Then, the Shephelah sites seem to have prospered in the later Iron I, with Tell Miqne-Ekron the dominant centre and smaller surrounding settlements dependent on it (Koch 2017: 185–6; Bloch-Smith/Nakhai 1999: 102–3). A number of lowland features of Iron I later became characteristic of highland Iron II, primarily the collared-rim store jars, the four-room house, and the bench tombs. This indicates a movement of some lowland peoples to the east and north (Bloch-Smith/Nakhai 1999: 103). Y. Dagan (2004: 2680–1) concluded that in Iron IIA the sites developed slowly as the process of Judaean settlement began, with many 'dispersed' and 'isolated' structures, a situation unknown in earlier periods, indicating a period of stability.

It is often assumed that Judah controlled the Shephelah from an early time, but a number of scholars have recently argued that this important foothill region remained a source of contention until well into the ninth century BCE or even later. N. Na'aman (2013: 263–4) argued that Judah was already making inroads by perhaps the first half of the ninth century. However, a recent study by G. Lehmann and M. H. Niemann (2014) argued that the Shephelah settlements show a material culture independent of both Philistia and the highlands; however, as the largest city in the region Gath dominated the area, including the Shephelah (Maeir 2012b). It was only after the destruction of Gath by Hazael about 835 BCE that Judah was able to expand into the Shephelah. Na'aman (2013) is quite correct that Judah probably had a non-aggression pact with Gath, but such an agreement is unlikely to have allowed Judah to expand at Philistine expense.

With regard to the central Shephelah site of Lachish, it was rebuilt after a long habitation gap in Iron I (Ussishkin [ed.] 2004: 1:76–87). Although little remains of this city (level V), the inhabitants seem to be a new people with a new material culture. Some have wanted to date level V to the tenth century and connect it with the invasion of Shoshenq, but the latter's inscription does not mention Lachish (nor any place in Judah proper except Arad in the Negev), nor has any destruction layer been uncovered. Based on A. Zimhoni's study of the pottery (2004: 4:1707) Ussishkin dated level IV to the mid-ninth century BCE and level V to the first half of the ninth. (This incidentally supports the LC, but Ussishkin notes that the interpretation is not conclusive.) If Lachish V dates to the ninth, Rehoboam could not have fortified the site (2 Chron. 11:5-12, 23) nor would Shoshenq have destroyed it.

The recently excavated Khirbet Qeiyafa has been the occasion of much discussion, in large part because of the claims of the excavators that the site was Judahite and disproved those who doubted the biblical account of David (Garfinkel 2011; Garfinkel/Ganor/Hasel 2012a, 2012b; Garfinkel et al. 2012). Their conclusions about the archaeology of the site was criticized by Y. Dagan (2009) who had done a surface survey of the area. (Although Dagan's objections are well-taken, there is the caveat that surface surveys have some problems of their own.) The excavators noted that Qeiyafa seemed to be a short-lived site that was in existence only for some decades before being destroyed or abandoned (and not revived until the Hellenistic period). Based on ^{14}C dating, they put it in the period of Iron IIA, about 1025–975 BCE (Garfinkel/Kang 2011; Garfinkel et al. 2012; Garfinkel et al. 2015); however, this dating has been attacked on methodological grounds with the argument that raw ^{14}C dates need to be integrated with all the data, including pottery and other aspects of material culture. Based on this approach, Finkelstein and Fantalkin (2012) have argued for a broader dating of about 1050–915 BCE; they even suggest that the site might have been brought to an end by Shoshenq I's invasion. L. Singer-Avitz (2012, 2016) also contended that the excavators dated the site too late and argued for an Iron I dating, pointing out that the closest comparable pottery assemblage is found at nearby Beth-Shemesh. Yet the Beth-Shemesh level is dated to Iron I, as the Qeiyafa excavators themselves seemed to accept. Singer-Avitz also argues that radiometric dates ultimately support the Iron I dating.

There is also controversy over whether the site is Judahite, as the excavators claimed, or whether it might be Israelite (Finkelstein/Fantalkin 2012) or even Canaanite (Na'aman 2010). The argument that it is to be identified with biblical Shaaraim has also been opposed, with others identifying it as Gob (Na'aman 2008; Finkelstein/Fantalkin 2012: 46–8). A recent study brings together a lengthy statement and interpretation of the chief excavator with a critique from both archaeologists and biblical scholars (Schroer/Münster 2017). A. M. Maeir points out the unsatisfactory nature of the way in which the excavators question the whole methodological basis of modern biblical interpretation in their reconstruction: 'The complex nature of the biblical texts – and for sure those dealing with the "Davidic cycle" – cannot be collapsed into a monolithic, "Sunday School" understanding of early biblical history!' (in Schroer/Münster [eds] 2017: 68). Similarly, T. Römer advises that 'one should not "personalize" the site too much by relating all kinds of buildings and finds to David and Solomon. It could be that the historical reality of the tenth century in Judah and Philistia is quite different from a biblical historicist reconstruction' (in Schroer/Münster [eds] 2017: 81). In short, the implications of the site are still hotly disputed, and it is likely to take some time for any sort of consensus to develop. But as should be clear, one's view of the biblical tradition is as important as archaeology for some archaeologists.

In the Negev there was a settlement gap throughout the LB but a renewal in population came in Iron I. The Beersheba Valley is normally too arid for farming, but there have been a few periods of sufficient rainfall, including the period from the thirteenth to the tenth centuries (Herzog 1994: 125–6). This increased fertility and peaceful conditions (apparently), and led to population growth (*c.* 1000 in the eleventh century). New settlements included Tel Masos, Arad, Tel Haror, Tel Sera', Tel Esdar, Tel Beersheba, Naḥal Yattir, and other sites. Some sites (e.g., Tel Sera' and Tel Haror) were apparently settled by Philistines, but the identity of those moving into other sites is controversial (see the survey in Herzog 1994: 146–8). The biblical text mentions a number of groups associated with this region: Judah and related groups, Simeon, Amalekites, Canaanites, Kenites, Calebites, and so on, though how seriously to take this list is a question.

A large number of sites were identified in the Negev Highlands around Qadesh-Barnea in archaeological surveys, about 50 of which were identified as 'Israelite fortresses', perhaps built by Solomon (e.g., Aharoni 1967). However, a number of scholars have now questioned this interpretation, arguing that they were desert settlements of local people who were possibly changing from a nomadic to a more settled lifestyle (see the summary in Finkelstein 1995a: 103–14; also Na'aman 1992c). The main reason is that the location of the sites and their construction do not fit with what would be expected of fortresses; furthermore, there was no renewal of them at a later time when Judah definitely controlled this area.

Another important site is Tel Masos in the Beersheba Valley which had been excavated in 1972–75 (Fritz/Kempinski 1983). Finkelstein developed the thesis of a polity, perhaps a 'chiefdom', centred on Tel Masos that grew up when the population took control of trade in the region (Finkelstein 1995a: 114–26; 2013: 126–7; Fantalkin/Finkelstein 2006). An important aspect of the economy at this time was copper production and the regional commerce involving it. But when the copper trade declined, the 'Tel Masos polity' also declined. The Tel Masos 'chiefdom' was not conquered by Shoshenq I, according to Finkelstein; on the contrary, Egyptian evident interest in the copper trade (cf. §6.3.3.5) led to its expansion for a time, until production in Cyprus resumed in about the ninth century. For further on the copper production in this region, see the discussion at §6.3.3.5.

The transition from Iron I to Iron IIA was marked by a significant abandonment of settlements. Tel Masos was destroyed or abandoned, but it was rebuilt as a small fortress, and a number of other fortresses were also established. It has been argued that these changes were the result of intervention by the Jerusalem monarchy, but 'the spatial distribution of the sites in the valley and the demographic estimates does not support this model'; rather, a good case can be made that the cause was environmental (Herzog 1994: 143–5). Other suggestions are expanding highland settlements or Shoshenq's invasion (Finkelstein 2003a: 78–9). Certainly, the sites most uncontroversially associated with the campaign of Shoshenq are found in the Negev. The 'Greater Arad' of Shoshenq is generally agreed to be Tel Arad (Finkelstein 1999a: 38–9). Arad has been much debated over the years, with later studies substantially disagreeing with the original excavator's. Stratum XI had been identified with Shoshenq's invasion, but Zimhoni (1985) and A. Mazar and E. Netzer (1986) concluded that XI must be later than the tenth century, which would make stratum XII the Shoshenq level. The latest excavator Z. Herzog (2001; 2002: 58–72) agrees with this. Thus Arad XI and Beersheba V (with the first Iron Age fortifications in Judah) must be in the ninth century.

8.2.2 Analysis and Conclusions on Archaeology

There is wide agreement that Arad XII and related Negev sites are to be related to Shoshenq's invasion (Mazar 2007, 2008). The use of Shoshenq's list of cities provided a chronological anchor of crucial importance (Ussishkin 2007b). Albright's assumption that Shoshenq destroyed the whole country has been widely accepted, but his actions might have been varied: the erection of a royal stela at Megiddo shows that Shoshenq aimed to hold the city, not destroy it. Thus, his list is useless as a secure archaeological and chronological anchor, the only possible exception being Arad XII. If Arad XII dates to the second half of the tenth century and not later, this affects the dating of Lachish V, Tel Beit Mirsim B, and Tel Beersheba VII; however, Ussishkin (2007b) has some doubts about the reliability even of this synchronization.

Here we get into controversy over the so-called low chronology. The main advantage of the 'low chronology' is that it closes the 'Dark Age' of the ninth century (Finkelstein 1996a: 184–5). Its main disadvantage is that it changes the entire understanding of the emergence of the Israelite state. The monuments previously associated with the United Monarchy are redated from the second half of the tenth century to the early ninth. The 'low chronology' forces reconsideration of several issues relating to the archaeology of proto-Israel. In the hill country settlements of the tenth century are not much different from those of the eleventh; thus, the real transformation came about 900 BCE rather than about 1000 BCE, which has consequences for a United Monarchy. In the northern highlands this transformation brought significant growth in the number and size of sites and expansion into new frontiers and niches, while the southern highlands were only sparsely settled in early Iron II.

'Accepting the Low Chronology means stripping the United Monarchy of monumental buildings' (Finkelstein 1996a: 185). According to Finkelstein (1999b: 39) many of the strata conventionally dated to eleventh century should now be the tenth (Megiddo VIA; Beth-shean Upper VI, Tel Hadar

IV, Jokneam XVII, Beersheba VII, Arad XII). Important for our purposes are those redated to the ninth century according to the LC: Megiddo VA-IVB, Beersheba V, Arad XI. (Those strata dated to the eighth and seventh centuries are not affected.) The main mounds in both the north and the south (Megiddo, Gezer, Beersheba, Lachish) would be dated to the ninth century BCE or even later. Although inscribed seals and impressions are known from mid-ninth century, they are mainly found in the eighth century onwards.

Finally, the LC closes the unexplained gap between the monumental architecture traditionally assigned to the tenth century and the evidence of public administration for which we have clues in the late ninth to the eighth. In sum, the LC puts the tenth century closer to the previous period of Iron I than to the Iron II; the real revolution then came in the ninth century, more in the north than the south. The line between Iron I and Iron II came in the early ninth century rather than about 1000 BCE. The kingdom of David and Solomon would have been a chiefdom or early state but without monumental construction or advanced administration (cf. the early Ottoman Turks or Shechem in the Amarna age).

Mazar's MCC seems to have been fairly widely accepted, but its extended Iron IIA spanning both the tenth and ninth centuries means that 'it would make the position of those who wish to utilize archaeology for secure historical interpretation of the tenth–ninth centuries BCE harder to sustain' (Mazar 2007; cf. 2008). It also means that events that were dated to the tenth century in conventional chronology – and which the LC dates to the ninth century – are left unspecific in the MCC. Ussishkin has expressed his pessimism about resolving the issues about chronology by normal archaeological methods, referring to the

> ambiguity of clear stratigraphic evidence in many sites, and the difficulty of comparing pottery from different regions of the country. Hence there are possibilities for different interpretations and different chronologies. In my view, as long as no new additional data are available it would be impossible to solve the chronological differences being debated at present. [Ussishkin 207b: 139]

He goes on to refer to radiocarbon dating, a 'method that has been enthusiastically adopted' by some scholars on both sides of the debate, but 'this method is far from providing conclusive and perfect results', for 'the interpretation of the same ^{14}C tests can be fitted to different ideologies' (Ussishkin 2007b: 139). As quoted above, Mazar has noted the problems with radiocarbon dating but, nevertheless, refers to the results that he feels supports his case. It may be that radiocarbon data will lead to a resolution or partial resolution of the debate, but this is likely to be only after a substantial database has been established (Sharon et al. 2005).

Another conclusion (only partially divorced from the chronology debate) is the difference between the development in northern Palestine as contrasted with southern Palestine. This was largely due to geographical factors: topography, geology, soil, rainfall, climate in general. The northern region, both the hill country and the lowlands, was much more suited to settlement, farming, and fertility in general. The region of Judah was less fertile, had a lower density of population, and developed economically more slowly than Samaria. When one considers the *longue durée*, it would have been extraordinary for the Judaean highlands to dominate the north in the Iron I or IIA. A number of archaeologists argue that the archaeology does not support the text, which depicts a Judaean-

Highland-centred United Monarchy. Those who do argue for archaeological support for the United Monarchy generally do so by explicit – or implicit – appeal to the text as the guide for interpreting the archaeology. As will be argued below (§8.5.6), the United Monarchy indeed existed but was considerably different from the biblical picture.

Jerusalem remains an area of considerable controversy, but those who maintain that Jerusalem did not develop into a substantial city until Iron IIB have current archaeology on their side (the building recently found by E. Mazar has intriguing possibilities but currently has widely different interpretations among archaeologists). Those who maintain an earlier development must argue on the basis of what has presumed to have disappeared or what might be found in the future. This is why a substantial argument is now made that the Northern Kingdom (in the form of the Omride dynasty) was the prior development to a state in the ninth century, with Judah coming along more slowly, reaching its height only in the eighth century. Needless to say, the debate continues.

8.3 COMING OF THE PHILISTINES

M. Artzy (2013) 'On the Other "Sea Peoples"', in A. E. Killebrew and G. Lehmann (eds), *The Philistines and Other 'Sea Peoples' in Text and Archaeology*: 329–44; **S. Bunimovitz** (1990) 'Problems in the "Ethnic" Identity of the Philistine Material Culture', *TA* 17: 210–22; **E. H. Cline** (2016) Review of E. Stern, *The Material Culture of the Northern Sea Peoples in Israel*, *JAOS* 136: 197–9; **B. Davis, A. M. Maeir, and L. A. Hitchcock** (2015) 'Disentangling Entangled Objects: Iron Age Inscriptions from Philistia as a Reflection of Cultural Processes', *IEJ* 65: 140–66; **W. Dietrich** (2007) *The Early Monarchy in Israel: The Tenth Century B.C.E.*; **idem** (2012) 'David and the Philistines: Literature and History', in G. Galil, A. Gilboa, A. M. Maeir, and D. Kahn (eds), *The Ancient Near East in the 12th–10th Centuries BCE: Culture and History*: 79–98; **Eliyahu-Behar et al.** (2012) 'Iron and Bronze Production in Iron Age IIA Philistia: New Evidence from Tell es-Safi/Gath, Israel', *Journal of Archaeological Science* 39: 255–67; **I. Finkelstein** (1998) 'The Rise of Early Israel: Archaeology and Long-Term History', in S. Ahituv and E. D. Oren (eds), *The Origin of Early Israel – Current Debate: Biblical, Historical and Archaeological Perspectives*: 7–39; **idem** (2002a) 'The Philistines in the Bible: A Late-Monarchic Perspective', *JSOT* 27: 131–67; **idem** (2003) 'City-States to States: Polity Dynamics in the 10th–9th Centuries B.C.E.', in W. G. Dever and S. Gitin (eds), *Symbiosis, Symbolism, and the Power of the Past: Canaan, Ancient Israel, and their Neighbors from the Late Bronze Age through Roman Palaestina*: 75–83; **K. Galling** (1966) 'Goliath und seine Rüstung', in *Volume du Congrès Genève 1965*: 150–69; **A. H. Gardiner** (1947) *Ancient Egyptian Onomastica: Text and Plates*; **A. Gilboa** (2005) 'Sea Peoples and Phoenicians along the Southern Phoenician Coast – A Reconciliation: An Interpretation of Šikila (*SKL*) Material Culture', *BASOR* 337: 47–78; **S. Gitin, T. Dothan, and J. Naveh** (1997) 'A Royal Dedicatory Inscription from Ekron', *IEJ* 47: 1–16; **Y. Gottlieb** (2010) 'The Advent of the Age of Iron in the Land of Israel: A Review and Reassessment', *TA* 37: 89–110; **L. G. Herr** (1997) 'Emerging Nations: The Iron Age II Period', *BA* 60: 114–83; **L. A. Hitchcock** (2018) '"All the Cherethites, and All the Pelethites, and All the Gittites (Samuel 2:15-18)" – An Up-to-Date Account of the Minoan Connection with the Philistines', in I. Shai et al. (eds), *Tell It in Gath: Studies in the History and Archaeology of Israel: Essays in Honor of Aren M. Maeir on the Occasion of his Sixtieth Birthday*: 304–21; **L. A. Hitchcock and A. M. Maeir** (2013) 'Beyond Creolization and Hybridity: Entangled and Transcultural Identities in Philistia', *Archaeological Review from Cambridge* 28: 43–65; **D. Kaniewski, E. Van Campo, K. Van Lerberghe, T. Boiy, K. Vansteenhuyse, G. Jans, K. Nys, H. Weiss, C. Morhange, T. Otto, and J. Bretschneider** (2011) 'The Sea Peoples, from Cuneiform Tablets to Carbon Dating', *PLoS One* 6, issue 6: 1–7; **A. E. Killebrew and G. Lehmann (eds)** (2013) *The Philistines and Other 'Sea Peoples' in Text and Archaeology*; **G. A. Lehmann** (1979) 'Die Šikalāju – ein neues Zeugnis zu den "Seevölker"-Heerfahrten im späten 13. Jh. v. Chr. (RS 34.129)', *UF* 11: 481–94; **A. M. Maeir** (2012) 'Insights on the Philistine Culture and Related Issues: An Overview of 15 Years of Work at Tell eṣ-Ṣafi/Gath', in G. Galil, A. Gilboa, A. M. Maeir, and D. Kahn (eds), *The Ancient Near East in the 12th–10th Centuries BCE: Culture and History: Proceedings of the International Conference held at the University of Haifa, 2-5 May, 2010*: 345–404; **idem** (2017a) 'Philistine Gath after 20 Years: Regional Perspectives on the Iron Age', in O. Lipschits and A. M. Maeir (eds), *The Shephelah during the Iron Age: Recent Archaeological Studies*: 133–54; **idem** (2017b) Review of S. Rodan, *Aegean Mercenaries in Light of the Bible*, *Journal of Eastern Mediterranean Archaeology & Heritage Studies* 5: 246–7; **idem** (2019a) 'Iron Age I Philistines: Entangled Identities in a Transformative Period', in A. Yasur-Landau, E. H. Cline, and Y. M. Rowan (eds), *The Social Archaeology of the Levant: From Prehistory to the Present*: 310–23; **A. M. Maeir (ed.)** (2012) *Tell es-Ṣafi/Gath I: The 1996–2005 Seasons: Part 1: Text*.; **A. M. Maeir and J. Uziel** (2007) 'A Tale of Two Tells: A Comparative Perspective on Tel Miqne-Ekron and Tell eṣ-Ṣâfi/Gath in Light of Recent Archaeological Research', in S. White Crawford (eds), *'Up to the Gates of Ekron': Essays on the Archaeology and History of the Eastern Mediterranean in Honor of Seymour Gitin*: 29–42; **J. Maran** (2018) 'Goliath's Peers: Interconnected Polyethnic Warrior Elites in the Eastern Mediterranean of the 13th and 12th Centuries BCE', in I. Shai et al. (eds), *Tell It in Gath: Studies in the History and Archaeology of Israel: Essays in Honor of Aren M. Maeir on the Occasion of his Sixtieth Birthday*: 223–41; **J. M. Millek** (2014) Review of E. Stern, *The Material Culture of the Northern Sea Peoples in Israel*, *ZDPV* 130: 110–11; **N. Na'aman** (1996c) 'Sources and Composition in the History of David', in V. Fritz and P. R. Davies (eds), *The Origins of the Ancient Israelite States*: 170–86; **idem** (2002) 'In Search of Reality Behind the Account of David's Wars with Israel's Neighbours', *IEJ* 52: 200–224; **H. M. Niemann** (2003) 'Pentapolis', *RGG*[4] 6: 1087–8; **idem** (2013) 'Neighbors and Foes, Rivals and Kin: Philistines, Shepheleans, Judeans between Geography and Economy, History and Theology', in A. E. Killebrew and G. Lehmann (eds), *The Philistines and Other 'Sea Peoples' in Text and Archaeology*: 243–64; **S. Rodan** (2015) *Aegean Mercenaries in Light of the Bible: Clash of Cultures in the Story of David and Goliath*; **A. Rofé** (2015) 'David Overcomes Goliath (1 Samuel 17): Genre, Text, Origin and Message of the Story', *Henoch* 37: 66–100; **B. U. Schipper** (2005) *Die Erzählung des Wenamun: Ein Literaturwerk im Spannungsfeld von Politik,*

Geschichte und Religion; **I. Sharon and A. Gilboa** (2013) 'The *SKL* Town: Dor in the Early Iron Age', in A. E. Killebrew and G. Lehmann (eds), *The Philistines and Other 'Sea Peoples' in Text and Archaeology*: 393–468; **I. Singer** (2000) 'New Evidence on the End of the Hittite Empire', in E. D. Oren (ed.), *The Sea Peoples and their World: A Reassessment*: 21–33; **T. Stech-Wheeler, J. D. Muhly, K. R. Maxwell-Hyslop, and R. Maddin** (1981) 'Iron at Taanach and Early Iron Metallurgy in the Eastern Mediterranean', *AJA* 85: 245–68; **E. Stern** (2013) *The Material Culture of the Northern Sea Peoples in Israel*; **J. Van Seters** (2010) 'David the Mercenary', in L. L. Grabbe (ed.), *Israel in Transition: From Late Bronze II to Iron IIA (c. 1250–850 BCE): Volume 2 The Text*: 199–219; **J. R. Zorn** (2010) 'Reconsidering Goliath: An Iron Age I Philistine Chariot Warrior', *BASOR* 360: 1–22.

The settlement of some of the Sea Peoples in south Palestine and along the coast created a new element within Canaan that was to have profound significance for the developing state of Israel. The Philistines were one of the components of the Sea Peoples who migrated from the wider Mediterranean area in the late second millennium BCE. The Sea Peoples were discussed in the previous chapter (§7.2). However, as indicated there it is difficult to separate analysis of the Philistines from the broader question of the Sea Peoples. Thus, the discussion here will of necessity overlap to some extent that already recorded for the Sea Peoples. According to the biblical text the Philistines were the main enemy of Israel through much of its early history. This picture is manifestly wrong in certain parts; for example, the Philistines have been anachronistically projected back as settled in the land in the early second millennium BCE (Gen. 21:22-34; 26:1-18; Finkelstein [2002a: 152–4] suggests that this reflects an eighth or seventh century context). Yet other parts of the biblical picture may be correct; we can know only after looking at it carefully.

Beginning about 1200 BCE, various waves of Sea Peoples arrived in southern Palestine. But the total added up probably only to a few thousand. Rameses III's attempts to check them seems to have been unsuccessful, even if he won a battle or two against them. The new sites established in Iron I and their total built-up area confirms that the number of new settlers was small. The Philistines and other tribes of the Sea Peoples settled along the coast and in the coastal plain but seem to have been essentially independent of one another (some of the other tribes are noted below).

The major LB sites of southern Palestine were divided between Philistines (Tell eṣ-Ṣâfī-Gath, Tel Miqne-Ekron, Ashkelon, Ashdod, Gaza) and what are usually identified as Judahites (Gezer and Lachish), and Yurza. These continued into Iron I, with two exceptions: Lachish was abandoned (as was Tel Ḥarasim), but Tel Miqne-Ekron had grown considerably. Ashdod and Ekron appear to be the strongest towns in the region, with Ashkelon and Gath the weakest (unless Ashkelon controlled Jaffa). The estimated population is 35,000 for LB and 30,000 for Iron I. This compares with 44,000 for the central hill country in Iron I (but only 2200 of these were in the Judaean Hills). Considering that few new sites were established in Iron I, and the total built-up area was also very similar, this suggests that the number of new settlers – the Philistines – were few, which confirms what a number of scholars had been arguing: the Philistines settled among the indigenous Canaanite population, perhaps as an elite.

A. M. Maeir has been among those who have argued for looking at the Philistine settlement in all its complexity. He and several colleagues have recently tackled the question of the Philistine invasion/settlement from the point of view of 'acculturation', 'hybridization', or whatever term one wishes to use (Davis, Maeir, and Hitchcock 2015; Hitchcock and Maeir 2013). This recognizes the complicated product that arose from the Philistine settlement in Canaan. Maeir and his colleagues have adopted the term 'entangled' to describe the way in which the cultures of native Canaanites and the incoming Philistines affected each other to produce the culture that is sometimes called Philistine but which also includes clear Canaanite aspects. It helps to explain the complex nature of the cultural processes reflected in the literary and archaeological records.

Maeir cites with approval the scenario suggested by Assaf Yasur-Landau (2010: 315–34), which resolves the problem of chronology by proposing that the Philistine settlement took place over a lengthy period of time, with different phases, as is normal for migration and settlement processes that have been studied. According to Yasur-Landau (cf. also Killebrew 2005: 230–1), the immediate origin of the Sea Peoples may have been Cyprus and perhaps even Asia Minor (even if the ultimate origin was the eastern Aegean), and the settlements there may not have been many years before those in Palestine. The number migrating was probably only a few thousand, far fewer than the 25,000 to 30,000 often proposed. The first wave of a small number of scout or pioneering immigrants could have come shortly after 1200 BCE, to be followed by much larger waves. When Ramesses III realized what was happening, he attempted to stem the flow about 1175 BCE (though this was probably not a single event in that year but took place over a period of time) but is likely to have had only small success.

One result of this migration and settlement is that the material culture in the region included both Philistine and Canaanite elements (Bunimovitz 1990). But if the Philistines were so few, this argues against a major invasion force or even a large-scale migration. When we ask where the Philistines came from, A. M. Maeir points out that

> one cannot speak of a single place of origin; rather, the early Philistine population is comprised of peoples of mixed origins, from various places in the eastern and central Mediterranean, who settled among local Canaanites. This is exemplified by many different cultural influences seen in early Iron Age Philistia – not Mycenaean, Cypriote, Anatolian, or a single other cultural origin, but a combination of many…an 'entangled' culture…. [Maeir 2017: 134]

Whether some portion of the Sea Peoples destroyed the Hittite empire, Ugarit, and other kingdoms along the Mediterranean is perhaps a separate question, though not unrelated, but this is discussed elsewhere (§5.4).

When we try to track the Philistines into Iron IIA, we run into difficulties because, as L. Herr (1997: 129, 131) points out, our archaeological information is poor. We are thrown back on the biblical text with all the problems noted for it elsewhere. If we follow it, the Philistines threatened Israel and Judah. Here we must give a reinterpretation of the data compared to the biblical text and the conventional view. It is probable that the Philistines controlled the Shephelah during this period, but it is unlikely that they were interested in moving into the hill country, since the 'carrying capacity' of the coastal plain had not been reached (Finkelstein 1998: 24). If there was a clash between the people of the hill country and the Philistines, it is likely that Israel/Judah initiated it. When we note similar situations, such as the Assyrians and the inhabitants of the Zagros mountains, or the Babylonians and the Kassite mountain tribes, it is the mountain tribes who are the aggressors and make raids on the 'more civilized' peoples, i.e., those in the settled agricultural areas.

Would the highlanders have had the strength or resources for a wholesale invasion of Philistine territory? It seems unlikely (cf. Finkelstein 1998: 24; 2003: 78). Instead, they would have made the occasional raid to carry off livestock, stored grain, and other spoil. The Philistines in their turn would have periodically retaliated by a concerted campaign into the hill country to stop this constant irritant. It would have helped for a time but would not have stopped it permanently. This was the history of relations between the Philistines and the Israelites and Judahites until the time of Saul.

At this point, there is potential engagement between biblical text and archaeology. Israel Finkelstein (2002a), for example, has argued that the actual context for the main Philistine narrative in 1 Samuel is the seventh century BCE. Others see evidence of some earlier memory there (Na'aman 1996: 2002); for example, the Ark Narrative is not intrinsically unbelievable overall. Unfortunately, many of the welcome recent archaeological finds do not impinge directly on the Bible. For example, the pebbled hearth that Aren Maeir (2012a: 354–5) has noted as characteristic of the Philistine area for many centuries seems not to be reflected in the biblical text. There are several examples where text and archaeology interact which we can survey briefly.

Several lists of Philistine cities are found (Josh. 11:22; 19:43; Judg. 1:18; 1 Sam. 6:17; Jer. 25:20; 2 Chron. 26:6). 1 Samuel 6:17 lists five cities that have become known as the Philistine Pentapolis: Ashdod, Gaza, Ashkelon, Gath, and Ekron. Gath was destroyed by the Aramaean king Hazael about 830 BCE and ceased to be a major Philistine site (2 Kgs 2:18; Maeir/Uziel 2007: 31–5). The biblical text seems to remember the original importance of Gath, which suggests an early memory (Na'aman 2002: 210–12). Whether the cities were united into some sort of Pentapolis, with a council of *seranim* making decisions for it as pictured in the text (e.g., 1 Sam. 5:8, 11), is a separate question. With Gath and Ekron both roughly the same size but also much larger than the other three cities in the Iron I and early Iron IIA (Maeir/Uziel 2007), would they have been content to share power and authority equally with the smaller cities? Would they not have been rivals in at least certain ways? These data do not seem to be reflected in the text in any way. As Niemann notes, 'The treatment of the five Philistine main sites as a unified block was not historical: it was an element of "theological historical writing" projected back' (Niemann 2003, my translation).We also have the statement in 1 Sam. 7:14 that the cities of Gath to Ekron were returned to Israel after the ark incident. This is clearly unhistorical in the light of archaeology: we have no evidence of Israelite/Judahite occupation in the material culture of this time. Indeed, 1 Sam. 17:52 evidently has Ekron in Philistine hands when David was young, not too many years afterward.

The architecture of Philistine temples is known from excavations, but there is one feature also found in the text: the placement of the pillars supporting the roof in the Philistine temple. In Judg. 16:25-30 the pillars look like a match to those found in archaeological excavations, where pillars placed closely side by side support the roof (Maeir [ed.] 2012: 29–30). Yet we must qualify this positive statement with two more negative ones. First, the statement that there were people on the roof who could observe events on the ground floor of the temple (as if overlooking an unroofed courtyard) is not confirmed by anything so far found. Secondly, this description of a Philistine temple could be quite late, since temples existed in Philistine towns until very late (note 1 Macc. 10:84; 11:4).

A number of biblical passages refer to Achish, king of Gath (מלך גת: 1 Sam. 21:11, 13; 27:2-4, 11; 1 Kgs 2:39). This is the only evidence for such a person; however, we have an inscription from the seventh century that reads partially as follows (in the translation of the publishers: Gitin/Dothan/ Naveh 1997: 9):

1. The temple (which) he built, *'kyš* son of Padi, son of
2. *Ysd*, son of Ada, son of Ya'ir, ruler of Ekron,
3. for *Ptgyh* his lady....

Thus, in the seventh century there was an Achish (אכיש) who was ruler (שר) of Ekron. Finkelstein (2002a: 133–6) suggests that the author of the narrative (written in the seventh century) made use of the name of a contemporary ruler in the area of Philistia, but because Gath was already strongly in the David tradition, he made Achish a ruler of Gath. This is a reasonable argument, but it seems to me that those who see Achish as a ruler of Gath in an early tradition about David also present a reasonable picture. W. Dietrich (2012: 94) argues against Finkelstein's interpretation, citing the label of Achish as *king* of Gath (1 Kgs 2:39). However, the reference to the figure of Achish in the Ekron inscription as שר, which seems to me likely to be equivalent to מלך, would actually bolster Finkelstein's argument. At the moment, I see no way of demonstrating for certain whether Achish is a late introduction into the narrative or an early element in the tradition.

One passage that is often mentioned, though seldom discussed in proper depth, is 1 Sam. 13:19-21. The translation of the passage is quite different in modern translations from traditional ones, such as the Luther Bibel and the Authorized Version, partly because of archaeology (though the text is difficult and probably corrupt), primarily because of the finding of weights of two thirds of a shekel with the word *pym* on them, which seems to be the import of the word *pîm* in this passage. Basically, this passage says that the Philistines control the working of metal, and that for repair or sharpening of farming implements Israelites had to travel to the Philistines and pay them. The passage is somewhat difficult, partly because it may be corrupt and partly because the instruments listed are not all clearly identified, though their status as metal farm tools seems obvious from the context. What is done to them by the Philistine metal workers is also not certain. To renew a ploughshare that had been blunted or even damaged by stones would probably cost two-thirds of a sheqel (the value of a *pîm*), but this would seem extremely expensive simply to sharpen a sickle. Moreover, the Israelite farmer could easily have found appropriate whet stones in the environment to use to sharpen a sickle or mattock.

In the last few years several excavations have turned up data about metalworking in the Levant at the end of the Bronze and beginning of the Iron Age. The basic situation that emerges from what is presently known is that bronze dominated metal usage until about 1000 BCE, at which point the balance shifted heavily to iron. Yet in the Late Bronze Age and the early Iron Age, both copper-based and iron-based tools and weapons were in use. Carburized steel technology had developed by the twelfth century, so what had changed around 1000 BCE was one of proportions of use, not a change of technology (Gottlieb 2010: 89–90).

It was once claimed that the Hittites first monopolized iron production and that the Philistines then took that position in the Levant; however, it is now widely believed that that position has been disproved (Stech-Wheeler et al. 1981). Yet quite a few commentators have still accepted the view that 1 Sam. 13:19-21 was basically true and showed that the Philistines controlled or limited Israelite metallurgical skills (cf. Niemann 2013: 262–3; Dietrich 2007: 156, 213). It should be noted that 1 Sam. 13:19-22 does not specify iron; the tools and weapons in the passage could just as well have been bronze. A recent survey by Y. Gottlieb (2010), which takes into account a variety of earlier studies, looks at the beginnings of the use of iron in Palestine in the early Iron Age. It is only in the Iron IIA (tenth century) that iron begins to displace bronze as the technology to make carburized steel develops. However, she notes that our data for the Shephelah and the highlands are sparse, and her statistics are primarily reliable for the North (especially Megiddo and Beth Shean) and the South (the Negev and the Beersheba Valley). In the central highlands the stratigraphy is problematic, but in Iron I and early Iron IIA bronze seems to have prevailed for agricultural implements in sites like Khirbet Raddana, though iron is predominant at Bethel and et-Tell. Interestingly, older settled areas seem to have been more conservative and continued to prefer bronze even while newer settlements (such as in the Negev) had focused on iron.

For the Shephelah, copper-based artefacts predominate until late Iron IIA, while for the area of Philistia, the first iron tools seem to be as late as Iron IIB. Gottlieb's article was written before the important metal-working facility was found at Gath/Tel eṣ-Ṣafi (Maeir 2012a: 367–8; Maeir [ed.] 2012: 27–8; Eliyahu-Behar et al. 2012). Gath has provided the first physical evidence on the state of metallurgy technology in Philistia in the early Iron Age. Both bronze and iron working are attested for the early Iron IIA, once again indicating the importance of both metals at this time. But what we do not find is any indication that the Philistines controlled metal technology. As Aren Maeir notes, 'one cannot speak of a Philistine monopoly on metal production in the late Iron I and early Iron IIA (the available evidence from the ancient Levant does not support this supposition)' (Maeir 2012a: 367). It seems to me an absurd notion that Israelites had to go to Philistia just to sharpen their farm implements, not only paying a very high price but also taking the time and trouble to travel there and back. What we find in 1 Sam. 13:19-22 is a statement of theology, not contemporary metal technology.

An important question relates to Goliath's armour. Although there are a few who argue that it reflects Iron Age I (Singer 2013: 20, 25, 27), many have followed Kurt Galling (1966) in maintaining that 'the narrator…has put together the wholly singular weaponry of Goliath from diverse elements of military equipment known to him' at a rather later time. Finkelstein (2002a: 145–6) has argued that Goliath's armoury represents a Greek hoplite soldier of the seventh century, though he also recognizes that some parts of the description fit Assyrian equipage. This last point complicates matters: is an actual soldier with his weaponry being described, or is the image of Goliath simply made up eclectically (as Galling seems to be saying)? In either case, though, a later time than the Iron I or early Iron II is being represented. J. R. Zorn (2010) recently argued that Goliath's armour fitted that of a Philistine chariot warrior of the IA I period. Whether he has made his case regarding the armour description can be left to specialists, but one specialist, J. Maran (2010: 223), is sceptical, arguing that a literary work is not concerned with historical accuracy but 'often freely combines non-contemporary features in order to emphasize specific issues and have a particular effect on the reader'. He goes to observe, 'the fascinating description of Goliath's armor cannot be used as a trustworthy source for determining the origin of the warrior' (Maran 2010: 232).

A recent study is that of S. Rodan (2015) who believes the background of the story relates to the Greek mercenaries in the armies of Saite Egypt during the seventh and sixth centuries BCE. The Jews exiled in Egypt opposed the ethos of the Greek mercenaries and sought to contrast their culture and beliefs with them. The name Goliath was derived from the Greek term γυαλαθώραξ, which was the name of the hoplite armour. However, Goliath's scale coat is a problem because hoplites did not normally wear such armour. In his review of her work, A. M. Maeir (2017b) points out that the name 'Goliath' seems to have been introduced into the story at a rather late stage. This would nullify her emphasis on the type of armour giving the name to Goliath. But the idea that hoplite armour is being described here is essentially the same as Finkelstein, even though her Egyptian context is different. Finally, as A. Rofé (2015) proposes, the composition of the story probably dates from Persian times and is unlikely to preserve accurate memories of the IA I.

As for the Cherethites and Pelethites (2 Sam. 8:18), they are associated with the Philistines (Ezek. 25:16); indeed, Pelethite is interpreted as 'Philistine' by some. The Philistines are alleged to have come from Crete (Caphtor) in Amos 9:7. In Ezek. 25:16, where the MT has 'Cherethites', the LXX has 'Cretans'. L. A. Hitchcock (2018) points out that many connect the Philistines with Mycenae and Cyprus but goes on to emphasize the Minoan/Cretan connection. Finkelstein (2002a: 148–50) notes that Cherethites and Pelethites do not occur explicitly among the groups of Sea Peoples, but he follows Albright in interpreting Pelethites as a reference to Greek peltasts (*peltastai*) or light infantry (from their *pelte* or light shield). Again, he relates them to the Greek mercenary troops widely used in the seventh century, as does John Van Seters (2010: 214–17; see also §8.5.6.2).

As well as the Philistines in the southern coastal plain, Sea Peoples tribes were said to be settled elsewhere in Canaan (Artzy 2013; Stern 2013). *Wenamun* (1.8) states that the city of Dor was a town of the Tjeker (cf. Schipper 2005), though it should be noted that it literally is a 'harbour of the Tjeker' (*w' dmj.t n T̠-k-r* [Schipper 2005: 45]). Whether this shows an area where the Tjeker settled or was only a city with a harbour somehow identified with the Tjeker is a matter of debate. We also have the geographical list in the *Onomasticon of Amenope* (Gardiner 1947). What we find is that a number of the tribes of the Sea Peoples are listed, along with other geographical names (listed according to Gardiner 1947: 119*–205*, using his numbering of the names):

252	*Qdš(w)*	Qadesh on the Orontes (İrnt̠)
253	*İrr*	Alalah?
254-6		(lost)
257	*Kpn(y)*	Byblos
258	*T̠ḫsy*	(corrected from *Tsḫ*) Takhsy (near Qadesh?)
259	*N'ryn*	?
260	*Nhryn*	Nahrin (area to the east of the Euphrates)
261		(lost)
262	*İsqnrn*	Ashkelon
263	*İsdd*	Ashdod
264	*Gd̠t*	Gaza
265	*İsr*	Assyria (or possibly Asher)
266	*Sbry?*	Shubaru? (an Assyrian people?)
267		(lost)
268	*Šrdn*	Sherden
269	*T̠kr*	Tjeker
270	*Prst*	Philistines
271	*Ḥrm*	Hurma? (a Hittite city)

Although most of the Sea Peoples occur here, it will be clear that there is no particular pattern to the individual names that might allow one to deduce the location of their settlement.

E. Stern (2013) describes the material culture which he associates with the Sea Peoples settled in the area between the Yarkon River and the Plain of Akko. Putting together the Egyptian statements, the biblical text (e.g., 1 Sam. 28:4; 29:1, 11), and the archaeology, he concludes that the 'Sikils' (Tjeker) lived to the north of the Yarkon, in the Sharon, and on Carmel, while the Sherden lived north of them in the Plain of Akko. He thinks their culture reflects the Aegean region. Stern's survey of the material culture is exemplary, based on long experience. He acknowledges, however, that a number of other excavators in the region disagree (Stern 2003: 7). Some reviewers also lodged caveats about Stern's conclusions (Millek 2014; Cline 2016). They especially note the controversy over the assumption that 'pots equal people' (see further at §8.4.1). J. M. Millek (2014: 111) sums up the situation: 'how do we know archaeologically that the Sikil people were not living in the South or Philistines were not living in the North as either group could have used whichever material was available locally?'

I. Sharon and A. Gilboa (2013) have also carried out fieldwork on Dor. They concluded (in explicit disagreement with Stern) that the material culture of Dor was 'Phoenician'. In spite of theories that have seen the site change hands at the end of the LB (Canaanite to Sikil), the mid-Iron I (Sikil to Phoenician), and finally late Iron I (Phoenician to Israelite), no destruction occurred between LB and Iron I. A destruction did take place at the end of Iron IA, but there is no real evidence of a change in material culture, only the natural evolution that one would expect in a local site. Twenty years of excavating at Dor has produced only one complete vessel and a few additional sherds for what would have been a century of 'Sikil pottery' production on the site. They point out that were it not for the single statement in Wenamun, no one would have suggested a connection of Iron I Dor with the Sea Peoples. Thus, at this stage to assign specific settlement areas to Sea Peoples other than the Philistines seems speculative at best.

To conclude the discussion of the Philistines, A. M. Maeir summarizes their situation as follows:

> During the early Iron Age, the Philistines were a group of very mixed origins (entangled), deriving from various regions and origins, including non-local and local Canaanite elements. A variety of evidence hints that substantial parts of the Philistine population may have derived from pirate-like groups.... Thus, it would appear that early Philistine culture was not modeled on the Bronze Age Aegean palace structure but rather on that of a society led by a charismatic leader.... The repertoire of Philistine material culture seems to indicate that while Aegean-oriented symbols and behaviors were of importance (and perhaps even dominated), other traditions existed, too. This may very well indicate that while this society was eclectic in nature, the cultural memory of this group, throughout the Iron Age, stressed the supposed Aegean origins of this group...and suppressed other origin components of this culture.... Thus, while one cannot accept the earlier suppositions of a monolithic migration as the explanation for the appearance of Philistine culture, nevertheless, migration and the arrival of substantial elements of the Philistine populace can be sustained. [Maeir 2019a: 318–19]

8.4 THE SETTLEMENT (OF 'ISRAEL'?)

I. Finkelstein (2019) 'First Israel, Core Israel, United (Northern) Israel', *NEA* 82: 8–15; **A. E. Knauf** (2008) *Josua*; **idem** (2010a) 'History in Joshua', in L. L. Grabbe (ed.), *Israel in Transition: From Late Bronze II to Iron IIA (c. 1250–850 BCE): Volume 2 The Text*: 130–9; **idem** (2016a) *Richter*; **J. M. Miller** (1977) 'Archaeology and the Israelite Conquest of Canaan: Some Methodological Observations', *PEQ* 109: 87–93; **N. Na'aman** (1994c) 'The "Conquest of Canaan" in the Book of Joshua and in History', in I. Finkelstein and N. Na'aman (eds), *From Nomadism to Monarchy: Archaeological and Historical Aspects of Early Israel*: 218–81; **idem** (2005b) 'The Kingdom of Judah under Josiah', in L. L. Grabbe (ed.), *Good Kings and Bad Kings: The Kingdom of Judah in the Seventh Century BCE*: 189–247; **J. Van Seters** (1990) 'Joshua's Campaign of Canaan and Near Eastern Historiography', *SJOT* 2: 1–12.

The two biblical books that ostensibly describe the settlement are Joshua and Judges, and they were once given a fair amount of credence. Yet now both books have been critically examined for historical data and are generally found wanting (e.g, Knauf 2008, 2016a). The book of Joshua describes how the Israelites crossed the Jordan (Joshua 1–5) and conquered the land in only five years, the major cities taken being Jericho and Ai, while Gibeon and Kiriath-jearim submitted without a fight (Joshua 9). Other cities are enumerated in Joshua 10. The surprising thing is that when the reader moves from Joshua – where the land was conquered and divided up – to Judges, there is something of a shock, since the land seems far from being under Israelite control. Granted, here and there are statements in Joshua that suggest that everything was not conquered all at once (e.g., Josh. 17:14-17), which means that something of a mixed message comes across. Nevertheless, the dominant impression is that it was all settled after five years. This is especially the impression left by Josh. 11:23; 14:15; 21:41-43, and Joshua 13–19 where the land is divided up among the various tribes.

Some decades ago the broad picture of the conquest of Canaan by the Israelites was widely accepted in parts of scholarship. Now that this is no longer the case, the question to be asked is whether any of the book of Joshua can be taken as historical. Many would answer this in the negative (e.g., Na'aman 1994c: 249–81; Van Seters 1990; Miller 1977). Some lists seem, however, to relate to a much later time and situation and to still have value as historical sources, at least according to some (cf. Na'aman 2005b on Josh. 15:21-62; 18:21-28; 19:2-8, 40-46; Finkelstein 2019). For another assessment of some bits of data in Joshua that seem to represent a genuine historical memory, see Knauf 2010a. Further on Joshua and Judges is given below (§8.4.5).

8.4.1 Who Settled in the Hill Country?

F. Barth (ed.) (1969*) Ethnic Groups and Boundaries: The Social Organization of Culture Difference*; **E. Bloch-Smith** (2003) 'Israelite Ethnicity in Iron I: Archaeology Preserves What Is Remembered and What Is Forgotten In Israel's History', *JBL* 122: 401–25; **M. G. Brett (ed.)** (1996) *Ethnicity and the Bible*; **D. V. Edelman**

(1996b) 'Ethnicity and Early Israel', in M. G. Brett (ed.), *Ethnicity and the Bible*: 42–7; **I. Finkelstein** (1998a) 'The Great Transformation: The "Conquest" of the Highlands Frontiers and the Rise of the Territorial States', in T. E. Levy (ed.), *The Archaeology of Society in the Holy Land*: 349–65; **C. Geertz** (1973) *The Interpretation of Cultures*; **A. K. Grayson** (1996) *Assyrian Rulers of the Early First Millennium BC II (858–745 BC)*; **B. Hesse and P. Wapnish** (1997) 'Can Pig Remains Be Used for Ethnic Diagnosis in the Ancient Near East?' in N. A. Silberman and D. B. Small (eds), *The Archaeology of Israel: Constructing the Past, Interpreting the Present*: 238–70; **J. Hutchinson and A. D. Smith (eds)** (1996*) Ethnicity*; **S. Jones** (1997) *The Archaeology of Ethnicity*; **K. A. Kamp and N. Yoffee** (1980) 'Ethnicity in Ancient Western Asia during the Early Second Millennium B.C.: Archaeological Assessments and Ethnoarchaeological Prospectives', *BASOR* 237: 85–104; **C. F. Keyes** (1997) 'Ethnic Groups, Ethnicity', in T. Barfield (ed.), *The Dictionary of Anthropology*: 152–4; **A. E. Killebrew** (2005) *Biblical Peoples and Ethnicity*; **R. Kletter** (2006) 'Can a Proto-Israelite Please Stand Up? Notes on the Ethnicity of Iron Age Israel and Judah', in A. M. Maeir and P. de Miroschedji (eds), *'I Will Speak the Riddles of Ancient Times'*: 573–86; **A. M. Maeir** (2019b) 'Philistine and Israelite Identities: Some Comparative Thoughts', *WO* 49: 151–60; **idem** (2021) 'On Defining Israel: Or, Let's Do the *Kulturkreislehre* Again!', *HeBAI* 10: 106–48; **L. Monroe and D. E. Fleming** (2019) 'Earliest Israel in Highland Company', *NEA* 82: 16–23; **O. Sergi** (2019a) 'The Formation of Israelite Identity in the Central Canaanite Highlands in the Iron Age I–IIA', *NEA* 82: 42–51; **idem** (2019b) 'Israelite Identity and the Formation of the Israelite Polities in the Iron I–IIA Central Canaanite Highlands', *WO* 49: 206–35; **S. J. Shennan (ed.)** (1989*) Archaeological Approaches to Cultural Identity*; **M. Skjeggesald** (1992) 'Ethnic Groups in Early Iron Age Palestine: Some Remarks on the Use of the Term "Israelite" in Recent Research', *SJOT* 6: 159–86; **S. Sokolovskii and V. Tishkov** (1996) 'Ethnicity', in A. Barnard and J. Spencer (eds), *Encylopedia of Social and Cultural Anthropology*: 190–3; **K. L. Sparks** (1998) *Ethnicity and Identity in Ancient Israel*.

As was clear in the discussion of archaeology (§8.2) and will be clear in the discussion below, there was a significant settlement and increase in population in the central hill country (and a bit later in the Judaean hills) in the Iron I. The question is, what was the identity of the community created by the settlement? The issue of ethnic identity is one that has been extensively discussed in recent literature (see most recently Maeir 2021; cf. also the discussion in Grabbe 2017: 19–22). It is not the aim of the present section to debate the issue at length but to draw attention to some recent studies, especially those that comment on the question of determining ethnic identity from archaeology. The following brief points will summarize much of the discussion relevant for our purposes:

- There have been different approaches to ethnicity, extensively in anthropological study (Barth [ed.] 1969; Shennan [ed.] 1989; Hutchinson and Smith [eds] 1996; Sokolovskii and Tishkov 1996; Keyes 1997), but also in biblical scholarship (Brett 1996; Sparks 1998; Killebrew 2005: 8–16). A view that the ethnicity should be seen mainly in biological terms (ethnic groups have a common ancestry or kinship or genetic pool) is widely rejected in

modern study. Yet it has contributed the important insight that ethnic groups generally define themselves in kinship or quasi-kinship terms, which was also true in antiquity. There is also the fact that there is a 'primordial' quality to ethnic identity in which the group's distinctiveness – 'we/they' – is essential (Geertz 1973: 255–310; Keyes 1997).
- Some – even a few recent writers – have seen the question in terms of distinct cultures, but this is problematic in that cultural groups do not always develop an ethnic identity or group consciousness, nor do some ethnic groups have specific cultural features (especially those that show up in archaeology).
- O. Sergi (2019a, 2019b) has suggested that 'Israel' was a kinship term (cf. further at §8.4.2 below). This seems to be correct, at least originally – for example, in the Merenptah stela they seem to be a 'people' – but the point at which the name designated a territorial state can be debated. Sergi suggests that when Ahab was called an 'Israelite', this was a kinship designation since he was not also called king (see the inscription in Grayson 1996: 17). However, the term 'Israelite' is preceded by the KUR 'country' determinative. Also, Assyrian inscriptions often omit giving the title 'king' to the heads of states they fought. More frequent is 'son/man of X' ('DUMU/*mar* X') or 'house of X' ('*bīt* X') or simply the name (see discussion in Grabbe 2017: 185). It seems likely that 'Ahab the Israelite' (ᵐ*A-ha-ab-bu* KUR *Sir-'-la-a-a*) in this case is the equivalent of 'man of Israel' or even 'king of Israel'. Ahab's kingdom might already have been a territorial state with the name 'Israel'.
- Very much disputed at the present is the question of whether ethnic identity can be determined from material culture – archaeology – also known as the 'pots equal people' debate. Relating material culture to ethnicity is fraught with problems (Edelman 1996b; Skjeggesald 1992). It is interesting that the elements accepted by many researchers to describe ethnic identity (e.g., Kletter 2006: 574) leave no trace in the archaeological record. Also, differences or similarity in material culture do not necessarily show differences or identity in ethnicity: they may be the result of similar or diverse environments (Finkelstein 1998a: 359, 365) or similar or diverse lifestyles.
- Any list of particular traits in the material culture is likely to be problematic, whether we think of pottery, architecture, diet, or even language. What is clear is that there 'is no list of material traits that can cause "ancient Israel to stand up" independently, without the help of written sources' (Kletter 2006: 579). As already noted in the discussion with regard to archaeology (§8.2), the traditional list of 'Israelite ethnic markers' has evaporated as exclusive indicators: four-room pillared house, collared-rim jar, abstinence from pork (Maeir 2021: 134–40; Bloch-Smith 2003: 406–11; Kamp and Yoffee 1980; Kletter 2006: 579; Hesse and Wapnish 1997).
- Because our knowledge of groups in antiquity is based on texts rather than a direct study of living peoples, we are limited by what the texts tell us. This means that the task of penetrating to identity and ethnicity is often very complicated.

What we can say about the settlement in the hill country in the Iron I are two things: first, an 'Israel' had already been attested with Merenptah's account of his supposed campaign against various groups, which means that we should not be surprised to find an Israel in Canaan in subsequent centuries; secondly, in textual sources relating to the early Iron IIa we seem to find an

Israel concentrated in the central hill country. This suggests that we can talk about an 'Israelite settlement' in that region in the Iron I and early Iron IIa, but this can only be provisional. A connection between the Israel of Merenptah and the later Israel of the biblical text is plausible but not certain: the name could have been taken up and reapplied to another group for a variety of possible reasons. Further, the texts themselves are much later than IA I and even IA IIa, and our use of the term 'Israel' to designate the entity might be overturned by subsequent finds in the archaeology. We must also keep in mind that the original settlement in the hill country appears to have been a loose collection of farmsteads and villages and only later be conceived of as a somewhat unified community, much less called a state.

To conclude, there is still much disputed about what is constituted by the designation 'Israel' in our textual sources, as well as how to identify it in the material culture. In the discussion below, references to 'Israelite settlement' depend on projecting back from the later kingdom of Israel to earlier stages in its development, a reasonable (or so it seems to me) but nevertheless hypothetical process. In any case, it should be clear that 'Israel' refers to a somewhat different entity in each stage of its development, whether in terms of territory, organization, demography, or religious practice. There might be a thread connecting Merenptah through IA I and IA IIA to Omri, but that remains to be demonstrated.

8.4.2 Recent Models for the Settlement

D Ben-Ami (2001) 'The Iron Age I at Tel Hazor in Light of the Renewed Excavations', *IEJ* 51: 148–70; **A. Ben-Tor** (1998) 'The Fall of Canaanite Hazor – The "Who" and "When" Questions', in S. Gitin, A. Mazar, and E. Stern (eds), *Mediterranean Peoples in Transition: Thirteenth to Early Tenth Centuries BCE, in Honor of Professor Trude Dothan*: 456–67; **W. G. Dever** (2017) *Beyond the Texts: An Archaeological Portrait of Ancient Israel and Judah*; **J. H. Hayes and J. M. Miller (eds)** (1977) *Israelite and Judaean History*; **A. E. Killebrew** (2006) 'The Emergence of Ancient Israel: The Social Boundaries of a "Mixed Multitude" in Canaan', in A. M. Maeir and P. de Miroschedji (eds), *'I Will Speak the Riddles of Ancient Times': Archaeological and Historical Studies in Honor of Amihai Mazar on the Occasion of his Sixtieth Birthday*: 555–72; **J. J. McDermott** (1998) *What Are They Saying about the Formation of Israel?*; **G. E. Mendenhall** (1962) 'The Hebrew Conquest of Palestine', *BA* 25: 66–87; **J. M. Miller** (1979) 'W. F. Albright and Historical Reconstruction', *BA* 42: 37–47; **G. W. Ramsey** (1981) *The Quest for the Historical Israel*; **Y. Yadin** (1979) 'The Transition from a Semi-Nomadic to a Sedentary Society in the Twelfth Century B.C.E.', in F. M. Cross (ed.), *Symposia: Celebrating the Seventy-Fifth Anniversary of the Founding of the American Schools of Oriental Research (1900–1975)*: 57–68; **idem** (1982) 'Is the Biblical Account of the Israelite Conquest of Canaan Historically Reliable?', *BAR* 8, no. 2: 16–23.

Over the past thirty to forty years a great deal of debate has centred on the question of how an 'Israel' got into the land and eventually became a nation (see the survey in Ramsey 1981; McDermott 1998; Killebrew 2006, as well as recent histories of Israel). Until the 1960s most scholars favoured one of two models, the 'Conquest Model' of the Albright school and the 'Peaceful Infiltration Model' of the Alt–Noth school. Then, in 1963 a programmatic article by G. E. Mendenhall in a semi-popular journal outlined a third theory, but its real development came in the late 1970s: the Mendenhall–Gottwald theory of an internal revolt. Much deliberation has centred on these, and understanding them is still important for getting at the historical situation, yet as we shall see the debate has moved on the past several decades.

The Albright model of a unified conquest was heavily influenced by the biblical text, though it would be incorrect to conclude that it was only a paraphrase of Joshua. Albright initially dated the conquest to the fifteenth century BCE, but then N. Glueck conducted a survey of the Transjordanian region in the years 1938–40. Since Glueck concluded that these regions were uninhabited until the thirteenth century, Albright redated the conquest to the thirteenth century, a position he continued to maintain until his death. Although ostensibly based on archaeology, it had an uncanny resemblance to the first half of Joshua. In some ways, this was more apparent than real, but it allowed the conservative tendency to maintain academic respectability while still really following the biblical text.

In 1977 J. M. Miller gave a thorough critique of the Albright position and ultimately rejected it (Hayes/Miller 1977: 254–62, 270–7; also Miller 1979). His conclusions presented a picture emphasizing the development of Israel from internal populations and also from the Sea Peoples or tribes forced to migrate in their wake, and expressed some scepticism toward the significance of nomadic incursions. The position continued to be stoutly defended by Y. Yadin, even in some of his last articles to be published (Yadin 1979, 1982), but by then it was being widely abandoned by scholars. Thus, one is somewhat disconcerted to find a mainstream archaeologist trot out the thesis again, apparently without realizing that biblical scholarship has abandoned the position (Ben-Tor 1998, but cf. Ben-Ami 2001). The 'Conquest' model is now only of historical interest, but it should alert scholars to the fact that vociferous adherence by large numbers of academics is no guarantee that a particular theory will stand the test of time.

There have been a few die-hard defences by conservative-evangelicals (e.g., Wood 1990; Bimson 1981). There has even been a move to postulate an exodus from Egypt in the fifteenth century BCE, against the Albright dating of it to the thirteenth century BCE – and against the standard scholarly view to downplay or even deny any such event. It is true that one can and should demonstrate the fragility of the archaeological support for the Albright thesis, but this was done only to undermine Albright's dating of 'the exodus' rather than the conquest model as such. This attempt to date Joshua to the end of the Middle Bronze Age, while going back to Albright's original position, has gained no following in mainstream scholarship.

The 'Peaceful Infiltration' model of Alt and Noth has better stood the test of time in certain ways than Albright's. It continued to find adherents among archaeologists in the 1980s and even the 1990s (e.g., Zertal 1994). Yet a number of several criticisms had been levelled at it that rendered the thesis in its original form questionable. One was that the desert could not produce sufficient nomads to populate the hill country in the Iron I (see Chaney 1983; but this is disputed by Finkelstein [1988: 308] on a different basis). Another was that nomads adopt this lifestyle out of necessity and want nothing more than the chance to settle down: in fact, the 'nomadic' mode of life takes many forms, and those who engage in it are no more likely to change than those in other forms of subsistence agrarian activity (see the discussion in Lemche 1985: 136–47).

The 'Mendenhall–Gottwald thesis' is widely used to designate the internal revolt model. Gottwald's 1979 study was the academic underpinning for Mendenhall's programmatic article (1962) almost two decades earlier. A collection strongly espousing the Mendenhall–Gottwald thesis was notable for the trenchant essay by Mendenhall attacking and disowning Gottwald's approach! (Mendenhall/Graf 1983: 91–103). Although some genuine differences can be shown to exist between the two scholars, it has not stopped the hyphenated designation for this model. N. P. Lemche, while expressing his appreciation of Gottwald's use of sociology, presented a major critique of his work (1985; also Finkelstein 1988: 306–14). Although differing from Gottwald on many points, including the concept of an internal revolt, Lemche's final picture was of an internal development of the indigenous population. In his view, though, it was not urban residents who fled oppression of the city-states but members of the rural peasantry who went up into the hill country to escape taxes (Lemche 1985: 427–32). As V. Fritz (1981: 69–72) argued the highland material culture does not suggest that those settling there were individuals formerly employed in urban occupations.

The three models that dominated the twentieth century are no longer the main alternatives. An examination of their strengths and weaknesses has already suggested which way scholarship has moved. The Albright thesis of a unified conquest has all but been abandoned by mainstream critical scholarship and continues to be pressed only by a few conservative scholars. The reason is that much of the support has simply evaporated, in particular the evidence that was once seen as its main strength: the archaeology. In the past half century most of the discussion has revolved around the Alt–Noth and the Mendenhall–Gottwald theories and has focused on the archaeology and on social-scientific models.

Some new suggestions for models have combined aspects of both Alt–Noth and Mendenhall–Gottwald but also new considerations, especially derived from work in the social sciences and further developments in archaeology. The 'symbiosis theory' of V. Fritz (1981, 1987) is really a variant of the Alt–Noth thesis, though it also incorporates insights from Mendenhall–Gottwald. Fritz points to the similarity of the material culture of the highland settlers to that found in the territories of the Canaanite city-states, but also differences. This shows that the new population (assumed to be pastoralists) was not the same as the Canaanites but was in close contact with them over several generations. This population eventually settled down, their material culture showing a lot in common with Canaanite culture but also with enough differences to distinguish them. However, his concept of 'Canaanite' is problematic, as shown in a previous discussion (§6.3.3.2).

I. Finkelstein produced what seems to be a true merging of Alt–Noth and Mendenhall–Gottwald, with a firm archaeological base (Finkelstein 1988). Much of his study is on the archaeology of developments during the Iron I and documents the unprecedented growth of population in the hill country through this period. Although accepting that the new population included a number of elements, he especially argued that the spectacular growth came about because a large nomadic population settled down. The nomads did not come from the 'deep' desert region, however, but were the descendants of those who left settled life for a pastoral lifestyle in the Middle Bronze because of adverse conditions. He argues that the region went through a regular long-term cycle of people moving from settled life to nomadic life and back again, depending on climatic and economic cycles. Thus, the new population of the hill country was made up of nomadic pastoralists different from the Canaanites (as Alt–Noth proposed) but they were part of the indigenous population (as argued by

Mendenhall–Gottwald). He notes that the earliest settlements in the areas of Ephraim, Manasseh, and Benjamin were on the desert fringe; they also often settled near Canaanite cities (1988: 310).

Finkelstein's thesis has been critiqued mainly on the basis that the archaeology of the Iron I hill country settlements does not indicate nomadic influence on the material culture (Dever 1998a, 1992a; 2017: 255–7). Also, the studies of pastoralists indicate that pastoralism is often not an exclusive lifestyle but one activity of people who also engage in agriculture (Lemche 1985: 136–47; Killebrew 2006: 565). This is true, but it does not strike at the heart of Finkelstein's proposal – indeed, he knows and accepts that. More important are studies of Palestinian nomads in recent times who lived and moved freely among the settled areas and peasant farmers. Dever refers to these in his criticisms of Finkelstein (Dever 1998a: 222–9). As G. Lehmann (2003: 155) points out, however, 'It is impossible to estimate the number or the impact of nomadic pastoralists in Iron Age Judah'. More important is the context argued for by Finkelstein: the alternating cycles of sedentary agriculture and pastoralism that he sees as determining settlement and the lifestyle of the inhabitants in Palestine from at least the third millennium BCE and studies on other periods, such as Palestine under Ottoman rule.

Finkelstein's basic thesis has been widely accepted in recent study and lies at the core of what seems to be a new consensus emerging. Although there are a number of variants to this consensus, it clusters around the view that Israel emerged in the highlands of Canaan largely from native inhabitants. Yet it has become widely accepted that the inhabitants settling in the hill country came from a variety of backgrounds. A. E. Killebrew (2005: 149–96; 2006) has used the term 'mixed multitude' for this thesis, which serves as a good description for many of the views. Although most accept that early Israel was made up of a variety of groups, some tend to favour a single group as making up the bulk of the people. Specific debate about the origins of Israel, in the context of models and evidence, will be discussed below (§8.4.6), which will help to illustrate both the common core and the diversity of the specific theories.

8.4.3 Israelite Tribes

E. Blum (2020) 'The Israelite Tribal System: Literary Fiction or Social Reality?', in J. J. Krause, O. Sergi, and K. Weingut (eds), *Saul, Benjamin, and the Emergence of Monarchy in Israel: Biblical and Archaeological Perspectives*: 201–22; **F. W. Dobbs-Allsopp, J. J. M. Roberts, C. L. Seow, and R. E. Whitaker (eds)** (2005) *Hebrew Inscriptions: Texts from the Biblical Period of the Monarchy with Concordance*; **M. H. Fried** (1968) 'On the Concepts of "Tribe" and "Tribal Society"', in June Helm (ed.), *Essays on the Problem of Tribe: Proceedings of the 1967 Annual Spring Meeting of the American Ethnological Society*: 3–20; **idem** (1975) *The Notion of Tribe*; **C. H. J. de Geus** (1976) *The Tribes of Israel: An Investigation into Some of the Presuppositions of Martin Noth's Amphictyony Hypothesis*; **N. Gottwald** (1979) *The Tribes of Yahweh: A Sociology of the religion of Liberated Israel, 1250–1050 B.C.E.*; **idem** (1993) 'Recent Studies of the Social World of Premonarchic Israel', *CR:BS* 1: 163–89; **J. Helm (ed.)** (1968) *Essays on the Problem of Tribe: Proceedings of the 1967 Annual Spring Meeting of the American Ethnological Society*; **M. D. Johnson** (1988) *The Purpose of the Biblical Genealogies*; **Z. Kallai** (1995) 'The Twelve-Tribe Systems of Israel', *VT* 47: 53–90; **idem**

(1999) 'A Note on the Twelve-Tribe Systems of Israel', *VT* 49: 125–7; K. **A. Kamp and N. Yoffee** (1980) 'Ethnicity in Ancient Western Asia during the Early Second Millennium B.C.: Archaeological Assessments and Ethnoarchaeological Prospectives', *BASOR* 237: 85–104; **P. S. Khoury and J. Kostiner** (1990) 'Introduction: Tribes and the Complexities of State Formation in the Middle East', in P. S. Khoury and J. Kostiner (eds), *Tribes and State Formation in the Middle East*: 1–22; **P. S. Khoury and J. Kostiner (eds)** (1990) *Tribes and State Formation in the Middle East*; **N. P. Lemche** (1977) 'The Greek "Amphictyony" – Could it Be a Prototype for the Israelite Society in the Period of the Judges?', *JSOT* 4: 48–59; **idem** (1985) *Early Israel: Anthropological and Historical Studies on the Israelite Society Before the Monarchy*; **C. Levin** (1995) 'Das System der zwölf Stämme Israels', in J. A. Emerton (ed.), *Congress Volume Paris 1992*: 163–78; **Y. Levin** (2001) 'Understanding Biblical Genealogies', *CR:BS* 9: 11–46; **J.-D. Macchi** (1999) *Israël et ses tribus selon Genèse 49*; **P. McNutt** (1999) *Reconstructing the Society of Ancient Israel*; **A. D. H. Mayes** (1974) *Israel in the Period of the Judges*; **M. Noth** (1930) *Das System der zwölf Stämme Israels*; **idem** (1960) *The History of Israel*; **J. W. Rogerson** (1978) *Anthropology and the Old Testament*; **idem** (1986) 'Was Early Israel a Segmentary Society?', *JSOT* 36: 17–26; **K. Weingart** (2014) *Stämmesvolk – Staatsvolk – Gottesvolk? Studien zur Verwendung des Israel-Namens im Alten Testament*; **idem** (2019) '"All These Are the Twelve Tribes of Israel": The Origins of Israel's Kinship Identity', *NEA* 82: 24–31; **H. Weippert** (1973) 'Das geographische System der Stämme Israels', *VT* 23: 76–89; **M. Weippert** (2010) *Historisches Textbuch zum Alten Testament*; **R. R. Wilson** (1977) *Genealogy and History in the Biblical World*.

It is easy to dismiss the matter of tribes from the history of ancient Israel as a late and insignificant addition to the tradition, but that would be to forget the importance of tribalism's place in ancient societies. Even in the first century when it was a great honour to be a Roman citizen, Roman citizens were all members of one of Rome's ancient tribes. Any outsider becoming a Roman citizen also joined one of the tribes. The stress of the biblical text on the tribes of Israel sometimes is simply a literary fossil within the text, but here and there are passages in which tribes as such play an important role.

Several issues debated among social anthropologists have been intertwined with the discussions on the origins of Israel, including 'tribes/tribalism'. First, 'tribes' and 'tribalism' are an aspect of the debate over ethnicity (Rogerson 1978: 86–101; Lemche 1985: 202–44; McNutt 1999: 75–94; Gottwald 1979: 293–341). 'Ethnic group' is now often used where 'tribe' would have been used in the past. 'Tribe' is of course the English word but is frequently the translation of Hebrew שבט *šēveṭ* and מטה *maṭṭeh*. The term has been widely discussed in anthropology (Helm [ed.] 1968; Fried 1968, 1975; Kamp/Yoffee 1980: 88–9; Lemche 1985: 202–44; Khoury/Kostiner [eds] 1990) without any consensus, except that the term is problematic. M. H. Fried (1968: 4–5) stated that the 'single most egregious case of meaninglessness' was the word 'race', but 'tribe' was not far behind: thus, many anthropologists avoid using the term.

Yet because of its frequent application in the context of Hebrew Bible study, the word 'tribe' cannot be avoided. Many seem to agree that ancient Israel was a segmentary society, that is, one organized according to (supposed) descent and kinship (but see Rogerson 1986, though he suggests that Israel might have been closer to a segmentary state). The relationship between various Israelites (and also other peoples) was expressed by the creation and use of genealogies (Wilson 1977; Johnson 1988; Levin 2001). In most societies, ancient and modern, genealogies do not necessarily show actual biological relationship or descent but social relationships between members and sections of society. Biblical genealogies also seem to have had this function.

A theory once popular among biblical scholars was that pre-monarchic Israel was organized as an 'amphictyony' (Noth 1930; 1960: 85–109; Gottwald 1979: 345–57), a tribal league organized around a central shrine. After considerable critique of the thesis in the 1960s and especially the 1970s (e.g., de Geus 1976; Mayes 1974; Lemche 1977), this model was generally abandoned. Both it and Gottwald's alternative model placed a great deal of emphasis on tribes and a specific confederation of Israelite tribes (Gottwald 1979: 358–86; but see the more cautious view in Gottwald 1993: 177–82). One of the problems is making the tribe the key social unit. Apart from the book of Judges, the text gives little collective function to the tribes. Most collective action is carried out by small groups, and the tribes appear to be mainly territorial units (Weippert 1973; de Geus 1976: 211; Lemche 1985: 71). That is, references to tribes were usually a reference to geography; this clarifies most of the Bible references to Israelite tribes. The people within a specific territory were generally assumed to be of a common lineage, but since property was seen as belonging by right to a specific lineage (Lev. 25:13-16, 23-28), the two went together.

The essential problem is that 'tribe' has come to be used of social and/or political units of different sorts. The difficulty is not unique to English usage but extends to the biblical text itself. A variety of terms are used in Hebrew to designate divisions of the Israelites, and their significance is widely assumed to be the following (Rogerson 1978: 93–4): שבט *šēveṭ*; מטה *maṭṭeh* 'tribe'; משפחה *mišpāḥāh* 'family, clan'; בית אב *bêt-'āv* 'extended family'. Yet the terms are often used interchangeably, as Rogerson points out (cf. Exod. 6:16-25; Judg. 17:7; Amos 3:1). Furthermore, an entity that would be called a tribe in the modern context of any East African ethnic group would correspond to the entirety of the Israelites, not the individual members of each of the 'twelve tribes' (Mojola 1998: 26). What this means is that we should be careful about making any social assumptions about the individual Israelite 'tribes'.

Here we come to another controversial point. Was the system of twelve tribes in the biblical tradition a late development, perhaps as late as the sixth century or even later (Macchi 1999: 272–80; Levin 1995)? M. Noth's (1930; 1960: 85–7) analysis of the various lists, showing two types of lists (one with Levi and Joseph, another without Levi but with Ephraim and Manasseh instead of Joseph), has been quite influential. More recent study confirms that there are two systems, but argues that they have been edited together into the scheme of 12 tribes (Macchi 1999; Kallai 1995, 1999). Everyone seems to agree that the 12-fold system is an artificial creation, but that does not mean that the tribes as such are an artificial creation. For one thing we have a partial list of tribes in one of the earliest passages in the Bible, Judges 5. This suggests that the development of the Israelite tribes is complicated. For example, some have argued that the tribe of Gad may originally have been a Moabite tribe because of the Mesha stela (Weippert 2010: 242–8; opposed by Blum 2020: 210–13). Yet those who reject the information in Judges 5 must argue that it is late. Granted that the tribal list there might have been redacted in its transmission, most would still see this as an early – and valuable – source of information, including on the tribes.

Most recently E. Blum (2020) has argued for the reality of the tribes (see also Weingart 2014, 2019). He notes the importance of genealogy to many ancient and modern peoples. The biblical genealogies, while artificial from a modern point of view, match the function of genealogies in many tribal peoples known to anthropologists. More important, the names in the Samaria Ostraca, which come from the ancient region ascribed to Manasseh in the text, contain all the male clan names and two of the female clan names given in Josh. 17:2-3 (cf. Num. 26:30-33). Although Blum does not list the correspondences, they are as follows (drawing on the text and reconstructions in Dobbs-Allsopp/Roberts/Seow/Whitaker 2005: 423–97):

Abiezer	Ostraca 13.1; 28.1
Helek	Ostraca 22.1; 24.1; 25.1; 27.1; 26.1
Asriel	Ostraca 42.1; 48.1 (in the form שראל)
Shechem	Ostracon 44.1
Hepher	Ostracon 44.2?
Shemida	Ostraca 3.2; 29.1; 30.1; 33.1; 34.1; 35.1, 36.1, etc.
Noah	Ostraca 50.1; 52.1; 64
Hoglah	Ostraca 43.1; 45.1; 46.1; 47.1; 66

He suggests that the tribes of Eshbaal's kingdom listed in 2 Sam. 2:8-9 may have included more or less those of Judges 5, if Jezreel is taken to include Issachar, Naphtali, and Zebulun, and Ephraim would take in Machir/Manasseh (except for Dan – and presumably Reuben, which he does not mention). See below for a similar conclusion by E. A. Knauf (§8.4.5).

Some general comments will summarize the discussion:

- Identity among ancient peoples (as among many moderns) was often expressed in terms of kinship and genealogy. Although this was usually expressed in biological terms (what we today might refer to as 'DNA connections'), this was often a fiction. That is, identity and ethnicity was often a geographical matter, in which groups in the same territory saw themselves as the same kinship group – and expressed it as such in kinship terms – even though they were not in fact biologically related. Genealogies were fluid and could be adjusted to take into account new additions or losses from the ethnic groups.
- The ubiquitous reference to 'tribes' in the Bible, including in some possibly early passages, suggest that Israelite society was 'tribalized'. Yet if Israel and Judah grew out of a coalescing of various elements (pastorialists, agriculturalists, Tranjordanians, etc.), the named tribes may have developed over time. But a number of the Israelite tribal names occur in what seem to be early passages.
- In many cases, tribalization seems to have had little practical effect, since we see little evidence that society was organized by tribes for administrative purposes or collective action. The 12-tribe scheme, known from many biblical passages, is likely to be a late development, created for ideological purposes. Yet at times in the early history of Israel, some of the tribes did act together for a common purpose (or were at least expected to join their fellow tribes in a united action).

- The once-common assumption that early Israel consisted of a tribal league (whether Noth's 'amphictyony' or something related) is still influential in some circles, even though generally thought to have been refuted.

8.4.4 Israel versus Judah

G. Lehmann (2003) 'The United Monarchy in the Countryside: Jerusalem, Judah, and the Shephelah during the Tenth Century B.C.E.', in Andrew G. Vaughn and Ann E. Killebrew (eds), *Jerusalem in Bible and Archaeology: The First Temple Period*: 117–62; **A. Ofer** (1994) '"All the Hill Country of Judah": From a Settlement Fringe to a Prosperous Monarchy', in I. Finkelstein and N. Na'aman (eds), *From Nomadism to Monarchy: Archaeological and Historical Aspects of Early Israel*: 92–121.

One of the factors of historical development often forgotten is the difference between Israel in the north and Judah in the south. This is an element in the *longue durée* which must always be recognized and given an essential part in the historical interpretation. There was a considerable disparity of natural resources and economy between the two, with Judah continually the poorer. There are reasons for this (Lehmann 2003: 149–62; Ofer 1994: 93–5). In Judah the agriculture was largely subsistence and disadvantaged by lack of good soil for grain-growing and rainfall of 300–500 mm per annum. The better soils around Hebron had their value reduced by low rainfall. This meant that pastoralism was an important pursuit. In competition with Israel, Judah definitely came off second best. When Palestine entities enter the inscriptions of other nations, such as the Assyrians in the first millennium BCE, there is already a division between Israel and Judah.

This long-term division is also hinted at in a number of biblical passages (2 Sam. 2:4; 5:4; Judges 5), in spite of a supposed 12-tribe nation. The most important of these is Judges 5 (also discussed below [§8.4.5]). As one of the earliest passages in the Hebrew Bible, it seems to have been written not long after the events it describes. It lists a number of tribes of Israel that cooperated in opposing the predations of Sisera. To what extent names have been added to the list in the course of literary transmission can be debated, but the important point is that Judah was absent, even though from other biblical passages we would have expected it to be here. Another passage is 2 Sam. 2:3-4 which states that David and his family settled in Hebron, along with the men of his band and their families. Then, 'the men of Judah' (אנשי יהודה) came and made him king 'over the house of Judah' (על־בית יהודה). Clearly, the 'house of Judah' was separate from Saul's kingdom of Israel, as is further made clear when Abner schemed to transfer the kingdom of Israel ('the house of Saul') to David's rule (in 2 Sam. 3–4). This finally happened when 'all the elders of Israel' (כל־זקני ישראל) came and made David king over Israel (2 Sam. 5:1-3). This (temporary) uniting of what had been a division between the two peoples is acknowledged in 2 Sam. 5:5: 'he reigned over all Israel and Judah' (מלך ... על כל־ישראל ויהודה).

8.4.5 The Book of Judges and the 'Song of Deborah' (Judges 5)

B.-J. Diebner (1995) 'Wann sang Deborah ihr Lied? Überlegungen zu zwei der ältesten Texte des TNK (Ri 4 und 5)', *ACEBT* 14: 106–30; **I. Finkelstein** (2016a) 'The Old Jephthah Tale in Judges: Geographical and Historical Considerations', *Bib* 97: 1–15;

idem (2016b) 'Comments on the Abimelech Story in Judges 9', *UF* 46: 69–84; **idem** (2017a) 'Compositional Phases, Geography and Historical Setting behind Judges 4–5 and the Location of Harosheth-ha-goiim', *SJOT* 31: 80–91; **idem** (2017b) 'Major Saviors, Minor Judges: The Historical Background of the Northern Accounts in the Book of Judges', *JSOT* 41: 431–49; **I. Finkelstein and O. Lipschits** (2017) 'Geographical and Historical Observations on the Old North Israelite Gideon Tales in Judges', *ZAW* 129: 1–18; **J. C. L. Gibson** (1975) *Textbook of Syrian Semitic Inscriptions: Volume I, Hebrew and Moabite Inscriptions*; **P. D. Guest** (1998) 'Can Judges Survive without Sources? Challenging the Consensus', *JSOT* 78: 43–61; **P. Guillaume** (2004) *Waiting for Josiah: The Judges*; **B. Halpern** (1988) *The First Historians: The Hebrew Bible and History*; **R. de Hoop** (2009) 'Judges 5 Reconsidered: Which Tribes? What Land? Whose Song?', in J. van Ruiten and J. C. de Vos (eds), *The Land of Israel in Bible, History, and Theology: Studies in Honour of Ed Noort*: 151–66; **E. A. Knauf** (1991b) 'Eglon and Ophrah: Two Toponymic Notes on the Book of Judges', *JSOT* 51: 25–44; **idem** (2005) 'Deborah's Language: Judges ch. 5 in its Hebrew and Semitic Context', in B. Burtea, J. Tropper, and H. Younansardaround (eds), *Studia Semitica et Semitohamitica*: 167–82; **idem** (2010b) 'History in Judges', in L. L. Grabbe (ed.), *Israel in Transition: From Late Bronze II to Iron IIA (c. 1250–850 BCE): Volume 2 The Text* : 140–9; **idem** (2016a) *Richter*; **B. Lindars** (1995) *Judges 1–5: A New Translation and Commentary*; **N. Na'aman** (1990a) 'Literary and Topographical Notes on the Battle of Kishon (Judges IV–V)', *VT* 40: 423–36; **H. Niehr** (1994) 'שפט šāpaṭ', *TDOT* 15: 411–31; **D. A. Robertson** (1972) *Linguistic Evidence in Dating Early Hebrew Poetry*; **L. E. Stager** (1988) 'Archaeology, Ecology, and Social History: Background Themes to the Song of Deborah', in J. A. Emerton (ed.), *Congress Volume Jerusalem 1986*: 221–34.

The book of Judges comes across quite differently from Joshua: far from being conquered and under Israelite rule, the lowlands and many of the main cities were still controlled by the Canaanites who fought with chariots of iron (Judges 1). As noted above, if one had read Joshua for the first time and then moved to Judges without knowing anything about its contents, it would have produced considerable consternation, because a number of the things supposedly accomplished in Joshua had to be done again (e.g., Judg. 1:19-36 versus Joshua 16–19). On the face of it, the book of Judges seems to reflect in a general way the state of Canaan in the Early Iron Age, especially the presence of a number of small, semi-independent polities fighting for status and even survival among themselves. But this picture is illusionary if one assumes it reflects genuine historical memory. For the book reflects an overall theological, rather than historical, design. It is mainly made up of a series of episodes which follow a common theological pattern: Israel sins, is punished by being made subjects of a foreign people, cries to Yhwh, has a deliverer sent who leads them in throwing off the foreign yoke – following a 40/80 year cycle. This structure is clear through much of the book. These stories, in addition to their entertainment value, had an important content relating to morality, which is probably the main reason they were told. But our concern is with their historicity.

As has long been recognized, the narrative of Judges is divided between heroic deliverers ('major judges') and civic leaders ('minor judges') (cf. Finkelstein 2017b). The latter get little actual space but are presented in two brief lists (Judg. 10:1-5; 12:7-15). Shamgar ben Anath has a curious name, because it suggests a worshiper of the goddess Anat (Judg. 3:31; 5:6). The judge named Jerubbaal is only later identified with Gideon (Judges 6–8; 6:32 gives an nonsensical etymology of his name; it means something like 'Let Baal be great'). Abimelech (son of Gideon) looks like the king of a Canaanite city-state (Judges 9). Jephthah occurs in the list of 'minor judges' but also appears as a heroic figure, whereas Samson seems independent of the other deliverer stories. One cannot rule out that some actual historical core can be found in some of the 'deliverer' stories, but when we turn the statement around, demonstrating such a core of history is very difficult. B. Halpern (1988) argued for such a core of historicity in the Ehud/Eglon story, but E. A. Knauf (1991) has cast considerable doubt on his argument by showing that 'Ehud' was a Benjaminite clan, and Eglon, a town in the Judaean foothills. Despite references to 'all Israel' only one or two tribes are normally involved in the action in an episode; the Song of Deborah (Judges 5) is the only passage with more than two tribes. The amount of confirmed historical data in Judges seems small (cf. Knauf 2010b).

I. Finkelstein has looked at various of the tales within Judges and sees some glimpses of historical events in them. He and O. Lipschits (2017) reconstruct an original oral tale about Gideon. Whether the person of Gideon is just an invention of the story teller or not, the story is about military action against the Midianites west of Shechem in the tenth century. With regard to Jephthah, Finkelstein (2016a) suggests that an old (and short) Saviour Tale lies at the heart of this story. It was about a border dispute with the Ammonites, conducted by an apiru group led by Jephthah, between the town of Gilead (south of the Jabbok River) and the town of Mizpah (north of the Jabbok) no later than the tenth century BCE. As for the Abimelech story in Judges 9, Finkelstein (2016b) traces it through various redactional layers to the presumed oldest tradition. He proposes that it dealt with a struggle between two apiru groups over control of Shechem that ended in the destruction of stratum XI (late eleventh or early tenth century BCE); later insertions into the account relate to persons and events in the history of the Northern Kingdom. Finally, he summarizes his conclusions about the 'Saviour Tales' and examines the 'Minor Judges' accounts (Finkelstein 2017b). He sees five such accounts (Othniel and Shamgar being Deuteronomistic insertions) with origins in heroic tales of the North; their geographical distribution shows a deliberate attempt to fill in the territory of the Northern Kingdom to cover the Israelite hill country, Gilead, Jezreel, and the northern border areas (remarkably similar to the description in 2 Sam. 2:9).

We can now focus on the 'Song of Deborah' (Judges 5). This is an example of early poetry (Robertson 1972), which might suggest that it was written close to the events described (Stager 1988; see the summary of arguments in Lindars 1995: 212–17). E. A. Knauf (2005) dates it to the tenth century BCE. The list of Israelite tribes differs in several ways from all other lists (Machir instead of Manasseh [Judg. 5:14]; Gilead instead of Gad [Judg. 5:17]; Judah, Simeon, Levi are absent), which might demonstrate an independent tradition and one possibly earlier than other traditions. Nevertheless, a number of scholars have argued that the Song of Deborah shows signs of lateness (e.g., Diebner 1995; Lindars 1995: 213–15), and assuming that it is more trustworthy as a historical source is misplaced confidence. I. Finkelstein (2017a) hypothesizes two original traditions arising from separate events in the tenth century, one affecting the southwestern Jezreel Valley, the other taking place around Mt Tabor and Anaharath. He thinks these were written down in the eighth century, which is also when the Song of Deborah was composed. At that time, they were merged into a single event, with further editings in the seventh century. He says nothing, however, about the fact that Judges 5 is written in Archaic Biblical Hebrew and appears to be quite a bit earlier than the account in Judges 4. Therefore, Knauf's investigation, which shows a proper analysis based on principles of historical linguistics, will be followed here, and the story of Judges 5 will be accepted as representing in essence the situation in the tenth century.

The list of tribes is the following (Judg. 5:14-18), which can be compared with the contents of Israel under Ishbaal's (Ish-bosheth's) rule (2 Sam. 2:9):

Judges 5	*2 Sam. 2:9*
Ephraim	Ephraim
Benjamin	Benjamin
Machir	
Zebulun	
Issachar	
Reuben	
Gilead	Gilead
Dan	
Asher	Ashurites?
Naphtali	
	Jezreel

Gilead, which is a region across the Jordan, occurs in the list, whereas Gad does not; however, Gad seems to be a late addition to Israel, according to the Mesha Inscription, which suggests that it was taken over by Ahab from Moab (lines 10-14 [Gibson 1975: text no. 16]). Knauf (2005: 168–9) comments:

> Benjamin, Efraim, Makir, Issachar, Zebulon and Naftali. They represent approximately the Cisjordanian segment of Ishbaal's kingdom. In [Judges 5, verses] 15C-17, four more tribes are vituperated for inactivity: Dan, Asher, Gilead and Reuben. The first pair leads to the far north of the territory claimed for Biblical Israel, the second pair to Transjordan.... From the geographical point of view, Judges 5 represents pre-Omride Israel.

Knauf concludes that Judges 5 delineates a tribal Israel also found, more or less, in Saul's kingdom. A similar conclusion was reached by E. Blum, as already noted (§8.4.3 above).

Making use of chapter 5 does not give credence to the rest of Judges as a historical source. P. D. Guest (1998) has argued that far from being a compilation of different sources, the book of Judges shows the marks of unitary authorship that produced a 'crafted history' of the period: 'Although the text presents itself as history, it should not be mistaken for such' (1998: 61). In one area, however, Judges as a book may reflect an older linguistic usage: the title 'judge' (Hebrew שופט *šôfēṭ*). Although the word means 'judge' in a judicial sense in most Hebrew usage, the reference to persons by this title in Judges means something like 'political/military leader' (Niehr 1994). Thus, here and there may be reliable early traditions, but demonstrating them is difficult; the book is generally too problematic to use as a historical source.

8.4.6 The Settlement: An Overview

G. W. Ahlström (1986) *Who Were the Israelites?*; **D. G. Bates** (1973) *Nomads and Farmers: A Study of the Yörük of Southeastern Turkey*; **D. Ben-Ami** (2001) 'The Iron Age I at Tel Hazor in Light of the Renewed Excavations', *IEJ* 51: 148–70; **A. Ben-Tor** (1998) 'The Fall of Canaanite Hazor – The "Who" and "When" Questions', in S. Gitin, A. Mazar, and E. Stern (eds), *Mediterranean Peoples in Transition: Thirteenth to Early Tenth Centuries BCE, in Honor of Professor Trude Dothan*: 456–67; **J. J. Bimson** (1981) *Redating the Exodus and Conquest*; **M. L. Chaney** (1983) 'Ancient Palestinian Peasant Movements and the Formation of Premonarchic Israel', in D. N. Freedman and D. F. Graf (eds), *Palestine in Transition: The Emergence of Ancient Israel*: 39–90; **D. Chatty** (1980) 'The Pastoral Family and the Truck', in P. C. Salzman (ed.), *When Nomads Settle: Processes of Sedentarization as Adaptation and Response*: 80–94; **W. G. Dever** (1992a) 'How to Tell a Canaanite from an Israelite', in Hershel Shanks (ed.), *The Rise of Ancient Israel: Symposium at the Smithsonian Institution, October 26, 1991*: 27–60 (plus reply to responses, pp. 79–85); **idem** (1998) 'Israelite Origins and the "Nomadic Ideal": Can Archaeology Separate Fact from Fiction?', in S. Gitin, A. Mazar, and E. Stern (eds), *Mediterranean Peoples in Transition: Thirteenth to Early Tenth Centuries BCE, in Honor of Professor Trude Dothan*: 220–37; **idem** (2003) *Who Were the Early Israelites and Where Did They Come From?*; **idem** (2017) *Beyond the Texts: An Archaeological Portrait of Ancient Israel and Judah*; **I. Finkelstein** (1988) *The Archaeology of the Israelite Settlement*; **idem** (2019) 'First Israel, Core Israel, United (Northern) Israel', *NEA* 82: 8–15; **I. Finkelstein and N. Na'aman (eds)** (1994) *From Nomadism to Monarchy: Archaeological and Historical Aspects of Early Israel*; **V. Fritz** (1981) 'The Israelite "Conquest" in the Light of Recent Excavations at Khirbet el-Meshâsh', *BASOR* 214: 61–73; **idem** (1987) 'Conquest or Settlement? The Early Iron Age in Palestine', *BA* 50: 84–100; **W. Goldschmidt** (1980) 'Career Reorientation and Institutional Adaptation in the Process of Natural Sedentarization', in P. C. Salzman (ed.), *When Nomads Settle: Processes of Sedentarization as Adaptation and Response*: 48–61; **L. L. Grabbe** (2001) 'Sup-urbs or Only Hyp-urbs? Prophets and Populations in Ancient Israel and Socio-historical Method', in Lester L. Grabbe and Robert D. Haak (eds), *'Every City Shall Be Forsaken': Urbanism and Prophecy in Ancient Israel and the Near East*: 93–121; **B. Halpern** (1988) *The First Historians: The Hebrew Bible and History*; **J. H. Hayes and J. M. Miller (eds)** (1977) *Israelite and Judaean History*; **Z. Herzog** (2002) 'The Fortress Mound at Tel Arad: An Interim Report', *TA* 29: 3–109; **D. Ilan** (2019) 'The "Conquest" of the Highlands in the Iron Age I', in A. Yasur-Landau, Eric H. Cline, and Yorke M. Rowan (eds), *The Social Archaeology of the Levant: From Prehistory to the Present*: 283–309; **A. E. Killebrew** (2005) *Biblical Peoples and Ethnicity: An Archaeological Study of Egyptians, Canaanites, Philistines, and Early Israel 1300–1000 B.C.E.*; **idem** (2006) 'The Emergence of Ancient Israel: The Social Boundaries of a "Mixed Multitude" in Canaan', in A. M. Maeir and P. de Miroschedji (eds), *'I Will Speak the Riddles of Ancient Times': Archaeological and Historical Studies in Honor of Amihai Mazar on the Occasion of his Sixtieth Birthday*: 555–72;

A. E. Knauf (1991b) 'Eglon and Ophrah: Two Toponymic Notes on the Book of Judges', *JSOT* 51: 25–44; **idem** (2008) *Josua*; **idem** (2010a) 'History in Joshua', in L. L. Grabbe (ed.), *Israel in Transition: From Late Bronze II to Iron IIA (c. 1250–850 BCE): Volume 2 The Text*: 130–9; **idem** (2010b) 'History in Judges', in L. L. Grabbe (ed.), *Israel in Transition: From Late Bronze II to Iron IIA (c. 1250–850 BCE): Volume 2 The Text*: 140–9; **idem** (2016a) *Richter*; **G. Lehmann** (2003) 'The United Monarchy in the Countryside: Jerusalem, Judah, and the Shephelah during the Tenth Century B.C.E.', in A. G. Vaughn and A. E. Killebrew (eds), *Jerusalem in Bible and Archaeology: The First Temple Period*: 117–62; **N. P. Lemche** (1985) *Early Israel: Anthropological and Historical Studies on the Israelite Society Before the Monarchy*; **T. E. Levy** (2009a) 'Ethnic Identity in Biblical Edom, Israel, and Midian: Some Insights from Mortuary Contexts in the Lowlands of Edom', in J. David Schloen (ed.), *Exploring the* Longue Durée: *Essays in Honor of Lawrence E. Stager*: 251–61; **idem** (2009b) 'Pastoral Nomads and Iron Age Metal Production in Ancient Edom', in J. Szuchman (ed.), *Nomads, Tribes, and the State in the Ancient Near East: Cross-Disciplinary Perspectives*: 147–77; **T. E. Levy, R. B. Adams, and A. Muniz** (2004) 'Archaeology and the Shasu Nomads: Recent Excavations in the Jabal Hamrat Fidan, Jordan', in R. E. Friedman and W. H. C. Propp (eds), *Le-David Maskil: A Birthday Tribute for David Noel Freedman*: 63–89; **J. J. McDermott** (1998) *What Are They Saying about the Formation of Israel?*; **G. E. Mendenhall** (1983) 'Ancient Israel's Hyphenated History', in D. N. Freedman and D. F. Graf (eds), *Palestine in Transition: The Emergence of Ancient Israel*: 91–103; **J. M. Miller** (1977) 'Archaeology and the Israelite Conquest of Canaan: Some Methodological Observations', *PEQ* 109: 87–93; **idem** (1979) 'W. F. Albright and Historical Reconstruction', *BA* 42: 37–47; **N. Na'aman** (1994c) 'The "Conquest of Canaan" in the Book of Joshua and in History', in I. Finkelstein and N. Na'aman (eds), *From Nomadism to Monarchy: Archaeological and Historical Aspects of Early Israel*: 218–81; **idem** (2005) *Canaan in the Second Millennium B.C.E.: Collected Essays, Volume 2*; **H. Niehr** (1994) 'שפט *šāpaṭ*', *TDOT* 15: 411–31; **H. M. Niemann** (2002) 'Taanach und Megiddo: Überlegungen zur strukturell-historischen Situation zwischen Saul und Salomo', *VT* 52: 93–102; **G. W. Ramsey** (1981) *The Quest for the Historical Israel*; **P. C. Salzman** (1980b) 'Processes of Sedentarization among the Nomads of Baluchistan', in P. C. Salzman (ed.), *When Nomads Settle: Processes of Sedentarization as Adaptation and Response*: 95–110; **O. Sergi** (2019a) 'The Formation of Israelite Identity in the Central Canaanite Highlands in the Iron Age I–IIA', *NEA* 82: 42–51; **E. van der Steen** (2004) *Tribes and Territories in Transition: The Central East Jordan Valley in the Late Bronze Age and Early Iron Ages: A Study of the Sources*; **J. Van Seters** (1990) 'Joshua's Campaign of Canaan and Near Eastern Historiography', *SJOT* 2: 1–12; **B. G. Wood** (1990) 'Did the Israelites Conquer Jericho? A New Look at the Archaeological Evidence', *BAR* 16, no. 2: 44–58; **Y. Yadin** (1979) 'The Transition from a Semi-Nomadic to a Sedentary Society in the Twelfth Century B.C.E.', in Frank M. Cross (ed.), *Symposia: Celebrating the Seventy-Fifth Anniversary of the Founding of the American Schools of Oriental Research (1900–1975)*: 57–68; **idem** (1982) 'Is the Biblical Account of the Israelite Conquest of Canaan Historically Reliable?', *BAR* 8, no. 2: 16–23; **A. Zertal** (1994)

'"To the Land of the Perizzites and the Giants": On the Israelite Settlement in the Hill Country of Manasseh', in I. Finkelstein and N. Na'aman (eds), *From Nomadism to Monarchy: Archaeological and Historical Aspects of Early Israel*: 47–69.

The archaeology relating to the settlement in the hill country was described above (§8.2) and will not be repeated here. Instead, this section will focus on views about what factors led to the settlement and who in fact settled there. The central hill country seems to have been settled first, after going most of the LBA with few inhabitants, with the Judaean hills being settled later. The question is what caused the settlement, after so many centuries with hardly any population. The Egyptians are sometimes brought into the equation, though some have seen them as a negative force, pushing people into remote areas, whereas others see them as a positive influence that aided the settlers.

D. Ilan (2019) argues that Egyptian imperial strategy was a critical factor in the initiation of the settlement. The settlement began when Egypt still had a network of administrative centres and military garrisons (thirteenth and early twelfth centuries). Those who manned these were often foreigners brought in to do the job. They might have married local women in many cases, and when they completed their service, many would have been encouraged to retire locally. The collared-rim pithoi, produced with a standard volume according to Egyptian requirements, might in some cases be evidence of aid offered to such individuals to get started in a local settlement. The Egyptian administration and 'retirement' policy thus would have been an important factor in commencing the highland settlement. Ilan does not suggest what percentage of the settlers this might have included, but it is a reasonable contributing group.

N. Na'aman (1994c) associates the origins of Israel with the wider developments in the eastern Mediterranean. The thirteenth to eleventh centuries brought the settlement of peripheral areas contemporary with the collapse of urban culture in the entire Aegean-Anatolian-Syro-Palestinian region and the migration of large groups on the boundaries of Mesopotamia. At no other time was the disruption of urban culture in Anatolia and Syro-Palestine (reaching as far as the Aegean and the Balkans) so complete as in the twelfth century. The Aramaeans gradually took over large tracts in Mesopotamia and Syria. Migration in Iron I because of destruction in Asia Minor means that various groups reached Canaan and played an important part in settlement: Hittites in Hebron; Hivites in western Benjamin and perhaps around Shechem; Jebusites from the Hittite empire; Girgashites from Anatolia. Only two of the alleged seven pre-Israelite nations were autochthonous.

These groups (or 'tribes') may have helped break Egyptian rule. Traditions about patriarchal migrations to Egypt are best understood against this background (so Na'aman); similarly, stories of coming out of Egypt such as the exodus should be understood as vaguely remembered background rather than routine migration of pastoral groups. Thus, the overall picture does not support the assumption that the Iron I settlement was only an internal Palestinian one or settlers only from local Canaanite elements. The various groups entering Canaan joined the local uprooted and pastoral groups, which led to an increase in pastoral and bandit splinter groups that upset the urban–nomad balance and induced the nomads to settle down: 'The model that emerges from my analysis is of small and larger groups of variegated ethnic and cultural background who settled during a long period and slowly and gradually started cooperating in the new environment' (Na'aman 1994c: 246).

Z. Herzog (2002: 89–92) draws attention to the current 'fluid' concept of ethnicity that undermines attempts to identify ethnic borders. In the Beersheba Valley in the Iron I a variety of different groups seem to have lived (according to the biblical text), with a relatively uniform material culture. Here the groups mixed and combined in a complex social composition. Using the Beersheba Valley as a model, Herzog argues that the larger settlement and the emergence of an Israelite identity should be understood from an 'interactive-combined model' in which 'a community identity is created from the development and combination of various social groups. Clearly, in different regions there were different combinations of communities, simultaneous with inter-regional mixing and blending' (2002: 92).

As already noted above (§8.4.2) A. E. Killebrew (2005: 149–96; 2006) has argued for the origins of Israel as a 'mixed multitude'. Although she gives a succinct and persuasive argument for her case, she admits that the thesis is not original with her. Indeed, it has been adumbrated in some form or other (though often briefly and without supporting argumentation) by a number of researchers going back at least to the mid-1980s (Ahlström 1986: 57–83; cf. Dever 1992a; Finkelstein/Na'aman 1994: 13–14). According to this theory, the population that became Israel was made up of a diverse group of people:

> ...demographic redistribution and an increase in the settled population, especially in the central hill country and Transjordanian highlands. These inhabitants most likely comprised different elements of Late Bronze Age society, namely, the rural Canaanite population, displaced peasants and pastoralists, and lawless *'apiru* and *shasu*. Outside elements probably included other marginal groups, such as fugitive or 'runaway' Semitic slaves from Twentieth-Dynasty New Kingdom Egypt.... Other nonindigenous groups, such as Midianites, Kenites, and Amalekites, perhaps connected with the control of camel caravan trade routes between Arabia and Canaan, may have constituted an essential element of this 'mixed multitude'. [Killebrew 2006: 571]

The recent study of E. van der Steen (2004: 306–10) lends support to this thesis. She argues that the trading collapse in Ammon caused inhabitants to migrate not only into Moab but also into the Jordan Valley. There the pressure of population caused further migration into the hill country west of the Jordan. It may be that there was a partial vacuum there at this time because Merenptah (or Rameses II) had 'laid waste Israel' (Merenptah Stela) who may have been living in the northern hill country (as noted previously [§8.4.1], this can only be speculation because the Merenptah inscription does not actually tell us where 'Israel' lived).

Accepting the 'mixed multitude' thesis for the origin of Israel still leaves a number of questions unanswered. Some researchers have argued that the early Israelites were primarily from one particular group. At the moment, there is a considerable debate between those who say that the early Israelites were mainly 'Canaanite' and those who argue that they arose from the Shasu. For example, although differing from Gottwald on many points, including the concept of an internal revolt, Lemche's (1985: 427–32) final picture was of an internal development of the indigenous population. In his view, though, it was not urban residents who fled oppression of the city-states but members of the Canaanite rural peasantry who went up into the hill country to escape taxes. A question, though, would be whether taxes were so oppressive that people felt inclined to leave their farms for life in the highlands to escape them.

More recently, Dever has been a major voice in urging the case for postulating the Canaanite origin of the highland settlers who became Israel (his 'Proto-Israelites'). In his view, the basis of the highland settlements were farmers and others withdrawing from the systems collapse of the Canaanite lowlands (see especially Dever 2003: 167–89). The idea that these new settlers were 'nomads' or 'semi-nomads' settling down is anathema to him. He argues that there is no evidence that nomadic types are generally willing to become agriculturalists; also, there would not have been sufficient nomadic pastoralists in the region to account for the population growth. This position is somewhat surprising in light of Dever's recent archaeological report on two Early Bronze IV sites (Dever [ed.] 2014). Although the sites are some centuries before IA I and Dever ascribes them to nomadic pastoralists, he notes that pastoral nomadism covers a broad spectrum of habitation styles, including those who planted crops in their summer pasture area and returned to harvest them, as well as engaging in trade and perhaps even metallurgy (Dever [ed.] 2014: 231–5). He also suggests that the pastoral nomads who occupied these sites were Canaanites who left a sedentary lifestyle for particular reasons.

But if they could become pastoral nomads, could not they revert to a more settled lifestyle? Modern anthropological studies have shown that there are a variety of examples of a shift from a nomadic lifestyle to a sedentary one (see §6.3.3.1 on the whole question). This is not theoretical but comes from study of societies which have actually made the voluntary move from nomadism to sedentarianism. To give three examples of different forms of adaptation, the first example is of the Sebei of East Africa who made the shift from nomadic pastoralism to sedentary cultivation (Goldschmidt 1980). This was not from coercion but done voluntarily because it was seen as advantageous to themselves. For the second example, some of the Yörük (or Yuruk or Yoruk) of southeast Turkey remained pastoralists but others chose to settle down and become village cultivators (Bates 1973). This was because of economic circumstances which militated against the entire group's remaining pastoralists. Although the process was subject to adverse conditions, the shift in lifestyle was entered into voluntarily by those who left pastoralism for cultivation. A third example is nomadic groups who drastically reduced their adherence to the nomadic way of life while not giving it up entirely. This includes the Bedouin of the Beqa Valley of Lebanon (Chatty 1980) and nomads of Baluchistan (Salzman 1980b). Thus, to argue that pastoralists do not settle down is to ignore many known examples where this has precisely taken place.

Others have argued that the Israelites arose from the Shasu. Such has been proposed by A. F. Rainey (2001) and D. B. Redford (1990: 73–5; 1992: 267–80), plus a number of others. This is partly based on the reliefs associated with Merenptah's supposed conquests. Some argue that the 'Israel' of the inscription is to be identified with the Shasu of the reliefs. This appears to go far beyond the evidence. The equation of the reliefs with entities in the inscription is more ingenious than convincing. In any case, it seems that the texts distinguish the Israelites, Canaanites, and Shasu. This does not mean that both Shasu and Canaanites could not have joined the settlers who became Israel, but once Israel had its own identity (as indicated by the Merenptah inscription) it was apparently seen as separate from both the Canaanites and Shasu. (See §6.3.4 for a detailed discussion of the Merenptah inscriptions.)

Avraham Faust (e.g., 2006) has been another outspoken defender of the Shasu thesis. His position is that the highland culture shows mainly discontinuity, which militates against the settlers being Canaanites. Rather, they are mainly the Shasu who have changed their lifestyle because of various circumstances. Faust is quite right to argue that some of the settlers in the highlands could have been Shasu settling down (in opposition to Dever). Yet his rejection of the importance of Canaanites in the settlement process seems misplaced, based mainly on the argument of discontinuity between LB material culture and that of the IA I. The general view among other archaeologists seems to be that there is a great deal of continuity (see especially Killebrew 2005: 171–81).

The most important of these continuities is in the pottery: 'Iron I highland pottery…is remarkable for its continuity with Late Bronze Age ceramic traditions', including the collared-rim jar which is a continuation of the Canaanite jar tradition (Killebrew 2005: 177–81). Also, contrary to Faust, many argue with regard to the three- or four-room house that 'its roots go back to Late Bronze Age Canaanite architecture' (Killebrew 2005: 174 plus n. 65). The main discontinuity Faust can point to is that of burials, but this is a disputed area (cf. Kletter 2002; the IA cemetery at Wadi Fidan 40 [Levy/Adams/Muniz 2004; Levy 2009a]); in any case, one expects a certain amount of discontinuity in light of the different environment and circumstances of the highland settlers.

Furthermore, Faust discounts or ignores some important continuities pointed out by Dever (2003a: 168). Two of these are language (the Israelites spoke a form of Canaanite) and religion (Israelite religion was essentially the Northwest Semitic religion shared by Canaanites and others in the region). Finally, we need to consider the arguments of Hasel about the Shasu. He draws up a comparison of Israel as described in the Merenptah inscription and the characteristics of the Shasu, and concludes that they differ from each other in three main points (Hasel 1998: 236–9):

1. Each is given a separate name by the Egyptians.
    An important point, but Israel could have originated with the Shasu, even if later it had its own separate identity
2. They occupy different areas, Israel in Canaan and the Shasu in Edom/Seir.
    The difference between the hill country and Edom/Seir is not great; in any case, the Shasu are connected with a number of different locations.
3. The Shasu appear to be nomadic while Israel is a settled people.
    The Mereptah stela is not that specific about the lifestyle of Israel, while the Shasu – at least, some of them – are in some cases apparently described as settled.

While these points have merit and might seem to support Israel's origins from Canaanites, they are not conclusive (for the reasons noted; see further at §6.3.3.4 for information supporting the objections). Each characteristic is based on slender evidence and can be debated. What his arguments do not seem to do is rule out that Israel could (whether in part or as a whole) have originated from a Shasu population settling down.

However, an important fact must be emphasized with regard to the two main authors being compared above – Dever and Faust: each author undermines his own argument! This is because Dever accepts that some of the new settlers were likely to have been pastoral nomads, including Shasu (Dever 2003a: 181–2). Likewise, Faust allows that some of the settlers came from the Canaanite lowlands: 'it seems as if ancient Israel was composed of peoples who came from various backgrounds: …[including] settled Canaanites who for various reasons changed their identity…. In the end it is likely that many, if not most, Israelites had Canaanite origins' (Faust 2006: 186). So, in making such a concession in the individual positions, each actually negates his main argument which focuses only on one group. From a broader perspective, though, these two positions reinforce the 'mixed multitude' thesis because each concedes that there is more than one component to the original highland settlements.

In sum, who were those who settled in the central highlands at the end of the Late Bronze and beginning of the Iron I? The identity of a number of potential settlers has been indicated, and can be listed as follows:

- Agriculturalists from the lowlands who wanted unclaimed land; this could have included inhabitants of Canaanite cities whose occupation was farming.
- Rural settlers around urban centres (including Egyptian fortresses and administrative centres) who engaged in symbiotic relations with the urban entities and did not see themselves as independent from their urban colleagues.
- Transhumance pastoralists who wanted to practise agriculture as well.
- Nomadic pastoralists who wanted a more settled life (such as some of the Shasu).
- Foreigners brought in as administrators and garrison troops for Egyptian centres in Canaan, who settled there after their service was complete.
- Migrants from abroad who saw opportunities in the Canaanite highlands.

It seems a reasonable conclusion that the highlands settlers included Shasu, either because the Shasu were less monocultural in their way of living than often assumed or because some of them moved from mobile pastoralism to a more settled way of living (or perhaps both). Yet it is also likely that the settlers included people of the Canaanite lowlands who left their villages and farms, and even the Canaanite cities, and made these remote regions their home. Those who fled to the highlands were often designated as *'apiru* in Egyptian sources, but that tells us little other than that they were seen as displaced persons and potential troublemakers. The term is not necessarily a designation of a particular lifestyle nor of an ethnic identification. It is true that the *'apiru* might well be raiders or mercenaries, and some of those living in the highlands might well have taken up both occupations. But just as the medieval Vikings were also farmers and settlers, as well as warriors and raiders, so those called *'apiru* pursued more than one way of making a living. Many or perhaps even most of them engaged in raising crops and livestock instead of or even in addition to those activities that the Egyptians objected to.

Yet we still face a further problem: the large expansion of settlement in the highlands took place in IA I, yet Israel seems to have originated *before* this, in the LBA. If an 'Israel' was already in existence by 1208 BCE or possibly even earlier, then where was it located? Could the highland population already be called 'Israel' even before this significant expansion? This seems unlikely. Thus, we have to assume either that a population associated with the highlands was already called Israel before the IA I settlement or that Israel actually originated elsewhere and only subsequently became associated with the population of the hill country. In the former case, it might be that some of the Shasu or related groups were called 'Israel'. So far, no such group is attested in our literary or archaeological sources, but we might need to look harder. With regard to the latter case, we are hard put to find a group, in the Egyptian realm but outside the Palestinian highlands, that could identified with Israel.

Faust has suggested that the settlement process already started in the thirteenth century (2006: 160). A recent study by Yitzhak Meitlis (2008) seems to go even further. Based on LB pottery found in IA I contexts, he argues that LB pottery was not easily distinguished from early IA I pottery. He concludes that IA I began much earlier than often dated. If he is right, it may be that the highland settlement was underway earlier than the time of Merenptah. This would also fit with those Egyptologists who think they have found references to Israel perhaps even as early as the fourteenth century BCE (§6.3.4). Thus, either the highland settlements began much earlier than normally dated, or the Israel of the early Egyptian sources was located elsewhere. This is a case where new archaeological (or perhaps even textual) discoveries may help us to resolve what remains a difficulty in our historical reconstruction.

To conclude this discussion, several observations that are relevant to the highland settlements and the rise of Israel need to be made:

- 'Israel' did not begin with the settlement of the hill country in the Iron I. An entity called Israel was already in existence in the LBA, even if we know little about it. Presumably it gave its name to the settlement that developed, but this is an inference based both on the Merenptah stela and the state that first arose in the central hill country in the late Iron I/Iron II period. We have no certain evidence.
- Although the rural population was important in the settlement, recent studies have shown the significance of urban developments, some of which survived from the LBA and some of which developed in the Iron I (Sergi 2019a). There was a symbiosis between the urban areas and the surrounding countryside: they were not primarily in opposition (contrary to some theories) but each depended on the other for certain aspects and needs of life.
- Many of the inhabitants of Canaanite cities were not 'urbanites' as we think of the term. That is, they were not scribes or administrators or members of the upper class but simply agriculturalists who lived in the city. We have plenty of evidence of this even in modern times (e.g., in quite large Third World cities where the majority of the inhabitants leave each day to tend their cultivated areas [Grabbe 2001]). Therefore, some of those settling the highlands would logically have been Canaanite peasants and farmers from villages and farmsteads surrounding the Canaanite cities, but also those who had lived within the city walls.
- As discussed above with regard to the Shasu, the assumption that they were all 'nomads' or 'semi-nomads' is not at all established from the few texts that we have of them (§6.3.3.4). They do not just wander around indiscriminately but make up a Shasu country or territory. Although we know that pastoralism was characteristic of some or possibly even most, we cannot say that this was the sole means of livelihood of all of them: pastoralism is part of the general way of living among settled peoples as well. Some inscriptions indicate that Shasu are also associated with certain cities.
- Although the idea that nomads naturally settle down or even want to settle down has been shown to be an outdated concept, this does not mean that pastoralists do not sometimes move to cultivation and a settled lifestyle. It is true that among modern examples, we often find that pastoralists who give up their lifestyle do so because of governmental coercion. Yet it is also a fact that we have many examples in which pastoralists change – without government coercion – to a more settled way of living (§6.3.3.1).

8.5 RISE OF THE ISRAELITE STATE

W. Dietrich (2007) *The Early Monarchy in Israel: The Tenth Century B.C.E.*; **idem** (2011) *Samuel: Teilband 1: 1 Sam 1–12*; **idem** (2012) 'David and the Philistines: Literature and History', in G. Galil, A. Gilboa, A. M. Maeir, and D. Kahn (eds), *The Ancient Near East in the 12th–10th Centuries BCE: Culture and History: Proceedings of the International Conference held at the University of Haifa, 2-5 May, 2010*: 79–98; **idem** (2015) *Samuel: Teilband 2: 1 Sam 13–26*; **idem** (2019) *Samuel: Teilband 3: 1 Sam 27–2 Sam 8*; **I. Finkelstein** (2002b) 'The Campaign of Shoshenq I to Palestine: A Guide to the 10th Century BCE Polity', *ZDPV* 118: 109–35; **idem** (2013) *The Forgotten Kingdom: The Archaeology and History of Northern Israel*; **idem** (2020) 'Saul and Highlands of Benjamin Update: The Role of Jerusalem', in J. J. Krause, O. Sergi, and K. Weingut (eds), *Saul, Benjamin, and the Emergence of Monarchy in Israel: Biblical and Archaeological Perspectives*: 33-56; **L. L. Grabbe** (2016) 'The Mighty Men of Israel: 1–2 Samuel and History', in W. Dietrich, C. Edenburg, and P. Hugo (eds), *The Books of Samuel: Stories - History - Reception History*: 83–104; **idem** (2017b) *1 and 2 Kings: History and Story in Ancient Israel: An Introduction and Study Guide*; **E. A. Knauf** (2016b) *1 Könige 1–14*; **idem** (2019) *1 Könige 15–22*.

8.5.1 Models of Statehood

T. J. Barfield (1990) 'Tribe and State Relations: The Inner Asian Perspective', in Philip S. Khoury and Joseph Kostiner (eds), *Tribes and State Formation in the Middle East*: 153–82; **S. C. Caton** (1990) 'Anthropological Theories of Tribe and State Formation in the Middle East: Ideology and the Semiotics of Power', in P. S. Khoury and J. Kostiner (eds), *Tribes and State Formation in the Middle East*: 74–108; **G. M. Feinman and J. Marcus (eds)** (1998) *Archaic States*; **M. Fortis and E. Evans-Pritchard** (1940) *African Political Systems*; **E. Gellner** (1981) 'Cohesion and Identity: the Magreb from Ibn Khaldun to Emile Durkheim', in *Muslim Society*: 86–98; **M. Godelier** (1986) *The Making of Great Men: Male Domination and Power among the New Guinea Baruya*; **C. Gosden** (1999) 'The Organization of Society', in G. Barker (ed.), *Companion Encyclopedia of Archaeology*: 470–504; **L. L. Grabbe** (2004) *A History of the Jews and Judaism in the Second Temple Period 1: Yehud: A History of the Persian Province of Judah*; **A. H. Joffe** (2002) 'The Rise of Secondary States in the Iron Age Levant', *JESHO* 45: 425–67; **M. Liverani** (1983) 'Political Lexicon and Political Ideologies in the Amarna Letters', *Berytus* 31: 41–56; **idem** (2021b) 'Contrasts and Confluences of Political Conceptions in the Amarna Period', in M. Liverani, *Historiography, Ideology and Politics in the Ancient Near East and Israel*: 185–201; **D. M. Master** (2001) 'State Formation Theory and the Kingdom of Ancient Israel', *JNES* 60: 117–31; **R. D. Miller II** (2005) *Chieftains of the Highland Clans: A History of Israel in the 12th and 11th Centuries B.C.*; **W. Moran** (1995) 'Some Reflections on Amarna Politics', in Z. Zevit, S. Gitin, and M. Sokoloff (eds), *Solving Riddles and Untying Knots: Biblical,*

Epigraphic, and Semitic Studies in Honor of Jonas C. Greenfield: 559–72; **E. Pfoh** (2009) *The Emergence of Israel in Ancient Palestine: Historical and Anthropological Perspectives*; **idem** (2016) *Syria-Palestine in the Late Bronze Age: An Anthropology of Politics and Power*; **C. L. Redman** (1999) 'The Development of Archaeological Theory: Explaining the Past', in G. Barker (ed.), *Companion Encyclopedia of Archaeology*: 48–80; **C. Renfrew and P. Bahn** (2004) *Archaeology: Theories, Methods and Practice*; **J. W. Rogerson** (1986) 'Was Early Israel a Segmentary Society?', *JSOT* 36: 17–26; **B. Routledge** (2004) *Moab in the Iron Age: Hegemony, Polity, Archaeology*; **D. Schloen** (2001) *The House of the Father as Fact and Symbol: Patrimonialism in Ugarit and the Ancient Near East*; **E. Service** (1962) *Primitive Social Organization*; **A. W. Southall** (1956) *Alur Society: A Study in Processes and Types of Domination*; **L. E. Stager** (1985a) 'The Archaeology of the Family in Ancient Israel', *BASOR* 260: 1–36; **R. Tapper** (1990) 'Anthropologists, Historians, and Tribespeople on Tribe and State Formation in the Middle East', in P. S. Khoury and J. Kostiner (eds), *Tribes and State Formation in the Middle East*: 48–73; **B. G. Trigger** (2003) *Understanding Early Civilizations: A Comparative Study*; **N. Yoffee** (2005) *Myths of the Archaic State: Evolution of the Earliest Cities, States, and Civilizations*.

The question of statehood for Israel and Judah cannot easily be disassociated from that of the settlement: the settlement and the rise of the monarchy seem ultimately to be part of the same process. This does not suggest that, once those who became Israel settled down, a state was inevitable, but the settlement – its nature, its development, the resources available – are all determining factors in the progress toward statehood. One followed from and presupposed the other.

In recent years there has been much discussion among anthropologists and archaeologists about the nature of states, the types of states, how states develop, and what precedes them. It is not unusual for discussions about the rise of Israel to make some reference to this discussion, but it must be said that most writings by biblical scholars do not give a thorough treatment of the subject. It is fair to say that when anthropological studies on state development are mentioned, it is not infrequently to expound one and follow it without serious discussion of other possibilities or critique of the one being followed. The literature on the subject is quite substantial, especially if one takes into account everything written since the seminal work by M. Fortis and E. Evans-Pritchard (1940). No attempt will be made here to trace the discussion over the decades, but several points can be made in order to summarize the most important consideration for discussion in the present:

- Much of the discussion, at least until recently, has been based on evolutionary models (Redman 1999: 49–53; Gosden 1999: 476–82; Renfrew/Bahn 2004: 178–82; Yoffee 2005: 22–41). A popular one has been the model of E. R. Service (1962) in which civilization developed through the stages of bands, tribes, chiefdoms, and finally states. Evolutionary models do not have to force everything into a rigid pattern nor suggest inevitability (Feinman/Marcus 1998: 5–6). N. Yoffee fully accepts the concept of social evolution, but his recent study is a sustained critique of the widely regarded 'neo-evolutionary model' (Yoffee 2005: 22–41).

- The various models of statehood are ideal types, but there is a danger of elevating ideal types to reality. Reality is always much more complicated, while ideal types (borrowed from Max Weber) only serve as a means of investigation and comparison. Within the various types there is a great deal of variation. To pick one sociological model and argue from it without considering others or without critiquing the models themselves is to be naive and uncritical.
- The concept of chiefdom – so beloved of studies on the development of statehood in Israel and Judah – has been much criticized (Yoffee 2005: 22–31). See further on this below.

The types of early states have been discussed in the anthropological literature, with a bewildering variety of models: city-states, territorial states, regional states, segmentary states, tribal states, ethnic states. The term 'city-state' frequently comes up in discussions relating to ancient Palestine, yet a recent collection found the term problematic (Feinman/Marcus 1998: 8–10). Still, B. Trigger (2003: 92–113) divides early states into the 'city-state' and 'the territorial state'; yet, disconcertingly, toward the end of his discussion he suddenly introduces the 'regional state/kingdom' without discussing what it is or how it relates to the other two. 'Regional state' is also used by T. J. Barfield (1990), but he seems to be using the term in a different sense from Trigger.

A number of the recent theorists on the rise of the Israelite and Judahite states have worked with the model of the chiefdom. Of recent works R. D. Miller II (2005: especially 6–14) argues that Israel began as a 'complex chiefdom', by which he means 'those having an intermediate level or levels of "subchiefs" between the paramount and the people'; he goes on to assert, it 'is complex chiefdoms that develop into states and that one would expect to find in Israel on the threshold of Monarchy' (Miller 2005: 8). Three main characteristics are said to be associated with complex chiefdoms: (1) tribute mobilization, (2) cycling (between two or three levels of control), and (3) sacralization. Unfortunately, Miller does not appear to take account of the debate. For example, he makes little reference to the critique of the chiefdom concept (e.g., Yoffee 2005: 22–31) and none to those who argue that the chiefdom is an alternative to the state, i.e., that chiefdoms do not develop into states (cf. Yoffee 2005: 26–7). His statement that it is the complex chiefdom that develops into the state also does not seem to recognize that the complex chiefdom might well cycle into a 'simple chiefdom'.

N. Yoffee (2005) both critiques the 'neo-evolutionary' thesis and also makes his own proposals about the development of the state. His thesis seems to be expressed in the following statement:

> …new social roles and new forms of social relations emerged alongside, and to an extent supplanted, exclusive kinship rules (of marriages and the status of children) that also functioned as the framework for relations of production. Leadership, exercised by shamans, expert hunters, and charismatic individuals, gave way to formalized ideologies in which the accumulation of wealth and high status were seen as rightfully belonging to leaders whose roles were, among other things, to 'make inequality enchant'. As social relations were transformed into relations of domination, new ideologies led to the acquiescence of subjects in their own domination and the production of their own subordination (Godelier 1986). The new ideologies of state, which were inextricable from the changing social relations that gave them birth, thus depicted how dominant leaders 'served' those who daily and perpetually served them…. The earliest

states, thus, consisted of a political center with its own leadership structure, specialized activities, and personnel, but also included numerous differentiated groups. These social groups continuously changed in their organization and membership in relation to the needs and goals, strengths and weaknesses of the political center. [Yoffee 2005: 32–4]

According to Yoffee (2005: 34–8) the critical processes of social and economic differentiation and political integration come about through the various forms of power that had to be in place before the earliest states could evolve: economic power (agricultural production, mercantile activity), social power (elites at both the state and local level, creation or adaptation of symbols of cultural commonality), and political power (bureaucratic administration, military organization, legal system, taxation structure). Although ancient states were unlikely to have passed through a chiefdom-like stage, he accepts and even presses the concept of city-state (2005: 42–62). He mentions in passing 'Yoffee's rule': 'If you can argue whether a society is a state or isn't, then it isn't' (2005: 41).

A. H. Joffe (2002) proposes the model of the 'ethnic state' for the rise of secondary states in the southern Levant, meaning Israel, Judah, Ammon, Moab, and finally Edom. By 'ethnic state' he means

polities integrated by means of identity, especially ethnicity, and which are territorially based.... they are novel and historically contingent political systems which appear in the Levant during the first millennium BCE thanks to the confluence of several factors, not least of all the collapse of imperial domination and the longstanding city-state system. [Joffe 2002: 426]

Joffe focuses on the archaeology and extra-biblical texts rather than the biblical accounts.

Based on fragmented evidence from the material culture (e.g., a series of palatial structures in *bit-ḫilani* style; proto-Aeolic capitals; red-burnished Phoenician-style tableware) Joffe identifies a state in the Cis-Jordan region already in the tenth century (Joffe 2002: 440–6). The similarity of construction styles at Megiddo, Hazor, and Gezer indicates they were part of a larger political unit, but all three seem to be in border areas. What the centre might be is not known. In spite of some marks of royal ideology, other significant ones are missing: representational art, monumental inscriptions, inscribed or decorated objects, inscribed or uninscribed seals, or weights. Although Joffe insists on calling it a state, he admits it was fragile, hardly integrated, and had little in the way of meaningful ethnic unity. In any case, much depends on following the conventional dating: if the 'low chronology' turns out to be correct, the postulated development of the ethnic states will be somewhat different.

Other types of early state are sometimes postulated. The term 'segmentary state' seems to have been coined by A. W. Southall (1956). In a more recent article, J. W. Rogerson (1986) argued that ancient Israel was not a segmentary society but approached being a segmentary state. The concept has come under considerable criticism, and Southall himself eventually gave it up (Marcus/Feinman 1998: 7–8). Another is 'tribal state', of which three sorts are proposed: (1) one tribal elite or dynasty conquers and rules over a heterogeneous population; (2) a nontribal dynasty is brought to power by and depends on tribal support; (3) the rulers attempt to eliminate tribalism but promote a national ideology of integration that resembles tribal ideology (Tapper 1990: 69). Inspired by M. Weber,

L. E. Stager (1985a: 25–8), followed by D. Schloen (2001) and D. M. Master (2001), proposed the archetype of the patrimonial state. This is modelled on the household, in which leadership is vested by tradition in the patriarchal figure (yet this seems to be more like what Pfoh calls a 'patronage' state). In a recent book on the rise of Moab as a state B. Routledge (2004: 115–23) considered but rejected both the popular 'local models' of state formation, i.e., 'tribal states' and 'patrimonial states'.

Although perhaps not providing a model as such, M. Liverani (1983, 2021b) argued for two essential approaches to subordinate kingdoms by their overlords. The 'Asiatic model', sometimes referred to as the 'feudal model' (especially expressed in the Hittite vassal treaties), placed obligations on the vassal kingdoms to support their overlord with tribute and military assistance when needed. In return the vassal ruler was given the right to rule his kingdom and would be assisted if attacked from outside. In other words, loyalty worked both ways: the vassal must be loyal to his overlord, but the overlord in turn had obligations of loyalty toward the vassal. The other was the 'Egyptian model' in which the vassal had obligations of tribute and military assistance, but as the divine king the pharaoh had no obligations to the vassal. His gift to his underlings was 'life'. Many of the Egyptian vassals misunderstood this because they worked with the 'Asiatic' understanding of their relationship to the pharaoh, though it is evident that some began to understand the situation and adapt to it. W. Moran (1995) accepts the first part of Liverani's thesis but challenged the argument that the vassals misunderstood; rather, he thinks the problem is the difference between political ideas (which the Egyptians never gave up) and political realities (in which the vassals sometimes acted in ways contrary to Egyptian ideology).

This model was taken up by E. Pfoh (2016; cf. also Pfoh 2009 on the patronage model) and developed into what he referred to as the 'patronage' and the 'patrimonial' models (though his 'patrimonial state' seems in many ways the opposite of Stager's!). Of particular interest here is the 'patronage model', most clearly expressed by E. Pfoh but seems to apply *in nuce* to several of the models; at heart, it is essentially the imprinting of the model of kinship and the extended family onto the kingdom. The king acts as the senior family member toward his subjects. Clan and family leaders support the ruler but also act as a sort of electoral college in choosing the king and advising and supporting him. The king is thus dependent on the tribes of his kingdom for his authority and must listen to and meet the basic needs of the tribes, expressed through the tribal leaders. The ruler is fundamentally a *primus inter pares*:

> Political power in Syria-Palestine is better defined as dependent on a network of interpersonal relations, a hierarchy of personal loyalties.... In sum, patron–client relations constituted the conceptual, symbolic and socio-political matrix of the Syro-Palestinian societies' ontology. [Pfoh 2016: 170]

To sum up, a variety of models are currently being proposed and used, yet they are not necessarily mutually exclusive. The 'patronage model' works well for the early Israelite monarchy, as we shall see, but it can be combined with other models.

One of the points made in a number of studies is the importance of ideology to the founding of states (Caton 1990; also to ethnic identity: §8.4.1). 'Ideology' can of course cover a number of different perspectives, including that of religion. For example, E. Gellner (1981) has demonstrated the significance of saints and religious leaders for the development or maintenance of chiefdoms in early Islamic history (also Tapper 1990: 65). In this light, the suggestion of Gottwald and others that Yahwism was important to the development of early Israel takes on a new significance. We also have to consider the place of law, which can play a similar role. In Israel law included not just civil law but moral and religious law (on law, see Grabbe 2004: 173–83). Unfortunately, it becomes a matter of speculation at this point because we have so little evidence.

8.5.2 Beginnings of the Kingdom of Israel

M. Broshi and I. Finkelstein (1992) 'The Population of Palestine in Iron Age II', *BASOR* 287: 47–60; **R. Coote and K. W. Whitelam** (1987) *The Emergence of Early Israel in Historical Perspective*; **I. Finkelstein** (1998b) 'The Rise of Early Israel: Archaeology and Long-Term History', in S. Aḥituv and E. D. Oren (eds), *The Origin of Early Israel – Current Debate: Biblical, Historical and Archaeological Perspectives*: 7–39; **idem** (1999a) 'State Formation in Israel and Judah: A Contrast in Context, A Contrast in Trajectory', *NEA* 62: 35–52; **M. Noth** (1981) *The Deuteronomistic History*, ET of chaps 1–13 of Noth (1943) *Überlieferungsgeschichtliche Studien: Die sammelnden und bearbeitenden Geschichtswerke im Alten Testament*.

The reasons for the development of a state in the highlands are no doubt complex, but there are a number of factors to be taken into account:

- The settlement of the Philistines and other Sea Peoples in the south of Palestine and along the coast which added a new element to the population of Canaan.
- The rapid settlement of the hill country, followed by collapse toward the end of IA I.
- The general increase in population in the areas of the Israelite tribes.
- The successful cooperation of several tribes against a common enemy (e.g., against Sisera in Judges 4–5).
- Gradual removal of Egyptian control, whether in manned fortresses or the threat of raids against Canaan's inhabitants.
- Competition with other groups in the region, including the Philistines.

Eventually the kingdoms of Israel and Judah developed in this region. What was the process? Perhaps one important factor was a growth in population: a critical mass of settlers was reached without which certain things could not happen, but this was more significant in the north and decreased as one went south, with the area south of Jerusalem still being mainly pastoral. It seems that at some point a dominant ethnic consciousness came about in this region. Part of the reason might be by force: an 'Israelite' group might have conquered or otherwise taken over some other smaller groups and assimilated them (as suggested in Joshua and Judges). But it is doubtful if that was sufficient.

Here the suggestion of Mendenhall, Gottwald, and others might have some theoretical validity, even if they provided no concrete evidence: Yahwism. One of the characteristics – and constituents – of an ethnic group is a set of common myths and ideologies, which can include religion (§8.4.1). Israelite society was long polytheistic, but Yhwh did function in some way as a national god and seems to have been the most widely honoured deity. Thus, it is possible that Israel partly coalesced around Yhwh but, even if true, this would have been only one factor; it would be simplistic to suggest that this was the only factor. Indeed, we do not know for certain to what extent the hill peoples saw themselves as a single ethnic group, but the question becomes relevant if we start discussing Israel as an 'ethnic state'.

We can now ask how and why Israel and Judah developed into states, for we almost all agree that they eventually became states. The problem is that the current debate makes it difficult to come to firm conclusions about the archaeology (§8.2), especially with the debate over the 'low chronology' (§1.3), but the archaeology does put limits on what can and cannot have happened. For many anthropologists, the formation of the Israelite and Judahite states would probably be explained from impersonal social and political forces, but others would allow a personal element into the mix, such as the presence of a dynamic charismatic leader. For example, Coote and Whitelam (1987) explain the rise of Israel as a state from the combination of pressure on highland resources as the population expanded and the pressure from the Philistines in the lowlands. This follows a long line of scholars seeing the 'Philistine threat' as in some way pressing the Israelites into initiating a monarchy.

Yet there are some objections to these proposals. First, there is no evidence that the 'bearing capacity' of the highlands had been reached; in other words, archaeological surveys suggest that the highland population could still have been sustained by local resources without having to expand: the same population or greater could be found there in other periods (cf. Finkelstein 1999a; Broshi/Finkelstein 1992). Secondly, was there any impetus for the lowlanders to expand into the highlands since they also still had room to grow (Finkelstein 1998b: 24)? As already noted in the discussion about the Philistines (§8.3), there was little reason for the Philistines to want to expand their territory into the highlands. They already had control of the coastal plain and the Shephelah. If there was friction between the Israelites and Philistines, it is likely to have been the Israelites who initiated it. That is, it would have been expected that the highlanders would have made raids into the more prosperous areas of the lowlands.

This has already been noted in Mesopotamia, with tribes from the Zagros mountains and elsewhere bothering Assyria and Babylonia with periodic raids for booty and resources (e.g., §3.2; §7.3.1). The developing Israelite tribes in the highlands may well have organized raiding parties against the Philistines until finally the people demanded retaliation by their leaders. At this point, the Philistines would have campaigned against the Israelites – to punish them and to discourage further raids. But the highland tribes might well have reacted as the tribes in the Zagros had done and countered with further aggression and even an aim to expand their settlements in the lowlands at the expense of the Philistine cities who controlled the region.

But considering this explanation – a 'Philistine threat' – inadequate does not answer the question of why the highland settlements coalesced into a state. By rights we would expect the first state in Palestine to arise in the coastal plain, but here the individual Philistine city-states were successful, and there seems to have been no impetus to form a larger unit. The next area would be the northern region, perhaps the northern valleys or hill country. It is precisely in this area that the Omride kingdom emerged, which is one of the reasons that some scholars think this was the first Israelite state. The problem is what to do with the biblical traditions about the rise of the Israelite kingship. The idea that Israel was under divine rule but had Samuel anoint a king chosen by Yhwh is of course pure theology, not history. Should we simply dismiss the whole of the biblical account as too difficult to deal with? This is perhaps tempting, and some have certainly followed this approach. Yet more considered analyses suggest that there is history behind the stories of the 'United Monarchy', even if precisely what sort of history is a matter of debate.

It has often been assumed in the past that with the reigns of Saul and David we begin to do get into the historical period. In Noth's classic theory, 1 Samuel 13 to 2 Kings 2 was thought to have been made up of several blocks of tradition that were given only minor editing (including some formulaic introductions and transitional passages) before being incorporated into the Dtr-H (Noth 1981: 54–7). More recent analysis has not been as optimistic about finding early narratives, but the stories of Saul and David show evidence of a variety of traditions: there is pro-Saul bias in the Saul traditions and anti-David perspectives in the Davidic material. There are also some essential differences between them and the Solomon narrative.

Although the Judges narrative is suspect as a historical source as such, it shows a fragmented Canaan divided between tribes and cities, some of which seem to have charismatic leaders. There is a certain resemblance between some of the 'judges' in the book and the Canaanite kinglets known from the Amarna period. For example, Abimelech son of Gideon looks like the king of a Canaanite city-state (Judges 9). There is also the figure of Shamgar ben Anath who appears in the narrative section as one who 'also saved/delivered Israel' (Judg. 3:31), but he seems to have been an embarrassment for the narrator, perhaps because of being apparently a worshiper of the goddess Anat. He is given only a couple of sentences, but he seems to have been someone who could not be overlooked. Furthermore, he is known from the Song of Deborah. If the statement in Judg. 5:6 is original, he seems to be attested as some sort of leader, perhaps a tribal leader or mayor of the city. He reminds one of Abdi-Heba of Amarna Jerusalem who was a local leader and also had a goddess as part of his name.

As we shall see with Saul, what we seem to find is the natural development of a 'patronage' or 'tribal' entity in the highlands, perhaps for mutual self-protection and self-interest. That is, it possibly wanted to exploit the trade links across its territory but also to protect itself against the reaction of the Philistines to this exploitation. The 'chiefdom' or 'kingdom' was not initially large or complicated, but ambitious individuals (such as Saul, Eshbaal, and David) seized opportunities to expand and develop this inchoate state, a process perhaps eventually reached in the time of Omri and following reigns.

At this point, it would be useful to examine the proposal of I Finkelstein (2002b; 2013; 2020) about the development of the kingdoms of Israel and Judah. He argues for the importance of the invasion of Pharaoh Shoshenq I. According to his reconstruction, there was a political entity centred on the Gibeon-Bethel plateau led by Saul. This polity looked to be expanding to the north and also south and southwest. The problem was that this appeared to threaten vital Egyptian interests, especially the trade route(s) through the region and the copper industry which the Egyptians depended on (because the copper supply from Cyprus had dried about 1200 BCE). From Shoshenq's own inscription, we know that his invasion targeted the Gibeon-Bethel region (not Jerusalem, as 1 Kgs 14:25-28 has it). After destroying the Gibeon polity (Saul was killed by the Egyptians, not the Philistines) Shoshenq then set up a Northern political entity at Shechem (headed by Jeroboam) and a Southern one at Jerusalem (headed by David). Having taken control of this region, Egypt continued to dominate it until about 850 BCE.

Various aspects of this scenario, which is admittedly given in highly summary form here, will be examined in the sections that follow, along with my own interpretation and reconstruction of the development of the early Israelite kingdoms. But first several points about Finkelstein's interpretation – and my reaction to it – can be made:

- Finkelstein's scenario is plausible and may well be correct. Yet while some aspects of it are well supported by archaeology and other sources, other aspects are highly hypothetical and hardly the only reconstruction possible.
- Finkelstein is no doubt correct that the writing of literary accounts probably developed in Israel much later than this time (cf. §2.5), and 1–2 Samuel and the early part of 1 Kings are not necessarily reliable historiographical sources.
- Although Finkelstein takes up a number of the biblical names/figures, his reconstruction essentially ignores the picture given by the text. For example, he has Saul eliminated by the Egyptians, not the Philistines, and essentially excludes Solomon from his account. He also ignores the implied chronology of the text, making Saul and David contemporary with Shoshenq I.
- I fully agree that the biblical text describing the reigns of Saul, David, and Solomon are problematic, but my view is that there is more historical memory in the biblical text than Finkelstein allows for (see Grabbe 2016; 2017a: 138–50). For example, we should keep in mind that a court chronicle was probably already being drawn on for some aspects of the reigns of Jeroboam and Rehoboam (cf. 1 Kgs 14:19-21, 29-31). Surprisingly, Finkelstein (2013: 64) accepts that the order and even approximate length of the reigns of kings from Jeroboam and Rehoboam are roughly reliable. Yet his interpretation assumes that the biblical writers had completely forgotten the order and actions of the slightly earlier kings, Saul to Jeroboam/Rehoboam.
- Specifically, some of the main outline features of Saul and David – and even Solomon – in the text may be reliable, in my opinion. Especially important is that the narratives of Saul and David are intertwined and cannot be separated into two independent accounts (Grabbe 2016: 97–9; 2017a: 144–6). This seems to rule out the death of Saul at the hands of the Egyptians and the separate installation of David over a polity alongside Jeroboam. And problematic as the narrative is about Solomon, it looks unlikely that his place as the successor to David and predecessor of Rehoboam/Jeroboam has been invented.

8.5.3 Samuel

W. Dietrich (2011) *Samuel: Teilband 1: 1 Sam 1–12*; **idem** (2015) *Samuel: Teilband 2: 1 Sam 13–26*; **idem** (2019) *Samuel: Teilband 3: 1 Sam 27–2 Sam 8*.

The story of Samuel is in many ways a continuation of the line of judges described in the book of Judges. Samuel is said to have 'judged' Israel (1 Sam. 7:15). He was both priest and prophet, but he was also a political leader, at least for the first part of his life. We do not normally expect either priest or prophet to be the king (or a similar figure), yet after the fall of the monarchy the high priest of Judah was also a political leader of the Jewish community and sometimes had prophetic functions.

One would have expected a religious figure – priest or prophet – to have been associated with the rise of the monarchy in Israel. You might think of the archbishop of Canterbury in English history. Although the archbishop was a religious figure, he had considerable power, including the power to crown the monarch. We also know that some archbishops were very political, even holding political office along with their ecclesiastical duties. Just as the history of the English monarchy includes the activities of many of the Canterbury archbishops, Samuel who had both priestly and prophetic functions, as well as a community leadership role, would have been a necessary figure.

In the present text Samuel is in many ways the linchpin that connects the Saul and David traditions. He anointed the first king but, after Saul was rejected by Yhwh, he then anointed David. Yet many literary critics have argued that the prophetic figure who first anointed Saul (1 Sam. 10:1) was originally an anonymous figure. The question is whether Samuel is a historical figure. Samuel seems to fill the role in the narratives about Saul and David that Merlin does in the King Arthur story. Although his activities are sometimes centre stage, his purpose is to choose and anoint the person to be king. Merlin was a sort of shaman figure, which means that he functioned in both prophetic and priestly activities, much as Samuel did.

It might be suggested that Samuel should be better associated with David, and that he has been brought into the Saul tradition secondarily. Yet Samuel's original circuit of cities where he carried out his priestly duties were Bethel, Gilgal, Mizpah, and Ramah, all places in the North, and not everyone wants to replace the Samuel anointing Saul with an anonymous holy man. Whether Samuel should be inserted into 1 Samuel 9–10 (as he is now) or not, he could well have been an important shamanistic figure and king maker in the period at the beginnings of an Israelite state. He could then have been active in the rise of Saul but became disillusioned with him, at which point he would have looked around for a replacement.

In that sense, his general activities in both the Saul and David traditions are plausible. However, some of the activities ascribed to Samuel are unlikely to be historical. His function as a mouthpiece for anti-monarchic speeches is one of these. Many of the passages that express hostility toward kingship for Israel (e.g., 1 Samuel 8) are probably late (though as so often, the matter is complicated [cf. Dietrich 2011: 42*–3*).

8.5.4 Saul

W. Creamer and J. Haas (1985) 'Tribe versus Chiefdom in Lower Central America', *American Antiquity* 50: 738–54; **D. Edelman** (1986) 'Saul's Battle Against Amaleq (1 Sam. 15)', *JSOT* 35: 71–84; **idem** (1991) *King Saul in the Historiography of Judah*; **idem** (1996a) 'Saul ben Kish in History and Tradition', in V. Fritz and P. R. Davies (eds), *The Origins of the Ancient Israelite States*: 142–59; **I. Finkelstein** (2013) *The Forgotten Kingdom: The Archaeology and History of Northern Israel*; **S. Shalom Brooks** (2005) *Saul and the Monarchy: A New Look*.

Perhaps the best reason for believing that Saul was a historical personage is that he was plainly a problem for the narrator of 1–2 Samuel. It seems clear that the narrator wanted to tell the story of David but had to deal with Saul as well, even though he would rather have ignored or forgotten about him. According to narrative logic, the rulership and dynasty should have begun with David.

The whole story of the monarchy is of the legitimacy of the Davidic dynasty and the illegitimacy of the northern kingship. The Northern Kingdom should not have existed, and the northern kings were presented as usurpers. But how is this is to be explained, if David was also a usurper – not part of the dynasty originally chosen by God? The narrator of 1 Samuel has to present it that Saul's dynasty was not just wiped out, but that his descendants were declared null and void as far as kingship was concerned – a rather strange concept, if it was the king and dynasty originally chosen and anointed by Yhwh. If Saul's rulership and dynasty could be overturned, why not that of David? Why should not his throne have been overthrown with Solomon who also went astray? Yet the narrative insists on treating David's line quite differently from that of Saul.

Thus, it seems that the narrator was stuck with Saul and his family. The existence of Saul as the first king of Israel does not strike the critical reader as a likely fictional scenario, even if some aspects of the relationship and interaction between Saul and David could easily find their place in a work of fiction. The tradition was too firmly settled and known to the people to have been given major changes, such as dropping Saul altogether. Even though there is absolutely no evidence for Saul apart from the biblical text, there is good reason to believe there was a historical Saul.

What else can we say with more or less confidence about this figure? As has long been observed, 2 Samuel 2–9 describes Eshbaal (or Ishbosheth) as ruling over 'Gilead, the Ashurites, Jezrel, Ephraim, and Benjamin'. This is reasonably the territory ascribed to Saul. It is especially important because it does not include Judah, for reasons already noted above (§8.4.4). Apart from some territory on the other side of the Jordan, the core of the fiefdom is the central hill country, which archaeology suggests is the centre of the Iron I settlement area. Many of Saul's activities could have been accomplished in two years (cf. 1 Sam. 13:1).

Much of the Saul tradition involves fighting against the Philistines. Yet he was supposed to have originally made his name by fighting the Amalekites (1 Samuel 15). On the surface, this appears unlikely, since the territory of the Amalekites was presumed to have been in the Negev (Num. 13:29). That is a valid objection, since Saul's territory does not appear to have included Judah, much less the areas to the south of it. D. Edelman (1986) has argued, however, that Saul attacked Amalekites who were living in the region of Samaria. This is much more credible as a historical event.

It is plausible that Saul fought the Philistines, but it is more likely that Saul attacked them than the other way round. Philistines had lived happily in the coastal region for well over a century. The Shephelah acted as a transition zone, and there was opportunity for Philistines to expand if they had wanted to do so, without moving into the highlands. The ones aiming to expand their territory seem to have been the Israelites. Probably, the highlanders made periodic raids into the prosperous lowlands, though that may have forced the Philistines to send troops occasionally on retaliatory incursions into the highlands. But the idea that the Philistines were wanting to expand their territory into the highlands at this time looks unlikely. If Saul arose to defend Israel, it may be because the Philistines were seeking to put a stop to highland raids once and for all by a major campaign against Israel.

In sum, we should not think of an Israelite David being threatened by a Philistine Goliath; rather, the Philistine cities and Israel were simply rivals in the same narrow region of Palestine. This interpretation seems to be supported by the archaeology. The Galilee region and northern valleys prospered during the Iron I for the most part, but some of the main sites were destroyed in the later Iron I (Finkelstein 2013: 32–6). Radiocarbon dating now suggests that these destructions were not a unitary event but happened over a period of some decades. The subsequent material culture suggests that invaders from the highlands were the cause of the destructions. This would seem to confirm the view that the highlanders – Israel – were expanding out of their core territory. If so, they would probably have also been expanding south, into Philistine territory. Rather than being the victims in the clash with the Philistines, Israel may have been the instigators. It has been suggested that Saul gained his finances by controlling the trade between the Jordan Valley and the Philistine cities, even perhaps robbing trade caravans on occasion (Knauf/Guillaume 2016: 67; Knauf/Niemann 2021: 123). If so, this would have been a good reason for the Philistines to want to 'sort him out' to protect their trade route.

Here are some salient points about the Saul tradition. First of all, Saul looks like chieftain, with a court that meets under a tree (1 Sam. 22:6). We have two versions of how he became king: one is that he was anointed by Samuel (1 Sam. 9:1–10:16 [23] + 13:2–14:52), which looks like a biased account from a prophetic source that wants to make Saul subordinate to Samuel; the other – more likely to be reliable – is that he arose as a deliverer (1 Sam. 11:1-15). A recent analysis of the Saul tradition finds a historical core, though this has been filtered through the distorting lenses of Davidic court circles, prophetic circles, Deuteronomistic perspectives, and anti-monarchic views (Shalom Brooks 2005). The stories of killing the priests of Nob or the Gibeonites are probably later calumnies.

According to Shalom Brooks (2005) the population in the central highlands was already moving toward a new socio-economic situation characterized by a developing centralization. This was the background for the rise of the monarchy. Saul was a successful leader, the first to develop a standing army, who had the support of the people (she includes – less convincingly – the Judahite hill country). Saul was not only able to unite the Israelite tribes but also to incorporate Canaanites and other minority groups into the emerging state. Loyalty to Saul continued after his death, creating rebellions and other problems for David; indeed, David almost wrecked the monarchy by his sabotage of Saul's rule in order to gain the throne for himself. Similarly, D. Edelman (1996, 1991) sees the historical Saul as the petty king of Gibeon with Benjaminite roots who expanded into surrounding territory to create a state called 'Israel'. Attempts to control local trade routes and find markets brought him in conflict with the Philistines and other independent states. He died trying to expand into the Jezreel–Beth She'an corridor.

I. Finkelstein (2002b; 2013; 2020) sees Saul as the leader of a polity that had its centre in the Gibeon-Bethel plateau. This polity – and Saul's life with it – was brought to an end by the Egyptian conquest of Shoshenq I. While much of Finkelstein's Saulide polity agrees with the picture presented here, he also inserts Egypt which is completely absent from the text at this point. It is not unprecedented for the biblical text to omit an important historical actor: for example in the account of Ahab (in which the king interacts with the Aramaeans), his actual confrontation with the Assyrians is ignored (cf. Grabbe 2017a: 181–4). But even though the Assyrians are missed from the biblical account of Ahab, other aspects of the text are nevertheless supported by the Assyrian inscriptions. Yet in the case of Saul and the Egyptians, there is no place for them in Saul's lifetime, according to the text; moreover, the Egyptians are also absent from the David narrative (contrary to Finkelstein's scenario).

Saul's kingdom seems to have been an example of a chiefdom (if such exist; see objections at §8.5.1), but also of a tribal state; how these two differed and how they functioned is a matter of debate (cf. Creamer/Haas 1985): in Saul's case either term seems appropriate. Saul seems to have been a charismatic leader, but also the leading families (i.e., the tribes) chose Saul as their leader. He functioned as a chiefdom, with a simple governing structure (1 Sam. 22:6: under a tree), but power was apparently invested for the most part in various clan leaders. Further discussion of Saul will occur in the account of David (§8.5.6).

8.5.5 Eshbaal

Eshbaal, son of Saul, also seems to have been a problem for the narrator. He is not necessary: David could have become king of Israel on the death of Saul, a simpler and more straightforward scenario. Yet the writer seems to have been stuck with an Ishbaal tradition too strong to be ignored; he called him Ish-Bosheth ('man of shame') instead of his proper name, 'man of Baal', another embarrassing part of the tradition (cf. 1 Chron. 8:33). Furthermore, Eshbaal's own relative Abner conspired to deliver Saul's – Eshbaal's – kingdom to David. It is also here that the narrator notes the territory ruled by Eshbaal, which was evidently also some of that ruled by Saul (2 Sam. 2:9); however, Eshbaal seems to have expanded his area of control somewhat, moving into Gilead, the Jezreel Valley, and the Lower Galilee (Knauf/Guillaume 2016: 70–1; Knauf/Niemann 2021: 126). The brief rivalry between David's and Eshbaal's kingdoms does not take up much narrative space, until Abner brings Israel over to David. The reality may have been different: Eshbaal may have ruled for a couple of decades or more. He is given two years by 2 Sam. 2:10, but this is at the same time as David is said to have ruled seven years in Hebron, while there was a 'long war' between the two kingdoms. It may be that a number has dropped out before the 'two' in 2 Sam. 2:10.

8.5.6 David

D. Ben-Ami (2014) 'Notes on the Iron IIA Settlement in Jerusalem in Light of Excavations in the Northwest of the City of David', *TA* 41: 3–19; **M. Brettler** (1995) *The Creation of History in Ancient Israel*; **J. M. Cahill** (2003) 'Jerusalem at the Time of the United Monarchy: The Archaeological Evidence', in A. G. Vaughn and A. E. Killebrew (eds), *Jerusalem in Bible and Archaeology: The First Temple Period*: 13–80; **idem** (2004) 'Jerusalem in David and Solomon's Time', *BAR* 30, no. 6: 20–31, 62–3; **W. Dietrich** (2007) *The Early Monarchy in Israel: The Tenth Century B.C.E.*; **idem** (2012) 'David and the Philistines: Literature and History', in G. Galil, A. Gilboa, A. M. Maeir, and D. Kahn (eds), *The Ancient Near East in the 12th–10th Centuries BCE: Culture and History*: 79–98; **I. Finkelstein** (2001) 'The Rise of Jerusalem and Judah: The Missing Link', *Levant* 33: 105–15; **I. Finkelstein and N. A. Silberman** (2006) *The Bible Unearthed: Archaeology's New Vision of Ancient Israel and the Origin of its Sacred Texts*; **I. Finkelstein, Z. Herzog, L. Singer-Avitz, and D. Ussishkin** (2007) 'Has King David's Palace in Jerusalem Been Found?', *TA* 34: 142–64; **L. L. Grabbe** (2003c) 'Ethnic Groups in Jerusalem', in T. L. Thompson (ed.), *Jerusalem in Ancient History and Tradition*: 145–63; **B. Halpern** (2001) *David's Secret Demons: Messiah, Murderer, Traitor, King*; **L. A. Hitchcock** (2018) '"All the Cherethites, and All the Pelethites, and All the Gittites (Samuel 2:15-18)" – An Up-to-Date Account of the Minoan Connection with the Philistines', in I. Shai et al. (eds), *Tell It in Gath: Studies in the History and Archaeology of Israel: Essays in Honor of Aren M. Maeir on the Occasion of his*

Sixtieth Birthday: 304–21; **A. E. Killebrew** (2003) 'Biblical Jerusalem: An Archaeological Assessment', in A. G. Vaughn and A. E. Killebrew (eds), *Jerusalem in Bible and Archaeology: The First Temple Period*: 329–45; **S. L. McKenzie** (2000) *King David: A Biography*; **A. Mazar** (2007) 'The Spade and the Text: The Interaction between Archaeology and Israelite History Relating to the Tenth-Ninth Centuries BCE', in H. G. M. Williamson (ed.), *Understanding the History of Ancient Israel*: 143–71; **E. Mazar** (2006) 'Did I Find King David's Palace?', *BAR* 32, no. 1: 16–27, 70; **idem** (2009) *The Palace of King David: Excavations at the Summit of the City of David: Preliminary Report of Seasons 2005–2007*; **N. Na'aman** (1996c) 'Sources and Composition in the History of David', in V. Fritz and P. R. Davies (eds), *The Origins of the Ancient Israelite States*: 170–86; **idem** (2002) 'In Search of Reality Behind the Account of David's Wars with Israel's Neighbours', *IEJ* 52: 200–224; **idem** (2010) 'Khirbet Qeiyafa in Context', *UF* 42: 497–526; **idem** (2013) 'Khirbet Qeiyafa in Context', *UF* 42: 497–526; **R. Ngo** (2014) *Canaanite Fortress Discovered in the City of David, Biblical Archaeology Sites, News*; **H. M. Niemann** (2013) 'Neighbors and Foes, Rivals and Kin: Philistines, Shepheleans, Judeans between Geography and Economy, History and Theology', in A. E. Killebrew and G. Lehmann (eds), *The Philistines and Other 'Sea Peoples' in Text and Archaeology*: 243–64; **R. Reich** (2011) *Excavating the City of David: Where Jerusalem's History Began*; **S. Shalom Brooks** (2005) *Saul and the Monarchy: A New Look*; **M. Steiner** (1994) 'Re-dating the Terraces of Jerusalem', *IEJ* 44: 13–20; **idem** (1998) 'The Archaeology of Ancient Jerusalem', *CR:BS* 6: 143–68; **idem** (2001) 'Jerusalem in the Tenth and Seventh Centuries BCE: From Administrative Town to Commercial City', in A. Mazar (ed.), *Studies in the Archaeology of the Iron Age in Israel and Jordan*: 280–8; **idem** (2003a) 'Expanding Borders: The Development of Jerusalem in the Iron Age', in T. L. Thompson (ed.), *Jerusalem in Ancient History and Tradition*: 68–79; **idem** (2003b) 'The Evidence from Kenyon's Excavations in Jerusalem: A Response Essay', in A. G. Vaughn and A. E. Killebrew (eds), *Jerusalem in Bible and Archaeology: The First Temple Period*: 347–63; **J. Van Seters** (2010) 'David the Mercenary', in L. L. Grabbe (ed.), *Israel in Transition: From Late Bronze II to Iron IIA (c. 1250–850 BCE): Volume 2 The Text*: 199–219.

The first thing to notice about David is that he is inextricably associated with Judah. This is important, because the relationship of Judah with Israel is one of the areas in which the data clash strongly with the surface narrative of the biblical text. It has long been known and accepted that Judah had its own national identity and was separate from and a rival of Israel from an early period, as was discussed above (§8.4.4). A number of recent studies attempts to analyse the David story (Brettler 1995: 91–111; McKenzie 2000; Halpern 2001; Finkelstein/Silberman 2006). The David traditions are in part bound up with the Saul traditions, and they need to be evaluated together.

One of the concerns in the early part of the story is to legitimate David – strongly suggesting that David was a usurper (Shalom Brooks 2005: 69–88). To take one analysis, N. Na'aman (1996c) argues for some written material (lists, extracts from a chronicle of kings), though not all necessarily from David's time. It was not customary at this time to cite documents. These probably came from the scribal milieu where such documents were used for training. For example, the story of Shishak's invasion may have been based on an actual account, though it was interpreted by a later writer (but see other interpretations at §8.5.8). A notable historical point is that David seems to have ruled over a united Kingdom of Israel that included Judah. However, whether he ruled over a large kingdom is probably to be answered in the negative. David's (and Solomon's) 'United Monarchy' is quite different from the one portrayed in the biblical text and seems not to have been much of an advance on Saul's chiefdom or tribal kingdom.

8.5.6.1 Origin/Early Life of David
Saul may have had connections with the tribal and clan leaders of Judah, even though he did not rule over Judahite territory. Two stories are given about David's rise to power and to being the son-in-law of Saul. According to one he was a musician who came to Saul's court and helped him to appease his demons by playing on the lyre. The other story is that David secured his place in Saul's court by his military exploits. The idea that Saul was able to draft in soldiers from Judah, including David's brothers, is an unlikely one. On the other hand, Saul's army might have attracted young men from Judah as volunteers who wanted the mercenary pay and the excitement. While the David-and-Goliath story is not credible (further on Goliath can be found at §8.3), the idea that David impressed with his military prowess fits the image of David throughout much of his adult life, when he was a military commander. The saying, 'Saul has slain his thousands, and David his tens of thousands' might be an actual historical memory, in which David was fated in Saul's court because he was a great soldier hero (on this saying, see further below [§8.5.6.5]).

Although Saul did not rule over the Judaean territory, he seems to have had quite a bit of influence – or possibly it was just a matter if intimidation. When David was supposedly on the run from him, he was able to chase him through the southern area without hindrance (1 Samuel 22–26), and some of the local people reported on him to Saul (1 Sam. 23:7-13; 24:2; 26:1). It may be that the Judahites did not wish to bring Saul's wrath down on themselves and did not support David so that Saul would leave them alone. But it may well be that David – acting as an *apiru* leader – was regarded with suspicion by the local people, even if they were fellow Judahites. According to the biblical text, he only raided Philistine territory but left the Judahites alone (1 Samuel 26). Yet this could simply be the bias of the surviving text, whereas David may have actually taken what his band needed from all sides, including from the people and villages of the Judahite people. If so, he would have had his supporters but also those who feared him and would not help him unless they were forced to.

8.5.6.2 David's Wars
According to the text of 2 Samuel, David continued Saul's fight with the Philistines, especially in 5:17-25 and 8:1. Yet several scholars have argued that the reality was different, and that David may not have fought with the Philistines but arranged a truce that allowed a peaceful co-existence throughout his reign (Niemann 2013: 259–60; Dietrich 2012: 95–8). There are a number of arguments in support of this. First, David's wars with the Philistines in 2 Sam. 5:17-25 seem only a passing episode, with little consequence; indeed, taking little space to describe. The motive for the Philistines to attack him also looks rather trumped up. Niemann notes that these campaigns (and the statement in 2 Sam. 5:25) fit Saul better and were probably borrowed from the Saulide tradition.

Secondly, David does not defeat the Philistines (only the tacked on summary statement in 2 Sam. 5:25 claims this), yet the threat simply disappears from the text. Thirdly, we also have the reference to the 600 warriors from Gath, under the command of Itai, who assist David at the time of Absalom's rebellion (2 Sam. 15:18-22). Fourthly, Achish king of Gath is clearly at peace with Solomon after the time of David (1 Kgs 2:39-40). Finally, Judah seems to have expanded into the Shephelah in the first half of the ninth century, yet there is no evidence of conflict with Gath which would have dominated the area as a large city at this time (Na'man 2010: 516–17; 2013: 264). This indicates that an earlier agreement (presumably the one made in the time of David) was still in effect.

Yet if David did not fight with the Philistines, was he seeking an essential expansion of his territory? According to 2 Samuel, David fought a variety of the surrounding peoples. Essentially, he expanded his territory to the north and east and south, into Moab, Ammon, Edom, and the region of Aramaean rule (2 Sam. 8; 10:1–11.1; 12:26-31). The extension of control into Edom and Transjordan is credible, but defeat of the Aramaeans – even placing a garrison in Damascus (2 Sam. 8:6) – looks contrived. Now, N. Na'aman has presented a compelling case that this fight against and defeat of Hadadezer of Zobah is a literary creation, based on the Aramaean king Hazael in the ninth century (Na'aman 2002: 207–10). However, he goes on to argue that David's conquest of Moab was also a literary creation, aiming to counter the defeat of Israel by Moab under Mesha; that the defeat of Ammon was devised to compensate for the cruelty inflicted by the Ammonites on Israel as outlined in Amos 1:13; and David's defeat of Edom was borrowed from Amaziah's later victory over the Edomites (2 Kgs 14:7; Na'aman 2002: 212–14). In the end, Na'aman (2002: 215) sees in the story of David's conquests only a few historical elements, viz., the conquest of Jerusalem and the subjugation of the Philistines. As we have seen above, however, it looks as if the driving of the Philistines from the central hill country is also a literary creation! This leaves us with the taking of Jerusalem, though here we do appear to have a genuine historical datum. Also, some excursions into Transjordanian territory are not incredible, though Na'aman has a point.

John Van Seters (2010) argues for an even later time, that the accounts of David as a leader show a dating of the narrative to the late Persian period at the earliest. He points out that in the Davidic narrative David shows considerable reliance on mercenaries in his time; on the other hand, there is hardly any mention of them in the later narratives of Kings. The Saite dynasty seems to have used a variety of mercenaries, including Jews, and Greek mercenaries appear to have been stationed at Mesad Hashavyahu and Arad. This account of the Davidic monarchy fits the militaristic regimes of the late Persian period because it is only from the fourth century onwards that Persian rulers and satraps made use of these particular Greek professional mercenaries, the Cretans and the peltasts, with their specialized skills.

Van Seters concludes that the references to mercenaries in the David Saga are so pervasive that they cannot be removed by redaction-critical methods: the narrator has freely invented a portrayal of David modelled on the monarchs of his own day. One cannot use any of it to reconstruct the Davidic monarchy of the tenth century. Van Seters makes a good case, though his explanation is not entirely convincing. After all, it seems that David and similar *'apiru* leaders hired themselves out as bands of mercenary soldiers, fighting for pay or for booty, which is the same thing. However, his basic point that *Greek* mercenaries were a feature of the Persian and Hellenistic periods is well taken.

8.5.6.3 Jerusalem

With regard to Jerusalem, the stories in Judges seem to remember a Jerusalem that came into Israelite hands only relatively late and continued to have the earlier people as a part of the population for some time afterward. What the various traditions suggest, therefore, is that there was a collective folk memory of a time when Jerusalem was not Israelite, and even that it came into Israelite hands much later than some of the surrounding territory. This is a remarkable memory, especially if we keep in mind that it would have been more convenient to believe that Jerusalem was conquered with the rest of the territory and divided up by the Israelites without any complications.

Yet the text acknowledges complications: Jerusalem is sometimes the property of Judah (Josh. 15:63; cf. Judg. 1:8) and sometimes within the territory of Benjamin (Josh. 18:28; Judg. 1:21). In both cases, it recognizes that some of the original inhabitants, the Jebusites, continued to live in the city, alongside the Judahites (Josh. 15:63; Judg. 1:21) or Benjaminites (Judg. 1:21). In spite of this tradition, 2 Sam. 5:6-9 requires David to conquer the city from the Jebusites again. David took the city and renamed it 'the city of David'. What sort of entity Jerusalem was is not clear: the account suggests a type of fortress, though this does not mean a large or grand settlement, as is confirmed by the image given by the passage.

The story in 2 Sam. 24:16-25 is part of an incident in which a plague was devastating Israel because of David's sin. In order to stay the plague, David was told to set up an altar on the threshing floor of 'Araunah (הארונה) the Jebusite' which he purchased. The name 'Araunah' is curious. It does not look like a typical Hebrew name, and in 2 Sam. 24:16 the word occurs with the article which is not normal with names. It has been explained as a Hittite word meaning 'aristocrat' or a Hurrian word meaning 'lord'. Either explanation suggests that the owner of the threshing floor was the (former?) king or lord of the city, which is also one way of reading the Hebrew text of 2 Sam. 24:23: 'Araunah the king gives all to the king (David)'. The proposal is that it was this threshing floor which later became the site of the temple built by Solomon, but the episode suggests the size of the Jebusite city was not large. Two further points put David crossways with the general trend of teaching and piety in the Hebrew Bible. First, David's sons acted as priests at this time, possibly even before he took Jerusalem (2 Sam. 8:17). Secondly, David made the Jebusite priest Zadok one of his two chief priests. It has long been recognized that Zadok was formerly a priest from the Jerusalem cult (cf. Grabbe 2003c). But just these two incidents show that David's rule has not been totally assimilated to later religious sensibilities.

8.5.6.4 Archaeology

Archaeology especially as it relates to Jerusalem is discussed here (see §8.2 for a general archaeological survey). The dating of archaeology here is according to the 'modified conventional chronology' (for convenience, without implying that the 'low chronology' has been rejected [cf. §1.3]). When we come to the Iron Age, the questions start to multiply. According to the text, we should find a Jebusite city for Iron I, which was then replaced in Iron IIA-B by an expanding city that functioned as an administrative centre and a capital of a considerable kingdom, under David and Solomon. A. E. Killebrew refers to the two 'bookends' of monumental architecture in the Middle Bronze, on one side, and in the eighth to seventh centuries BCE, on the other. She argues that the lack of other finds relating to fortification suggests that Jerusalem was unwalled and unfortified between the LB and Iron IIB (sixteenth to mid-eighth centuries BCE), and thus Jerusalem was 'at best modest'

(Killebrew 2003: 334). This of course differs from the picture of the text. Yet it is supported by a recent study by D. Ben-Ami which argued that excavations at the Givati parking lot showed that there were no Iron IIA fortifications on the southeast ridge ('City of David' settlement); rather, 'all Iron Age fortification components unearthed in Jerusalem are the outcome of one comprehensive building operation that took place at the close of the 8th century BCE' (Ben-Ami 2014: 3–19).

Nevertheless, we find major disputes among archaeologists over this period. One of the main contentions is that we should expect monumental architecture, if the text is correct, but do we find that? Some have pointed to the Stepped Stone Structure. That does not fit what one would normally call 'monumental architecture', but E. Mazar (2006, 2009) has recently argued that a building at the top of the Stepped Stone Structure dates to David's time and could be his palace. This appears to be an important site and the first potential evidence for monumental architecture from the time of David. Acceptance of Mazar's interpretation is by no means universal, however.

The main problem with the Stepped Stone Structure and 'David's palace' is its dating. On the one hand, J. M. Cahill (2003, 2004) dates it to the Late Bronze/Early Iron transition, arguing that both the stepped mantle and the terraces below it were built together as a single architectural unit. In contrast, M. Steiner (1994, 1998; 2003b: 351–61) argues from Kenyon's excavations that the Stepped Stone Structure as such was quite different in extension and construction method from the terrace system. Where the terraces existed, only a mantle of stones was added, but where there were no terraces the structure was built up from bedrock. For confirmation of the dating and construction, she points to the pottery in the fill of the terraces which was Iron I, with no mix of later material. Steiner would date its construction to the tenth or early ninth century. In sum, according to Steiner the terrace and Stepped Structure Systems do not have similar boundaries, identical pottery, or the same construction techniques. Apart from considerable dispute about the Stepped Stone Structure, E. Mazar's claims about the 'David's palace' building have been critiqued in an article by Israel Finkelstein, Ze'ev Herzog, Lily Singer-Avitz, and David Ussishkin (2007). They give quite a different interpretation of the site, eventually concluding that the building is most likely late Hellenistic. We should batten down the hatches for a long debate.

Newspaper columns beginning in early March 2014 reported that the Jebusite fortress taken by David in the conquest of Jerusalem (2 Sam. 5:6-9) had been found near the Gihon spring (e.g., Ngo 2014). This was something of a surprise, because the lead excavator of that area, Ronny Reich (2011), had not reported it in his recently published book, *Excavating the City of David*. One might assume that it was a new excavation, made after Reich had left his post at Gihon, but this was not the case. Instead, the MB building known as the 'Spring Tower' had been identified to reporters as the fortress captured by David. The argument was that it was still in existence and being used at the beginning of Iron IIA, about 1000 BCE. We await proper archaeological reports, but according to newspaper reports Reich has not accepted this new interpretation of 'the Spring Fortress'.

In sum, M. L. Steiner's (2001, 2003a, 2003b) view is that Jerusalem of the tenth and ninth centuries was a small town occupied mainly by public buildings, not exceeding 12 hectares and approximately 2000 inhabitants. It exhibited the characteristics of a regional administrative centre or the capital of a small, newly established state, the towns of Megiddo, Hazor, Gezer, and Lachish showing similar characteristics at the same time. For the Jerusalem settlement to be little more than a village at the time of David is not a problem. This was probably all that was needed for David's state, considering its small size and complexity. It was certainly an advance on Saul's open-air court under a large tree!

8.5.6.5 Relationship of Saul and David Traditions
Having argued that there is a historical core to both the Saulide and Davidide traditions, we must now ask whether there is any connection between them. The David traditions in the present narrative are in part bound up with the Saul traditions, and they need to be evaluated together. Granted, the present redacted text has the traditions heavily intertwined, but was that the case in the beginning? Can we simply see two sets of traditions, one of which described in some way the first northern king, while the other independently had the first southern king at its core? Such an interpretation is quite believable in itself and has the merit of being simple. Why must we complicate the story more than is necessary, even though the redactors certainly did?

Yet a closer examination exposes greater complexity. Note the following: There is first of all the saying, 'Saul has slain his thousands, but David his tens of thousands' (1 Sam. 18:7; 21:12; 29:5). Not a major datum but nevertheless one worth noting, and one likely to be early according to some commentators (Dietrich 2007: 264–5). If this is an early saying, where did it come from if the David and Saul traditions were originally separate? Secondly, one of the major characteristics of the David tradition is the extent to which his reign is legitimated (strongly suggesting that David was a usurper [Shalom Brooks 2005: 69–88]).

- Comes as an apprentice to Saul's court (1 Sam. 16:14-23).
- Performs personal duties for Saul's health (1 Sam. 16:14-23).
- Fights as a champion against Israel's enemies (1 Sam. 17).
- Marries the king's daughter (1 Sam. 18:17-27).
- Wins her hand by warrior-worthy deeds (1 Sam. 18:25-27).
- Anointed by a prophet-priest (1 Sam. 16:1-13).
- Even the king's son and heir recognizes David's right to rule (1 Sam. 18:1; 20:12-17; 23:16-18).

Why go to all this trouble to make David's rule legitimate if he had been accepted as the first king of Judah by the tradition? This suggests that the present picture of the text (that he was not the first king but actually effected a change of dynasty) was not a secondary creation but one already there in the tradition when the text was redacted.

Thirdly, one could take the example of Michal. She could have been added to the tradition simply to give a further negative picture of Saul, since her story is ultimately a negative one in which she is rejected and childless, though remaining David's wife. But her story is more complicated and interesting than this. For example, she helps David escape from her father by a clever deception (1 Sam. 19:11-17). After she was married to another man, David expended some effort to get her back (2 Sam. 3:12-16).

Fourthly, there is also the story of Jonathan. Again, he could serve just as another reason to bolster David's legitimacy: even the heir to the throne supports David's right instead of his own. But why make him such an integral part of the story, if that were his only purpose? Not least is the question of why Jonathan did not succeed his father. The many hazards to an heir not only growing up but acquiring the necessary military prowess and confidence of the troops meant that prime heirs did not always gain the throne. But we might have expected a different sort of story, if it was simply a literary invention to enhance David's right to the throne.

Finally, we have to ask: if the Saul tradition was simply about the first king of Israel, separate from Judah, what happened to his dynasty? We know that at a later time, kings well attested in historical sources ruled over Israel. But if the Saul tradition was completely independent of the David one, what happened to the Israelite monarchy that had begun with Saul? Did it simply peter out? If so, what filled the vacuum, and how did it get started up again? It is such questions that make us turn to the David tradition and ask whether it is perhaps correct that David in some way was the successor on the throne of the inchoate state of Israel begun by Saul.

It is as if the Davidic and Solomonic traditions are *necessary* to fill the gap between Saul and the history of the two kingdoms or monarchies of Israel and Judah. If so, then the concept of the 'United Monarchy' is perhaps correct, after all – but only in a particular sense. That is, the first king Saul ruled over a portion of the central highlands, though apparently not Judah. The Judahite David – possibly a tribal leader of Judah but perhaps being appointed as a sort of king of Judah, as the text suggests – took over from Saul (or Saul's son), establishing some sort of rule over both the northern highlands and the Judaean highlands.

8.5.6.6. Conclusions about David

What we find in 1–2 Samuel is the story of a young Judahite warrior made good. He seems to have grown up in a society that was not heavily stratified; nevertheless, there was no doubt tribal leadership, with Judahite elders and perhaps even a tribal chieftain or chieftains. Was David the heir of one of these tribal leaders? There are also some hints that his family was not so humble. After all, he was brought into Saul's court, unlikely to happen to a complete nobody. In any case, David became some sort of *Apiru* leader: surprisingly, this image appears to be agreed on by two archaeologists who otherwise take somewhat different views on the 'United Monarchy' (Mazar 2007: 164–5; Finkelstein 2001: 107–8).

In the biblical story, David fits the image of the hero figure; there are many folkloristic elements and a variety of traditions; yet there are also traditions with some interesting twists, such as the willingness to acknowledge some of David's weaknesses, the need to legitimate David from a variety of angles – suggesting that he was not seen as legitimate by everyone – and the admission that David did not do certain things that we might have expected. One of the interesting points about the Davidic tradition is how 'lumpy' it is. That is, it often disagrees with what we would expect from the biblical text as a whole. To summarize, we can note some of the points that emerge from a look at the Saul and David traditions:

- The tradition recognizes that David was not the first king.
- Saul came to the throne probably as a military leader by popular acclaim (1 Sam. 11:1-15), whereas the prophetic tradition that the king was subject to Samuel's choice and censure is unrealistic (1 Sam. 9:1–10:16; 10:23; 13:2–14:52).
- The apparent boundaries of Saul's kingdom (2 Sam. 2:9) is reasonably in line with the natural and demographic resources in Cis-Jordan.
- A strong link is made between David's rise and Saul's court, but much of this looks like a deliberate attempt to legitimate David as king from a variety of angles: anointing by Samuel (1 Sam. 16:1-13); armour-bearer in Saul's court who plays the lyre for him personally (1 Sam. 16:14-23); slaying of Goliath (1 Sam. 17); marriage to Saul's daughter (1 Sam. 18:17-27).

- Contrary to expectations David does not build a temple (though a strenuous effort is made for him to do everything short of the actual building).
- Both Saul and David were mainly military leaders.
- The text itself does not suggest an extensive administrative apparatus in the case of either Saul or David.

8.5.7 Solomon

P. S. Ash (1999) *David, Solomon and Egypt: A Reassessment*; **F. C. Conybeare, J. R. Harris, and A. Smith Lewis** (1913) *The Story of Aḥiḳar from the Aramaic, Syriac, Arabic, Armenian, Ethiopic, Old Turkish, Greek and Slavonic Versions*; **L. L. Grabbe** (2006b) 'Mighty Oaks from (Genetically Manipulated?) Acorns Grow: The Chronicle of the Kings of Judah as a Source of the Deuteronomistic History', in R. Rezetko, T. H. Lim and W. B. Aucker (eds), *Reflection and Refraction: Studies in Biblical Historiography in Honour of A. Graeme Auld*: 154–73; **L. Jonker** (2008) 'The Chronicler's Portrayal of Solomon as the King of Peace within the Context of the International Peace Discourses of the Persian Era', *Old Testament Essays* 21: 653–9; **K. A. Kitchen** (1997) 'Sheba and Arabia', in L. K. Handy (ed.), *The Age of Solomon: Scholarship at the Turn of the Millennium*: 126–53; **E. A. Knauf** (1997) 'Le roi est mort, vive le roi! A Biblical Argument for the Historicity of Solomon', in L. K. Handy (ed.), *The Age of Solomon: Scholarship at the Turn of the Millennium*: 81–95; **M. Liverani** (2005) *Israel's History and the History of Israel*; **A. Malamat** (1982) 'A Political Look at the Kingdom of David and Solomon and its Relations with Egypt', in T. Ishida (ed.), *Studies in the Period of David and Solomon and Other Essays: Papers Read at the International Symposium for Biblical Studies, Tokyo, 5-7 December, 1979*: 189–204; **N. Na'aman** (1997b) 'Sources and Composition in the History of Solomon', in L. K. Handy (ed.), *The Age of Solomon: Scholarship at the Turn of the Millennium*: 57–80; **idem** (2019) 'Hiram of Tyre in the Book of Kings and in the Tyrian Records', *JNES* 78: 75–85; **H. M. Niemann** (1997) 'The Socio-Political Shadow Cast by the Biblical Solomon', in L. K. Handy (ed.), *The Age of Solomon: Scholarship at the Turn of the Millennium*: 252–99; **T. Römer** (2008) 'Salomon d'apres les deuteronomistes – un roi ambigu', in C. Lichtert and D. Nocquet (eds), *Le roi Salomon, un héritage en question: Hommage à Jacques Vermeylen*: 98–130; **B. U. Schipper** (1999) *Israel und Ägypten in der Königszeit: Die kulturellen Kontakte von Salomo bis zum Fall Jerusalems*; **idem** (2000) 'Salomo und die Pharaonentochter – zum historischen Kern von 1 Kön 7,8', *BN* 102: 84–94; **idem** (2002) 'Noch einmal zur Pharaonentochter – ein Gespräch mit Karl Jansen-Winkeln', *BN* 111: 90–8; **H. Tadmor** (1994) *The Inscriptions of Tiglath-Pileser III King of Assyria: Critical Edition, with Introductions, Translations and Commentary*.

Solomon's kingdom could not be more different from Saul and David's! The narrative about Solomon's reign (1 Kings 2–11) strikes the reader as quite unlike those about Saul and David. Almost from start to finish Solomon fits the image of the great 'Oriental emperor'. It is essentially a folktale about an Eastern potentate – it is royal legend or *Königsnovelle*. He controls a vast territory and possesses great wealth, with absolute sovereignty over his subjects. Of course, he marries the daughter of a country of similar power – suggesting equality with Egypt in this case – and harnesses the best craftsmen and materials from legendary Tyre to build his city. His capital city consists of great palaces and a magnificent temple, with gold like dust and silver so abundant it is of little account.

His household overflows with luxuries, his table groans under the weight of exotic fruits, meats from rare animals, and every sort of desirable food for consumption. He boasts a harem of a thousand women, all of whom he apparently services. His wisdom is legendary, and he exceeds all others in intellectual skills. His reputation reaches far and wide, and rulers from distant lands travel to see such a supreme example of power, wealth, and wisdom – only to find that the reports were understated. His ships travel to the ends of the earth for rare and astonishing goods. Unlike David's 'lumpy' story, one is immediately struck by how uniform the tale about Solomon is. It looks like the product of a master creator of sagas about great men. Much of it looks and feels like a fairy tale.

Thus, it looks difficult to discover much in the Solomon story that strikes the critical reader as likely to be historical. Although the story of David has him expanding his territory via conquests, there is nothing to suggest that he rules all the land between Egypt and the Euphrates, yet this is the territory that Solomon controls – even though he fought no battles (1 Kgs 5:1, 4)! There is not a hint that David could monopolize the trade in horses between Egypt and Mesopotamia, as Solomon does (1 Kgs 10:28-29). As for the wealth invested in the House for Yhwh, this is commensurate with the quantity of gold that Solomon receives each year: 666 talents plus the revenue from trade, etc. (1 Kgs 10:14-15). Only a great empire, such as that of the later Persians, could collect so much wealth: according to Herodotus (3.91) the Persians collected 14,560 talents of silver in tribute annually – the equivalent of 1120 talents of gold. The idea that Solomon could raise 666 talents of gold plus much additional wealth each year is a gross flight of fancy on the part of the writer. It has been suggested that a number of the achievements of later kings are here ascribed to Solomon (Knauf/Guillaume 2016: 76; Knauf/Niemann 2021: 174). There are also a number of parallels with achievements by Assyrian kings in the latter part of the Neo-Assyrian empire. As Na'aman (2019: 79) notes, 'the shape of Solomon's Kingdom as the golden age in Israel's history and his figure as an imperial ruler was borrowed from that of the Assyrian Empire, probably at the time of Sargon II'.

In this story, though, the height of marvels is Solomon's great wisdom (1 Kgs 10:3, 68, 23-24), even if there is precious little in the way of examples of how this is demonstrated. The one example of the two prostitutes claiming the same child is a facile one, in no way comparable to examples found, e.g., in the story of Ahiqar (Conybeare/Harris/Smith Lewis 1913) where the king responds to a challenge to build a city in the sky.

Of course, this is only part of the story, since there are also passages in which a negative picture of Solomon is painted (1 Kings 11 has many such statements or examples). The account of Solomon has been edited from different perspectives over the centuries (Römer 2008). N. Na'aman (e.g., 2019: 75–80) has argued the biblical writer made use of an 'Acts of Solomon' as a source; from internal references and data it appears to have been composed during Assyrian control of Judah, perhaps about 707 BCE. In any case it was long after the time of Solomon. The existence of a King Solomon is not to be discounted, however. His name echoing the old god of Jerusalem (Shalim/Shalem) is suggestive of reality rather than simply the piety of the David story. Also, he began his reign with the bloody elimination of rivals, though the idea that he took his throne in the midst of adversity which he overcame could be a part of the stereotype. The writer probably saw nothing bad in this.

Overall, there is little in the Solomon story that looks on the face of it to be historically reliable. Yet one cannot help being intrigued by the story that he built the Jerusalem temple. This sort of story is what we might expect, and the description of the wealth and rare construction of the temple fits well the legend. Yet David – the expected temple-builder – did not construct it, and we find nothing in the stories of the later kings that might hide such a building (with the possible exception of Jehoash who is said to collect money to repair the temple: 2 Kings 12). This suggests that a temple was built in Jerusalem at a fairly early time. If David did not build it, who? Possibly here we have a genuine remembrance that has been expanded into a great legend. Yet an oblique reference to a temple in the time of David is found in 2 Sam. 22:7, and it seems unlikely that Jerusalem had no temple when it was captured by David. If so, Solomon might have only enhanced a pre-existing temple, though he could also have constructed a new one.

We further have the ascription of materials supplied by Hiram of Tyre. How credible is this? Early annals of Tyre have been alleged to exist. For example, Josephus refers to them, though it is clear that he cites them from more recent Greek historians, such as Menander (of Pergamum?) and an unknown writer named Dius (*Ag. Ap.* 1.17-18 §106-27). To what extent these writings preserve ancient tradition and to what extent they are typical Hellenistic invention and misunderstanding is a question. For example, the *Phoenician History* of Philo of Byblos supposedly drew on an ancient account of Sanchuniathon (see especially Barr 1973–74; Baumgarten 1981). This is possible, but Philo's account has nevertheless been clearly influenced by the Greek literary tradition, showing that whatever ancient material might have been used, it was recast in a Greek literary form. We should also keep in mind that some of Josephus's statements are based on his own deductions and not necessarily on the actual statements of the sources (see the discussion with regard to the Hyksos at §4.3.3).

N. Na'aman (2019) has investigated the Hiram account. Although he argues for some genuine cultural memory in Menander's account, he suggests that the original Phoenician writer from whom Menander took the details would have been writing long after the Hiram of the tenth century BCE. This Hiram's reign is blown up into a Golden Age of Tyrian history, parallel to Solomon's in Israel. This is why the eighth-century biblical writer was able to draw on the Hiram story, which he got from somewhere, as contemporary with Solomon. But most of the details are the invention of the writer. Possibly he even drew on the historical Hiram of the eighth century (usually called Hiram II), known from the Assyrian inscriptions of Tiglath-pileser III (Tadmor 1994: 89). From several considerations, therefore, the temple story has been inflated into a legendary extravaganza.

E. A. Knauf (1997) thinks that Solomon was historical but that he differed considerably from the biblical picture. The king's name shows that he was non-Judaean in origin. The Bathsheba story was not suppressed because there was a worse story: Solomon was not David's son. Knauf has tried to reconstruct some early sources. He sees 1 Kgs 8:12-13 as an early text quoting an incomplete royal building inscription which confirms Solomon's place in association with the temple (though perhaps only establishing a cult in a pre-existent temple rather a temple builder as such). In 1 Kings 1–2 (a text probably from the seventh century) he sees glimpses of Solomon as the puppet of the Jerusalem elite on whom he turns and whom he eliminates. He concludes that Solomon was the son of a Jerusalem mother but not necessarily of a Judaean father. He became king through a *coup d'état* by getting rid of the Jerusalem elite. He was no monotheist, because the Judaean tribal deity Yhwh had only a subordinate position in the Jerusalem pantheon. More recently, Knauf (2016: 290–2; also Knauf/Niemann 2021: 171–8) has proposed that Solomon is to be identified with Rehoboam. The idea is not that radical and has some interesting arguments in favour of it; however, I find myself drawn more to Knauf's original arguments outlined above. It also seems difficult to believe that the historical memory was so defective that it was possible to invent a Solomon – much of the details of his reign invented, yes, but not the person.

In a long survey of the Solomonic tradition M. H. Niemann (1997) argues that Solomon's alleged building programme of cities and monumental buildings cannot be confirmed archaeologically. Instead, we find evidence of a series of representatives (often relatives) who were sent to the northern areas as the first attempt to build a network of loyalty in an area that had not yet declared support for Solomon's rule. Solomon might indeed have married the daughter of an Egyptian pharaoh, according to Niemann, but this would have been because he was a vassal of that pharaoh (Shoshenq?). This could be the reason that Jerusalem is not found on the Shoshenq inscription (but see below on Solomon's alleged marriage).

N. Na'aman (1997d) also analysed the account of Solomon for the existence of sources. He accepts that the early 'chronicle of Israelite kings' was created in the eighth century and thus rather later than Solomon; however, the Deuteronomist also had the 'Book of the Acts of Solomon' (1 Kgs 11:41), which Na'aman tries to reconstruct. Some episodes were invented by the post-Dtr redactor, including the one of the Queen of Sheba and the description of the temple (based on a description of the temple of his own times). Na'aman concludes that only in the late redaction do we have a picture of a ruler of an empire and a great sage. Although agreeing that there was a 'Chronicle of the Kings of Judah' (Grabbe 2006b), I find it difficult to characterize a 'Book of the Acts of Solomon'; on the other hand, Na'aman argues it is a later creation of the eighth century and thus long after the historical Solomon. Thus, here and there might be a verse that reflects the historical Solomon, but the Solomon story is the most problematic of those relating to the early Israelite kings, providing the thickest cloud of obscurity over the history that lies behind it. The Chronicler continued to develop the story to address issues of his own time (cf. Jonker 2008).

The episode relating to the Queen of Sheba illustrates the historical problem (1 Kgs 10:1-13). Although the Solomon story was characterized as on the whole an 'Oriental tale', the Sheba story has all the marks of a folktale (though it has been incorporated into the text by a literary writer). The main figure has no name: she is simply 'the Queen of Sheba'. She herself is a representative of wealth, wisdom, and power. Yet her function in the story is to marvel at all that Solomon and Jerusalem have to show her: in spite of all her own wealth and wisdom, Solomon's are much greater. He leaves her speechless. The story is often defended as historical by explaining it as a journey to establish trade relations between southern Arabia and Israel (e.g., Malamat 1982: 191, 204; Kitchen 1997), yet the biblical text says not a word about such a purpose. On the contrary, according to 1 Kgs 10:1, the Queen of Sheba came to Solomon 'to test him with riddles'. Attempts have been made to authenticate the story by appealing to developments in southern Arabia by the tenth century. However, Mario Liverani encapsulates the problem in a nutshell:

> It was easy to decorate details that were otherwise authentic, but far more banal, with colourful fictional features. For examples, opening up trading links with the Yemen in the tenth century is not anachronistic; but the story of the Queen of Sheba's visit is too much like a fairy-tale in style and in use of narrative themes to be regarded as anything other than a romance from the Persian era. [Liverani 2005: 315]

A major question relating to Solomon is the Israelite relations with Egypt. Solomon is not only said to marry Pharaoh's daughter but to have received Gezer as a wedding gift from her father. Some have identified the king in question as Siamun (*c.* 986–968), the next to last king of the 21st Dynasty. There are a number of arguments against this interpretation (Schipper 1999: 19–35; Ash 1999: 37–46). Briefly, an Egyptian relief that some have interpreted as showing an incursion into Palestine by Siamun has probably been misinterpreted, and Siamun is not likely to have made any such expedition to the east. Although there are some destruction layers in Gezer and elsewhere in Philistia, the cause is not known, and no indication of Egyptian involvement is found in the material culture. It also seems rather unlikely that the Pharaoh would have given a *destroyed* city as a wedding gift to Solomon. Finally, the main destruction layer in Gezer is probably to be ascribed to Shoshenq I. Indeed, some argue that Shoshenq's invasion was actually during Solomon's reign rather than after his death (see the discussion in the next section [§8.5.8]). As for Solomon's marriage to Pharaoh's daughter, many Egyptologists are of the opinion that it is very unlikely since it was clearly the custom for the reigning king to marry his daughters only to those within Egypt itself, not foreigners (Ash 1999: 112–19). Although some have claimed to find examples in which this was done during the Third Intermediate Period, no examples of the marriage of a reigning Egyptian king's daughter to a foreign ruler have in fact been found (Schipper 1999: 84–90; 2002). B. U. Schipper (2000) mentions two possibilities that might explain this biblical tradition (either the reference was to a building, not a person, or the person was someone from the court perhaps distantly related to the Pharaoh), but neither allows a literal reading of the biblical tradition or supports the view that Solomon was seen as an equal with the Egyptian king. As Ash concludes, 'it is best at this time to avoid placing any weight on the reports of Solomon's marriage to an Egyptian princess' (Ash 1999: 119).

8.5.8 Shoshenq I's Palestinian Raid(s)

P. S. Ash (1999) *David, Solomon and Egypt: A Reassessment*; **S. Ben-Dor Evian** (2011) 'Shishak's Karnak Relief – More Than Just Name-Rings', in S. Bar, D. Kahn, and J. J. Shirley (eds), *Egypt, Canaan and Israel: History, Ideology, Imperialism and Literature: Proceedings of a Conference at the University of Haifa, 3–7 May 2009*: 11–22; **A. Fantalkin and I. Finkelstein** (2006) 'The Sheshonq I Campaign and the 8th-Century BCE Earthquake – More on the Archaeology and History of the South in the Iron I–IIA', *TA* 33: 18–42; **E. Feucht** (1981) 'Relief Scheschonqs I. Beim Erschlagen der Feinde aus El-Hibe', *SAK* 9: 105–17; **I. Finkelstein** (2002b) 'The Campaign of Shoshenq I to Palestine: A Guide to the 10th Century BCE Polity', *ZDPV* 118: 109–35; **idem** (2013) *The Forgotten Kingdom: The Archaeology and History of Northern Israel*; **W. Helck** (1971) *Die Beziehungen Ägyptens zu Vorderasien im 3. und 2. Jahrtausend v. Chr.*; **S. Herrmann** (1964) 'Operationen Pharao Schoschenks I. im östlichen Ephraim', *ZDPV* 80: 55–79; **K. A. Kitchen** (1986) *The Third Intermediate Period in Egypt (1100–650 BC)*; **E. A. Knauf** (2008a) 'From Archaeology to History, Bronze and Iron Ages with Special Regard to the Year 1200 BCE and the Tenth Century', in L. L. Grabbe (ed.), *Israel in Transition: From Late Bronze II to Iron IIA (c. 1250–850 BCE): The Archaeology*: 72–85; **A. Mazar** (2008) 'From 1200 to 850 BCE: Remarks on Some Selected

Archaeological Issues', in L. L. Grabbe (ed.), *Israel in Transition: From Late Bronze II to Iron IIA (c. 1250-850 BCE): The Archaeology*: 86–120; **N. Na'aman** (2006) 'Israel, Edom and Egypt in the 10th Century B.C.E.', in *Ancient Israel's History and Historiography: The First Temple Period; Collected Essays Volume 3*: 120–38; **H. M. Niemann** (1997) 'The Socio-Political Shadow Cast by the Biblical Solomon', in L. K. Handy (ed.), *The Age of Solomon: Scholarship at the Turn of the Millennium*: 252–99; **M. Noth** (1938) 'Die Wege des Pharaonenheere in Palästina und Syrien: Untersuchungen zu den hieroglyphischen Listen palästinischer und syrischer Städte: IV. Die Schoschenkliste', *ZDPV* 61: 277–304; **D. B. Redford** (1973) 'Studies in Relations between Palestine and Egypt during the First Millennium B.C.: II. The Twenty-Second Dynasty', *JAOS* 93: 3–17; **B. U. Schipper** (1999) *Israel und Ägypten in der Königszeit: Die kulturellen Kontakte von Salomo bis zum Fall Jerusalems*; **D. Ussishkin** (2008) 'The Date of the Philistine Settlement in the Coastal Plain: The View from Megiddo and Lachish', in L. L. Grabbe (ed.), *Israel in Transition: From Late Bronze II to Iron IIA (c. 1250–850 BCE): The Archaeology*: 203–16; **M. Weippert** (2010) *Historisches Textbuch zum Alten Testament*; **K. A. Wilson** (2005) *The Campaign of Pharaoh Shoshenq I into Palestine*.

The supposed raid of Shishak has been seen as a major event in Israel's history and a means of determining its early chronology, as well as allegedly providing evidence within the archaeology (because of assumed destruction of various Palestinian sites). According to 1 Kgs 14:25-28 a king Shishak of Egypt came up against Jerusalem in Rehoboam's fifth year and took all the treasures of the temple. When an inscription of Shoshenq I (*c.* 943–923 BCE), founder of the 22nd Dynasty, was found at Karnak listing many topographical sites in Palestine, a connection was made with the passage in the Bible and has been the standard view ever since. All seem to agree that Shoshenq's expedition was a signal event in Israel's history, but precisely what happened on the ground and even when the invasion took place is considerably disputed. The conventional view is heavily informed by the Bible. According to it, Shoshenq's army made a number of destructive raids on various parts of Palestine, destroying many sites in the Negev and even as far north as Megiddo; however, Jerusalem did not fall because the Pharaoh was bought off by Rehoboam.

A number of studies have addressed the issue of Israel/Judah and Shoshenq's 'invasion' beginning with M. Noth's study in 1938 (for a survey of earlier studies, see Wilson 2005; also Schipper 1999: 119–32; Ash 1999: 50–6; Helck 1971: 238–45; Na'aman 2006; Finkelstein 2002b). Most past treatments have assumed that Shoshenq conducted an invasion of Palestine, that the chronology fits with Rehoboam's reign, that the inscription gives some sort of invasion route, that the inscription can be reconciled with the biblical text, and that the archaeology matches the inscription. There have, nevertheless, been some problems (not always acknowledged), especially the fact that Israel and Judah are not mentioned specifically, that no site in Judah occurs in the inscription (except perhaps for Arad in the Negev), that the toponyms cannot be worked into any sort of itinerary sequence, and that the biblical text says nothing about an invasion of the Northern Kingdom.

It might not be surprising if a Jerusalem scribe did not record the details of Shoshenq's raids on Israel, but why omit the destructive attacks on the Negev, which was a part of Judah – at least, in the eyes of the biblical writers? Leaving aside the Jerusalem question, there is still considerable disagreement how to interpret Shoshenq's inscription. Was it a raid or primarily an occupation – albeit temporary – of the land? Various explanations have been given of the order of toponyms as they might relate to the progress of the invasion, but none has been completely convincing. Now, however, K. Wilson (2005) has investigated Shoshenq's inscription in the context of other Egyptian triumphal inscriptions. He concludes:

- Triumphal inscriptions were designed to extol the Pharaoh's exploits, not provide historical data.
- The reliefs glorify all the exploits of the king rather than a particular campaign.
- The topographical lists are not laid out according to any system that allows a reconstruction of the military route.
- The sites listed may in some cases be those attacked, but others not attacked – indeed, friendly towns and allies – might be listed as well.
- The lists were apparently drawn in part from military records and onomastical lists, which means that some data of value for certain purposes may be included.

The implications of these conclusions are considerable. Rather than recording a particular campaign into Palestine, Shoshenq's inscription may include more than one (as maintained by Knauf 2008a). This would help to explain the vague nature of the inscriptions that accompany the topographical lists, without clarifying the reasons for or objectives of the 'invasion'. In any case, the precise nature and progress of the campaign(s) cannot be worked out.

More puzzling is the lack of any reference to Judah or Jerusalem as such. The argument is that this was in a section of the inscription that is no longer readable. This argument is still maintained by the latest study of the Shoshenq inscription by Wilson. It must be said that this argument, while possible, is not compelling. Another obvious interpretation is that Shoshenq bypassed Judah – or at least, the Judaean highlands – because it did not suit his purpose, and the biblical writer got it wrong. Interestingly, the solution that seems to be agreed on by both A. Mazar (2008: 107–10) and A. Fantalkin and I. Finkelstein (2008: 37–9) is that Shoshenq was indeed interested in coming up against Judah because of the copper trade. This could make Jerusalem not just a stage in the invasion but its main object (though not Finkelstein's view). This is an interesting interpretation, yet one might ask why Shoshenq then pushed on north as far as the Jezreel Valley if he had already reached his objective.

Fantalkin and Finkelstein, among others, argue that the main phase of prosperity was post-Shoshenq and that the sites in the south were primarily not destroyed but abandoned (Fantalkin/Finkelstein 2008). They point out that Shoshenq also does not mention the Philistine cities, which could be significant. Finkelstein interprets it as evidence for their control of the copper trade. But whether or not that is right, we have to ask why the Philistines were omitted. If the Egyptian expedition was a general attack on Palestinian cities in Israel and Judah, why should the Philistine plain be omitted? Could these cities have a particular relationship with Egypt? Or was the Shoshenq operation a more complex one? D. Ussishkin (2008: 205–6) makes the reasonable argument that Shoshenq would hardly set up his stela in a ruined city, but suggests that Megiddo was not just attacked but was occupied to become a regional headquarters. This calls for a rethink as to whether Shoshenq's raid may have actually achieved dominance and intimidation more than destruction.

Shoshenq's campaign(s) may have had an effect on other regional polities. Finkelstein (2002b; also Finkelstein 2013: 41–9; Fantalkin/Finkelstein 2006) had drawn attention to the development of the 'Tel Masos chiefdom' in the Beersheba region into a prosperous settlement in the eleventh–tenth centuries, with a number of smaller sites in its circle. This polity – whatever form it took, though not a state – reached its peak about the same time as the mining operation in Khirbet en-Nahas. The inhabitants of the region were pastoralists but seem to have been involved in transporting copper to the coast and were in the process of settling down. Shoshenq's aim was not destruction (there is no evidence of destruction in the region) but in taking control of the copper trade and providing support for it. Shoshenq may have attacked the Philistine city of Ekron, however, since it shows some evidence of this, and Gath came to prominence in Ekron's place afterwards.

N. Na'aman (2006) had a different take on Shoshenq'a campaign. He followed Redford's view (1973: 10–11) that Shoshenq marched into Canaan because of a desire to support Rehoboam (or even a request from him) against the 'rebellion' of the north. That's why there are no toponyms of Judah are listed in the inscription; that is also why Rehoboam paid off Shoshenq in gold (cf. 1 Kgs 14:26). Thus, there was no invasion of the hill country (contrary to Finkelstein). Na'aman agrees with Finkelstein about how the Negev settlements emerged from former pastoralists:

> The collapse of the urban culture in Canaan and the subsequent need for grain formerly obtained from the sedentary population, the Egyptian withdrawal from Canaan after the mid-12th century BCE, the development of mining activity and metallurgy along the Jordan Valley and the Arabah, and the growing participation of the local population in the overland trade – these factors combined to bring about the gradual sedentarization of the local pastoral population. [Na'aman 2006: 133–4]

On the other hand, Na'aman disagrees with Finkelstein on several points. He argues that far from Egypt's supporting the Negev settlements, Shoshenq's troops plundered and destroyed the area. This dealt the region a severe blow from which it was not able to recover, and they reverted to their pastoral way of life. There is also no evidence that Egypt attempted to regain control of the trade in the region: they made no attempt to establish permanent control or to act as middlemen in trade.

Na'aman's comments draw attention to the view that Shoshenq concentrated on destroying the polity concentrated on the Gibeon-Bethel plateau. As noted above, Finkelstein (2020) argued that Shoshenq used the opportunity to create vassaldoms in Shechem and Jerusalem. With a different but parallel interpretation, Knauf (2016: 290; cf. Knauf/Guillaume 2016: 81–2; Knauf/Niemann 2021: 164–6) thought that the polities of Jerusalem and Shechem were already vassals of Egypt and were spared destruction by Shoshenq. A careful examination of the toponyms named on Shoshenq's inscription does indeed suggest that Judah was spared since none of the toponyms named are located there (the Negev was probably not part of Judah at this time). But what about the tribute taken from Rehoboam according to 1 Kgs 14:25-28? Nothing supports the biblical statement. If Jerusalem paid tribute, it seems paramount that Shoshenq would have mentioned it, yet the place for Jerusalem to be mentioned in the list in such a case has no obliterated or questionable names. Also, the argument that the tribute was paid to the Pharaoh at Gibeon goes nowhere – he still would have listed Jerusalem. Knauf (2016: 405) has suggested that this was simply a creation of the biblical writer, as a way of explaining what happened to Solomon's alleged enormous wealth that was clearly no longer there in subsequent centuries.

Yet when we look at the toponyms, it appears that more of the North is implicated than just the Gibeon region. It is mainly rows II–V (toponyms 13–65) that seem to be concerned here (for details of the sites, see Wilson 2005: 102–18; Kitchen 1986: 432–9; Schipper 1999: 125–8; Weippert 2010: 233–8):

Row I: Shephelah?
12   Gezer? Makkedah?
13   Rubūtu (Khirbet Ḥamīde?)

Row II: central hill country and eastern Jezreel Valley
14   Taanach
15   Shunem
16   Beth-shean
17   Rehov
18   Hapharaim (eṭ-Ṭayyibe?)
22   Mahanaim
23   Gibeon
24   Beth-horon
26   Aijalon

Row III: Carmel and Sharon
27   Megiddo
32   Khirbet Ara?
33   Khirbet Burin?
38   Socho
39   Beth-Tappuah?

Row IV: mostly obliterated

Row V: both east and west of the Jordan River
53   Penuel
56   Adama
57   Zemaraim
58   Migdal
59   Tirza?
65   Jezreel?

There is much uncertainty here, both in the reading of the names and their identification with geographical sites. Yet not only the Gibeon region but also the region of Samaria (Tirzah, Zemaraim) and the Transjordan territory (Mahanaim, Penuel) that may have been a part of Jeroboam I's kingdom also appear to be included. How we are to interpret this is not immediately clear.

One could conclude that Judah/Rehoboam was spared but that Samaria/Jeroboam was attacked, but this could be a facile deduction, considering the considerable difficulties in interpretation of the inscription. However, if my interpretation here is correct, it seems to create difficulties for both the theses of Finkelstein and Knauf on this particular point.

The supposed date of Shoshenq's raid has had a major influence on the chronology of early Israel (cf. §1.3); therefore, a final question is, when did this raid take place? The biblical text places it under Rehoboam, but some have wanted to put it earlier, in Solomon's time (see the discussion and references in Finkelstein 2002b: 110; also Niemann 1997: 297–9). In fact, we do not know within Shoshenq's reign when the excursion took place: some want to place it early in his reign (e.g., Ben-Dor Evian 2011), but others prefer later. Too many simply project into Egyptian history the date they have calculated for Rehoboam's reign. Thus, the lack of knowledge about the date of Shoshenq's campaign, its precise nature, and the dating of Solomon's rule all contribute to a great deal of uncertainty. His raid – the crutch on which many historians and archaeologists have leaned – sadly does not provide the solid support that many had hoped.

8.5.9 Reversion to Two Kingdoms

L. L. Grabbe (2006a) '"Mighty Oaks from (Genetically Manipulated?) Acorns Grow: The Chronicle of the Kings of Judah as a Source of the Deuteronomistic History', in R. Rezetko, T. H. Lim and W. B. Aucker (eds), *Reflection and Refraction: Studies in Biblical Historiography in Honour of A. Graeme Auld*: 154–73; **idem** (2017c) 'Jeroboam I? Jeroboam II? Or Jeroboam 0? Jeroboam in History and Tradition', in O. Lipschits, Y. Gadot, and M. J. Adams (eds), *Rethinking Israel: Studies in the History and Archaeology of Ancient Israel in Honor of Israel Finkelstein*: 115–24; **H. M. Niemann** (1993) *Herrschaft, Königtum und Staat: Skizzen zur soziokulturellen Entwicklung im monarchischen Israel*; **idem** (2007) 'Royal Samaria – Capital or Residence? or: The Foundation of the City of Samaria by Sargon II', in L. L. Grabbe (ed.), *Ahab Agonistes: The Rise and Fall of the Omri Dynasty*: 184–207.

With the death of Solomon, the pressures of traditional ethnic identity and pride, desire to return to an older autonomy, and dissatisfaction with the state leadership led to the United Monarchy splitting once more into the original two peoples, now two states, Israel and Judah. One can debate the details of the confrontation between Rehoboam and Jeroboam (cf. Grabbe 2017c), but the basic split into the older division between Israel and Judah clearly took place. But we should also note that the author of 1 Kings at this point begins to use what seems to be a *Chronicle of the Kings of Judah* (Grabbe 2006a).

H. M. Niemann has produced a model, in which he argues that the kingdom of Omri was the first state in Palestine (1993, 2007). David was only a tribal chief, while Solomon functioned much as the lord of a Canaanite city. It was Jeroboam I who consolidated the tradition of mountain rulers in the Northern Kingdom, but Israel never managed to fuse the various tribal and cultural elements into a unity. Niemann interprets Omri and his successors as mobile warrior leaders, which is reflected in the structure of the Northern Kingdom. Less emphasis was placed on a permanent centre (Samaria was not a capital city, for example), but society remained largely tribal (as it had traditionally been) and precedent was put on maintaining the military strength. Samaria served as an administrative unit, but administrative structures were not well developed (e.g., no network of civil servants across the country). There were a few specialized centres with differentiated functions (trade, cult, defence), but these formed only a loose network of (mainly military) sites, primarily on the borders. Samaria was the only royal foundation in the heartland (though the traditional cultic sites of Dan [if this cult site existed – see Grabbe 2017c] and Bethel received royal support).

But we have now passed the date of 900 BCE, and the story of the two kingdoms of Israel and Judah is told elsewhere (e.g., Grabbe [2017a] and the other histories of Israel listed at the head of this chapter). At this point, we come to the end of our story of Israel's origins.

8.6 CONCLUSIONS

E. Bloch-Smith and B. A. Nakhai (1999) 'A Landscape Comes to Life: The Iron I Period', *NEA* 62: 62–92, 101–27; **I. Finkelstein** (2001) 'The Rise of Jerusalem and Judah: the Missing Link', *Levant* 33: 105–15; **A. Mazar** (2007) 'The Spade and the Text: The Interaction between Archaeology and Israelite History Relating to the Tenth-Ninth Centuries BCE', in H. G. M. Williamson (ed.), *Understanding the History of Ancient Israel*: 143–71.

The context for this chapter has been the eastern Mediterranean and ancient Near East during the early Iron Age. It was remarkable in that Palestine became to some extent isolated for a short time. The late Bronze Age had seen the Mediterranean world expand into an interconnected cosmopolis, but the end of the LBA presided over a general collapse of trade and communication, with many cities destroyed along the Mediterranean coast and sometimes further inland. This collapse had a far-reaching effect on the various cultures in the region from about 1200 BCE. Mesopotamia and Anatolia ceased to have contact with the Levant by the end of the LBA (except that certain of the Anatolian population may have migrated south). Toward the beginning of Iron I Egypt withdrew from Palestine. Some of the Sea Peoples had settled in southern Palestine, beginning about 1200 BCE. But then external contacts faded, including trade links. This left the inhabitants of Canaan to develop more or less as they saw fit without outside interference.

Many questions remain about the archaeology of Canaan, especially over such matters as chronology; this is despite the greater use of C14 dating. After the LBA had left many sites destroyed or abandoned at its end, the IA I saw an astonishing recovery. Ceramic continuity in the Jezreel and Beth-Shean Valleys indicates that it was the indigenous inhabitants whose population increased, rather than this being new settlers from outside. In the country between the Jezreel and Beersheba Valleys it was mainly in the north that one sees continuity, with many of the LBA sites continuing into IA I. But the settlement gap of the LBA comes to an end in IA I, even if the increase was much slower in the Judaean Hills and south than in the north. In the Ephraimite and Manassite regions population increase was unprecedented. The Shephelah had shown a momentous decline in the transition from the LBA to the IA I but significant growth in the later IA I. Similarly, in the Negev the settlement gap of the LBA was met by much new settlement in IA I.

The city-state system of Palestine and Syria had not come to an end as such. The rural sector certainly experienced continuity, with the peasants in the vicinity of the ruined LB cities living as they always had. Especially in the northern valleys the population remained dense. Then, in Iron I the main urban centres began to recover, including the development of trade with Phoenicia, Cyprus and beyond. In a few cases, even new city-states emerged, especially to replace those that had declined or disappeared. Concomitant with this was a remarkable increase in settlement in the highlands, mainly small sites.

The singular most significant point arising from the archaeology is the rapid expansion of settlement in IA I, especially in the northern hill country. The Judaean hill country lagged behind, and its growth came primarily in IA IIA. This helps to explain why the kingdom of Judah had fewer resources and was generally eclipsed in population and resources by the kingdom of Israel. This is why the idea that Judah dominated the north in the IA I or IIA is absurd. But the settlement in the Judaean hills and in the Negev did eventually reach a prosperous level.

The Philistines were a prominent component of Canaan in the Iron Age. The population seems to have been a synthesis of immigrating Sea Peoples from various places in the Mediterranean and the indigenous Canaanite inhabitants. This conclusion arises from the material culture in the areas considered Philistine. On the other hand, it seems unlikely that the Philistines were trying to expand into the hill country. They appeared to be happy with their lowland home, which had by no means reached 'carrying capacity' which would have put pressure on them to expand. Their clash with Israel was more likely the result of Israelite raids into their territory for plunder and food stuffs, as well as perhaps an attempt to control the trade routes that crossed Israelite territory.

We associate the settlement in the hill country with Israel, but this is based on the fact that the later kingdom of Israel arose in this part of the region. We have no confirmation from archaeology or texts, nor can we be sure that the later Israel had anything to do with the Israel of the Merenptah inscription. It is plausible that a line stretched from the 'Israel' mentioned by Merenptah to the kingdom of Israel several centuries later, but plausibility is not proof. In any case, the settled Israel may have been rather different in various ways from the 'people' referred to by Merenptah. The Israel that settled in the highlands probably had a variety of origins: pastoralists (including *Shasu*) settling down, farmers migrating from other parts of Canaan, migrants from outside Canaan, and any number of people seeking a better life by cultivating land in a sparsely settled countryside. These gradually coalesced into tribes of people related by ancestral descent (whether actual or fictional). A number of innovations in technology have long been ascribed to this settlement in the central highlands: terracing, plastered cisterns, the 'Israelite house', collared-rim jars, and the use of iron; also the absence of pig husbandry has been seen as significant. Unfortunately, it seems there is no list of technologies or practices that is exclusive to this region and time or that can serve as 'Israelite ethnic markers'.

The book of Judges describes a Canaan made up of a variety of independent tribes and peoples, often squabbling among themselves. Judges 5 seems to describe an Israel in which independent tribes sometimes worked together for a common good but pursued their own ends for the most part. Some of the tribal and other groups known to us from biblical genealogies might have originated in this period, though we know that others are probably much later creations. Local leaders might have given rise to some of the stories in the book of Judges, but it is doubtful if much historical memory remains here, even if the general picture of a disunited series of autonomous (or partially autonomous) peoples is quite believable.

The situation was described by E. Bloch-Smith and B. A. Nakhai (1999: 62) in this way: 'Perhaps, then, what characterized the Iron I is that it was the era in which the peoples of the southern Levant begin to develop their own individual identities, identities that would provide the basis for nationhood in subsequent centuries'.

Why then did the disparate tribes decide to unite into one people or unit? The answer is not simple and would probably involve a number of considerations. The 'Philistine threat' has often been invoked, though, as discussed above, the Israelites may well have brought this 'threat' down upon themselves because of becoming a thorn in the side of the Philistines. But however important this was, there were likely other considerations. In any case, if they were to fight a common enemy, it would have made sense to unite under a military leader that all had confidence in. By rights we would expect the first state in Palestine to arise in the coastal plain. In fact, the Philistine city-states were quite successful in the coastal plain, yet there seems to have been no impetus to form a larger unit. The next area would be the northern region, perhaps the northern valleys or hill country. It is precisely in this area that the Omride kingdom emerged, which is one of the reasons that some scholars think this was the first Israelite state.

The problem is what to do with the biblical traditions about the rise of the Israelite kingship. The idea that Israel was under divine rule but had Samuel anoint a king chosen by Yhwh is of course pure theology, not history. Should we simply dismiss the whole of the biblical account as too difficult to deal with? This is perhaps tempting, and some have certainly followed this approach. Yet more considered analyses suggest that there is history behind the stories of the 'United Monarchy', even if precisely what sort of history is a matter of debate. There seems to be sufficient evidence to assert that Saul, David, and Solomon existed as historical individuals. Saul was evidently the first king, was primarily a military leader, and was overthrown by David who subsequently met a lot of opposition, including from Judah.

If anything resembling a united Israel – a territorial state – came about under David, it would have been an unusual development. One can hardly claim that it would be impossible, but it seems reasonable to conclude that in the light of all circumstances it would not be very likely. On the other hand, perhaps a city-state, much like the city-states of Shechem under Lab'aya or of Jerusalem under Abdi-Heba, would be feasible. Much in the David tradition would be compatible with that. But a Jerusalem city-state or a Davidic chiefdom or a David tribal state is not the same as the 'United Monarchy' of the Bible. It seems unlikely that David controlled anything beyond a limited territory centred on the southern hill country and Jerusalem. This appears to have overlapped with territory earlier controlled by Saul. A. Mazar summarizes the situation as he sees it, based on the available archaeology:

> It is certain that much of the biblical narrative concerning David and Solomon is mere fiction and embellishment written by later authors.... I would compare the potential achievements of David to those of an earlier hill country leader, namely Labayu, the *habiru* leader from Shechem.... David can be envisioned as a ruler similar to Labayu, except that he operated in a time free of intervention by the Egyptians or any other

foreign power, and when the Canaanite cities were in decline. In such an environment, a talented and charismatic leader, politically astute, and in control of a small yet effective military power, may have taken hold of large part of a small country like the Land of Israel and controlled diverse population groups under his regime from his stronghold in Jerusalem, which can be identified archaeologically. Such a regime does not necessitate a particularly large and populated capital city. David's Jerusalem can be compared to a medieval Burg, surrounded by a medium-sized town, and yet it could well be the centre of a meaningful polity. The only power that stood in David's way consisted of the Philistine cities, which, as archaeology tells us, were large and fortified urban centres during this time. Indeed the biblical historiographer excludes them from David's conquered territories. [Mazar 2007: 164–5]

As was argued above, it is likely that David formed some sort of pact with the Philistines. This is why the few clashes with Philistines alleged for his rule in the Bible were probably borrowed from Saul's deeds. Saul seems to have presided over a small amount of territory centred on the central highlands. Ethbaal appears to have expanded this, moving into Gilead, the Jezreel Valley, and Lower Galilee. David added the area of Judah to this, but it still formed only a small state in central Canaan. I. Finkelstein gives a summary of his views:

…we may still be able to identify in them [the stories of David] the action of a local chieftain who moves with his gang to the south of Hebron, in the Judean Desert and in the Shephelah, far from the control of the central government in the highlands further to the north. David takes over Hebron, the second most important Iron Age town in the highlands of Judah and the centre of his theatre of operations, and then expands to the north and conquers Jerusalem, the traditional centre of government in the southern hill country. David, according to these stories, is a typical Apiru leader, who manages to establish a new dynasty in Jerusalem. [Finkelstein 2001: 107–8]

Thus, in spite of their many differences Mazar and Finkelstein give a picture of the rise of the Israelite state that is remarkably similar. In the interpretation given here the 'United Monarchy' under David did indeed encompass both Israel and Judah, but it was nothing like the kingdom described in the Bible. What is surprising is that without any description of new conquests or major changes to David's state, Solomon suddenly presides over a huge empire, stretching from Asia Minor to Egypt, over which he establishes economic and commercial control and brings in unheard-of wealth. There is nothing in the text to prepare for the sudden change with Solomon's kingdom. It soon becomes obvious that we are dealing with a typical tale of an Oriental potentate with great wisdom, enormous wealth, and many women.

There are reasons to think Solomon existed (including his name, from a local deity of Jerusalem), but much of the description of his kingdom and his reign are incredible. Even the demonstration of his wisdom depends on a banal tale of two prostitutes. It is hardly surprising that after his undistinguished reign, the kingdom broke up into its natural parts: Israel and Judah, which had long existed separately. The history of these two kingdoms is another story which must be told elsewhere.

Part V
Conclusions

CHAPTER 9

The Origins of Israel – A Holistic Perspective

The aim of this study was to illuminate the origins of Israel. The best way to look for evidence is to work backwards, at least initially. We know there was an entity called 'Judah' (Yehud, Judaea) in the Second Temple period because many Greek and Roman sources tell us about it. We can trace this back to the Persian period without any problem, and in the Neo-Babylonian period we also have Mesopotamian sources that mention Judah in one form or another. But they do not mention Israel. We know of Israel first from the Bible. In the period before 600 BCE we appear to have evidence that almost everyone accepts of a kingdom called Judah, and before 725 BCE, of a kingdom alongside Judah called Israel. The name Israel seldom occurs outside the Bible at this time; instead, we have names like *Bit-Ḫumri* and 'Samaria', though Ahab is called an 'Israelite' in one Assyrian inscription (but it is the equivalent of 'king of Israel', as argued at §8.4.1).

It is at this point that we start to run into difficulties, because our only source explicitly using the name Israel is the Bible, and the accounts of Israel in it were clearly written long after the events being described. This is why a study such as the present one is needed, in order to look for evidence of where the Israelite kingdom – attested by consensus in the eighth century BCE – came from. What was the origin of Israel? In which source(s) was it first attested, and what is the history of that Israel between its original attestation and the kingdom of Israel known from the eighth century BCE? Our pivotal piece of information is the reference to an 'Israel' in an inscription of the Egyptian pharaoh named Merenptah about 1200 BCE. This is the place to begin, going both forwards and backwards. It has recently been proposed that the name Israel is found on an even earlier Egyptian inscription, but this is very uncertain – some Egyptologists reject it outright; yet even if accepted, this would take us only a couple of centuries further back.

So Israel is first attested in the last part of the LBA. What can we say about this Israel? Very little, beyond its existence. The hieroglyphic determinative used with the name suggests that 'Israel' is a people. The name is used alongside several topographical names: *pa-Canaan* (either the region Canaan or the city Gaza), the cities Ashkelon and Gezer (in southern Canaan), the city Yenoam (perhaps near Beth-Shean), and Kharu (apparently a synonym for Canaan). This suggests that Israel was somewhere in Canaan, though Transjordan cannot be ruled out. Beyond that we cannot go, at least from the inscription. Some have tried to relate the battle scenes of the same monument to Israel and other groups named in the inscription, but there is no consensus of how to interpret these.

The best procedure seems to be to go further into the past to try to determine where this Israel of the Merenptah stela came from. A good place to start would be the EBA or third millennium BCE. Around the year 3000 BCE writing seems to have been invented in both Mesopotamia and Egypt. What was originally a form of picture writing as a way of keeping accounts of livestock and the like became a means of expressing speech in writing. The earliest writing was not used to describe events (what we might call 'historiography'), but by about the middle of the third millennium, some kings were recounting their deeds in writing, which constitutes a predecessor of history writing. We can write history before the use of writing by drawing on archaeology: although sometimes called 'pre-history', it is as much history as that based on documents. But history based solely on archaeology lacks a certain dimension that access to documents can give (of course, history without archaeology also lacks important aspects, especially the ability to correct a picture derived from available written sources alone).

The EBA encompasses the Egyptian Old Kingdom and the initial Mesopotamian civilization in the region of Sumer. As the Sumerian cities declined in power in the latter part of the third millennium, a dynamic king in the form of Sargon I arose further north in Mesopotamia and conquered Sumer, to found the Akkadian empire. This lasted perhaps two centuries before being brought to an end by the people of the Zagros mountains called the Gutians. The Sumerian cities gradually regained their independence from the Gutians and established the Ur III period in which the city of Ur dominated from about 2100 to 2000 BCE. But connections between Mesopotamia and Palestine seem not to have existed at this time.

One people making its appearance in Syria and Mesopotamia at this time were the Amorites. We have many references to them in the Ur III texts, though much of our information in fact comes from Mari texts in the MBA. Who the Amorites were is an important question. They are presented as a nomadic, unsophisticated, primitive people in many texts, lacking in all the refinements of civilization, even burial after death. Yet we find that there were various groups, perhaps the equivalent of tribes. Yes, they tended to inhabit the steppes, but as pastoralists they moved their flocks and herds seasonally, and some seemed to live in permanent settlements. More importantly, Amorite dynasties came to rule in a number of Mesopotamian and Syrian cities, showing that they were as 'civilized' and 'sophisticated' as the native inhabitants, even though their Amorite identity was still in some way known to scribes. We shall come back to Amorites below when we talk about Mari.

The Egyptian Old Kingdom, sometimes called the 'Pyramid Age', lasted for six dynasties before a period of fragmentation, called the First Intermediate Period during which Egypt had split into sections ruled by several different rulers at the same time from Memphis, Heracleopolis, and Thebes. One of the perennial fears of the Egyptians was that of disorder, which is what prevailed in the First Intermediate Period. Associated with disorder was the encroachment of people from the north and east of Egypt who were called *Amu* or 'Asiatics', among other designations. These various terms seem to have been applied to the inhabitants of Palestine/Canaan (often called *Retenu*). Egypt developed trade relations to the north and south. This included Nubia which had a number of products needed by Egypt. Sinai was a source of turquoise and other precious stones. Byblos on the Syrian coast was an important partner from the third millennium, especially for timber from the cedar forests but also other products. The peoples of the desert were seen as a problem, though their occasional encroachment on Egyptian territory does seems to have been more an imagined rather than an actual problem.

We have a number of references to excursions into Palestine, though the language of these does not make it easy to differentiate a peaceful journey to receive gifts or collect tribute from a military attack. Only a couple of accounts of military campaigns into Syria-Palestine have come down to us (e.g., Weni). Yet we also have indications that foreign workers were widely employed in Egypt at this time. Some evidently came from immigration of those looking for employment as a means of living. But others were enslaved persons captured in war, either enemy soldiers or 'civilian' inhabitants who were taken captive during military excursions. This meant a substantial population of Semites in Egypt from territories to the north and east of the Delta. It is possible that some of Israel's ancestors were among them.

The excavations of the city of Ebla at Tell Mardikh in the 1960s and 1970s yielded evidence of a notable urban centre in Syria in the later third millennium BCE. Because of some sensational statements about these finds connecting them with the biblical account of the patriarchs, some biblical scholars even suggested pushing the patriarchal age back into the third millennium (though it had traditionally been dated to the early second millennium BCE). Unfortunately, these alleged references to places and events also known from the Bible mainly evaporated, and Ebla ceased to be cited as evidence in support of the biblical account. It remains, of course, an important window into Syria in the mid-to-late third millennium.

The Middle Bronze Age ushered in the Egyptian Middle Kingdom about 2000 BCE. Once more united under a single ruler, Egyptian experienced a golden age. The language and literature of the Middle Kingdom remain the 'classical' expression of Egyptian culture. A number of texts show us that 'Asiatics' migrated temporarily or permanently into Egyptian territory, especially in the Delta. But the Middle Kingdom was followed by the Second Intermediate Period which brought in another phenomenon that has been related to the origins of Israel. These were the Hyksos. At one time, it was believed that the Hyksos were an invading people who conquered and set up their rule over Lower Egypt. More recently it is argued that various Semitic people(s) had long lived in the Delta and on the margins of northern Egypt. When Egypt became fragmented during the Second Intermediate Period (c. 1750–1550 BCE), a Hyksos dynasty (Dynasty 15) arose in the Delta with its capital at Avaris (Tell el-Dab'a).

The Hyksos ruled for about a century or so before the country became united once more under the new Dynasty 18. Hyksos rule was brought to an end, and the Hyksos were allegedly driven from the country. It seems clear that some individuals relating to the Hyksos dynasty left Egypt and moved to Sharuhen in southern Palestine (perhaps Tel Haror/Tell Abû Hureirah). But this would probably have been some of the elite, in any case only a small population: the bulk of the population of Avaris and the Hyksos kingdom remained where they were, though now under rule from Thebes. The archaeology shows no break in the material culture or a large emigration from the region. Some have seen Israel's ancestors among the Hyksos. This might be the case, but the supposition (entertained, e.g., by Josephus) that the Hyksos were the exodus group is to be rejected.

In Mesopotamia the Old Assyrian Period (*c.* 2000–1750 BCE) saw important trade connections between Assyria and Kanesh in Anatolia. Shamshi-Adad I (*c.* 1800 BCE) brought the various major Assyrian cities under his control. He was an older contemporary of Hammurabi of Babylon (*c.* 1775 BCE), and the two were rivals. He conquered Mari and attempted to take Yamhad but apparently without success. Shamshi-Adad's empire collapsed after his death, removing a threat to Babylon. Hammurabi continued to expand, taking Mari which had recovered after Shamshi-Adad's death and was ruled by Zimri-Lim.

The city of Mari on the western edge was an important player until conquered by Hammurabi (*c.* 1775 BCE) of Babylon. Because of a large archive of texts we know a lot about Mari in the last few decades before Hammurabi's taking of the city. What we find is that both Shamshi-Adad and Hammurabi were of Amorite ancestry, and an Amorite dynasty ruled in Mari. Amorites were also an important constituent of the Mari kingdom. We know of several Amorite tribes, but two of special importance were the Yaminites and Simalites. The Yaminites ('sons of the south' or southerners) inhabited the areas on the south side of the Euphrates, while the Simalites ('sons of the north' or northerners) plied their pastoral activities on the north side of the river. The name of the Yaminites first attracted attention since it was interpreted as equivalent to 'Benjaminites'; however, the reading has been disputed. The last part of the name, *Yamīna*, apparently referring to the right-hand (or southern) bank of the Euphrates, is clear, but the first part of the name is written in Sumerograms DUMU.MEŠ 'sons (of)'. The question is whether it should be read as Akkadian *marū(-yamīna)* or as Northwest Semitic *bini(-yamīna)*. There was also the parallel tribe of DUMU.MEŠ-*si-im-a-al* 'sons of the north', which has no connection to Israel or any name in the Bible. One suggestion was that 'sons' is only a semantic indicator of a tribal name and that it is appropriate to refer only to Yaminites or Simalites. In any case, the similarity to the biblical Benjaminites seems coincidental, even if the name is read *Bini-Yamīna* and not *Marū-Yamīna* or just *Yamīna*.

Many Amorites were well integrated into Babylonian, Assyrian, etc. society. Probably there were many of Amorite ancestry who no longer identified or were identified as Amorite. Yet the Amorites – or at least some of them – were also associated with specific territory. The centre of Amorite habitation and culture seems to have been in northern Syria, around Jebel Bišri, to the northeast of Palmyra. This is where the cuneiform sources of the Early and Middle Bronze Age put them, and the later kingdom of Amurru of the LBA was also located in this region. This suggests that the Amorites were more than just people of a particular lifestyle (especially pastoralism) but were actually a specific ethnic group. On the other hand, we cannot exclude the possibility that Mesopotamian scribes lumped a number of different peoples into their label 'Amorite'. There is also the linguistic problem. Their language (and often their identity) is derived mainly from personal names. This has led to their being categorized as Northwest Semitic, and many would put them in with Canaanites, Aramaeans, and even the people of Ugarit. But although the Ugarit dynasty also seems to have been Amorite, the latest study of the language has not been able to place it in Northwest Semitic, since it also has strong features of East Semitic (the language type of Mesopotamia).

The Amorites then remain to some extent an enigma. They cannot certainly be classified as Northwest Semitic. Some Amorites seem to have lived in or near Canaan. A few scholars have wanted to make these 'Asiatic' peoples (as they were known to the Egyptians), largely Amorites, but there is no evidence that such a simple identity prevailed. No doubt some Amorites migrated southward from their north Syrian (and Mesopotamian?) home, but there is no evidence that the bulk of the Palestinian inhabitants were Amorite. The name consistently used, whenever there is a generic reference, is 'Canaan/Canaanite'. The Egyptian texts do not use the term 'Amorite' until the LBA when they refer to the kingdom of Amurru well known from the Amarna letters.

The so-called Patriarchal Narratives (*c.* Gen. 11:22–50:26) have conventionally been set in the early second millennium BCE, though over the years a number of different periods of time have been proposed. Through the 1950s and 1960s it was customary, at least in the USA, to argue that these chapters in Genesis contained 'substantial historicity'. A leading proponent, W. F. Albright, died in 1971. A few years later in the mid-1970s two studies (by T. L. Thompson and J. Van Seters) appeared that argued the narratives were written much later than the first century or so after 2000 BCE. These two studies had a major influence on opinion, and within a few years the patriarchal period became assigned to the legendary period of the previous chapters in Genesis (containing the story of Adam and Eve, the flood, and so on). As we shall see, it began a process in which the story of Israel in the Bible from Exodus to Judges began to be questioned, revised, and rewritten.

The argument was that the patriarchal narratives were filled with anachronisms, references, and allusions to events, customs, and culture of much later times. For example, the ancestors given for Abraham are simply the names of cities (Gen. 11:22-26). Abraham is said to come from Ur of the Chaldees (אור כשדים: Gen. 11:28), yet the Chaldeans are first attested a thousand years later, about the ninth century BCE. The alleged parallels from Nuzi and other second-millennium texts (though the Nuzi texts were centuries after the time ascribed to Abraham) have not stood up to scrutiny, a number of them being better paralleled from the seventh or sixth centuries BCE. Archaeology shows that a number of the important sites in the stories of the patriarchs were actually not inhabited at the time; on the other hand, many of the main cities known to have existed in the MBA are absent from the text. No period in the early or middle second millennium BCE is known when all the sites in the patriarchal narratives were settled.

But then came the Ebla texts about 1975, and claims were made by the epigrapher (or were allegedly made, since he later denied them) that found surprising confirmation of details in the patriarchal narratives in some of these texts. Some of the traditional scholars waxed lyrical about how their view of 'substantial historicity' in the text was confirmed. Then the bottom fell out – other Assyriologists expressed scepticism toward the finds (often they did not yet have direct access to the texts) and then the epigrapher withdrew or denied these claims. Further philological work on the texts did not bear up the supposed biblical parallels, and newly deciphered texts also gave no support. The result has been that as important as the Ebla texts are for the history of Syria in the third millennium, they provide little in the way of illumination of Genesis. Doubting the historical veracity of the patriarchal texts (though they have great value for areas other than history, such as theology and literature) has remained the trend in scholarly circles.

It is in the LBA that our knowledge of Syria and Palestine suddenly increases greatly, primarily because of the Amarna letters but also inscriptions from Egypt and cuneiform texts from the Hittites, Ugarit, and Mitanni. Babylonia, Assyria, Elam, and other Mesopotamian peoples have left a fair amount of information about their history as well, but their activities do not seem to have affected Syria-Palestine very much. Babylonia was ruled by a Kassite dynasty for much of the LBA, and the Middle Assyrian Kingdom asserted itself for a time toward the end of the LBA. But these did not have a major interaction with the regions further west and south except for some arrangements and communications with Egypt.

The story that we should be witnessing in our various texts is that of the biblical books of Exodus, Numbers to Deuteronomy, Joshua, and Judges. If the events described there occurred, they could not have failed to leave a mark in Egyptian royal inscriptions, the Amarna letters, or the archaeology of the LBA in Palestine. First of all, a large population arising from Canaanite migrants was said to be settled in the Delta. After a series of disasters affecting them to some extent but mainly the population of Egypt to the south of the Delta, they all marched out of their Delta home and across the desert to cross a large body of water (called the *Yam Suph* in Hebrew, but thought to designate the Reed Sea, a branch of the Red Sea, or the Red Sea itself). The pursuing Egyptian army was drowned in the sea, though the Israelites got across successfully. They then spent forty years in the wilderness, mainly around Qadesh-Barnea before marching up the east side of the Dead Sea, crossing the Jordan into northern Palestine, and conquering the various Canaanite tribes. Once this was done the tribes were assigned portions of the territory, which was then divided up among the people to give each family an inheritance of land. Yet because there was no king, the various tribes had to contend with indigenous peoples living there, such as the surviving Canaanites and the Philistines, or other nearby peoples such as the Amalekites and Midianites.

A study of the exodus and settlement narratives reveals many problems, however. Apart from the size of the Israelite migration (600,000 young fighting men, meaning several million people as a whole), there are a number of late references in the text, such as the 'store houses' that the Israelites were supposed to have constructed. If 'Pithom' is Tell el-Maskhuta, as many think, it was not settled between the sixteenth and the seventh centuries BCE. The name of 'Ramesses' is given a late spelling, putting it long after the Egyptian New Kingdom. On the other hand, the important site of Sile, which was on the Israelites' alleged march out of Egypt, is not mentioned at all, suggesting the writer of the account knew nothing about it. There is also the problem of the 'land of Goshen' which is not attested until the Saite period. As for the itinerary out of Egypt to the east side of the Dead Sea, it makes no sense, probably because different traditions about the route have been combined. More importantly, the various sites named in the text do not reflect the fifteenth or thirteenth centuries BCE but the seventh or eighth. Only at the end of IA II were most of the sites that can be identified actually occupied. As for the archaeology, the huge Israelite population is said not only to have marched across the wilderness of Sinai but to have spent several decades in the region of Qadesh-Barnea. A group this size staying this long in the same place should have left clear remains in the archaeology. Yet Qadesh (Tell el-Qudeirat), which has been extensively excavated, shows no habitation between the Middle Bronze Age and the tenth century BCE or possibly even later.

Some have attempted to explain the exodus account in naturalistic terms: for example, that the Ten Plagues were natural phenomena in the Nile valley, or that the Egyptians were drowned by a storm as they pursued Israelites in boats across the Red Sea. True, Exod. 14:21-29 may be describing local wind and tidal conditions, but the Israelites marching through the waters dryshod and the water returning to drown the Egyptians is a supernatural miracle. Similarly, the water from the rock and manna from heaven are supernatural miracles. There is no question but that the exodus from Egypt was an event with supernatural elements in it. Which is why it is problematic when the mummy of the pharaoh alleged to be ruling at the time shows no signs of drowning.

The question of the settlement will be discussed later, but an exodus as described in the Pentateuch did not take place. There are, of course, several scenarios that might well have given rise to a greatly expanded and developed exodus narrative full of imagined and anachronistic detail. One possibility, long argued, is that a small group of slaves escaped from Egypt, perhaps pursued by a unit of soldiers who were unaccountably thwarted or even destroyed in their pursuit, an event which then became blown up into the story found in the book of Exodus. Another is that in his fight against Israel, Merenptah captured and enslaved a number of Israelites. Over time they or their descendants were freed and even allowed to make their way back home (presumably Palestine). Their experience was developed into a story of gaining miraculously their freedom from Egypt. Other proposals are possible, though some still insist that there was no historical basis for the exodus but that the story was invented at a much later time when there were many Jews living in Egypt.

To return to the crucial Amarna archive, it consisted mainly of letters to the Egyptian king from the petty kings of Syro-Palestinian city-states, plus some kingdoms such as Byblos and Ugarit. Apart from a few letters from Egyptian officials and some letters from the pharaoh to Babylon and Assyria, the letters are by and large to the Egyptian king, without replies. We know of what the king himself said almost entirely from references to this in letters by the Canaanite kinglets. Yet for a few decades we have unprecedented information on the main cities and rulers in Syria-Palestine and their interactions with one another. We know who the major players were and the game(s) they played.

The bulk of the letters relate to northern Syria. This was because of Abdi-Ashirta who usurped the throne of Amurru, apparently by enlisting *Apiru* and others to give military aid. He then proceeded to threaten his neighbours, especially Byblos. After his death his son Aziru continued to pursue the same goals of expansion of territory and takeover of city-states in the region. But much of the correspondence comes from Rib-Hadda, the ruler of Byblos, who continually points out to the pharaoh what Abdi-Ashirta and Aziru were getting up to and how they threatened him and other neighbours. There were also letters relating to Ugarit, Tyre, and other kingdoms in the region. These letters give us information on events in northern Syria and also a general idea of the ethos of the Syro-Palestinian rulers in relation to the Egyptian administration; however, they do not tell us much about Canaan.

But we also have letters from Canaan itself: a number of letters relating to different city-states, including Hazor, Akko, Pella, Shechem, Jerusalem, Lachish, Megiddo, Gezer, Gath, Ashkelon. For example, we have about six letters from Abdi-Heba the ruler of Jerusalem (at a time when archaeology has not yet identified his city/fortress/stronghold). We have a number of letters from Lab'ayu the ruler of Shechem, the views of his neighbours on his activities (nefarious from their point of view), and the actions of his sons after his death. Like so many others, they are seeking to defend their power and territory from the rulers around them but also to extend their power and territory at the expense of those same neighbours – all the time complaining to pharaoh about how they are being mistreated by their fellow 'mayors' and asking for Egyptian help to defend themselves (apparently not normally forthcoming, to judge from the follow-up correspondence). Lab'ayu was especially aggressive and may have been executed by the Egyptians themselves, though that apparently did not deter his sons from continuing down the same path.

The Amarna letters confirm in detail what we already knew from the series of documents on Egyptian rulers and Egyptian history: Egypt was firmly in control of Palestine throughout the Egyptian New Kingdom. There is hardly a period when campaigns were not being made into Syria and Palestine, or at least tribute was not being collected from there. The biblical narratives from Exodus to Judges do not square in any way with Egyptian history at this time. There was no place for plagues to devastate Egypt or a large group to emigrate from the Delta through the desert to the

Negev, up the east side of the Dead Sea, and then into Palestine by crossing the Jordan in the north. We have many inscriptions telling us about the pharaohs of the 18th and 19th Dynasties. None has anything remotely to say that parallels the story of the biblical text at this time. The Amarna letters show a Canaan quite different from that depicted in Joshua and Judges. There are no Israelites in the Amarna letters, and the situation with the various city-states and their interactions are incompatible with the picture given in the biblical books.

But then a little over a century after the last extant Amarna tablet was written, Merenptah reports of his defeat and destruction of Israel. The name 'Israel' appears for the first time in history, only to be described as plundered and its 'seed' eradicated (whether this refers to 'offspring' or to 'grain supplies'). Nothing of the proud story of deliverance from Egypt, destruction of the Egyptian army in the Red/Reed Sea, or triumphant conquest of the Canaanite tribes in Palestine. What we seem to have is a small people in his inscription (listed alongside several cities and a reference to the region of Canaan) who were subjugated, but their home and location is not specified. Judging from the various toponyms in the text we presume that this 'Israel' lived somewhere in Canaan, but exactly where is uncertain. Arguments based on reliefs of battle scenes at Karnak have not been decisive.

Much speculation has been expended about the makeup of this Israel. A number of different groups are known from texts in the LBA. These include the *Apiru* and the *Shasu*. The *Apiru* seem to be a social group, made up of those on the margins of society who have left their people to make their living as outcasts or migrants or even outlaws. They were sometimes hired by rulers as mercenaries when fighters were needed. The term *Shasu* ('Sutaean' seems to be used in the same way) looks primarily to refer to a particular lifestyle, pastoralism. Yet here and there are texts that talk about tribes and settlements and seem to suggest an ethnic group. It may of course be that the Egyptians were lumping more than one group together under the name.

Because *Apiru* is almost certainly a cognate of the word 'Hebrew', it was once thought that the two could be equated, and the *Apiru* of the Amarna texts were the 'Hebrews' or 'Israelites'. Further study now suggests that the term 'Hebrew' as an ethnic term for Israelites was a development from the original social usage. This would suggest a connection between *Apiru* and Israel, but an indirect one, so that while some of Israel's ancestors might have been *Apiru*, one should not equate the term with all Israelites. Perhaps more relevant is the term *Shasu*. They are often associated with Edom and the area around the southern end of the Dead Sea. We also have one reference to *Yhw3 Š3sw*, which has been seen as the origin of the divine name *Yhwh*, the primary Israelite deity. Some have argued that the battle reliefs of Merenptah show that 'Israel' is pictured as *Shasu*; unfortunately, others argue that the battle scenes of Egyptians fighting Canaanites are the ones that picture Israel. Thus, some see Israel as having its origins among the *Shasu*, but others have just as seriously denied this.

What seems clear is that a variety of peoples made contributions to Israel. Israelites were certainly Canaanites, but that does not exclude *Shasu*, some of whom may have settled in the central highlands. It has been demonstrated that some of those settling in the hill country were former pastoralists, but others may have been farmers moving to less settled areas, migrants from outside Canaan, and people in general seeking land and a new life. This was because the highlands had been largely uninhabited in the LBA and offered land for those willing to put in the effort to make it productive. The evidence looks convincing that there was a cyclical process in Palestine, with the inhabitants shifting from settled agrarians to pastoralists as the climate became more or less favourable to growing crops.

Pastoralism took a variety of forms, but pastoralists seldom wandered aimlessly with their flocks and herds. The normal process was seasonal transhumance movement between pastures. This could even mean that some of the population could be settled and even planting and harvesting while the rest herded their animals. But there were and are many forms of pastoralism. The archaeology suggests that those who settled in the hill country had a pastoralist background but one in which they had lived near settled communities for many generations, perhaps forming a symbiotic relationship with the agrarian communities in which they traded their animals for grain and each population generally supported the other.

But this picture arises from examining the archaeology of Canaan – none of this comes from Merenptah's brief comments on his inscription. What we find from archaeology is greatly increased settlement during the IA I, especially in the hill country. This is the area that became the centre of the kingdom of Saul and Eshbaal. It is therefore plausible that the IA I settlement in the hill country was the basis for the later kingdom of Israel. Yet it is too soon to say this is a certainty. Above all, we have no way of asserting that this was the basis of Merenptah's Israel. It is always possible – even if unlikely – that the earlier name of Merenptah's Israel was picked up and appropriated by the later kingdom of Israel and that the two had no organic relationship, only the same name. Plausibility is one thing; dogmatic assertion is quite another.

Literary sources make Israel a tribal entity. This is the state of things in one of the earliest passages in the Hebrew Bible, the 'Song of Deborah' in Judges 5. Although the tribes always add up to twelve, this is done by two ways of counting. One names Joseph as one tribe but also includes the Levites as a tribe; however, another divides Joseph into two tribes (Ephraim and Manasseh) and usually omits Levi. In Judges 5, however, we find a number of the tribes named, some positively as participating in opposing Sisera and some negatively as avoiding the summons to provide assistance. Yet two tribes are listed (Machir and Gibeon) who occur nowhere else, while Levi and especially Judah are not named at all. What this suggests is what emerges from other passages: Judah was separate from Israel and had its own distinct identity; it was not one of the tribes of Israel, despite being listed in many passages. But the names found in Judges 5 might more or less include the same areas mentioned in Saul's and Eshbaal's kingdom, and the poem refers to these people as Israel (Judg. 5:2, 3, 5, 7, 9, 11), for the first time bringing together a people, region, and name – even if it is in a literary context.

The situation reminds one of the multiple city-states of the Amarna period, but there are also essential differences. Instead of people organized around cities to form a city-state, a territorial and citizenship concept, they are brought together into tribes organized as kinship groups (whether fictional or actual). These tribes seem to control certain parcels of land and are independent of one another. They might nevertheless cooperate in some cases, especially where there was a mutual threat from an outside force. The idea that they are somehow related appears to exercise a strong influence on how they act toward their neighbours. This ideology of kinship was no doubt one impulse (among many) that pushed the tribes to unite into some sort of state.

Some have blamed pressure from the Philistines; others have argued for other factors, but all agree that Israel eventually came together into a state. The relationship of the Israelites with the Philistine cities was evidently a complicated one. Far from the Philistines attempting to spread their settlement into the hill country, they seem to have been happy with their lives in the lowlands (which had not by any means reached 'carrying capacity' and put pressure on them to expand). It seems more likely that the highland people periodically raided the lowland areas for plunder and especially to steal livestock and grain supplies; they also seem to have wanted to control the trade routes across their territories. But this constant irritant may have led to a call to confront the Israelites of the hill country to punish them and make them think twice about further excursions against the Philistines. Conversely, the Israelites would not have taken this reaction lying down: hence, the confrontation between the two peoples.

The story of Saul as the first king is plausible because 1 and 2 Samuel are so focused on idolizing the figure of David. But Saul's rise to leadership was most probably based on military skills and potential. It is unlikely that he arose simply because it was claimed that 'God/the gods' had chosen him. Yet his choice might well have been confirmed and legitimated by the ritual actions of a senior priestly/prophetic figure such as Samuel. Again, the narrator could have told David's story without Saul, but he seems to have been stuck with an entangled narrative in which David was not the first king and whose dynasty was legitimated only because another dynasty was cut off.

David himself also rose to prominence as a warrior. Although the David-and-Goliath story is incredible and seems to have originally been a statement about another Israelite hero, David's prowess as a fighter looks genuine. But he was also an inventive and ruthless politician who first gained rulership over the tribe of Judah and then kingship over a united Israel and Judah. This was not done without bloodshed: it included deals with those on the other side, such as Abner, a member of the Saulide family. Once he occupied the throne, he also seems to have made a deal with the Philistines and neutralized that threat (his battles with them are probably appropriated from Saul in some cases). But not everyone was reconciled with his rule, which is why several rebellions took place in the latter part of his reign. He apparently went on to expand his territory, probably being the one to take Jerusalem into his domain, but this is unlikely to have included the Aramaeans who were far north of his kingdom.

The exaggerated legend of Solomon does not fit well with David. Although David controlled a certain amount of territory, gained in part through his personal military ability and leadership, Solomon suddenly – though he fights no battles nor leads an army – controls land from Egypt to Anatolia, monopolizes trade in the region, sends his ships to far-off lands, and brings in vast sums of gold that match those of later great empires such as Persia. His wealth and wisdom are so great that the Queen of Sheba must travel to Israel to meet him. When she does, she finds that they were even greater than the legend had claimed! Yet the one account we have of his wisdom is a banal story about two prostitutes, nothing like the great Oriental tales of cleverness and wisdom about Ahiqar or Alexander. Solomon probably existed, but he was evidently a minor local ruler whose domain covered only a portion of Palestine, which he had inherited from David.

Solomon had managed to hold together the kingdom he had inherited. But after his death it reverted to the natural division that had been there from the beginning: it split back into a kingdom of Israel and a kingdom of Judah, once again rivals with one another as they apparently had been in the past. It is during the reigns of Rehoboam and Jeroboam I that we first find evidence that the narrator has used a source, probably a court daybook or chronicle. This appears to have been the backbone of the story of the kings of Judah and Israel. This chronicle was brief, giving the name of the king and recounting a few military exploits and building projects. Much else found in the narrative is legend or religious invention.

So, what can we say about the origins of Israel? We saw that Semitic peoples lived in or migrated into Palestine from an early time. 'Canaan' was a topographical region, and the Canaanites were not necessarily a monolithic people. The biblical text gives various 'tribes' of Canaanites, which suggests a diverse origin, as an examination of some of the alleged tribes indicates. One group with its own identity was the Phoenicians. Although the Phoenicians made their name as seafarers, most Canaanites seem to have been small farmers and herders. For various reasons (including poverty, misfortune, or laziness) a few people left agriculture to become renegades and made their living in bands of raiders and brigands, known as *Apiru*. Some of these even hired themselves out as mercenaries. Another group named in Egyptian sources were the *Shasu*, who seem to have been mainly herders with a location often placed east of the Dead Sea. Although their name has not yet been identified in the Bible, they were probably also part of the Canaanite picture. The description in the text sometimes seems to identify them as simply those with a particular mode of life (i.e., pastoralism), but at other times it suggests an ethnic group. Some texts suggest that at least some of them were settled in towns or cities. They may have been part of the cyclical process, powered by the climate, in which the inhabitants of Canaan pursued agriculture when rainfall was abundant but reverted to pastoralism when drought prevailed.

When it comes to Israel, various proposals have been made for the origin of the name, but whether we know where the name came from is doubtful. From its first appearance in the inscription of Merenptah it appears to designate a section of the population in Palestine, but exactly where this entity was settled or how many of the inhabitants made it up is unknown. The most likely conclusion is that these were Canaanites – a section of the Canaanite population living on the land and subsisting by agrarian activities. It had some sort of coherence and a specific identity, however, which caused others to refer to it by the specific name of Israel. The chances are that in the time of Merenptah, the people known as 'Israel' lived somewhere in Palestine and were in some way (part of?) the ancestors of the Israel of the Iron Age.

What is plain is the Canaanite origins of Israel. By the time much of the Bible was written, Israel had its own identity – in fact, it saw itself as distinct from the Canaanites who were even categorized as opponents – but its Canaanite heritage was still very much in evidence. Some early passages (such as the poetic passages of the 'Song of the Sea' and the 'Song of Deborah') are closer to its Canaanite roots, but the Canaanite origins of Israelite language, ethnic identity, and religion remain clearly evident in the literary and archaeological remains of ancient Israel and Judah. Israel's Canaanite identity is in part manifested by its language, which is referred to in earlier texts as the 'lip of Canaan' and its heimat in the 'land of Canaan'. The language is only later given the name of 'Hebrew' (עברית). Hebrew is of course closely related to Phoenician (though differing from it in several grammatical features) and other Canaanite dialects (such as Moabite). It has often been said that we have little in the way of Canaanite literature, but this seems incorrect: our chief example of Canaanite literature is the Hebrew Bible! Israel had a typical Canaanite religion, with the divinity El at the head of the pantheon. She eventually moved to a focus on Yhwh who was probably brought in from outside; however, El was not given up but simply identified with Yhwh.

Israel does not seem to have been made up of a single group. This is indicated by later sources which refer to 12 or 13 tribes. While some of these may well be legendary creations, others appear to have diverse origins. For example, the Danites look like the Danae known from the Aegean region.

The Benjaminites bore a name well attested for Amorite groups on the Euphrates: a connection of some sort seems possible but it would have been remote. Judah, as a careful study shows, was a separate group that had its own identity and was grouped with the Israelites only on a temporary basis in the Early Iron Age. Whether they had a common ethnic origin with Israel or only later became associated with them is at present only a matter of speculation.

At some point an entity developed in Canaan that took the name Israel (or was given it by outsiders). This was probably in the LBA, since the name occurs first during this period. It could of course be that the entity arose earlier but that the name does not occur earlier by chance. This would be especially the case if 'Israel' was their name for themselves but was not widely known to outsiders. Yet the chances are that the entity developed not long before it had an encounter with Merenptah. What was this entity? It seems to have been a group of people, judging by how it is treated in the 'Israel stela'. Where they grew up and how they came together is, however, not clear from LBA sources. It is unlikely that they arose in the Palestine hill country since this area was largely empty of settlement until the very end of the LBA and the beginning of Iron I.

The fact that in the Merenptah inscription 'Israel' is associated with several cities suggests that the number making up Israel was not great. On the other hand, it was sufficiently large to merit Merenptah's attention. A group which periodically raided Egyptian territory or supply routes would certainly attract the attention of the Egyptian administration. Considering the division between Israel and Judah attested in later sources, 'Israel' probably did not include those identified as 'Judah(ites)'. That a number of Israelite tribes are named in the 'Song of Deborah' (Judges 5) indicates that Israel was initially a tribal entity but not particularly unified. That is, the individual tribes were independent, though they could sometimes work together by agreement, especially when faced with an external threat. But Israel was not a state of any kind, only a collection of tribes, though they may have seen themselves as a kinship group.

Exactly how or why they came to form a state is uncertain, though there were probably multiple causes. Opposition to the Philistines was one possible reason but only one. The earliest state had the characteristics of what is often described as a chiefdom but also of a tribal state, headed by a military leader. A brief union of Israel with Judah took place under David but quickly evaporated after the death of his successor Solomon. This brings us to the end of our study. We have just begun the history of the two kingdoms, Israel and Judah, but that is another story. For it, one needs to consult histories of Israel.

Bibliography

Abbas, Mohamed Raafat. 2017. 'The Town of Yenoam in the Ramesside War Scenes and Texts of Karnak', *Cahiers de KARNAK* 16: 329–41.
Abbas, Mohamed Raafat. 2020. 'The Canaanite and Nubian Wars of Merenptah: Some Historical Notes', *Égypte Nilotique et Méditerranéenne* 13: 133–49.
Adler, William, and Paul Tuffin (ed. and trans.). 2002. *The Chronography of George Synkellos: A Byzantine Chronicle of Universal History from the Creation*. Oxford: Oxford University Press.
Agranat-Tamir, Lily, et al. 2020. 'The Genomic History of the Bronze Age Southern Levant', *Cell* 181 (28 May 2020): 1146–57.
Aharoni, Yohanan. 1960. 'Some Geographical Remarks concerning the Campaigns of Amenhotep II', *JNES* 19: 177–83.
Ahituv, Shmuel. 1984. *Canaanite Toponyms in Ancient Egyptian Documents*. Jerusalem: Magnes Press.
Ahlström, Gösta W. 1986. *Who Were the Israelites?* Winona Lake, IN: Eisenbrauns.
Ahlström, Gösta W. 1993a. *The History of Ancient Palestine from the Palaeolithic Period to Alexander's Conquest*. JSOTSup 146. Sheffield: Sheffield Academic Press.
Ahlström, Gösta W. 1993b. 'Pharaoh Shoshenq's Campaign to Palestine', in André Lemaire and Benedikt Otzen (eds), *History and Traditions of Early Israel: Studies Presented to Eduard Nielsen, May 8th 1993*, 1–16. VTSup 50. Leiden: Brill.
Ahlström, Gösta W., and Diana Edelman. 1985. 'Merneptah's Israel', *JNES* 44: 59–61.
Akkermans, Peter M. M. G., and Glenn M. Schwartz. 2003. *The Archaeology of Syria: From Complex Hunter-Gatherers to Early Urban Societies (ca. 16,000–300 BC)*. Cambridge World Archaeology. Cambridge: Cambridge University Press.
Albertz, Rainer. 1992. *A History of Israelite Religion in the Old Testament Period*. 2 vols. London: SCM Press. ET of *Geschichte der israelitischen Religion*. 2 vols. Das Alte Testament Deutsch Ergänzungsreihe 8. Göttingen: Vandenhoeck & Ruprecht, 1992.
Albright, William F. 1961. 'Abram the Hebrew: A New Archaeological Interpretation', *BASOR* 163: 36–54.
Albright, William F. 1964. 'The Eighteenth-century Princes of Byblos and the Chronology of Middle Bronze', *BASOR* 176: 38–46.
Albright, William F. 1965. 'Further Light on the History of Middle-Bronze Byblos', *BASOR* 179: 38–43.
Albright, William F. 1966. 'Remarks on the Chronology of Early Bronze IV–Middle Bronze IIA in Phoenicia and Syria-Palestine', *BASOR* 184: 26–35.
Allen, James P. 2008. 'The Historical Inscription of Khnumhotep at Dahshur: Preliminary Report', *BASOR* 352: 29–39.

Alt, Albrecht. 1954. 'Neue Berichte über Feldzüge von Pharaonen des Neuen Reiches nach Pälestina', *ZDPV* 70: 33–75.

Alt, Albrecht. 1966. 'The God of the Fathers', in Albrecht Alt, *Essays on Old Testament History and Religion*, 1–77. Oxford: Blackwell. ET of *Der Gott der Väter: Ein Beitrag zur Vorgeschichte der israelitischen Religion*. BWANT 48. Stuttgart: Kohlhammer, 1929.

Altman, Amnon. 1977. 'The Fate of Abdi-Ashirta', *UF* 9: 1–11.

Altman, Amnon. 2001. 'EA 59:27–29 and the Efforts of Mukiš, Nuḫašše and Niya to Establish a Common Front against Šuppiluliuma I', *UF* 33: 1–25.

Altman, Amnon. 2008. 'Ugarit's Political Standing in the Beginning of the 14th Century BCE Reconsidered', *UF* 40: 25–64.

Anbar, Moshé. 1991. *Les tribus amurrites de Mari*. OBO 108. Freiburg: Universitätsverlag. Göttingen: Vandenhoeck & Ruprecht.

Andrason, Alexander, and Juan-Pablo Vita. 2018. 'Amorite: A Northwest Semitic Language?', *JSS* 63: 19–58.

Anon. 2011. *Hittites, Mittanis and Aryans; Indo-Aryan Superstrate in Mitanni*. Http://docshare02.docshare.tips/files/5716/57160696.pdf (accessed 20 May 2021).

Archi, Alfonso. 1979. 'The Epigraphic Evidence from Ebla and the Old Testament', *Bib* 60: 556–66.

Archi, Alfonso. 1985. 'Mardu in the Ebla Texts', *Or* 54: 7–13.

Archi, Alfonso. 2015. *Ebla and its Archives: Texts, History, and Society*. Studies in Ancient Near Eastern Records 7. Berlin: de Gruyter.

Archi, Alfonso, and Maria Giovanna Biga. 2003. 'A Victory over Mari and the Fall of Ebla', *JCS* 55: 1–44.

Arnaud, Daniel. 1997. 'Prolégomènes à la rédaction d'une histoire d'Ougarit 1. Ougarit avant Suppiluliuma 1er', *SMEA* 39: 151–61.

Arnaud, Daniel. 1998. 'Prolégomènes à la rédaction d'une histoire d'Ougarit II: Les bordereaux de rois divinisés', *SMEA* 41: 153–73.

Artzy, Michal. 2013. 'On the Other "Sea Peoples"', in Ann E. Killebrew and Gunnar Lehmann (eds), *The Philistines and Other 'Sea Peoples' in Text and Archaeology*, 329–44. Society of Biblical Literature Archaeology and Biblical Studies 15. Atlanta, GA: Society of Biblical Literature.

Ash, Paul S. 1999. *David, Solomon and Egypt: A Reassessment*. JSOTSup 297. Sheffield: Sheffield Academic Press.

Aston, David A. 2004. 'Amphorae in New Kingdom Egypt', *Ägypten und Levante* 14: 175–213.

Astour, Michael C. 1963. 'Place-Names from the Kingdom of Alalaḫ in the North Syrian List of Thutmose III: A Study in Historical Topography', *JNES* 22: 220–41.

Astour, Michael C. 1972. 'Ḫattušiliš, Ḫalab, and Ḫanigalbat', *JNES* 31: 102–9.

Astour, Michael C. 1981. 'Ugarit and the Great Powers', in Gordon D. Young (ed.), *Ugarit in Retrospect: Fifty Years of Ugarit and Ugaritic*, 3–29. Winona Lake, IN: Eisenbrauns.

Astour, Michael C. 1992. 'An Outline of the History of Ebla (Part 1)', in Cyrus H. Gordon and Gary A. Rendsburg (eds), *Eblaitica: Essays on the Ebla Archives and Eblaite Language 3*, 3–82. Winona Lake, IN: Eisenbrauns.

Astour, Michael C. 2002. 'A Reconstruction of the History of Ebla (Part 2)', in Cyrus H. Gordon and Gary A. Rendsburg (eds), *Eblaitica: Essays on the Ebla Archives and Eblaite Language 4*, 57–95. Winona Lake, IN: Eisenbrauns.

Baer, Klaus. 1963. 'An Eleventh Dynasty Farmer's Letters to his Family', *JAOS* 83: 1–19.

Baines, John. 1982. 'Interpreting *Sinuhe*', *JEA* 68: 31–44.

Baines, John. 1995. 'Kingship, Definition of Culture, and Legitimation', in D. O'Connor and D. P. Silverman (eds), *Ancient Egyptian Kingship*, 3–47. Probleme der Ägyptologie 9. Leiden: Brill.

Barako, Tristan J. 2013. 'Philistines and Egyptians in Southern Coastal Canaan during the Early Iron Age', in Ann E. Killebrew and Gunnar Lehmann (eds), *The Philistines and Other 'Sea Peoples' in Text and Archaeology*, 37–51. Society of Biblical Literature Archaeology and Biblical Studies 15. Atlanta, GA: Society of Biblical Literature.

Barfield, Thomas J. 1990. 'Tribe and State Relations: The Inner Asian Perspective', in Philip S. Khoury and Joseph Kostiner (eds), *Tribes and State Formation in the Middle East*, 153–82. Berkeley: University of California Press.

Barkay, Gabriel. 1992. 'The Iron Age II-III', in Amnon Ben-Tor (ed.), *The Archaeology of Ancient Israel*, 302–73. Translated by R. Greenberg. New Haven, CT: Yale University Press.

Barr, James. 1974–75. 'Philo of Byblos and his "Phoenician History"', *BJRL* 57: 17–68.

Bartelmus, Alexa. 2010. 'Restoring the Past. A Historical Analysis of the Royal Temple Building Inscriptions from the Kassite Period', *Kaskal* 7: 143–71.

Bartelmus, Alexa, and Katja Sternitzke (eds). 2017. *Karduniaš: Babylonia under the Kassites, Volumes 1–2*. Untersuchungen zur Assyriologie und Vorderasiatischen Archäologie 11/1–2. Berlin: de Gruyter.

Bates, Daniel G. 1973. *Nomads and Farmers: A Study of the Yörük of Southeastern Turkey*. University of Michigan Museum of Anthropology Anthropological Papers Series 52. Ann Arbor: University of Michigan Press.

Becher, Rabbi Mordechai. n.d. 'The Ten Plagues – Live from Egypt'. *Ohr Somayach*: ohr.edu/yhiy/article.php/838 (accessed 6 June 2013).

Beckerath, Jürgen von. 1964. *Untersuchungen zur politischen Geschichte der Zweiten Zwischenzeit in Ägypten*. Ägyptologische Forschungen 23. Glückstadt: J. J. Augustin.

Beckerath, Jürgen von. 1984. *Handbuch der ägyptische Königsnamen*. Münchner Ägyptologische Studien 20. Munich: Deutscher Kunstverlag.

Beckman, Gary M. 1995. 'The Siege of Uršu Text (CTH 7) and Old Hittite Historiography', *JCS* 47: 23–34.

Beckman, Gary M. 1996. *Hittite Diplomatic Texts*. Edited by Harry A. Hoffner, Jr. SBLWAW 7. Atlanta, GA: Scholars Press.

Beckman, Gary M. 2001. 'Sargon and Naram-Sin in Hatti: Reflections of Mesopotamian Antiquity among the Hittites', in Dieter Kuhn and Helga Stahl (eds), *Die Gegenwart des Altertums: Formen und Funktionen des Altertumsbezugs in den Hochkulturen der Alten Welt*, 85–91. Heidelberg: edition forum.

Bell, Barbara. 1971. 'The Dark Ages in Ancient History. I. The First Dark Age in Egypt', *AJA* 75: 1–26.

Ben-Ami, Doron. 2001. 'The Iron Age I at Tel Hazor in Light of the Renewed Excavations', *IEJ* 51: 148–70.

Ben-Ami, Doron. 2014. 'Notes on the Iron IIA Settlement in Jerusalem in Light of Excavations in the Northwest of the City of David', *TA* 41: 3–19.

Ben-Dor Evian, Shirly. 2011. 'Shishak's Karnak Relief – More Than Just Name-Rings', in Shay Bar, Dan'el Kahn, and Judith J. Shirley (eds), *Egypt, Canaan and Israel: History, Ideology, Imperialism and Literature: Proceedings of a Conference at the University of Haifa, 3–7 May 2009*, 11–22. CHANE 51. Leiden: Brill.

Ben-Dor Evian, Shirly. 2016. 'The Battles between Ramesses III and the "Sea-Peoples": When, Where and Who? An Iconic Analysis of the Egyptian Reliefs', *ZÄS* 143: 151–68.

Ben-Dor Evian, Shirly. 2017. 'Ramesses III and the "Sea-Peoples": Towards a New Philistine Paradigm', *OJA* 36: 267–85.

Ben-Tor, Amnon. 1982. 'The Relations between Egypt and the Land of Canaan during the Third Millennium B.C.', *JJS* 33: 3–18.

Ben-Tor, Amnon. 1986. 'The Trade Relations of Palestine in the Early Bronze Age', *JESHO* 29: 1–27.

Ben-Tor, Amnon. 1991. 'New Light on the Relations between Egypt and Southern Palestine during the Early Bronze Age', *BASOR* 281: 3–10.

Ben-Tor, Amnon. 1998. 'The Fall of Canaanite Hazor – The "Who" and "When" Questions', in Seymour Gitin, Amihai Mazar, and Ephraim Stern (eds), *Mediterranean Peoples in Transition: Thirteenth to Early Tenth Centuries BCE, in Honor of Professor Trude Dothan*, 456–67. Jerusalem: Israel Exploration Society.

Ben-Tor, Amnon. 2000. 'Hazor and the Chronology of Northern Israel: A Reply to Israel Finkelstein', *BASOR* 317: 9–15.

Ben-Tor, Amnon (ed.). 1992. *The Archaeology of Ancient Israel*. Translated by R. Greenberg. New Haven, CT: Yale University Press.

Ben-Tor, Amnon, Sharon Zuckerman, Shlomit Bechar, and Débora Sandhaus (eds). 2017. *Hazor VII: The 1990–2012 Excavations, The Bronze Age*. Edited by Tsipi Kuper-Blau. Jerusalem: Israel Exploration Society, 2017.

Ben-Tor, Daphna, Susan J. Allen, and James P. Allen. 1999. 'Seals and Kings' [review of K. S. B. Ryholt, *The Political Situation in Egypt during the Second Intermediate Period c. 1800–1550 B. C.*], *BASOR* 315: 47–74.

Ben-Yosef, Erez. 2010. *Technology and Social Process: Oscillations in Iron Age Copper Production and Power in Southern Jordan*. PhD thesis at the University of California at San Diego. Https://escholarship.org/uc/item/5t72d1xp (accessed 1 September 2021).

Ben-Yosef, Erez. 2012. 'Environmental Constraints on Ancient Copper Production in the Aravah Valley: Implications of the Newly Discovered Site of Khirbet Manaʻiyah in Southern Jordan', *TA* 39: 186–202.

Ben-Yosef, Erez. 2019. 'The Architectural Bias in Current Biblical Archaeology', *VT* 69: 361–87.

Ben-Yosef, Erez, Thomas E. Levy, Thomas Higham, Mohammad Najjar, and Lisa Tauxe. 2010. 'The Beginning of Iron Age Copper Production in the Southern Levant: New Evidence from Khirbat al-Jariya, Faynan, Jordan', *Antiquity* 84: 724–46.

Ben-Yosef, Erez, Ron Shaar, Lisa Tauxe, and Hagai Ron. 2012. 'A New Chronological Framework for Iron Age Copper Production at Timna (Israel)', *BASOR* 367: 31–71.

Benz, Brendon C. 2016. *The Land before the Kingdom of Israel: A History of the Southern Levant and the People Who Populated It*. History, Archaeology, and Culture of the Levant 7. Winona Lake, IN: Eisenbrauns.

Betancourt, Philip P. 1997. 'Relations between the Aegean and the Hyksos at the End of the Middle Bronze Age', in Eliezer D. Oren (ed.), *The Hyksos: New Historical and Archaeological Perspectives*, 429–32. University Museum Monograph 96. University Museum Symposium Series 8. Philadelphia, PA: University of Pennsylvania, The University Museum.

Bienkowski, Piotr. 1992a. 'The Beginning of the Iron Age in Southern Jordan: A Framework', in Piotr Bienkowski (ed.), *Early Edom and Moab: The Beginning of the Iron Age in Southern Jordan*, 1–12. Sheffield Archaeological Monographs 7. Sheffield: J. R. Collis Publications.

Bienkowski, Piotr. 1992b. 'The Date of Sedentary Occupation in Edom: Evidence from Umm el-Biyara, Tawilan and Buseirah', in Piotr Bienkowski (ed.), *Early Edom and Moab: The Beginning of the Iron Age in Southern Jordan*, 99–112. Sheffield Archaeological Monographs 7. Sheffield: J. R. Collis Publications.

Bienkowski, Piotr (ed.). 1992. *Early Edom and Moab: The Beginning of the Iron Age in Southern Jordan*. Sheffield Archaeological Monographs 7. Sheffield: J. R. Collis Publications.

Bietak, Manfred. 1987. 'Comments on the "Exodus"', in Anson F. Rainey (ed.), *Egypt, Israel, Sinai: Archaeological and Historical Relationships in the Biblical Period*, 163–71. Tel Aviv University Kaplan Project on the History of Israel and Egypt. Tel Aviv University.

Bietak, Manfred. 1996. *Avaris, The Capital of the Hyksos: Recent Excavations at Tell el-Dabʻa*. The First Raymond and Beverly Sackler Foundation Distinguished Lecture in Egyptology. London: British Museum Press.

Bietak, Manfred. 1997. 'Avaris, Capital of the Hyksos Kingdom: New Results of Excavations', in Eliezer D. Oren (ed.), *The Hyksos: New Historical and Archaeological Perspectives*, 87–139. University Museum Monograph 96. University Museum Symposium Series 8. Philadelphia, PA: University of Pennsylvania, The University Museum.

Bietak, Manfred. 2001. 'Hyksos', *OEAE* 2:136–43.

Bietak, Manfred. 2006. 'The Predecessors of the Hyksos', in Seymour Gitin, J. Edward Wright, and J. P. Dessel (eds), *Confronting the Past: Archaeological and Historical Essays on Ancient Israel in Honor of William G. Dever*, 285–93. Winona Lake, IN: Eisenbrauns.

Bietak, Manfred. 2010. 'From Where Came the Hyksos and Where Did They Go?', in Marcel Marée (ed.), *The Second Intermediate Period (Thirteenth–Seventeenth Dynasties): Current Research, Future Prospects*, 139–81. OLA 192. Leuven: Peeters.

Bietak, Manfred. 2011. 'The Aftermath of the Hyksos in Avaris', in Rakefet Sela-Sheffy and Gideon Toury (eds), *Culture Contacts and the Making of Cultures: Papers in Homage to Itamar Even-Zohar*, 19–46. Tel Aviv University Press.

Bimson, John J. 1981. *Redating the Exodus and Conquest*. 2nd edn. JSOTSup 5. Sheffield: Sheffield Academic Press.

Bin-Nun, S. R. 1974. 'Who Was Tahurwaili, the Great Hittite King?', *JCS* 26: 112–20.

Bloch-Smith, Elizabeth. 2003. 'Israelite Ethnicity in Iron I: Archaeology Preserves What Is Remembered and What Is Forgotten In Israel's History', *JBL* 122: 401–25.

Bloch-Smith, Elizabeth, and Beth Alpert Nakhai. 1999. 'A Landscape Comes to Life: The Iron I Period', *NEA* 62: 62–92, 101–27.

Blum, Erhard. 2020. 'The Israelite Tribal System: Literary Fiction or Social Reality?', in J. J. Krause, O. Sergi, and K. Weingut (eds), *Saul, Benjamin, and the Emergence of Monarchy in Israel: Biblical and Archaeological Perspectives*, 201–22. Ancient Israel and its Literature 40. Atlanta, GA: SBL.

Boivin, Odette. 2018. *The First Dynasty of the Sealand in Mesopotamia*. Studies in Ancient Near Eastern Records 20. Berlin: de Gruyter.

Bordreuil, Pierre (ed.). 1991. *Une bibliotheque au sud de la ville: les textes de la 34e campagne (1973)*. RSO 7. Paris: Editions Recherche sur les Civilisations.

Bordreuil, Pierre, and Dennis Pardee. 1982. 'Le rituel funéraire ougaritique RS. 34.126', *Syria* 59: 21–8.

Brand, Peter J. 2000. *The Monuments of Seti I: Epigraphic, Historical and Art Historical Analysis*. PdÄ 16. Leiden: Brill.

Breasted, James Henry. 1906–7. *Ancient Records of Egypt: Historical Documents from the Earliest Times to the Persian Conquest, Edited and Translated with Commentary, Vols 1–5*. Chicago: University of Chicago Press. Reprinted London: Histories and Mysteries of Man, 1988.

Brettler, Marc Zvi. 1995. *The Creation of History in Ancient Israel*. London/New York: Routledge.

Bright, John. 1980. *A History of Israel*. 3rd edn. Philadelphia, PA: Westminster.

Brinkman, John A. 1963. 'Provincial Administration in Babylonia under the Second Dynasty of Isin', *JESHO* 6: 233–42.

Brinkman, John A. 1968. *A Political History of Post-Kassite Babylonia 1158–722 B.C.* AnOr 43. Rome: Pontifical Biblical Institute.

Brinkman, John A. 1976. *Materials and Studies for Kassite History, Vol. 1: A Catalogue of Cuneiform Sources Pertaining to Specific Monarchs of the Kassite Dynasty*. Chicago: Oriental Institute of the University of Chicago.

Brinkman, John A. 1980. 'Kasitten (*Kaššû*)', *RlA* 5:464–73.

Brinkman, John A. 1997. 'Meerland (Sealand)', *RlA* 8:6–10.

Brinkman, John A. 1998–2001. 'Nebukadnezar I', *RlA* 9:192–4.

Brooke, George J. 1979. 'The Textual, Formal and Historical Significance of Ugaritic Letter RS 34.124 (= *KTU* 2.72)', *UF* 11: 69–87.

Brooke, George J., Adrian H. W. Curtis, and John F. Healey (eds). 1994. *Ugarit and the Bible: Proceedings of the International Symposium on Ugarit and the Bible, Manchester, September 1992*. Ugaritisch-Biblische Literatur 11. Münster: Ugarit-Verlag.

Broshi, Magen, and Israel Finkelstein. 1992. 'The Population of Palestine in Iron Age II', *BASOR* 287: 47–60.

Broshi, Magen, and Ram Gophna. 1986. 'Middle Bronze Age II Palestine: Its Settlements and Population', *BASOR* 261: 73–90.

Bryan, Betsy M. 1991. *The Reign of Thutmose IV*. Baltimore: Johns Hopkins University Press.

Bryan, Betsy M. 2000. 'The Egyptian Perspective on Mittani', in Raymond Cohen and Raymond Westbrook (eds). 2000. *Amarna Diplomacy: The Beginnings of International Relations*, 71–84. Baltimore: Johns Hopkins University Press.

Bryce, Trevor R. 1979. 'The Role of the Lukka People in Late Bronze Age Anatolia', *Antichthon* 13: 1–11.

Bryce, Trevor R. 1981. 'Ḫattušili I and the Problems of the Royal Succession in the Hittite Kingdom', *AS* 31: 9–17.

Bryce, Trevor R. 2005. *The Kingdom of the Hittites*. Oxford: Oxford University Press, 2nd edn.

Bryce, Trevor R. 2012. *The World of the Neo-Hittite Kingdoms: A Political and Military History*. Oxford: Oxford University Press.

Bryce, Trevor. 2014. *Ancient Syria: A Three Thousand Year History*. Oxford: Oxford University Press.

Buccellati, Giorgio. 1966. *The Amorites of the Ur III Period*. Pubblicazioni del Seminario di Semitistica: Richerche 1. Naples: Istituto Orientale di Napoli.

Buccellati, Giorgio. 1992. 'Ebla and the Amorites', in Cyrus H. Gordon and Gary A. Rendsburg (eds), *Eblaitica: Essays on the Ebla Archives and Eblaite Language 3*, 83–104. Winona Lake, IN: Eisenbrauns.

Buccellati, Giorgio. 1997. 'Amorites', *OEANE* 1: 107–11.

Buck, Mary E. 2020. *The Amorite Dynasty of Ugarit: Historical Implications of Linguistic and Archaeological Parallels*. Studies in the Archaeology and History of the Levant 8. Leiden: Brill.

Bunimovitz, Shlomo. 1990. 'Problems in the "Ethnic" Identity of the Philistine Material Culture', *TA* 17: 210–22.

Bunimovitz, Shlomo. 1998. 'On the Edge of Empires – Late Bronze Age (1500–1200 BCE)', in Thomas E. Levy (ed.), *The Archaeology of Society in the Holy Land*, 320–31. New Approaches in Anthropological Archaeology. London: Leicester University Press, 2nd edn.

Bunimovitz, Shlomo. 2019. '"Canaan is your Land and its Kings Are your Servants": Conceptualizing the Late Bronze Age Egyptian Government in the Southern Levant', in Assaf Yasur-Landau, Eric H. Cline, and Yorke M. Rowan (eds), *The Social Archaeology of the Levant: From Prehistory to the Present*, 265–79. Cambridge: Cambridge University Press.

Bunimovitz, Shlomo, and Avraham Faust. 2003. 'Building Identity: The Four Room House and the Israelite Mind', in William G. Dever and Seymour Gitin (eds), *Symbiosis, Symbolism, and the Power of the Past: Canaan, Ancient Israel, and their Neighbors from the Late Bronze Age through Roman Palaestina: Proceedings of the Centennial Symposium W. F. Albright Institute of Archaeological Research and the American Schools of Oriental Research Jerusalem, May 29–31, 2000*, 411–23. Winona Lake, IN: Eisenbrauns.

Bunimovitz, Shlomo, and Zvi Ledermann. 2008. 'A Border Case: Beth-Shemesh and the Rise of Ancient Israel', in Lester L. Grabbe (ed.), *Israel in Transition: From Late Bronze II to Iron IIA (c. 1250–850 BCE), Volume 1 The Archaeology*, 21–31. LHBOTS 491 = ESHM 7. London/New York: T&T Clark International.

Bunimovitz, Shlomo, and Zvi Lederman. 2013. 'Solving a Century-Old Puzzle: New Discoveries at the Middle Bronze Gate of Tel Beth-Shemesh', *PEQ* 145: 6–24.

Burke, Aaron A. 2021. *The Amorites and the Bronze Age Near East: The Making of a Regional Identity*. Cambridge: Cambridge University Press.

Burke, Aaron A., Krystal V. Lords, Martin Peilstöcker, Kyle H. Keimer, and George A. Pierce. 2010. 'Egyptians in Jaffa: A Portrait of Egyptian Presence in Jaffa during the Late Bronze Age', *NEA* 73: 2–30.

Burke, Aaron A., Amy B. Karoll, George A. Pierce, Nadia Ben-Marzouk, Jacob C. Damm, Andrew J. Danielson, Brett Kaufman, Krystal V. Lords Pierce, Felix Höflmayer, Brian Damiata, and Heidi Dodgen Fessler. 2016. 'Excavations of the New Kingdom Fortress in Jaffa, 2011–2014: Traces of Resistance to Egyptian Rule in Canaan', *AJA* 121: 85–133.

Burstein, Stanley M. 1978. *The Babyloniaca of Berossus*. SANE 1/5. Malibu, CA: Undena.

Cahill, Jane M. 2003. 'Jerusalem at the Time of the United Monarchy: The Archaeological Evidence', in Andrew G. Vaughn and Ann E. Killebrew (eds), *Jerusalem in Bible and Archaeology: The First Temple Period*, 13–80. SBLSymS 18. Atlanta, GA: Society of Biblical Literature.

Cahill, Jane M. 2004. 'Jerusalem in David and Solomon's Time', *BAR* 30, no. 6: 20–31, 62–3.

Cancik-Kirschbaum, Eva, Nicole Brisch, Jesper Eidem (eds). 2014. *Constituent, Confederate, and Conquered Space; The Emergence of the Mittani State*. Topoi – Berliner Studien der Alten Welt 17. Berlin: de Gruyter.

Caquot, André, Jean-Michel de Tarragon, and Jesús-Luis Cunchillos. 1989. *Textes ougaritiques, Tome II: Textes religieux et rituels; Correspondance*. Littératures anciennes du Proche-Orient 14. Paris: Cerf (= LAPO 14).

Caton, Steven C. 1990. 'Anthropological Theories of Tribe and State Formation in the Middle East: Ideology and the Semiotics of Power', in Philip S. Khoury and Joseph Kostiner (eds), *Tribes and State Formation in the Middle East*, 74–108. Berkeley, CA: University of California Press.

Chaney, Marvin L. 1983. 'Ancient Palestinian Peasant Movements and the Formation of Premonarchic Israel', in David Noel Freedman and D. F. Graf (eds), *Palestine in Transition: The Emergence of Ancient Israel*, 39–90. Social World of Biblical Antiquity Series 2. Sheffield: Sheffield Academic Press.

Charpin, Dominique, and Jean-Marie Durand. 1986. '"Fils de Sim'al": Les origines tribales des rois de Mari', *RdA* 80: 141–83.

Chatty, Dawn. 1980. 'The Pastoral Family and the Truck', in Philip Carl Salzman (ed.), *When Nomads Settle: Processes of Sedentarization as Adaptation and Response*, 80–94. New York: Praeger.

Chavalas, Mark W. (ed.). 2006. *The Ancient Near East: Historical Sources in Translation*. Blackwell Sourcebooks in Ancient History. Oxford: Blackwell.

Childs, Brevard S. 1970. *Biblical Theology in Crisis*. Philadelphia, PA: Westminster Press.

Clark, W. Malcolm. 1977. 'The Patriarchal Traditions: The Biblical Traditions', in John H. Hayes and J. Maxwell Miller (eds), *Israelite and Judaean History*, 120–48. OTL. Philadelphia, PA: Westminster Press).

Clements, Ronald E. 1974. 'אברהם *'abhrāhām'*, *TDOT* 1:52–8.

Cline, Eric H. 2014. *1177 B.C.: The Year Civilization Collapsed*. Turning Points in Ancient History. Princeton, NJ: Princeton University Press.

Cline, Eric H. 2016. Review of E. Stern, *The Material Culture of the Northern Sea Peoples in Israel, JAOS* 136: 197–9.

Cline, Eric H., and David O'Connor (eds). 2006. *Thutmose III: A New Biography* (Ann Arbor, MI: University of Michigan Press).

Cline, Eric H., and David O'Connor. 2003. 'The Mystery of the "Sea Peoples"', in David O'Connor and Stephen Quirke (eds), *Mysterious Lands*, 107–38. Encounters with Ancient Egypt. London: UCL Press.

Cline, Eric H., and David O'Connor (eds). 2012. *Ramesses III: The Life and Times of Egypt's Last Hero*. Ann Arbor, MI: University of Michigan Press.

Cohen, Raymond, and Raymond Westbrook (eds). 2000. *Amarna Diplomacy: The Beginnings of International Relations*. Baltimore: Johns Hopkins University Press.

Cohen, Rudolf. 1981. 'Excavations at Kadesh-barnea 1976–1978', *BA* 44: 93–107.

Cohen, Rudolf. 1997. 'Qadesh-barnea', in *The Oxford Encyclopedia of Archaeology in the Near East*, 4:365–7. Edited by Eric M. Meyers. 5 vols. Oxford: Oxford University Press.

Cohen, Susan L. 2002. *Canaanites, Chronologies, and Connections: The Relationship of Middle Bronze IIA Canaan to Middle Kingdom Egypt*. Harvard Semitic Museum Publication 3. Winona Lake, IN: Eisenbrauns.

Coldstream, Nicolas. 2003. 'Some Aegean Reactions to the Chronological Debate in the Southern Levant', *TA* 30: 247–58.

Collins, Billie Jean. 2007. 'The Bible, the Hittites, and the Construction of the "Other"', in Detlev Groddek and Marina Zorman (eds), *Tabularia Hethaeorum: Hethitologische Beitrage, Silvin Kosak zum 65. Geburtstag*, 153–61. Dresdner Beitrage zur Hethitologie 25. Wiesbaden: Harrassowitz.

Conybeare, F. C., J. Rendel Harris, and Agnes Smith Lewis. 1913. *The Story of Aḥiḳar from the Aramaic, Syriac, Arabic, Armenian, Ethiopic, Old Turkish, Greek and Slavonic Versions*. 2nd edn. Cambridge: Cambridge University Press.

Cooper, Lisa. 2010. 'States of Hegemony: Early Forms of Political Control in Syria during the Third Millennium BC', in Diane Bolger and Louise C. Maguire (eds), *The Development of Pre-State Communities in the Ancient Near East: Studies in Honour of Edgar Peltenburg*, 87–94. British Association for Near Eastern Archaeology 2. Oxford: Oxbow Books.

Coote, Robert, and Keith W. Whitelam. 1987. *The Emergence of Early Israel in Historical Perspective*. Social World of Biblical Antiquity 5. Sheffield: Sheffield Academic Press.

Cornelius, Friedrich. 1976. *Geschichte der Hethiter: mit besonderer Berücksichtigung der geographischen Verhältnisse und der Rechtsgeschichte*. Darmstadt: Wissenschaftliche Buchgesellschaft.

Couroyer, B. 1971. 'Ceux-qui-sont-sur-le-sable: Les Hériou-Shâ', *RevB* 78: 558–75.

Creamer, Winifred, and Jonathan Haas. 1985. 'Tribe versus Chiefdom in Lower Central America', *American Antiquity* 50: 738–54.

Croatto, J. Severino. 1966. '*'Abrek* "Intendant" dans Gén. XLI 41, 43', *VT* 16: 113–15.

Cross, Frank M., Jr. 1973. *Canaanite Myth and Hebrew Epic*. Cambridge, MA: Harvard University Press.

Cross, Frank M., Jr, and David Noel Freedman. 1955. 'The Song of Miriam', *JNES* 14: 237–50.

Cumming, Barbara (trans. and ed.). 1982. *Egyptian Historical Records of the Later Eighteenth Dynasty, Fascicle I*. From the Original Hieroglyphic Text as Published in W. Helck, *Urkunden der 18.Dynastie*, Heft 17–19. Warminster: Aris & Phillips.

Cumming, Barbara (trans. and ed.). 1984a. *Egyptian Historical Records of the Later Eighteenth Dynasty, Fascicle II*. From the Original Hieroglyphic Text as Published in W. Helck, *Urkunden der 18.Dynastie*, Heft 17–19. Warminster: Aris & Phillips.

Cumming, Barbara (trans. and ed.). 1984b. *Egyptian Historical Records of the Later Eighteenth Dynasty, Fascicle III*. From the Original Hieroglyphic Text as Published in W. Helck, *Urkunden der 18.Dynastie*, Heft 17–19. Warminster: Aris & Phillips.

Dagan, Yehuda. 2004. 'Results of the Survey: Settlement Patterns in the Lachish Regions', in David Ussishkin (ed.), *The Renewed Archaeological Excavations at Lachish (1973–1994)*, 2672–90. Vols. 1–5. Tel Aviv University Ronia and Marco Nadler Institute of Archaeology, Monograph Series 22. Tel Aviv: Emery and Claire Yass Publications in Archaeology.

Dalley, Stephanie. 2002. *Mari and Karana: Two Old Babylonian Cities*. Piscataway, NJ: Gorgias Press, 2nd edn.

Davies, Benedict G. (trans. and ed.). 1992. *Egyptian Historical Records of the Later Eighteenth Dynasty, Fascicle IV*. From the Original Hieroglyphic Text as Published in W. Helck, *Urkunden der 18.Dynastie*, Heft 20. Warminster: Aris & Phillips.

Davies, Benedict G. (trans. and ed.). 1994. *Egyptian Historical Records of the Later Eighteenth Dynasty, Fascicle V*. From the Original Hieroglyphic Text as Published in W. Helck, *Urkunden der 18.Dynastie*, Heft 21. Warminster: Aris & Phillips.

Davies, Benedict G. (trans. and ed.). 1995. *Egyptian Historical Records of the Later Eighteenth Dynasty, Fascicle VI*. From the Original Hieroglyphic Text as Published in W. Helck, *Urkunden der 18.Dynastie*, Heft 22. Warminster: Aris & Phillips.

Davies, Benedict G. 1997. *Egyptian Historical Inscriptions of the Nineteenth Dynasty*. Documenta Mundi: Aegyptiaca 2. Jonsered, Sweden: Paul Åström.

Davies, David Peter. 2003. *The Taking of Joppa*. A thesis submitted for the degree of MPhil in Archaeology at the University of Durham. Http://etheses.dur.ac.uk/3997/ (accessed 13 September 2021).

Davies, Graham I. 1979. *Way of the Wilderness: A Geographical Study of the Wilderness Itineraries in the Old Testament*. Society for Old Testament Study Monograph Series 5. Cambridge: Cambridge University Press.

Davies, Graham I. 1983. 'The Wilderness Itineraries and the Composition of the Pentateuch', *VT* 33: 1–13.

Davies, Graham I. 1990. 'The Wilderness Itineraries and Recent Archaeological Research', in J. A. Emerton (ed.), *Studies in the Pentateuch*, 161–75. Vetus Testamentum Supplement 41. Leiden: Brill.

Davies, Graham I. 2004. 'Was There an Exodus?', in John Day (ed.), *In Search of Pre-exilic Israel: Proceedings of the Oxford Old Testament Seminar*, 23–40. JSOTSup 406. London/New York: T&T Clark International.

Davis, Brent, Aren M. Maeir, and Louise A. Hitchcock. 2015. 'Disentangling Entangled Objects: Iron Age Inscriptions from Philistia as a Reflection of Cultural Processes', *IEJ* 65: 140–66.

Dearman, J. Andrew. 1992. 'Settlement Patterns and the Beginning of the Iron Age in Moab', in Piotr Bienkowski (ed.), *Early Edom and Moab: The Beginning of the Iron Age in Southern Jordan*, 65–75. Sheffield Archaeological Monographs 7. Sheffield: J. R. Collis Publications.

Dever, William G. 1977. 'The Patriarchal Traditions: Palestine in the Second Millennium BCE: The Archaeological Picture', in John H. Hayes and J. Maxwell Miller (eds), *Israelite and Judaean History*, 70–120. OTL. Philadelphia, PA: Westminster Press.

Dever, William G. 1987. 'The Middle Bronze Age – The Zenith of the Urban Canaanite Era', *BA* 50: 148–77.

Dever, William G. 1992a. 'How to Tell a Canaanite from an Israelite', in Hershel Shanks (ed.), *The Rise of Ancient Israel: Symposium at the Smithsonian Institution, October 26, 1991*, 27–60 (plus reply to responses, pp. 79–85). Smithsonian Resident Associate Program. Washington, DC: Biblical Archaeology Society.

Dever, William G. 1992b. 'Israel, History of (Archaeology and the Israelite "Conquest")', *ABD* 3:545–58.

Dever, William G. 1997. 'Is There any Archaeological Evidence for the Exodus?', in Ernest S. Frerichs and Leonard H. Lesko (eds), *Exodus: The Egyptian Evidence*, 67–86. Winona Lake, IN: Eisenbrauns.

Dever, William G. 1998. 'Israelite Origins and the "Nomadic Ideal": Can Archaeology Separate Fact from Fiction?', in Seymour Gitin, Amihai Mazar, and Ephraim Stern (eds), *Mediterranean Peoples in Transition: Thirteenth to Early Tenth Centuries BCE, in Honor of Professor Trude Dothan*, 220–37. Jerusalem: Israel Exploration Society.

Dever, William G. 2001. *What Did the Biblical Writers Know and When Did They Know it? What Archaeology Can Tell Us about the Reality of Ancient Israel*. Grand Rapids, MI: Eerdmans.

Dever, William G. 2003. *Who Were the Early Israelites and Where Did They Come From?* Grand Rapids, MI: Eerdmans.

Dever, William G. 2009. 'Merenptah's "Israel," the Bible's, and Ours', in J. David Schloen (eds), *Exploring the Longue Durée: Essays in Honor of Lawrence E. Stager*, 89–96. Winona Lake, IN: Eisenbrauns.

Dever, William G. 2017. *Beyond the Texts: An Archaeological Portrait of Ancient Israel and Judah*. Atlanta, GA: SBL Press.

Diebner, B.-J. 1995. 'Wann sang Deborah ihr Lied? Überlegungen zu zwei der ältesten Texte des TNK (Ri 4 und 5)', *ACEBT* 14: 106–30.

Dietrich, Manfried. 2001. 'Der Brief des Kommandeurs Šumiyānu an den ugaritischen König Niqmepaʻ (RS 20.33): Ein Bericht über Aktivitäten nach der Schlacht bei Qadeš 1275 v. Chr.', *UF* 33: 117–91.

Dietrich, Walter. 2007. *The Early Monarchy in Israel: The Tenth Century B.C.E.* Society of Biblical Literature Biblical Encyclopedia 3. Translated by Joachim Vette. Atlanta, GA: Society of Biblical Literature. Revised and expanded from *Die frühe Königszeit in Israel: 10. Jahrhundert v. Chr.* Biblische Enzyklopädie 3. Stuttgart: Kohlhammer, 1997.

Dietrich, Walter. 2011. *Samuel: Teilband 1: 1 Sam 1–12*. BKAT VIII/1. Neukirchen-Vluyn: Neukirchener Theologie.

Dietrich, Walter. 2012. 'David and the Philistines: Literature and History', in Gershon Galil, Ayelet Gilboa, Aren M. Maeir, and Dan'el Kahn (eds), *The Ancient Near East in the 12th–10th Centuries BCE: Culture and History: Proceedings of the International Conference held at the University of Haifa, 2–5 May, 2010*, 79–98. AOAT 392. Münster: Ugarit-Verlag.

Dietrich, Walter. 2015. *Samuel: Teilband 2: 1 Sam 13–26*. BKAT VIII/2. Neukirchen-Vluyn: Neukirchener Theologie.

Dietrich, Walter. 2019. *Samuel: Teilband 3: 1 Sam 27–2 Sam 8*. BKAT VIII/3. Neukirchen-Vluyn: Neukirchener Theologie.

Dijkstra, Meindert. 2011. 'Origins of Israel between History and Ideology', in Bob Becking and Lester L. Grabbe (eds), *Between Evidence and Ideology: Essays on the History of Ancient Israel Read at the Joint Meeting of the Society for Old Testament Study and the Oud Testamentisch Werkgezelschap, Lincoln, July 2009*, 41–82. OTS 59. Leiden: Brill.

Dijkstra, Meindert. 2016. 'Canaan in the Transition from the Late Bronze to the Early Iron Age from an Egyptian Perspective', in Lester L. Grabbe (ed.), *The Land of Canaan in the Late Bronze Age*, 59–89. LHBOTS 636. ESHM 10. London and New York: Bloomsbury T&T Clark.

Dinçol, Ali M., Belkis Dinçol, J. David Hawkins, and Gernot Wilhelm. 1993. 'The "Cruciform Seal" from Boğazköy-Hattusa', *Istanbuler Mitteilungen* 43: 87–106.

Dion, Paul E. 1997. *Les Araméens à l'âge du fer: histoire politique et structures sociales*. Etudes bibliques, nouvelle série no. 34. Paris: Librairie Lecoffre, Gabalda.

Dobbs-Allsopp, F. W., J. J. M. Roberts, C. L. Seow, and R. E. Whitaker (eds). 2005. *Hebrew Inscriptions: Texts from the Biblical Period of the Monarchy with Concordance*. New Haven, CT: Yale University Press.

Donner, Herbert. 1969. 'Adoption oder Legitimation? Erwägungen zur Adoption im Alten Testament auf dem Hintergrund der altorientalischen Rechte', *Oriens Antiquus* 8: 87–119.

Dossin, Georges. 1938. 'Les Archives épistolaires du Palais de Mari', *Syria* 19: 105–26.

Dossin, Georges. 1939a. 'Iamḫad et Qatanum', *RdA* 36: 46–54.

Dossin, Georges. 1939b. 'Les archives économiques du palais de Mari', *Syria* 20: 97–113.

Dossin, Georges. 1955. 'L'inscription de fondation de Iaḫdun-Lim, roi de Mari', *Syria* 32: 1–28.

Dossin, Georges. 1956. 'Une lettre de Iarîm-Lim, roi d'Alep, à Iašûb-Iaḫad, roi de Dîr', *Syria* 33: 63–9.

Dossin, Georges. 1973. 'Une mention de Cananéens dans une lettre de Mari', *Syria* 50: 277–82.

Dothan, Trude, and David Ben-Shlomo. 2013. 'Mycenaean IIIC:1 Pottery in Philistia: Four Decades of Research', in Ann E. Killebrew and Gunnar Lehmann (eds), *The Philistines and Other 'Sea Peoples' in Text and Archaeology*, 29–35. Society of Biblical Literature Archaeology and Biblical Studies 15. Atlanta, GA: Society of Biblical Literature.

Dothan, Trude, and Alexander Zukerman. 2004. 'A Preliminary Study of the Mycenaean IIIC:1 Pottery Assemblages from Tel Miqne-Ekron and Ashdod', *BASOR* 333: 1–54.

Drews, Robert. 1988. *The Coming of the Greeks: Indo-European Conquests in the Aegean and the Near East*. Princeton, NJ: Princeton University Press.

Drews, Robert. 1993. *The End of the Bronze Age: Changes in Warfare and the Catastrophe ca. 1200 B.C.* Princeton, NJ: Princeton University Press.

Drews, Robert. 1998. 'Canaanites and Philistines', *JSOT* 81: 39–61.

Drews, Robert. 2000. 'Medinet Habu: Oxcarts, Ships, and Migration Theories', *JNES* 59: 161–90.

Dunand, Maurice. 1937. *Fouilles de Byblos: tome 1, 1926–1932: Atlas*. Bibliothéque Archéologique et Historique 24. Paris: Paul Geuthner.

Durand, Jean-Marie. 1997. *Documents épistolaires du palais de Mari,1*. Littératures anciennes du Proche-Orient 16. Paris: Cerf (= LAPO 16).

Durand, Jean-Marie. 1998. *Documents épistolaires du palais de Mari, 2*. Littératures anciennes du Proche-Orient 17. Paris: Cerf (= LAPO 17).

Durand, Jean-Marie. 2000. *Documents épistolaires du palais de Mari, 3*. Littératures anciennes du Proche-Orient 18. Paris: Cerf (= LAPO 18).

Durand, Jean-Marie. 2012. 'Sargon a-t-il détruit la ville de Mari ?', *RdA* 106: 117–32.

Dušek, Jan, and Jana Mynářová (eds). 2019. *Aramaean Borders: Defining Aramaean Territories in the 10th–8th Centuries B.C.E.* CHANE 101. Leiden: Brill.

Ebeling, Erich, Bruno Meissner, et al. (eds). 1932–2018. *Reallexikon der Assyriologie und Vorderasiatischen Archäologie, Vols 1–16*. Berlin/Boston: de Gruyter.

Edel, Elmar. 1953. 'Die Stelen Amenophis' II. aus Karnak und Memphis mit dem Bericht über die asiatischen Feldzüge des Königs', *ZDPV* 69: 97–176.

Edelman, Diana V. 1986. 'Saul's Battle Against Amaleq (1 Sam. 15)', *JSOT* 35: 71–84.

Edelman, Diana V. 1991. *King Saul in the Historiography of Judah*. JSOTSup 121. Sheffield: Sheffield Academic Press.

Edelman, Diana V. (ed.). 1995. *You Shall not Abhor an Edomite for he is your Brother: Edom and Seir in History and Tradition*. SBLABS 3. Atlanta, GA: Scholars Press.

Edelman, Diana V. 1996a. 'Saul ben Kish in History and Tradition', in Volkmar Fritz and Philip R. Davies (eds), *The Origins of the Ancient Israelite States*, 142–59. JSOTSup 228. Sheffield: Sheffield Academic Press.

Edelman, Diana V. 1996b. 'Ethnicity and Early Israel', in Mark G. Brett (ed.), *Ethnicity and the Bible*, 42–7. BIS 19; Leiden: Brill.

Edelman, Diana V. 1998. 'The Creation of Exodus 14–15', in Irne Shirun-Grumach (eds), *Jerusalem Studies in Egyptology*, 137–58. Ägypten und Altes Testament 40. Wiesbaden: Harrassowitz.

Ehrlich, Carl S. 1996. *The Philistines in Transition: A History from ca. 1000–730 B.C.E.* SHCANE 10. Leiden: Brill.

Eichler, B. L. 1977. 'Another Look at the Nuzi Sistership Contracts', in Maria de Jong Ellis (ed.), *Essays on the Ancient Near East in Memory of Jacob Joel Finkelstein*, 45–59. Memoirs of the Connecticut Academy of Arts and Sciences 19. Hamden, CT: Archon Books.

Eissfeldt, Otto. 1975. 'Palestine in the Time of the Nineteenth Dynasty: (a) The Exodus and Wanderings', in I. E. S. Edwards, C. J. Gadd, N. G. L. Hammond and E. Sollberger (eds), *The Cambridge Ancient History: Volume II, Part 2 History of the Middle East and the Aegean Region c. 1380–1000 B.C.*, 307–30. 3rd edn. Cambridge: Cambridge University Press.

Elayi, Josette. 2018. *The History of Phoenicia*. Translated by Andrew Plummer. Atlanta, GA: Lockwood Press. ET of *Hisoire de la Phénicie*. Rev. edn. Paris: Perrin, 2018.

Eliyahu-Behar, Adi, Naama Yahalom-Mack, Sana Shilstein, Alexander Zukerman, Cynthia Shafer-Elliott, Aren M. Maeir, Elisabetta Boaretto, Israel Finkelstein, and Steve Weiner. 2012. 'Iron and Bronze Production in Iron Age IIA Philistia: New Evidence from Tell es-Safi/Gath, Israel', *Journal of Archaeological Science* 39: 255–67.

Enmarch, Roland. 2008. *A World Upturned: Commentary on and Analysis of* The Dialogue of Ipuwer and the Lord of All. Oxford: Oxford University Press, for the British Academy.

Epstein, Claire. 1963. 'A New Appraisal of Some Lines from a Long-Known Papyrus', *JEA* 49: 49–56.

Erman, Adolf, and Hermann Grapow (eds). 1926–63. *Wörterbuch der ägyptischen Sprache*. 6 vols. Leipzig: Hinrichs.

Fantalkin, Alexander, and Israel Finkelstein. 2006. 'The Sheshonq I Campaign and the 8th-Century BCE Earthquake – More on the Archaeology and History of the South in the Iron I–IIA', *TA* 33: 18–42.

Farino, Giulio. 1938. *Papiro dei re, restaurate*. Pubblicazione Eggitologiche del R. Museo di Torino. Rome: Giovanni Bardi.

Faulkner, Raymond O. 1962. *A Concise Dictionary of Middle Egyptian*. Oxford: Oxford University Press for the Griffith Institute.

Feinman, Gary M., and Joyce Marcus (eds). 1998. *Archaic States*. School of American Research Advanced Seminar Series. Santa Fe, NM: School of American Research Press.

Feucht, Erika. 1981. 'Relief Scheschonqs I. Beim Erschlagen der Feinde aus El-Hibe', *SAK* 9: 105–17.

Fieger, Michael, and Sigrid Hodel-Hoenes. 2007. *Der Einzug in Ägypten: Ein Beitrag zur alttestamentlichen Josefsgeschichte*. Das Alte Testament im Dialog 1. Bern: Peter Lang.

Finkelstein, Israel. 1988. *The Archaeology of the Israelite Settlement*. Jerusalem: Israel Exploration Society.

Finkelstein, Israel. 1988–89. 'The Land of Ephraim Survey 1980–1987: Preliminary Report', *TA* 15–16: 117–83.

Finkelstein, Israel. 1992a. 'Edom in the Iron I', *Levant* 24: 159–66.

Finkelstein, Israel. 1992b. 'Stratigraphy, Pottery and Parallels: A Reply to Bienkowsky', *Levant* 24: 171–2.

Finkelstein, Israel. 1992c. 'The Middle Bronze Age "Fortifications": A Reflection of Social Organization and Political Formations', *TA* 19: 201–20.

Finkelstein, Israel. 1993. 'The Sociopolitical Organization of the Central Hill Country in the Second Millennium B.C.E.', in Avraham Biran and Joseph Aviram (eds), *Biblical Archaeology Today, 1990. Proceedings of the Second International Congress on Biblical Archaeology*: Supplement: *Pre-Congress Symposium: Population, Production and Power, Jerusalem, June 1990*, 110–31. Jerusalem: Israel Exploration Society.

Finkelstein, Israel. 1995a. *Living on the Fringe: The Archaeology and History of the Negev, Sinai and Neighbouring Regions in the Bronze and Iron Ages*. Monographs in Mediterranean Archaeology 6. Sheffield: Sheffield Academic Press.

Finkelstein, Israel. 1995b. 'The Date of the Settlement of the Philistines in Canaan', *TA* 22: 213–39.

Finkelstein, Israel. 1996a. 'The Archaeology of the United Monarchy: An Alternative View', *Levant* 28: 177–87.

Finkelstein, Israel. 1996b. 'The Philistine Countryside', *IEJ* 46: 225–42.

Finkelstein, Israel. 1996c. 'The Territorial-Political System of Canaan in the Late Bronze Age', *UF* 28: 221–55.

Finkelstein, Israel. 1998a. 'The Great Transformation: The "Conquest" of the Highlands Frontiers and the Rise of the Territorial States', in Thomas E. Levy (ed.), *The Archaeology of Society in the Holy Land*, 349–65. New Approaches in Anthropological Archaeology. 2nd edn. London: Leicester University Press.

Finkelstein, Israel. 1998b. 'The Rise of Early Israel: Archaeology and Long-Term History', in Shmuel Aḥituv and Eliezer D. Oren (eds), *The Origin of Early Israel – Current Debate: Biblical, Historical and Archaeological Perspectives*, 7–39. Beer-Sheva 12. Beersheba: Ben-Gurion University of the Negev Press.

Finkelstein, Israel. 1999a. 'State Formation in Israel and Judah: A Contrast in Context, A Contrast in Trajectory', *NEA* 62: 35–52.

Finkelstein, Israel. 1999b. 'Hazor and the North in the Iron Age: A Low Chronology Perspective', *BASOR* 314: 55–70.

Finkelstein, Israel. 2001. 'The Rise of Jerusalem and Judah: The Missing Link', *Levant* 33: 105–15.

Finkelstein, Israel. 2002a. 'The Philistines in the Bible: A Late-Monarchic Perspective', *JSOT* 27: 131–67.

Finkelstein, Israel. 2002b. 'The Campaign of Shoshenq I to Palestine: A Guide to the 10th Century BCE Polity', *ZDPV* 118: 109–35.

Finkelstein, Israel. 2003. 'City-States to States: Polity Dynamics in the 10th–9th Centuries B.C.E.', in William G. Dever and Seymour Gitin (eds), *Symbiosis, Symbolism, and the Power of the Past: Canaan, Ancient Israel, and their Neighbors from the Late Bronze Age through Roman Palaestina: Proceedings of the Centennial Symposium W. F. Albright Institute of Archaeological Research and the American Schools of Oriental Research Jerusalem, May 29–31, 2000*, 75–83. Winona Lake, IN: Eisenbrauns.

Finkelstein, Israel. 2005a. 'A Low Chronology Update: Archaeology, History and Bible', in Thomas E. Levy and Thomas Higham (eds), *The Bible and Radiocarbon Dating: Archaeology, Text and Science*, 31–42. London: Equinox.

Finkelstein, Israel. 2005b. 'Khirbet en-Nahas, Edom and Biblical History', *TA* 32: 119–25.

Finkelstein, Israel. 2013. *The Forgotten Kingdom: The Archaeology and History of Northern Israel*. Society of Biblical Literature Ancient Near East Monographs 5. Atlanta, GA: Society of Biblical Literature.

Finkelstein, Israel. 2016a. 'The Old Jephthah Tale in Judges: Geographical and Historical Considerations', *Bib* 97: 1–15 (reprinted in Israel Finkelstein, *Essays on Biblical Historiography: From Jeroboam II to John Hyrcanus* [FAT 148; Tübingen: Mohr Siebeck, 2022], 219–32).

Finkelstein, Israel. 2016b. 'Comments on the Abimelech Story in Judges 9', *UF* 46: 69–84 (reprinted in Israel Finkelstein, *Essays on Biblical Historiography: From Jeroboam II to John Hyrcanus* [FAT 148; Tübingen: Mohr Siebeck, 2022], 233–47).

Finkelstein, Israel. 2017a. 'Compositional Phases, Geography and Historical Setting behind Judges 4–5 and the Location of Harosheth-ha-goiim', *SJOT* 31: 80–91 (reprinted in Israel Finkelstein, *Essays on Biblical Historiography: From Jeroboam II to John Hyrcanus* [FAT 148; Tübingen: Mohr Siebeck, 2022], 185–201).

Finkelstein, Israel. 2017b. 'Major Saviors, Minor Judges: The Historical Background of the Northern Accounts in the Book of Judges', *JSOT* 41: 431–49 (reprinted in Israel Finkelstein, *Essays on Biblical Historiography: From Jeroboam II to John Hyrcanus* [FAT 148; Tübingen: Mohr Siebeck, 2022], 249–63).

Finkelstein, Israel. 2019. 'First Israel, Core Israel, United (Northern) Israel', *NEA* 82: 8–15.

Finkelstein Israel. 2022a. *Essays on Biblical Historiography: From Jeroboam II to John Hyrcanus*. FAT 148. Tübingen: Mohr Siebeck.

Finkelstein, Israel. 2020b. 'The Appearance and Dissemination of Writing in Judah' [revised version]', in Israel Finkelstein, *Essays on Biblical Historiography: From Jeroboam II to John Hyrcanus*, 25–43. FAT 148. Tübingen: Mohr Siebeck.

Finkelstein, Israel, and Alexander Fantalkin. 2012. 'Khirbet Qeiyafa: An Unsensational Archaeological and Historical Interpretation', *TA* 39: 38–63.

Finkelstein, Israel, and Oded Lipschits. 2017. 'Geographical and Historical Observations on the Old North Israelite Gideon Tales in Judges', *ZAW* 129: 1–18 (reprinted in Israel Finkelstein, *Essays on Biblical Historiography: From Jeroboam II to John Hyrcanus* [FAT 148; Tübingen: Mohr Siebeck, 2022], 203–18).

Finkelstein, Israel, and Nadav Na'aman (eds). 1994. *From Nomadism to Monarchy: Archaeological and Historical Aspects of Early Israel.* Jerusalem: Israel Exploration Society.

Finkelstein, Israel, and Nadav Na'aman. 2005. 'Shechem of the Amarna Period and the Rise of the Northern Kingdom of Israel', *IEJ* 55: 172–93.

Finkelstein, Israel, and Eli Piasetzky. 2008. 'Radiocarbon and the History of Copper Production at Khirbet en-Naḥas', *TA* 35: 82–95.

Finkelstein, Israel, and Eli Piasetzky. 2003. 'Wrong and Right: High and Low – ^{14}C Dates from Tel Reḥov and Iron Age', *TA* 30: 283–95.

Finkelstein, Israel, and B. Sass. 2013. 'The West Semitic Alphabetic Inscriptions, Late Bronze II to Iron IIA: Archeological Context, Distribution and Chronology', *HBAI* 2: 149–220.

Finkelstein, Israel, and Benjamin Sass. 2021. 'The Exceptional Concentration of Inscriptions at Iron IIA Gath and Rehob and the Nature of the Alphabet in the Ninth Century BCE', in Thomas Römer, Hervé Gonzalez, Lionel Marti, and Jan Rückl (eds), *Oral et écrit dans l'Antiquité orientale: les processus de rédaction et d'édition: Actes du colloque organisé par le Collège de France, Paris, les 26 et 27 mai 2016*, 127–73. OBO 291; Leuven: Peeters.

Finkelstein, Israel, and Neil Asher Silberman. 2001. *The Bible Unearthed: Archaeology's New Vision of Ancient Israel and the Origin of its Sacred Texts*. New York: Free Press.

Finkelstein, Israel, Ze'ev Herzog, Lily Singer-Avitz, and David Ussishkin. 2007. 'Has King David's Palace in Jerusalem Been Found?', *TA* 34: 142–64.

Finkelstein, Israel, David Ussishkin, and Baruch Halpern (eds). 2000. *Megiddo III: The 1992–1996 Seasons*. 2 vols. Tel Aviv University Institute of Archaeology Monograph Series 18. Tel Aviv: Institute of Archaeology.

Finkelstein, J. J. 1961. 'Ammiṣaduqa's Edict and the Babylonian "Law Codes"', *JCS* 15: 91–104.
Finkelstein, J. J. 1969. 'The Edict of Ammiṣaduqa: A New Text', *RdA* 63: 45–64.
Fischer, Henry G. 1959. 'A Scribe of the Army in a Saqqara Mastaba of the Early Fifth Dynasty', *JNES* 18: 233–72.
Fischer, Peter M. 1999. 'Chocolate-on-White Ware: Typology, Chronology, and Provenance: The Evidence from Tell Abu al-Kharaz, Jordan Valley', *BASOR* 313: 1–29.
Fleming, Daniel E. 2012. '"People without Town": The *'apiru* in the Amarna Evidence', in Rebecca Hasselbach and Na'ama Pat-El (eds), *Language and Nature: Papers Presented to John Huehnergard on the Occasion of his 60th Birthday*, 39–50. SAOC 67. Chicago: Oriental Institute.
Fleming, Daniel E. 2016. 'The Amorites', in Bill T. Arnold and Brent A. Strawn (eds), *The World around the Old Testament: The Peoples and Places of the Ancient Near East*, 1–30. Grand Rapids, MI: Baker Academic.
Fleming, Daniel E., and Sara J. Milstein. 2010. *The Buried Foundation of the Gilgamesh Epic: The Akkadian Huwawa Narrative*. Cuneiform Monographs 39. Leiden: Brill. Atlanta, GA: SBL Press.
Fortes, M., and E. Evans-Pritchard. 1940. *African Political Systems*. Oxford: Oxford University Press.
Frahm, Eckart. 2011. *Babylonian and Assyrian Text Commentaries: Origins of Interpretation*. Guides to the Mesopotamian Textual Record 5. Münster: Ugarit-Verlag.
Frayne, Douglas R. 1990. *Old Babylonian Period (2003–1595 BC)*. RIME 4. Toronto: University of Toronto Press.
Frerichs, Ernest S., and Leonard H. Lesko (eds). 1997. *Exodus: The Egyptian Evidence*. Winona Lake, IN: Eisenbrauns.
Freu, Jacques. 2003. *Histoire du Mitanni*. Collection KUBABA 3. Paris: l'Harmattan.
Freu, Jacques. 2006. *Histoire politique du royaume d'Ugarit*. Collection KUBABA, Série Antiquité 11. Paris: L'Harmattan.
Frevel, Christian. 2016. *Geschichte Israels*. Kohlhammer Studienbücher Theologie. Stuttgart: Kohlhammer.
Fried, Morton H. 1968. 'On the Concepts of "Tribe" and "Tribal Society"', in June Helm (ed.), *Essays on the Problem of Tribe: Proceedings of the 1967 Annual Spring Meeting of the American Ethnological Society*, 3–20. Seattle/London: University of Washington Press.
Fried, Morton H. 1975. *The Notion of Tribe*. Menlo Park, CA: Cummings Publishing.
Fritz, Volkmar. 1981. 'The Israelite "Conquest" in the Light of Recent Excavations at Khirbet el-Meshâsh', *BASOR* 214: 61–73. ET of 'Die kulturhistorische Bedeutung der früheisenzeitlichen Siedlung auf der *Ḥirbet el-Mšāš* und das Problem der Landnahme', *ZDPV* 96 (1980): 121–35.
Fritz, Volkmar. 1987. 'Conquest or Settlement? The Early Iron Age in Palestine', *BA* 50: 84–100.
Fritz, Volkmar, and Aharon Kempinski (eds). 1983. *Ergebnisse der Ausgrabungen auf der Ḥirbet el-Mšāš (Tel Māśōś) 1972–1975: Teil I: Textband; Teil II: Tafelband; Teil III: Pläne*. 2 vols. Abhandlungen des Deutschen Palästinavereins. Wiesbaden: Harrassowitz, 1983.
Galling, Kurt. 1966. 'Goliath und seine Rüstung', in *Volume du Congrès Genève 1965*, 150–69. VTSup 15. Leiden: Brill.
Gardiner, Alan H. 1909. *The Admonitions of an Egyptian Sage from a Hieratic Papyrus in Leiden (Pap. Leiden 344 recto)*. Leipzig: Hinrichs.
Gardiner, Alan H. 1918a. 'The Delta Residence of the Ramessides', *JEA* 5: 127–38, 242–71.
Gardiner, Alan H. 1918b. 'The Supposed Egyptian Equivalent of the Name of Goshen', *JEA* 5: 218–23.
Gardiner, Alan H. 1920. 'The Ancient Military Road between Egypt and Palestine', *JEA* 6: 99–116.
Gardiner, Alan H. 1924. 'The Geography of the Exodus: An Answer to Professor Naville and Others', *JEA* 10: 87–96.
Gardiner, Alan H. 1927. 'An Administrative Letter of Protest Author(s)', *JEA* 13: 75–8.
Gardiner, Alan H. 1933. 'Tanis and Pi-Ra'messe: A Retraction', *JEA* 19: 122–8.
Gardiner, Alan H. 1947. *Ancient Egyptian Onomastica: Text and Plates*. 3 vols. Oxford: Oxford University Press.
Gardiner, Alan H. 1961. *Egypt of the Pharaohs: An Introduction*. Oxford: Oxford University Press.

Gardiner, Alan H., and T. Eric Peet. 1917. *The Inscriptions of Sinai, Part I Introduction and Plates*. London: Egypt Exploration Society.
Gardiner, Alan H., T. Eric Peet, and Jaroslave Černý. 1955. *The Inscriptions of Sinai, Part II Translations and Commentary*. From the Manuscripts of Alan H. Gardiner and T. Eric Peet, edited and completed by Jaroslave Černý. London: Egypt Exploration Society.
Garfinkel, Yosef. 2011. 'The Davidic Kingdom in Light of the Finds at Khirbet Qeiyafa', *City of David Studies of Ancient Jerusalem* 6: 14*–35*.
Garfinkel, Yosef, and Hoo-Goo Kang. 2011. 'The Relative and Absolute Chronology of Khirbet Qeiyafa: Very Late Iron Age I or Very Early Iron Age IIA?' *IEJ* 61: 171–83.
Garfinkel, Yosef, Saar Ganor, and Michael G. Hasel. 2012a. 'The Iron Age City of Khirbet Qeiyafa after Four Seasons of Excavations', in Gershon Galil, Ayelet Gilboa, Aren M. Maeir, and Dan'el Kahn (eds), *The Ancient Near East in the 12th–10th Centuries BCE: Culture and History*, 149–74. AOAT 392. Münster: Ugarit-Verlag.
Garfinkel, Yosef, Saar Ganor, and Michael G. Hasel. 2012b. 'Khirbat Qeiyafa 2010–2011', *Hadashot Arkheologiyot* 124 (19/4/2012): 1–12.
Garfinkel, Yosef, Mitka R. Golub, Haggai Misgav, and Saar Ganor. 2015. 'The ʾIšbaʿal Inscription from Khirbet Qeiyafa', *BASOR* 373: 217–33.
Garfinkel, Yosef, Katharina Streit, Saar Ganor, and Michael G. Hasel. 2012. 'State Formation in Judah: Biblical Tradition, Modern Historical: Theories, and Radiometric Dates at Khirbet Qeiyafa', *Radiocarbon* 54: 359–69.
Garfinkel, Yosef, Katharina Streit, Saar Ganor, and Paula J. Reimer. 2015. 'King David's City at Khirbet Qeiyafa: Results of the Second Radiocarbon Dating Project', *Radiocarbon* 57: 881–90.
Gelb, Ignace J. 1954. 'Two Assyrian King Lists', *JNES* 13: 209–30.
Gelb, Ignace J. 1961. 'The Early History of the West Semitic Peoples', *JCS* 15: 27–47.
Gelb, Ignace J. 1968. 'An Old Babylonian List of Amorites', *JAOS* 88: 39–46.
Gelb, Ignace J. 1980. *Computer-Aided Analysis of Amorite*. Assyriological Studies 21. Chicago: Oriental Institute of the University of Chicago.
Gelb, Ignace J. 1984. 'The Inscription of Jibbit.Lïm, King of Ebla', *Studia Orientalia* 55: 213–29.
Gellner, Ernest. 1981. 'Cohesion and Identity: The Magreb from Ibn Khaldun to Emile Durkheim', in *Muslim Society*, 86–98. Cambridge: Cambridge University Press.
Genz, Hermann, and Dirk Paul Mielke (eds). 2011. *Insights into Hittite History and Archaeology*. Colloquia Antiqua 2. Leuven: Peeters.
Geraty, Lawrence T., and Øystein Sakala LaBianca (eds). 1987–98. *Hesban*. Vols 1–10. Berrien Springs, MI: Andrews University Press.
Geus, C. H. J. de. 1976. *The Tribes of Israel: An Investigation into Some of the Presuppositions of Martin Noth's Amphictyony Hypothesis*. Studia Semitica Neerlandica 18. Assen/Amsterdam: Van Gorcum.
Gibson, John C. L. 1975. *Textbook of Syrian Semitic Inscriptions: Volume I Hebrew and Moabite Inscriptions*. Oxford: Clarendon.
Gibson, Shimon. 2001. 'Agricultural Terraces and Settlement Expansion in the Highlands of Early Iron Age Palestine: Is There any Correlation between the Two?', in Amihai Mazar (ed.), *Studies in the Archaeology of the Iron Age in Israel and Jordan*, 113–46. JSOTSup 331. Sheffield: Sheffield Academic Press.
Gilan, Amir. 2004. 'Der Pūḫanu Text – Theologischer Streit und politische Opposition in der Althethitischen Literatur', *AoF* 31: 263–96.
Gilan, Amir. 2008. 'Were There Cannibals in Syria? History and Fiction in an Old Hittite Literary Text', in Ettore Cingano and Lucio Milano (eds), *Papers on Ancient Literatures: Greece, Rome and the Near East: Proceedings of the "Advanced Seminar in the Humanities", Venice International University 2004–2005*, 267–84. Quaderni del Dipartimento di Scienze dell'Antichità e del Vicino Oriente, Università Ca' Foscari, Venezia 4. Padua: S.A.R.G.O.N. Editrice e Libreria.
Gilan, Amir. 2013. 'Hittites in Canaan? The Archaeological Evidence', *BN* 156: 39–52.
Gilboa, Ayelet. 2005. 'Sea Peoples and Phoenicians along the Southern Phoenician Coast – A Reconciliation: An Interpretation of Šikila (*SKL*) Material Culture', *BASOR* 337: 47–78.

Gitin, Seymour, Trude Dothan, and Joseph Naveh. 1997. 'A Royal Dedicatory Inscription from Ekron', *IEJ* 47: 1–16.
Giveon, Raphael. 1965. 'The Shosu of Egyptian Sources and the Exodus', *Proceedings of the World Congress of Jewish Studies, 1965, Volume 1*, 193–6. Jerusalem: World Union of Jewish Studies.
Giveon, Raphael. 1969. 'Thutmosis IV and Asia', *JNES* 28: 54–9.
Giveon, Raphael. 1971. *Les bédouins Shosou des documents égyptiens*. Documenta et Monumenta Orientis Antiqui 22. Leiden: Brill.
Giveon, Raphael. 1975. 'Asiaten', *LdÄ* 1: 462–71.
Giveon, Raphael. 1978. *The Impact of Egypt on Canaan: Iconographical and Related Studies*. OBO 10. Freiburg: Universitätsverlag; Göttingen: Vandenhoeck & Ruprecht.
Giveon, Raphael. 1984. 'Scharuhen', *LdÄ* 5: 532.
Glassner, Jean-Jacques. 2004. *Mesopotamian Chronicles*. Edited by Benjamin R. Foster. SBL Writings from the Ancient World 19. Atlanta, GA: Society of Biblical Literature.
Godelier, Maurice. 1986. *The Making of Great Men: Male Domination and Power among the New Guinea Baruya*. Translated by Rupert Sawyer. Cambridge Studies in Social Anthropology 56. Cambridge: Cambridge University Press.
Goedicke, Hans. 1963. 'The Alleged Military Campaign in Southern Palestine in the Reign of Pepi I', *RDSO* 38: 187–97.
Goedicke, Hans. 1975. *The Report of Wenamun*. Baltimore: Johns Hopkins University Press.
Goedicke, Hans. 1968. 'The Capture of Joppa', *Chronique d'Egypte* 43: 219–33.
Goedicke, Hans. 1986. 'The End of the Hyksos in Egypt', in Leonard H. Lesko (ed.), *Egyptological Studies in Honor of Richard A. Parker, Presented on the Occasion of his 78th Birthday, December 10, 1983*, 37–47. Hanover, NH: University Press of New England.
Goedicke, Hans. 1987. 'Anastasi VI 51–61', *SAK* 14: 83–98.
Goedicke, Hans. 1992. 'Amenophis II in Samaria', *SAK* 19: 133–50.
Goedicke, Hans. 2004. 'Remarks on the "Israel-Stela"', *Wiener Zeitschrift für die Kunde des Morgenlandes* 94: 53–72.
Goetze, Albrecht. 1933. *Die Annalen des Muršiliš*. Mitteilungen der Vorderasiatisch-Ägyptischen Gesellschaft 38. Hethitische Texte, Heft 6. Leipzig. Reprinted Darmstadt: Wissenschaftliche Buchgesellschaft, 1967.
Goetze, Albrecht. 1957a. 'On the Chronology of the Second Millennium B. C.', *JCS* 11: 53–61.
Goetze, Albrecht. 1957b. 'On the Chronology of the Second Millennium B. C. (Concluded)', *JCS* 11: 63–73.
Goldschmidt, Walter. 1980. 'Career Reorientation and Institutional Adaptation in the Process of Natural Sedentarization', in Philip Carl Salzman (ed.), *When Nomads Settle: Processes of Sedentarization as Adaptation and Response*, 48–61. New York: Praeger.
Golinets, Viktor. 2018. *Das amurritische Onomastikon der altbabylonischen Zeit: Band 2 Verbalmorphologie des Amurritischen und Glossar der Verbalwurzeln*. AOAT 271/2. Münster: Ugarit-Verlag.
Gonen, Rivka. 1984. 'Urban Canaan in the Late Bronze Period', *BASOR* 253: 61–73.
Gophna, Ram. 1976. 'Egyptian Immigration into Southern Canaan during the First Dynasty?', *TA* 3: 31–7.
Gophna, Ram. 1984. 'The Settlement Landscape of Palestine in the Early Bronze Age II–III and Middle Bronze Age II', *IEJ* 34: 24–31.
Gordon, Andrew. 2001. 'Foreigners', *OEAE* 1: 544–8.
Gordon, Cyrus H. 1958. 'Abraham and the Merchants of Ura', *JNES* 17: 28–31.
Gordon, Cyrus H. 1962. *Before the Bible*. New York: Collins.
Goren, Yuval, Israel Finkelstein, and Nadav Na'aman. 2003. 'The Expansion of the Kingdom of Amurru According to the Petrographic Investigation of the Amarna Tablets', *BASOR* 329: 1–11.
Goren, Yuval, Israel Finkelstein, and Nadav Na'aman. 2004. *Inscribed in Clay: Provenance Study of the Amarna Tablets and Other Ancient Near Eastern Texts*. Tel Aviv: Tel Aviv University Press.
Görg, Manfred. 1997. *Die Beziehungen zwischen dem Alten Israel und Ägypten: Von den Anfängen bis zum Exil*. Erträge der Forschung 290. Darmstadt: Wissenschaftliche Buchgesellschaft, 1997.
Görg, Manfred. 2001 'Israel in Hieroglyphen', *BN* 106: 21–7.

Gosden, Chris. 1999. 'The Organization of Society', in Graeme Barker (ed.), *Companion Encyclopedia of Archaeology*, 470–504. London and New York: Routledge.

Gottlieb, Yulia. 2010. 'The Advent of the Age of Iron in the Land of Israel: A Review and Reassessment', *TA* 37: 89–110.

Gottwald, Norman. 1979. *The Tribes of Yahweh: A Sociology of the Religion of Liberated Israel, 1250–1050 B.C.E.* Maryknoll, NY: Orbis Books.

Gottwald, Norman. 1993. 'Recent Studies of the Social World of Premonarchic Israel', *CR:BS* 1: 163–89.

Grabbe, Lester L. 1993. 'Comparative Philology and Exodus 15,8: Did the Egyptians Die in a Storm?', *SJOT* 7: 263–9.

Grabbe, Lester L. 1994. '"Canaanite": Some Methodological Observations in Relation to Biblical Study', in George J. Brooke, Adrian H. W. Curtis, and John F. Healey (eds), *Ugarit and the Bible: Proceedings of the International Symposium on Ugarit and the Bible, Manchester, September 1992*, 113–22. Ugaritisch-Biblische Literatur 11. Münster: Ugarit-Verlag.

Grabbe, Lester L. 1997. 'The Book of Leviticus', *CR:BS* 5: 91–110.

Grabbe, Lester L. 2000. '*Adde Praeputium Praeputio Magnus Acervus Erit*: If the Exodus and Conquest Had Really Happened', in J. Cheryl Exum (ed.), *Virtual History and the Bible*, 23–32. Biblical Interpretation 8. Leiden: Brill.

Grabbe, Lester L. 2001. 'Sup-urbs or Only Hyp-urbs? Prophets and Populations in Ancient Israel and Socio-historical Method', in Lester L. Grabbe and Robert D. Haak (eds), *'Every City Shall Be Forsaken': Urbanism and Prophecy in Ancient Israel and the Near East*, 93–121. JSOTSup 330. Sheffield: Sheffield Academic Press.

Grabbe, Lester L. 2003a. 'Of Mice and Dead Men: Herodotus 2.141 and Sennacherib's Campaign in 701 BCE', in Lester L. Grabbe (ed.), *'Like a Bird in a Cage': The Invasion of Sennacherib in 701 BCE*, 119–40. JSOTSup 363 = ESHM 4. Sheffield: Sheffield Academic Press.

Grabbe, Lester L. 2003b. 'Ethnic Groups in Jerusalem', in Thomas L. Thompson, with the collaboration of Salma Khadra Jayyusi (eds), *Jerusalem in Ancient History and Tradition*, 145–63. JSOTSup 381. Copenhagen International Seminar 13. London/New York: T&T Clark International.

Grabbe, Lester L. 2003c. 'Were the Pre-Maccabean High Priests "Zadokites"?', in J. Cheryl Exum and H. G. M. Williamson (eds), *Reading from Right to Left: Essays on the Hebrew Bible in Honour of David J. A. Clines*, 205–15. JSOTSup 373. Sheffield: Sheffield Academic Press.

Grabbe, Lester L. 2004. *A History of the Jews and Judaism in the Second Temple Period 1: Yehud: A History of the Persian Province of Judah*. LSTS 47. London/New York: T&T Clark International.

Grabbe, Lester L. 2006a. '"Mighty Oaks from (Genetically Manipulated?) Acorns Grow: The Chronicle of the Kings of Judah as a Source of the Deuteronomistic History', in R. Rezetko, T. H. Lim and W. B. Aucker (eds), *Reflection and Refraction: Studies in Biblical Historiography in Honour of A. Graeme Auld*, 154–73. VTSup 113. Leiden: Brill.

Grabbe, Lester L. 2006b. 'The Law, the Prophets, and the Rest: The State of the Bible in Pre-Maccabean Times', *DSD* 13: 319–38.

Grabbe, Lester L. 2013. 'Elephantine and the Torah', in Alejandro F. Botta (ed.), *In the Shadow of Bezalel: Aramaic, Biblical, and Ancient Near Eastern Studies in Honor of Bezalel Porten*, 125–35. Culture and History of the Ancient Near East 60. Leiden/Boston: Brill.

Grabbe, Lester L. 2014. 'The Exodus and Historicity', in Thomas B. Dozeman, Craig A. Evans, and Joel N. Lohr (eds), *The Book of Exodus: Composition, Reception, and Interpretation*, 61–87. VTSup 164. Leiden: Brill.

Grabbe, Lester L. 2016. 'The Mighty Men of Israel: 1-2 Samuel and History', in Walter Dietrich, Cynthia Edenburg, and Philippe Hugo (eds), *The Books of Samuel: Stories - History - Reception History*, 83–104. Bibliotheca Ephemeridum Theologicarum Lovaniensium 284: Leuven: Peeters, 2016.

Grabbe, Lester L. 2017a. *Ancient Israel: What Do We Know and How Do We Know It?* 2nd edn. London/New York: Bloomsbury T&T Clark.

Grabbe, Lester L. 2017b. *1 and 2 Kings: History and Story in Ancient Israel: An Introduction and Study Guide*. T & T Clark Study Guides to the Old Testament. London/New York: Bloomsbury T&T Clark.

Grabbe, Lester L. 2017c. 'Jeroboam I? Jeroboam II? Or Jeroboam 0? Jeroboam in History and Tradition', in Oded Lipschits, Yuval Gadot, and Matthew J. Adams (eds), *Rethinking Israel: Studies in the History and Archaeology of Ancient Israel in Honor of Israel Finkelstein*, 115–24. Winona Lake, IN: Eisenbrauns.

Grabbe, Lester L. (ed.) 2016. *The Land of Canaan in the Late Bronze Age*. LHBOTS 636. ESHM 10. London and New York: Bloomsbury T&T Clark.

Grajetzki, Wolfram. 2006. *The Middle Kingdom of Ancient Egypt: History, Archaeology and Society*. Duckworth Egyptology. London: Duckworth.

Grandet, Pierre. 1993. *Ramsès III: Histoire d'un règne*. Paris: Gérard Watelet.

Grayson, Albert Kirk. 1972. *Assyrian Royal Inscriptions, Volume I: From the Beginning to Ashur-resha-ishi I*. Records of the Ancient Near East. Wiesbaden: Harrassowitz.

Grayson, Albert Kirk. 1976. *Assyrian Royal Inscriptions, Volume II: From Tiglath-pileser I to Ashur-nasir-apli II*. Records of the Ancient Near East. Wiesbaden: Harrassowitz.

Grayson, Albert Kirk. 1991. *Assyrian Rulers of the Early First Millennium BC I (1114–859 BC)*. Royal Inscriptions of Mesopotamia: Assyrian Periods 2. Toronto: University of Toronto Press.

Grayson, Albert Kirk. 1996. *Assyrian Rulers of the Early First Millennium BC II (858–745 BC)*. Royal Inscriptions of Mesopotamia: Assyrian Periods 3. Toronto: University of Toronto Press.

Greenberg, Moshe. 1955. *The Ḫab/piru*. American Oriental Series 39. New Haven, CT: American Oriental Society.

Greenfield, Haskel J., Tina L. Greenfield, Elizabeth Arnold, Itzick Shai, Shira Albaz, and Aren M. Maeir. 2020. 'Evidence for Movement of Goods and Animals from Egypt to Canaan During the Early Bronze of the Southern Levant: A View from Tell Eṣ-Ṣâfi/Gath', *Ägypten und Levante* 30: 377–97.

Greengus, Samuel. 1975. 'Sisterhood Adoption at Nuzi and the "Wife-Sister" in Genesis', *HUCA* 46: 5–31.

Grimal, Nicolas. 1992. *A History of Ancient Egypt*. Translated by Ian Shaw. Oxford: Blackwell. ET idem, *Histoire de l'Egypte ancienne*. Paris: Librarie Arthème Fayard, 1988.

Groddek, Detlev. 2002. 'Muršili II., die großen Feste und die "Pest" Überlegungen zur Anordnung der Fragmente der späteren Jahre seiner Regierung in den AM', in Stefano De Martino and Franca Pecchioli Daddi (eds), *Anatolia antica: studi in memoria di Fiorella Imparati*, 1:329–38. 2 vols. Eothen: Studi sulle Civiltà dell'Oriente Antico 11. Firenze: LoGisma.

Groll, Sarah I. 1998. 'The Egyptian Background of the Exodus and the Crossing of the Reed Sea: A New Reading of Papyrus Anastasi VIII', in Irne Shirun-Grumach (ed.), *Jerusalem Studies in Egyptology*, 173–92. Ägypten und Altes Testament 40. Wiesbaden: Harrassowitz.

Guest, P. Deryn. 1998. 'Can Judges Survive without Sources? Challenging the Consensus', *JSOT* 78: 43–61.

Guillaume, Philippe. 2004. *Waiting for Josiah: The Judges*. JSOTSup 385. London: T & T Clark.

Gurney, O. R. 1990. *The Hittites*. London: Penguin Books.

Güterbock, Hans G. 1967. 'The Hittite Conquest of Cyprus Reconsidered', *JNES* 26: 73–81.

Güterbock, Hans G. 1983. 'The Hittites and the Aegean World: Part 1, The Ahhiyawa Problem Reconsidered', *AJA* 87: 133–8.

Haber, Marc. 2017. 'Continuity and Admixture in the Last Five Millennia of Levantine History from Ancient Canaanite and Present-Day Lebanese Genome Sequences', *Journal of Human Genetics* 101 (3 August 2017): 274–82.

Halayqa, Issam K. H. 2010. 'The Demise of Ugarit in the Light of its Connections with Ḫatti', *UF* 42: 297–330.

Halpern, Baruch. 1988. *The First Historians: The Hebrew Bible and History*. San Francisco: Harper & Row.

Halpern, Baruch. 1993. 'The Exodus and the Israelite Historians', *EI* 24: 89*–96*.

Halpern, Baruch. 2001. *David's Secret Demons: Messiah, Murderer, Traitor, King*. Grand Rapids, MI: Eerdmans.

Haran, Menahem. 1976. 'Exodus, The', *IDBSup*: 304–10.

Harrison, Timothy P., and Celeste Barlow. 2005. 'Mesha, the Mishor, and the Chronology of Iron Age Mādabā', in Thomas E. Levy and Thomas Higham (eds), *The Bible and Radiocarbon Dating: Archaeology, Text and Science*, 179–90. London: Equinox.

Hart, Stephen. 1992. 'Iron Age Settlement in the Land of Edom', in Piotr Bienkowski (ed.), *Early Edom and Moab: The Beginning of the Iron Age in Southern Jordan*, 93–8. Sheffield Archaeological Monographs 7. Sheffield: J. R. Collis Publications.

Hasel, Michael G. 1994. 'Israel in the Merneptah Stela', *BASOR* 296: 45–61.
Hasel, Michael G. 1998. *Domination and Resistance: Egyptian Military Activity in the Southern Levant, ca. 1300–1185 BC.* PdÄ 11. Leiden: Brill.
Hasel, Michael G. 2003. 'Merenptah's Inscription and Reliefs and the Origin of Israel', in Beth Alpert Nakhai (ed.), *The Near East in the Southwest: Essays in Honor of William G. Dever*, 19–44. AASOR 58. Boston: American Schools of Oriental Research).
Hasel, Michael G. 2004. 'The Structure of the Final Hymnic-Poetic Unit on the Merenptah Stela', *ZAW* 116: 75–81.
Hasel, Michael G. 2008. 'Merenptah's Reference to Israel: Critical Issues for the Origin of Israel', in Richard S. Hess, Gerald A. Klingbell, and Paul J. Ray Jr (eds), *Critical Issues in Early Israelite History*, 47–59. Bulletin for Biblical Research Supplements 3. Winona Lake, IN: Eisenbrauns.
Hasel, Michael G. 2009. 'Pa-Canaan in the Egyptian New Kingdom: Canaan or Gaza?', *JAEI* 1, no. 1: 8–17.
Hasel, Michael G. 2011. 'The Battle of Kadesh: Identifying New Kingdom Polities, Places, and Peoples in Canaan and Syria', in Shay Bar, Dan'el Kahn, and Judith J. Shirley (eds), *Egypt, Canaan and Israel: History, Ideology, Imperialism and Literature: Proceedings of a Conference at the University of Haifa, 3–7 May 2009*, 65–86. CHANE 51. Leiden: Brill.
Hayes, John H., and J. Maxwell Miller (eds). 1977. *Israelite and Judaean History*. OTL. Philadelphia, PA: Westminster Press.
Hayes, William C. 1949. 'The Career of the Great Steward Ḥenenu under Nebḥepetrē' Mentuḥotpe', *JEA* 35: 43–9.
Heimpel, Wolfgang. 2003. *Letters to the King of Mari: A New Translation, with Historical Introduction, Notes, and Commentary*. Mesopotamian Civilizations. Winona Lake, IN: Eisenbrauns.
Helck, Wolfgang. 1956. *Untersuchungen zu Manetho und den Ägyptischen Königslisten*. Untersuchungen zur Geschichte und Altertumskunde Ägypte NS Band 18. Berlin: Akademie-Verlag.
Helck, Wolfgang. 1963. 'Urḫi-Tešup in Ägypten', *JCS* 17: 87–97.
Helck, Wolfgang. 1965. 'Ṯkw und die Ramses-Stadt', *VT* 15: 35–48.
Helck, Wolfgang. 1971. *Die Beziehungen Ägyptens zu Vorderasien im 3. und 2. Jahrtausend v. Chr.* 2nd edn. Ägytololgische Abhandlungen 5. Wiesbaden: Harrassowitz.
Helck, Wolfgang. 1984. 'Die Sukzija-Episode im Dekret des Telepinus', *WO* 15: 103–8.
Helck, Wolfgang, and Eberhard Otto (eds). 1975–92. *Lexikon der Ägyptologie. Vols. 1–7.* Wiesbaden: Harrassowitz.
Helm, June (ed.). 1968. *Essays on the Problem of Tribe: Proceedings of the 1967 Annual Spring Meeting of the American Ethnological Society*. Seattle/London: University of Washington Press.
Heltzer, M. 1976. 'Mortgage of Land Property and Freeing from It in Ugarit', *JESHO* 19: 89–95.
Heltzer, M. 1982. 'The Yaureans and the Yaīrites', *Rivista degli studi orientali* 56: 17–20.
Herr, Larry G. 1997. 'Emerging Nations: The Iron Age II Period', *BA* 60: 114–83.
Herr, Larry G. 2001. 'The History of the Collared Pithos at Tell el-'Umeiri, Jordan', in Samuel R. Wolff (ed.), *Studies in the Archaeology of Israel and Neighboring Lands in Memory of Douglas L. Esse*, 237–50. The Oriental Institute of the University of Chicago Studies in Ancient Oriental Civilization 59. ASOR Books 5. Chicago: Oriental Institute.
Herr, Larry G., and M. Najjar. 2001. 'The Iron Age', in B. MacDonald, R. Adams, and P. Bienkowski (eds), *The Archaeology of Jordan*, 323–45. Sheffield: Sheffield Academic Press.
Herr, Larry G., et al. (eds). 1989–2002. *Madaba Plains Project. Vols 1–5.* Berrien Springs, MI: Andrews University Press.
Herrmann, Siegfried. 1964. 'Operationen Pharao Schoschenks I. im östlichen Ephraim', *ZDPV* 80: 55–79.
Herzog, Ze'ev. 1994. 'The Beer-Sheba Valley: From Nomadism to Monarchy', in Israel Finkelstein and Nadav Na'aman (eds), *From Nomadism to Monarchy: Archaeological and Historical Aspects of Early Israel*, 122–49. Jerusalem: Israel Exploration Society.
Herzog, Ze'ev. 1997. 'Beersheba', *OEANE* 1: 287–91.

Herzog, Ze'ev. 2001. 'The Date of the Temple of Arad: Reassessment of the Stratigraphy and the Implications for the History of Religion in Judah', in Amihai Mazar (ed.), *Studies in the Archaeology of the Iron Age in Israel and Jordan*, 156–78. JSOTSup 331. Sheffield: Sheffield Academic Press.

Herzog, Ze'ev, and Lily Singer-Avitz. 2004. 'Redefining the Centre: The Emergence of State in Judah', *TA* 31: 209–44.

Hess, Richard S. 1998. 'Occurrences of "Canaan" in Late Bronze Age Archives of the West Semitic World', in Shlomo Izre'el, Ithamar Singer and Ran Zadok (eds), *Past Links: Studies in the Languages and Cultures of the Ancient Near East*, 365–72 (= *IOS* 18). Winona Lake, IN: Eisenbrauns.

Hesse, Brian, and Paul Wapnish. 1997. 'Can Pig Remains Be Used for Ethnic Diagnosis in the Ancient Near East?' in Neil A. Silberman and David B. Small (eds), *The Archaeology of Israel: Constructing the Past, Interpreting the Present*, 238–70. JSOTSup 239. Sheffield: Sheffield Academic Press.

Higham, Thomas, Johannes van der Plicht, Christopher Bronk Ramsey, Hendrik J. Bruins, Mark A. Robinson and Thomas E. Levy. 2005. 'Radiocarbon Dating of the Khirbat en-Nahas Site (Jordan) and Bayesian Modeling of the Results', in Thomas E. Levy and Thomas Higham (eds), *The Bible and Radiocarbon Dating: Archaeology, Text and Science*, 164–78. London: Equinox.

Hitchcock, Louise A. 2018. '"All the Cherethites, and All the Pelethites, and All the Gittites (Samuel 2:15–18)" – An Up-to-Date Account of the Minoan Connection with the Philistines', in Itzhaq Shai, et al (eds), *Tell It in Gath: Studies in the History and Archaeology of Israel: Essays in Honor of Aren M. Maeir on the Occasion of his Sixtieth Birthday*, 304–21. Ägypten und Altes Testament 90. Münster: Ugarit-Verlag.

Hitchcock, Louise A., and Aren M. Maeir. 2013. 'Beyond Creolization and Hybridity: Entangled and Transcultural Identities in Philistia', *Archaeological Review from Cambridge* 28: 43–65.

Hitchcock, Louise A., and Aren M. Maeir. 2016. 'A Pirate's Life for Me: The Maritime Culture of the Sea Peoples', *PEQ* 148: 1–20.

Hitchcock, Louise A., and Aren M. Maeir. 2017. 'Fifteen Men on a Dead Seren's Chest: Yo Ho Ho and a Krater of Wine', in A. Batmaz, G. Bedianashvili, A. Michalewicz and A. Robinson (eds), *Context and Connection: Essays on the Archaeology of the Ancient Near East in Honour of Antonio Sagona*, 147–59. OLA 268. Leuven: Peeters.

Hjelm, Ingrid, and Thomas L. Thompson. 2002. 'The Victory Song of Merneptah, Israel and the People of Palestine', *JSOT* 27: 3–18.

Hoch, James E. 1994. *Semitic Words in Egyptian Texts of the New Kingdom and Third Intermediate Period*. Princeton, NJ: Princeton University Press.

Hoffman, Yair. 1989. 'A North Israelite Typological Myth and a Judaean Historical Tradition: The Exodus in Hosea and Amos', *VT* 19: 169–82.

Hoffman, Yair. 1998. 'The Exodus – Tradition and Reality: The Status of the Exodus Tradition in Ancient Israel', in Irene Shirun-Grumach (ed.), *Jerusalem Studies in Egyptology*, 193–202. Ägypten und Altes Testament 40. Wiesbaden: Harrassowitz.

Hoffmeier, James K. 1997. *Israel in Egypt: The Evidence for the Authenticity of the Exodus Tradition*. Oxford: Oxford University Press.

Hoffmeier, James K. 2005. *Ancient Israel in Sinai: The Evidence for the Authenticity of the Wilderness Tradition*. Oxford: Oxford University Press.

Hoffmeier, James K. 2007. 'What Is the Biblical Date for the Exodus? A Response to Bryant Wood', *JETS* 50: 225–47.

Hoffmeier, James K., Thomas W. Davis, and Rexine Hummel. 2016. 'New Archaeological Evidence for Ancient Bedouin (Shasu) on Egypt's Eastern Frontier at Tell el-Borg', *Ägypten und Levante* 26: 285–311.

Hoffner, Harry A. 1969. 'Some Contributions of Hittitology to Old Testament Study', *Tyndale Bulletin* 20: 27–55.

Hoffner, Harry A. 1973. 'The Hittites and Hurrians', in D. J. Wiseman (ed.), *Peoples of Old Testament Times*, 197–228. Oxford: Clarendon Press.

Hoffner, Harry A. 2009. *Letters from the Hittite Kingdom*. Edited by Gary M. Beckman. SBLWAW 15. Atlanta, GA: Society of Biblical Literature.

Höflmayer, Felix. 2015. 'Egypt's "Empire" in the Southern Levant in the Early 18th Dynasty', in Birgitta Eder and Regine Pruzsinszky (eds), *Policies of Exchange: Political Systems and Modes of Interaction in the Aegean and the Near East in the 2nd Millennium B.C.E.: Proceedings of the International Symposium at the University of Freiburg Institute for Archaeological Studies, 30th May–2nd June 2012*, 191–206. Österreichische Akademie der Wissenschaften, Philosophisch-historische Klasse, Oriental and European Archaeology 2. Vienna: Austrian Academy of Sciences.

Höflmayer, Felix. 2019. 'The Expulsion of the Hyksos and the End of the Middle Bronze Age: A Reassessment in Light of Recent Chronological Research', *JAEI* 21: 20–30.

Holladay, John S., Jr. 2001. 'Pithom', *OEAE* 2: 50–3.

Hoop, Raymond de. 2009. 'Judges 5 Reconsidered: Which Tribes? What Land? Whose Song?', in Jacques van Ruiten and J. Cornelis de Vos (eds), *The Land of Israel in Bible, History, and Theology: Studies in Honour of Ed Noort*, 151–66. VTSup 124. Leiden: Brill.

Hornung, Erik, Rolf Krauss, and David A. Warburton (eds). 2006. *Ancient Egyptian Chronology*. HdO Section One, Volume 83. Leiden: Brill.

Hort, Greta. 1957. 'The Plagues of Egypt', *ZAW* 69: 84–103.

Hort, Greta. 1958. 'The Plagues of Egypt', *ZAW* 70: 48–59.

Huehnergard, John. 1991. 'Remarks on the Classification of Northwest Semitic Languages', in J. Hoftijzer and G. van der Kooij (eds), *The Balaam Text from Deir 'Alla Re-evaluated: Proceedings of the International Symposium Held at Leiden 21–24 August 1989*, 282–93. Leiden: Brill.

Huehnergard, John, and Na'ama Pat-El. 2019. 'Introduction to the Semitic Languages and their History', in John Huehnergard and Na'ama Pat El (eds), *The Semitic Languages*, 1–21. 2nd edn. Routledge Language Family Series. Abingdon/New York: Routledge.

Huehnergard, John, and Christopher Woods. 2004. 'Akkadian and Eblaite', in Roger D. Woodard (ed.), *The Cambridge Encyclopedia of the World's Ancient Languages*, 218–80. Cambridge: Cambridge University Press.

Huffmon, Herbert Bardwell. 1965. *Amorite Personal Names in the Mari Texts: A Structural and Lexical Study*. Baltimore: Johns Hopkins University Press.

Iggers, Georg G. 1997. *Historiography in the Twentieth Century: From Scientific Objectivity to the Postmodern Challenge*. Hanover, NH: University Press of New England.

Ilan, David. 1998. 'The Dawn of Internationalism – The Middle Bronze Age', in Thomas E. Levy (ed.), *The Archaeology of Society in the Holy Land*, 297–319. 2nd edn. New Approaches in Anthropological Archaeology. London: Leicester University Press.

Ilan, David. 2019. 'The "Conquest" of the Highlands in the Iron Age I', in Assaf Yasur-Landau, Eric H. Cline, and Yorke M. Rowan (eds), *The Social Archaeology of the Levant: From Prehistory to the Present*, 283–309. Cambridge: Cambridge University Press.

Imparati, Fiorella. 1965. 'L'Autobiografia di Ḫattušili I', *Studi Classici e Orientali* 14: 40–76.

Irons, William, and Neville Dyson-Hudson (eds). 1972. *Perspectives on Nomadism*. International Studies in Sociology and Social Anthropology 13. Leiden: Brill.

Izre'el, Shlomo. 1991. *Amurru Akkadian: A Linguistic Study*. With an Appendix on the History of Amurru by Itamar Singer. Vols 1–2. HSS 40–41. Atlanta, GA: Scholars Press.

Izre'el, Shlomo, and Itamar Singer. 1990. *The General's Letter from Ugarit: A Linguistic and Historical Evaluation of RS 20.33 (Ugaritica V, No. 20)*. Tel Aviv: Tel Aviv University.

Jacobsen, Thorkild. 1939. *The Sumerian King List*. Assyriological Studies 11. Chicago: Oriental Institute of the University of Chicago.

Jacoby, Felix. 1926–58. *Die Fragmente der griechischen Historiker*. Parts 1–17. Berlin: Weidman.

James, Peter. 1991. *Centuries of Darkness: A Challenge to the Conventional Chronology of Old World Archaeology*. London: Pimlico.

James, Peter, and Peter G. van der Veen. 2015. *Solomon and Shishak: Current Perspectives from Archaeology, Epigraphy, History and Chronology: Proceedings of the Third BICANE Colloquium held at Sidney Sussex College, Cambridge 26–27 March, 2011*. BAR International Series 2732. Oxford: BAR Publishing.

James, Peter, I. J. Thorpe, Nikos Kokkinos, Robert Morkot, and John Frankish. 1992. 'Centuries of Darkness: A Reply to Critics', *Cambridge Archaeological Journal* 2: 127–44.
James, T. G. H. 2002. *Ramesses II*. Vercelli: White Star Publishers.
Jamieson-Drake, David W. 1991. *Scribes and Schools in Monarchic Judah: A Socio-Archeological Approach*. JSOTSup 109. Social World of Biblical Antiquity 9. Sheffield: Almond Press.
Joffe, Alexander H. 2002. 'The Rise of Secondary States in the Iron Age Levant', *JESHO* 45: 425–67.
Johnson, Marshall D. 1988. *The Purpose of the Biblical Genealogies*. 2nd edn. Cambridge: Cambridge University Press.
Jonker, Louis. 2008. 'The Chronicler's Portrayal of Solomon as the King of Peace within the Context of the International Peace Discourses of the Persian Era', *Old Testament Essays* 21: 653–9.
Joosten, Jan. 2005. 'The Distinction between Classical and Late Biblical Hebrew as Reflected in Syntax', *Hebrew Studies* 46: 327–39.
Joosten, Jan. 2019. 'The Linguistic Dating of the Joseph Story', *HeBAI* 8: 1–20.
Kahn, Dan'el. 2011. 'One Step Forward, Two Steps Backward: The Relations between Amenhotep III, King of Egypt and Tushratta, King of Mitanni', in Shay Bar, Dan'el Kahn, and Judith J. Shirley (eds), *Egypt, Canaan and Israel: History, Ideology, Imperialism and Literature: Proceedings of a Conference at the University of Haifa, 3–7 May 2009*, 136–54. CHANE 51. Leiden: Brill.
Kallai, Zecharia. 1995. 'The Twelve-Tribe Systems of Israel', *VT* 47: 53–90.
Kallai, Zecharia. 1999. 'A Note on the Twelve-Tribe Systems of Israel', *VT* 49: 125–7.
Kamp, Kathryn A., and Norman Yoffee. 1980. 'Ethnicity in Ancient Western Asia During the Early Second Millennium B.C.: Archaeological Assessments and Ethnoarchaeological Prospectives', *BASOR* 237: 85–104.
Kamrin, Janice. 2009. 'The Aamu of Shu in the Tomb of Khnumhotep II at Beni Hassan', *JAEI* 1: 22–36.
Kamrin, Janice. 2013. 'The Procession of "Asiatics" at Beni Hasan', in Joan Aruz, Sarah B. Graff, and Yelena Rakic (eds), *Cultures in Contact: From Mesopotamia to the Mediterranean in the Second Millennium B.C.*, 156–69. The Metropolitan Museum of Art Symposia. New York: Metropolitan Museum of Art.
Kaniewski, David, Elise Van Campo, Karel Van Lerberghe, Tom Boiy, Klaas Vansteenhuyse, Greta Jans, Karin Nys, Harvey Weiss, Christophe Morhange, Thierry Otto, and Joachim Bretschneider. 2011. 'The Sea Peoples, from Cuneiform Tablets to Carbon Dating', *PLoS ONE* 6, issue 6: 1–7.
Kaniewski, David, Elise Van Campo, Joël Guiot, Sabine Le Burel, Thierry Otto, and Cecile Baeteman. 2013. 'Environmental Roots of the Late Bronze Age Crisis', *PLoS ONE* 8, issue 8: 1–10.
Katzenstein, H. Jacob. 1997. *The History of Tyre: From the Beginning of the Second Millennium B.C.E. until the Fall of the Neo-Babylonian Empire in 539 B.C.E.* 2nd edn. Jerusalem: Negev Press.
Kempinski, Aharon, and Silvin Košak. 1982. '*CTH* 13: The Extensive Annals of Hattušili I (?)', *TA* 9: 87–116.
Kenyon, Kathleen M. 1966. *Amorites and Canaanites*. The Schweich Lectures of the British Academy 1963. London: OUP for the British Academy.
Khazanov, A. M. 1994. *Nomads and the Outside World*. Translated by Julia Crookenden. Cambridge: Cambridge University Press.
Khoury, Philip S., and Joseph Kostiner. 1990. 'Introduction: Tribes and the Complexities of State Formation in the Middle East', in Philip S. Khoury and Joseph Kostiner (eds), *Tribes and State Formation in the Middle East*, 1–22. Berkeley, CA: University of California Press.
Khoury, Philip S., and Joseph Kostiner (eds) 1990. *Tribes and State Formation in the Middle East*. Berkeley, CA: University of California Press.
Kienast, Burkhart. 1980. 'Die altbabylonischen Kaufurkunden aus Alalaḫ', *WO* 11: 35–63.
Killebrew, Ann E. 2000. 'Aegean-Style Early Philistine Pottery in Canaan During the Iron I Age: A Stylistic Analysis of Mycenaean IIIC:1b Pottery and its Associated Wares', in Eliezer D. Oren (ed.), *The Sea Peoples and their World: A Reassessment*, 233–53. University Museum Monograph 108. University Museum Symposium Series 11. Philadelphia, PA: University of Pennsylvania, The University Museum.

Killebrew, Ann E. 2001. 'The Collared Pithos in Context: A Typological, Technological, and Functional Reassessment', in Samuel R. Wolff (ed.), *Studies in the Archaeology of Israel and Neighboring Lands in Memory of Douglas L. Esse*, 377–98. The Oriental Institute of the University of Chicago Studies in Ancient Oriental Civilization 59. ASOR Books 5. Chicago: Oriental Institute.

Killebrew, Ann E. 2003. 'Biblical Jerusalem: An Archaeological Assessment', in Andrew G. Vaughn and Ann E. Killebrew (eds), *Jerusalem in Bible and Archaeology: The First Temple Period*, 329–45. SBLSymS 18. Atlanta, GA: Society of Biblical Literature.

Killebrew, Ann E. 2005. *Biblical Peoples and Ethnicity: An Archaeological Study of Egyptians, Canaanites, Philistines, and Early Israel 1300–1000 B.C.E.* SBLABS 9. Atlanta, GA: Society of Biblical Literature.

Killebrew, Ann E. 2006. 'The Emergence of Ancient Israel: The Social Boundaries of a "Mixed Multitude" in Canaan', in Aren M. Maeir and Pierre de Miroschedji (eds), *'I Will Speak the Riddles of Ancient Times': Archaeological and Historical Studies in Honor of Amihai Mazar on the Occasion of his Sixtieth Birthday*, 555–72. Winona Lake, IN: Eisenbrauns.

Killebrew, Ann E. 2007. 'The Canaanite Storage Jar Revisited', in Sidnie White Crawford (eds), *'Up to the Gates of Ekron': Essays on the Archaeology and History of the Eastern Mediterranean in Honor of Seymour Gitin*, 166–88. Jerusalem: Israel Exploration Society.

Killebrew, Ann E. 2008. 'Aegean-Style Pottery and Associated Assemblages in the Southern Levant: Chronological Implications Regarding the Tradition from the Late Bronze Age II to the Iron I and the Appearance of the Philistines', in Lester L. Grabbe (ed.), *Israel in Transition: From Late Bronze II to Iron IIA (c. 1250–850 BCE): The Archaeology*, 54–71. LHBOTS 491. ESHM 7. London and New York: T&T Clark International.

Killebrew, Ann E., and Gunnar Lehmann (eds). 2013. *The Philistines and Other 'Sea Peoples' in Text and Archaeology*. Society of Biblical Literature Archaeology and Biblical Studies 15. Atlanta, GA: Society of Biblical Literature.

Kitchen, K. A. 1964. 'New Light on the Asiatic Wars of Rameses II', *JEA* 50: 47–70.

Kitchen, K. A. 1967. 'Byblos, Egypt, and Mari in the Early Second Millennium B.C.', *Or* 36: 39–54.

Kitchen, K. A. 1982. *Pharaoh Triumphant: The Life and Times of Ramesses II, King of Egypt*. Monumenta Hannah Sheen dedicata II. Warminster, Wilts.: Aris & Phillips.

Kitchen, K. A. 1986. *The Third Intermediate Period in Egypt (1100–650 BC)*. 2nd edn. Warminster, Wiltshire: Aris & Philips.

Kitchen, K. A. 1992a. 'The Egyptian Evidence on Ancient Jordan', in Piotr Bienkowski (ed.), *Early Edom and Moab: The Beginning of the Iron Age in Southern Jordan*, 21–34. Sheffield Archaeological Monographs 7. Sheffield: J. R. Collis Publications.

Kitchen, K. A. 1992b. 'Exodus, The', *ABD* 2:700–708.

Kitchen, K. A. 1993. *Ramesside Inscriptions: Translated and Annotated: Translations Volume I: Ramesses I, Sethos I and Contemporaries*. Oxford: Blackwell.

Kitchen, K. A. 1996. *Ramesside Inscriptions: Translated and Annotated: Translations Volume II: Ramesses II, Royal Inscriptions*. Oxford: Blackwell.

Kitchen, K. A. 1997. 'Sheba and Arabia', in Lowell K. Handy (ed.), *The Age of Solomon: Scholarship at the Turn of the Millennium*, 126–53. SHCANE 11. Leiden: Brill.

Kitchen, K. A. 1998. 'Egyptians and Hebrews, from Ra'amses to Jericho', in Shmuel Aḥituv and Eliezer D. Oren (eds), *The Origin of Early Israel – Current Debate: Biblical, Historical and Archaeological Perspectives*, 65–131. Beer-Sheva 12. Beersheba: Ben-Gurion University of the Negev Press.

Kitchen, K. A. 2004. 'The Victories of Merenptah, and the Nature of their Record', *JSOT* 28: 259–72.

Klengel, Horst. 1992. *Syria 3000 to 300 B.C.: A Handbook of Political History*. Berlin: Akademie Verlag.

Klengel, Horst. 1998. *Geschichte des Hethitischen Reiches*. HdO I/34. Leiden: Brill.

Kletter, Raz. 2006. 'Can a Proto-Israelite Please Stand Up? Notes on the Ethnicity of Iron Age Israel and Judah', in Aren M. Maeir and Pierre de Miroschedji (eds), *'I Will Speak the Riddles of Ancient Times': Archaeological and Historical Studies in Honor of Amihai Mazar on the Occasion of his Sixtieth Birthday*, 573–86. Winona Lake, IN: Eisenbrauns.

Knapp, Andrew. 2015. *Royal Apologetic in the Ancient Near East*. SBLWAWS 4. Atlanta, GA: SBL.

Knauf, Ernst Axel. 1988. *Midian: Untersuchungen zur Geschichte Palästinas und Nordarabiens am Ende des 2. Jahrtausends v. Chr.* ADPV 7. Wiesbaden: Harrassowitz.

Knauf, Ernst Axel. 1991a. 'From History to Interpretation', in Diana V. Edelman (ed.), *The Fabric of History: Text, Artifact and Israel's Past*, 26–64. JSOTSup 127. Sheffield: Sheffield Academic Press.

Knauf, Ernst Axel. 1991b. 'Eglon and Ophrah: Two Toponymic Notes on the Book of Judges', *JSOT* 51: 25–44.

Knauf, Ernst Axel. 1992. 'The Cultural Impact of Secondary State Formation: The Cases of the Edomites and Moabites', in Piotr Bienkowski (ed.) *Early Edom and Moab: The Beginning of the Iron Age in Southern Jordan*, 47–54. Sheffield Archaeological Monographs 7. Sheffield: Sheffield Academic Press.

Knauf, Ernst Axel. 1997. 'Le roi est mort, vive le roi! A Biblical Argument for the Historicity of Solomon', in Lowell K. Handy (ed.), *The Age of Solomon: Scholarship at the Turn of the Millennium*, 81–95. SHCANE 11. Leiden: Brill.

Knauf, Ernst Axel. 2000. 'Jerusalem in the Late Bronze and Early Iron Ages: A Proposal', *TA* 27: 75–90.

Knauf, Ernst Axel. 2005. 'Deborah's Language: Judges ch. 5 in its Hebrew and Semitic Context', in B. Burtea, Josef Tropper, and Helen Younansardaround (eds), *Studia Semitica et Semitohamitica*, 167–82. Festschrift Rainer Voigt. AOAT 317. Münster: Ugarit-Verlag.

Knauf, Ernst Axel. 2008a. 'From Archaeology to History, Bronze and Iron Ages with Special Regard to the Year 1200 BCE and the Tenth Century', in Lester L. Grabbe (ed.), *Israel in Transition: From Late Bronze II to Iron IIA (c. 1250–850 BCE): The Archaeology*, 72–85. LHBOTS 491. ESHM 7. London and New York: T&T Clark International.

Knauf, Ernst Axel. 2008b. *Josua*. Züricher Bibelkommentare, Altes Testament 6. Zürich: Theologischer Verlag.

Knauf, Ernst Axel. 2010a. 'History in Joshua', in Lester L. Grabbe (ed.), *Israel in Transition: From Late Bronze II to Iron IIA (c. 1250–850 BCE): Volume 2 The Text*, 130–9. LHBOTS 521 = ESHM 8. London/New York: T&T Clark International.

Knauf, Ernst Axel. 2010b. 'History in Judges', in Lester L. Grabbe (ed.), *Israel in Transition: From Late Bronze II to Iron IIA (c. 1250–850 BCE): Volume 2 The Text*, 140–9. LHBOTS 521 = ESHM 8. London/New York: T&T Clark International.

Knauf, Ernst Axel. 2010c. 'Exodus and Settlement'. in Lester L. Grabbe (ed.) *Israel in Transition: From Late Bronze II to Iron IIA (c. 1250–850 BCE): Volume 2 The Text*, 241–50. LHBOTS 521. ESHM 8. London/New York: T&T Clark International.

Knauf, Ernst Axel. 2016a. *Richter*. Züricher Bibelkommentare, Altes Testament 7. Zürich: Theologischer Verlag.

Knauf, Ernst Axel. 2016b. *1 Könige 1–14*. Herders Theologischer Kommentar zum Alten Testament. Freiburg: Herder.

Knauf, Ernst Axel. 2016c. 'The Impact of the Late Bronze III on the Origins of Israel', in Lester L. Grabbe (ed.), *The Land of Canaan in the Late Bronze Age*, 125–32. LHBOTS 636; European Seminar in Historical Methodology 10. London/New York: Bloomsbury T&T Clark.

Knauf, Ernst Axel. 2019. *1 Könige 15–22*. Herders Theologischer Kommentar zum Alten Testament. Freiburg: Herder.

Knauf, Ernst Axel, and Philippe Guillaume. 2016. *A History of Biblical Israel: The Fate of the Tribes and Kingdoms from Merenptah to Bar Kochba*. Worlds of the Ancient Near East and Mediterranean. London: Equinox.

Knauf, Ernst Axel, and Hermann Michael Niemann. 2021. *Geschichte Israels und Judas im Altertum*. Berlin: de Gruyter.

Knudtson, J. A. 1907–15. *Die El-Amarna Tafeln*. Vorderasiatische Bibliotek 2. Berlin: Hinrichs.

Koch, Ido. 2017. 'Settlements and Interactions in the Shephelah during the Late Second through Early First Millennia BCE', in Oded Lipschits and Aren M. Maeir (eds), *The Shephelah during the Iron Age: Recent Archaeological Studies*, 181–207. Winona Lake, IN: Eisenbrauns.

Koch, Ido. 2018. 'The Egyptian-Canaanite Interface as Colonial Encounter: A View from Southwest Canaan', *JAEI* 18: 24–39.

Koch, Ido. 2019. 'Southwestern Canaan and Egypt during the Late Bronze Age I-IIA', in Aren M. Maeir, Itzhaq Shai, and Chris McKinny (eds), *The Late Bronze and Early Iron Ages of Southern Canaan*, 262–82. Archaeology of the Biblical Worlds 2. Berlin: de Gruyter.

Kohl, Philip L. 1995. Review of P. James, *Centuries of Darkness*, *Journal of Interdisciplinary History* 26: 274–5.

Kossian, Aram V. 1997. 'The Mushki Problem Reconsidered', *SMEA* 39: 253–66.

Krahmalkov, C. R. 1994. 'Exodus Itinerary Confirmed by Egyptian Evidence', *BAR* 20, no. 5: 55–62, 79.

Kramer, Samuel Noah. 1949. 'Schooldays: A Sumerian Composition Relating to the Education of a Scribe', *JAOS* 69: 199–215.

Krause, Joachin J., Omer Sergi, and Kristin Weingut (eds). 2020. *Saul, Benjamin, and the Emergence of Monarchy in Israel: Biblical and Archaeological Perspectives*. Ancient Israel and its Literature 40. Atlanta, GA: SBL.

Krebernik, Manfred. 1996. 'The Linguistic Classification of Eblaite: Methods, Problems, and Results', in Jerrold S. Cooper and Glenn M. Schwartz (eds), *The Study of the Ancient Near East in the Twenty-First Century: The William Foxwell Albright Centennial Conference*, 233–51. Winona Lake, IN: Eisenbrauns.

Kuhrt, Amélie. 1995. *The Ancient Near East c. 3000–300 BC, Volumes 1–2*. Routledge History of the Ancient World. London/New York: Routledge.

LaBianca, Øystein S. 1997. 'Palestine in the Bronze Age', *OEANE* 4: 212–17.

LaBianca, Øystein S., and Randall W. Younker. 1998. 'The Kingdoms of Ammon, Moab and Edom: The Archaeology of Society in Late Bronze/Iron Age Transjordan (ca. 1400–500 BCE)', in Thomas E. Levy (ed.), *The Archaeology of Society in the Holy Land*, 399–415. 2nd edn. New Approaches in Anthropological Archaeology. London: Leicester University Press.

Lacheman, Ernest R., and M. P. Maidman (eds). 1989. *Joint Expedition with the Iraq Museum at Nuzi VII: Miscellaneous Texts*. Studies on the Civilization and Culture of Nuzi and the Hurrians 3. Winona Lake, IN: Eisenbrauns.

Lacheman, Ernest R., Martha A. Morrison, and David I. Owen (eds). 1993. *The Eastern Archives of Nuzi and Excavations at Nuzi 9/2*. Studies on the Civilization and Culture of Nuzi and the Hurrians 4. Winona Lake, IN: Eisenbrauns.

Lackenbacher, Sylvie. 1982. 'Nouveaux documents d'Ugarit: I. Une lettre royale', *RdA* 76: 141–56.

Lackenbacher, Sylvie. 2002. *Textes akkadiens d'Ugarit: Textes provenant des vingt-cinq premières campagnes*. Littératures anciennes du Proche-Orient 20. Paris: Cerf (= LAPO 20).

Lambert, W. G. 1957–58. Review of F. Gössmann, *Das Era-Epos*, *AfO* 18: 395–401.

Lambert, W. G. 1962. 'The Reign of Nebuchadnezzar I: A Turning Point in the History of Ancient Mesopotamian Religion', in W. S. McCullough (ed.), *The Seed of Wisdom: Essays in Honour of T. J. Meek*, 3–13. Toronto: University of Toronto Press.

Laroche, Emmanuel. 1971. *Catalogue des textes hittites*. Paris: Klincksieck [standard reference, referred to by *CTH*].

Larson, Mogens Trolle. 1976. *The Old Assyrian City-State and its Colonies*. Mesopotamia: Copenhagen Studies in Assyriology 4. Copenhagen: Akademisk Forlag.

Leahy, Anthony. 2001. 'Foreign Incursions', *OEAE* 1: 548–52.

Leclant, Jean. 1984. 'T. P. Pépi Ier VII: Une nouvelle mention des *FNḪW* dans Les Textes des Pyramides', *SAK* 11: 455–60.

Leemans, W. F. 1960. 'The Trade Relations of Babylonia and the Question of Relations with Egypt in the Old Babylonian Period', *JESHO* 3: 21–37.

Lehmann, G. A. 1979. 'Die Šikalājū – ein neues Zeugnis zu den "Seevölker"-Heerfahrten im späten 13. Jh. v. Chr. (RS 34.129)', *UF* 11: 481–94.

Lehmann, Gunnar. 2003. 'The United Monarchy in the Countryside: Jerusalem, Judah, and the Shephelah during the Tenth Century B.C.E.', in Andrew G. Vaughn and Ann E. Killebrew (eds), *Jerusalem in Bible and Archaeology: The First Temple Period*, 117–62. SBLSymS 18. Atlanta, GA: Society of Biblical Literature.

Lehmann, Gunnar, and Hermann Michael Niemann. 2014. 'When Did the Shephelah Become Judahite?' *TA* 41: 77–94.

Lemche, Niels Peter. 1977. 'The Greek "Amphictyony" – Could it Be a Prototype for the Israelite Society in the Period of the Judges?' *JSOT* 4: 48–59.

Lemche, Niels Peter. 1985. *Early Israel: Anthropological and Historical Studies on the Israelite Society before the Monarchy.* VTSup 37. Leiden: Brill.

Lemche, Niels Peter. 1991. *The Canaanites and Their Land: The Tradition of the Canaanites*. JSOTSup 110. Sheffield: Sheffield Academic Press.

Lemche, Niels Peter. 1992. 'Ḫabiru, Ḫapiru', *ABD* 3:6–10.

Lemche, Niels Peter. 1996. 'Where Should We Look for Canaan? A Reply to Nadav Na'aman', *UF* 28: 767–72.

Lemche, Niels Peter. 1998a. *Prelude to Israel's Past: Background and Beginnings of Israelite History and Identity*. Translated by E. F. Maniscalco. Peabody, MA: Hendrickson.

Lemche, Niels Peter. 1998b. 'Greater Canaan: The Implications of a Correct Reading of EA 151:49–67', *BASOR* 310: 19–24.

Levin, Christoph. 1995. 'Das System der zwölf Stämme Israels', in J. A. Emerton (ed.), *Congress Volume Paris 1992*, 163–78. VTSup 61. Leiden: Brill.

Levy, Thomas E. 2009a. 'Ethnic Identity in Biblical Edom, Israel, and Midian: Some Insights from Mortuary Contexts in the Lowlands of Edom', in J. David Schloen (ed.), *Exploring the* Longue Durée: *Essays in Honor of Lawrence E. Stager*, 251–61. Winona Lake, IN: Eisenbrauns.

Levy, Thomas E. 2009b. 'Pastoral Nomads and Iron Age Metal Production in Ancient Edom', in Jeffrey Szuchman (ed.), *Nomads, Tribes, and the State in the Ancient Near East: Cross-Disciplinary Perspectives*, 147–77. University of Chicago Oriental Institute Seminars 5. Chicago: Oriental Institute.

Levy, Thomas E., Russell B. Adams, and Adolfo Muniz. 2004. 'Archaeology and the Shasu Nomads: Recent Excavations in the Jabal Hamrat Fidan, Jordan', in Richard Elliott Friedman and William H. C. Propp (eds), *Le-David Maskil: A Birthday Tribute for David Noel Freedman*, 63–89. Biblical and Judaic Studies 9. Winona Lake, IN: Eisenbrauns.

Levy, Thomas E., Russell B. Adams, Mohammad Najjar, Andreas Hauptmann, James D. Anderson, Baruch Brandl, Mark A. Robinson and Thomas Higham. 2004. 'Reassessing the Chronology of Biblical Edom: New Excavations and ^{14}C Dates from Khirbat en-Nahas (Jordan)', *Antiquity* 302: 865–79.

Levy, Thomas E., Mohammad Najjar, Johannes van der Plicht, Neil G. Smith, Hendrik J. Bruins and Thomas Higham. 2005. 'Lowland Edom and the High and Low Chronologies: Edomite State Formation, the Bible and Recent Archaeological Research in Southern Jordan', in Thomas E. Levy and Thomas Higham (eds), *The Bible and Radiocarbon Dating: Archaeology, Text and Science*, 129–63. London: Equinox.

Levy, Thomas E. (ed.). 1998. *The Archaeology of Society in the Holy Land*. 2nd edn. New Approaches in Anthropological Archaeology. London: Leicester University Press.

Levy, Thomas E., and Thomas Higham (eds). 2005. *The Bible and Radiocarbon Dating: Archaeology, Text and Science*. London: Equinox.

Levy, Thomas E., Mohammad Najjar, and Erez Ben-Yosef (eds). 2014. *New Insights into the Iron Age Archaeology of Edom, Southern Jordan: Surveys, Excavations, and Research from the University of California, San Diego & Department of Antiquities of Jordan, Edom Lowlands Regional Archaeology Project (ELRAP)*. 2 vols. Monumenta Archaeologica 35. Los Angeles, CA: Cotsen Institute of Archaeology Press.

Levy, Thomas E., Thomas Schneider, and William H. C. Propp (eds). 2015. *Israel's Exodus in Transdisciplinary Perspective: Text, Archaeology, Culture, and Geoscience*. Quantitative Methods in the Humanities and Social Sciences. Cham, Switzerland: Springer.

Lichtheim, Miriam. 1973. *Ancient Egyptian Literature, Volume I: The Old and Middle Kingdoms*. Berkeley/Los Angeles: University of California Press.

Lichtheim, Miriam. 1976. *Ancient Egyptian Literature, Volume II: The New Kingdom*. Berkeley/Los Angeles: University of California Press.

Lichtheim, Miriam. 1980. *Ancient Egyptian Literature, Volume III: The Late Period*. Berkeley/Los Angeles: University of California Press.

Lichtheim, Miriam. 1988. *Ancient Egyptian Autobiographies, Chiefly of the Middle Kingdom: A Study and an Anthology*. OBO 84. Freiburg/Schweiz: Universitätsverlag.

Lindars, Barnabas. 1995. *Judges 1–5: A New Translation and Commentary*. Edited by A. D. H. Mayes. Edinburgh: T & T Clark.

Lipinska, Jadwiga. 2001. 'Hatshepsut', *OEAE* 2:85–7.

Lipiński, Edward. 2000. *The Aramaeans: Their Ancient History, Culture, Religion*. OLA 100. Leuven: Peeters.

Lipschits, Oded, and Aren M. Maeir (eds). 2017. *The Shephelah during the Iron Age: Recent Archaeological Studies*. Winona Lake, IN: Eisenbrauns.

Liverani, Mario. 1973. 'The Amorites', in D. J. Wiseman (ed.), *Peoples of Old Testament Times*, 100–33. Oxford: Clarendon Press.

Liverani, Mario. 1983. 'Political Lexicon and Political Ideologies in the Amarna Letters', *Berytus* 31: 41–56. Reprinted in Mario Liverani, *Historiography, Ideology and Politics in the Ancient Near East and Israel*, 202–20. Edited by Niels Peter Lemche and Emanuel Pfoh. Changing Perspectives 5. London/New York: Routledge, 2021.

Liverani, Mario. 1990. *Prestige and Interest: International Relations in the Near East ca. 1600–1100 B.C.* History of the Ancient Near East Studies 1. Padua: Sargon.

Liverani, Mario. 2004. *Myth and Politics in Ancient Near Eastern Historiography*. Edited by Zainab Bahrani and Marc Van De Mieroop. Studies in Egyptology and the Ancient Near East. London: Equinox.

Liverani, Mario. 2005. *Israel's History and the History of Israel*. Translated by Chiara Peri and Philip R. Davies. London: Equinox.

Liverani, Mario. 2014. *The Ancient Near East: History, Society and Economy*. Translated by Soraia Tabatabai. London/New York: Routledge. ET of *Antico Oriente*. 2nd edn. Milan: Gius, Laterza and Figh, 2011.

Liverani, Mario. 2017. *Assyria: The Imperial Mission*. Translated by Andrea Trameri and Jonathan Valk. Mesopotamian Civilizations 21. Winona Lake, IN: Eisenbrauns. ET of Mario Liverani, *Assiria. La preistoria dell'imperialismo*. Rome: Editori Laterza, 2017.

Liverani, Mario. 2021a. *Historiography, Ideology and Politics in the Ancient Near East and Israel*. Edited by Niels Peter Lemche and Emanuel Pfoh. Changing Perspectives 5. London/New York: Routledge.

Liverani, Mario. 2021b. 'Contrasts and Confluences of Political Conceptions in the Amarna Period', in Mario Liverani, *Historiography, Ideology and Politics in the Ancient Near East and Israel*. Edited by Niels Peter Lemche and Emanuel Pfoh. Changing Perspectives 5. London/New York: Routledge. ET of 'Contrasti e confluenze de concezioni politiche nell'età di El-Amarna', *RdA* 61(1967): 1–18.

Liverani, Mario (ed.). 1993. *Akkad: The First World Empire: Structure, Ideology, Traditions*. History of the Ancient Near East I Studies 5. Padua: Sargon.

Liverani, Mario (ed. and trans.). 1998. *Le lettere di el-Amarna: vol. 1. Le lettere dei 'Piccoli Re'*. Testi del Vicino Oriente antico 1. Brescia: Paideia.

Liwik, Rüdiger. 1992. 'Sharuhen', *ABD* 5:1163–5.

Lloyd, Alan B. 1970. 'The Egyptian Labyrinth', *JEA* 56: 81–100.

Loretz, Oswald. 1984. *Habiru-Hebräer: Eine sozio-linguistische Studie über die Herkunft des Gentiliziums 'ibrî vom Appellativum ḫabiru*. BZAW 160. Berlin/New York: de Gruyter.

Loretz, Oswald. 1995. 'Les Šerdanū et la fin d'Ougarit: À propos des documents d'Égypte, de Byblos et d'Ougarit relatifs aux Shardana'; Annexe de Jochem Kahl: 'Les témoignages textuels égyptiens sur les Shardana', in Marguerite Yon, Maurice Sznycer, and Pierre Bordreuil (eds), *Le pays d'Ougarit autour de 1200 av. J.-C.: Histoire et archéologie, Actes du Colloque International, Paris, 28 juin–1er juillet 1993*, 125–36. Ras Shamra-Ougarit 11. Paris: Editions Recherche sur les Civilisations.

Lorton, David. 1973. 'The So-called "Vile" Enemies of the King of Egypt (in the Middle Kingdom and Dyn. XVIII)', *JARCE* 10: 65–70.

Lucas, Christopher J. 1979. 'The Scribal Tablet-House in Ancient Mesopotamia', *History of Education Quarterly* 19: 305–32.

Macchi, Jean-Daniel. 1999. *Israël et ses tribus selon Genèse 49*. OBO 171. Freiburg (Schweiz): Universitätsverlag; Göttingen: Vandenhoeck & Ruprecht.

MacDonald, Burton. 2000. *'East of the Jordan': Territories and Sites of the Hebrew Scriptures*. ASOR Books 6. Boston, MA: American Schools of Oriental Research.

MacDonald, Burton, Russell Adams, and Piotr Bienkowski (eds). 2001. *The Archaeology of Jordan*. Levantine Archaeology 1. Sheffield: Sheffield Academic Press.

Maeir, Aren M. 2012. 'Insights on the Philistine Culture and Related Issues: An Overview of 15 Years of Work at Tell eṣ-Ṣafi/Gath', in Gershon Galil, Ayelet Gilboa, Aren M. Maeir, and Dan'el Kahn (eds), *The Ancient Near East in the 12th–10th Centuries BCE: Culture and History: Proceedings of the International Conference held at the University of Haifa, 2–5 May, 2010*, 345–404. AOAT 392. Münster: Ugarit Verlag.

Maeir, Aren M. 2017a. 'Philistine Gath after 20 Years: Regional Perspectives on the Iron Age', in Oded Lipschits and Aren M. Maeir (eds), *The Shephelah during the Iron Age: Recent Archaeological Studies*, 133–54. Winona Lake, IN: Eisenbrauns.

Maeir, Aren M. 2017b. Review of S. Rodan, *Aegean Mercenaries in Light of the Bible*, *Journal of Eastern Mediterranean Archaeology & Heritage Studies* 5: 246–7.

Maeir, Aren M. 2019a. 'Iron Age I Philistines: Entangled Identities in a Transformative Period', in Assaf Yasur-Landau, Eric H. Cline, and Yorke M. Rowan (eds), *The Social Archaeology of the Levant: From Prehistory to the Present*, 310–23. Cambridge: Cambridge University Press.

Maeir, Aren M. 2019b. 'Philistine and Israelite Identities: Some Comparative Thoughts', *WO* 49: 151–60.

Maeir, Aren M. 2021. 'On Defining Israel: Or, Let's Do the *Kulturkreislehre* Again!', *HeBAI* 10: 106–48.

Maeir, Aren M. (ed.). 2012. *Tell es-Safi/Gath I: The 1996–2005 Seasons: Part 1: Text*. Ägypten und Altes Testament 69. Wiesbaden: Harrassowitz.

Maeir, Aren M., and Joe Uziel. 2007. 'A Tale of Two Tells: A Comparative Perspective on Tel Miqne-Ekron and Tell eṣ-Ṣâfî/Gath in Light of Recent Archaeological Research', in Sidnie White Crawford (eds), *'Up to the Gates of Ekron': Essays on the Archaeology and History of the Eastern Mediterranean in Honor of Seymour Gitin*, 29–42. Jerusalem: Israel Exploration Society.

Maidman, Maynard Paul. 1994. *Two Hundred Nuzi Texts from the Oriental Institute of the University of Chicago, Part I*. Studies on the Civilization and Culture of Nuzi and the Hurrians 6. Bethesda, MD: CDL Press.

Maidman, Maynard Paul. 1995. 'Nuzi: Portrait of an Ancient Mesopotamian Provincial Town', in Jack M. Sasson (ed.), *Civilizations of the Ancient Near East*, 2:931–47. New York: Scribner's.

Malamat, Abraham. 1971. 'Syro-Palestinian Destinations in a Mari Tin Inventory', *IEJ* 21: 31–8.

Malamat, Abraham. 1982. 'A Political Look at the Kingdom of David and Solomon and its Relations with Egypt', in Tomoo Ishida, *Studies in the Period of David and Solomon and Other Essays: Papers Read at the International Symposium for Biblical Studies, Tokyo, 5–7 December, 1979*, 189–204. Winona Lake, IN: Eisenbrauns.

Malamat, Abraham. 1997. 'The Exodus: Egyptian Analogies', in Ernest S. Frerichs and Leonard H. Lesko (eds), *Exodus: The Egyptian Evidence*, 15–26. Winona Lake, IN: Eisenbrauns.

Malko, Helen O. 2014. *Investigation into the Impacts of Foreign Ruling Elites in Traditional State Societies: The Case of the Kassite State in Babylonia (Iraq)*. PhD thesis at Stony Brook University, New York. Https://search.proquest.com › openview › 1.pdf (accessed 15 April 2021).

Maran, Joseph. 2018. 'Goliath's Peers: Interconnected Polyethnic Warrior Elites in the Eastern Mediterranean of the 13th and 12th Centuries BCE', in Itzhaq Shai et al. (eds), *Tell It in Gath: Studies in the History and Archaeology of Israel: Essays in Honor of Aren M. Maeir on the Occasion of his Sixtieth Birthday*, 223–41. Ägypten und Altes Testament 90. Münster: Ugarit-Verlag.

Mareno Garcia, Juan Carlos (ed.). 2013. *Ancient Egyptian Administration*. HdO I/104. Leiden: Brill.

Margalith, Othniel. 1990. 'On the Origin and Antiquity of the Name "Israel"', *ZAW* 102: 225–37.

Márquez Rowe, Ignacio. 1996. 'An Akkadian Letter of the Amarna Period at Ugarit', *Aula Orientalis* 14: 107–26.

Márquez Rowe, Ignacio. 2000. 'The King of Ugarit, his Wife, her Brother, and her Lovers: The Mystery of a Tragedy in Two Acts Revisited', *UF* 32: 365–72.

Martin, Geoffrey T. 1968. 'A New Prince of Byblos', *JNES* 27: 141–2.

Master, Daniel M. 2001. 'State Formation Theory and the Kingdom of Ancient Israel', *JNES* 60: 117–31.

Matthiae, Paolo. 2020. *Ebla: Archaeology and History*. Translated by Richard Bates, Mattia Bilardello, and Anita Weston. Cities of the Ancient World. London: Routledge. English translation and revision of idem, *Ebla, la città del trono: Archeologia e storia*. Turin: Einaudi, 2010.

Matthiae, Paolo, Frances Pinnock, and Marta d'Andrea (eds). 2018. *Ebla and Beyond: Ancient Near Eastern Studies after Fifty Years of Discoveries at Tell Mardikh: Proceedings of the International Congress Held in Rome, 15th–17th December 2014*. Wiesbaden: Harrassowitz.

Mayes, A. D. H. 1974. *Israel in the Period of the Judges*. Studies in Biblical Theology, 2nd series 29. London: SCM Press.

Mayrhofer, Manfred. 1982. 'Welches Material aus dem Indo-arischen von Mitanni verbleibt für eine selektive Darstellung?', in Erich Neu (ed.), *Investigationes philologicae et comparativae: Gedenkschrift für Heinz Kronasser*, 72–90. Wiesbaden: Harrassowitz.

Mazar, Amihai. 1993. *Archaeology of the Land of the Bible 10,000–586 B.C.E.* New York: Doubleday; Cambridge: Lutterworth Press.

Mazar, Amihai. 2004. 'Greek and Levantine Iron Age Chronology: A Rejoinder', *IEJ* 54: 24–36.

Mazar, Amihai. 2005. 'The Debate over the Chronology of the Iron Age in the Southern Levant: Its History, the Current Situation, and a Suggested Resolution', in Thomas E. Levy and Thomas Higham (eds), *The Bible and Radiocarbon Dating: Archaeology, Text and Science*, 15–30. London: Equinox.

Mazar, Amihai. 2007. 'The Spade and the Text: The Interaction between Archaeology and Israelite History Relating to the Tenth-Ninth Centuries BCE', in H. G. M. Williamson (ed.), *Understanding the History of Ancient Israel*, 143–71. Proceedings of the British Academy 143. Oxford: Oxford University Press for the British Academy.

Mazar, Amihai. 2008. 'From 1200 to 850 BCE: Remarks on Some Selected Archaeological Issues', in Lester L. Grabbe (ed.), *Israel in Transition: From Late Bronze II to Iron IIA (c. 1250–850 BCE): The Archaeology*, 86–120. LHBOTS 491. ESHM 7. London and New York: T&T Clark International.

Mazar, Amihai, and Ehud Netzer. 1986. 'On the Israelite Fortress at Arad', *BASOR* 263: 87–91.

Mazar, Amihai, Hendrik J. Bruins, Nava Panitz-Cohen and Johannes van der Plicht. 2005. 'Ladder of Time at Tel Reḥov: Stratigraphy, Archaeological Context, Pottery and Radiocarbon Dates', in Thomas E. Levy and Thomas Higham (eds), *The Bible and Radiocarbon Dating: Archaeology, Text and Science*, 193–255. London: Equinox.

Mazar, Eilat. 2006. 'Did I Find King David's Palace?' *BAR* 32, no. 1: 16–27, 70.

Mazar, Eilat. 2009. *The Palace of King David: Excavations at the Summit of the City of David: Preliminary Report of Seasons 2005–2007*. Jerusalem: Shoham Academic Research and Publication.

McDermott, John J. 1998. *What Are They Saying about the Formation of Israel?* Mahwah, NJ: Paulist Press.

McGovern, Patrick E., and Garman Harbottle. 1997. '"Hyksos" Trade Connections Between Tell el-Dabʻa (Avaris) and the Levant: A Neutron Activation Study of the Canaanite Jar', in Eliezer D. Oren (ed.), *The Hyksos: New Historical and Archaeological Perspectives*, 141–57. University Museum Monograph 96. University Museum Symposium Series 8. Philadelphia, PA: University of Pennsylvania, The University Museum.

McKenzie, Stephen L. 2000. *King David: A Biography*. Oxford: Oxford University Press.

McNutt, Paula. 1999. *Reconstructing the Society of Ancient Israel*. Library of Ancient Israel. Louisville, KY: Westminster John Knox Press. London: SPCK.

Melchert, Craig. 1978. 'The Acts of Hattusili I', *JNES* 37: 1–22.

Mendenhall, George E. 1962. 'The Hebrew Conquest of Palestine', *BA* 25: 66–87.

Mendenhall, George E. 1983. 'Ancient Israel's Hyphenated History', in David Noel Freedman and D. F. Graf (eds), *Palestine in Transition: The Emergence of Ancient Israel*, 91–103. Social World of Biblical Antiquity Series 2. Sheffield: Sheffield Academic Press.

Michałowski, Kazimierz. 1968. 'The Labyrinth Enigma: Archaeological Suggestions', *JEA* 54: 219–22.

Michalowski, Piotr. 1985. 'Third Millennium Contacts: Observations on the Relationships between Mari and Ebla', *JAOS* 105: 293–302.

Michalowski, Piotr. 2011. *The Correspondence of the Kings of Ur: An Epistolary History of an Ancient Mesopotamian Kingdom*. Mesopotamian Civilizations 15. Winona Lake, IN: Eisenbrauns.

Mieroop, Marc Van De. 2000. 'Sargon of Agade and his Successors in Anatolia', *Studi Micenei ed Egeo-Anatolici* 42: 133–59.

Mieroop, Marc Van De. 2003. *A History of the Ancient Near East, ca. 3000–323 BC*. Blackwell History of the Ancient World 1. Oxford: Blackwell.

Millek, Jesse Michael. 2014. Review of E. Stern, *The Material Culture of the Northern Sea Peoples in Israel*, *ZDPV* 130: 110–11.

Millek, Jesse Michael. 2017. 'Sea Peoples, Philistines, and the Destruction of Cities: A Critical Examination of Destruction Layers "Caused" by the "Sea Peoples"', in Peter M. Fischer and Teresa Bürge (eds), *'Sea Peoples' Up-to-Date: New Research on Transformations in the Eastern Mediterranean in the 13th–11th Centuries BCE: Proceedings of the ESF-Workshop held at the Austrian Academy of Sciences, Vienna, 3–4 November 2014*, 113–40. Contributions to the Chronology of the Eastern Mediterranean 81. Vienna: Verlag der Österreichischen Akademie der Wissenschaften.

Millek, Jesse Michael. 2020–21. '"Our City Is Sacked. May You Know it!" The Destruction of Ugarit and its Environs by the "Sea People"', *Archaeology and History in the Lebanon* 52–53: 102–32.

Millek, Jesse Michael. 2021. 'Just What did They Destroy? The Sea Peoples and the End of the Late Bronze Age', in J. Kamlah and A. Lichtenberger (eds), *The Mediterranean Sea and the Southern Levant: Archaeological and Historical Perspectives from the Bronze Age to Medieval Times*, 59–98. Abhandlungen des Deutschen Palästina-Vereins 48. Wiesbaden: Harrassowitz.

Millek, Jesse Michael. Forthcoming. *The Fall of the Bronze Age*.

Miller, J. Maxwell. 1977. 'Archaeology and the Israelite Conquest of Canaan: Some Methodological Observations', *PEQ* 109: 87–93.

Miller, J. Maxwell. 1979. 'W. F. Albright and Historical Reconstruction', *BA* 42: 37–47.

Miller, J. Maxwell. 1992. 'Early Monarchy in Moab?' in Piotr Bienkowski (ed.), *Early Edom and Moab: The Beginning of the Iron Age in Southern Jordan*, 77–91. Sheffield Archaeological Monographs 7. Sheffield: J. R. Collis Publications.

Miller, J. Maxwell (ed.). 1991. *Archaeological Survey of the Kerak Plateau, Conducted during 1978–1982 under the Direction of J. Maxwell Miller and Jack M. Pinkerton*. ASOR Archaeological Reports. Atlanta, GA: Scholars Press.

Miller, Robert D., II. 2004. 'Identifying Earliest Israel', *BASOR* 333: 55–68.

Miller, Robert D., II. 2005. *Chieftains of the Highland Clans: A History of Israel in the 12th and 11th Centuries B.C.* Grand Rapids, MI: Eerdmans.

Mohammed, Abbas. 1973. 'The Nomadic and the Sedentary: Polar Complementaries – Not Polar Opposites', in Cynthia Nelson (ed.), *The Desert and the Sown: Nomads in the Wider Society*, 97–112. Institute of International Studies. Berkeley, CA: University of California Press.

Monier-Williams, Monier. 1899. *A Sanskrit-English Dictionary: Etymologically and Philologically Arranged with Special Reference to Cognate Indo-European Languages*. Revised by E. Leumann, C. Cappeller, et al. Oxford: Clarendon Press.

Monroe, Lauren, and Daniel E. Fleming. 2019. 'Earliest Israel in Highland Company', *NEA* 82: 16–23.

Montet, Pierre. 1928. *Byblos et l'Égypte: Quatre campagnes de fouilles à Gebeil, 1921–1922–1923–1924: Texte*. Bibliothéque Archéologique et Historique 11. Paris: Paul Geuthner.

Moran, William L. 1992. *The Amarna Letters*. Baltimore: Johns Hopkins University Press.

Moran, William L. 1995. 'Some Reflections on Amarna Politics', in Ziony Zevit, Seymour Gitin, and Michael Sokoloff (eds), *Solving Riddles and Untying Knots: Biblical, Epigraphic, and Semitic Studies in Honor of Jonas C. Greenfield*, 559–72. Winona Lake, IN: Eisenbrauns. Reprinted in William L. Moran, *Amarna Studies: Collected Writings*, 327–41. Edited by John Huehnergard and Shlomo Izre'el. HSS 54. Winona Lake, IN: Eisenbrauns, 2003.

Moran, William L. 2003. *Amarna Studies: Collected Writings*. Edited by John Huehnergard and Shlomo Izre'el. HSS 54. Winona Lake, IN: Eisenbrauns.

Morris, Ellen Fowles. 2005. *The Architecture of Imperialism: Military Bases and the Evolution of Foreign Policy in Egypt's New Kingdom*. PdÄ 22. Leiden: Brill.

Morrison, Martha A., and David I. Owen (eds). 1981. *In Honor of Ernest R. Lacheman on His Seventy-fifth Birthday, April 29, 1981.* Studies on the Civilization and Culture of Nuzi and the Hurrians 1. Winona Lake, IN: Eisenbrauns.

Moscati, Sabatino (ed.). 1988. *i Fenici.* Milan: Bompiani.

Mourad, Anna-Latifa. 2013. 'Asiatics and Abydos: From the Twelfth Dynasty to the Early Second Intermediate Period', *Bulletin of the Australian Centre for Egyptology* 24: 31–58.

Mourad, Anna-Latifa. 2015. *Rise of the Hyksos: Egypt and the Levant from the Middle Kingdom to the Early Second Intermediate Period.* Archaeopress Egyptology 11. Oxford: Archaeopress.

Mumford, Gregory Duncan. 1998. *International Relations between Egypt, Sinai, and Syria-Palestine during the Late Bronze Age to Early Persian Period (Dynasties 18–26: c. 1550–525 B.C.).* A Thesis Submitted for the Degree of Doctor of Philosophy in the Graduate Department of Near and Middle Eastern Civilizations, University of Toronto. Available from https://tspace.library.utoronto.ca/handle/1807/12551 (accessed 1 July 2021).

Murnane, William J. 1990. *The Road to Kadesh: A Historical Interpretation of the Battle Reliefs of King Sety I at Karnak.* 2nd edn. Studies in Ancient Oriental Civilization 42. Chicago: Oriental Institute of the University of Chicago.

Murnane, William J. 1995. *Texts from the Amarna Period in Egypt.* SBLWAW 5. Atlanta, GA: Scholars Press.

Na'aman, Nadav. 1977. 'Yeno'am', *TA* 4: 168–77. Reprinted in *Canaan in the Second Millennium B.C.E.: Collected Essays Volume 2,* 195–203. Winona Lake, IN: Eisenbrauns, 2005.

Na'aman, Nadav. 1979. 'The Origin and Historical Background of Several Amarna Letters', *UF* 11: 673–84. Reprinted in *Canaan in the Second Millennium B.C.E.: Collected Essays Volume 2,* 65–81. Winona Lake, IN: Eisenbrauns, 2005.

Na'aman, Nadav. 1985. 'Historical-Geographical Aspects of the Amarna Tablets', in *Proceedings of the World Congress of Jewish Studies: Panel Session Bible Studies and Ancient Near East,* 17–26. Jerusalem: World Congress of Jewish Studies.

Na'aman, Nadav. 1986a. 'Ḫabiru and Hebrews: The Transfer of a Social Term to the Literary Sphere', *JNES* 45: 271–88.

Na'aman, Nadav. 1986b. 'The Canaanite City-States in the Late Bronze Age and the Inheritances of the Israelite Tribes', *Tarbiz* 55: 463–88 (Heb.) + I (Eng. abstract).

Na'aman, Nadav. 1988a. 'Canaanites and Perizzites', *BN* 45: 42–7.

Na'aman, Nadav. 1988b. Review of O. Loretz, *Habiru-Hebräer, JNES* 47: 192–4.

Na'aman, Nadav. 1990a. 'Literary and Topographical Notes on the Battle of Kishon (Judges IV–V)', *VT* 40: 423–36.

Na'aman, Nadav. 1990b. 'Praises to the Pharaoh in Response to his Plans for a Campaign to Canaan', in Tzvi Abusch, John Huehnergard, and Piotr Steinkeller (eds), *Lingering over Words: Studies in Ancient Near Eastern Literature in Honor of William L. Moran,* 73–104. HSS 37. Atlanta, GA: Scholars Press. Reprinted in *Canaan in the Second Millennium B.C.E.: Collected Essays Volume 2,* 99–109. Winona Lake, IN: Eisenbrauns, 2005.

Na'aman, Nadav. 1992a. 'Amarna Letters', *ABD* 1:174–81.

Na'aman, Nadav. 1992b. 'Canaanite Jerusalem and its Central Hill Country Neighbours in the Second Millennium B.C.E.', *UF* 24: 275–91. Reprinted in *Canaan in the Second Millennium B.C.E.: Collected Essays Volume 2,* 173–94. Winona Lake, IN: Eisenbrauns, 2005.

Na'aman, Nadav. 1994a. 'The Canaanites and their Land: A Rejoinder', *UF* 26: 397–418. Reprinted in *Canaan in the Second Millennium B.C.E.: Collected Essays Volume 2,* 110–33. Winona Lake, IN: Eisenbrauns, 2005.

Na'aman, Nadav. 1994b. 'The Hurrians and the End of the Middle Bronze Age in Palestine', *Levant* 26: 275–91. Reprinted in *Canaan in the Second Millennium B.C.E.: Collected Essays, Volume 2,* 1–24. Winona Lake, IN: Eisenbrauns.

Na'aman, Nadav. 1994c. 'The "Conquest of Canaan" in the Book of Joshua and in History', in Israel Finkelstein and Nadav Na'aman (eds), *From Nomadism to Monarchy: Archaeological and Historical Aspects of Early Israel,* 218–81. Jerusalem: Israel Exploration Society.

Na'aman, Nadav, 1996a. 'The Contribution of the Amarna Letters to the Debate on Jerusalem's Political Position in the Tenth Century B.C.E.', *BASOR* 304: 17–27.

Na'aman, Nadav. 1996b. 'Ammishtamru's Letter to Akhenaten (EA 45) and Hittite Chronology', *AuOr* 14: 251–57. Reprinted in *Canaan in the Second Millennium B.C.E.: Collected Essays Volume 2*, 40–9. Winona Lake, IN: Eisenbrauns, 2005.

Na'aman, Nadav. 1996c. 'Sources and Composition in the History of David', in Volkmar Fritz and Philip R. Davies (eds), *The Origins of the Ancient Israelite States*, 170–86. JSOTSup 228. Sheffield: Sheffield Academic Press.

Na'aman, Nadav. 1997a. 'The Network of Canaanite Late Bronze Kingdoms and the City of Ashdod', *UF* 29: 599–626. Reprinted in *Canaan in the Second Millennium B.C.E.: Collected Essays Volume 2*, 145–72. Winona Lake, IN: Eisenbrauns, 2005.

Na'aman, Nadav. 1997b. 'Sources and Composition in the History of Solomon', in Lowell K. Handy (ed.), *The Age of Solomon: Scholarship at the Turn of the Millennium*, 57–80. SHCANE 11. Leiden: Brill.

Na'aman, Nadav. 1999. 'Four Notes on the Size of Late Bronze Canaan', *BASOR* 313: 31–7. Reprinted in *Canaan in the Second Millennium B.C.E.: Collected Essays Volume 2*, 134–44. Winona Lake, IN: Eisenbrauns, 2005.

Na'aman, Nadav. 2000. 'The Egyptian-Canaanite Correspondence', in Raymond Cohen and Raymond Westbrook (eds), *Amarna Diplomacy: The Beginnings of International Relations*, 125–38. Baltimore: Johns Hopkins University Press.

Na'aman, Nadav. 2002. 'In Search of Reality Behind the Account of David's Wars with Israel's Neighbours', *IEJ* 52: 200–224.

Na'aman, Nadav. 2005a. *Canaan in the Second Millennium B.C.E.: Collected Essays, Volume 2*. Winona Lake, IN: Eisenbrauns.

Na'aman, Nadav. 2005b. 'The Kingdom of Judah under Josiah', in Lester L. Grabbe (ed.), *Good Kings and Bad Kings: The Kingdom of Judah in the Seventh Century BCE*, 189–247. JSOTSup 393. ESHM 5. London and New York: T&T Clark International.

Na'aman, Nadav. 2006. 'Israel, Edom and Egypt in the 10th Century B.C.E.', in *Ancient Israel's History and Historiography: The First Temple Period; Collected Essays Volume 3*, 120–38. Winona Lake, IN: Eisenbrauns. Slightly revised from the original version in *TA* 19 (1992): 71–93.

Na'aman, Nadav. 2008. 'In Search of the Ancient Name of Khirbet Qeiyafa', *Journal of Hebrew Scriptures* 8/21.

Na'aman, Nadav. 2010. 'Khirbet Qeiyafa in Context', *UF* 42: 497–526.

Na'aman, Nadav. 2011. 'The Shephelah according to the Amarna Letters', in Israel Finkelstein and Nadav Na'aman (eds), *The Fire Signals of Lachish: Studies in the Archaeology and History of Israel in the Late Bronze Age, Iron Age, and Persian Period in Honor of David Ussishkin*, 281–99. Winona Lake, IN: Eisenbrauns.

Na'aman, Nadav. 2013. 'The Kingdom of Judah in the 9th Century BCE: Text Analysis versus Archaeological Research', *TA* 40: 247–76.

Na'aman, Nadav. 2015. 'Literacy in the Negev in the Late Monarchical Period', in Brian Schmidt (ed.), *Contextualizing Israel's Sacred Writing: Ancient Literacy, Orality, and Literary Production*, 47–70. SBLAIL 22. Atlanta: Society of Biblical Literature.

Na'aman, Nadav. 2019. 'Hiram of Tyre in the Book of Kings and in the Tyrian Records', *JNES* 78: 75–85.

Na'aman, Nadav. 2021. 'Dating the Renaming of Cities Referred to in the Biblical Conquest and Settlement Accounts', *VT* 71: 653–64.

Nelson, Cynthia (ed.). 1973. *The Desert and the Sown: Nomads in the Wider Society*. Institute of International Studies. Berkeley, CA: University of California Press.

Nestor, Dermot. 2015. 'Merneptah's 'Israel' and the Absence of Origins in Biblical Scholarship', *CBR* 13: 293–329.

Newberry, Percy E. 1893. *Beni Hasan, Parts I-II*. 2 vols. Archaeological Survey of Egypt. London: Kegan Paul.

Newberry, Percy E. 1938. 'Three Old-Kingdom Travellers to Byblos and Pwenet', *JEA* 24: 182–4.

Ngo, Robin. 2014. *Canaanite Fortress Discovered in the City of David, Biblical Archaeology Sites, News*, posted on 7 April 2014. Http://www.biblicalarchaeology.org/daily/news/canaanite-fortress-discovered-in-the-city-of-david/ (accessed 27 June 2014).

Nibbi, Alessandra. 1989. *Canaan and Canaanite in Ancient Egypt*. Oxford: Discussions in Egyptology.

Niccacci, Alviero. 1997. 'La stèle d'Israël: grammaire et stratégie de communication', in *Études égyptologiques et bibliques à la mémoire du Père B. Couroyer*, 43–107. Cahiers de la Revue Biblique 36. Paris: Gabalda.

Nicholson, Ernest W. 1973. *Exodus and Sinai in History and Tradition*. Oxford: Blackwell.

Niehr, Herbert. 1994. 'שפט šāpaṭ', *TDOT* 15: 411–31.

Niemann, Hermann Michael. 1993. *Herrschaft, Königtum und Staat: Skizzen zur soziokulturellen Entwicklung im monarchischen Israel*. FAT 6. Tübingen: Mohr Siebeck.

Niemann, Hermann Michael. 1997. 'The Socio-Political Shadow Cast by the Biblical Solomon', in L. K. Handy (ed.), *The Age of Solomon: Scholarship at the Turn of the Millennium*, 252–99. Studies in the History and Culture of the Ancient Near East 11. Leiden: Brill. Reprinted in Hermann Michael Niemann, *History of Ancient Israel, Archaeology, and Bible: Collected Essays/Geschichte Israels, Archäologie und Bibel: Gesammelte Aufsätze*, 91–126. Edited by Meik Gerhards. AOAT 418. Münster: Ugarit-Verlag, 2015.

Niemann, Hermann Michael. 2002. 'Taanach und Megiddo: Überlegungen zur strukturell-historischen Situation zwischen Saul und Salomo', *VT* 52: 93–102.

Niemann, Hermann Michael. 2003. 'Pentapolis', *RGG*[4] 6: 1087–8.

Niemann, Hermann Michael. 2007. 'Royal Samaria – Capital or Residence? or: The Foundation of the City of Samaria by Sargon II', in Lester L. Grabbe (ed.), *Ahab Agonistes: The Rise and Fall of the Omri Dynasty*, 184–207. LHBOTS 421. ESHM 6. London/New York: T&T Clark International.

Niemann, Hermann Michael. 2013. 'Neighbors and Foes, Rivals and Kin: Philistines, Shepheleans, Judeans between Geography and Economy, History and Theology', in Ann E. Killebrew and Gunnar Lehmann (eds), *The Philistines and Other "Sea Peoples" in Text and Archaeology*, 243–64. Society of Biblical Literature Archaeology and Biblical Studies 15. Atlanta, GA: Society of Biblical Literature.

Nigro, Lorenzo, Lucio Calcagnile, Jehad Yasin, Elisabetta Gallo, and Gianluca Quarta. 2019. 'Jericho and the Chronology of Palestine in the Early Bronze Age: A Radiometric Re-Assessment', *Radiocarbon* 61: 211–41.

Noort, Ed. 1994. *Die Seevölker in Palästina*. Palaestina Antiqua 8. Kampen: Kok Pharos.

Noth, Martin. 1930. *Das System der zwölf Stämme Israels*. BWANT 4/1. Stuttgart: Kohlhammer.

Noth, Martin. 1938. 'Die Wege des Pharaonenheere in Palästina und Syrien: Untersuchungen zu den hieroglyphischen Listen palästinischer und syrischer Städte: IV. Die Schoschenkliste', *ZDPV* 61: 277–304.

Noth, Martin. 1943. *Überlieferungsgeschichtliche Studien: Die sammelnden und bearbeitenden Geschichtswerke im Alten Testament*, 43–266. Schriften der Königsberger Gelehrten Gesellschaft, Geisteswissenschaftliche Klass 18. Jahr, Heft 2. Halle: Max Niemeyer Verlag. ET of chapters 1–13: *The Deuteronomistic History*. JSOTSup 15. Sheffield: JSOT Press, 1981.

Noth, Martin. 1960. *The History of Israel*. Revised translation. London: A. & C. Black. New York: Harper & Row. ET of *Geschichte Israels*. 3rd edn. Berlin: Evangelisch Verlagsanstalt, 1956.

Noth, Martin. 1962. *Exodus*. Translated by J. S. Bowden. OTL. Philadelphia, PA: Westminster Press. ET of *Das zweite Buch Mose (Exodus)*. Das Alte Testament Deutsch: Neues Göttinger Bibelwerk, Band 5. Göttingen: Vandenhoeck & Ruprecht, 1958.

Nuzzolo, Massimiliano, and Jaromír Krejčí. 2017. 'Heliopolis and the Solar Cult in the Third Millennium BC', *Ägypten und Levante* 27: 357–80.

O'Callaghan, Roger T. 1948. *Aram Naharaim: A Contribution to the History of Upper Mesopotamia in the Second Millennium B.C.* Rome: Pontifical Biblical Institute.

O'Connor, David. 2000. 'The Sea Peoples and the Egyptian Sources', in Eliezer D. Oren (ed.), *The Sea Peoples and the World: A Reassessment*, 85–102. University Museum Monograph 108. University Museum Symposium Series 11. Philadelphia, PA: University of Pennsylvania, The University Museum.

O'Connor, David, and Eric H. Cline (eds). 1998. *Amenhotep III: Perspectives on his Reign*. Ann Arbor, MI: University of Michigan Press.

O'Connor, David, and David P. Silverman (eds). 1995. *Ancient Egyptian Kingship*. Probleme der Ägyptologie 9. Leiden: Brill.

Odorico, Marco de. 1995. *The Use of Numbers and Quantifications in the Assyrian Royal Inscriptions*. SAAS 3. Helsinki: The Neo-Assyrian Text Corpus Project.
Ofer, Avi. 1994. '"All the Hill Country of Judah": From a Settlement Fringe to a Prosperous Monarchy', in Israel Finkelstein and Nadav Na'aman (eds), *From Nomadism to Monarchy: Archaeological and Historical Aspects of Early Israel*, 92–121. Jerusalem: Israel Exploration Society.
Ofer, Avi. 2001. 'The Monarchic Period in the Judaean Highland: A Spatial Overview', in Amihai Mazar (ed.), *Studies in the Archaeology of the Iron Age in Israel and Jordan*, 14–37. JSOTsup 331. Sheffield: Sheffield Academic Press.
Oren, Eliezer D. 1973. 'The Overland Route Between Egypt and Canaan in the Early Bronze Age (Preliminary Report)', *IEJ* 23: 198–205.
Oren, Eliezer D. 1984. 'Migdol: A New Fortress on the Edge of the Eastern Nile Delta', *BASOR* 256: 7–44.
Oren, Eliezer D. (ed.). 1997. *The Hyksos: New Historical and Archaeological Perspectives*. University Museum Monograph 96. University Museum Symposium Series 8. Philadelphia, PA: University of Pennsylvania, The University Museum.
Oren, Eliezer D. (ed.). 2000. *The Sea Peoples and the World: A Reassessment*. University Museum Monograph 108. University Museum Symposium Series 11. Philadelphia, PA: University of Pennsylvania, The University Museum.
Owen, David I. 1995. *General Studies and Excavations at Nuzi 9/3*. Studies on the Civilization and Culture of Nuzi and the Hurrians 5. Winona Lake, IN: Eisenbrauns.
Owen, David I., and Martha A. Morrison (eds). 1987. *General Studies and Excavations at Nuzi 9/1*. Studies on the Civilization and Culture of Nuzi and the Hurrians 2. Winona Lake, IN: Eisenbrauns.
Pardee, Dennis. 1983–84. 'Ugaritic', *AfO* 29–30: 321–9.
Pardee, Dennis. 1988. *Les textes para-mythologiques de la 24ᵉ Campagne (1961)*. RSO 4. Paris: Editions Recherche sur les Civilisations.
Pardee, Dennis. 2002. *Ritual and Cult at Ugarit*. SBLWAW 10. Atlanta, GA: Society of Biblical Literature.
Parker, Simon B. 1997. *Ugaritic Narrative Poetry*. SBLWAW 9. Atlanta, GA: Scholars Press.
Parkinson, Richard B. 1991. *Voices from Ancient Egypt: An Anthology of Middle Kingdom Writings*. London: British Museum Press.
Parkinson, Richard B. 1997. *The Tale of Sinuhe and Other Ancient Egyptian Poems 1940–1640 BC*. Oxford: Oxford University Press.
Parkinson, Richard B. 2001. 'Ipuwer', *OEAE* 2: 182.
Paulus, Susanne, and Tim Clayden (eds). 2020. *Babylonia under the Sealand and Kassite Dynasties*. Studies in Ancient Near Eastern Records 24. Berlin: de Gruyter.
Payne, Annick. 2012. *Iron Age Hieroglyphic Luwian Inscriptions*. Edited by H. Craig Melchert. SBLWAW 29. Atlanta, GA: Society of Biblical Literature.
Pearce, Laurie E. 1995. 'The Scribes and Scholars of Ancient Mesopotamia', in Jack M. Sasson (ed.), *Civilizations of the Ancient Near East*, 4:2265–91. New York: Scribner's.
Peckham, J. Brian. 2014. *Phoenicia: Episodes and Anecdotes from the Ancient Mediterranean*. Winona Lake, IN: Eisenbrauns.
Peden, A. J. 1994. *Egyptian Historical Inscriptions of the Twentieth Dynasty*. Documenta Mundi: Aegyptiaca 3. Jonsered, Sweden: Paul Åström.
Peet, Eric. 1914. *Stela of Sebek-khu: The Earliest Record of an Egyptian Campaign in Asia*. The Manchester Museum Handbooks. Manchester University Press.
Petschow, Herbert. 1965. 'Die neubabylonische Zwiegesprächsurkunde und Genesis 23', *JCS* 19: 103–20.
Pettinato, Giovanni. 1991. *Ebla: A New Look at History*. Translated by C. Faith Richardson. Baltimore: Johns Hopkins University Press. ET of *Ebla: Nuovi orizzonti della storia*. Milan: Rusconi Libri, 1986.
Pfoh, Emanuel. 2009. *The Emergence of Israel in Ancient Palestine: Historical and Anthropological Perspectives*. CIS. London: Equinox.
Pfoh, Emanuel. 2016. *Syria-Palestine in the Late Bronze Age: An Anthropology of Politics and Power*. CIS. London: Routledge.

Piasetzky, Eli, and Israel Finkelstein. 2005. '¹⁴C Results from Megiddo, Tel Dor, Tel Reḥov and Tel Hadar', in Thomas E. Levy and Thomas Higham (eds), *The Bible and Radiocarbon Dating: Archaeology, Text and Science*, 294–309. London: Equinox.

Pitard, Wayne T. 1987. *Ancient Damascus: A Historical Study of the Syrian City-State from Earliest Times until its Fall to the Assyrians in 732 B.C.E.* Winona Lake, IN: Eisenbrauns.

Poebel, A. 1942a. 'The Assyrian King List from Khorsabad', *JNES* 1: 247–306.

Poebel, A. 1942b. 'The Assyrian King List from Khorsabad (Continued)', *JNES* 1: 460–92.

Poebel, A. 1943. 'The Assyrian King List from Khorsabad (Concluded)', *JNES* 2: 56–90.

Posener, Georges. 1940. *Princes et pays d'Asie et de Nubie: Textes hiératiques sur des figurines d'envoûtement du Moyen Empire*. Brussels: Fondation égyptologique Reine Élisabeth.

Posener, Georges. 1957. 'Les Asiatiques en Égypte sous les XIIe et XIIIe dynasties (À propos d'un livre récent)', *Syria* 34: 145–63.

Powell, Barry B. 2009. *Writing: Theory and History of the Technology of Civilization*. Chichester: Wiley-Blackwell.

Pruitt, Madeline Lawson. 2019. *Cultural Identity, Archaeology, and the Amorites of the Early Second Millennium BCE: An Analytical Paradigmatic Approach*. University of California at Berkeley PhD thesis. Available at escholarship.org/content/qt9pn561nn/qt9pn561nn_noSplash_a7bcaf22383cdec0ff03ae8b34ac6324.pdf?t=pwzt6k; accessed 1 April 2021.

Pusch, Edgar B. 2001. 'Piramesse', *OEAE* 2: 48–50.

Quirke, Stephen G. J. 2001. 'Second Intermediate Period', in *OEAE* 3: 260–5.

Raban, Avner. 2001. 'Standardized Collared-Rim Pithoi and Short-Lived Settlements', in Samuel R. Wolff (ed.), *Studies in the Archaeology of Israel and Neighboring Lands in Memory of Douglas L. Esse*, 493–518. The Oriental Institute of the University of Chicago Studies in Ancient Oriental Civilization 59. ASOR Books 5. Chicago: Oriental Institute.

Rabinowitz, Isaac. 1956. 'Aramaic Inscriptions of the Fifth Century B.C.E. from a North-Arab Shrine in Egypt', *JNES* 15: 1–9.

Rad, Gerhard von. 1965. 'The Form-Critical Problem of the Hexateuch', in *The Problem of the Hexateuch and other Essays*, 1–78. Translated by E. W. Trueman Dicken. Edinburgh: Oliver & Boyd.

Rainey, Anson F. 1972. 'The World of Sinuhe', *IOS* 2: 369–408.

Rainey, Anson F. 1973. 'Amenhotep II's Campaign to Takhsi', *JARCE* 10: 71–5.

Rainey, Anson F. 1982. 'Toponymic Problems (cont.)', *TA* 9: 130–6.

Rainey, Anson F. 1984. 'Early Historical Geography of the Negeb', in Ze'ev Herzog (ed.), *Beer-Sheba II: The Early Iron Age Settlements*, 88–104. Publications of the Institute of Archaeology 7. Tel Aviv: Tel Aviv University Institute of Archaeology.

Rainey, Anson F. 1993. 'Sharḫân / Sharuhen – The Problem of Identification', in *Eretz-Israel 24: Avraham Malamat Volume*, 178*–87*. Jerusalem: Israel Exploration Society.

Rainey, Anson F. 1996. 'Who Is a Canaanite? A Review of the Textual Evidence', *BASOR* 304: 1–15.

Rainey, Anson F. 2001. 'Israel in Merenptah's Inscription and Reliefs', *IEJ* 51: 57–75.

Rainey, Anson F. 2015a. *The El-Amarna Correspondence: A New Edition of the Cuneiform Letters from the Site of El-Amarna based on Collations of all Extant Tablets, Volume 1*. Edited by William Schniedewind and Zipora Cochavi-Rainey. HdO I/110. Leiden: Brill.

Rainey, Anson F. 2015b. *The El-Amarna Correspondence: A New Edition of the Cuneiform Letters from the Site of El-Amarna based on Collations of all Extant Tablets, Volume 2*. Edited and completed by Zipora Cochavi-Rainey. HdO I/110. Leiden: Brill.

Rainey, Anson F. (ed.). 1987. *Egypt, Israel, Sinai: Archaeological and Historical Relationships in the Biblical Period*. Tel Aviv: Tel Aviv University.

Rainey, Anson F., and R. Steven Notley (eds). 2014. *The Sacred Bridge: Carta's Atlas of the Biblical World*. 2nd emended and enhanced edn. Jerusalem: Carta.

Ramsey, George W. 1981. *The Quest for the Historical Israel*. Atlanta, GA: John Knox Press.

Raulwing, Peter. 2005. 'The Kikkuli Text (CTH 284). Some Interdisciplinary Remarks on Hittite Training Texts for Chariot Horses in the Second Half of the 2nd Millennium B.C.', in Armelle Gardeisen (ed.), *Les Équidés dans le monde méditerranéen antique: Actes du colloque organisé par l'École française d'Athènes, le Centre Camille Jullian, et l'UMR 5140 du CNRS, Athènes, 26–28 Novembre 2003*, 61–75. Monographies d'archéologie méditerranéenne 1. Lattes: Éd. de l'Association pour le développement de l'archéologie en Languedoc-Rousillon.

Raulwing, Peter. 2009. 'The Kikkuli Text: Hittite Training Instructions for Chariot Horses in the Second Half of the 2nd Millennium B.C. and Their Interdisciplinary Context'. Http://www.lrgaf.org/Peter_Raulwing_The_Kikkuli_Text_MasterFile_Dec_2009.pdf (accessed 20 May 2021).

Raulwing, Peter, and Rüdiger Schmitt. 1998. 'Zur etymologischen Beurteilung der Berufsbezeichnung aššuššanni des Pferdetrainers Kikkuli von Mittani', in Peter Anreiter et al. (eds), *Man and the Animal World: Studies in Archaeozoology, Archaeology, Anthropology and Paleolinguistics in memoriam Sándor Bökönyi*, 675–704. Archaeolingua 8. Budapest: Archaeolingua.

Rawlinson, George. 1889. *History of Phoenicia*. London: Longmans, Green & Co.

Redford, Donald B. 1963. 'Exodus I 11', *VT* 13: 401–18.

Redford, Donald B. 1970a. *A Study of the Biblical Story of Joseph (Genesis 37–50)*. VTSup 20. Leiden: Brill.

Redford, Donald B. 1970b. 'The Hyksos in History and Tradition', *Or* 39: 1–51.

Redford, Donald B. 1973a. 'New Light on the Asiatic Campaigning of Ḥoremheb', *BASOR* 211: 36–49.

Redford, Donald B. 1973b. 'Studies in Relations between Palestine and Egypt during the First Millennium B.C.: II. The Twenty-Second Dynasty', *JAOS* 93: 3–17.

Redford, Donald B. 1979. 'A Gate Inscription from Karnak and Egyptian Involvement in Western Asia during the Early 18th Dynasty', *JAOS* 99: 270–87.

Redford, Donald B. 1982. 'Mitanni', *LdÄ* 4: 149–52.

Redford, Donald B. 1984. *Akhenaten: The Heretic King*. Princeton, NJ: Princeton University Press.

Redford, Donald B. 1986a. *Pharaonic King-Lists, Annals and Day-Books: A Contribution to the Study of the Egyptian Sense of History*. Society for the Study of Egyptian Antiquities Publication 4. Mississauga, Ontario: Benben Publications.

Redford, Donald B. 1986b. 'The Ashkelon Relief at Karnak and the Israel Stela', *IEJ* 36: 188–200.

Redford, Donald B. 1986c. 'Egypt and Western Asia in the Old Kingdom', *JARCE* 23: 125–43.

Redford, Donald B. 1987. 'An Egyptological Perspective on the Exodus Narrative', in Anson F. Rainey (ed.), *Egypt, Israel, Sinai: Archaeological and Historical Relationships in the Biblical Period*, 137–61. Tel Aviv University Kaplan Project on the History of Israel and Egypt. Tel Aviv: Tel Aviv University.

Redford, Donald B. 1990. *Egypt and Canaan in the New Kingdom*. Edited by Shmuel Aḥituv. Beer-Sheva 4. Beer-Sheva: Ben-Gurion University of the Negev Press.

Redford, Donald B. 1992a. *Egypt, Canaan, and Israel in Ancient Times*. Princeton, NJ: Princeton University Press.

Redford, Donald B. 1992b. 'Execration and Execration Texts', *ABD* 2:681–2.

Redford, Donald B. 2000. 'Egypt and Western Asia in the Late New Kingdom: An Overview', in Eliezer D. Oren (ed.), *The Sea Peoples and their World: A Reassessment*, 1–20. University Museum Monograph 108. University Museum Symposium Series 11. Philadelphia, PA: University of Pennsylvania, The University Museum.

Redford, Donald B. 2003. *The Wars in Syria and Palestine of Thutmose III*. CHANE 16. Leiden: Brill.

Redford, Donald B. 2009. 'The Land of Ramesses', in Peter J. Brand and Louise Cooper (eds), *Causing his Name to Live: Studies in Egyptian Epigraphy and History in Memory of William J. Murnane*, 175–7. Leiden: Brill.

Redford, Donald B. (ed.). 2001. *Oxford Encyclopedia of Ancient Egypt*. Oxford: Oxford University Press.

Redford, Donald B., and James M. Weinstein. 1992. 'Hyksos', *ABD* 3:341–8.

Redman, Charles L. 1999 'The Development of Archaeological Theory: Explaining the Past', in Graeme Barker (ed.), *Companion Encyclopedia of Archaeology*, 48–80. London/New York: Routledge.

Redmount, Carol A. 1995. 'The Wadi Tumilat and the "Canal of the Pharaohs"', *JNES* 54: 127–35.

Reinhold, Gotthard G. G. 1989. *Die Beziehungen Altisraels zu den aramäischen Staaten in der israelitisch-judäischen Königszeit*. Europaische Hochschulschriften, Reihe 23, Band 368. Frankfurt am Main: Peter Lang.

Rendtorff, Rolf. 1997. 'Directions in Pentateuchal Studies', *CR:BS* 5: 43–65.

Renfrew, Colin, and Paul Bahn. 2004. *Archaeology: Theories, Methods and Practice*. 4th edn. London: Thames & Hudson.

Robertson, David A. 1972. *Linguistic Evidence in Dating Early Hebrew Poetry*. SBLDS 3. Missoula, MT: SBL.

Robinson, Andrew. 2007. *The Story of Writing: Alphabets, Hieroglyphs and Pictograms*. London: Thames & Hudson.

Rodan, Simona. 2015. *Aegean Mercenaries in Light of the Bible: Clash of Cultures in the Story of David and Goliath*. Oxford: Archaeopress.

Rofé, Alexander. 2015. 'David Overcomes Goliath (1 Samuel 17): Genre, Text, Origin and Message of the Story', *Henoch* 37: 66–100. Revision of the article, 'The Battle of David and Goliath: Folklore, Theology, Eschatology', in Jacob Neusner, B. A. Levine, and Ernest S. Frerichs (eds), *Judaic Perspectives on Ancient Israel*, 117–51. Philadelphia, PA: Fortress Press.

Rogerson, John W. 1978. *Anthropology and the Old Testament*. Oxford: Blackwell.

Rogerson, John W. 1986. 'Was Early Israel a Segmentary Society?' *JSOT* 36: 17–26.

Römer, Thomas. 2008. 'Salomon d'apres les deuteronomistes – un roi ambigu', in Claude Lichtert and Dany Nocquet (eds), *Le roi Salomon, un héritage en question: Hommage à Jacques Vermeylen*, 98–130. Brussels: Lessius.

Roskop, Angela R. 2011. *The Wilderness Itineraries: Genre, Geography, and the Growth of Torah*. History, Archaeology, and Culture of the Levant 3. Winona Lake, IN: Eisenbrauns.

Routledge, Bruce. 2004. *Moab in the Iron Age: Hegemony, Polity, Archaeology*. Archaeology, Culture, and Society. Philadelphia, PA: University of Pennsylvania Press.

Routledge, Bruce. 2008. 'Thinking "Globally" and Analysing "Locally": South-Central Jordan in Transition', in Lester L. Grabbe (ed.), *Israel in Transition: From Late Bronze II to Iron IIA (c. 1250–850 BCE): The Archaeology*, 144–76. LHBOTS 491. ESHM 7. London and New York: T&T Clark International.

Russell, Brian D. 2007. *The Song of the Sea: The Date of Composition and Influence of Exodus 15:1–21*. Studies in Biblical Literature 101. New York: Peter Lang.

Russell, Stephen C. 2009. *Images of Egypt in Early Biblical Literature: Cisjordan-Israelite, Transjordan-Israelite, and Judahite Portrayals*. BZAW 403. Berlin/New York: de Gruyter.

Ryholt, K. S. B. 1997. *The Political Situation in Egypt 'during the Second Intermediate Period c. 1800–1550 B. C.* With an Appendix by Adam Bülow-Jacobsen. Carsten Niebuhr Institute Publications 20. Copenhagen: Museum Tusculanum Press.

Sader, Hélène S. 1987. *Les états araméens de Syrie depuis leur fondation jusqu'à leur transformation en provinces assyriennes*. Beiruter Texte und Studien 36. Wiesbaden: Steiner Verlag.

Sader, Hélène. 2019. *The History and Archaeology of Phoenicia*. SBL Archaeology and Biblical Studies 25. Atlanta, GA: SBL.

Saleen, Sahar N., and Zahi Hawass. 2021. 'Computed Tomography Study of the Mummy of King Seqenenre Taa II: New Insights Into His Violent Death', *Frontiers in Medicine* (21 February 2021). www.frontiersin.org/articles/10.3389/fmed.2021.637527/full; accessed 1 April 2021.

Salzman, Philip Carl. 1980a. 'Introduction: Processes of Sedentarization as Adaptation and Response', in Philip Carl Salzman (ed.), *When Nomads Settle: Processes of Sedentarization as Adaptation and Response*, 1–19. New York: Praeger.

Salzman, Philip Carl. 1980b. 'Processes of Sedentarization Among the Nomads of Baluchistan', in Philip Carl Salzman (ed.), *When Nomads Settle: Processes of Sedentarization as Adaptation and Response*, 95–110. New York: Praeger.

Salzman, Philip Carl. 2002. 'Pastoral Nomads: Some General Observations Based on Research in Iran', *Journal of Anthropological Research* 58: 245–64.

Salzman, Philip Carl. 2004. *Pastoralists: Equality, Hierarchy, and the State*. Boulder, CO/Oxford: Westview Press.

Salzman, Philip Carl (ed.) 1980. *When Nomads Settle: Processes of Sedentarization as Adaptation and Response*. New York: Praeger.

Sapir-Hen, Lidar, and Erez Ben-Yosef. 2013. 'The Introduction of Domestic Camels to the Southern Levant: Evidence from the Aravah Valley', *TA* 40: 277–85.

Saporetti, Claudio. 1965. ['L'Autobiografia di Ḫattušili I:] Versione Accadica', *Studi Classici e Orientali* 14: 77–85.

Saretta, Phyllis. 2016. *Asiatics in Middle Kingdom Egypt: Perceptions and Reality*. Bloomsbury Egyptology. London: Bloomsbury Academic.

Sasson, Jack M. 1984. 'Biblical Archaeologist Update: Zimri-Lim Takes the Grand Tour', *Biblical Archaeologist* 47: 246–51.

Sasson, Jack M. 2008. 'Text, Trade, and Travelers', in Joan Aruz (ed.), *Beyond Babylon: Art, Trade, and Diplomacy in the Second Millennium B.C.*, 95–100. New York: Metropolitan Museum of Art/Yale University Press.

Sasson, Jack M. 2015. *From the Mari Archives: An Anthology of Old Babylonian Letters*. Winona Lake, IN: Eisenbrauns.

Sasson, Jack M. (ed.). 1995. *Civilizations of the Ancient Near East. Vols 1–4*. New York: Scribner.

Sauer, James A. 1986. 'Transjordan in the Bronze and Iron Ages: A Critique of Glueck's Synthesis', *BASOR* 263: 1–26.

Säve-Söderbergh, T. 1951. 'The Hyksos Rule in Egypt', *JEA* 37: 53–71.

Sawyer, John F. A., and David J. A. Clines (eds). 1983. *Midian, Moab and Edom: The History and Archaeology of Late Bronze and Iron Age Jordan and North-West Arabia*. JSOTSup 24. Sheffield: Sheffield Academic Press.

Schipper, Bernd Ulrich. 1999. *Israel und Ägypten in der Königszeit: Die kulturellen Kontakte von Salomo bis zum Fall Jerusalems*. OBO 170. Freiburg: Universitätsverlag. Göttingen: Vandenhoeck & Ruprecht.

Schipper, Bernd Ulrich. 2000. 'Salomo und die Pharaonentochter – zum historischen Kern von 1 Kön 7,8', *BN* 102: 84–94.

Schipper, Bernd Ulrich. 2002. 'Noch einmal zur Pharaonentochter – ein Gespräch mit Karl Jansen-Winkeln', *BN* 111: 90–8.

Schipper, Bernd Ulrich. 2005. *Die Erzählung des Wenamun: Ein Literaturwerk im Spannungsfeld von Politik, Geschichte und Religion*. OBO 209. Freiburg: Universitätsverlag. Göttingen: Vandenhoeck & Ruprecht.

Schipper, Bernd Ulrich. 2011. 'Gen 41:42 and the Egyptian Background to the Investiture of Joseph', *RevB* 118: 331–8.

Schipper, Bernd Ulrich. 2015. 'Raamses, Pithom, and the Exodus: A Critical Evaluation of Ex 1:11', *VT* 65: 265–88.

Schipper, Bernd Ulrich. 2018. 'Joseph, Ahiqar, and Elephantine: The Joseph Story as a Diaspora Novella', *JAEI* 18: 71–84.

Schloen, David. 2001. *The House of the Father as Fact and Symbol: Patrimonialism in Ugarit and the Ancient Near East*. SAHL 2. Winona Lake, IN: Eisenbrauns.

Schlott, Adelhard. 1989. *Schrift und Schreiber im Alten Ägypten*. Beck's Archäologische Bibliothek. Munich: Beck.

Schneider, Hans D. 2001. 'Horemheb', *OEAE* 2: 114–16.

Schneider, Nik. 1952. 'Patriarchennamen in zeitgenössischen Keilschrifturkunden', *Bib* 33: 516–22.

Schneider, Thomas. 2003. 'Foreign Egypt: Egyptology and the Concept of Cultural Appropriation', *Ägypten und Levante* 13: 155–61.

Schroer, Silvia, and Stefan Münster (eds). 2017. *Khirbet Qeiyafa in the Shephelah: Papers Presented at a Colloquium of the Swiss Society for Ancient Near Eastern Studies Held at the University of Bern, September 6, 2014*. OBO 282. Fribourg: Academic Press. Göttingen: Vandenhoeck & Ruprecht.

Schulman, Alan R. 1987. 'The Great Historical Inscription of Merneptaḥ at Karnak: A Partial Reappraisal', *JARCE* 24: 21–34.

Scolnic, Benjamin Edidin. 2004. 'A New Working Hypothesis for the Identification of Migdol', in James K. Hoffmeier and Alan Millard (eds), *The Future of Biblical Archaeology: Reassessing Methodologies and Assumptions*, 91–120. Grand Rapids, MI: Eerdmans.

Seidl, Ursula. 1989. *Die babylonischen Kudurru-Reliefs: Symbole mesopotamischer Gottheiten*. OBO 87. Freiburg: Universitätsverlag. Göttingen: Vandenhoeck & Ruprecht.

Seidlmayer, Stephan J. 2001. 'Execration Texts', *OEAE* 1: 487–9.

Sergi, Omer. 2019a. 'The Formation of Israelite Identity in the Central Canaanite Highlands in the Iron Age I–IIA', *NEA* 82: 42–51.

Sergi, Omer. 2019b. 'Israelite Identity and the Formation of the Israelite Polities in the Iron I–IIA Central Canaanite Highlands', *WO* 49: 206–35.

Sergi, Omer, Oded Lipschits, and Ido Koch. 2019. 'Memories of the Early Israelite Monarchy in the Books of Samuel and Kings', in Ido Koch, Thomas Römer, and Omer Sergi (eds), *Writing, Rewriting, and Overwriting in the Books of Deuteronomy and the Former Prophets: Essays in Honour of Cynthia Edenburg*, 173–94. BETL 304. Leuven: Peeters.

Service, Elman. 1962. *Primitive Social Organization*. New York: Random House.

Shalom Brooks, Simcha. 2005. *Saul and the Monarchy: A New Look*. Society for Old Testament Study Monographs. Aldershot, Hampshire: Ashgate.

Sharon, Ilan, and Ayelet Gilboa. 2013. 'The *SKL* Town: Dor in the Early Iron Age', in Ann E. Killebrew and Gunnar Lehmann (eds), *The Philistines and Other 'Sea Peoples' in Text and Archaeology*, 393–468. Society of Biblical Literature Archaeology and Biblical Studies 15. Atlanta, GA: Society of Biblical Literature.

Sharon, Ilan, Ayelet Gilboa, and Elisabetta Boaretto. 2008. 'The Iron Age Chronology of the Levant: The State-of-Research at the ^{14}C Dating Project, Spring 2006', in Lester L. Grabbe (ed.), *Israel in Transition: From Late Bronze II to Iron IIA (c. 1250–850 BCE): The Archaeology*, 177–92. LHBOTS 491. ESHM 7. London/New York: T&T Clark International.

Sharon, Ilan, Ayelet Gilboa, Elisabeth Boaretto, and A. J. Timothy Jull. 2005. 'The Early Iron Age Dating Project: Introduction, Methodology, Progress Report and an Update on the Tel Dor Radiometric Dates', in Thomas E. Levy and Thomas Higham (eds) *The Bible and Radiocarbon Dating: Archaeology, Text and Science*, 65–92. London: Equinox.

Shaw, Garry J. 2009. 'The Death of King Seqenenre Tao', *JARCE* 45: 159–76.

Shea, William H. 1981. 'Artistic Balance among the Beni Hasan Asiatics', *BA* 44: 219–28.

Sherrett, Susan. 2003. 'The Mediterranean Economy: "Globalization" at the End of the Second Millennium B.C.E.', in William G. Dever and Seymour Gitin (eds), *Symbiosis, Symbolism, and the Power of the Past: Canaan, Ancient Israel, and their Neighbors from the Late Bronze Age through Roman Palaestina: Proceedings of the Centennial Symposium W. F. Albright Institute of Archaeological Research and the American Schools of Oriental Research Jerusalem, May 29–31, 2000*, 37–62. Winona Lake, IN: Eisenbrauns.

Shortland, A. J. 2005. 'Shishak, King of Egypt: The Challenges of Egyptian Calendrical Chronology', in Thomas E. Levy and Thomas Higham (eds) *The Bible and Radiocarbon Dating: Archaeology, Text and Science*, 43–54. London: Equinox.

Singer, Itamar. 1985. 'The Battle of Niḫriya and the End of the Hittite Empire'. *ZA* 75: 100–123. Reprinted in *The Calm before the Storm: Selected Writings of Itamar Singer on the Late Bronze Age in Anatolia and the Levant*, 353–73. SBLWAW 1. Atlanta, GA: Society of Biblical Literature, 2011.

Singer, Itamar. 1988. 'Merneptah's Campaign to Canaan and the Egyptian Occupation of the Southern Coastal Plain of Palestine in the Ramesside Period', *BASOR* 269: 1–10.

Singer, Itamar. 1991a. 'Appendix III: A Concise History of Amurru', in Shlomo Izre'el, *Amurru Akkadian: A Linguistic Study, vol. 2*, 2:135–95. HSS 41. Atlanta, GA: Scholars Press.

Singer, Itamar. 1991b. 'The "Land of Amurru" and the "Lands of Amurru" in the Šaušgamuwa Treaty', *Iraq* 53: 69–74.

Singer, Itamar. 1999. 'A Political History of Ugarit', in Wilfred G. E. Watson and Nicolas Wyatt (eds), *Handbook of Ugaritic Studies*, 603–733. Handbuch der Orientalistik: Erste Abteilung, Der Nahe und Mittlere Osten 39. Band. Leiden: Brill.

Singer, Itamar. 2000. 'New Evidence on the End of the Hittite Empire', in Eliezer D. Oren (ed.), *The Sea Peoples and their World: A Reassessment*, 21–33. University Museum Monograph 108. University Museum Symposium Series 11. Philadelphia, PA: University of Pennsylvania, The University Museum.
Singer, Itamar. 2006. 'The Hittites and the Bible Revisited', in Aren M. Maeir and Pierre de Miroschedji (eds), *'I will Speak the Riddles of Ancient Times': Archaeological and Historical Studies in Honor of Amihai Mazar on the Occasion of His Sixtieth Birthday*, 723–56. Winona Lake, IN: Eisenbrauns.
Singer, Itamar. 2011. *The Calm before the Storm: Selected Writings of Itamar Singer on the Late Bronze Age in Anatolia and the Levant*. SBLWAW 1. Atlanta, GA: Society of Biblical Literature.
Singer-Avitz, Lily. 2012. 'Khirbet Qeiyafa: Late Iron Age I in Spite of It All', *IEJ* 62: 177–85.
Singer-Avitz, Lily. 2016. 'Khirbet Qeiyafa: Late Iron Age I in Spite of It All – Once Again', *IEJ* 66: 232–44.
Sjöberg, Åke W. 1976. 'The Old Babylonian Eduba', in *Sumerological Studies in Honor of Thorkild Jacobsen on his 70th Birthday*, 159–79. AS 20. Chicago: University of Chicago Press.
Skjeggesald, Marit. 1992 'Ethnic Groups in Early Iron Age Palestine: Some Remarks on the Use of the Term "Israelite" in Recent Research', *SJOT* 6: 159–86.
Soggin, J. Alberto. 2000. 'Dating the Joseph Story and Other Remarks', in Friedemann W. Golka and Wolfgang Weiß (eds), *Joseph: Bibel und Literatur: Symposion Helsinki/Lathi 1999*, 13–24. Oldenburg: Bibliotheks- und Informationssystem der Universität Oldenburg.
Soldt, Wilfred H. van. 2002. 'Studies on the *sākinu*-Official (2): The Functions of the *sākinu* of Ugarit', *UF* 34: 805–28.
Soldt, Wilfred H. van. 2014–16. 'Ugarit. A. Geschichte und Literatur', *RlA* 14: 280–3.
Sommerfeld, Walter. 1995. 'The Kassites of Ancient Mesopotamia: Origins, Politics, and Culture', in Jack M. Sasson (ed.), *Civilizations of the Ancient Near East*, 2:917–30. New York: Scribner's.
Southall, Aiden W. 1956. *Alur Society: A Study in Processes and Types of Domination*. Cambridge: Heffers.
Soysal, Oğuz. 1989a. *Mursili I – Eine historische Studie*. Doctoral thesis in the Philosophischen Fäkultät der Julius-Maximilians-Universität zu Würzburg. Available under the author's name on Academia.edu, accessed 17 February 2021.
Soysal, Oğuz. 1989b. '"Der Apfel möge die Zähne nehmen!"', *Or* 58: 171–92.
Soysal, Oğuz. 1990. 'Noch einmal zur Šukziya-Episode im Erlaß Telipinus', *Or* 59: 271–9.
Spalinger, Anthony. 1977. 'A Critical Analysis of the "Annals" of Thutmose III (Stücke V-VI)', *JARCE* 14: 41–54.
Spalinger, Anthony. 1978. 'New Reference to an Egyptian Campaign of Thutmose III in Asia', *JNES* 37: 35–41.
Spalinger, Anthony. 1979. 'The Northern Wars of Seti I: An Integrative Study', *JARCE* 16: 29–47.
Speiser, E. A. 1964. *Genesis: A New Translation and Commentary*. AB 1. Garden City, NY: Doubleday.
Stager, Lawrence E. 1985a. 'The Archaeology of the Family in Ancient Israel', *BASOR* 260: 1–36.
Stager, Lawrence E. 1985b. 'Merenptah, Israel and Sea Peoples: New Light on an Old Relief', *EI* 18: 56*–64*.
Stager, Lawrence E. 1988. 'Archaeology, Ecology, and Social History: Background Themes to the Song of Deborah', in J. A. Emerton (ed.), *Congress Volume Jerusalem 1986*, 221–34. VTSup 40. Leiden: Brill.
Stager, Lawrence E. 1998a. 'The Impact of the Sea Peoples in Canaan (1185–1050 BCE)', in Thomas E. Levy (ed.), *The Archaeology of Society in the Holy Land*, 332–48. London/Washington: Leicester University Press.
Stager, Lawrence E. 1998b. 'Forging an Identity: The Emergence of Ancient Israel', in Michael D. Coogan (ed.), *The Oxford History of the Biblical World*, 123–75. Oxford: Oxford University Press.
Stantis, Chris, Arwa Kharobi, Nina Maaranen, Geoff M. Nowell, Manfred Bietak, Silvia Prell, Holger Schutkowski. 2020. 'Who were the Hyksos? Challenging Traditional Narratives Using Strontium Isotope ($^{87}Sr/^{86}Sr$) Analysis of Human Remains from Ancient Egypt', *PLoS ONE* 15/7: 1–14. Https://doi.org/10.1371/journal.pone.0235414 (accessed 24 September 2021).
Staubli, Thomas. 1991. *Das Image der Nomaden im Alten Israel und in der Ikonographie seiner sesshaften Nachbarn*. OBO 107. Freiburg: Universitätsverlag. Göttingen: Vandenhoeck & Ruprecht.
Stech-Wheeler, T., J. D. Muhly, K. R. Maxwell-Hyslop, and R. Maddin. 1981. 'Iron at Taanach and Early Iron Metallurgy in the Eastern Mediterranean', *AJA* 85: 245–68.

Steen, Eveline J. van der. 2004. *Tribes and Territories in Transition: The Central East Jordan Valley in the Late Bronze Age and Early Iron Ages: A Study of the Sources*. OLA 130. Leuven: Peeters.
Steen, Eveline J. van der. 2016. 'The Archaeology of the Late Bronze Age in Palestine', in L. L. Grabbe (ed.), *The Land of Canaan in the Late Bronze Age*, 159–75. LHBOTS 636. ESHM 10. London and New York: Bloomsbury T&T Clark.
Steen, Eveline J. van der, and Piotr Bienkowski. 2005. 'Radiocarbon Dates from Khirbat en-Nahas: A Methodological Critique'. Http://antiquity.ac.uk/ProjGall/levy/index.html.
Steen, Eveline J. van der, and Piotr Bienkowski. 2005–6. 'How Old Is the Kingdom of Edom?'. Http://www.wadiarabahproject.man.ac.uk.
Steen, Eveline J. van der, and Piotr Bienkowski. 2006. 'Radiocarbon Dates from Khirbat en-Nahas: A Methodological Critique', *Antiquity* 80 (no. 307): [no pagination].
Stein, Diana L. 1989. 'A Reappraisal of the "Sauštartar [*sic*] Letter" from Nuzi', *ZA* 79: 36–60.
Steindorff, Georg (founding editor). 1906–58. *Urkunden des ägyptischen Altertums*. 4 vols. Berlin: Akademi Verlag.
Steiner, Margreet L. 1994. 'Re-dating the Terraces of Jerusalem', *IEJ* 44: 13–20.
Steiner, Margreet L. 1998. 'The Archaeology of Ancient Jerusalem', *CR:BS* 6: 143–68.
Steiner, Margreet L. 2001. 'Jerusalem in the Tenth and Seventh Centuries BCE: From Administrative Town to Commercial City', in Amihai Mazar (ed.), *Studies in the Archaeology of the Iron Age in Israel and Jordan*, 280–8. JSOTSup 331. Sheffield: Sheffield Academic Press.
Steiner, Margreet L. 2003a. 'Expanding Borders: The Development of Jerusalem in the Iron Age', in Thomas L. Thompson, with the collaboration of Salma Khadra Jayyusi (ed.), *Jerusalem in Ancient History and Tradition*, 68–79. JSOTSup 381. CIS 13. London/New York: T&T Clark International.
Steiner, Margreet L. 2003b. 'The Evidence from Kenyon's Excavations in Jerusalem: A Response Essay', in Andrew G. Vaughn and Ann E. Killebrew (eds), *Jerusalem in Bible and Archaeology: The First Temple Period*, 347–63. SBLSymS 18. Atlanta, GA: Society of Biblical Literature.
Steiner, Margreet L., and Ann E. Killebrew (eds). 2014. *The Oxford Handbook of the Archaeology of the Levant, c. 8000–332 BCE*. Oxford: Oxford University Press.
Stern, Ephraim. 2013. *The Material Culture of the Northern Sea Peoples in Israel*. HSM 5. Winona Lake, IN: Eisenbrauns.
Stiebing, William H., Jr. 1989. *Out of the Desert? Archaeology and the Exodus-Conquest Narratives*. Buffalo, NY: Prometheus.
Streck, Michael P. 2000. *Das amurritische Onomastikon der altbabylonischen Zeit: Band 1 Die Amurriter, die onomastische Forschung, Orthographie und Phonologie, Nominalmorphologie*. AOAT 271/1. Münster: Ugarit-Verlag.
Streit, Katharina. 2017. 'A Maximalist Interpretation of the Execration Texts – Archaeological and Historical Implications of a High Chronology', *JAEI* 13: 59–69.
Szuchman, Jeffrey (ed.) 2009. *Nomads, Tribes, and the State in the Ancient Near East: Cross-Disciplinary Perspectives*. University of Chicago Oriental Institute Seminars 5. Chicago: Oriental Institute.
Tadmor, Hayim. 1958. 'Historical Implications of the Correct Rendering of Akkadian *dâku*', *JNES* 17: 129–41.
Tadmor, Hayim. 1994. *The Inscriptions of Tiglath-Pileser III King of Assyria: Critical Edition, with Introductions, Translations and Commentary*. Jerusalem: Israel Academy of Sciences and Humanities.
Tammuz, Oded. 2001. 'Canaan – A Land without Limits', *UF* 33: 501–43.
Tapper, Richard. 1990. 'Anthropologists, Historians, and Tribespeople on Tribe and State Formation in the Middle East', in Philip S. Khoury and Joseph Kostiner (eds), *Tribes and State Formation in the Middle East*, 48–73. Berkeley, CA: University of California Press.
Thieme, Paul. 1960. 'The "Aryan" Gods of the Mitanni Treaties', *JAOS* 80: 301–17.
Thompson, Thomas L. 1974. *The Historicity of the Patriarchal Narratives: The Quest for the Historical Abraham*. BZAW 133. Berlin: de Gruyter.
Tigay, Jeffrey H. 1982. *The Evolution of the Gilgamesh Epic*. Philadelphia, PA: University of Pennsylvania Press.
Tinney, Steve. 1995. 'A New Look at Naram-Sin and the "Great Rebellion"', *JCS* 47: 1–14.

Trigger, Bruce G. 2003. *Understanding Early Civilizations: A Comparative Study*. Cambridge: Cambridge University Press.
Tucker, Gene. 1966. 'Legal Background of Genesis 23', *JBL* 85: 77–84.
Tufnell, O., and W. A. Ward. 1966. 'Relations between Byblos, Egypt and Mesopotamia at the End of the Third Millennium B.C.: A Study of the Montet Jar', *Syria* 43: 165–241.
Tyldesley, Joyce. 1996. *Hatchepsut: The Female Pharaoh*. London: Penguin Books.
Tyldesley, Joyce. 2000. *Ramesses: Egypt's Greatest Pharaoh*. London: Penguin Books.
Tyson, Craig W. 2014. *The Ammonites: Elites, Empires, and Sociopolitical Change (1000–500 BCE)*. LHBOTS 585. London/New York: Bloomsbury T&T Clark.
Uphill, Edward P. 1968. 'Pithom and Raamses: Their Location and Significance', *JNES* 27: 291–316.
Uphill, Edward P. 1969. 'Pithom and Raamses: Their Location and Significance', *JNES* 28: 15–39.
Ussishkin, David. 1995. 'The Rectangular Fortress at Kadesh-Barnea', *IEJ* 45: 118–27.
Ussishkin, David. 2003. 'Solomon's Jerusalem: The Text and the Facts on the Ground', in Andrew G. Vaughn and Ann E. Killebrew (eds), *Jerusalem in Bible and Archaeology: The First Temple Period*, 103–15. SBLSymS 18. Atlanta, GA: Society of Biblical Literature.
Ussishkin, David. 2007a. 'Samaria, Jezreel and Megiddo: Royal Centres of Omri and Ahab', in Lester L. Grabbe (ed.), *Ahab Agonistes: The Rise and Fall of the Omri Dynasty*, 293–309. LHBOTS 421. ESHM 6. London and New York: T&T Clark International.
Ussishkin, David. 2007b. 'Archaeology of the Biblical Period: On Some Questions of Methodology and Chronology of the Iron Age', in Hugh G. M. Williamson (ed.), *Understanding the History of Ancient Israel*, 131–41. Proceedings of the British Academy 143. Oxford: Oxford University Press for the British Academy.
Ussishkin, David. 2008. 'The Date of the Philistine Settlement in the Coastal Plain: The View from Megiddo and Lachish', in Lester L. Grabbe (ed.), *Israel in Transition: From Late Bronze II to Iron IIA (c. 1250–850 BCE): The Archaeology*, 203–16. LHBOTS 491. ESHM 7. London and New York: T&T Clark International.
Ussishkin, David (ed.). 2004. *The Renewed Archaeological Excavations at Lachish (1973–1994). Vols. 1–5*. Tel Aviv University Ronia and Marco Nadler Institute of Archaeology, Monograph Series 22. Tel Aviv: Emery and Claire Yass Publications in Archaeology.
Van Seters, John. 1966, *The Hyksos: A New Interpretation*. New Haven, CT: Yale University Press.
Van Seters, John. 1972. 'The Terms "Amorite" and "Hittite" in the Old Testament', *VT* 22: 64–81.
Van Seters, John. 1975. *Abraham in History and Tradition*. New Haven, CT: Yale University Press.
Van Seters, John. 1990. 'Joshua's Campaign of Canaan and Near Eastern Historiography', *SJOT* 2: 1–12.
Van Seters, John. 2010. 'David the Mercenary', in Lester L. Grabbe (ed.), *Israel in Transition: From Late Bronze II to Iron IIA (c. 1250–850 BCE): Volume 2 The Text*, 199–219. LHBOTS 521 = ESHM 8. London/New York: T&T Clark International.
Van Seters, John. 2011. 'The Geography of the Exodus', in *Changing Perspectives I: Studies in the History, Literature and Religion of Biblical Israel*, 115–33. With an Introduction by Thomas L. Thompson. London: Equinox. Reprint of J. A. Dearman and M. P. Graham (eds), *The Land that I Will Show You: Essays on the History and Archaeology of the Ancient Near East in Honor of J. Maxwell Miller*, 255–76. JSOTSup 343. Sheffield: Sheffield Academic Press, 1997.
Vandersleyen, C. 1987. 'L'étymologie de Phoïnix, "Phénicien"', in Edward Lipiński (ed.), *Phoenicia and the Eastern Mediterranean in the First Millennium B.C.: Proceedings of the Conference held in Leuven from the 14th to the 16th of November 1985*, 19–22. Studia Phoenicia 5. OLA 2. Leuven: Peeters.
Vassiliev, Alexandre. 2006. 'The Localization of the Shasu-Land of Ramses II's Rhetorical Texts', in Maria Cannata (ed.), *Current Research in Egyptology: Proceedings of the Seventh Annual Symposium*, 162–8. Oxford: Oxbow Books.
Vassiliev, Alexandre. 2020. 'Upper Retenu and Lower Retenu', in C. Graves (ed.), *BEC 4: Proceedings of the Fourth British Egyptology Congress University of Manchester, 7–9 September 2018*, 159–67. London: EES.
Veen, Peter van der. 2012. 'Berlin Statue Pedestal Reliefs 21687 and 21688: Ongoing Research', *JAEI* 4.4: 41–2.
Veen, P. van der, Christoffer Theis, and Manfred Görg. 2010. 'Israel in Canaan (Long) before Pharaoh Merneptah? A Fresh Look at Berlin Statue Pedestal Relief 21687', *JAEI* 2.4: 15–25.

Velikovsky, Immanuel. 1952. *Ages in Chaos*. Garden City, NY: Doubleday.
Verbrugghe, Gerald P., and John M. Wickersham. 1996. *Berossos and Manetho, Introduced and Translated: Native Traditions in Ancient Mesopotamia and Egypt*. Ann Arbor, MI: University of Michigan Press.
Vergote, J. 1959. *Joseph en Égypte: Genèse Chap. 37–50 à la Lumière des Études Égyptologiques Récentes*. OBL 3. Leuven: Publications Universitaires.
Vidal, Jordi. 2000. 'King Lists and Oral Transmission: From History to Memory', *UF* 32: 555–66.
Vidal, Jordi. 2006. 'The Origins of the Last Ugaritic Dynasty', *AoF* 33: 168–75.
Villard, Pierre. 1986. 'Un roi de Mari à Ugarit', *UF* 18: 387–412.
Vita, Juan-Pablo. 2005. 'The Town of Mušiḫuna and the Cities of the "Beqaʿ Alliance" in the Amarna Letters', *SEL* 22: 1–7.
Wachsmann, Shelley. 1982. 'The Ships of the Sea Peoples (IJNA, 10.3: 187–220): Additional Notes', *The International Journal of Nautical Archaeology and Underwater Exploration* 11: 291–304.
Wachsmann, Shelley. 2000. 'To the Sea of the Philistines', in Eliezer D. Oren (ed.), *The Sea Peoples and their World: A Reassessment*, 103–43. University Museum Monograph 108. University Museum Symposium Series 11. Philadelphia, PA: University of Pennsylvania, The University Museum.
Waddell, W. G. 1940. *Manetho*. LCL. London: Heinemann. Cambridge, MA: Harvard University Press.
Wallenfels, Ronald. 2019. 'Shishak and Shoshenq: A Disambiguation', *JAOS* 139: 487–500.
Wapnish, Paula. 1997. 'Camels', *OEANE* 1:407–8.
Ward, William A. 1961. 'Egypt and the East Mediterranean in the Early Second Millennium B. C.', *Orientalia* 30: 22–45; 129–55.
Ward, William A. 1963. 'Egypt and the East Mediterranean from Predynastic Times to the End of the Old Kingdom', *JESHO* 6: 1–57.
Ward, William A. 1972. 'The Shasu "Bedouin": Notes on a Recent Publication', *JESHO* 15: 35–60.
Ward, William A. 1992a. 'Shasu', *ABD* 5:1165–7.
Ward, William A. 1992b. 'Goshen', *ABD* 2:1076–7.
Ward, William A., and Martha Sharp Joukowsky (eds). 1992. *The Crisis Years: The 12th Century B.C. from Beyond the Danube to the Tigris*. Dubuque, IL: Kendall/Hunt Publishing.
Watson, Wilfred G. E., and Nicolas Wyatt (eds). 1999. *Handbook of Ugaritic Studies*. Handbuch der Orientalistik: Erste Abteilung, Der Nahe und Mittlere Osten: 39. Band. Leiden: Brill.
Weeks, Kent R. (ed.). 1986. *Reliefs and Inscriptions at Karnak, Volume 4: The Battle Reliefs of King Sety I*. University of Chicago Oriental Institute Publications 107. Chicago: Oriental Institute.
Wegner, Ilse. 2007. *Einführung in die hurritische Sprache*. 2nd edn. Wiesbaden: Harrassowitz.
Wei, Tom F. 1992. 'Pithom', *ABD* 5:376–7.
Weidner, Ernst. 1963. 'Assyrische Epen über die Kassiten-Kämpfe', *AfO* 20: 113–16.
Weingart, Kristin. 2014. *Stämmesvolk – Staatsvolk – Gottesvolk? Studien zur Verwendung des Israel-Namens im Alten Testament*. FAT 2/68. Tübingen: Mohr Siebeck.
Weingart, Kristin. 2019. '"All These Are the Twelve Tribes of Israel": The Origins of Israel's Kinship Identity', *NEA* 82: 24–31.
Weinstein, James. 1997a. 'Exodus and Archaeological Reality', in Ernest S. Frerichs and Leonard H. Lesko (eds), *Exodus: The Egyptian Evidence*, 87–103. Winona Lake, IN: Eisenbrauns.
Weinstein, James M. 1997b. 'Hyksos', *OEANE* 3:133–6.
Weippert, Helga. 1973. 'Das geographische System der Stämme Israels', *VT* 23: 76–89.
Weippert, Helga. 1988. *Palästina in vorhellenistischer Zeit*. HdA II/1. Munich: Beck.
Weippert, Manfred. 1971. *The Settlement of the Israelite Tribes in Palestine: A Critical Survey of Recent Scholarly Debate*. Studies in Biblical Theology, 2nd Series 21. London: SCM Press. ET of *Die Landnahme der israelitischen Stämme in der neueren wissenschaftlichen Diskussion: Ein kritischer Bericht*. Göttingen: Vandenhoeck & Ruprecht, 1967.
Weippert, Manfred. 1974. 'Semitische Nomaden des zweiten Jahrtausends: Über die Š3św der ägyptischen Quellen', *Bib* 55: 265–80, 427–33.

Weippert, Manfred. 1979. 'The Israelite "Conquest" and the Evidence from Transjordan', in Frank M. Cross (ed.), *Symposia: Celebrating the Seventy-Fifth Anniversary of the Founding of the American Schools of Oriental Research (1900–1975)*, 15–34. Cambridge, MA: American Schools of Oriental Research.

Weippert, Manfred. 2010. *Historisches Textbuch zum Alten Testament*. Grundrisse zum Alten Testament 10. Göttingen: Vandenhoeck & Ruprecht.

Whiting, Robert M. 1995. 'Amorite Tribes and Nations of Second-Millennium Western Asia', in Jack M. Sasson (ed.), *Civilizations of the Ancient Near East*, 2:1231–42. New York: Scribner's.

Whybray, R. Norman. 1987. *The Making of the Pentateuch: A Methodological Study*. JSOTSup 53. Sheffield: JSOT Press.

Wilhelm, Gernot. 1987–90. 'Marijannu', *RlA* 7:419–21.

Wilhelm, Gernot. 1989. *The Hurrians*. Translated by Jennifer Barnes, with a chapter by Diana L. Stein. Ancient Near East Series. Warminster: Aris & Phillips. ET and expansion of *Grundzüge der Geschichte und Kultur der Hurriter*. Darmstadt: Wissenschaftliche Buchgesellschaft, 1982.

Wilhelm, Gernot, and Diana L. Stein. 1993–97. 'Mittan(n)i, Mitanni, Maitani', *RlA* 8:286–99.

Wilhelm, Gernot, and Diana L. Stein. 1998–2001. 'Nuzi', *RlA* 8:636–47.

Wilson, Kevin A. 2005. *The Campaign of Pharaoh Shoshenq I into Palestine*. FAT 2/9. Tübingen: Mohr Siebeck.

Wilson, Robert R. 1977. *Genealogy and History in the Biblical World*. Yale Near Eastern Researches 7. New Haven, CT: Yale University Press.

Wimmer, S. J. 2009–11. 'Seevölker', *RlA* 12: 340–1.

Wiseman, Donald J. 1953. *The Alalakh Tablets*. Occasional Publications of the British School of Archaeology at Ankara 2. London: British School of Archaeology at Ankara.

Witzel, Michael. 2001. 'Autochthonous Aryans? The Evidence from Old Indian and Iranian Texts', *Electronic Journal of Vedic Studies* 7, no. 3: 1–93.

Wood, Bryant G. 1990. 'Did the Israelites Conquer Jericho? A New Look at the Archaeological Evidence', *BAR* 16, no. 2: 44–58.

Wood, Bryant G. 2003. 'From Ramesses to Shiloh: Archaeological Discoveries Bearing on the Exodus-Judges Period', in David M. Howard, Jr. and Michael A. Grisanti (eds), *Giving the Sense: Understanding and Using Old Testament Historical Texts*, 256–82. Leicester: Apollos.

Worschech, Udo. 1997. 'Egypt and Moab', *BA* 60: 229–36.

Wright, G. Ernest. 1950. *The Old Testament Against its Environment*. London: SCM Press.

Wright, G. Ernest. 1952. *The God Who Acts*. London: SCM Press.

Yadin, Yigael. 1979. 'The Transition from a Semi-Nomadic to a Sedentary Society in the Twelfth Century B.C.E.', in Frank M. Cross (ed.), *Symposia: Celebrating the Seventy-Fifth Anniversary of the Founding of the American Schools of Oriental Research (1900–1975)*, 57–68. Cambridge, MA: American Schools of Oriental Research.

Yadin, Yigael. 1982. 'Is the Biblical Account of the Israelite Conquest of Canaan Historically Reliable?' *BAR* 8, no. 2: 16–23.

Yasur-Landau, Assaf. 2010. *The Philistines and Aegean Migration at the End of the Late Bronze Age*. Cambridge: Cambridge University Press.

Yasur-Landau, Assaf, Eric H. Cline, and Yorke M. Rowan (eds). 2019. *The Social Archaeology of the Levant: From Prehistory to the Present*. Cambridge: Cambridge University Press.

Yeivin, Sh. 1967. 'Amenophis II's Asianic Campaigns', *JARCE* 6: 119–28.

Yeivin, Sh. 1968. 'Additional Notes on the Early Relations between Canaan and Egypt', *JNES* 27: 37–50.

Yoffee, Norman. 2005. *Myths of the Archaic State: Evolution of the Earliest Cities, States, and Civilizations*. Cambridge: Cambridge University Press.

Yon, Marguerite. 1992. 'The End of the Kingdom of Ugarit', in William A. Ward and Martha Sharp Joukowsky (eds), *The Crisis Years: The 12th Century B.C. from Beyond the Danube to the Tigris*, 111–22. Dubuque, IL: Kendall/Hunt Publishing.

Yon, Marguerite, Maurice Sznycer, and Pierre Bordreuil (eds). 1995. *Le pays d'Ougarit autour de 1200 av. J.-C.: Histoire et archéologie, Actes du Colloque International, Paris, 28 juin–1er juillet 1993*. Ras Shamra-Ougarit 11. Paris: Editions Recherche sur les Civilisations.

Young, Gordon D. (ed.). 1981. *Ugarit in Retrospect: Fifty Years of Ugarit and Ugaritic*. Winona Lake, IN: Eisenbrauns.

Young, Gordon D. (ed.). 1992. *Mari in Retrospect: Fifty Years of Mari and Mari Studies*. Winona Lake, IN: Eisenbrauns.

Younger, K. Lawson, Jr. 2007. 'The Late Bronze Age/Iron Age Transition and the Origins of the Arameans', in K. Lawson Younger, Jr. (ed.), *Ugarit at Seventy-Five*, 131–74. Winona Lake, IN: Eisenbrauns.

Younger, K. Lawson, Jr. 2016. *A Political History of the Arameans: From their Origins to the End of their Politics*. Archaeology and Biblical Studies 13. Atlanta, GA: SBL.

Younger, K. Lawson, Jr. (ed.). 2007. *Ugarit at Seventy-Five*. Winona Lake, IN: Eisenbrauns.

Yuhong, Wu. 1994. *A Political History of Eshnunna, Mari and Assyria during the Early Old Babylonian Period (from the End of Ur III to the Death of Šamši-Adad)*. The Institute for the History of Ancient Civilizations 2. Supplement to *Journal of Ancient Civilizations* 1. Changchun, China: Institute of History of Ancient Civilizations, Northeast Normal University.

Yurco, Frank J. 1986. 'Merenptah's Canaanite Campaign', *JARCE* 23: 189–215.

Yurco, Frank J. 1997. 'Merenptah's Canaanite Campaign and Israel's Origins', in Ernest S. Frerichs and Leonard H. Lesko (eds), *Exodus: The Egyptian Evidence*, 27–55. Winona Lake, IN: Eisenbrauns.

Zarins, Juris. 1978. 'The Camel in Ancient Arabia: A Further Note', *Antiquity* 52: 44–6.

Zarzeki-Peleg, Anabel. 1997. 'Hazor, Jokneam and Megiddo in the 10th Century B.C.E.', *TA* 24: 258–88.

Zertal, Adam. 1994. '"To the Land of the Perizzites and the Giants": On the Israelite Settlement in the Hill Country of Manasseh', in Israel Finkelstein and Nadav Na'aman (eds), *From Nomadism to Monarchy: Archaeological and Historical Aspects of Early Israel*, 47–69. Jerusalem: Israel Exploration Society.

Zimhoni, Orna. 1985. 'The Iron Age Pottery of Tel 'Eton and its Relation to the Lachish, Tell Beit Mirsim and Arad Assemblages', *TA* 12: 63–90.

Zimhoni, Orna. 2004. 'Chapter 25 The Pottery of Levels V and IV and its Archaeological and Chronological Implications', in David Ussishkin (ed.), *The Renewed Archaeological Excavations at Lachish (1973–1994), vols. 1–5*, 4:1643–1788. Tel Aviv University Ronia and Marco Nadler Institute of Archaeology, Monograph Series 22. Tel Aviv: Emery and Claire Yass Publications in Archaeology.

Zorn, Jeffrey R. 2010. 'Reconsidering Goliath: An Iron Age I Philistine Chariot Warrior', *BASOR* 360: 1–22.

Index of References

Hebrew Bible/Old Testament		41:43	77	Leviticus		
Genesis		45:10	157	18:3	140	
11–50	73, 78	45:20	157	25:13-16	221	
11:10-26	4	46:28	157	25:23-28	221	
11:20-32	76	46:29	157			
11:22-26	275	46:34	157	Numbers		
11:25–50:26	275	47:1	157	2:32	160	
11:26	73	47:4	157	10:11	159	
11:28	78, 275	47:6	157	12:16	159	
12–50	75	47:11	158	13:26	159	
12:6	141	47:27	157	13:29	57, 245	
12:10-20	76			13:33	159	
14:6	141	Exodus		13:35	159	
15:19-21	141	1:11	158	20:1	159	
15:21	57	3:8	141	20:22	159	
19:24-29	64, 75	6:16-25	221	21:10-20	159	
20:1-2	76	8:22	157	21:13	57	
21–22	64, 75	9:26	157	21:26	57	
21:22-34	206	12:37	158, 159	21:33-35	159	
22:21	78	13:5	57	26:30-33	222	
22:24	125	14:8	155	33	159	
23	76	14:21-29	276	33:1-49	159	
24:10	78	14:21	156	33:3	158	
26:1-18	206	14:22-29	156	33:36	159	
26:1-11	76	15	156, 162			
26:12-18	78	15:7	156	Deuteronomy		
36	147	21:2	142	1:4	159	
36:20-30	141	23:23	140, 141	1:7	57	
36:31	147	23:28	140	1:28	159	
40:15	77	33:2	140	1:44	57	
41:42	77	34:11	140, 141	2:1-25	159	

Deuteronomy (cont.)		*Judges*		15	245
2:10	159	1	224	16:1-13	253, 254
2:11	159	1:8	251	16:14-23	253, 254
2:12	141	1:9-17	141	17	253, 254
2:21	159	1:18	208	17:52	208
2:22	141	1:19-36	224	18:1	253
3:10-11	159	1:21	251	18:7	253
6:21-23	155	1:27-33	141	18:17-27	253, 254
7:1	141	3:5	141	18:25-27	253
9:2	159	3:31	225, 242	19:11-17	253
11:30	141	4–5	240	20:12-17	253
12:29-31	140	4	226	21:11	208
15:12	142	5	5, 191, 221–3, 225, 226, 266, 279	21:12	253
18:9	140			21:13	208
20:17	141	5:2	279	22–26	249
21:1	141	5:3	279	22:6	246, 247
26:5-9	155	5:5	279	23:7-13	249
		5:6	225, 242	23:16-18	253
Joshua		5:7	279	24:2	249
1–5	213	5:9	279	26:1	249
3:10	141	5:11	279	27:2-4	208
5:1	141	5:14-18	226	27:11	208
9:1	141	5:14	225	28:4	212
9:10	159	5:17	225	29:1	212
10	213	6–8	225	29:5	253
11:21-22	159	6:32	225	29:11	212
11:22	208	9	225, 242		
11:23	213	10:1-5	224	*2 Samuel*	
12:4	159	12:7-15	224	2–9	245
12:8	140	16–19	224	2:3-4	223
13:12	159	16:25-30	208	2:4	5, 223
14:12	159	17:7	221	2:8-9	222
14:15	159, 213			2:9	225, 226, 247, 254
15:14	159	*1 Samuel*		2:10	247
15:21-62	213	5:8	208	3–4	223
15:63	251	5:11	208	3:12-16	253
17:2-3	222	6:17	208	5:1-3	223
17:14-17	213	7:14	208	5:4	5, 223
17:16	141	7:15	243	5:5	223
17:18	141	8	244	5:6-9	251, 252
18:21-28	213	9–10	244	5:17-25	249
18:28	251	9:1–10:16	246, 254	5:25	250
19:2-8	213	10:1	244	8	250
19:6	85	10:23	254	8:1	249
19:24-48	119	11:1-15	254	8:6	250
19:40-46	213	13	242	8:17	251
19:43	208	13:1	245	8:18	211
21:41-43	213	13:2–14:52	246, 254	10:1–11:1	250
24:2-13	155	13:19-22	210	11	141
24:11	140, 141	13:19-21	209	12:26-31	250

15:18-22	250	*Nehemiah*		**APOCRYPHA**		
22:7	257	2:19	157	*1 Maccabees*		
24:16-25	251	6:1-2	157	10:84	208	
24:16-24	141	6:6	157	11:4	208	
24:16	251	9:8	140			
24:23	251			**OTHER ANCIENT SOURCES**		
		Job		Herodotus		
1 Kings		26:5	159	*Histories*		
1–2	257			2.102-11	37	
2–11	255	*Psalms*		3.91	256	
2:39-40	250	88:11-13	159	7.73	180	
2:39	208, 209					
5:1	256	*Proverbs*		Josephus		
5:4	256	9:18	159	*Against Apion*		
8:12-13	257			1.14 §§73-92	67	
10:1-13	258	*Isaiah*		1.14 §§79-92	70	
10:1	258	19:18	140	1.14 §84	70	
10:3	256	19:19-25	160	1.16 §103	67	
10:14-15	256	26:14	159	1.17-18 §§106-27	257	
10:23-24	256	26:19	159	1.26 §228	67	
10:28-29	256	29:22	77			
10:68	256	39:1	92	Xanthus		
11:41	258			*Lydiaka*		
13:36	77	*Jeremiah*		765, frags. 14-15	180	
14:19-21	243	25:20	208			
14:25-28	9, 242, 260, 262	33:26	77	**OSTRACA**		
14:26	262	34:9	142	3.2	222	
14:29-31	243	34:14	142	13.1	222	
18:36	77	42–44	160	22.1	222	
		47:4	173	24.1	222	
2 Kings		52:25	29	25.1	222	
2	242			26.1	222	
2:18	208	*Ezekiel*		27.1	222	
12	257	16:3	57	28.1	222	
13:23	77	25:16	211	29.1	222	
14:7	250			30.1	222	
20:12	92	*Hosea*		33.1	222	
25:19	29	12:1	155	34.1	222	
		13:4	155	35.1	222	
1 Chronicles				36.1	222	
8:33	247	*Amos*		42.1	222	
		3:1	221	43.1	222	
2 Chronicles		7:9	77	44.1	222	
11:5-12	200	7:16	77	44.2	222	
11:23	200	9:7	173, 211	45.1	222	
26:6	208			46.1	222	
		Micah		47.1	222	
Ezra		7:20	77	48.1	222	
9:1	140, 141			50.1	222	
				52.1	222	

Ostraca (cont.)

64	222	171	91	85.69-71	126
66	222	172	102, 107	86	101
		173	91	88	130, 135
		181	177	89	129
INSCRIPTIONS AND		182	95	90	101
OTHER TEXTUAL				92	129
ARM		*CTA*		95	101, 130
28.16	61	1.113	55	97-98	130, 181
				98	129, 182
Anastasi		*EA*		99	130
5 19.2–20.6	160	1-50	129	100	101, 130
		1-11	129	101-38	100, 130, 181
CTH		1	129	101	100, 101, 129, 182
4	47, 98	8	135, 140	103	129, 182
6	47	12	129	104	101, 182
7	47, 98	13-25	129	105	101, 182
10	47	16	143, 183	106	101, 182
11	47, 48	19-20	99	107.28	136
13	47, 48, 98	26	129	109	101
16	98	27-29	129	111	135
17	98	29	99	114	101, 129
19	46, 98	29.16-20	99	118	101
20	48	29.16-18	99, 125	122-23	177
22	48	30	140	122	143, 183
40	95	31-32	129	123	143, 183
45	106	33-40	129	126	101, 129
46	106	45-50	129	129	115
47	106	45	112, 129	131	140
49	101	49	106, 112	136-38	101
54	101	51-62	130	137	140
61	177	51	130	139-40	130, 181
62	101	52-57	130	140	101
64	107	53	130	141-43	130, 181
65	107	53.63	136	144-49	129
66	107	56	130	144-45	130, 182
75	47	58	130	146-55	130, 182
77	106	59	101, 130	146	182
81	95	60-62	100, 129, 130	148	135
88	95	63-65	130, 133	149	182
91	95	66-96	100, 130, 181	151	129, 177, 182
92	102	66-214	130	152	182
93	107	67-140	129, 130	154	182
94	107	68	142	156-71	130
95	108	73-76	129	156-61	101
105	102	73	130	159	101
107	108	75	130	160	101
108	108	77	129	161	101
110	109	81	130	162	101, 126
121	95	83	129, 181, 182	164-67	101
142	177	85	129, 135, 181	164	101

INDEX OF REFERENCES

165	101	244-46	131, 135	307-12	133		
168	101	244	131	313	133		
169-70	101	245	131, 132, 135	314-16	133		
169	143, 183	246	132, 183	317-18	131		
171	101	248	131, 133, 135	318	143, 183		
175	130	249-50	131, 135	319	131, 133		
182-84	130	249	135	320-26	133, 135		
185-86	130	250	131, 132, 135	320-21	115		
185	142	251	133	322	115		
186	142	252-54	135	326	140		
187	115, 130	253	115, 132, 135	327	131		
188	130	254	115, 132, 135	328	115, 133, 135		
189-90	129	255-56	131, 135	329	115, 133, 135		
189	130	255	131, 135	330-32	133		
190	130	256	135	333	133, 135		
191-92	130	257-60	131	335	115, 133		
193	130	257-59	135	336-37	133		
194-97	130	261-62	133	338-39	133		
195	143, 183	263-66	135	362	100, 130, 140, 181		
196-97	131, 135	263	131, 133, 135	363	130		
197	131	264-66	131	364	131, 135		
197.21	136	267-71	133, 135	365	135		
199-200	130	271	135	366-67	131		
201	130	272	131, 133, 140	366	115, 134, 135		
203	130	273-74	133	367	135		
204	131	275-77	133	369	135		
205	131	278-84	133, 135	370	115, 135		
206	131	280	131, 132, 134, 135	378	135		
207	130	281	140				
208	130	284	115, 133, 134	*KTU*			
209-10	130	285-91	133	1.108	159		
211-14	130	285-90	115, 134, 135, 141	1.113	105, 106		
215-337	130	286	140, 142	1.161	110		
215-16	133	287	115, 131, 132, 134, 135, 142	1.161, 1.32	109		
221-22	133			2.16	109		
223	135	288	115, 131, 135, 142	2.36	109		
224-25	131	289	131, 132, 135, 142	2.37	109		
225-26	135	290	131, 135	2.39	110		
227-28	130, 135	292-94	135	2.61	110		
227	140	292	135	2.73	109		
232-35	131, 135	293-93	133	2.74	109		
236	131	294	133				
237-38	135	295	133, 182	*KUB*			
237	131, 133, 135, 140	296-300	133	XXI 38	102		
238	133	296	115, 133				
239	133	297-300	133, 135	*Mari texts*			
240	133	297	143, 183	23.556	55		
241	131	298	133	A.2966	55		
242-47	131	301-6	133				
242-46	135	306	133				

RS

4.449	106
11.732	106
15.8	109
15.14	109
16.146	101, 107
16.161	101, 107
16.249	107
16.270, ll. 22-25	109
17.18	109
17.35	108
17.59	108
17.62	107
17.130	107
17.132	106
17.133	108
17.159	108
17.189	109
17.226	110
17.227	106
17.229	107
17.235	107
17.237	107
17.238	107
17.247	109, 110
17.292	109
17.328	107
17.334	106
17.335	107
17.338	107
17.340	106
17.341	109
17.352	108
17.355	110
17.368	107
17.369	106
17.379	107
17.380	107
17.381	107
17.385	109
17.396	108
17.423	109
18.21	110
18.38	110
19.11	110
19.68	101, 106
20.33	107
20.162	103
20.212	110
20.216	110
20.237	109
20.238	110
24.257	55, 105
32.204	109
34.126	109
34.129	110, 177
34.136	110
34.138	109
34.143	110
34.150	109
34.152	110
34.165	109
94.2518	55, 105, 106

Summary Inscription
7:10' 186

Suppiluliuma Treaty
iii 4'-5' 101

Urk.

IV 744: 3-5	24
IV 780: 4	24
IV 780: 16	24
IV 1296: 13-1297: 4	24
IV 1556	126

Wenamun
1.8   177, 211

Index of Authors

Abbas, M. R. 148, 150
Adler, W. 35, 38
Adams, R. B. 117, 121, 143, 145, 147, 185, 228, 232
Aharoni, Y. 125, 201
Ahituv, S. 116, 125, 148, 150, 184, 204
Ahlström, G. 227, 230
Albertz, R. 153, 155
Albright, W. F. 19, 56, 57, 62, 64, 73, 74, 78, 191, 202, 211, 216–18, 228, 275
Allen, J. P. 35, 39
Allen, S. J. 35, 39
Alt, A. 71, 73, 137, 217, 218
Altman, A. 100, 103, 106, 108
Anbar, M. 56, 59
Anderson, J. D. 145
Andrason, A. 56, 59
Archi, A. 16, 18, 22, 56, 59, 71, 74
Arnaud, D. 54, 55, 103, 105, 106
Artzy, M. 204, 211
Ash, P. S. 6, 9, 255, 259, 260
Aston, D. A. 116, 121
Astour, M. C. 60, 62, 96–8

Baer, K. 35, 36
Baeteman, C. 117
Bahn, P. 236
Baines, J. 12, 13, 51, 52
Barako, T. J. 169, 174, 176
Barfield, T. J. 214, 235, 237
Barkay, G. 6, 9
Barlow, C. 185
Barr, J. 257

Bartelmus, A. 90
Bates, D. G. 227, 231
Beckerath, J. von 35, 65, 70
Beckman, G. M. 18, 45, 47, 90, 91, 93, 95, 96, 98, 100–3, 106–10
Bell, B. 12, 15
Ben-Ami, D. 116, 120, 191, 195, 216, 217, 227, 247, 252
Ben-Dor Evian, S. 8, 169, 172, 174, 259, 264
Ben-Tor, A. 6, 18, 20, 21, 26, 27, 35, 116, 191, 195, 216, 217, 227
Ben-Yosef, E. 72, 78, 145–7
Benz, B. C. 136, 143
Betancourt, P. P. 65, 69
Bienkowski, P. 116, 117, 145–7, 184, 185, 187, 188
Bietak, M. 65, 67, 69, 153, 158
Bimson, J. J. 217, 227
Bin-Nun, S. R. 94
Bloch-Smith, E. 116, 119, 186, 187, 191, 195–8, 200, 213, 215, 265, 267
Blum, E. 219, 221, 222, 226
Boivin, O. 90
Boiy, T. 205
Bordreuil, P. 103, 110, 170
Brand, P. J. 122, 126, 154
Brandl, B. 145
Breasted, J. H. 123, 124
Bretschneider. J. 205
Brettler, M. Z. 247, 248
Bright, J. 71, 73, 75, 76
Brinkman, J. A. 90, 178
Brisch, N. 96

Brooke, G. J. 51, 53, 103, 104, 109, 139
Broshi, M. 53, 240, 241
Bryan, B. M. 83, 87, 96, 99, 125, 126
Bryce, T. R. 18, 45–7, 94, 95, 169, 177, 180, 181
Buccellati, G. 16, 17, 56–60
Buck, M. E. 53–6, 58, 60
Bunimovitz, S. 53, 62, 64, 116, 119, 120, 128, 133, 169, 175, 191, 196, 204, 207
Burke, A. A. 56, 58
Burstein, S. M. 27, 30

Cahill, J. M. 191, 198, 199, 247, 252
Cancik-Kirschbaum, E. 96
Caquot, A. 54
Caton, S. C. 235, 239
Chaney, M. L. 137, 217, 227
Charpin, D. 57
Chatty, D. 227, 231
Chavalas, M. W. 45, 47, 96, 98, 178, 179
Childs, B. S. 71, 73
Clark, W. M. 62, 64, 71, 73
Clayden, T. 90
Clements, R. E. 72, 77
Cline, E. H. 83, 86, 87, 116, 121, 122, 126, 167–9, 177, 204, 205, 212, 227
Clines, D. J. A. 185
Cohen, R. 96, 153, 159
Coldstream, N. 6, 9
Collins, B. J. 72, 139, 141
Conybeare, F. C. 255, 256
Cooper, L. 19, 154
Coote, R. 240, 241
Cornelius, F. 45, 94
Couroyer, B. 18, 24, 149
Creamer, W. 244, 246
Croatto, J. S. 72, 77
Cross, F. M., Jr. 21, 99, 115, 117, 137, 143, 145, 153, 156, 216, 228, 276
Cumming, B. 124, 126
Cunchillos, J.-L. 54

Dagan, Y. 45, 70, 191, 200
Dalley, S. 40
d'Andrea, M. 16, 19
Davies, D. P. 122, 123
Davies, G. I. 153, 156, 158, 159
Davis, B. 143, 204, 207
Dearman, J. A. 116, 184, 186, 187

Dever, W. G. 62–4, 72, 73, 116, 118, 148, 152, 153, 158–60, 191, 192, 196, 197, 204, 216, 219, 227, 230–2
Diebner, B.-J. 223, 225
Dietrich, W. 103, 107–9, 204, 209, 235, 243, 244, 247, 249, 253
Dijkstra, M. 148, 152
Dion, P. E. 183
Donner, H. 72, 76
Dossin, G. 40, 56, 57, 60, 61
Dothan, T. 63, 116, 169, 171, 174, 191, 204, 209, 216, 227
Drews, R. 96, 116, 121, 167, 169, 173, 177, 181
Dunand, M. 19
Durand, J.-M. 40, 57
Dušek, J. 183
Dyson-Hudson, N. 137

Edel, E. 125
Edelman, D. V. 4, 153, 184, 185, 213, 215, 244–6
Ehrlich, C. S. 169, 171, 173
Eichler, B. L. 72, 76
Eidem, J. 96
Eissfeldt, O. 148, 150
Elayi, J. 181, 182
Eliyahu-Behar, A. 204, 210
Epstein, C. 122, 123

Fantalkin, A. 191, 192, 200, 201, 259, 261, 262
Farino, G. 65
Faulkner, R. O. 19, 23, 24, 122, 123
Faust, A. 116, 191, 196, 197, 231, 232, 234
Feinman, G. M. 235–8
Feucht, E. 259
Fieger, M. 153
Finkelstein, I. 3, 6–11, 27, 28, 30, 31, 62–4, 72, 78, 116, 117, 119–21, 128–34, 139, 145–8, 153, 154, 159, 169, 174–6, 181, 182, 184, 185, 187, 188, 191, 192, 194–202, 204, 206–11, 213–15, 217–19, 223–5, 227–30, 235, 240–8, 252, 254, 259–62, 264, 265, 268
Finkelstein, J. J. 40, 43
Fischer, P. M. 53
Fleming, D. E. 27, 30, 57, 214
Frahm, E. 28, 29
Frankish, J. 6, 8
Frayne, D. R. 40, 62
Frerichs, E. S. 149, 153–6
Freu, J. 46, 96, 103, 107, 108, 110
Frevel, C. 3, 4, 190

Fried, M. H. 219, 220
Fritz, V. 192, 201, 205, 218, 227, 244, 248

Galling, K. 204, 210
Gardiner, A. H. 19, 24, 27, 57, 58, 122, 123, 153, 157, 204, 211
Garfinkel, Y. 192, 200
Geertz, C. 214, 215
Gelb, I. J. 40, 42, 53, 54, 57, 59, 60, 90
Gellner, E. 235, 239
Genz, H. 46, 94
Geraty, L. T. 185
Geus, C. H. J. de 219, 221
Gibson, J. C. L. 117, 192, 196, 224, 226
Gilan, A. 72, 94, 96, 98, 139, 141
Gilboa, A. 7, 137, 141, 192, 194, 204–6, 212, 235, 247
Gitin, S. 116–18, 191, 192, 204, 205, 209, 216, 227, 236
Giveon, R. 23, 83, 85, 86, 143, 144
Glassner, J.-J. 90, 93, 178, 179, 184
Godelier, M. 235, 237
Goedicke, H. 65, 122, 123, 125, 136, 143, 144
Goetze, A. 94, 96
Goldschmidt, W. 227, 231
Golinets, V. 57
Gonen, R. 117, 120
Gophna, R. 19, 21, 26, 53
Gordon, C. H. 72, 73, 78
Goren, Y. 120, 128–31, 133, 134, 181, 182
Görg, M. 148, 149, 153
Gosden, C. 235, 236
Gottlieb, Y. 204, 209, 210
Gottwald, N. 136, 137, 142, 218–21, 230, 240
Götze, A. 46, 170, 177
Grabbe, L. L. 3–7, 30, 35, 38, 40, 41, 51–3, 103, 104, 116, 118, 139, 141, 148, 153–6, 170, 171, 185, 190, 191, 193, 194, 206, 213–15, 224, 227, 28, 234, 235, 240, 243, 246–8, 251, 255, 258–60, 264, 265
Grandet, P. 167, 168
Grayson, A. K. 40, 90, 91, 93, 178, 179, 184, 214, 215
Greenberg, M. 142
Greenfield, H. J. 19, 26, 27, 236
Greengus, S. 72, 76
Grimal, N. 3, 4, 7, 12, 35, 36, 83, 167
Groddek, D. 72, 139, 170, 177
Groll, S. I. 153, 157, 160
Guest, P. D. 224, 226

Guillaume, P. 3, 4, 190, 224, 246, 247, 256, 262
Guiot, J. 117,
Gurney, O. R. 46, 94
Güterbock, H. G. 94, 95, 170, 177

Haas, J. 244, 246
Halpern, B. 116, 119, 192, 195, 224, 225, 227, 247, 248
Haran, M. 76, 153, 159
Harris, J. R. 255, 256
Harrison, T. P. 185
Hart, S. 185, 187
Hasel, M. G. 136, 143, 144, 148, 150, 151, 153, 192, 200, 232
Hauptmann, A. 145
Hawass, Z. 66, 70
Hawkins, J. D. 46
Hayes, J. H. 216, 217, 227
Hayes, W. C. 19, 27, 65
Heimpel, W. 40, 60, 61
Helck, W. 12, 13, 19, 27, 46, 48, 51–3, 55, 57, 58, 99, 100, 102, 122, 123, 125, 129, 132, 153, 158, 259, 260
Helm, J. 219, 220
Heltzer, M. 104
Herr, L. G. 117, 145, 147, 185, 187, 188, 192, 196, 204, 207
Herrmann, S. 259
Herzog, Z. 63, 64, 117, 192, 193, 197–9, 201, 202, 227, 229, 230, 247, 252
Hess, R. S. 139, 140, 148
Hesse, B. 117, 193, 196, 214, 215
Higham, T. 6, 7, 145, 146, 185, 192–4
Hitchcock, L. A. 204, 205, 207, 211, 247
Hjelm, I. 148, 150, 151, 154
Hoch, J. E. 154, 158
Hodel-Hoenes, S. 153
Hoffman, Y. 154
Hoffmeier, J. K. 143, 148, 149, 154, 155, 157–9, 161
Hoffner, H. A. 46, 47, 72, 76, 94, 95, 139, 141, 170, 177
Holladay, J. S., Jr 154, 158
Hoop, R. de 224
Hornung, E. 3, 4, 7, 13, 14, 35, 38, 39, 70, 83, 89, 167, 169
Hort, G. 154, 156
Huehnergard, J. 19, 22, 104
Huffmon, H. B. 57

Iggers, G. G. 4, 5
Ilan, D. 63, 64, 117, 118, 120, 227, 229
Imparati, F. 46, 47, 96, 98, 170
Irons, W. 137
Izre'el, S. 57, 100, 101, 103, 104, 106, 108, 139

Jacobsen, T. 16, 28
Jacoby, F. 180
James, P. 6, 8, 83, 84
Jamieson-Drake, D. W. 193, 198
Jans, G. 205
Joffe, A. H. 235, 238
Johnson, M. D. 219, 221
Jonker, L. 255, 258

Kahn, D. 83, 96, 192, 204, 205, 235, 247, 259
Kallai, Z. 219, 221
Kamp, K. A. 57, 60, 137, 138, 214, 215, 220
Kang, H.-G. 192, 200
Kaniewski, D. 117, 119, 205
Katzenstein, H. J. 181
Kempinski, A. 46, 47, 94, 96, 98, 192, 201
Kenyon, 57, 194, 199, 248, 252
Khazanov, A. M. 137, 138
Khoury, P. S. 220
Kienast, B. 60, 62
Killebrew, A. E. 3, 4, 6, 9, 10, 19–21, 23, 51, 58, 63, 117–21, 133, 136, 137, 140, 141, 169, 170, 172, 174, 176, 177, 186, 191, 193, 194, 196, 199, 204–7, 214, 216, 219, 223, 227, 228, 230, 232, 247, 248, 251, 252
Kitchen, K. A. 40, 56, 83, 84, 88, 117, 122, 126, 127, 148–52, 154, 167, 168, 185, 186, 255, 258, 259, 263
Klengel, H. 12, 35, 46, 47, 51, 55, 61, 62, 83, 94, 100, 108, 110, 167
Kletter, R. 117, 193, 196, 214, 215, 232
Knauf, E. A. 3–5, 145, 147, 154, 160, 190, 193, 199, 213, 222, 224–6, 228, 235, 246, 247, 255–9, 261, 262, 264
Knudtson, J. A. 114, 115
Koch, I. 193, 199, 200
Kohl, P. L. 6, 8
Kokkinos, N. 6, 8
Košak, S. 46, 47, 94, 96, 98, 192, 201
Kossian, A. V. 178, 180, 181
Kostiner, J. 220
Krahmalkov, C. R. 154, 159
Kramer, S. N. 28, 29

Krause, J. J. 219, 235
Krauss, R. 3, 4, 7, 13, 14, 35, 38, 39, 70, 83, 89, 167, 169
Krebernik, M. 19, 22
Krejčí, J. 13, 14
Kuhrt, A. 3, 4, 7, 12, 35, 42, 46, 51, 83, 167, 173

LaBianca, Ø. S. 63, 117, 185–7
Lacheman, E. R. 96
Lackenbacher, S. 54, 104, 109
Lambert, 178, 179, 183, 184
Larson, M. T. 40, 42
Le Burell, S. 117
Leclant, J. 19, 23
Ledermann, Z. 116
Leemans, W. F. 40
Lehmann, G. A. 3, 5, 104, 110, 137, 169, 170, 176, 177, 193, 197–200, 204–6, 219, 223, 228, 248
Lemche, N. P. 137–40, 142, 151, 217–21, 228, 230
Lesko, L. H. 153, 156
Levin, C. 220, 221
Levy, T. E. 6, 7, 19, 20, 62, 63, 116, 117, 121, 143, 145–7, 154, 155, 185, 187, 192–4, 214, 228, 232
Lichtheim, M. 13, 15, 35, 83, 127
Lindars, B. 224, 225
Lipinska, J. 83, 86
Lipiński, E. 19, 183, 184
Lipschits, O. 193, 205, 224, 225, 264
Liverani, M. 3, 4, 7, 12, 16, 35, 46, 51, 57, 59, 68, 83, 97, 99, 107, 110, 178, 181, 182, 235, 239, 255, 258
Lloyd, A. B. 38
Loretz, O. 142, 170, 177
Lorton, D. 19, 25
Lucas, C. J. 28, 29

Macchi, J.-D. 220, 221
MacDonald, B. 145, 154, 159, 185–7
Maeir, A. M. 72, 117, 139, 170, 176, 192, 193, 200, 201, 204–8, 210–12, 214–16, 227, 235, 247
Maidman, M. P. 96
Malamat, A. 41, 66, 154, 156, 255, 258
Malko, H. O. 90
Maran, J. 205, 210
Margalith, O. 148, 150
Márquez Rowe, I. 104, 107–9
Martin, G. T. 56, 219
Master, D. M. 235, 239, 256
Matthiae, P. 16, 19, 22
Mayes, A. D. H. 220, 221

Mayrhofer, M. 96, 97
Mazar, A. 6, 8–11, 19, 20, 72, 116, 117, 139, 170, 175, 191–5, 198, 199, 202–4, 216, 227, 248, 252, 254, 259, 261, 265, 267, 268
McDermott, J. J. 216, 228
McGovern, P. E. 65, 67
McKenzie, S. L. 248
McNutt, P. 220
Mendenhall, G. E. 137, 216–19, 228, 240
Michałowski, K. 35, 38
Mielke, D. P. 46, 94
Mieroop, M. V. De 3, 4, 7, 18, 41, 178
Millek, J. M. 100, 103, 104, 111, 167, 170, 173, 205, 212
Miller, J. M. 117, 185–7, 213, 216, 217, 227, 228
Miller, R. D., II 235, 237
Milstein, S. J. 27, 30
Mohammed, A. 137, 138
Monier-Williams, M. 96, 98
Monroe, L. 214
Montet, P. 19
Moran, W. L. 114, 115, 129, 131–4, 182, 235, 239
Morhange, C. 205
Morkot, R. 6, 8
Morris, E. F. 154, 158, 170–4
Morrison, M. A. 96
Moscati, S. 181
Mourad, A.-L. 9, 23, 35, 51, 65–71
Mumford, G. D. 83, 122, 125–7, 167
Münster. S. 194, 201
Murnane, W. J. 88, 96, 99, 122, 126, 127

Na'aman, N. 3, 28, 31, 65, 78, 96, 97, 104, 106, 117, 118, 120, 128–34, 139–42, 148, 150, 152, 154, 181, 182, 192–4, 200, 201, 205, 208, 213, 223, 224, 227–30, 248, 250, 255–8, 260, 262
Najjar, M. 145, 146, 147, 185
Nakhai, B. A. 116, 119, 148, 153, 184, 186, 187, 191, 195–8, 200, 265, 267
Naveh, J. 204, 209
Nelson, C. 137, 186
Nestor, D. 148
Ngo, R. 248, 252
Niccacci, A. 149, 150
Nicholson, E. W. 154, 155
Niehr, H. 224, 226, 228
Niemann, H. M. 3, 4, 190, 193, 200, 205, 208, 209, 228, 246–9, 255, 256, 257, 260, 262, 264
Nigro, L. 19, 20

Noort, E. 170, 172, 224
Noth, M. 73, 137, 154, 156, 217–21, 223, 240, 242, 260
Nuzzolo, M. 13, 14
Nys, K. 205

O'Callaghan, R. T. 183
O'Connor, D. 83, 86, 87, 122, 126, 167–71, 177
Odorico, M. de 154, 159
Ofer, A. 3, 5, 193, 197, 198, 223
Oren, E. D. 19, 26, 63, 65–7, 71, 94, 116, 154, 170, 171, 204, 206, 240
Otto, T. 117, 205
Owen, D. I 96

Panitz-Cohen, N. 6
Pardee, D. 54, 55, 103–6, 109, 110
Parker, S. B. 51, 52, 65
Parkinson, R. B. 19, 25, 36, 37
Paulus, S. 90
Payne, A. 180
Pearce, L. E. 28, 29
Peckham, J. B. 181
Peet, E. 19, 27, 66, 69
Petschow, H. 72, 76
Pettinato, G. 19, 22, 74
Pfoh, E. 236, 239
Piasetzky, E. 6, 11, 145, 146
Pinnock, F. 16, 19
Pitard, W. T. 183
Plicht, J. van der 6, 145, 146, 185
Poebel, A. 41, 90
Posener, G. 51, 52, 66
Powell, B. B. 28
Pruitt, M. L. 53, 57
Pusch, E. B. 154, 158

Quirke, S. G. J. 36, 39, 169

Raban, A. 118, 194, 196
Rabinowitz, I. 154, 157
Rad, G. von 154, 155
Rainey, A. F. 51, 52, 63, 64, 66, 71, 114, 115, 125, 129, 131–3, 139, 140, 143, 144, 149, 151–4, 170, 177, 181, 182, 231
Ramsey, C. B. 145
Ramsey, G. W. 72, 75, 76, 78, 216, 228
Raulwing, P. 96–8
Rawlinson, G. 181

Redford, D. B. 3, 4, 12–15, 19, 23, 24, 26, 51, 52, 65–9, 72, 77, 83–7, 97, 99, 100, 114, 122–4, 126, 143, 144, 149–52, 154, 156–8, 170–3, 231, 260, 262
Redman, C. L. 236
Redmount, C. A. 66, 67, 154
Reinhold, G. G. G. 183
Rendtorff, R. 52, 53
Renfrew, C. 236
Robertson, D. A. 154, 156, 224, 225
Robinson, A. 28, 145
Robinson, M. A. 145
Rodan, S. 205, 210
Rofé, A. 205, 211
Rogerson, J. W. 220, 221, 236, 238
Römer, T. 27, 201, 255, 256
Roskop, A. R. 155
Routledge, B. 185, 236, 239
Russell, S. C. 155
Ryholt, K. S. B. 35, 36, 38–40, 66, 68–70

Sader, H. 181–4
Saleen, S. N. 66, 70
Salzman, P. C. 137, 138, 227, 228, 231
Sapir-Hen, L. 72, 78
Saporetti, C. 46, 47, 97, 98
Saretta, P. 19, 23, 26, 57, 58, 66
Sasson, J. M. 28, 41, 54, 55, 60, 61, 90, 96
Sauer, J. A. 118, 185–7
Säve-Söderbergh, T. 66, 68
Sawyer, J. F. A. 185
Schipper, B. U. 72, 77, 155, 158, 205, 211, 255, 259, 260, 263
Schloen, D. 117, 153, 228, 236, 239
Schlott, A. 13, 14, 28, 29
Schmitt, R. 97, 98
Schneider, N. 72, 76, 84, 87, 154, 155
Schneider, H. D. 84, 87
Schneider, T. 154, 155
Schroer, S. 194, 201
Schulman, A. R. 149
Scolnic, B. E. 155
Seidl, U. 90
Seidlmayer, S. J. 52
Sergi, O. 214, 215, 219, 228, 234, 235
Service, E. 14, 177, 229, 233, 236
Shalom Brooks, S. 244, 246, 248, 253
Sharon, I. 7, 10, 11, 137, 141, 194, 203, 206, 212
Shaw, G. J. 66, 70
Shortland, A. J. 7, 9

Singer, I. 54, 55, 57, 72, 90, 91, 94, 100, 101, 104, 106–11, 125, 139, 141, 149, 175, 192–4, 197, 198, 200, 201, 206, 210, 247, 252
Singer-Avitz, L. 192–4, 197, 198, 200, 201, 247, 252
Sjöberg, Å. 28, 29
Smith Lewis, A. 255, 256
Soggin, J. A. 72, 77
Soldt, W. H. van 104, 110, 181, 182
Sommerfeld, W. 90
Southall, A. W. 236, 238
Soysal, O. 46–8, 94, 97, 98
Spalinger, A. 97, 100, 122, 126, 127
Speiser, E. A. 72, 76
Stager, L. E. 117, 153, 175, 194, 197, 224, 225, 228, 236, 239
Stantis, C. 66, 68
Staubli, T. 137, 138
Stech-Wheeler, T. 206, 209
Steen, E. J. van der 118, 119, 146, 147, 185–7, 228, 230
Stein, D. L. 97, 99
Steiner, M. L. 3, 4, 19–21, 23, 51, 58, 63, 119, 121, 133, 186, 194, 198, 199, 248, 252
Stern, E. 116, 191, 204–6, 211, 212, 216, 227
Stiebing, W. H., Jr 155
Streck, M. P. 57
Streit, K. 52, 96, 192
Szuchman, J. 117, 137, 138, 143, 145, 228

Tadmor, H. 57, 59, 61, 72, 185, 186, 255, 257
Tapper, R. 236, 238, 240
Tarragon, J.-M. de 54
Theis, C. 149
Thieme, P. 97, 98
Thompson, T. L. 72, 74, 76, 148, 150, 151, 154, 194, 247, 248, 275
Thorpe, I. J. 6, 8
Tigay, J. H. 28, 30
Tinney, S. 18
Trigger, B. G. 28, 236, 237
Tucker, G. 72, 76
Tuffin, P. 35, 38
Tyldesley, J. 84, 86, 88
Tyson, C. W. 118, 185, 186

Uphill, E. P. 155
Ussishkin, D. 7–9, 116, 118–20, 155, 159, 171, 173–6, 191, 192, 194, 195, 198–200, 202, 203, 247, 252, 260, 261

INDEX OF AUTHORS

Van Campo, E. 117, 205
Van Lerberghe, K. 205
Van Seters, J. 66–8, 72, 74, 139, 141, 155, 206, 211, 213, 228, 248, 250, 275
Vandersleyen, C. 19
Vansteenhuyse, K. 205
Vassiliev, A. 19, 24, 122, 123
Veen, P. van der 6, 8, 149
Velikovsky, I. 84, 86
Vergote, J. 155, 157
Vidal, J. 104, 106
Villard, P. 54, 55
Vita, J.-P. 56, 59, 128, 130

Wachsmann, S. 171
Waddell, W. G. 13, 36, 38, 66, 67, 70
Wallenfels, R. 7, 8
Wapnish, P. 72, 78, 117, 193, 196, 214, 215
Warburton, D. A. 3, 4, 7, 13, 14, 35, 38, 39, 70, 83, 89, 167, 169
Ward, W. A. 19, 26, 27, 118, 121, 143, 144, 155, 157, 167
Watson, W. G. E. 104, 105
Weeks, K. R. 122, 126
Wegner, I. 97
Wei, T. F. 155, 158
Weidner, E. 90, 93
Weingart, K. 220, 222
Weinstein, J. 66, 67, 155
Weippert, H. 3, 4, 20, 23, 63, 220, 221

Weippert, M. 143, 220, 221, 260
Weiss, H. 205
Whitelam, K. W. 240, 241
Whybray, R. N. 52, 53
Wilhelm, G. 46, 97, 98
Wilson, K. A. 260, 261, 263
Wilson, R. R. 220, 221
Wiseman, 54, 57, 60–2, 139
Witzel, M. 97, 98
Wood, B. G. 20, 22, 23, 27, 32, 65, 148, 217, 228
Worschech, U. 185
Wright, G. E. 72, 73
Wyatt, N. 104, 105

Yadin, Y. 195, 216, 217, 228
Yasur-Landau, A. 167, 168, 171, 173, 174, 177, 205, 207, 227
Yeivin, Sh. 122, 124, 125
Yoffee, N. 57, 60, 137, 138, 214, 215, 220, 236–8
Yon, M. 170
Young, G. D. 41, 96, 98, 208, 249, 254, 276
Younger, K. L., Jr 88, 183
Yuhong, Wu 41
Yurco, F. J. 144, 149–52

Zarins, J. 72, 78
Zarzeki-Peleg, A. 194, 195
Zertal, A. 217, 228
Zimhoni, O. 194, 200, 202
Zorn, J. R. 206, 210

Index of Subjects

Abba-El 62
Abdi-Ashtarti 133
Abdi-Heba 120, 131–4, 141, 242, 267, 277
Abdi-Milki 130
Abdi-Resha 130
Abdi-Shullim 130
Abdi-Tirši/Abdi-Tirshi 130, 135
Abiezer 222
Abimelech 224, 225, 242
Abimilki 130, 182
Abishemu 56
Abram/Abraham/Abhrāhām 4, 62, 72, 73, 76, 78, 80, 275
Abrek 72, 77
Absalom 250
Acco/Akko/Akka/Acre 65, 121, 127, 132, 135, 136, 183, 196, 212, 277
acculturation 207
Achaea 177
Achish 208, 209, 250
Achshaph 123, 131, 132, 135, 136
Ada 209
Adab 16
Adad-apla-iddina 184
Adad-nirari 91, 93, 95, 113, 179, 183
Adad-shum-usur 93
Adam and Eve 73, 275
Adanawa 180
Adda-Danu 135
Addu-nirari 130
adoption 72, 76

adultery 108, 109
Aegean 6, 8–10, 55, 65, 69, 94–6, 124, 148, 167, 170–3, 176, 205, 207, 212, 229, 281
Aeolic 238
Africa/African 138, 221, 231, 235
Agade 17, 18
agrarian 22, 217, 279, 281
agricultural/agriculturalist/agriculture 5, 20–2, 44, 117, 138, 146, 180, 182, 186, 192, 208, 210, 219, 223, 233, 238, 281
Agum 92
Aha 13
Ahab 7, 194, 215, 226, 246, 264, 271
Ahat-Milku 101, 108
Ahhiyawa 94, 95, 102, 170, 177
Aḥiḳar/Ahiqar 72, 255, 256, 280
Ahlamu 179, 183
Ahmose/Ahmose Pennekheb 39, 40, 71, 85, 86, 89, 99, 123, 128, 160
Aramaeans/Ahtiashna/Ahtirumna 131, 133
Ai 21, 77, 197, 213
'Ain Na'am 88
Akawash 89
Akhenaten/Akhenaton 83–5, 87, 89, 90, 92, 99, 104, 106, 112, 113, 115, 122, 126, 128, 129, 160
Akheperenre 86
Akhetaten 133
Akizzi 130
Akkad 16–18, 20, 21, 28, 31, 42, 43, 91, 178
Akshak 16
Akšapa 132, 135

INDEX OF SUBJECTS

Alalakh/Alalah 47, 53, 54, 60–2, 70, 79, 98, 106, 142, 211
Alashiya/Alashia 95, 129, 171
Aleppo 22, 47, 49, 54, 61, 62, 79, 94, 95, 124
alliance 23, 45, 61, 79, 97, 128, 132
alphabet 27, 52, 54, 55
altar 251
Aluwamna 94
Ama'e 142
Amalek/Amaleq/Amalekites 201, 230, 244, 245, 276
Amarna 52, 53, 60, 73, 84, 87, 89, 92, 96, 100, 101, 104, 107, 108, 111, 112, 114, 115, 119, 120, 126, 128–30, 132–6, 140–3, 157, 160, 162, 163, 181–3, 203, 235, 242, 275–9
Amar-Suen 56
Amawashe 130
Amayashe 131
Amenemhet 36–8, 49, 56, 68, 99
Amenhotep 83–7, 89, 90, 92, 96, 99, 106, 112, 122–6, 129, 140, 183
Amenmesses 168, 169
Amenophis 84, 87, 89, 122
Ameny 25
Ammenemes 36, 37
Ammia 142
Ammisaduqa/Ammishtamru/Ammistamru/Ammiṯtamru 43, 102, 104–6, 108, 109, 112, 129
Ammiya 100, 130
Ammon/Ammonite 117, 185–7, 230, 238, 250
Ammuna 48
Ammunenshi 25
Ammunira 130, 181
Ammurapi 105, 109, 110, 113
Ammu-šamar 105
Amnanūm 59
Amor/Amorite/Amorites 16, 17, 21, 22, 26, 41, 42, 44, 50, 53–61, 64, 65, 68, 78, 79, 100, 104, 139, 141, 171, 179, 184, 272, 274, 275, 282
amphictyony 219–21, 223
amphora/amphorae 67, 116, 121
Amu/*3mw*/Aamu 15, 23, 25, 26, 32, 58, 66–8, 272
Amun 88, 123
Amurru/Amurrite/Amorite 57, 58, 60, 83, 88, 95, 100–4, 106–12, 115, 126–30, 135, 136, 140, 173, 179, 181, 182, 274, 275, 277
Anaharath 125, 132, 133, 135, 136, 225
Anakim 159
Anastasi 136, 143, 153, 160
Anat/Anath 69, 88, 224, 225, 242

Anatolia 12, 17, 18, 31, 42, 45, 46, 49, 60, 93, 95, 98, 111, 119, 129, 141, 169, 170, 172, 177, 178, 180, 184, 229, 265, 274, 280
Andurārum 43
Anitta 43, 46, 49
annals 13, 46, 47, 94, 96, 98, 100, 179, 257
anoint/anointed/anointing 241, 244–6, 253, 254, 267
anthropologist/anthropology 97, 214, 220, 236
Apachnan 70
Apapi/Apepi 70
'Aper-'Anati 70
Aphek 65, 125
Apiru 100, 115, 119, 127, 130, 132, 134, 136, 142, 147, 183, 225, 230, 233, 249, 250, 254, 268, 277, 278, 281
Apophis 13, 39, 70
Apu 130
Aqaba 132
Ar'anu 124
Arabah 143, 146–8, 187, 188, 262
Arabia/Arabs 72, 78, 115, 157, 185, 230, 255, 258
Arad 31, 192–4, 197, 200–3, 227, 250, 260
Aramaic/Aram/Aramaean 52, 78, 91, 104, 154, 179, 180, 183, 184, 189, 208, 229, 246, 250, 255, 274, 280
Arasha 130
Araunah 141, 251
Aravah Valley 72, 78, 145
Arazik 62
Arbel 143
arboriculture 138, 144
archaeozoology 97
archers 134
archive 36, 115, 129, 133, 274, 277
Ardata 100, 101, 124
Ar-Halba/Ar-Ḫalba 105, 107
Ari-Teshub 101
Ark-den-ili 93
Armant Stela 123
Armenian 255
Arnon 186
Arnuwanda 95
Arqa 119
Arsawuya 130
Artamanya 130
Artashumara 98
Artatama 90, 98, 99, 125
Artatarna 113
Arwad 101, 179, 181, 182
Aryan 97, 98, 111

Arzawa 94, 95, 129, 171
Ashdod 9, 10, 118, 121, 123, 128, 133, 136, 169, 175, 176, 206, 208, 211
Asher 211, 226
Ashirta 100, 101, 106, 108, 112, 128, 130, 181, 277
Ashkelon 65, 115, 123, 128, 130, 132, 133, 135, 136, 149–52, 168, 175, 206, 208, 211, 271, 277
Ashtarot/Ashtaroth/Ashtartu/Aštartu 65, 130–2, 135, 136, 159
Ashur/Ashurites 40, 42, 90–3, 113, 129, 178, 179, 183, 226, 245
Ashurbanipal 187
Ashur-bel-kala 183
Ashur-Dan 91, 93, 178, 183
Ashur-nadin-apli 91
Ashurnasirpal 180
Ashur-nirari 91
Ashur-resh-ishi 179
Ashur-uballit 90–3, 113, 129
Asriel 222
Assis 70
aššu-ššanni 98
Assyria/Assyrians 5, 17, 18, 41–6, 61, 79, 90, 91, 93, 95, 98, 99, 102, 103, 108, 109, 111–13, 119, 124, 126, 127, 129, 178–81, 183–5, 188, 207, 211, 223, 241, 246, 255, 274, 275, 277
Astarte 23
Aśva 98
Asy 124
Asyut 36
Aten 84
Atlantic 73
Atum 158
Atuna 180
Avaris 39, 49, 64, 65, 67, 69–71, 79, 85, 112, 123, 273
Ay 126
Aya 36, 40, 87, 89, 115, 267
Ayyab 131, 135
Aziru 101, 107, 108, 112, 126, 128, 130, 181, 182, 277

Baal 69, 182, 225, 247
Baalbek 125
Baal-Shiptu 182
Babylon/Babylonia/Babylonians 29, 40–5, 47, 50, 54, 61, 62, 79, 87, 91–3, 102, 107, 111, 129, 140, 178, 179, 184, 188, 208, 241, 274, 275, 277
Baduzana 133
Bahrain 17

Balaam 104
Baltil 29
Baluchistan 137, 228, 231
Baʻlu-Dani
Baʻlu-Meher/Baʻlu-Meḫir 131, 135
Baʻlu-Shipti 133
bandit/brigand 130, 142, 229
Barattarna/Barrattarna 98, 99, 112
Ba-sa-ar' 59
Bashan 130, 131, 136, 159
Bathsheba 257
Batruna 100
Bay 168
Bayadi 133, 135
Bayawa 133
Bayt-ʻAnath 88
Bazi 179
bedouin 24, 143, 231
Beersheba/Beer-Sheba 10, 31, 63, 64, 75, 117, 120, 192, 195, 197, 201–3, 210, 229, 230, 262, 265
Beni-Hasan/Beni-Hassan
Benjamin/Benjaminites 59, 60, 76, 198, 219, 226, 229, 235, 245, 251, 263, 265, 271
Benteshina 102, 108, 112, 127
Berossus/Berossos 27, 30
Berytus/Beirut 100, 101, 119, 130, 140, 181, 182, 235
Beth Yerah 21
Bethel 133, 210, 242, 244, 246, 262, 265
Beth-Shean 65, 119, 121, 126, 127, 131, 132, 150, 168, 195, 196, 202, 263, 265, 271
Beth-Shemesh 53, 65, 116, 128, 133, 196, 201
Beth-zur 63
Bin-ʻAnu 70
bini-yamina/*bini-yamīna* 60, 274
Biridashwa 130, 131, 135
Biridiya 131, 135
Biryawaza 130
Bit-Adini 184
Bit-Agusi 184
Bitarha 100
bit-ḫilani 238
Bit-Ḫumri 271
Bit-Rehob 184
Bnōn 70
Boğazköy 60
border 9, 16, 58, 91, 93, 95, 102, 107, 109, 116, 126, 128, 130, 135, 143, 144, 158, 175, 179, 186, 187, 191, 225, 238
bureaucracy 13, 14, 28, 29, 31, 41

INDEX OF SUBJECTS

burial 20, 121, 272
Burna-Buriash 92, 93
Burraburiash 129
Busruna 130, 136
Byblos 14, 19–21, 23, 25–7, 32, 37, 38, 40, 49, 54–6, 64, 65, 70, 79, 100, 101, 111, 115, 119, 125–7, 129, 130, 136, 170, 173, 177, 179, 181, 182, 211, 257, 273, 277
Byzantine 35

camel 72, 78, 230
Canaanite 9, 22, 24, 26, 28, 39, 40, 51–3, 62, 64, 65, 67, 103, 104, 116–19, 121, 128, 129, 134, 136, 139–41, 147–9, 151, 153, 163, 175–7, 184, 191, 194, 201, 206–7, 212, 214, 216, 218. 219, 225, 227–34, 242, 248, 264, 266, 268, 275–8, 281
Caphtor 173, 211
Cappadocia 183
caravan/caravaneer 78, 230
Carchemish 42, 61, 62, 79, 95, 106–9, 126, 171, 180
Carmel 26, 86, 124, 196, 197, 212, 263
cattle 14, 25, 66, 143
cedar 23, 27, 65, 273
cemetery 121, 182, 232
ceramic 52, 119, 121, 196, 197, 232, 265
Chalcolithic 20, 26, 64
Chaldeans/Chaldees 78, 275
chariot/charioteer/chariotry 85, 86, 96, 98, 102, 125, 142, 151, 206, 210
Cherethites 204, 211, 247
chiefdom 201–3, 237, 238, 242, 244, 246, 247, 249, 262, 267, 282
chronicle 35, 47, 93, 179, 243, 248, 255, 258, 264, 280
chronography 35
Cilicia 99, 172
Cisjordan 114, 155, 189, 196
cisterns 196, 266
clan 159, 221, 222, 225, 239, 247, 249
Colchis 37
copper 18, 20, 26, 27, 32, 38, 55, 78, 91, 109, 121, 144–8, 188, 189, 201, 202, 210, 242, 261, 262
Cretan/Crete 37, 54, 55, 119, 173, 211
cult 13–15, 54, 84, 104, 251, 257, 265
cuneiform 5, 28, 29, 45, 46, 52, 54–7, 60, 78, 79, 90, 114, 115, 142, 181, 205, 274–5
Cyprus/Cypriot 9, 52, 54, 55, 69, 87, 94, 95, 108, 110, 118, 119, 121, 124, 129, 133, 146, 147, 172, 183, 202, 207, 211, 242, 266

Djahi/Djahy/D3hy/Ḏahy 123, 124, 126, 171, 173
Dagan 45, 70, 191, 200
Dagantakala 131
Damascus 60, 65, 119, 127, 130, 132, 136, 140, 183, 184, 250
Dan 91, 93, 177, 178, 183, 192, 222, 226, 265
Danae 281
Danaoi 176
Danites 281
Danuna 177
Dapur 127
Dashru 133
David 6, 8, 10, 116, 117, 120, 143, 145, 184, 187, 189, 191–3, 199–201, 203–6, 208, 209, 223, 235, 242, 257, 259, 264, 267, 268, 280, 282
daybook 280
Debir 133
Deborah 191, 223–5, 242, 279, 281, 282
Deir el-Ballas 70
Delta 13, 15, 16, 24, 26, 27, 36–40, 49–50, 58, 66, 68–71, 79, 80, 85, 89, 127, 143, 144, 153, 154, 156, 157, 173, 273, 276, 277
Demotic 28
Denye/Denyen 171, 176, 177
Deuteronomist/Deuteronomistic/Deuteronomy 53, 225, 240, 246, 255, 258, 264, 276
Dialect 18, 28, 41, 104
Dilbat 42
Dilmun 17
dimorphic 44, 59
Ditanu 55
Dius 257
divorce 108, 110
Djehuty 123, 163
Djoser 14
Dor 6–8, 133, 137, 169, 172–4, 177, 183, 189, 194, 196, 206, 211, 212, 259
Drehem 58
Duppi-Teshub 101, 102
Dur-Kurigalzu 93

earthquake 191, 259
easterners 24
Ebla 16–23, 32, 53, 54, 56, 59, 61, 71, 74, 75, 78, 80, 124, 183, 273, 275
economy 3, 5, 12, 17, 22, 35, 36, 43, 44, 51, 83, 118, 146, 178, 196, 197, 201, 205, 223, 248
edict 40, 43, 46, 98
Edom/Edomite 116–18, 125, 127, 141, 143–7, 159, 184, 189, 193, 228, 232, 238, 250, 260, 278

Edrei 159
education 28
'Egel 56
'Egliya 56
Eglon 224, 225, 228
Egypt/Egyptian 3, 4, 6–9, 12–15, 18–21, 23–32, 31, 32, 35–40, 48, 49, 51, 52, 55–8, 62, 64–72, 77, 79, 80, 83–90, 92, 93, 95–7, 99–102, 106–8, 111–17, 119–36, 140, 142–4, 146, 148–50, 152–63, 167–74, 176, 177, 181–6, 190, 193, 195, 199, 202, 204, 210–12, 217, 229, 230, 233, 234, 239, 240, 242, 246, 255, 256, 258–62, 264, 265, 271–3, 275–8, 280–2
Ehli-Nikkalu 110
Ehli-Tešub 105
Ehud 225
Ekallatum 42
Ekron 65, 117, 169, 175, 176, 200, 204–6, 208, 209, 262
Ekwesh 177
Elam/Elamite 17, 41, 43, 45, 93, 178, 179, 275
Elephantine 72
Eleutherus 140
elite 41, 69–71, 79, 97, 111, 119, 175, 180, 188, 206, 238, 257, 273
Elohist 53
Emar 44, 61, 62, 98, 142
emigration/immigration 19, 64, 66, 69, 174, 176, 273
empire 16–18, 21, 28, 31, 41–4, 47, 49, 51, 87, 90, 92, 94–6, 102, 104, 112, 127, 172, 173, 180, 181, 188, 206, 207, 229, 256, 258, 268, 272, 274
Endaruta/Intaruta 131, 132, 135
Eni-Shasi/Enishazi 130, 136
Enkidu 30
Enkomi 133
Enlil-kudurri-usur 91, 93
Enlil-nirari 93
Entin 56
Enuma Eliš/Enuma Elish 29, 179
Ephraim/Ephraimite 63, 65, 116, 192, 196–8, 219, 221, 222, 226, 245, 259, 265, 279
epic 17, 28–30, 153, 179
epigraphy 6, 154
Esarhaddon 187
Eshbaal/Ishbaal 222, 226, 242, 245, 247, 279
Eshnuna/Eshnunna 41–3, 45, 61, 79, 92
Etakkama 129, 130
Ethiopia/Ethiopic 37, 255
Etruscans 177

Euphrates 16, 18, 23, 32, 43, 44, 47, 59–62, 78, 86, 87, 91, 95, 99, 112, 123, 124, 179, 184, 211, 256, 274, 282
Europe 37
Eusebius 13
Execration Texts 52, 56, 65, 66, 79, 134, 163
exodus 67, 84, 88, 89, 115, 136, 143, 148, 149, 153–63, 217, 227, 229, 273, 275–7

famine 15, 17, 110, 118
farmsteads 216, 234
Faynan/Feinan 121, 145–7, 188
Fayum 37, 38
Fenkhu 123, 124, 126
feudal 76, 239
Fidan 117, 143, 145, 228, 232
figurines 51
flood 4, 15, 16, 30, 73, 275
fortification 120, 198, 199, 251, 252
fortress 37, 71, 107, 120, 123, 124, 143, 146, 147, 154, 155, 158, 193, 202, 227, 248, 251, 252, 277
Freedman 74, 75, 117, 137, 143, 145, 153, 156, 227, 228
frontier 87, 91, 93, 107, 143, 158, 160, 171

Gad 221, 225, 226
Galilee 119, 120, 125, 129, 131, 136, 152, 245, 247, 268
Gandash 92
Gath/Gimtu 19, 27, 115, 130–3, 135, 136, 170, 174, 175, 196, 200, 204–6, 208–10, 247, 250, 262, 277
Gath-padalla 131, 136
Gaza 85, 115, 126, 127, 143, 148, 150, 151, 175, 206, 208, 211, 271
Gebel Barkal 99
genealogy 220, 222
Genesis 16, 32, 53, 64, 72–6, 78–80, 147, 151, 275
Geshem 157
Gezer/Gazru 10, 115, 126, 128, 130, 132–6, 150–2, 175, 195, 199, 203, 206, 238, 252, 259, 263, 271, 277
Gibeon 213, 242, 246, 262, 263, 279
Giboa-Saman 125
Gideon 224, 225, 242
Gilead 225, 226, 245, 247, 268
Gilgal 244
Gilgamesh 17, 28–30
Ginta 132
Ginti-Ashna 131, 133
Ginti-Kirmil 131, 132, 135

INDEX OF SUBJECTS

Girgashites 141, 229
Gittites 205, 247
Giza 14
God 13, 15, 67, 69, 71–3, 123, 132, 159, 240, 245, 256, 280
goddess 23, 69, 134, 225, 242
Golan 120, 129
Goliath 204–6, 210, 211, 245, 249, 254, 280
Gomorrah 74, 75
Goshen 153, 155, 157, 276
governor 178
grain 5, 22, 110, 138, 151, 197, 208, 223, 262, 278–80
Greece 94, 96, 121
Gubla 56, 129
Gungunum 42
Gurgum 180
Gutian 17
Guzana 184

Ḫaberu/Habiru/Ḫabiru/Ḫabiru/Hapiru 142, 267
Hadadezer 250
Halab/Ḫalab 22, 61, 96, 142
Ḫālmu'di 70
Halunnu 130, 136
Ham 123
Hamath 126, 180, 184
Hammath 88
Hammurabi 41–5, 49, 61, 62, 92, 274
Hana 92
Hanigalbat/Ḫanigalbat 90, 91, 96, 98, 111, 113
Hantili 48, 94
Haran 76, 153, 159
Harapshi 48
Harosheth-ha-goiim 224
Hashabu 125, 136
Hasi 130, 136
Hasrurum 56
Haṣura 135
Hathor 23, 69
Hatshepsut 83, 84, 86, 89, 123
Hatti/Ḫatti/Hattušili/Ḫattušili/Hattusili 18, 43, 45, 46–9, 58, 62, 79, 88, 91–8, 101–2, 106–8, 110, 112, 113, 127, 129, 171, 177, 179, 180
Hauran 130
Hawara 38
Hazael 195, 200, 208, 250
Ḫazannu 134
Hazor 10, 21, 53, 58, 64, 65, 79, 86, 116, 121, 123, 130, 132, 135, 136, 191, 192, 194–6, 199, 216, 227, 238, 252, 277

Hebrew/Hebrews 11, 22, 29, 52, 62, 72, 73, 77, 97, 104, 123, 140–2, 144, 147, 153–5, 158, 163, 182, 191, 193, 216, 219–21, 223–7, 251, 276, 278, 279, 281
Hebron 5, 63, 76, 79, 132, 197, 223, 229, 247, 268
Hebua 158
Helek 222
Heliopolis 13
Helladic 9
Hellespont 180
Henenu/Ḥenenu 19, 27, 65
Hephaestus 37
Hepher 222
Heqanakht 36
Heracleopolis/Herakleopolis 15, 36, 272
Herodotus 35, 37, 38, 49, 180, 256
Heshbon/Hesban 127, 185
Hetjera 125
hieratic 19, 28
hieroglyphs 28
Hieropolis 70
highland 65, 123, 187, 194, 198, 200, 202, 204, 214, 218, 229, 231–5, 241, 245, 280
Hilakku 180
Hiram 182, 255, 257
historian 12, 191
historiography 4, 27, 32, 45, 73, 93, 96, 98, 228, 235, 244, 255, 260, 264, 272
Hittites 18, 45, 46, 48, 49, 72, 76, 84, 87, 88, 90, 91, 93, 95, 98, 102, 103, 106–9, 112, 113, 119, 126–8, 139, 141, 144, 169, 170, 179, 180, 184, 209, 229, 275
Hivites 141, 229
Hizziri 133
Hoglah 222
holy 19, 62, 63, 116, 117, 185, 192, 214, 244
Hoplite 210, 211
Horemhab/Horemheb/Ḥoremheb 84, 87–9, 122, 126
Horites 97, 141
horse 86, 142
Horus 13
Hosea 154, 155
household 69, 77, 85, 139, 173, 239, 256
ḥq3w.ḫ3swt 23, 67
Ḥrm 211
ḥrt 123
ḥryw-šʿ 24, 25
Hu'aket 125
Huleh 127
Ḫumri 271

Hupishna 180
Hurba-tilla 93
Huriya 129
Hurma 211
Hurrians 18, 47, 48, 64, 68, 96–8, 112, 139, 179
Hutwaret 69
Huwawa 28, 30
Huzziya 46, 48, 94
Hyksos 19, 23, 35, 36, 38–40, 49–51, 58, 64–71, 79, 80, 84–6, 89, 112, 123, 160, 257, 273

Iannas 70
Išar-Damu 22
Ibira 106
Ibiranu/Ibirānu 105, 106, 109, 110
Ibi-Zikir 23
Iblul 23
Ibrium 23
iconography 157, 162
Idrimi 98, 142
Igriš-Ḫalab 22
Ildayyi 130
Ilima-yapi(i) 56
Ili-Rapih 130, 181
Ilu-Dayyani 130
Ilushuma 42
image 137, 210, 249, 251, 254, 255
immigrants/immigration 19, 64, 66, 69, 119, 163, 174, 176, 196, 207, 273
India/Indians 97, 140
Indo-Aryan 97, 98, 111
Indo-European 18, 46, 96, 97
Indo-Iranian 65
Indra 98
Indus 17
inscription 3, 26, 28, 40, 46, 53, 60, 69, 70, 78, 89, 98, 99, 122–6, 143, 144, 148–53, 156, 157, 162, 173, 174, 177–9, 186, 190, 192, 200, 204, 208–9, 215, 226, 230–2, 242, 257, 258, 260–2, 264, 266, 271, 272, 278, 279, 281, 282
Ionic 10
Ipte 130
Ipuwer 16, 24, 27, 29, 157
Iran/Iranian 17, 43, 65, 97, 137
Iraq 90, 96, 100
Irkab-Damu 22
Irkabtum 62
Irkata/Irqata 100, 101, 124, 127, 130
İrnṯ 211
İrr 211

Irride 62
Isaac 76, 77
Isaiah 157
İsdd 211
Ishbi-Erra 41
Ish-Bosheth 226, 247
Ishme-Dagan 45
Ishtar 93
Ishtunda 180
Isin 41–3, 48, 58, 178, 179
İsqnrn 211
İsr 211
Issachar 222, 226
Itai 250
Italy 177
Itj-tawy 37, 39
Ituryn 125
Izbet-Ṣartah 197

Jabbok 186, 225
Jaffa 125, 175, 206
Jatt 131, 196
Jebel Bishri/Jebel Bišri 59, 78, 100, 184, 274
Jebel ed-Druz 131
Jebusite 251, 252
Jehoash 257
Jemma 125
Jemnet Nasr 16, 31
Jephthah 223, 225
Jeremiah 157, 160
Jericho 19, 21, 154, 213, 228
Jeroboam 27, 242, 243, 263, 264, 280
Jerubbaal 225
Jerusalem 3, 10, 63, 65, 67, 79, 115, 116, 118, 120, 128, 130–6, 141, 153, 154, 163, 191–4, 197–9, 202, 204, 223, 224, 228, 235, 240, 242, 247, 248, 250–2, 256–8, 260–2, 265, 267, 268, 277, 280
Jew 11
Jezreel 7, 9, 10, 63, 64, 119, 120, 125, 130–3, 136, 150, 152, 194–7, 222, 225, 226, 246, 247, 261, 263, 265, 268
Jibbit-Lîm 54
Jinaśśi'-Ad/Jinaśśi-Ad 70
Jonathan 253
Joppa 122, 123, 163
Jordan 53, 65, 116–18, 120, 127, 129, 132, 140, 143, 145, 146, 150, 152, 154, 184, 187, 192–4, 196, 197, 213, 226, 228, 230, 238, 245, 246, 248, 254, 262, 263, 276, 278
Joseph 72, 77, 80, 155, 162, 221, 235, 279

INDEX OF SUBJECTS

Josephus 13, 67, 70, 257, 273
Joshua 128, 129, 136, 139, 148, 154, 157, 191, 213, 217, 224, 228, 240, 276, 278
Josiah 213, 224
Judaea/Judaean 11, 62, 72, 120, 133, 154, 175, 194, 197, 198, 200, 203, 206, 214, 216, 225, 227, 229, 249, 254, 257, 261, 265, 266, 271
Judah/Judahite 3–5, 10, 27, 31, 40, 51, 116, 117, 139, 142, 155, 160, 163, 184, 192, 193, 197, 198, 200–4, 207, 208, 213, 214, 216, 219, 222, 223, 225, 227, 228, 235–8, 240–6, 247, 251, 253–6, 258, 260–2, 264–8, 271, 279–82
Judaism 40, 51, 155, 235
Judges 5, 43, 128, 157, 191, 213, 220–6, 228, 240, 242, 243, 251, 266, 275–9, 282
Julius Africanus 13, 67

Kadash-Enlil 93
Kadashman-Enlil 102, 129
Kadashman-Harbe 93
Kadesh 122, 125, 153, 155
Kadmonites 141
Kamid el-Loz 119
Kamose 39, 40, 71, 85, 89
Kanesh 42, 43, 46, 49, 274
Kara-indash 92
Karana 40, 44
Karatepe 77
Karduniaš/Karduniash 90, 92
Karnak 122, 123, 126, 148–50, 152, 259, 260, 278
Karpu[n/m]a 88
Kar-Tukulti-Ninurta 91
Kārum 43
Kashtiliash 91–3
Kaska 94, 95, 112
Kassite 44, 90–3, 95, 111, 113, 178, 179, 208, 275
Keilah 132
Kenites 141, 201, 230
Kenizzites 141
Kerak 21, 185
Kfar Hasidim 125
Khamudi 70
Kharu 150, 151, 271
Khaʻsekhemwy 23
Khatte 150, 151
Khayan 70
Khirbat al-Jariya 145
Khirbat Umm ad-Dananir 187
Khirbet en-Nahas 145, 262
Khirbet Manaʻiyah 145, 146

Khirbet Qeiyafa 192–4, 200, 248
Khirbit Raddana 197
Khufu 14
Khu-sobek 69
Kikkuli 96–8
Kinneret 123, 196
Kiriath-jearim 213
Kirta 99
Kish 16, 42, 244
Kizzuwadna/Kizzuwatna 48, 94, 95, 99, 107, 180
Kode 171
Königsnovelle 255
Koptos 36
Kumidi 127, 130, 136
Kummah 180
Kurigalzu 91, 93
Kurkh Monolith 186
Kussara 43, 46
Kutir-Nahhunte 178

Labʼayu/Labayu 131, 132, 134, 135, 267, 277
Laban 143
Labana 130
Labarna 46
Lacharēs 38
Lachish 9, 10, 31, 115, 118, 121, 130, 132, 133, 135, 136, 168, 169, 171, 174, 175, 191, 194, 199, 200, 202, 203, 206, 252, 260, 277
Lagaš/Lagash 16, 58
Lagish 17
Laish 65
Lakiša 135
Lamarēs/Lamaris 38
Lapana 136
Larsa 16, 41–3, 48, 92
law code 41, 43
Lebanon 25, 27, 60, 65, 104, 119, 124, 125, 130, 132, 134, 150, 170, 179, 231
Lebu 89
Levant 3, 4, 6, 7, 19–21, 26, 27, 35, 51, 52, 54, 55, 60, 65, 66, 68–72, 78, 79, 96, 100, 104, 111, 114, 115, 119, 136, 139, 143, 145, 146, 148, 152, 153, 170, 172, 179, 184, 192, 193, 205, 209, 210, 227, 235, 238, 247, 265, 267
Levites 160, 279
Leviticus 51
Libya/Libyan 14, 27, 36, 89, 152, 168, 177
Lim-il-Malik 105
lowland/lowlanders 146, 185, 200, 241, 266, 280
Luash 180, 184

Lukka 110, 169, 176, 177
Luwian 18, 180
Lycia 110, 176, 177

Maat 13
Mabu'u 105
Machir 222, 225, 226, 279
Madaba 185
Magidda 135
Malatya 180
malikum 22
Manasseh/Manassite 63, 152, 197, 198, 219, 221, 222, 225, 229, 265, 279
Manetho 12, 13, 15, 36, 38, 39, 49, 66–8, 70
Manna 276
Marduk 29, 92, 93, 179
Marduk-apla-iddina 92
Marduk-nadin-ahhe 179
Mari 16–18, 22, 23, 32, 40–5, 48–50, 53–7, 59–62, 76, 78, 79, 272, 274
Marijannu 97
Marom 88
Martu 43
mārū-yamīna 60, 274
maryannu/maryanu 98, 123, 171, 173
Masuwari 180
Mawatalli 127
maximalist 52, 171
Mayarzana 130
Medinet Habu 169, 171, 172, 177
Megiddo 6–10, 21, 28, 58, 65, 86, 97, 117, 119, 121, 123, 130–2, 135, 136, 163, 168, 169, 171, 173, 192, 194, 195, 199, 202, 203, 210, 228, 238, 252, 260, 261, 263, 277
Mektilyn 125
Memphis 14, 15, 85, 122, 125, 126, 133, 272
Menander 257
Mendjat 125
Menes 13
Menkaure 23
Mentuhotep 36, 49
mercenary 206, 211, 248–50
Merenptah/Merneptah 3, 84, 89, 114, 115, 127, 128, 143–5, 148–57, 160–3, 168, 186, 190, 215, 216, 230–2, 234, 266, 271, 272, 277–9, 281, 282
Merkare 27
Merneferre Aya 36, 40
Merodach-baladan 92
Mersa Gawasis 36
Mesad Hashavyahu 250

Mesha 185, 221, 226, 250
Meshwesh 89
Mesopotamia 4, 7, 12, 16, 17, 21–3, 26, 28, 29, 31, 32, 35, 40, 41, 43, 44, 48, 49, 53, 55, 57, 59–61, 64, 79, 90, 97, 111, 115, 144, 178, 183, 184, 229, 241, 256, 265, 272, 274
metal/metallurgy 20, 22, 27, 42, 117, 143, 145–7, 206, 209, 210, 228, 231, 262
Mḥtyw 24
Midian/Midianites 117, 145, 154, 185, 225, 228, 230, 276
Migdol 154, 155, 158
migrant 142
Milawata 95
Milkilu 133–5
minimalist 172
mining 26, 27, 32, 38, 146, 147, 188, 262
Minoan 205, 211, 247
Mīšarum 43
Mishal 123, 133
Mita 181
Mitanni 46, 48, 53, 58, 83, 84, 86, 87, 90, 91, 94–9, 101, 111–13, 119, 122, 129, 135, 140, 188, 275
Mitra 98
Mittani 95–7
Mizpah 225, 244
Mnṯw 24, 25
Moab/Moabites 116–18, 127, 141, 145, 184–8, 226, 230, 236, 238, 239, 250
monotheism 84
Montu 24
mortuary 14, 15, 38, 85, 86, 117, 126, 228
Moses 156, 162
Mukiš/Mukish 103, 106, 107, 112, 180
Mukishkhi 142
Muršili/Muršiliš/Mursili 44, 46–50, 62, 79, 92, 94, 95, 97, 98, 106, 107, 111, 113, 127, 170
Mushihuna 130
Mushki 178, 180, 181
Mut-Baḫlu 135
Mut-Ba'lu 131
Muwatalli/Muwattalli 47, 94, 95, 112
Mycenae 102, 119, 211
myth 54, 153, 154, 159

Naḥal Yattir 201
Naharin 99, 124–6
Nahor 76
Nahr el-Kebir 140
Nahrin 86, 211

Nairi 91
Naphtali 222, 226
Naram-Sin 17, 18, 23, 93, 178
Nar-mer 13
Nāsatya 98
Nashtarbi 62
Naṣib 131
Nasiba 131
Nazi-Marutash 91, 93
Nebḥepetrē/Nebhepetre Mentuhotep 19, 36, 65
Nebuchadnezzar 178, 179
Neferhotep 38, 56
Nefernefruaten 87, 89, 126
Neferti/Neferty 25, 27, 29, 37
Nefrusobk 38
Negeb/Negev 10, 26–8, 63, 64, 71, 75, 78, 85, 120, 129, 136, 145, 146, 152, 159, 185, 197, 200–2, 210, 245, 260, 262, 265, 266, 278
Nekhbet 123
Nesa 43, 46, 49
Nesite 18
netherworld 30
neutron activation 65, 67
Nhryn 211
Nihriya 91, 109
Nile 14, 15, 26, 32, 36, 50, 154, 173, 276
Nineveh 42
Ninurta-apil-Edur 91
Nippur 41, 58
Niqmaddu/Niqmadu 101, 105, 107, 109, 110, 112, 129
Niqmepa 101, 103, 105, 107, 108, 112
Niqmi-epuh 62
Nishin 62
Nitocris 15
Niy 125
Nob 246
nomad/nomadism 3, 117, 137–9, 144, 148, 154, 192, 194, 213, 223, 227–9, 231
nome 36
N'ryn 211
Nubia 14, 36–9, 49, 84, 86, 87, 150, 168, 172, 272
Nuhashe 101, 106, 112
Nuhasse 130
Nukhashshe 124
Nuzi 53, 72, 76, 96, 97, 99, 275

Omri/Omride 7, 10, 194, 195, 204, 216, 226, 241, 242, 264, 267
Ophel 199

oracle 77
Orontes 88, 100, 124, 125, 211
Osiris 13
ostracon/ostraca 31, 222

Pa'api 133
Padi 209
Palaian 18
Palmyra 59, 274
papyrus 19, 122, 143, 153, 157, 160
Parattarna 98
Parshatatar 98
Parsu 103
Passover 161
Patin 180
patriarchs 16, 22, 53, 64, 71, 73–6, 79, 273, 275
Pehel 132, 136
Pekana'an 150, 151
Pelasgoi 176
Peleg 76, 194, 195
Peleset 171, 176
Pelethite 211
Pella 65, 88, 127, 131, 132, 135, 277
Peltastai/Peltasts 211, 250
Pelte 211
Pentapolis 205, 208
Pentateuch 52, 53, 73, 115, 153, 161, 162, 276
Pepi-Nakht/Pepy-Nakht 15, 26
Pepi/Pepy 15, 20, 23, 25, 26, 32
Pergamum 257
Perizzites 139, 141, 229
Persia 280
pharaoh 13–15, 20, 23, 36, 58, 83–5, 87, 99–101, 106, 115, 122, 126, 130, 133, 134, 142, 149, 151, 155–7, 163, 168, 172, 181, 182, 239, 242, 258–62, 271, 276, 277
Phasis 37
Philistia 9, 169, 172, 174–6, 200, 201, 204, 205, 207, 209, 210, 259
Philistines 6, 78, 117, 136, 137, 142, 167, 169–77, 193, 201, 204–12, 227, 235, 240–3, 245–50, 261, 266–8, 276, 279, 280, 282
Philo of Byblos 257
Phoenicia/Phoenicians 19, 23, 65, 88, 111, 121, 127, 130, 140, 147, 181–3, 188, 204, 266, 281
Phrygians 179–81
pig 117, 193, 196, 214, 266
Pihawalwi 109
Piḫilu 132, 135
Pi-Ramasse 158

Pisheni 48
Pithana 43, 46
Pithom 154, 155, 158, 276
pithos/pithoi 117, 118, 188, 192–4, 229
Pîm 209
plague 95, 251
poem/poetry 51, 150, 155, 156, 224, 225, 279
population 21, 26, 32, 44, 53, 58, 59, 63, 64, 67–9, 71, 79, 89, 97, 100, 119, 159, 160, 168, 172, 174–7, 180, 181, 186, 188, 189, 195–8, 201, 203, 206, 207, 212, 214, 218, 229–34, 238, 240, 241, 246, 251, 262, 265, 266, 268, 273, 276, 279, 281
pork 196, 215
Potiphar 77
pottery 6, 8–10, 26, 27, 66, 169, 170, 172, 174–6, 184, 187, 188, 194, 195, 199–201, 203, 212, 215, 232, 234, 252
prehistory 4, 205, 227
priest/priesthood 13, 14, 84, 243, 244, 251, 253
prince 37, 56, 73, 88, 108, 109
prisoner 107
propaganda 43, 151, 172
prophecy/prophet 25, 27, 227, 243, 244, 253
province 40, 51, 140, 163, 235
Psammetichus 77
Puduhepa 108, 109
Punt 15, 36, 37, 49, 86
Pwenet 26
pyramid 14, 15, 272
Pyspys 143

Qadeš/Qadesh 24, 84, 88, 95, 102, 103, 107, 108, 112, 123, 124, 126, 127, 129, 130, 135, 140, 144, 153, 159, 162, 201, 211, 276
ha-Qain 197
Qana 88
Qanawat 131
Qantir 158
Qanu 131
Qatna 42, 45, 61, 79, 124, 125, 130
Qedarite 157
Qedem 25, 123
Qeltu 132
Qiryat Ata 21
Qos-Gabr 187
queen 15, 48, 86, 103, 108, 109, 129, 182, 258, 280
Qurn-Ḥaṭṭin 125

Raamses 155
radiocarbon/radiometric 6–8, 10, 11, 19, 78, 145–7, 185, 192–4, 201, 203, 245

Ramah 244
Rameses/Ramesses 8, 83, 84, 88, 89, 95, 102, 103, 108, 112, 122, 123, 126, 127, 143, 144, 149, 151, 152, 154, 157, 158, 160, 167–9, 171–4, 176, 186, 190, 206, 207, 230, 276
Rap'ānu 105
Rapha'u 159
Raphia 126
Ras Ibn Hani 111
Ras Shamra 37, 52, 55, 111
rebel/rebellion 18, 62, 92, 101, 106, 123, 124, 132, 135, 250, 262
refuge/refugee 92, 98, 101, 107, 127, 130, 142, 160, 181
Rehoboam 9, 200, 243, 257, 260, 262, 264, 280
Rehov/Reḥov/Rehob/Reḥob 27, 65, 88, 131–3, 135, 136, 184, 196, 263
religion 15, 52, 69, 71, 73, 79, 136, 153, 155, 178, 183, 193, 206, 219, 232, 239, 240, 281
Rephaim 55, 141, 159
Retenu/Reṯenu/Retjenu 19, 24, 25, 32, 69, 86, 99, 122–5, 272
Reuben 222, 226
revolt/revolution 36, 45, 150, 203, 217, 218, 230
Rib-Eddi (see Rib-Hadda) 130, 181
Rib-Hadda 100, 101, 130, 181, 182, 277
rite/ritual 54, 58, 104, 110, 280
river 17, 25, 87, 100, 125, 140, 171, 173, 186, 212, 225, 263, 274
Ṛta-dhāman 98
Ruhizzi 130, 136
rural 21, 63, 64, 79, 119, 121, 138, 175, 186, 218, 230, 233, 234, 266
Rusmanya 131

saga 250
Saite 77, 158, 161–3, 210, 250, 276
Sakir-Har 70
Salitis 67, 70
Sam'al 180, 184
Samaria 7, 9, 10, 194, 203, 222, 245, 263–5, 271
Samath 143
Samsu-ditana 92
Samsuiluna/Samsu-iluna 44, 62, 92
Samuel 117, 141, 191, 205, 208, 235, 241–7, 249, 250, 254, 267, 280
Sanchuniathon 257
Sanskrit 96, 98
Saqqara 14
Sarā-Dagan 70
Sardinia 176, 177

INDEX OF SUBJECTS

Sarepta 111, 182
Sargon 17, 18, 31, 40, 93, 256, 264, 272
Satatna 131
Saul 208, 219, 223, 226, 228, 235, 242–9, 252–5, 267, 268, 279, 280
scarabs 40, 67, 69, 70, 168, 169
scholar 75, 156
scribe 14, 28, 29, 152, 260
seal 46, 94, 99, 106–8, 179, 187
Sealand 44, 90, 92, 179
Sebek-khu Stela/Sebok-khu Stela 69
sedentarization 137, 138, 188, 227, 228, 262
segmentary 220, 221, 236–8
Sehetepibrē 56
Seir 127, 141, 143, 184, 186, 232
Sekmem 69
Semites 273
Sennacherib 29, 35
Senwosret 36–7
Septuagint 157
Seqenenra/Seqenenre 39, 66, 70
Serabit el-Khadim 38
Seranim 208
Serug 76
Sesostris 37, 38, 49, 65, 69
Seth 13, 69, 88
Sethnakhte 168, 169
Sethos/Seti/Sety 58, 88, 89, 95, 102, 112, 122, 126, 154, 163, 168, 169
settlement 3, 6, 9, 19, 20, 62–4, 75, 79, 116, 117, 119–21, 129, 136, 147, 154–6, 162, 167–9, 171, 172, 174–7, 184–93, 195–201, 203, 206, 207, 212–16, 219, 223, 227, 229, 230, 232–4, 236, 240, 245, 247, 251, 252, 260, 262, 265, 266, 276, 279, 282
settlers 68, 145, 175, 177, 184, 195, 196, 198, 206, 218, 229, 231–3, 240, 265
Shaaraim 201
Shakkanakku 44
Šakmu 135
Shalamu 88
Shalim/Shalem 256
Shalmaneser 91, 95, 109, 113, 127, 179, 180, 186
shaman 244
Shamash 125
Shamgar 224, 225, 242
Shamhuna/Shamḫuna/Šamḫuna 131, 132, 135
Shamshi-Adad 42–5, 49, 61, 79, 274
Šamu 135
Shamu-Adda 131
Šamuqēnu 70

Šāpaṭ 224, 228
Šaratu 135
Shardana 89, 170
Sharon 7, 10, 11, 123, 125, 131, 136, 137, 141, 152, 194, 203, 206, 212, 263
Sharuhen 66, 71, 79, 85, 86, 123, 273
Sharuna 131
Shashimi 130
Shasu/Shosu 86, 88, 89, 117, 119, 121, 123, 124, 126, 127, 136, 143–5, 147, 148, 151, 152, 156, 185, 188, 228, 230–4, 266, 278, 281
Shatiya 130
Shattura 91, 113
Shaushgamuwa/Šaušgamuwa 102, 103, 109, 112
Shaushtatar 90, 99, 112
Sheba 31, 63, 86, 117, 192, 255, 258, 280
Shechem 37, 63, 65, 69, 79, 115, 120, 128, 130–2, 135, 136, 152, 163, 203, 222, 225, 229, 242, 262, 267, 277
Shekelesh 89, 110, 171, 176, 177
Shemesh 53, 65, 116, 128, 133, 196, 201
Shemida 222
Shephelah 3, 9, 21, 26, 85, 175, 193, 194, 196, 197, 199, 200, 205, 207, 210, 223, 228, 241, 245, 250, 263, 268
Šerdanū 170
Sherden 171, 176, 177, 211, 212
Shigata 100, 101
Shikila(yu) 110
Shilhak-Inshushinak 178
Shiloh 63, 79, 197
Shimashki 17
Shimron 123, 132, 135
Shinutu 180
Shishak 6–9, 249, 259, 260
Shitti-Marduk Stela 179
Shoshenq/Sheshonq 7–9, 168, 190, 191, 195, 200, 202, 235, 242, 243, 246, 258–62, 264
Šuardatu 135
Shubandu 133
Shubaru 211
Shubat-Enlil 44
Shukziya 48
Shulgi 17
Šuma-Adda/Šum-Adda 135
Shutarna 130
Shutruk-Nahhunte 93, 178
Shuttarna 99
Shuwardata/Šuwardata 132, 133
Siamun 259
Sicily 176, 177

Sidon 100, 111, 119, 125–7, 129, 130, 136, 179, 181, 182
Ṣiduna 129
Sihathor 56
Sikil 177, 212
Sikru-Haddu 70
Sile 143, 158, 276
silver 37, 42, 102, 132, 256
Sim'al/Sim'alites 44, 57, 59, 61
Simeon 201, 225
sin 17, 18, 23, 42, 43, 92, 93, 107–9, 178, 251
Sinai 14, 19, 24, 26, 27, 32, 36, 38, 49, 83, 85, 122, 136, 145, 153, 154, 159, 167, 168, 185, 273, 276
Sinuhe 19, 25, 36, 37, 51, 52, 163
Sippar 42
Siptah 168, 169
Siribashani 130
Sisera 223, 240, 279
Siyannu 107, 109
Skmm 25, 69
slave 142, 160
Smenkhkare 87, 89, 126, 129
Sobah 184
Sobeknefern/Sobekneferu/Sebekkareʻ 38
Socho 125, 263
Sodom 74, 75
Solomon 6, 8, 10, 118, 182, 191, 195, 201, 203, 242, 243, 245, 247, 249–51, 255–60, 263, 264, 267, 268, 280, 282
stela 8, 9, 25, 66, 69, 84, 86, 99, 114, 115, 123, 127, 148, 149, 151, 156, 157, 163, 178, 179, 202, 215, 221, 230, 232, 234, 261, 272, 282
steppe 44, 60, 184
Sṯtyw 24, 68
Styw 25
Suhra 131
Sukkal-maḫ/Sukka-maḫ 45
Sumer 16, 17, 20, 28, 31, 41–4, 58, 60, 272
Sumerian 16, 17, 22, 26, 28–31, 41, 58–60, 78, 92, 272
Sumerogram 57
Sumu-abum 42
Sumu-epuh 45, 61
Sumur 100, 101
Suppiluliuma/Šuppiluliuma 90, 95, 99, 101, 103, 106, 112, 126, 129
Surashar 131, 133
Surata 131, 132, 135
Ṣurru 129
Susa 17, 178

Sutaean 278
Sutian 142
Sutu/Sutû 143, 148, 183
Suwardata 132, 135
Syncellus 38, 70
Syria 4, 12, 14, 15, 17, 18, 20–6, 31, 32, 35, 40, 44, 45, 47–53, 55–67, 69, 71, 73–5, 77–9, 83–9, 91, 93–7, 99–101, 103, 105, 107–9, 111, 113–14, 118, 119, 121–30, 132, 134–6, 144, 162, 163, 167, 168, 172, 174, 178, 180, 184, 190, 229, 236, 239, 266, 272–5, 277
Syriac 134, 255
Syrian 17, 21, 22, 42, 49, 54, 55, 57, 60, 61, 64, 79, 103, 119, 123, 124, 129, 172, 182, 183, 224, 272–4

Taanach 123, 131, 132, 135, 206, 228, 263
Tabal 180
Tagi 131, 135
Tahash 125
Taḫnaka 135
Takhsi/Takhsy/Tekhsy 24, 125, 211
Tall al-Umayri 186
Tall Sahab 186
Tanaju 177
Tanaya 124
Tarhundaradu 129
Taurus 23
Tausret 169
Tawilan 184, 187
tax/taxation 14, 37, 238
eṭ-Ṭayibeh 131
Tehu-Teshupa 130
Tekoah 197
Tel Bareqet 21
Tel Batash 9, 10
Tel Edar 197
Tel Esdar 201
Tel es-Safi/Tel eṣ-Ṣafi 210
Tel ʻEton 133, 194
Tel Hadar 6, 202
Tel Harasim/Tel Ḥarasim 175, 206
Tel Haror 10, 71, 79, 201, 273
Tel Jokneam 133
Tel Menorah 121
Tel Miqne 9, 10, 169, 175, 176, 205, 206
Tel Qasileh 197
Tel Rekhesh 133
Tel Yoqne 132, 135
Telipinu 46, 48, 50, 94, 98, 112
Tell Abu Hawam 182, 196

Tell Abû Hureirah 71, 79, 273
Tell Abu Sefeh 158
Tell Basta 69
Tell Beit Mirsim 10, 194
Tell ed-Dab'a/Tell et-Dab'a 39, 58, 67, 68
Tell el-Far'ah/Tell el-Farah 21, 63, 71, 85, 123
Tell el-Maskhuta 66, 158, 276
Tell el-Qudeirat 159, 276
Tell el-Ratabah 158
Tell eṣ-Ṣâfī 205, 206
Tell eṣ-Ṣarem 133
Tell Fekheriye 98
Tell Ḥašbe 125
Tell Halaf 184
Tell Halif 10
Tell Hizzin 130
Tell Jemmeh 78, 133
Tell Judeideh 133
Tell Kazel 103, 111
Tell Keisan 182
Tell Mardikh 16, 19, 22, 74, 273
Tell Qarnei-Ḥiṭṭin 133
temple 3, 14, 37, 38, 40, 51, 54, 58, 69, 103, 118, 123, 126, 150, 161, 171, 182, 191–4, 199, 208, 209, 223, 228, 235, 247, 248, 251, 255–8, 260, 271
Terah 76
Teresh 177
Terqa 44
terrace 199, 252
Tešub 105
Teye 129
Thebes 15, 36, 39, 70, 71, 85, 272, 273
Thracians 37
Thutmose 24, 29, 60, 62, 64, 83, 84, 86, 87, 89, 96, 97, 99, 100, 112, 122–6, 160, 163
Tianna/Tianni/Tienna/Tienni 123, 133, 136
Tiglath-pileser 178, 179, 183–6, 255, 257
Tigris 16, 32, 118, 167
Tikunani 47
Til Barsip 180
Timna 145, 146
Tin 18, 41, 42, 55
Tiwati 130
Tjalkhi 125
Tjehenu 150
Tjeker 171, 176, 177, 211, 212
Tobu 131
tomb 87, 123, 168
toponyms 24, 116, 144, 148, 161, 184, 260–3, 278
Torias 176

Towsre 168, 169, 182
trade 14, 17, 18, 20–3, 26, 27, 32, 36, 37, 40, 42, 43, 46, 49, 53–5, 64, 65, 69, 71, 79, 93, 102, 107, 108, 121, 132, 144, 146, 172, 177, 179, 180, 182, 183, 187–9, 201, 202, 230, 231, 242, 246, 256, 258, 261, 262, 265, 266, 272, 274, 280
transhumance 144, 184, 233, 279
Transjordan/Transjordanian 57, 64, 65, 75, 117, 118, 121, 127, 143, 146, 150, 152, 155, 159, 167, 184, 189, 196, 217, 226, 230, 250, 263, 272
treaty 17, 42, 47, 48, 84, 87, 88, 91, 94, 95, 99, 102, 106–8, 112, 113, 125, 127
Tresh 171
Treuci 176
tribe 5, 44, 59, 61, 140, 177, 179, 188, 219–23, 235, 236, 244, 274, 279, 280
tribute 14, 27, 32, 37, 38, 65, 101, 106–9, 113, 117, 123, 124, 126, 143, 145, 179, 228, 237, 239, 256, 262, 273, 277
troop 26, 108
Trw 158
Tubihu 136
Tudhaliya 91, 94, 95, 102, 109, 112, 113
Tuišeratta 98
Tukulti-Ninurta 91, 93, 109, 113
Tunip 47, 101, 123, 124, 127, 130
Turash 89
Turin Canon 69, 70
Tushratta 83, 96, 98, 99, 129
Tushultu 136
Tutankhamun 87, 89, 112, 126, 129
Tuthmosis 89, 99
Tutimaeus 67
Tuttul 44
Tuwana 180
Twosret 169
Tyre/Tyrian 65, 88, 100, 111, 119, 127, 129, 130, 136, 181, 182, 255, 257, 277
Tyrsenia 177

Ugarānu 105
Ugarit 20, 37, 45, 51–6, 58, 61, 62, 70, 78, 79, 83, 87, 88, 91, 95, 96, 99–115, 125, 127, 129, 135, 139, 140, 147, 170, 173, 177, 181, 183, 207, 236, 274, 275, 277
Ugarsallu 93
Ullasa 101
Ullaza 124
Umayri 185–8
Umm 184, 187

Umm al-Biyara 187
Umma 16, 17, 58
Umma-Gisha 16
Ur 16–18, 21, 30, 31, 41–3, 54, 56, 58–60, 78, 132, 272, 275
Ura 72, 107, 110
urbanism/urbanization 20, 21, 32, 63, 64, 79, 119, 227
Urhi-Teshub/Urḫi-Teshub 91, 95
Uriah 141
Ur-Nammu 17
Urshu 62
Uruk 16, 17, 30, 31, 41, 43
Urusalim 115, 133
Usha 47, 98, 182
Ushu 182
usurper 245, 248, 253
Utri-Sharrumma 108, 109
Utu-Hegal 17

Varuṅa 98
vassal 61, 69, 90, 91, 94, 95, 100, 106–8, 112, 127, 129, 180, 239, 258
Vedic 97, 98
village 14, 20, 29, 138, 198, 231, 252
vizier 36, 77, 84
votive 69, 158

Wadi al-Haba 187
Wadi al-Mujib 186, 187
Wadi az-Zarqa 186
Wadi Hisma 187
Wadi Tumilat 37, 154
Wahliya 101
Wartet 124
Wasashatta 91
Washshukkanni 98
Wenamun 115, 177, 205, 211, 212
Weni 15, 25, 27, 32, 273
Weshesh 171, 177
Wiktasu 133

Xanthus 180

Ya'ir 209
Yabni-Ilu 133, 135, 182

Yašdata 135
Yahdun-Lim 42, 44, 45, 61
Yaḥmadu 59
Yaḥmuṭum 59
Yahu/Yhw/Yhwh/Yahweh/Yahwism 136, 143, 156, 219, 224, 240, 241, 244, 245, 256, 257, 267, 278, 281
Yahzib-Hadda 133
Yakin-ilu 56
Yamhad 42, 45, 47, 49, 55, 60–2, 78, 79, 97, 98, 274
Yamina/Yaminite 44, 45, 59
Yamūtum 59
Yano'am 151, 152
Yantin 56
Yantin-Ammu 56
Yanuamma 130, 131, 136
Yapah-Hadda 130, 181
Yapaḫu 135
Yapai 133
Yapa'-shemu-abi/Yapi-shemu-abi 56
Yaqaru 105, 106
Yariḫūm 59
Yarim-Lim 45, 55, 61, 62
Yashdata 131–3
Yasmah-Addu 42, 45
Yatiri 133
Yehud/Yehuda 40, 51, 235, 271
Yemen 258
Yeno'am/Yenoam 24, 88, 126, 128, 131, 136, 148, 150, 151, 271
Yidya/Idiya 133, 135
Yiqdasu 133
Yokneam 131
Yörük/Yoruk/Yuruk 227, 231
Ysd 209
Yurza 133, 136, 175, 206

Zagros 17, 44, 91, 92, 207, 241, 272
Zebulun 222, 226
Zidan 129
Zidanta 48, 94
Zimri-Lim 45, 55, 56, 61, 79, 274
Zobah 250
Zuḫra/Suhra 131